# MASTERPLOTS II

## SHORT STORY SERIES
### REVISED EDITION

# MASTERPLOTS II

## SHORT STORY SERIES
### REVISED EDITION

## Volume 2
### Chi–Err

*Editor, Revised Edition*
**CHARLES MAY**
*California State University, Long Beach*

*Editor, First Edition*
**FRANK N. MAGILL**

SALEM PRESS
Pasadena, California     Hackensack, New Jersey

*Editor in Chief:* Dawn P. Dawson

*Editorial Director:* Christina J. Moose    *Assistant Editor:* Andrea E. Miller
*Project Editor:* R. Kent Rasmussen    *Research Supervisor:* Jeffry Jensen
*Production Editor:* Cynthia Beres    *Acquisitions Editor:* Mark Rehn
*Copy Editor:* Rowena Wildin    *Layout:* Eddie Murillo

Some of the essays in this work originally appeared in *Masterplots II, Short Story Series*, edited by Frank N. Magill (Pasadena, Calif.: Salem Press, Inc., 1986), and in *Masterplots II, Short Story Series Supplement*, edited by Frank N. Magill and Charles E. May (Pasadena, Calif.: Salem Press, Inc., 1996).

∞ The paper used in these volumes conforms to the American National Standard for Permanence of Paper for Printed Library Materials, Z39.48-1992 (R1997).

**Library of Congress Cataloging-in-Publication Data**
Masterplots II : Short story series / editor Charles May. — Rev. ed.
    p.    cm.
Includes bibliographical references and index.
    ISBN 1-58765-140-8 (set : alk. paper) — ISBN 1-58765-142-4 (vol. 2 : alk. paper) —
    1. Fiction—19th century—Stories, plots, etc. 2. Fiction—19th century—History and criticism. 3. Fiction—20th century—Stories, plots, etc. 4. Fiction—20th century—History and criticism. 5. Short story. I. Title: Masterplots 2. II. Title: Masterplots two. III. May, Charles E. (Charles Edward), 1941-
PN3326 .M27 2004
809.3′1—dc22

                                                                        2003018256

First Printing

PRINTED IN THE UNITED STATES OF AMERICA

# TABLE OF CONTENTS

# TABLE OF CONTENTS

# TABLE OF CONTENTS

# MASTERPLOTS II

## SHORT STORY SERIES
### REVISED EDITION

# THE CHILD OF QUEEN VICTORIA

*Author:* William Plomer (1903-1973)
*Type of plot:* Social realism
*Time of plot:* The early twentieth century
*Locale:* Lembuland, Africa
*First published:* 1933

> *Principal characters:*
> FRANT, the protagonist, a young English trader working in
>     Africa
> COLONEL MACGAVIN, his sponsor in Africa, a Scottish trader
> MRS. MACGAVIN
> SERAPHINA, a Lembu woman
> UMLILWANA, Seraphina's fiancé
> AN ELDERLY PROPHET

*The Story*

A young Englishman named Frant arrives in Africa to work as a volunteer in a trading post owned by Scottish-born Colonel MacGavin, who drives him to his store. Each man strains to maintain a hearty persona while imagining that the other resents him for representing values of another generation.

Frant stays in a room in the MacGavin's tiny house while serving in the trading post. The MacGavins treat him as a social inferior; however, as a white man, Frant is considered to be superior to his African customers, with whom he becomes friendly. In common with local Africans, Frant dislikes the MacGavins, who in turn dislike almost everybody. Frant's relatively jovial attitude increases sales, a fact for which the MacGavins are grudgingly grateful.

One day an attractive, young African woman named Seraphina enters the store and speaks with Frant. After she leaves, he fantasizes about sleeping with her and perhaps even marrying her. Because white people do not do such things with Africans, Frant worries about his desires and about the possible consequences of such a liaison. When MacGavin accuses him of being attracted to an African, Frant spews forth a diatribe against blacks so vitriolic that it frightens even himself.

After a long absence Seraphina returns with a huge snakeskin that she gives to Frant, explaining that she killed the snake herself. After Frant thanks her, he and Seraphina admit to liking each another, then Seraphina leaves. Frant hangs the snakeskin in his bedroom.

As Christmas approaches, the MacGavins invite Frant to accompany them as they visit other British residents in the region. Frant shocks them, however, by proposing to remain home alone. On Christmas Day he wanders about aimlessly before deciding to walk to Seraphina's village. Along his way he meets a young man named Umlilwana, who claims to be Seraphina's brother. Umlilwana tells him that he knows he and Seraphina like each other, adding in a friendly tone that such an attraction is not good because the races do not belong together. Frant is initially suspicious of Umlilwana's motives, but the young man's amiable manner persuades Frant to believe him when he says that Seraphina is away for two weeks visiting relatives.

After the holidays, heavy rains arrive and continue for weeks. In the middle of January Frant defies an impending storm by hiking to Seraphina's village. As he approaches her valley, he meets an elderly man who trades at MacGavin's store and who calls him "Child"—a diminution of "Child of Queen Victoria." Distraught, the man says that the storm has flooded the valley, drowning all its inhabitants. When Frant asks about Seraphina, who he believes to have been away visiting relatives, the man says that she never left the village and that Umlilwana was actually her fiancé. Frant considers running and plunging into the heavy waters to drown himself in the same torrent of water that swallowed Seraphina. Instead, he utters a single sob and heads home.

*Themes and Meanings*

William Plomer's "The Child of Queen Victoria" vividly illustrates race and class prejudices that dominated the historical period in which he sets his story. The tale's ironic theme suggests that human nature remains the sole constant in issues concerning social justice; despite the individual's desire to eradicate inequality, individual pride in righteousness will cause one to feel superior and therefore unequal to those whom one wishes to befriend. In addition, Plomer suggests that human nature, with all its flaws, resists redemption or transformation by man or woman alone. He further suggests that people are—by their very natures—destined to conquer one another, and implies that although such a truth is terrible, people can rise from their state of pathos and approach tragic nobility only when they fight what must be a losing battle against their natural, evil impulses.

At the beginning of the story, MacGavin and his wife appear pompous, prejudiced, and insensitive. Motivated by greed and insecurity, they must isolate themselves in their imagined superiority. Their notion that Africans are subhuman may be attributed to common white racial prejudices; however, their belittling of Frant—a fellow white man who gives them valuable free labor—proves that they have developed their prejudices even beyond those in vogue at the time.

Frant initially appears to be superior to the MacGavins in questioning the racial ideas with which he was reared. He is able to communicate honestly with Africans, who recognize his sincerity. One elderly African man, for example, pays Frant mock homage by calling him "Child of Queen Victoria." MacGavin cannot believe Frant allows an African to call him that, but Frant replies, "Why, he's old enough to be my grandfather!" His reply demonstrates his respect for both his elders and for people of another race—a deference that MacGavin lacks. Frant's sincerity diminishes, however, as he begins congratulating himself for his own open-mindedness. By catering to his own hubris, his selfless motives turn selfish and self-conscious, and he comes to regard himself as superior to those people he claims to respect.

Frant first sees Seraphina as a sylph-like woman surrounded by light, a vision of an angel. Their conversation is brief and mysterious, so that the image that stays with Frant is ethereal. Although MacGavin is used to having his way with African women who patronize his store, Frant is neither so boorish nor so indiscriminate. His attraction is to Seraphina alone, a woman named by a Christian missionary who said that God chose her identity. It is no coincidence that Seraphina means snakelike, for she is to Frant as the serpent is to Adam and Eve in the Garden of Eden.

Frant dares contemplating escape from the mold in which his Victorian era has cast him by turning his back on traditional attitudes and following his inherent instincts for freedom, fun, and adventure. In his diatribe to MacGavin condemning all blacks, he protests too much; it is not Frant, but his training speaking. His anger is toward the Victorian beliefs that still trap him, not toward blacks, as he pretends. Seraphina lures Frant with a real snakeskin, symbolic of the snake that taunts Eve in the Garden of Eden.

Frant's Christmas Day romp in the MacGavin's garden parallels his state of mind: He determines to renounce the societal prejudices that daunt him and to pursue his happiness—Seraphina—into a paradisiacal new era. His naïveté causes him to trust Umlilwana, just as Adam trusted Eve, and Frant returns home to brood while building tropical storms foreshadow his fate.

What Frant learns too late is that Umlilwana has lied to him, and Umlilwana's lie has shaped his sorrowful, if wiser, future. The fact that Umlilwana, an African, lies is important, as it underscores Plomer's point that all peoples are equal in their self-serving human natures. Frant wants to throw himself into the waters that drowned Seraphina. Against his will, his Victorian upbringing dominates his romantic nature, and as a dutiful representative of Everyman of his era, he turns back toward a life in which he is doomed to live as a true child of Queen Victoria.

*Style and Technique*

Plomer's choice of an omniscient narrator who reports primarily in the third person but occasionally speaks with the first-person "we" and the second-person "you" reinforces the story's theme by emphasizing that events happening to others are like those that occur in the lives of all human beings. The author avoids using the first-person "I," which would cause the reader to disassociate from experiences that would thereby seem personal instead of universal.

The tale's ironic tone mimics its ironic message. For example, Plomer writes, "We hear a great deal about sex nowadays; it is possible to overestimate its importance, because there are always people who pay it little attention or who apparently manage, like Sir Isaac Newton, to get along, without giving it a thought. Frant came of a susceptible family." The author's subtle-yet-constant humor acts as an essential lubricant to the story's somber theme.

Plomer's frequent allusions couched in figurative language define and enhance his style. Although his similes and metaphors foreshadow forthcoming events, they also personify emotions and conditions so the intangible becomes tangible and so the reader can see, touch, taste, hear, and smell what the people of Plomer's world feel. When Frant initially contemplates his African landscape, at first sight it seems, "like so many African landscapes, a happy mixture of the pastoral and the magnificent, but those who lived under its influence came to feel gradually a mingled sense of uneasiness and sorrow, so that what at first seemed grand became indifferent or menacing." Those sunny hills seem to "be possessed by a spirit that nursed a grievance." Similarly, when Frant congratulates himself for being better than the white people around him, Plomer writes that this attitude "shut him up in a cell of his own (as it were) closely barred with high principles."

*L. Elisabeth Beattie*

# THE CHILDHOOD OF LUVERS

*Author:* Boris Pasternak (1890-1960)
*Type of plot:* Coming of age
*Time of plot:* The early twentieth century
*Locale:* Perm and Ekaterinburg (modern Sverdlovsk), Russia
*First published:* "Detstvo Lyuvers," 1922 (English translation, 1945)

> *Principal characters:*
> ZHENIA LUVERS, a young girl
> MR. LUVERS, her father
> MRS. LUVERS, her mother
> LIZA DEFENDOVA, her friend, a neighbor girl
> SEREZHA, her brother
> DIKIKH, one of her tutors
> TSVETKOV, a friend of Dikikh

*The Story*

Zhenia Luvers's first memories are of Perm, a gloomy northern city not far removed from a state of nature: Bearskin rugs are made from local animals; during the spring, weeds sprout and trees bud overnight; ice floes pass by on the river. Mr. Luvers manages a mine and spends little time with his children. Occasionally he is seen playing cards or discussing his dealings with factory owners. A series of governesses tend to Zhenia. She is educated first by an Englishwoman she scarcely remembers and then by a French tutor who burdens her with the conjugation of difficult verbs. When Zhenia is thirteen, she feels strangely ill and inadvertently leaves bloodstains on a bearskin rug and on her clothes. She takes the maid's powder and attempts to efface the red marks, and a family confrontation takes place. Mrs. Luvers upbraids Zhenia at first and in the end dismisses the Frenchwoman. Subsequently, and quite more insistently than for previous visits, her mother arranges for a doctor to examine Zhenia. Some time later, and quite to her surprise, Zhenia learns that the family will move southeast to a city beyond the Urals.

At first, Zhenia is enchanted with her new surroundings, which she persistently regards as "Asian." Ekaterinburg is clear, clean, and spacious. The exotic and the commonplace mingle easily. Zhenia is entranced by Tatar children from the region; she makes friends with a local girl, Liza Defendova. When she is transferred from the city's lycee and is given private lessons at home, Zhenia is more upset than her friend that they will no longer meet in school. Zhenia's lessons do not always come easily— good-naturedly, she spells some words according to her own lights, and she confuses some terms for units of weight and measure. Her tutor, who has the improbable surname Dikikh, amuses her, and she is intrigued by his friend Tsvetkov, who walks with a limp. She competes half-seriously with her brother, Serezha, but fears that he may be steadily surpassing her in strength and endurance.

That autumn and winter are fixed in her mind more specifically and clearly than past changes of season; the days seem colder and darker than during previous years. Zhenia is aware that her mother does not leave the house, and rumors are afloat that she is pregnant. One night, as she lies in bed, Zhenia hears a scream and then another, rending, howling cries, and then she nearly runs into her father in the hallway. Hasty, disjointed questions and commands are exchanged among members of the family. Zhenia's intuition seems confirmed: Her mother has given birth again. Then she falls asleep and has some trouble convincing herself that she has not dreamed it all. The next day she is sent to stay with the Defendovs; on her way out Zhenia notices that, amid jumbled pots, pans, medical supplies, and towels, her mother lies in bed and is still moaning. While at the neighbors, Zhenia asks Liza Defendova whether she can have babies, and she is reassured when Liza tells her that all girls can.

After several weeks Zhenia returns home and resumes her lessons; she learns what has actually happened from the doctor and her tutor. One night, her mother and father were returning from the theater when their stallion inexplicably reared up and trampled a bypasser to death. The mother suffered what—in the doctor's euphemistic expression—was a "nervous upset." Zhenia infers that her little baby brother was born dead; the doctor can only confirm her worst fears. Dikikh, the tutor, finds Zhenia strangely changed; he declares that he too has lost a friend. Intuitively Zhenia associates Tsvetkov, or someone like him, with the accident outside the theater; she screams as Dikikh sets forth his recollections of that tragic evening. Later the tutor, who seemingly has accepted his friend's death, is taken aback at Zhenia's "excessive sensitivity." She seems under the power of impressions that cannot be described precisely in words. Zhenia's schoolbook must be put back on the shelf to await another day.

*Themes and Meanings*

The events of young Zhenia's life, both insubstantial and momentous, point to her development from a young girl to an adult woman. Largely this process takes her unawares: Continuous throbbing headaches and inexplicable effusions of blood beset her at the onset of sexual maturity. Transformation is also suggested, in quite another sense, by transportation beyond the Urals. Zhenia feels that she has reached a continental divide where much is similar, but the atmosphere seems changed somehow. The beginning of autumn seems more distinct than at other times she can recall. At one point she begins to use perfume; she becomes aware of physical differences between herself and boys her age.

Many transitions she grasps half-consciously and in passing: Her awareness of life's deeper concerns mingles with poignant everyday impressions that are still deeply felt. Her father is a remote figure and offers little in the way of guidance or understanding. Some basic issues she realizes only imperfectly and intuitively. Her mother's pregnancy, and the expectations and agonies of childbirth, are brought home to her only at a distance; only then does she understand that she, and other girls she knows, eventually will have babies of their own. During her discussions with Liza Defendova, she finds the other girl's knowledge remarkable and is shocked at the easy vulgarity with which Liza discusses procreation. The tragic end of life is revealed to Zhenia in broken, circuitous statements from the family doctor and her teacher: They cannot hold back news of the family's loss, or of the death of Dikikh's friend. Zhenia is at an awkward age: She can comprehend the beginning and end of life, but she cannot still her screams and uncontrollable outbursts of tears. She seems peculiarly sensitive to sorrow and suffering. The drama of her approaching adulthood seems darker and more profound because her character is still forming; she remains childlike in some respects even as in other ways physical and emotional maturity overtakes her.

*Style and Technique*

Young Zhenia's life and thoughts are presented in a rich, poetic language that, even for the most valiant and gifted translator, eludes precise rendition. The work originally was intended to be the opening portion of a novel, and it is often presented on its own as a story. The plot is uncomplicated and sometimes appears fragmented. The author tarries at some passages, whereas elsewhere time goes by unnoticed. The story is told in the third person but draws the reader directly into the world of feeling and experience that envelops young Zhenia. There are a few interventions in the narrative on the part of the author, mostly to trace the family's movements or to supply essential facts about their work or education.

Much of the work records Zhenia's own sensations and impressions of the world around her, some of which are imprinted most vividly on her memory. She recalls in detail lush, thick bearskin carpets of different colors. Mundane but discrete and clearly defined objects—budding trees, or ice floes on the river—are closely described and seem set in counterpoint to the more enduring transformations engulfing her. Climatic conditions, which foreshadow stages of Zhenia's own development, are recorded with a fine sense of feeling and atmosphere. Sometimes her French lessons, the chills of early spring, and throbbing headaches are inchoately intertwined. Perceptions that often seem scattered and kaleidoscopic during the first part of the story, which presents the girl's earliest memories, become more specific and lucid as Zhenia gains in maturity. Whole, connected conversations and episodes are set down, and Zhenia's view of the world takes on a somewhat sharper, clearer focus. Dikikh, the tutor, for example, is described more specifically and at greater length than any comparable characters from the first section of the work. All the while Zhenia still seems under the spell of powerful emotional forces; she perceives people and events at times as wordless impressions, producing sudden uncontrollable impulses that accompany her own unsteady but oncoming passage into adulthoood.

*J. R. Broadus*

# CHILDREN OF STRIKERS

*Author:* Fred Chappell (1936-    )
*Type of plot:* Social realism
*Time of plot:* The late twentieth century
*Locale:* A mill village in the South
*First published:* 1980

> *Principal characters:*
> A TWELVE-YEAR-OLD GIRL
> A YOUNGER BOY, her companion

## The Story

On a gray day, two poor children trudge along a riverbank path that leads away from their homes in Fiberville, a cluster of bungalows named for the paper mill where the adults work. The girl occasionally picks up pieces of trash from the ground and examines them. When the boy sees her put something in her pocket, he insists on seeing it. She refuses, however, and when he dashes at her, she slaps him. They walk on.

Eventually, the girl gives her companion a hint. She has found a baby's foot, she says. Excited, the boy begins to speculate about how the foot was cut off of the baby. Perhaps, he thinks, some girl was forced by a boyfriend to kill her baby and cut it up. Now that the girl has the boy's interest aroused, she tries to strike a bargain with him and asks what he will give her if she shows him her find. The boy admits that he does not have anything to offer. He suggests that she does not either and that she is making up her story about the baby's foot.

To prove the boy wrong, the girl shows him the foot. When the boy realizes that the foot belonged to a doll, not a real baby, he angrily knocks it out of her hand. After the girl picks it up again, the children examine it together, trying to guess why someone would mutilate a doll in this way. The cut is so clean that the boy insists that the act was carefully planned—not the result of an impulse—so that it must have been performed by an adult. With evident delight, he tries to imagine what tool was used—a knife or a meat cleaver—and he again insists that an adult was involved. Finally, the girl agrees with him.

Turning back toward the settlement, the children consider other mysteries in their lives, particularly their parents' unhappiness and the presence of angry outsiders in the neighborhood. Although they do not understand exactly what is happening in Fiberville, the children sense that the same kind of anger that would cause a man to cut off a doll's foot has now taken control of their families and their community.

## Themes and Meanings

At first glance, Fred Chappell's "Children of Strikers" may seem to be simply a story about violence. The central incident in the plot is the discovery of an amputated foot; although the foot belonged to a doll, not a person, the children see it as evidence of an unknown adult's fury. Moreover, the final paragraph describes the tension among labor strikers and leaves the impression that some violent action is inevitable. Such an interpretation, however, is too limited. This work is actually intended to demonstrate what modern industrial society does to nature and to human nature.

Chappell begins his story by showing how the paper mill has affected the local environment. The river has a noxious stench, the result of chemicals it collects when it flows through the mill. Its banks are black and covered with debris. How this pollution may have affected the health of the workers who live below the mill can only be guessed. Clearly this rape of the environment is not a new development, as the children do not even notice the foul odor. Ironically, to them the ruined river is a source of pleasure; the trash that it flings on the banks is their treasure trove.

Just as the mill owners are indifferent to nature, it is hardly surprising that they have no interest in the welfare of their workers. They have callously placed the workers' houses downriver from the polluting mill, and have obviously forgotten about them. The workers' cottages are not only small, they are also shabby and ill kept. Although the workers' misery has been intensified by their strike, it seems probable that they were driven to strike out of desperation. One can see evidence of the degree to which the workers were exploited in the pitiable condition of their children. The girl's sweater is so thin that it does not begin to keep her warm. Furthermore, both children look unhealthy, the boy pale and pasty, the girl sallow. The fact that they do not run, as one would expect children to do, but merely shuffle along the path, is further proof that they are malnourished.

Even more devastating than the physical results of grinding poverty is its emotional legacy. Young as she is, the girl has already surrendered to despair. When she looks ahead, the author reports, she sees only day after day of the same kind of misery. She has no dreams; her future holds no possibility of joy.

It is, of course, ironic that the macabre discovery of a baby's foot should bring the children brief pleasure. The primary significance of this central incident, however, can be seen in the way they react to their find. The girl's first impulse is to keep it from the boy, out of pure meanness; his response is to try to seize it. When she slaps him, he is not surprised. There are other telling details. When his imagination cuts loose, the boy speculates about a young mother forced to kill her unwanted baby. After he learns that the foot belonged to a doll, he invents another scenario for murder. Obviously, violence is part of the context of their lives.

When the author has the children think about the atmosphere in their homes in the last paragraph, he suggests an explanation for the violent impulses that he has recorded. To assume, however, that the strike is what brings about violence would be to miss the point of the story. If violence comes, it will be as a direct result not of the workers' protest but of the factory owners' systematic abuse of their employees and their contempt for the natural environment. There is nothing perfunctory about Chappell's choice of a title for his story. The plight of the two children does not only explain the reason for the strike; it also constitutes an indictment of twentieth century industrial society, which cares for nothing but production and profit.

*Style and Technique*

In writing, "Children of Strikers," Chappell keeps a considerable distance between himself and his subject. As an objective observer, he describes the landscape and the appearance of the children, and he continues to play this part as he reports their actions and their conversations. Even when he reveals their thoughts, as in the poignant passage when the girl looks into her dismal future, Chappell refrains from making the kind of comment that one might expect from an omniscient narrator. By thus restraining himself, he avoids the possibility of becoming sentimental or of showing his own feelings about such injustice. By simply outlining the situation and permitting readers to draw their own conclusions, he makes the story far more effective.

Although self-effacing, the author does not absent himself from his story. It is his voice that provides all the descriptions of the river, Fibertown with the factory towering over it, and of the children themselves. Without such details—which the children could scarcely be expected to provide—readers would have an incomplete picture. Moreover, the very difference between the perceptions of the adult observer and those of the inexperienced children emphasizes the latters' vulnerability. For example, the author reveals that the polluted river has a terrible odor. This in itself is bad enough, but when he goes on to say that the children are hardly aware of the smell, it is evident that they have lived with it so long that they simply take it for granted. They are too innocent to realize that they are being victimized.

Chappell's skill in juggling voices is also evident in his conclusion. Here he uses his own heightened lyrical style to reveal feelings that the children cannot express. Not until the final sentence, however, does Chappell finally make what might be considered an authorial comment, but even then the poetic quality of his prose leaves the words open to interpretation. Like the children themselves, Chappell's readers are left in a world that seems to be ruled by darkness.

*Rosemary M. Canfield Reisman*

# CHILDREN ON THEIR BIRTHDAYS

*Author:* Truman Capote (Truman Streckfus Persons, 1924-1984)
*Type of plot:* Fantasy
*Time of plot:* The 1940's
*Locale:* Alabama
*First published:* 1948

*Principal characters:*
MISS LILY JANE BOBBIT, a precocious, ambitious, ten-year-old girl
BILLY BOB, the boy next door
PREACHER STAR, his friend
ROSALBA CAT, a black girl befriended by Miss Bobbit

## The Story

Late one summer afternoon, an unusual-looking young girl, Miss Lily Jane Bobbit, arrives with her mother in a small, unidentified town in Alabama. The bus on which they arrive, the narrator of the story states in the opening lines, is the same one that will run over Miss Bobbit a year later as she prepares to move on, in pursuit of her dream of Hollywood stardom. Why she has chosen to settle briefly in this southern town is never revealed, and very little information about her earlier experiences is given. As for her family, her father is in a penitentiary in Tennessee; her mother is a strangely silent woman. Miss Bobbit herself, from first to last, remains an enigma, a funny, delightful, not real child-woman.

The particular day of her arrival in front of the house of a boy named Billy Bob is important: Billy Bob, his friends, his mother, and his cousin, Mr. C., the narrator of the story, are celebrating Billy Bob's birthday. Offered some of the party fare, Miss Bobbit refuses it in an adult fashion. Simultaneously little girl and adult, she is obviously different from any ordinary child. In many ways her conversation and behavior seem grown-up. Her face is made up as if she were a mature woman, although she is wearing a child's party dress. Both her dress and the occasion of Billy Bob's party symbolize Miss Bobbit's dream of what life should be: a world of beauty and happiness that is like a birthday party, particularly like children on their birthdays. Driven by her longings, she cannot take the time to be a child. She focuses all of her energy on the preparation for a dazzling existence in a place that she believes will turn her vision into reality.

During the year that she lives in a boardinghouse next door to Billy Bob and his family, Miss Bobbit becomes something of a celebrity because of her appearance, her mannerisms, and her behavior. Girls constantly walk past her house to catch glimpses of the elegant rival who keeps the boys fighting over her. Billy Bob and Preacher Star, competitors for her unavailable affection, wear themselves out trying to serve her. Rosalba Cat, the black girl whom she makes her "sister," brings further attention to her.

No matter what people think, Miss Bobbit always does as she chooses. She chooses not to go to church or school, in spite of community pressure. Neither is for her, she maintains, because her primary interest is the advancement of her career. In pursuit of her dreams of fame, she single-mindedly devotes herself to training for films. She practices her dancing, reads a dictionary, and dresses in one elegant outfit after another, made for her by her unobtrusive mother. To raise money for her travels, Miss Bobbit goes into business as an agent for magazines, putting Billy Bob and Preacher to work for her.

Miss Bobbit seems to be on her way to Hollywood, if not to the stardom that she assures her friends she will have, after she wins an amateur contest sponsored by a con man. Undaunted by the disappearance of the man who awarded her first prize—a screen test—and who also enticed a considerable number of young men to pay large sums of money in return for the promise of romantic-sounding jobs, Miss Bobbit shows her strength and ingenuity: She succeeds in tracking him down and getting the money restored. Her powers of persuasion prove to be as strong as her will when she convinces those same young men to invest their money in her future by sending her off to Hollywood.

However, Miss Bobbit is not destined to fulfill her heart's desire. As she rushes across the street to claim the roses that her two ardent admirers have picked for her, she is killed by the bus that delivered her to the town the summer before, when those same rose bushes were in bloom.

*Themes and Meanings*

Although the setting of the story is realistic, little else is. Miss Bobbit is a fantasy creature, unlike any ten-year-old girl who has ever existed. In her, Truman Capote created a type of child who reflected much of what he believed that children longed to be: beautiful, clever, and loved. Both in statements about his own childhood and in his fiction he brooded over the sadness and disappointments that children suffer. Happiness is evanescent: Most of the children of his stories begin their years in innocence and pleasure. Then the blow falls, usually with the loss of a much-loved person. However, his portrait of Miss Lily Jane Bobbit differs from the others in a very significant way: Like them, she lives with illusions and impossible dreams, but unlike the others, she dies before her hopes are vanquished.

Miss Bobbit is the forerunner of the more famous Holly Golightly of Capote's *Breakfast at Tiffany's* (1958). Miss Bobbit and Holly are restless females, with longings that will never be fulfilled. Each speaks of living in the sky, a metaphor that suggests both freedom and happiness but which also connotes separation from other people. Though the later story contains many of the same themes as the earlier one, it is ultimately more melancholy, for in it the heroine's dreams are blighted.

Capote portrayed a series of orphan characters, of whom Miss Bobbit is one, even though both of her parents are alive. She never hears from her imprisoned father, and her mother seems to play so small a role in her life that Miss Bobbit gives the impression of being completely responsible for herself. Furthermore, whatever attachments she forms are temporary, because she always plans and longs to move on. Thus, she is seen as a lone—though not lonely—and isolated figure, in spite of her popularity.

Capote often drew these "parentless" children as wanderers, seekers for a world unlike the one that they have known. Miss Bobbit has no home, no place (ironically, in a region that prides itself on place). Without roots, she imagines that she will gain both a home and glory once she crosses Hollywood's golden threshold.

Capote himself, as a boy, dreamed of becoming a famous tap dancer, a dream never realized, yet never forgotten. In this and other stories he reminds his readers, through his fantasy children, of the longings that all children have to be or do something extraordinary. The recognition that such yearnings cannot be fulfilled is a significant part of the impact of this story on readers, a reminder that all memories of childhood are a mixture of happiness and sadness. Miss Lily Jane Bobbit dies without achieving her desires, but she also dies before the disappointments and disillusionments of adulthood can touch her.

## Style and Technique

Here, as in a number of other stories, Capote has blended humor and nostalgia. Much that is humorous in his fiction comes through his variation of the "tall tale," that is, the exaggeration of details in both plot and character. With only a few exceptions, the characters in the story have humorous qualities. One comic episode follows another: Miss Bobbit's quaint mixture of French and English; her platonic massage of Billy Bob; the war that she and Rosalba conduct against the dogs of the town. The behavior of the boys is equally funny as they attempt to gain the love of the wondrous Miss Lily Jane Bobbit.

The comedy, though an integral part of the story, is finally less important than the sweet-sadness, the nostalgic element in the telling of the tale. Through the use of memory, the narrator captures, as if in a bottle or a glass, the perfect moment, the brief, lost world of childhood. However, at the same time that the past is caught forever, there is the counterpoint of the transient images, which add both joyfulness and melancholy to the story.

Typical of Capote's imagistic style, light and color flicker everywhere. At nightfall, birds swoop, fireflies dart among the leaves, and the swift movements and brief moments of light in darkness becoming symbolic of Miss Bobbit herself. The irises bloom only briefly. The scent of roses, sweet shrub, and wisteria perfumes the air. For a time it is as though summer will never end. Furthermore, the story is a summer story; in spite of the fact that a year passes, other seasons seem unimportant.

Miss Bobbit arrives in summer and dies at the same time the following year. Winter, symbolic of time and age, never touches her. Dressed in white as she runs toward her death, she has a Communion look, an image that captures purity and innocence in endless time. A fine mist of rain is falling as she moves joyfully toward twin bouquets of yellow roses, the rain the final emblem of nostalgia and irredeemable time.

*Helen S. Garson*

# THE CHILDREN'S CAMPAIGN

*Author:* Pär Lagerkvist (1891-1974)
*Type of plot:* Satire
*Time of plot:* 1978
*Locale:* An anonymous country
*First published:* "Det lilla falttget," 1935 (English translation, 1954)

> *Principal characters:*
> THE CHILDREN, who compose an army in a militaristic nation
> THE ADULTS, who compose the army and the civilian population
> of a neighboring country

## The Story

At the beginning of "The Children's Campaign," the reader is introduced to a nationalistic and militant society, in which children play an integral role in the country's defense. The children between the ages of six and fourteen constitute a highly respected and beloved children's army, which they command, train, and organize without adult intervention. The boys serve in the army corps, and the girls are allowed to volunteer as nurses.

An apparently inferior country insults, in some manner, this more powerful, unified nation, and the children's army receives permission to retaliate by launching an attack, which begins in the spring of that year.

As war is declared, the army of youths demonstrates its efficiency: Within a day, it is mobilized and ready to defend its country's honor. After a patriotic speech by the twelve-year-old commander in chief, the troops leave for the offending country, where their campaign begins victoriously.

By the summer, the children have nearly reached the enemy's capital, having won many battles and sustained comparatively few losses. Their heroism and discipline and their dedication to their mission are admired at home, where the media devotes specified times of day for reports on the progress of the popular war.

The bravery of the children is chronicled in detail: They defy death and bodily injury, and not a complaint is recorded. Moreover, the children's army is superior to the army of the enemy—a nonmilitaristic nation—in armed combat, military tactics, and troop discipline; only the physical size of the children prevents success in hand-to-hand combat and in the effective pursuit of defeated enemy forces.

As the strengths and weaknesses of the two armies are compared, it is clear that the children have important advantages: more soldiers, better organization and command, and superior skills and training. The enemy army's advantage is mainly the larger size of its soldiers, although the army's military skills do improve somewhat as the war continues.

Just before autumn, a simultaneous offensive strike results in a tragic battle in which the troops on both sides are annihilated. This battle indicates a stalemate because after it, neither army can truthfully declare victory, although both do. Both armies are forced to regroup and continue maneuvers from trenches, while the winter rains prevent further progress.

During this time, the morale of the children's army is decidedly higher than that of the enemy. The children endure great hardships, but not a complaint is uttered. Even during Christmas, the children remain dedicated to their cause, launching several attacks.

The stalemate continues until spring, when offensives are begun in preparation for the decisive battle. At one historic point in the war, the enemy discovers a weakness in the children's formation, enabling them to force a retreat of the children's army. The children, however, are able to turn this event to full advantage by encircling the advancing enemy and pressing for victory from all sides.

As the children gain the enemy's capital, the war is declared over, the children return home to a victory parade, and the troops are dismissed. A full account of the war is entered in the nation's annals, and the date of victory is to be commemorated forever after.

### Themes and Meanings

Themes of political and social nature intertwine in "The Children's Campaign" to issue a warning concerning the direction of human nature and society. Published before World War II, the story depicts a world obsessed by war, a world in which even war's tragedies are glorified.

In this setting, war is second nature, even to children. The prevailing image of childhood—innocent and free of the responsibilities of adult life—is quickly shattered as the fantasies of war games are replaced by the realities of military exercises. Indeed, these children need no adult supervision; they are proficient, exacting, and successful. Not only do they excel at military maneuvers but also they are well adapted to the physical hardships of army life. Although forced to live in mud-filled trenches during the winter months, they nevertheless "felt at home":

> Filthy and lousy, they lived there in the darkness as though they had never done anything else. With the adaptability of children they quickly got into the way of it. . . . When one saw them in their small gray uniforms, which were caked thick with mud, and their small gas masks, one could easily think they had been born to this existence.

In this subtle way, the author recalls images of boys at play in mud, sleet, or snow—in short, any activity in which the dirt becomes part of their youthful attire.

The war succeeds in seizing childhood away from the army of youths; "The war had hardened and developed them, made them men." However, the reader is often reminded that, despite their endeavors, these are still children; there are frequent references to their small size, an account of their love of chocolate, and a reference to an unhappy soldier, homesick at Christmastime, who is eventually court-martialed and shot.

The complex role of war in society is examined as the account of the campaign unfolds. War is viewed as the natural outlet for human cruelty, in which rules and regulations provide the acceptable manner for displaying aggressive tendencies. The enemy, a nonmilitaristic nation, is often denounced for its ignorance of the proprieties of war, an ignorance that leads its civilians to resort to acts of atrocity against the children. It must be remembered that the offense committed by the enemy is never revealed; its nature is ambiguous. One is told merely that the country has "behaved in a high-handed and unseemly way toward its powerful neighbor." Clearly, this is not an act of military provocation or overt aggression, yet the offended country is quick to rally its forces and launch a full-scale war.

In its final, senseless devotion to war's uncivilized accomplishments, the society in "The Children's Campaign" proves hungry enough for the spoils of war to sacrifice its most precious commodity: its children. Ultimately, one must question the high price of nationalism and the devotion to its ideals.

*Style and Technique*

The sociopolitical messages of "The Children's Campaign" are expressed in a deliberately understated style. Through straight narrative that chronicles both the military and the personal aspects of the campaign, the author satirizes war.

From the opening line ("Even the children at that time received military training . . . "), the reader is thrust immediately and forcefully into a hostile environment. There is no gradual introduction to the times or reasons offered for its nature; rather, the lack of alternatives is as arbitrary, as inevitable, as war itself.

War is, as are many highly serious topics, a subject that lends itself effectively to humor. In fact, the more intense, the more horrific, the effects of war are, the more absurd they appear. The story's imagery lends itself to this idea. The literary implications of spring—those of renewal, rebirth, the celebration of life—are recalled in a paradoxical manner: It is spring when the children's army first sets out to wield its destructive hand and, later, when the greatest loss of life is incurred.

Another image—that of the youths' size—becomes especially striking during battle descriptions, where the children are "so small . . . it was possible . . . to spit several of them on the bayonet at once." At other times, they are swarms of "little fiends," scurrying "over one and in between one's legs."

The story's most satiric description, indeed, accentuates childhood's ultimate representation: A female enemy civilian turns a child-lieutenant over her knee and gives him a spanking, declaring that he should be at home with his mother. The boy is consequently sent home to his family and forced to move with them to an obscure area of the country.

Although the language of "The Children's Campaign" is objective, the story nevertheless succeeds in re-creating individual beliefs and moral convictions concerning the polarities of human nature. The reader ends the narrative sadly recognizing the outlines of the familiar world in the grotesque world of this fable.

*Shelly Usen*

# A CHILD'S DRAWINGS

*Author:* Varlam Shalamov (1907-1982)
*Type of plot:* Social realism
*Time of plot:* The mid-1930's to the mid-1950's
*Locale:* A forced-labor camp in the Kolyma region of northeastern Siberia
*First published:* "Detskie kartinki," 1978 (English translation, 1980)

> *Principal characters:*
> THE NARRATOR, a political prisoner in one of Stalin's work camps
> TWO OTHER POLITICAL PRISONERS, members of his brigade

## *The Story*

The story begins as the routine day begins. The narrator, a nameless political pris-oner in a nameless Kolyma labor camp, is sent out with the other prisoners for the day's work. There is no checklist for the prisoners; they are simply lined up by fives so that the guards have an easy time of counting and multiplying. Today the narrator's brigade has an easy job—sawing wood with a circular saw, a task that usually falls to a more privileged prisoner group, the common criminals. The saw, like the prisoners, moves slowly, growling in the bitter cold of the far North. The third prisoner assigned to the woodpile works separately, splitting the brittle, frozen larch logs that fall apart easily, despite the fact that he can barely wield the hatchet.

The brigade has a few minutes of free time after stacking the wood because their guard has gone indoors to warm up and they have to wait for the remaining brigades to finish and gather for the collective march back to camp. They take advantage of the break to comb through a nearby garbage pile, a heap of trash they have been eyeing all day long. Picking through one layer after another, they collect the scraps and castoffs that may mean survival for another day—discarded socks, the odd crust of bread, left-over cutlets frozen hard.

The narrator keeps scratching because he alone of the three has not yet found any-thing useful. He turns up something he has not seen in years—a child's drawing tablet, filled with scenes from all four of Kolyma's cold seasons. As he begins flipping the pages, he recalls his own childhood and his own drawings of fantastic folk heroes and magical animals. The recollections are vivid—his white paint box, the kerosene lamp on the kitchen table, the drawings themselves. He remembers his Ivan-Tsarevich, Prince Ivan, loping through the forest astride his trusty gray wolf, smoke rising in a curlicue, birds like check marks. The more vivid his own recollection, the more acute the realization that his own childhood is gone and that he will find no trace of it in this child's drawings.

The world in this child's tablet is one of wooden fences and wooden walls, all iden-tical, all yellow ocher: fences, barbed wire, sentry boxes, guard towers, armed guards. The purity and brightness of the young artist's colors remind the narrator of a local

legend—that God created the taiga when he was still young, before he learned to create intricate designs or a variety of birds and beasts. When he grew up and learned
these things, he buried his stark taiga world in snow and left for the south.

The narrator concentrates on a winter scene, a northern hunt. Here Ivan-Tsarevich
wears a military-issue fur hat with earflaps, a thick sheepskin coat and a rifle at
his back. A German shepherd strains at the leash. The narrator realizes that the only
world this child knows or will ever recall is one where humans hunt one another and
where life is circumscribed by yellow buildings, wire fences, guards with guns, and
blue sky.

Another prisoner breaks the narrator's reverie. He tests the notebook paper, then
tosses it back onto the pile, remarking that newspaper works better for rolling cigarettes.

*Themes and Meanings*

"Nature in the north is not faceless, not indifferent—it is in league with those who
sent us here." Varlam Shalamov's narrator knows from experience that the fresh air regime of the Kolyma camps is more likely to kill a prisoner than save him, especially
because that prisoner is ill-clothed, ill-treated, overworked, and underfed.

Of all the "islands" in the Gulag Archipelago, the Kolyma camps were the most
frightful: the final, icy grave for millions of Joseph Stalin's victims. Barely populated
before the 1930's, this far corner of Siberia was "developed" for gold production in
order to accommodate the vast numbers of political prisoners arrested during the
purges. If the politicals provided the state with some gold, or lead, or furs, or fish before giving in to starvation, scurvy, dystrophy, or suicide—so much the better. Technically fiction, Shalamov's *Kolymskie rasskazy* (1978; *Kolyma Tales*, 1980) are both a
document and a testament.

"A Child's Drawings" bears witness to the fact that those inside the barracks and
barbed wire were not the only victims of Kolyma. As the narrator leafs through the
stiffened pages of the discarded notebook and remembers his own childhood, his remembrances are happy ones; although Russian folktales are far from always benign,
Ivan-Tsarevich, when in trouble, can call on a host of animal allies. The natural world,
in exchange for his kindness, comes to his aid—rocks, trees, rivers, winds alike. His
own native goodness, cleverness, and innocence, along with the magic provided him,
defeat evil sorcerers and wicked witches and, in the end, he is rewarded with prosperity and long life.

What the narrator experiences is not simply nostalgia for his own childhood, but
fear at the ominous vision that has replaced his own, and perhaps everyone's. This
child's vision is disturbing both in what it has and what it lacks: the bright primary
colors and triangle-larches, stark and uncompromising whatever the season, humankind's buildings repeated in the same color, surrounded by the same barbed wire—
nature and humankind, both hostile. Most frightening of all is Prince Ivan's transformation from the underdog hero to the pursuer and predator—this child's Ivan-
Tsarevich is on a hunt not for a fierce bear or shape-changing wizard but for men.

Nowhere in these drawings does the narrator find himself, the prisoner, for whom and by whom all these monotonous structures, these fences and towers, have been built. The hunt shows the pursuit but not the prey. In this child's world, the prisoners are simply not there—absent from his world as they are absent from the world of their own pasts—not yet dead but already gone.

## Style and Technique

Shalamov's semiautobiographical narrator is an insider, a veteran of camp life, an observer rather than an active participant. In this story, too, his only "act" is contemplative, when he stops digging through the trash heap for anything edible or useful and looks over the notebook. It is left to a fellow prisoner to judge the paper unfit for rolling cigarettes and toss the notebook back on the heap. Though not above the scene, this narrator is removed from it by his own reticence in act and speech.

What gives this story—and the rest of the *Kolyma Tales*—their impact is the dissonance between the unbelievable, nightmare absurdity of the labor camps and the narrator's calm reportage. He avoids dramatization, embellishment, sentimentality, even sympathy. He may explain, or clarify, but he never comments. What he leaves out reveals more than any description ever could.

For example, the story begins with a brief description of camp routine. The narrator tells the reader that the prisoners are marched out in fives to make counting easier because even the prisoner's patience wears thin if he has to wait in the cold. End of description. What the reader is left to figure out for himself is the ignorance and stupidity of those in control, and that the fear of violence—even violence by starving wrecks of men—controls the controllers.

The narrator's impartiality extends to himself as he relates how he systematically rummages through the garbage, envious of his companions' success in scavenging. His tone does not change when he describes his own reaction to the child's notebook: material boon, spiritual loss—seemingly equal value, redefined, redrawn by Kolyma.

The suggestive legend of the taiga god who discards his own crude, childish creation, covers it with snow and leaves forever, ends with a disclaimer—"So goes the legend." Once again, the narrator makes no connections, and the reader must link the god's abandoned, snow-covered world, the narrator's lost childhood, and the Kolyma child's tablet, coated with frost as soon as it returns to the garbage heap.

*Jane Ann Miller*

# CHILDYBAWN

*Author:* Seán O'Faoláin (John Francis Whelan, 1900-1991)
*Type of plot:* Domestic realism
*Time of plot:* Probably twentieth century
*Locale:* Ireland
*First published:* 1957

> *Principal characters:*
> BENJY SPILLANE, a forty-one-year-old bachelor who lives with
>     his mother
> MRS. SPILLANE, his apparently widowed mother
> ANGELA, his girlfriend, a fellow bank employee

*The Story*

Mrs. Spillane has received an anonymous letter telling her that her middle-aged bachelor son has been romantically involved for years with a young woman at the bank where he works. Horrified, she broods for a few weeks before questioning Benjy indirectly, by suggesting that a gossipy friend has implied that he is planning to marry someone. When he scoffs at her suggestion, she is placated and relieved. After Benjy's spring vacation in France, however, his mother receives another anonymous letter, informing her that the young lady at the bank, Angela, went to France with him. Unwilling to confront Benjy directly, she begins steaming open his letters until she finally finds one from Angela that confirms her worst fears.

Mrs. Spillane turns to a priest for guidance but is miffed when he only suggests that she pray for Benjy's early marriage. Certain that that idea would appeal no more to Benjy than it does to her, she takes another tack, attempting to involve Benjy in her devotion to Saint Monica, mother of the profligate-turned-saint, Augustine. Benjy, however, is more interested in the sinful chapters of Augustine's *Confessiones* (397-400; *Confessions*, 1620) than its redemptive sections. After an argument with his mother, he takes his dog for a walk, which quickly ends at the neighborhood pub. With Benjy out of the house, the sanctimonious Mrs. Spillane enjoys the interests that she hides so as not to trouble him: brandy and betting on the ponies.

Still unwilling to confront Benjy about Angela, Mrs. Spillane resorts to deep sighs, sad smiles, and thoughtfully heating his pants in the mornings and removing his galoshes when he gets home. After three months of enduring his mother's unexplained martyred air, Benjy is more than ready for his summer holiday. Convinced that Angela will accompany Benjy, Mrs. Spillane decides to report her son's indiscretions to the bank manager. The manager gives her no comfort, however. After telling her that his employees' personal lives are not his to control, he informs her that Benjy's future advancement at the bank is more likely to be impeded if he remains unmarried. Furious, Mrs. Spillane snarls that she would rather "see him in his pools of blood at my feet than see him married to that Jezebel!" The day after Benjy returns from his holiday, he collapses at his mother's feet in a puddle of blood from a burst ulcer and is rushed to the hospital.

Benjy barely survives physically; emotionally, he is a changed man. Now his evenings are spent quietly at home with his mother or doing charitable works for the church. Liquor and betting are exorcised from his life. His mother, however, continues to indulge in her bad habits, but now they are driven further underground. One night Benjy discovers evidence of his mother's other side: empty brandy bottles, old betting slips, grocery bills, and the anonymous letters. Convinced that his own dour behavior has driven her into secretly drinking and gambling, he begins encouraging her to have tiny drinks at night, and he insists on placing small bets for her. Later he is shocked to discover that her grocery and butcher bills are far in arrears and concludes that his vacations with Angela have prevented his mother from keeping up with the bills—until, that is, he learns that she also owes the betting office more than £125. After he returns to his office that afternoon to find Angela flirting with a teller, he can barely get through the rest of the day.

After dinner, he announces to his mother that he is considering marrying a woman from the bank. To his astonishment, she says that she wishes he had married a long time ago because his new piety is making her miserable. After pondering his situation, Benjy breaks the tension with a laughing riposte at his mother, and they begin planning his wedding over stiff shots of brandy. All that remains is for Benjy to convince Angela to take him back—which she agrees to after several hours of unspecified activities in her landlady's parlor.

Benjy and Angela finally marry five years later—after Mrs. Spillane's death.

*Themes and Meanings*

The two main characters in "Childybawn" live a life that is uncommon in modern Western urban society but one that was not terribly unusual in rural Ireland even in the twentieth century. Although the synergistic relationship between the middle-aged bachelor and his lonely mother appears exaggerated, it illustrates several themes: the interdependence underlying even dysfunctional relationships, the secret vices of apparently upstanding citizens, the consequences of lack of communication in relationships, and the ways in which a change in one person in a relationship forces a change in the other until balance is restored.

Although Mrs. Spillane is appalled by Benjy's secret relationship with Angela, she is equally dishonest with her son, waiting for him to leave the house in the evenings before she has her shot of brandy, "or if the poor heart was weak, or overexcited, maybe two." Both Benjy and his mother manage to maintain a comfortable domestic situation, while preserving a secret wild side. Mrs. Spillane's approach to confrontation with her son is no more direct than the communications of the anonymous letter writer who sets the plot in motion; rather than question him directly about his relationship with Angela, she resorts to sighing, then putting pictures of Saint Monica and Saint Augustine in his room, and finally going behind his back to the bank manager demanding that the young woman in question be fired. When Benjy finds the evidence of his mother's secret drinking and betting, he is convinced that his own behavior has driven her to such pursuits. Rather than discuss it with her directly, he unexpectedly begins to encourage her habits. She accedes but feigns reluctance, while continuing with her indulgences on an even larger scale when Benjy is out.

*Style and Technique*

"Childybawn" is filled with Irish expressions and spellings that firmly root the story in rural Ireland: "Wisha, I dunno now where did I get that?" "Amn't I his mother?" "You bloody ould rip of hell you!" Its title means "fair-haired child ("bawn" is an Irish word meaning "fair-haired"). Rural Ireland has changed so little over the years that the story could have been set as easily in the nineteenth century as in the twentieth; the few definitive clues to the fact that it takes place in the twentieth century include references to Angela's wearing seamed nylon stockings and slacks, and the fact that Benjy and his mother go to the movies.

"Childybawn" appeared in the 1950's, after Seán O'Faoláin had been publishing stories for approximately thirty years. O'Faoláin has said that his stories of that time were his first attempts to look at his countrymen with a more satirical eye. Although this story succeeds in highlighting its characters' foibles, it relies on several strained coincidences to advance the plot. In the apparently small town in which the Spillanes reside, for example, it is hard to believe that Benjy and Angela could be romantically involved for years, much less travel regularly together to the Continent, without either the bank manager or Mrs. Spillane being aware of it. The bleeding ulcer that brings on Benjy's near-deathbed conversion, coming shortly after his mother's curse that she would rather see him in a pool of his own blood than married to Angela, is another example of forced contrivance used to advance the plot.

It is appropriate that the two main characters are vividly and equally drawn, to the exclusion of the minor characters, because they exist and function as a couple, as Benjy points out, with no apparent self-consciousness, early in the story. By contrast, Angela's motives for staying in the lengthy relationship are never explained; in fact, she has no dialogue other than the brazen words in the letter Mrs. Spillane finds. Again, this fits the story: Angela understands that she will never replace Mrs. Spillane in Benjy's priorities; early in the story, the narrator recalls her saying it made Angela sick to see Benjy and his mother together; at the end, when Benjy asks her to marry him, she first suggests he marry his mother because he is so fond of her. Her perceptions are, of course, borne out by the fact that the engagement drags on for five years, until Mrs. Spillane dies.

*Irene Struthers Rush*

# CHINA BROWNE

*Author:* Gerald Vizenor (1934-    )
*Type of plot:* Social realism
*Time of plot:* Around the 1960's or 1970's
*Locale:* Beijing and Tianjin, China
*First published:* 1988

> *Principal characters:*
> CHINA BROWNE, a Native American woman visiting China
> AN OLD CHINESE WOMAN
> CINCH, an American teacher
> ANGEL, Cinch's wife, also a teacher

## The Story

China Browne is sitting in a railroad station lounge, reading and absorbing the sights, sounds, and smells of her surroundings. English-language travel posters on the wall behind the ticket counter reveal that she is in China. She has been in the country only three days, but the harried American couple who soon join her in the Beijing lounge are beginning their second year as teachers in China. When the heavily burdened teachers learn that China Browne—carrying only an overnight pack—is going their way, they impose on her to carry their heaviest piece of baggage.

As the three Americans head down the crowded stairs of the Beijing terminal for the departure platform to Tianjin, China finds herself behind an old Chinese woman. The woman, wearing peasant clothing and a visored cap with a red star, has traditionally bound feet; she is carefully descending the steps, not realizing that China is helping her by slowing the surging crowd behind them. A moment later China smiles at her, but the woman, who recognizes her as a foreigner, reacts with suspicion.

China continues her friendly overtures toward the old woman, introducing herself in Chinese and offering assistance, but is sorely repaid for her efforts: The old woman calls her a "foreign devil" and shouts irrational accusations at her. China feigns imperturbability and is admonished by the seasoned American couple not to befriend the Chinese. Inwardly, however, she wonders how to promote harmony in these unfamiliar circumstances. Her instincts ordinarily allow her to "overturn mistrust and suspicion"; but "with no natural cues to the humor" around her, she has to work harder than usual.

On arriving in Tianjin, China lags behind the two American teachers so that she may see the old woman again. She watches the woman cross the street and head down the rough concrete steps leading to the cool riverside. At the bottom level, the woman trips and falls into the river. Chinese passersby seem indifferent: As the woman struggles vainly to pull herself out onto the concrete walkway, no one moves to help her. China pulls the woman out herself, and this time is rewarded with a smile. She lovingly unbinds the woman's feet, massages her toes, and dries them with her bandanna, "the same cloth she [often] drew between her own toes in meditation." Both women rest briefly by the river. For the moment, time stands still, even moves backward. In this interlude, China finds harmony and relief from the crush of time. The two women part friends, and the old woman gives China two gifts: her cap with the red star and a small round metal herb box. Finally, China is rudely returned to the fast-paced time of the Americans' "measured world" when the two teachers find her and scold her for the delay and anxiety that she has caused them.

*Themes and Meanings*

The introduction of the two American teachers soon after China scans the grammatically tangled travel slogans draws attention to the slightly warped forms of English around her. Cinch's nonstandard spoken grammar (for example, "Angel and me are teachers here") would be insignificant were it not for the unstated assumption that American teachers overseas are hired, at least partly, to serve as models of standard American English as well as to promote good will. All of Cinch's initial dialogue (printed in run-on form, with comma splices), together with the couple's actions and frequently expressed lack of good will, reinforces two apparent aims of the author: to show that the couple's ideas are often wrong and to make China Browne shine by comparison. Angel, for example, is anything but an angel: In addition to unloading her heaviest piece of baggage on China, she crassly belittles China's Native American ancestry. The woman's "mock blonde" hair color intensifies the contrast between her and the millions of dark-haired Chinese around her. Finally, when they are not complaining, Angel and Cinch display the smugly superior condescending attitudes of the stereotypically ugly American cultural imperialist abroad. Unlike them, China speaks softly, looks more like the Chinese, and works at fitting in—even though she also is distinctively American, for both the abrasive American couple and the old Chinese woman immediately see that she is not Chinese.

The old Chinese woman's character, less fully defined than those of the others, befits her role as a symbolic link between past and present, a link suggested also within a subtitle that is sometimes used with the story: "Red Stars and Bound Lilies," both of whose nouns allude to the old woman. The red star on her Maoist army hat, symbolizing the revolutionary turmoil of twentieth century China, may explain her initial paranoia, for China's Cultural Revolution of the 1960's and 1970's caused great unrest and fear among the people. On the other hand, the woman's bound lilies—a common Chinese metaphor for bound feet—symbolize ancient tradition. Vizenor's sole fully contextualized use of the metaphor may not convey its dual meanings adequately to English-speaking readers, yet it is clear that the old woman's "golden lilies" (on which she "wobbled" unsteadily), the "bound lilies" on the cover of the herb box, and the "bound lilies" of the subtitle all signify the same thing—bound feet.

Feet, as well as people, are by tradition bound. In passing along the small herb box and its contents, the old woman symbolically connects China Browne to an old Chinese tradition—which the modern American teachers quickly disparage as worthless and possibly dangerous. The teachers obviously prefer their large burdensome box and the expensive modern device within, which will inevitably break down, become worthless, and be thrown away. Their box represents a value system based on new material possessions. The teachers, whose examples in this case should not be followed, exist in jarring contrast to China, her values, and her world.

China Browne's less materialistic ideals, like the small round herb box, take but small space and yet may be held, treasured, and passed on for generations. Similarly, her desire to make meaningful contact with those around her represents a universally esteemed human trait. In her encounter with the old woman, she demonstrates the life-sustaining and life-affirming rewards shared when two people meet and understand each other, despite linguistic and cultural traditions that are literally a world apart.

*Style and Technique*

Although Gerald Vizenor's understated humor in this story typifies his style, his language and plot here are more straightforward than usual. Vizenor's characters ordinarily act more strangely, his plots contain more bizarre twists, and his creative use of language leans far more toward the punningly incomprehensible. Some puns here are almost subtle enough to be dismissed as mere details: For example, the mangled English travel ads in the Beijing station (especially "Make Wind on a Phoenix Bicycle") may serve simply to identify the setting as non-English.

Vizenor's best extended pun, of the elusive sort that he often uses, may be his repeated reference to the capital-punishment article on the newspaper in which the teachers have wrapped a package. The joke is that the unending care for and carrying of their material possessions constitutes a form of punishment that the materialistic capitalists Cinch and Angel joylessly endure. Only the incident of China shouting into a "panic hole" eludes easy explanation; however, multiple references to the hot weather may suggest that the topsoil has dried and cracked under the stress of the summer heat. Despite this story's uncharacteristic clarity (relatively speaking), Vizenor's trademark word-play and tricks with names abound.

The characters are realistically drawn, with little overt mingling of fact and fiction. Only China's claim that her grandfather was "the Baron of Patronia" exemplifies the way in which Vizenor often blurs distinctions between the real and the imaginary. In another story in *The Trickster of Liberty* (1988), in which "China Browne" originally appeared, China reveals that her family lives on the White Earth Reservation—a real reservation in west-central Minnesota, where Vizenor spent much of his own childhood. As in many of Vizenor's stories, such distinctions underscore the oddly realistic and humorous ways in which reality and fantasy often blend indistinguishably.

*William Matta*

# CHRIST IN CONCRETE

*Author:* Pietro di Donato (1911-1992)
*Type of plot:* Social realism
*Time of plot:* The 1920's
*Locale:* New York City
*First published:* 1937

> *Principal characters:*
> GEREMIO, the leader of the construction crew
> ANNUNZIATA, his wife
> MURDIN, the construction boss who represents the company that exploits the workers and ultimately causes their deaths
> NINE ITALIAN AMERICAN IMMIGRANT WORKERS

*The Story*

First published as a short story, "Christ in Concrete" was the basis for the first two chapters of the novel by the same name published in 1939. The story is autobiographical, based on the death of the author's father in a construction accident in 1923. Paul, the oldest son of Geremio and Annunziata who is mentioned only briefly in the short story, becomes the protagonist in the novel. Paul represents Di Donato himself, who at the age of twelve, as the oldest son, was forced to go to work as a bricklayer to support the family after his father died.

The story covers the final two days in Geremio's life. The plot centers on the thoughts and actions of the Italian American construction workers in a realistic account of the hardships and dangers of their lives. Their dialogue, internal monologues, and the narrator-author's exposition show love of family as the driving force in the lives of these immigrant Italian peasants. They came to the United States early in the twentieth century to escape poverty and forced military service in the old country. Sustained by their strong Catholic faith, they are underpaid and exhausted but filled with hope for a future that will spare their children the hardships of their own lives.

The men exchange jokes about their wives, often coarse in their direct references to sex, but always with a rough affection and warmth. These workers are illiterate and hardworking, their lives centering on their families, the comforts of food and sex, and their religious faith. Physically strong but intellectually limited, they know that they are being exploited but cannot imagine any other kind of life. In the old country, they were accustomed to being dominated by church and government authorities, a traditional attitude that they have brought with them to the United States. They have a firm faith that God will protect them and their families.

Geremio, their spokesperson and crew leader, has earned their respect; they follow his orders willingly. The Job (sometimes referred to in the text with a capital "J"), is an antagonist in the narrative, the force against which the workers struggle. Murdin, the company boss (the name suggests his role as a murderer) is hard-driving and insensitive, treating the workers as little more than beasts who can be easily replaced. Nick the Lean stands apart from the other workers in his bitterness and lack of faith, representing a realistic view of these men's lives in the United States, in contrast to the naïve hopes of the others. Geremio fears the danger that looms on this job but knows he must follow Murdin's orders. Lacking job security, these men know that only their daily labor prevents them and their families from starving to death.

Geremio's wife is expecting another child, who both parents hope will be another boy to carry on the family name. Geremio has just bought a house, the achievement of his dream of success in the United States. The revelation that this dream will become a nightmare is foreshadowed throughout the text. The conversation among the men and their exchanges with Murdin show that the underpinnings of the building are based on old, unstable material, the shoddy construction caused by the company's cost-cutting efforts. There is an ominous undertone of doom in their own words and in the narrator's description of their thoughts. Geremio's wife Annunziata, in their bedtime conversation, worries because her husband, who always discusses with her the day's work, is silent about this job. The liturgical season is highly significant: Devout Catholics, they have been given two hours off work to mark Good Friday, the day of Christ's death.

The building collapses, and the death of each worker is described in ghastly detail. Geremio, the last to die, is impaled on a steel rod (literally, a crucifixion) and splinters his jawbone in a futile attempt to bite through a wooden beam to find breathing space. Still conscious, he calls on Jesus to save him but is smothered in a mass of drying concrete. The prolonged account of his death is horrifying in its detail. Critics cite this story as one of the most powerful in the social protest literature of its time.

*Themes and Meanings*

The nine workers in Geremio's crew are portrayed as crude and intellectually limited. The author overcomes stereotyping by humanizing them with descriptive nicknames such as Vincenzo the Snoutnose and Mike the Barrel-mouth. Despite their lack of full characterization, they project a strong physical identity. Their childlike qualities are foregrounded, along with their old-country superstitions. With the exception of the cynical Nick the Lean, they are filled with the immigrant's hope for a better life for the next generation. They depend on their comradeship and their faith to help them endure their hardships and assure them that their dreams will be realized. In contrast to their earthy humor and warm camaraderie stands Murdin, who demeans them with racist insults and drunken indifference, callously refusing to heed Geremio's warnings about impending disaster.

In the classic dichotomy of protest literature, innocence and goodness are opposed by corruption and evil. The construction site literally represents the material contribution of the immigrants to their new country and symbolically the blood sacrifice demanded of them as the building collapses. In the last moments of these men's lives, the American dream becomes a surrealistic nightmare. Geremio in his final agony calls on Jesus to save him but then realizes that he is dying and that he has been cheated of life by those in power. Echoing the last words of Jesus, he calls on God to receive his soul. The Christian symbolism in this conclusion is deeply ironic. In Christian theology, Jesus' death was redemptive, saving humankind from sin. Geremio's death on Good Friday is a useless sacrifice caused by the inhumanity of the men whose cold authority permits these deaths.

Although both the story and the novel have received mixed reviews, primarily for what some regard as its primitive language and characterizations, critics agree that the short story and the novel that it spawned are forceful documents of social protest in American literature.

*Style and Technique*

Pietro di Donato's unique handling of language, although more evident in the longer work, is nevertheless effectively developed in this short story. Critic Fred L. Gardaphe, in his introduction to the 1993 reprint of *Christ in Concrete*, notes that Di Donato's unique achievement is his ability to express the characters' thoughts and dialogue in both the immigrant's broken English and the speech rhythms of Italian translated into English.

In his view, Di Donato masterfully combines the elements of the two languages to represent the thought processes of the characters. The rough poetry of the language is often cited as a strength of both the story and the novel.

The omniscient narrator plays a prominent role, commenting on the often unrecognized contribution of these immigrants to the infrastructure of the United States, an insight that the characters themselves are incapable of reaching. However, the raw emotional power of the narrative comes through the dialogue among the characters and their interior monologues expressing their unspoken thoughts. Throughout the text descriptions of ethnic food and the loving warmth of the family, headed by the father as wage-earner and the earth-mother as the heart of the home, suggest a primitive innocence that contrasts with the knowing complicity of the society that exploits them.

The evolution of the short story into the novel reveals Di Donato's development as a writer. In addition to making name changes that allow the author to develop the characters in the longer work, he has deleted several passages of authorial commentary from the short story, letting the consciousness of his characters in their final agonies emphasize the horror of their deaths. The novel is the coming-of-age story of Geremio's son Paul. Having taken a stand against his exploitation and rejected the Catholic Church that has failed to help his family, he ultimately achieves freedom from exploitation and superstition. Nevertheless, the conclusion is an emotional scene at the hour of Annunziata's death in which Paul pays tribute to the warmth and strength of the Italian heritage that will be a gift to the life of the nation.

*Marjorie Podolsky*

# CHRISTMAS EVERY DAY

*Author:* Heinrich Böll (1917-1985)
*Type of plot:* Fable
*Time of plot:* 1947-1948
*Locale:* Probably Cologne, Germany
*First published:* "Nicht nur zur Weihnachtszeit," 1952 (English translation, 1986)

*Principal characters:*
THE UNNAMED NARRATOR
UNCLE FRANZ, a businessperson
AUNT MILLA, his wife, who loves Christmas
FRANZ, their son

## The Story

After World War II, apparently in Cologne, Uncle Franz Lenz's wholesale grocery business is bouncing back from a slight wartime interruption. The Lenz family—Uncle Franz, Aunt Milla, Johannes, Lucie, young Cousin Franz, and assorted grandchildren—have come through the conflict almost intact. Only Aunt Milla has been deeply unsettled by the recent bloodbath—because her Christmas celebrations were curtailed.

Cousin Franz is something of a conscience for the family, a young man of notable piety who scandalizes them by becoming a boxer. The first to notice how badly askew things are, he has little sympathy with his father, identified by the narrator as the kindest of men—who provided his wife a private bomb shelter and a car to take her to the country whenever air raids threatened—nor with his mother, who is still grieving that ornaments on her Christmas tree were damaged by nearby bomb explosions and that Christmas festivities were cancelled in 1940.

Now that those unpleasant times are over—the narrator can scarcely bring himself to mention the war by name—Aunt Milla is insisting that Christmas be restored right down to the angel at the tip of the tree, who actually whispers "peace." Uncle Franz is prosperous enough by 1946 to gratify his wife's wishes. He spares no expense to obtain the decorations, food, candies, and candles that Aunt Milla had enjoyed in the old days. When it comes time to take down the Christmas tree at Candlemas (February 2), the usually charming old lady begins to scream. Neurologists, priests, and psychiatrists are summoned to the house, but the shrieking goes on unabated for almost a week. Cousin Franz, who will not participate in indulging his mother, suggests a visit by an exorcist, but Uncle Franz comes up with a different solution: a new tree to replace the old and Christmas all over again.

Because it is nearly carnival time, Christmas decorations are not to be found in the city's shops, nor are trees for sale. Uncle Franz's connections allow extraordinary measures: An import license from Czechoslovakia is obtained; phone calls are made to toy companies; and grandchildren are dispatched to the forest with an ax. Soon arrangements are complete. When Aunt Milla is at last summoned to the Christmas room, everything appears normal, and she is able to call in the family to light the tree and sing carols.

To avoid upsetting Aunt Milla, Christmas Eve will become a permanent event. As other people sing "Come, Lovely May," "Silent Night" will resound from the Lenz house. In June, the parish priest refuses to continue taking part in the nightly ritual, but a replacement for him is easily found, and a firm contracted to replace old trees with fresh ones.

The enforced Christmases gradually begin to take their toll, and family members ask to be excused from attendance. Lucie, the first to succumb, suffers a nervous malady touched off by the sight of Christmas cookies.

Now Cousin Franz's earlier prognostications and the narrator's reluctant admission that symptoms of disintegration are appearing in his family come back to haunt the reader: Johannes has quit his choral society, sick to death of German songs; Uncle Franz has hired an actor to impersonate him at the nightly sessions around the Christmas tree, has taken a mistress, and is indulging in unethical business practices. He is even ready to pay professional actors to play the roles of family members in order to fool Aunt Milla.

As the two-year anniversary of this charade approaches, the narrator admits that Cousin Franz has been right. He sees that nightly singing and a diet of marzipan are having a bad effect on the smaller children and arranges to have the children replaced by wax dummies. He notes that his cousins have all suffered psychological disturbances. Johannes has joined the Communist Party. Lucie, a confirmed bar-hopper, is planning to leave Germany with her husband. The artificial Christmases continue, but the participants are drinking more than they should and indulging in petty thievery. Only Aunt Milla and the priest seem unaffected. When the narrator learns that the angel who whispers "peace" is activated by a phonograph in the next room, his disillusionment is complete. He visits his cousin Franz, now in a monastery, who tells him that life is punishment. Moral responsibility, Heinrich Böll seems to say, must be assumed; denial is poisonous.

*Themes and Meanings*

"Christmas Every Day" can be seen as an allegory of Germany's failure to accept responsibility for its past and a cautionary tale admonishing Germany—and, by extension, all humankind—to mind its moral house. Böll accuses his country of closing its eyes to the recent horrors of Adolf Hitler's Nazi repression. The new German Federal Republic, he says, is a bogus state, morally and ethically bankrupt, which attempts to present Germany to the world as a land of decent people with solid middle-class values, lovely music, and endearing traditions. Where, he asks in effect, is the penitent confession that this is a country in which millions of people still living supported the brutal invasion of their neighbors? Why are Christmas carols being sung by those who built death camps to destroy other human beings or, at the very best, by those who chose not to see what was going on?

In "Christmas Every Day," things stand for other things, but it is not always possible to identify them exactly. For example, it is hard to say with certainty what Böll means about one priest's taking another's place at the Christmas Eve festivities. Perhaps he is thinking of those clergymen, both Protestant and Roman Catholic, who resisted Nazi rule and the others who quietly acquiesced to it. In short, not even those well versed in modern German history and in literature will agree entirely on the meaning of the story, although its gist is startlingly clear.

## Style and Technique

As a satire highly critical of postwar German society, "Christmas Every Day" juxtaposes realistic details, such as accurate descriptions of everyday life, with strange, unlikely incidents and details. For example, while the Lenz family sings real songs and eats real Christmas cookies and candies around a real Christmas tree, such devices as individuals being replaced by actors or even wax figures alert one to the fact that there is more here than meets the eye.

This sort of juxtaposition suggests that there is something wrong and dangerous about refusing to recognize what a society has done. The Lenz family, gently bullied by a tyrannical wife and mother, indulges in preposterous make-believe verging on hypocrisy—just as Germany was doing, Böll implies, in the years of the Economic Miracle (the period of unparalleled prosperity that began only a few years after Germany's surrender to the Allies, and continued through the next two decades and beyond).

Böll likewise employs motifs that have become icons in much of his fiction to drive his point home. The pleasant qualities of middle-class German life serve Böll like a two-edged sword. In much of his fiction, loving families, little gifts, decorated birthday tables, and fresh flowers represent the civilizing elements of society that, fragile as they are, stand like mighty fortresses against totalitarianism and its armies of flunkies. Often a shared drink in a Hungarian tavern is more meaningful in his humanistic view than a troop movement. At other times, these same gestures, festive customs, and bourgeois ceremonies take on a threatening aspect. Such is certainly the case in "Christmas Every Day," in which German Christmas practices, which much of the Western world has embraced, become symbols of a sort of mass denial as an entire culture attempts to ignore its horrific past. If such a perspective seems confusing—two different ways of regarding the same thing—it is only because Böll himself has never quite resolved the contradiction. He has never decided if fallible humanity is capable of triumphing over the forces of selfishness, intolerance, and hate that constantly assault it. Even though he considers his country guilty of terrible crimes against humankind, he refuses to judge his people as collectively guilty. To do that would be to engage in a Nazi-like racism, to declare that Germans are racially moral inferiors, ethical "subhumans"—a notion that he positively rejects.

*James E. Devlin*

# A CHRISTMAS MEMORY

*Author:* Truman Capote (Truman Streckfus Persons, 1924-1984)
*Type of plot:* Domestic realism
*Time of plot:* The 1930's
*Locale:* Unspecified, but probably Monroeville, Alabama
*First published:* 1956

*Principal characters:*
BUDDY, the narrator, who recalls a Christmas when he was seven
HIS COUSIN, a woman in her sixties with the spirit of a child

*The Story*

The adult narrator of this story nostalgically remembers the last Christmas that he enjoyed as a seven-year-old boy with his "sixty-something" cousin, who called him Buddy in memory of a boy who had once been her best friend. Buddy lives with this cousin and other relatives in a spreading old house in a country town (which probably represents Monroeville, Alabama, where Truman Capote lived with his four unmarried adult cousins until he was about ten).

As they have done each year, Buddy and his favorite cousin inaugurate this Christmas season with a late November fruitcake baking, which entails gathering windfallen pecans and a visit to the dilapidated shack of Mr. Haha Jones to buy whiskey. They finance this operation with money that they have accumulated through the year in their Fruitcake Fund. After four days of baking, their fruitcakes are ready for delivery to friends—"persons we've met maybe once, perhaps not at all," who include President Roosevelt and the bus driver Abner Packer.

At this particular Christmas, the delivery of the fruitcakes is followed by a celebratory sharing of the last two inches of whiskey in the bottle used for the fruitcakes. Buddy, his cousin, and her dog Queenie all get slightly tipsy, moving two other relatives to scold Buddy's cousin for corrupting a child. The next morning's adventure heals all, however, as Buddy and his cousin search deep into the woods for their Christmas decorations. They gather wreaths, chop down a tree, laboriously drag everything home, and dress the tree with homemade decorations. They then wrap gifts, secretly making one another kites. On Christmas morning they wake early and make enough noise to rouse the others. After the presents are opened, Buddy and his cousin go to the pasture below the house to fly their new kites.

This is the last Christmas they spend together. The next year, Buddy is sent to a military school and then to a new home. Years later he receives news that his cousin has died—an event that he feels intuitively before the news arrives. As he grows older and feels winter coming on, he often thinks of "a lost pair of kites hurrying toward heaven."

## Themes and Meanings

There is an obvious sadness and sense of loss at the passing of the cousin in this story, but most important, "A Christmas Memory" reveals a preoccupation with the theme of children suffering from the dominance of unfeeling adults. As a seven-year-old, Buddy was an innocent young boy who would not realize the full impact of insensitive, adult domination until later in life. The real hero of his memoir is his cousin, who remains a child at heart even into her sixties. The villains of the story are their relatives, a shadowy group of adults who do not display the sensitivity and the joy for life that Buddy and his cousin share.

The story's villains are initially curtly described simply as the "other people [who] inhabit the house, relatives; and though they have power over us, and frequently make us cry, we are not, on the whole, too much aware of them." The point of the story, however, is that these adults cannot be ignored forever. The wonderful times that Buddy and his cousin enjoy are inevitably interrupted by reminders of the presence and domination of these unfeeling adults. Buddy and his cousin lack ready money for their annual fruitcakes because they only receive "skinflint sums [that] persons in the house occasionally provide (a dime is considered big money)." Two angry relatives burst into the whiskey-drinking scene, "potent with eyes that scold, tongues that scold," and their annoyance on rising so early on Christmas morning is followed by an artificially leisurely breakfast that delays the two "children" from opening their presents. The unimaginative and practical Christmas gifts that Buddy receives indicate the gulf between him and the other adults. Naturally, he is disappointed with socks, a Sunday-school shirt, handkerchiefs, a hand-me-down sweater and a subscription to *The Little Shepherd*. "It makes me boil," he recalls. Finally, these all-powerful adults, "Those who Know Best," send Buddy away to military school and a new home, separating him forever from his dear cousin.

Other adults in the story reinforce the theme—for example, the lazy wife of the rich mill owner who is offended because Buddy and his cousin will not sell their Christmas tree. Initially, Mr. Haha Jones, "a giant with razor scars across his cheeks," appears to be another unfeeling adult. He is called Haha because he never laughs; however, he ultimately shows a more playful side. He smiles at their request for whiskey and instead of charging them two dollars, asks only for a sample fruitcake in return. He is finally declared to be different, "a lovely man." Some of Buddy and his cousin's "friends" are adults, but they also are different from the adults of their immediate family circle. They are mostly strangers who display sensitivity and friendliness—such as the Roosevelts, who send thank you notes for the fruitcakes, and the Wistons, a young California couple who once spent a pleasant hour chatting with the family on the porch after their car broke down.

## Style and Technique

The most important stylistic feature of "A Christmas Memory" is the sense of immediacy that Capote creates by writing in the present tense. Although he writes as an adult remembering a childhood experience at least twenty years earlier, he avoids the feeling of distance that narrating a memoir in the past tense would create or the impersonal objectivity that a third-person narrator might lend. Anxious to create a strong emotional context, he favors the immediacy of the present tense, almost as if he would prefer the memoir to be a play. Indeed, in 1966 the story was adapted for television, with Capote reading the story as a voice-over narrator.

The story begins by asking readers to become an audience, almost as if they were sitting in a theater: "Imagine a morning in late November. A coming of winter morning more than twenty years ago." Before the first paragraph ends, the story slips into the present tense, thereby creating a dramatic quality: "Just today the fireplace commenced its seasonal roar. A woman with shorn white hair is standing at the kitchen window."

This immediate dramatic quality is maintained throughout the story. At times it describes past events that are important to the moment—"Once we won seventy-ninth prize, five dollars, in a national football contest"—but it is always quick to return the reader's attention to the dramatic present—"at the moment our hopes are centered on the fifty-thousand-dollar Grand Prize being offered to name a new brand of coffee." At times, Capote even includes what might be seen as stage directions—"Enter: two relatives. Very angry. Potent with eyes that scold, tongues that scold. Listen to what they have to say." At other times, he writes what sounds like directions in a film script: "Morning. Frozen rime lusters the grass" or "Home: Queenie slumps by the fire and sleeps till tomorrow, snoring loud as a human."

The story ends with "This is our last Christmas together. Life separates us," using "is" instead of "was." Even as Capote recalls the passage of time that eventually led to the death of his cousin, he holds on to the present tense as long as he can—"a morning arrives in November, a leafless, birdless coming of winter morning, when she cannot rouse herself to exclaim: 'Oh, my, it's fruitcake weather!'" In the last words of the story, Buddy is an adult again, but he still remembers in the present tense: "That is why, walking across a school campus on this particular December morning, I keep searching the sky. As if I expected to see, rather like hearts, a lost pair of kites hurrying toward heaven."

*Terry Nienhuis*

# CHRISTMAS MORNING

*Author:* Frank O'Connor (Michael Francis O'Donovan, 1903-1966)
*Type of plot:* Autobiographical
*Time of plot:* The early twentieth century
*Locale:* Ireland
*First published:* 1946

> *Principal characters:*
> LARRY, the narrator and restless older brother, who yearns for
> excitement
> SONNY, his smarter, younger brother
> HIS MOTHER, who must struggle to keep the father from drinking
> the household money
> HIS FATHER, who enjoys drinking and singing Latin hymns

*The Story*

The first-person narrator of this story, a young boy named Larry, learns an important lesson about growing up, about childhood beliefs, and about family relationships. Young Larry, who is not even ten years old, dislikes his younger, more studious brother, Sonny, because he believes that Sonny is mother's favorite child. Encouraged by their mother, Sonny concentrates on spelling words correctly, on displaying his learning in other subjects, and on attending school, whereas Larry, much to his mother's chagrin, dislikes his studies, favors playing with his boyhood "gang," and prefers skipping school. As the story unfolds, however, Larry discovers why his mother seems to favor Sonny and simultaneously discovers an important lesson about Christmas.

Instead of studying, Larry spends his time playing with the Doherty gang and dreaming of becoming a soldier. He believes that studying is not commendable and, perhaps, is better suited to sissies.

As Christmas approaches, Larry hears, but adamantly refuses to believe, that there is no Santa Claus. The neighborhood Doherty boys, who reveal this information, are a "rough class of children you wouldn't expect Santa to come to anyway," Larry observes.

Four days before the holidays, Larry is caught skipping school. Because he has not bothered to learn his required math lessons, he and Peter Doherty have cut classes and have been spending their time in a store on the quay. When his mother reprimands him for his truancy, Larry discovers that his lies have been more offensive to her than has been his failure to attend school. However, at this point in his life, he fails to understand why lying is such an important failing in a human being.

In contrast, Sonny behaves particularly well during the Christmas season. When the two boys retire for the night, Sonny warns Larry that Santa surely will not visit any boy who has skipped school and who has associated with the rough Doherty boys.

Larry, therefore, decides to remain awake on Christmas Eve to discuss his plight with Santa Claus—man to man. Surely Santa, because he is a man, will understand Larry's behavior. That evening, Larry rehearses several explanations of his behavior. Failing to realize that these explanations to Santa would simply be more lies, he awaits Christmas Eve and Santa's arrival.

Although the boys eagerly anticipate Christmas Eve, their mother is quite frustrated. When the father returns home after work and begrudgingly offers her only a few coins, the mother argues with him in an attempt to obtain extra housekeeping money for toys, cake, and a Christmas candle. However, the father tosses her only two extra half-crowns, shouts at her to make the best of the situation, and storms out of the house. An embittered woman, she takes the money and realizes that the father will spend the remainder of his salary on liquor.

Returning from her shopping trip on Christmas Eve, mother carries her cake, her Christmas candle, and a few packages. When father fails to return home, the three silently eat the cake, sip tea, light the candle, and hang Christmas stockings. Around eleven o'clock, a drunken father returns home. He attempts to sing Latin hymns but does not remember the correct words.

Although he struggles against sleep, Larry finally succumbs. When he awakens early the next morning, Larry is terribly dismayed to discover that Santa has made a grievous error. In his own stocking Larry unhappily discovers a book, a pen and pencil, and a bag of sweets. In Sonny's stocking Larry discovers a bag of sweets and a popgun. Larry knows that he can use the popgun but has absolutely no use for the book and writing instruments; therefore, a clever idea pops into his head. Perhaps he could switch the presents. Sonny would never be any good in a gang, Larry reasons, and could, at least, learn many new spellings from the book. Besides, only Santa knows what gifts each boy has received. Perhaps, Larry finally reasons, Santa has indeed made a mistake. Larry carefully makes the switch and returns to bed only to be awakened later by Sonny, who has discovered the presents, and who rushes to show mother and father. Because he has nothing to fear—only Santa and himself know of the switch—Larry joins Sonny in their parents' bedroom.

When his mother asks Larry where he got the gun, Larry answers that Santa brought it to him. Instantly, and perhaps without thinking, his mother accuses Larry of stealing the gun from Sonny. The father seems to understand the boys' plight and offers them a few coins. Mother, however, does not understand Larry's lying and mentions that she does not want her child to grow up to be a liar and a thief.

The climax of the story occurs when Larry suddenly realizes that the Dohertys were right after all: There is no Santa Claus. There are only the gifts that parents give their children. However, perhaps the most important lesson that Larry learns is that his mother has been relying on Larry to extricate her from her miserable existence. Larry painfully understands that the fear in his mother's eyes "was the fear that, like my father, I should turn out to be mean and common and a drunkard." Thus one Christmas morning a young boy grows up to understand adult relationships and adult hardships.

## Themes and Meanings

In this story, as in many of his stories, Frank O'Connor realistically treats the often harsh realities of life in rural Ireland. The story details a young boy's journey from innocence to maturity and depicts Larry's ultimate understanding of adult realities. The reader understands that Larry, the narrator and protagonist, did in fact learn important lessons on that Christmas morning, because early in the story Larry indicates that he was not very good in school until the age of nine or ten. In fact, before his epiphany on Christmas morning, Larry did not participate at all in his education: He did not understand math, he disliked reading and spelling, and he skipped school. Before the revelation that concludes the story, he is blinded by the natural selfishness of a child; because he plays with troublemakers, dreams of becoming a soldier, and is engaged in his own naïve world, he fails to see the difficulties that exist in his mother's world.

On Christmas morning, however, after he is admonished for exchanging his present for his brother's present, he suddenly realizes that his mother—a lonely, frightened woman—is at the mercy of his father, a brutal drunkard, who squanders the housekeeping money on liquor.

He also realizes that his mother's dreams of escape are focused directly on him, the older son. Although his discovery that Santa Claus is not real has been "almost more than [he] could bear," he has learned a more important lesson: The future of his family depends on his growing up with values different from his father's.

## Style and Technique

In this first-person narrative, O'Connor uses an informal, almost provincial style. Because the characters are Irish, as is O'Connor, many colloquialisms appear throughout the story to add authenticity to the realistic narration. For example, instead of skipping school, the boys "go on the lang" and engage in "mitching." Rather than say "my mother," the narrator always says "the mother." Moreover, Sonny, the "little prig," is "stuffed up" and tells the Dohertys that Larry "isn't left go out." Instead of drinking excessively, Larry's father "had a drop in." This conversational, provincial dialogue suggests a working-class Irish family.

O'Connor's deliberately repetitious use of the conjunction "and" intensifies the lesson that Larry learns at the end of the story: He sees that "Father was mean and common and a drunkard and that she [the mother] had been relying" on him. The last sentence reinforces the intensification: "And I knew . . . I should turn out to be mean and common and a drunkard."

*Bette Adams Reagan*

# CHROMA

*Author:* Frederick Barthelme (1943-    )
*Type of plot:* Neorealist
*Time of plot:* The 1980's
*Locale:* American suburbia
*First published:* 1987

> *Principal characters:*
> THE NARRATOR
> ALICIA, his wife
> JULIET and
> HEATHER, their neighbors

*The Story*

The unnamed narrator explains that his wife, Alicia, is not home this weekend; she is with her boyfriend, George. As part of their "new deal," Alicia spends every other weekend with him. The narrator is therefore spending Saturday with his attractive neighbor, Juliet, a fitness and health buff in her twenties. Juliet lives next door with her girlfriend, Heather, who is thirty-five. At a restaurant, Juliet tries to get the narrator to say what is bothering him, but he is unwilling to discuss it. She abruptly announces, "When we go back to the house I want to make love to you."

When they return to Juliet's house, she sits the narrator down on the sofa. Looking out the sliding doors, he notices that Heather and Juliet do not have a real Weber barbecue. Juliet tries to seduce him, but the narrator feels uncomfortable with the idea. They hug and kiss but do not have sex.

Later in the afternoon the narrator is out driving and comes on Heather, who has been shopping and is riding the bus. He gives her a ride home. As they talk, Heather urges the narrator to take a stand against Alicia's relationship with George. She also expresses concern about the narrator's and Juliet's interest in each other. On arriving home, they find Alicia working with some potted plants. Alicia invites Heather and Juliet to join them later for dinner. After Heather leaves, Alicia suggests that they go inside for a nap.

Juliet and Heather arrive at eight. There is a phone call from George in the middle of dinner, and Alicia goes into the other room to talk privately. Heather and Juliet become uncomfortable; Juliet gives the narrator a "sweet look out of the tops of her eyes." After Heather and Juliet leave, he tells Alicia about his earlier dalliance with Juliet. Unhappy, Alicia points out that their "deal" was that she would be free to go out while he stayed home and remained faithful to her. Pointing out that he looks unhappy, she asks if he will be okay if she goes out, clearly hinting that he should ask her to stay home. He does not pick up his cue. "Maybe I ought to stay?" she asks; he replies, "I'm O.K." Soon George arrives, honking his horn to summon Alicia.

The narrator watches television alone, fantasizes about Juliet, and eventually falls asleep. He is wakened by the doorbell. It is Heather, upset because Juliet has told her that she kissed him and offered to make love to him. The narrator tries to placate her, telling her that it was a sweet gesture, but one that nobody took seriously. Heather blurts out, "I don't want us in your mess." He admits that he feels "lousy" about the whole situation.

Alicia returns before midnight. She asks the narrator to talk to her while she takes a bath. He tells her that he did not sleep with Juliet but that they had a "terrific time." He stares at his wife, thinking that she is beautiful. They finally talk seriously, wondering aloud if they are "in trouble," as Heather had said, and wondering why he is becoming interested in Juliet, which was not part of the plan. Alicia guesses that they can save their marriage if they want to. Then she holds up her hands in a way that the narrator interprets to mean that she wants to straighten out something very important. Instead, she says that she is hungry for—"*dying for*"—cheese ball and has been thinking about it all night long. She will even make it herself. The story ends with the narrator trying to sort out his feelings as his wife has thrown him yet another curve. "She's so beautiful," he thinks.

*Themes and Meanings*

Among Frederick Barthelme's concerns in "Chroma" are the disconnectedness of modern American life, the inadequacy and unreliability of conversation and language, and the roles of the sexes. As in much of his fiction, the characters are given no histories beyond a few sketchy details. The reader never learns the protagonist's name or occupation or how long he has been married to Alicia. The locale is never identified, except that it is an American suburb. In neither the protagonist's thoughts nor his conversations does one get any sense of where he is from or where he wants to go. The story exists very much in its present moment (the narrator speaks in the present tense), in frequently trivial actions and conversations. Its suburbanites are disconnected both from their own histories and from one another. In Barthelme's modern America, people are more connected to the objects and surfaces of everyday life—a barbecue seen through a window, shirts and a plastic fish bought on a shopping trip, the cover of an *Artforum* magazine that the narrator likes "pretty much"—than to anything else.

Conversations in "Chroma" frequently confuse the characters and the reader alike. When Heather asks the narrator if he and his wife are "still playing Donkey Kong," he has no idea what she means; she does not either, it turns out—"I just said it." Twice other characters speak to the narrator using words or phrases so confusing that he simply echoes them. When his wife comments on his sad expression, for example, calling him "melancholy in the mug," he replies, "Mug?" Heather explicitly comments on the struggle to make oneself understood. Mimicking karate chops in the air, she says, "I don't even know what I'm talking about. . . . I'm having my ongoing struggle with the language."

More problematic than these language difficulties is Barthelme's distrust of people's very thoughts. Believing that people's views of the world are transitory and un-reliable, he generally has his characters say very little about their perspectives on life. As the story begins, for example, the narrator avoids telling Juliet what is bothering him for fear that he will say "a lot of junk now that won't be true this afternoon." Later, the narrator thinks about "how fast things fly through your head when you're think-ing, about how you see only key parts of stuff." This is a tantalizing idea, but Barthelme seldom gives readers a good look at those "things." Therefore—and this is the case with much neorealist or minimalist work—the reader never learns enough about the characters to decide how to feel about them. To a great extent, they remain ciphers, as disconnected from their own thoughts as they are from one another.

In Barthelme's stories, it is often the women characters who make things happen and who display the outward manifestations of strength and aggression. Whenever Alicia appears in the story, she calls the tune. It was her decision to have an affair (al-though that word is never used); her husband simply goes along with the idea. At one point, Alicia playfully pushes him a couple of times. Similarly, Juliet announces that she wants to make love to him, and he obligingly lets her "march" him to her house. He describes Juliet as having neck muscles that ripple prettily. Heather offers to have Juliet break George's nose, and Heather likes to spout her own version of tough-guy talk. Compared with these women, the narrator—and, one might guess, the unseen George, with his "discreet" beeps of the horn—is remarkably passive. Beyond this tweaking of stereotypes, there is another noteworthy aspect of sexuality. As in a num-ber of Barthelme's stories, sex is alluded to regularly and even offered, but it is not ac-tually engaged in—yet another example of the connections between people that are never made.

## Style and Technique

Barthelme is frequently called a minimalist (an identification that he does not rel-ish); his writing has also been classified as neorealism or pop realism. Rather than at-tempting to depict reality, he creates a fictive world that is at once an oblique reflec-tion and a reinterpretation of reality. Essential to the creation of this world is extreme specificity regarding visual details (gestures and objects) and, usually, extreme vague-ness regarding a larger sense of place and time. In the dialogue of "Chroma," Barthelme creates skewed phrases and expressions that do not quite belong to the world outside the story. Heather, with her hilariously offbeat slang, threatens the nar-rator by saying, "You touch the doughnut girl, I'll do your teeth in piano wire." Alicia refers to herself doing "the rope-a-dope all over the place."

One element of Barthelme's style that has attracted considerable comment is his tendency to describe scenes and actions through an accretion of brand names and proper nouns. Another is his detailed, almost hyper-real, descriptions of everyday ob-jects. In "Chroma," the brand names are relatively unobtrusive; on the other hand, the reader learns that Heather and Juliet do not have a "Weber barbecue" but never learn the narrator's name. A beautifully described scene that is almost a still life encapsu-lates Barthelme's ability to combine brand names and description to create a unique and somehow mysterious world. The narrator is home alone. In silence, he looks at a shadow cast on the wall by the "mercury vapor street lamp" shining through the Levolors; it is "broken by a gladiola on the pedestal where we always put outgoing mail." He is captivated; he sits there, watching the shadow ("it's gorgeous") and feeling like someone in an Obsession ad. Clearly Barthelme (who studied both art and architecture), as well as his characters, appreciates such sudden moments of beauty. Indeed, they are perhaps to be preferred to the uneasy, even vaguely threatening, human interactions that he describes. Barthelme criticizes but can also take delight in modern life, as when flowers, window blinds, and streetlights can produce a momentary respite from its uncertainties.

*McCrea Adams*

# THE CHRONICLE OF YOUNG SATAN

*Author:* Mark Twain (Samuel Langhorne Clemens, 1835-1910)
*Type of plot:* Fantasy
*Time of plot:* 1702
*Locale:* Imaginary Austrian village of Eseldorf
*First published:* 1969 (bowdlerized version published in 1916 as "The Mysterious Stranger")

*Principal characters:*
>THEODOR FISCHER, a village boy who narrates the story as an old man
>SATAN, an angel who assumes the name Philip Traum
>FATHER PETER, a kindly Roman Catholic priest
>FATHER ADOLF, an evil priest
>MARGET, Father Peter's adult niece
>WILHELM MEIDLING, Marget's sweetheart, a lawyer
>NIKOLAUS BAUMANN, Theodor's friend, a judge's son
>SEPPI WOHLMEYER, another friend, the son of the village's principal innkeeper

## The Story

After a brief prologue, this unfinished story opens with young Theodor Fischer, Nikolaus Baumann, and Seppi Wohlmeyer playing on a hillside, where a handsome young stranger joins them. The stranger, who seems to read Theodor's mind, impresses the boys with amazing tricks, including fashioning miniature people and animals out of clay and bringing them to life. He reveals that he is an angel named "Satan," a nephew of the great Satan, but as he is explaining that angels cannot commit sin, the tiny clay people begin to quarrel, and he quietly crushes them. Shortly after he leaves, the impoverished village priest Father Peter arrives, looking for his lost wallet. He finds it stuffed with gold coins, which the boys correctly guess were put there by young Satan.

Several days later, when another village priest, Father Adolf, learns about Peter's gold, he claims that Peter stole it from him and has him jailed, leaving Peter's niece Marget in financial trouble. One day Theodor and Satan find Marget's housekeeper, Ursula, comforting a stray kitten. Satan says it is a lucky cat that will provide for its owner. Afterward, silver coins regularly materialize in Ursula's pockets. As Marget appears increasingly prosperous, Father Adolf encourages villagers to spy on her. However, when he attends a party that she gives, he is possessed by Satan, who causes him to perform incredible and unnatural stunts and then disappear, leaving the villagers to think that God has deserted them.

Satan—who publicly calls himself Philip Traum—charms the villagers but causes such confusion that Theodor begins to regard his coming as a disaster. However, one night Satan takes him on an instantaneous trip to China and explains his views on human beings, whom he regards as mere machines without free will. Among his predictions is the disheartening revelation that Nikolaus will soon drown while trying to rescue a girl.

Later, Satan explains to Theodor and Seppi the history of human progress, showing them a panorama stretching from Cain's murder of Abel in the Garden of Eden through wars, murders, and massacres extending into the future. Afraid to ask Satan to predict his own future, Theodor instead asks for Seppi's future and gets it in a multivolume book that he will read through the rest of his own life. Theodor later learns that Seppi has a similar book about his (Theodor's) future. The boys often travel with Satan over great distances and times.

When Satan and Theodor witness the hanging of a suspected witch, Theodor joins the crowd in stoning her. Afterward, Satan says that sixty-two of the sixty-eight witnesses at the hanging did not want to throw stones but did so out of fear of being regarded as different. He explains that the human race is made up of sheep governed by minorities.

When Father Peter's trial finally begins, he is too feeble to attend, and Wilhelm Meidling represents him in court. Now back in the village, Father Adolf testifies against Peter, whose case appears hopeless until Satan—invisible to all but Theodor and Seppi—merges into Wilhelm's body and wins the case. Before anyone can reach Father Peter to report the good news, Satan visits him and tells him he has lost the case. The shock unsettles the priest and drives him mad; however, his madness leaves him happy—as Satan predicted he would become.

Afterward, Satan argues that humans live lives of uninterrupted self-deception and have scarcely a single fine quality. He takes Theodor to India, where he shows him a dramatic example of human greed and stupidity: A Portuguese farmer who refuses to share the limitless bounty of a fruit tree that Satan creates on his land. The narrative abruptly stops as Satan is about to expose a magician as a fake.

*Themes and Meanings*

Mark Twain worked on this story during the last years of the nineteenth century in the midst of writing other unfinished stories on closely related themes. One version, later published as "No. 44, The Mysterious Stranger," is set more than a century earlier than "The Chronicle of Young Satan" but opens with a nearly identical first chapter. A third version, later published as "Schoolhouse Hill," is placed in the nineteenth century Missouri setting of *The Adventures of Tom Sawyer* (1876) and uses several characters from that novel. The widely different chronological and geographical settings of these stories are strong indications of the relative unimportance of the early eighteenth century Austrian setting of "The Chronicle of Young Satan." What mattered to Twain were the story's universal themes.

One idea pervading "The Chronicle of Young Satan" is the difficulty of differentiating between reality and dreams—a theme that can be found in many unfinished stories that Twain wrote toward the end of his life. These include "The Great Dark" (first published in its entirety in 1962), which he wrote while working on "The Chronicle of Young Satan," "The Refuge of the Derelicts" (1972), and "Which Was the Dream?" (1967). In all these stories, successful middle-aged men find themselves in the midst of nightmares that seem so real that they begin to wonder if it is their normal lives that are the dreams.

"The Chronicle of Young Satan" opens with a description that sets a dreamlike mood for what follows:

> Yes, Austria was far from the world, and asleep, and our village was in the middle of that sleep, being in the middle of Austria. It drowsed in peace in the deep privacy of a hilly and woodsy solitude where news from the world hardly ever came to disturb its dreams, and was infinitely content.

After the arrival of the angel Satan, Theodor Fischer goes from one dreamlike experience to another, becoming increasingly unsure of the reality of his own senses. Significantly, the name that Satan uses when he is among other villagers is "Philip Traum"; *Traum* is a German word for "dream."

In 1916, six years after Twain died, his literary executor, Albert Bigelow Paine, with the help of magazine editor Frederick A. Duneka, published a condensed and bowdlerized version of "The Chronicle of Young Satan" as a magazine serial titled "The Mysterious Stranger" (also published in book form the same year). Paine presented this tale to the world as an authentic Twain story and even went so far as to tack onto it the last chapter of "No. 44, The Mysterious Stranger," claiming to have found the ending that Twain himself had lost. The extent of this literary fraud went undetected for nearly fifty years; meanwhile, "The Mysterious Stranger" grew famous for the bleak solipsistic ending that Paine had grafted onto the story; it ends with Satan telling Theodor that everything in the universe but his own existence is merely a dream. That ending is *not* part of "The Chronicle of Young Satan."

A more overt theme in "The Chronicle of Young Satan" is its exploration of God's indifference to humanity. This aspect of Twain's increasingly pessimistic philosophy is developed more extensively in another posthumously published work, "Letters from the Earth" (1962). In that epistolary story, the fallen archangel Satan visits Earth and writes back to his fellow archangels, Gabriel and Michael, to report his astonishment that humans seriously believe that God cares about them.

Visiting the earth on an unexplained mission, the Satan in "The Chronicle of Young Satan" is unimaginably old by Earth standards. He has been everywhere and seen everything and has godlike powers that allow him to move freely in time and space. Not constrained by the moral sense that afflicts mortal beings, he exists on a plane unimaginably higher than that of humans, whom he regards as inconsequential. Seeing humans as nothing more than machines with no ability to create, he laughs at the idea that human civilizations have achieved anything of which to be proud. As he weaves in and out of the lives of the villagers, he amuses himself by tampering with the fates of persons whom he encounters. During his very first appearance, he establishes that he is indifferent to human suffering when he shocks Theodor and his friends by callously destroying the village of miniature living people and animals he has created, as if they were still merely clay. When the boys express their dismay, his reaction is merely puzzled bewilderment.

*Style and Technique*

The structure of "The Chronicle of Young Satan" is similar to Twain's *The Personal Recollections of Joan of Arc* (1896), a thematically similar novel set in the fourteenth century. Both tales are related by elderly narrators recalling periods during their youth when they were close to remarkable beings that appeared not to be of this earth. The Joan of the novel is the historical French girl whose accomplishments in leading armies against English invaders made her seem divinely guided. The narrative technique in both these stories enabled Twain to balance the intimacy of first-hand observation against the distance of time.

All versions of Twain's so-called Mysterious Stranger stories are remarkable in their inventiveness and would have been regarded as pioneering works in science fiction and fantasy had they been published during his lifetime. Among the many literary innovations in "The Chronicle of Young Satan" are mind-reading, telekinesis, and teleportation. Although written more than a century ago, this comparatively unknown story is still capable of transporting readers into a world of ceaseless surprises and wonderment and is an important demonstration of the range of its author's creative powers.

*R. Kent Rasmussen*

# THE CHRYSANTHEMUMS

*Author:* John Steinbeck (1902-1968)
*Type of plot:* Domestic realism
*Time of plot:* 1937
*Locale:* The Salinas Valley in California
*First published:* 1938

> *Principal characters:*
> ELISA ALLEN, a woman in her thirties
> HENRY ALLEN, her husband
> MAN IN A WAGON, a tinker

*The Story*

Elisa Allen, a woman approaching middle age, is at a point in her life when she has begun to realize that her energy and creative drive far exceed the opportunities for their expression. Her marriage is reasonably happy—when she notices that her husband is proud of selling thirty head of steers he has raised, she gives him the compliment he hopes for, while he, in turn, appreciates her ability to grow flowers of exceptional quality. There is an easy banter between them, and while they have settled into a fairly familiar routine, they are still responsive to each other's moods, and eager to celebrate an achievement in each other's company with a night on the town. On the other hand, their marriage is childless, and Elisa generally wears bland, bulging clothes that tend to de-sex her. Their house is described as "hard-swept" and "hard-polished"; it is the only outlet for her talents and it is an insufficient focus for her energy. She has begun to sense that an important part of her is lying dormant and that the future will be predictable and rather mundane.

Although Elisa would never consider an actual affair, when a stranger appears at their farm offering to sharpen knives and mend pots, his singularity and unconventional appearance immediately arouse her interest. In contrast to her husband, he is a kind of adventurer who lives spontaneously, a man of the road not bound by standard measures of time and place. Because he has found it useful to be able to charm his potential customers into giving him work, he is accomplished at gauging a person's emotional needs, and he has developed a facility for the kind of conversation that verges on the suggestive. He is described as big, bearded, and graying, a man who has been around, who knows something about life and people: a man with a captivating presence whose eyes are dark and "full of brooding."

Elisa is fascinated by his way of life, overlooking the harshness and uncertainty of his existence in her eagerness to romanticize his style. When she tries to get him to discuss his travels, he steers the conversation back to the possibility of employment. When it is apparent that she has no work to give him, however, he cannily praises her flowers, and when Elisa responds to his "interest," he tells her that a woman he expects to see soon on his rounds has asked him to be on the watch for good seeds. Almost desperately eager to share the one thing she is actually doing, Elisa carefully gathers some shoots, and as she instructs the stranger on the proper care of the seedlings, her passionate involvement with the process of planting becomes an expression of all the suppressed romance in her life. The stranger senses this, and to show that he shares her vision, he offers just enough encouragement to lead her into a full-scale declaration of her profound sense of what planting means to her, a declaration that is presented in powerfully sensual terms. Elisa would like this moment of intensity to continue, but the tinker reminds her that hunger overcomes inspiration, and Elisa, somewhat abashed by her own openness, finds some useless, old pots for him to mend. She believes that the man has given her something intangible but valuable and that she is obliged to give him something he needs in return. As the man leaves, Elisa looks away after him, whispering to herself, "There's a bright direction. There's a glowing there."

The consequence of their conversation is very dramatic. Elisa feels energized and appreciated, delighted by her opportunity to share her special skill and excited by the chance to share, at least in her imagination, a totally different kind of life. As she prepares for the evening, the power she usually puts into scrubbing the house is redirected into her preparation to make herself as attractive as she now feels. Her husband is both surprised and pleased by her appearance, and their conversation is mixed with a pleasant uncertainty and a kind of unexpected delight as they both enjoy the animating effect of Elisa's encounter. Their mood remains distinctly elevated as they head for town, but then, Elisa sees a small speck on the road in the distance. Instantly, she realizes that this is the treasure she so avidly prepared. The tinker has discarded the flowers on the road to save the pot that contained them, the only object of value to him.

Elisa is shattered by the callous manner in which he has drawn something from her secret self and then completely betrayed her "gift" by not even taking the trouble to hide the flowers. She attempts to override her disappointment by maintaining a mood of gaiety, suggesting that they have wine at dinner, a bold gesture in the context of their lives. This, however, is not sufficient to help her restore her feelings of confidence and expectation, so she asks her husband if they might go to a prizefight, a request so completely out of character that her husband is totally baffled. She presses further, searching for that "special" feeling she held briefly, and asks if men "hurt each other very much." This is part of an effort to focus her own violent and angry feelings, but it is completely futile as an attempt to sustain and resurrect her sense of self-control and command. In a few moments, she completely gives up the pose, her whole body collapsing into the seat in an exhibition of defeat. As the story concludes, Elisa is struggling to hide her real feeling of pain from her husband. She is anticipating a dreadful future in which she pictures herself "crying weakly—like an old woman."

*Themes and Meanings*

John Steinbeck published "The Chrysanthemums" in a collection of stories called *The Long Valley* (1938). They are set in the Salinas Valley in California where he was born, the fertile farmland that the "Okies" settled after their flight from the Dust Bowl. Freed from the crushing burden of absolute poverty and social disintegration, Steinbeck's characters, like Henry Allen, are quite pleased to be able to make a decent living, but equally important, like Elisa Allen, they are beginning to sense that not everybody can be satisfied by bread alone.

In a subtle prefiguration of feminist philosophy, Steinbeck challenges the tradition of woman's "place"; although Henry Allen is well-meaning and basically decent, his concentration on his own role as provider, organizer, and decision-maker has blinded him to the fact that Elisa needs something more in her life than a neat house and a good garden. He is ready to offer what he can (a share in the work; brighter lights and bigger cities for occasional recreation), but Elisa's urgent need for someone to talk to who can understand the essential nature of her yearning for a poetic vision of the cosmos is, unfortunately, beyond Henry's range and insight. The question Steinbeck poses is whether one should settle for security and a lack of pain, or risk one's dreams in an attempt to live more completely and intensely. The retreat from action at the conclusion suggests that the risks are high, but there is a possibility that Elisa might not be permanently crushed by her pain.

The situation recalls D. H. Lawrence's story "The Shades of Spring," in which a woman reconciles herself to a steady man when the sparkling boy of her youth goes off to seek his fortune. However, she knows what she misses, and tells him on his return, "The stars are different with you." Elisa Allen is not ungrateful for her husband's kindness and for his provision of security, but the dark stranger brings thoughts of a life she has only sensed she was missing, and her response to his vague romantic encouragement startles her in its suddenness and its force. The paradox here is that the stranger has actually lost his spontaneity and manipulates her emotions not to satisfy his own romantic longings but to earn the money he needs for survival: money with which she no longer has to be concerned.

*Style and Technique*

It is clear from Steinbeck's epic novel of American experience, *The Grapes of Wrath* (1939), that he is particularly sensitive to the effect of landscape on a person's life. Because Elisa Allen's sense of her own self-worth is so closely tied to the land, Steinbeck has chosen to connect her psychic state to the season, the climate, and the terrain she inhabits. The mood of the story is set by his description of a fogbound valley in winter, a description that is also applicable to Elisa's mood. She is entering middle age, and when the valley is likened to a "closed pot" with "no sunshine . . . in December," there is a close parallel to the condition of her life at that point, a sealed vessel with little light available. Steinbeck calls it "a time of quiet and waiting," and the land, Elisa's only field of action, is dormant, with "little work to be done."

Elisa is earthbound, rooted securely in her garden but also held down by her connection to it. It is significant that her excitement in talking to the stranger is expressed by a vision of the stars and by her exclamation that "you rise up and up!" The stranger is not bound to a particular place, and although his freedom to roam is only a step removed from endless exile and rootlessness (as exemplified by Elisa's uprooting her plants, only to have them thrown away and left to die on the road), it is appealing in contrast to her chainlike connections to the earth.

Elisa is also seen alternately as a part of a larger landscape and as a small figure in an enclosed area. The story unfolds from an inventive cinematic perspective, as Steinbeck first describes the entire valley in a panoramic view, then moves closer to focus on the ranch in the valley, and then moves in for a close-up of Elisa working in her garden. Throughout the story, the perspective shifts from Elisa's narrow and cramped domain, walled or fenced in, to the entire ranch, and to the world beyond. Then, in a final shift, Elisa's shock is reflected by an image of multiple confinement, as she is enclosed by a wagon, surrounded by her seat and hidden within a coat that covers her face. It is not an image designed to create confidence in Elisa's prospects.

*Leon Lewis*

# CIMARRON

*Author:* Francine Prose (1947-    )
*Type of plot:* Domestic realism
*Time of plot:* 1983-1984
*Locale:* Cimarron Acres trailer park, near Oneonta, New York
*First published:* 1989

> *Principal characters:*
>> CORAL, a young expectant mother whose husband has been killed
>> MARGO, her mother-in-law
>> GENE, her father-in-law
>> LEE, a talkative neighbor
>> TRACY, Lee's "clairvoyant" daughter
>> PAUL, Coral's brother-in-law

*The Story*

Shortly after resigning herself to the fact that her husband, Kenny, will be absent from the birth of their first child, Coral sees a television news broadcast reporting that Kenny has been killed in Beirut, Lebanon. He is a victim of a terrorist car bomb attack on his military barracks. Over the ensuing weeks, Coral takes poor care of herself. Still numbed by Kenny's death, she exists only mechanically. She is thus relieved when her in-laws, Gene and Margo, take charge of her life by moving her to their somewhat unkempt rural trailer court at Cimarron Acres.

As more time passes Coral and Margo become closer. Coral also gets to know Lee, a single mother who lives in a neighboring trailer. Lee's conversations center on the perils of being a single mother and her conceited ten-year-old daughter, Tracy—who Lee believes is gifted with "second sight."

As Coral spends her free time taking walks, she notices the details of Cimarron Acres. At first she is uneasy with the ugly environment, especially a landfill behind the trailer. As she studies the mildly unpleasant children and mothers who inhabit the park, she worries about how her own child will turn out. Meanwhile, she also becomes acquainted with Kenny's brother Paul, who occasionally has dinner with his parents.

As the weather grows warmer, Coral gets bigger and her routine continues with little change. At times, Coral, Margo, and Gene laugh together at Coral's accurate impersonations of little Tracy and Margo's impersonations of Lee. One day Lee bursts in to announce that she has won five hundred dollars in a lottery with numbers that Tracy picked. Lee uses the money to prepare a special birthday party for Tracy.

Feeling relaxed on the day of Tracy's party, Coral is finally comfortable among her new neighbors and they are now used to her. As she and Paul sit together in Lee's yard, watching the festivities, Coral suddenly realizes that she has forgotten to buy Tracy a gift. Although she is not particularly fond of Tracy, she feels awful because she knows that each childhood birthday comes only once. Meanwhile, Tracy and Lee make a big production out of gathering presents from the guests. When Tracy sees that Coral has no gift for her, she calmly tells her of a "vision" she has had of Coral's baby in heaven, lying happily next to the Doberman who killed it. At first Coral is overcome by the fact that anyone—even a child like Tracy—can be so cruel to a pregnant mother. Then she realizes that her baby will be healthy, as Tracy is only being vindictive.

The story concludes with Paul's distant voice coming to Coral as she hugs her well-rounded stomach and thinks about her baby.

*Themes and Meanings*

"Cimarron" first appeared in a collection of short stories by twenty-two writers that was designed to benefit Share Our Strengths, a campaign against hunger, homelessness, and illiteracy. In some ways the tragic circumstances experienced by Francine Prose's character Coral might suggest a basis for the problems addressed by the campaign. After abruptly losing the emotional and physical support of her husband and pregnant with her first child, Coral becomes little more than an automaton. In deep shock she gazes repeatedly at pictures of Beirut in *Newsweek*, doing little more to care for herself than making mechanical trips to buy frozen dinners—one meal at a time. Though she realizes that this life is "unhealthy, and probably bad for the baby," she cannot break her cycle of despondency.

Though issues of poverty and homelessness are not central to this story, one senses that the root causes for these conditions—such as loss through death, isolation, or alienation—are being suggested. In that respect, it is not so much that Margo and Gene offer Coral a place to live but that they present her with safe haven, a place where she can reassess her life and heal. As the story progresses, it conveys a slow movement toward Coral's restoration of her strength and wits. Just as it is clear that Coral is a survivor, it is apparent that her willingness to live with Gene and Margo comes from her core of strength and knowledge of self. She is not presented as either self-destructive or foolish. At first Coral is disturbed by Cimarron Acres, with its "one frozen-solid brown road, rutted and covered with dog turds" and its "junk machinery everywhere," but gradually she understands that she needs the "solid presence" of Margo's shoulder on which to cry.

The characters of Lee and her daughter Tracy allow Prose to explore the further theme of coping in a sometimes hostile world. As Coral begins to become herself again, she thinks that she might be able to relate to the apparently independent Lee, only to realize that Lee is not quite the role model that she first appeared to be. For example, Lee's campaign to have a school-bus stop moved to the other side of the road reveals a selfish interest rather than one aimed at general betterment. When Lee is not boasting about Tracy, her conversations are limited to forceful declarations about the hard lives endured by single mothers, laced with horrific anecdotes. However, Lee's self-absorption (or her self-destructive chain smoking) may not necessarily be indictments. Lee may simply represent another kind of survivor—one whose circumstances force her in a different direction. The difference between Coral and Lee is that Coral has the support of people who care. However, Prose also leaves it clear—as ten-year-old Tracy chillingly predicts to Coral her baby's mutilation—that we remain prepared for the almost unlimited evil exhibited by those "just waiting . . . so they can drive into you and blow you up."

*Style and Technique*

Prose presents a realistic portrait of Coral's struggle to get on with her life. It succeeds because it first allows the reader to believe in what Coral has to endure. Coral's reactions immediately after hearing the news of her husband's death are not unlike those experienced by anyone who has abruptly lost a loved one. Coral's initial responses are almost surreal as the rituals of the funeral and visitors offering consolation take on the cartoonlike qualities of a wacky animated feature for her. Afterward, as she settles into a bare existence, Prose again hits the mark, achieving for the reader a feeling of sluggish inertia as Coral stares at her *Newsweek* magazines, heats frozen dinners, or lies awake nights worrying about her baby.

The next stage of Prose's story takes Coral from her nearly catatonic existence to one of renewed strength and hope. Though real change will take more time, the progression is discernible in gradual degrees. After relocating to Margo and Gene's trailer, Coral meekly submits to Margo's suggestions and commands. All the time she is conscious of her unborn baby, and it is evident by her concern about the landfill, for instance, that even before she begins to recover, her baby is foremost in her mind.

As Coral gradually reawakens to the world around her, the characters of Lee and Tracy are introduced. Because they are both odd figures, they initially provide a source of fun as Margo and Coral take turns mimicking them. Later, Lee becomes a yardstick by which Coral seems to measure her own fitness for motherhood. What this demonstrates is Coral's own gradually reawakening desire to be a mother. It is another step in her transition from shock to a state approaching normality.

Paul is little developed in the story; however, his function does not necessitate fully rounded characterization. Through his character the reader can further estimate the degree of Coral's own healing. At first, Paul's habits (such as throwing the dinner napkin into the trash after the meal) only remind Coral of Kenny, but gradually she begins once again to focus on her own physical and emotional needs concerning men. The character of Paul allows the reader to perceive Coral's slow movement away from withdrawal and toward integration. As if to focus attention on Coral's recovery, Prose allows only a minimal suggestion of romantic interest between Coral and Paul at the story's end. What is important is the fact that Coral is now finding her own strengths again.

*George T. Novotny*

# THE CINDERELLA WALTZ

*Author:* Ann Beattie (1947-      )
*Type of plot:* Character study, psychological
*Time of plot:* The late 1970's
*Locale:* Connecticut suburb and New York City
*First published:* 1979

> *Principal characters:*
> THE NARRATOR, a divorced woman and mother
> MILO, her self-centered former husband
> LOUISE, their nine-year-old daughter
> BRADLEY, Milo's homosexual lover

## The Story

"The Cinderella Waltz" consists of the memories, reflections, and insights of a divorced woman living with her nine-year-old daughter, Louise. The narration begins as she is waiting for her former husband Milo and his lover, Bradley, to pick up their daughter for her usual weekend visit. As she helps Louise pack her usual shopping bag of trinkets and toys, which give her security outside her mother's home, she thinks back to the final years of her marriage to Milo. She is trying to make the transition go smoothly for Louise, who has somewhat disconcertingly decided to pack a copy of a play by the modern existential playwright Samuel Beckett titled *Happy Days* (1961). However, she is always pulled back to the feelings of betrayal and abandonment she experienced in the dark period when her marriage to the arrogant Milo began to disintegrate.

She recalls how she and the empathic and considerate Bradley slowly became friends even as she and Milo maintained a cool emotional distance from each other. She has begun to realize, however, that Milo, a cold perfectionist, is finding flaws in Bradley as he once did with her. An even more disturbing issue for the narrator is the way in which Milo continually raises the possibility that he might relocate to San Francisco, a subject that inevitably makes both the narrator and her daughter apprehensive and fearful.

The next weekend, Milo begins to bicker with his daughter Louise, who expresses her growing sense of vulnerability by putting an old doll into her shopping bag. When Louise returns from New York City, where she played hostess for her father at his dinner party, Louise tells her mother that Bradley, who has been unwell and has lost his job, was absent. Later when Bradley phones the narrator and asks to come to talk to her about Milo, this unusual situation confirms the reality that, whether Bradley is friend or rival, their relationship to the touchy and self-involved Milo is essentially identical.

Soon after, the narrator is shocked to learn through a casual conversation with Milo's sister that her former husband is, indeed, going to California. When Milo proposes a champagne toast to his new life at a Sunday brunch that he has arranged for Bradley and his former wife, his daughter, Louise, bursts into tears and will not be consoled until Milo promises her magical visits to San Francisco, especially a ride in a glass elevator to the top of the Fairmont Hotel. This prospect leads the narrator to remember that Milo used to say that he wanted to give Louise glass slippers instead of bootees when she was a baby. With this memory comes a realization that her daughter is her husband's new Cinderella, while she and Bradley are discarded partners. The anguish of their rejection is contrasted with Louise's momentary "happy ending," which is itself complicated by an anxious recognition that soon Louise herself will know the pain of abandonment by the heartless Milo.

### Themes and Meanings

The central theme of this story is indicated by the Cinderella reference, which Ann Beattie uses as a contrast to her contemporary love story. Although Milo is the prince, promising fairy-tale happiness, his two previous partners have been rejected, each in his or her turn, as he moves on to someone else to play Cinderella to his Prince Charming. The ironic use of the Cinderella story points to the major themes of modern love, which does not promise a "happy ever after" but instead promises freedom from permanence or binding ties.

The use of the Cinderella story is perhaps the most prominent of the many ways in which Milo's euphoric sense of romantic possibilities is undermined by the story's disenchanted narrator, whose voice adds levels of skepticism and irony throughout the story, directed in the main at Milo, who must invest himself and everyone else with a magical glow and who will withdraw with icy fury when reality does not cooperate. Milo's presentation of himself as a free, modern, self-fulfilled individual is here debunked as in fact a form of toxic narcissism. His seductive charm and constant changing of partners—his Cinderella waltz—is exposed as an evil that makes him a dangerous new variation of the traditional Prince Charming of the fairy tale. Underneath Milo's perpetually youthful insouciance, Beattie suggests, is a sense of entitlement and a need for unlimited freedom that will leave in its wake a trail of damaged and disillusioned former partners.

This depiction of Milo's destructive narcissism is connected to a larger theme that pervades much of Beattie's fiction, namely the dubious lifestyle engendered by the baby boom generation who came of age during the 1960's and were forever altered by the experience. For Beattie, the members of this generation have cut their ties to any past models of family life or marriage and instead drift in and out of disposable relationships with little sense of obligation, preferring instead an ethic of personal liberty and pleasure that limits their ability to sustain relationships over time. Members of a generation that no longer lives within the stable world of family or community, Beattie's characters often seem trapped in a rootless present in which relationships are impermanent and shallow. For instance, although the narrator realizes that Bradley is her friend, she is also stunned that she does not know who Bradley's other friends are, how old he is, where he grew up, or what he really cares about. It is clear that Milo's job, residence, love life, and identity as a father are all surprisingly provisional.

Another major theme in this story is the precocious child. Louise is adjusting to her parent's divorce and her father's new lover with a degree of sophistication and perspicacity that suggests someone alarmingly wise beyond her years. This sense of a child hurried into adulthood is further exacerbated by Milo's use of Louise as a hostess for his dinner parties—she has somehow become the "woman of the house" in Milo's apartment. The blurring of the ordinary roles of parent and child adds to the disturbing quality of this story. Beattie points out, however, that Louise still retains a child's needs and vulnerability and that her need for love may by frustrated by a parent such as Milo. Bradley and the narrator also have emotional needs unmet by Milo, so that they too seem like abandoned children, bereft of secure affection or a safe harbor.

## Style and Technique

The story is shaped by the first-person perspective of the unnamed narrator. Suggesting the depressed sensibility of one who has been wounded or abandoned, this disenchanted perspective is the ground of "The Cinderella Waltz." Every character and situation is filtered through this tone of voice, which is flexible enough to include both ironic humor and deep sadness.

Another important aspect of Beattie's style is its economical understatement. Presenting her material in a low-key and even offhand series of episodes, Beattie requires the reader to draw emotional inferences that are not at first obvious. Satiric and detached, Beattie's narrative style is a counterpoise to subject matter that might be expected to induce more expressive and obvious emotion. This cool, quiet style is reinforced by Beattie's structure, which consists of a series of loose, episodic vignettes that seem to be composed of little more than an accretion of seemingly casual events, conversations, or observations. However, what seems an unconstructed, drifting narrative is in fact organized around details that are there for very specific and telling purposes. Details such as Louise's attachment to the bleak Samuel Beckett play or Milo's repainting his apartment stark, minimal white, allow the reader to draw wider inferences about character and situation. Perhaps the most important of these details is the image of the glass slippers mentioned at the end of the story—this image returns readers to the title of the story and serves to consolidate the Cinderella theme as a crucial one. Placing this image at the end of her story intensifies its impact and reminds readers to reflect on its meaning and the meaning of her title. In addition, Beattie's careful placement of the image of Milo and Louise riding euphorically up into the air in a magical glass elevator as the story's last sentence further develops the Cinderella theme, while touching once again on the resonant issue of disappearance, flight, and abandonment. What at first might appear to be a casual string of episodes is gathered into a final, unifying depiction of this story's two themes, that of Milo's world of magical escape and the listless depression of a discarded Cinderella whose romantic expectations have been dashed.

*Margaret Boe Birns*

# CINNAMON SHOPS

*Author:* Bruno Schulz (1892-1942)
*Type of plot:* Fantasy
*Time of plot:* The early twentieth century
*Locale:* A small city in Poland
*First published:* "Sklepy cynamanowe," 1934 (English translation, 1963)

> *Principal characters:*
> THE NARRATOR, a boy of high school age
> HIS FATHER
> HIS MOTHER
> PROFESSOR ARENDT, his drawing teacher
> AN OLD CAB HORSE

*The Story*

On winter days, the narrator's father communes with an invisible world that he shares with the family cat. To distract him, his mother arranges to have the family attend the theater. Before the curtain rises, however, the father notices that he has left at home his "wallet containing money and certain most important documents." The boy is sent home to fetch it.

He steps into a clear winter night and soon finds his imagination creating "illusory maps of the apparently familiar districts." Soon the town dissolves into "the tissue of dreams." He looks for his beloved cinnamon shops, replete with curiosities from and books about exotic places. He turns into a street he knows, but it presents him with an unknown vista of orchards, parks, and ornate villas—which metamorphose into the back of the high school building. He recalls the late-evening drawing classes taught there by Professor Arendt, an enthusiastic and inspiring teacher.

Seeking out the professor's classroom, the narrator instead finds himself in an unfamiliar wing of the school building, which houses the headmaster's magnificently luxurious apartment. Embarrassed to be caught prying into private quarters, he runs into the street and hails a horse-drawn cab, which circles the city. The cabdriver catches sight of a crowd of fellow cabbies gathered in front of an inn and jumps off the carriage to join them, abandoning his vehicle to the narrator and his old horse, which "inspired confidence—it seemed smarter than its driver." The narrator yields himself to the horse's will.

The cab leaves the city and enters a hilly landscape, while the boy enjoys the unforgettable sight of a starry sky and the haunting scent of the violet-perfumed night air. He is happy. At last the horse stops, panting. The narrator remarks tears in its eyes, a wound on its belly. He asks the horse why it did not reveal its injury sooner. The horse replies, "'My dearest, I did it for you' . . . and became very small, like a wooden toy."

The narrator leaves the horse, still feeling "light and happy," and runs most of the distance back to the city. He keeps admiring the changing shapes of the sky's many configurations. In the city's central square he meets people whose faces, like his, are uplifted with delight as they gaze at the sky's silvery magic and he "completely stop[s] worrying about Father's wallet," assuming that his father had most likely forgotten about it by now. Meeting with school friends who have been awakened by the brightly illuminated sky, the boy accompanies them, "uncertain whether it was the magic of the night which lay like silver on the snow or whether it was the light of dawn."

## Themes and Meanings

A thin, reclusive, shy, and sickly man, Bruno Schulz earned his living as a high school drawing instructor in his native southeastern Poland and wrote stories in his spare time but was too timid to submit them to publishers until friends arranged an introduction to Zofia Nalkowska, a highly regarded Warsaw novelist. She arranged for the publication of a slender volume of his short stories in 1934. Titled *Sklepy cynamanowe*, it was translated into English by Celina Wieniewska and published in 1963, in Britain under the title of *Cinnamon Shops* and in the United States as *The Street of Crocodiles*. Schulz was subsequently to produce one more collection of stories, a novella, and the manuscript of a novel before his death at the hands of the Nazis in 1942.

In Schulz's fiction, the narrator typically related phantasmagoric incidents wherein everyday reality is transfigured into a dream by the protagonist's surrealistic imagination. In an interview, Schulz termed the collection *Cinnamon Shops* "a biographical novel" whose spiritual genealogy vanishes into "mythological hallucination." This is evident in the title story, which lyrically celebrates a teenage boy's separation and individuation from his parents and commitment to a fictive family of animistic creatures and phenomena.

Central to most of the tales in *Cinnamon Shops* is the father, causing critics to compare Schulz to another Slavic-Jewish writer, Franz Kafka (1883-1924). However, whereas Kafka magnifies the progenitor to a potent, punitive, stern patriarch of God-like authority, Schulz reduces him to an eccentric but frail, antic and confused occultist dominated by his wife and maid. In "Cinnamon Shops," the father is a foolish fumbler, on speaking terms with an unseen world of imps and demons, escaping the demands of everyday routine and the needs of his family by engaging in interior monologues inaccessible to the outer world. The mother receives short, undefined shrift in this story; in other texts she is portrayed as energetic, practical, but unloving. Schulz's art can be more illuminatingly related to that of Isaac Bashevis Singer (1904-1991), another Polish Jew, with whom he shares an engrossment in folk motifs and supernatural powers. Although both Kafka and Singer are rooted in the tradition of Jewish religiosity, however, Schulz is a secularist whose mythological world is individualized, formless, fragmented, contingent, and isolated.

It is a world of animism in which reality is frequently irrational and fluid. Schulz is Platonic in rejecting the objective evidence of the senses. Matter and creatures can change shapes and faculties, can distort space or time. The father is more intimate with his cat than he is with his family; the boy's imagination accords credibility to fantasized streets, doorless houses, classic gods, mirrors exchanging glances, friezes panicking, and a horse addressing him intelligibly. The boy is the story's mythmaker: He is an artist of the fantastic, reminiscent of Marc Chagall (1887-1985), another Slavic Jew, in his glowing, occult visions that celebrate the ethereal manifestations of a magic universe in the landscape of the night sky.

*Style and Technique*

Schulz makes his hero's mythological hallucinations plausible by enveloping them in bold similes and metaphors brimming with intensely pictorial effects. Thus, midwinter is "edged on both sides with the furry dusk of mornings and evenings"; a park's bushes are "full of confusion, secret gestures, conniving looks"; cabs loom in the street "like crippled, dozing crabs or cockroaches"; the air "shimmered like silver gauze"; hills "rose like sighs of bliss"; the narrator is "touched by the divine finger of poetry." The imagery is sharp, immediate, and unforgettably lyrical.

Animism and anthropomorphism charge the story's texture. Gardens become parks that become forests. The night's stillness is interrupted by the "sighs and whispers of the crumbling gods" depicted in the statuary collected by the art professor. Mounted weasels and martens leave their school cabinets to mate nocturnally in park thickets. Schulz's language teems with a pan-masquerade of changed dimensions and roles, an intense hymn that expresses the narrator's delight with a universe alive with amazement and mystery. Although limited in scope and range, Schulz's talent is one of the most richly imaginative among European prose writers who matured between World Wars I and II.

*Gerhard Brand*

# THE CIRCULAR RUINS

*Author:* Jorge Luis Borges (1899-1986)
*Type of plot:* Fantasy
*Time of plot:* Unspecified
*Locale:* An unnamed jungle
*First published:* "Las ruinas circulares," 1940 (English translation, 1962)

> *Principal characters:*
> THE DREAMER, a worshiper of the fire god
> HIS SON

*The Story*

In "The Circular Ruins," from a nameless home in a time not marked on calendars, a figure known only as "the taciturn man" or "the gray man" beaches a bamboo canoe on the bank of a jungle river. When he lands, he kisses the mud and heads inland to the circular ruins: the ruins of an abandoned temple to a god no longer worshiped. He sleeps there in the ruins, and when he awakes, he will begin a task of creation.

He awakes in the morning and sees tracks around him, which inform him that the local residents of the area have observed him during the night. Those visitors suit his purpose: He has come to this region, as Jorge Luis Borges says, "to dream a man." He wants to dream this creation in every detail—every hair, every pore—and through the intensity and thoroughness of his dreaming, make it real. He has come to the ruins seeking their aid in the accomplishment of his task, seeking their loneliness and their barrenness. There will be less to distract him from his work. The local people will not intrude on him during the day but, filled with superstition, will supply his bodily needs with their offerings each night.

He begins by dreaming of an enormous lecture hall filled with students, candidates for the honor of being dreamed into reality. He considers all of them until he selects one, the likeliest, on whom to concentrate. After a few private lessons in his dreams, however, what he calls a catastrophe takes place. The dreamer is unable to sleep. After the dreamer begins to appreciate the difficulty of his task, he gives up conscious intention and no longer tries to direct his dreams. He abandons premeditation and lets the dreams come when they will.

On the night of the full moon, he falls asleep "with his heart throbbing"; it is of a heart that he dreams, a beating heart within a body whose form he cannot yet see. For two weeks he concentrates on that heart in his dreams, merely observing, not interfering. There is a hint that the dreamer is a magician: He lectures on magic to the imaginary students; he calls on the names of gods and planets. He works this sort of spell before dreaming of the next organ of his creation. When that one is finished, he goes on to another. A year passes before he comes to the skeleton. The "innumerable hair" is the hardest of all, but eventually he dreams an entire sleeping young man.

When the dreamer finally awakens his creation, it is crude and clumsy, like Frankenstein's monster, and the dreamer almost despairs. In his exhaustion, he throws himself before the strangely shaped statue of the god of the ruins and pleads with it to help him. Then, the fire god appears before the dreamer in his sleep and agrees to bring his creation to life in a special way: To all but the fire god and the dreamer, the creation will seem to be a normal man. However, there is a price for this gift. The dreamer must educate his creation in the ritual of the fire god, and when this child of his mind has learned the mysteries of that worship, he must be sent downstream to the next ruined temple to reestablish the worship of the fire god.

The dreamer agrees and, in the months that follow, instructs the created being whom he is now beginning to think of as his son. He cuts his waking hours down to an irreducible minimum, looking forward to sleep and the company of his creation.

He starts to introduce his son to "reality." For example, as always in a dream, he instructs the young man to place a flag on a mountaintop. When the dreamer awakes, he finds the flag where it was planted, flying in place in the waking world. After other such trials, he believes that his son is ready to be "born," to enter the waking world of the dreamer. In his dream that night, he kisses his son and sends him to the temple ruins downstream to take up his duties. He gives the youth one last gift, however: So that his creation will not think himself different from any other man, the dreamer erases from his mind the memory of his years of instruction.

Having achieved his greatest desire, the dreamer's life begins to interest him less and less. One night he is awakened by two local men who tell him of a man of strange powers in a nearby temple, a man who is able to walk on fire without being burned. He at once realizes that this man is his son, and he worries that his son's peculiar power might cause him to doubt his own reality. He imagines how humiliating it would be for one to realize that one is merely the creation of another's mind.

Eventually, these doubts of the dreamer pass. A night comes, however, on which the circular ruins, ages ago destroyed by fire, catch fire again. As the flames rise around him, the dreamer is not alarmed; his life's work is done and he is ready to die. Rather than try to escape, he walks toward the flames. When he enters them, however, they do not burn him. In a flash he realizes that this immunity to fire is the same as his son's, and he understands that he too is an illusion, the dream-child of another.

### Themes and Meanings

Borges was a great admirer of Lewis Carroll's comic fantasies, as seen in Borges's neatly summarizing the theme of "The Circular Ruins" with a quotation that stands at the head of the story: "And if he left off dreaming about you . . . " from Lewis Carroll's *Through the Looking-Glass and What Alice Found There* (1871). The reference is from a chapter of Carroll's book in which Tweedledee shows Alice the sleeping Red King, tells her that the king is dreaming about her, and asks, "And if he left off dreaming about you, where do you suppose you'd be?" Alice says she would be where she is now, but Tweedledee disagrees "contemptuously." He says, "You'd be nowhere. Why, you're only a sort of thing in his dream!"

Borges puts this notion, used for comedy in Carroll's book, to chilling effect in "The Circular Ruins" as the realization of the dreamer at the end of the story comes with enormous impact. Critics have called the story one of the most horrifying of Borges's works, yet it is simply the logical extension of a philosophical notion that informs the majority of Borges's fiction.

This notion, usually called "idealism" with various adjectives prefixed to it, can be traced to a number of philosophers whom Borges himself cites in various works. For example, the eighteenth century English philosopher George Berkeley developed a philosophy called "pluralistic idealism," which holds that the so-called real world perceived as around one exists only in one's consciousness. His German contemporary Immanuel Kant took this idea even further. Kant's "critical idealism" holds that matter does not exist if it is not sensed by the individual. The often-quoted question, "If a tree falls in the forest and no one hears it, does it make a sound?" is a question to which the idealist answers "No."

## Style and Technique

The word "circular" in the title accurately describes the form that Borges's story takes. At the end of the story the pieces fall neatly into place: Remembering that the dreamer erased all memories of his beginning from his son's mind, the reader recalls with new understanding the mysterious origin of the dreamer himself. The reader is never told where the dreamer comes from, except that it is upstream. His history is scanted, and the reader is never told how it is that he knows about the ritual of the fire god, or how he has acquired his magical powers. When the dreamer realizes that he is merely one revolution in a cycle, the reader realizes that the dreamer's memory has been wiped clean by his "father," just as the dreamer has done for his "son."

Borges's reliance on philosophical idealism in his fiction should not be taken as evidence that he seriously believed that human perception creates the universe. Rather, the philosophy is one that he could put to work in art; in "The Circular Ruins," it allows an ending of great power and surprise. Borges had a thorough familiarity with English and American literature, even with what is sometimes called "popular" literature—the detective story, for example. He often expressed an admiration for the classic detective story, especially for its ending, in which all the pieces of the mystery must fall into place in a revelation that is both surprising and satisfying to the reader. Just such a story, transposed into fantasy, is "The Circular Ruins."

*Walter E. Meyers*

# CITY BOY

*Author:* Leonard Michaels (1933-    )
*Type of plot:* Psychological
*Time of plot:* The mid-twentieth century
*Locale:* New York City, Upper East Side
*First published:* 1969

> *Principal characters:*
> PHILLIP, a young unemployed man, the narrator
> VERONICA, his girlfriend
> MORRIS COHEN, Veronica's wealthy father
> LUDWIG, the elevator operator

*The Story*

In Phillip's narrative, the thoughtless sexual behavior of Phillip and his girlfriend, Veronica, causes Veronica's father to have a heart attack. Though shamed, sorrowful, and vexed with Phillip, Veronica, on learning from her mother that her father will survive the attack, demands sex from Phillip.

At the outset of the story, Phillip and Veronica are having sex on the rug in the living room of her family home, surrounded in the dark by her family's expensive paintings and furnishings. Because her parents are in the next room, Veronica says what they are doing is crazy, but she responds eagerly to his touch. Phillip bites her neck, and she kisses his ear. While they are copulating, Phillip imagines that the furnishings are observing and reacting to them. Venting his lust, Phillip crushes Veronica's willing body under him, and—naked, satisfied, and exhausted—they both fall asleep.

Morris Cohen, Veronica's father, enters the living room to ask Veronica to tell her boyfriend to go home. From the other room, Veronica's mother can be heard complaining about her husband's lack of decisiveness. In the dark living room, Mr. Cohen accidentally steps on Phillip, pressing him into Veronica, who experiences a climax. Their secret tryst exposed, Phillip and Veronica fumble around as the outraged Mr. Cohen upbraids them. Phillip stumbles into the blinds, breaking some glass, and hearing the noise from the safe vantage of the other room, Veronica's mother threatens her husband if anything has been damaged. Phillip escapes naked.

While waiting for the elevator, Phillip decides to stand on his hands on the chance that his pubic hair will be mistaken for a beard and his penis for a nose. Ludwig, the elevator operator is not deceived but does not make an issue of Phillip's nakedness. Instead, he asks that Phillip treat Veronica more thoughtfully. Phillip is grateful.

Phillip proceeds naked down the street, climbs barefoot down the spit-spattered subway steps, and asks the neat African American man in the ticket booth to let him enter the train platform free. The ticket man refuses and, on noticing Phillip's nakedness, demands that he leave the station. At the head of the subway steps, Phillip encounters Veronica, who has chased after him with his clothes. She helps him dress.

Phillip walks her home, convinced that his feelings for her have vanished. He is prepared to tell her, but before he can act, however, he learns that Veronica's father has had a heart attack.

Ludwig takes the couple up in the elevator, and once in the apartment, Veronica rushes to the toilet, turns on the faucet, and urinates. Phillip wants to watch her, but annoyed, she tells him to wait in the living room. Her mother calls from the hospital and informs Veronica that her father is recovering and that they will be home in the morning. No sooner does Veronica hang up the phone and share the good news with Phillip than, sexually stimulated by tensions of their now relatively harmless adventure, she crudely orders him to have sex with her.

*Themes and Meanings*

The jobless Phillip lives alone, apart from his parents, in a shabby apartment in the slums, but his knowledge of the paintings of the French artists Maurice Utrillo and Maurice de Vlaminck indicates that he has been well educated. Utrillo painted Paris city scenes, and Vlaminck, a landscape artist, in his youth was a Fauvist, one of the early twentieth century "wild beasts" who experimented with vivid colors, avoiding realistic coloration and instead substituting different, often shocking, colors for natural hues. Phillip likes to think of himself as a sophisticated young man, a "city boy," but his hormones are still pumping out of control. Like Utrillo, he has an urban perspective, but like Vlaminck, he is a wild beast, a cauldron of hot passions. The degree of Veronica's sophistication is unclear, but she also bubbles with desire. What does it take, the story implicitly asks, to bring such heat under control?

As wild images explode in Phillip's mind, Phillip and Veronica clasp and sunder on the living room rug. Like untamed animals, they lie naked, one thin wall and door away from Veronica's parents. The young lovers are mortified when Veronica's father discovers them. However, when Phillip rises and he and Mr. Cohen look into each others' eyes, Philip recognizes them as "secret sharers." The phrase alludes to the 1912 novella of the same name by Joseph Conrad about a sailor who looks over the side of his ship and confronts his double in the water.

However, the simile Phillip invokes to characterize the place where he and Mr. Cohen confront each other is drawn neither from the New York City apartment in which the meeting takes place nor from the world where the events of "The Secret Sharer" happen. Rather, Phillip sees the confrontation as taking place in hell. Hell is the place the French existentialist philosopher Jean-Paul Sartre used to characterize the world in his play *Huis clos* (1944; *In Camera*, 1946, better known as *No Exit*, 1947). Existence precedes essence, Phillip thinks a little later, echoing Sartre. If so, it is possible to amend one's life. However, almost immediately Phillip recognizes that the opposite is true. He and Mr. Cohen, in this hell of daily life, are what they must be: Essence precedes existence.

In what sense are Phillip and Mr. Cohen images of each other? The question is never directly asked, but, clearly, at least once in their lives, Mr. and Mrs. Cohen clasped and sundered as Phillip and Veronica do. Late in life, as passions wane and the body moves toward death, it is possible to react with disgust to the passions of youth as Mr. Cohen does. However, the more profound insight of age into the problem of sexuality is reserved for another of the figures Phillip invokes. When naked, he sees himself as related to octogenarian King Lear, the hero of William Shakespeare's tragedy, first produced around 1605 or 1606. Lear, the father of three daughters, tore off his clothes to reveal the depraved animal that hides behind civilized cloaks.

Not even the horror of triggering Mr. Cohen's heart attack can save Phillip and Veronica from their lust. In fact, Veronica's desire is heightened by it. Civilized behavior—like clothing or the sound of a faucet flowing to cover the sound of urinating—masks but does not remove basic impulses. Veronica regrets the tryst that resulted in her father's heart attack, and Phillip desires to end the relationship; however, once Mr. Cohen is recovering, their story ends with Veronica's demand for raw sex.

On the basis of what Phillip saw in Veronica's father's eyes, the reader can guess that on the road to becoming like Mr. Cohen, Phillip will very willingly accede to Veronica's order. If he does not marry her eventually, he will nevertheless end up dominated by someone who will play Mrs. Cohen in his life, and if they have daughters, the reader can easily imagine what the result will be. Civilized trappings notwithstanding, humanity is controlled by the raw animal nature that has produced and will continue to control its world. Whatever people's aspirations, essence precedes existence in the world that Leonard Michaels here presents, and the essence of young adulthood is overwhelming lust.

*Style and Technique*

Michaels uses the youthful but sophisticated voice of Phillip, dominated by his frenetic perceptions, to track his protagonist's experiences from inside. Phillip, just emerging into adulthood, has been well schooled, but his still adolescent passions are out of control. Those of his girlfriend, Veronica, also smolder.

Michaels uses his characters' names to imply some of the history behind the story. The names of Phillip and Veronica are the self-consciously cultivated choices of upper-middle-class parents who have aspirations for social elegance. Phillip was Alexander the Great's father, and Veronica is the name of a flowering plant, but not your everyday rose, daisy, or lily. The veronica's flower, rarely seen in common gardens, blossoms in showy blue spikes, and Veronica in the contemporary comic strip *Archie* is an elegant, rich, and sophisticated young woman, contrasted with the friendly accessible Betty.

Generally, Veronica is a rich person's name. Phillip invokes a sophisticated sense of history. Such appellations and the fact that Veronica's home is decorated with paintings by great artists constitute clear declarations of wealth, cultivation, and taste. However, the dangerous and uncontrollable passions that course through the young are no more constrained by wealth, cultivation, and taste than they are by caution, common courtesy, and clothes.

*Albert Wachtel*

# CITY LIFE

*Author:* Mary Gordon (1949-    )
*Type of plot:* Domestic realism
*Time of plot:* The late 1990's
*Locale:* New York
*First published:* 1996

*Principal characters:*
PETER TALBOT, a college mathematics professor
BEATRICE TALBOT, his wife
A FORMER COLUMBIA CHEMISTRY PROFESSOR, their downstairs
apartment neighbor

## The Story

"City Life" is told in the third person through an omniscient narrator. The story begins with a description of Beatrice's childhood and follows her as she marries Peter Talbot, has three boys, and moves with her husband and children from Ithaca, New York, to an apartment in New York City. The young Beatrice's father is a gravedigger, and her mother is a housewife. Both are alcoholics. The family lives in a one-room, windowless house, down a dirt road in the middle of the woods. The single room serves as bedroom, kitchen, and living area and provides no privacy for any family member. In addition, the house is filthy and disorderly.

Beatrice learns about cleanliness and beauty from her teachers at school and stays away from home as much as possible. She moves out of her parents' house two days after she graduates from high school. She goes to Buffalo and works for five years in a tool-and-die factory while she attends night school at the community college. She then enrolls full time in the elementary education program at the University of Buffalo. She meets Peter at the university and eventually loses touch with her parents.

Peter, a mathematics major, sees in Beatrice clarity, simplicity, and thrift. Though she does not enjoy making love to Peter, Beatrice feels obligated to him for providing so well for her. During their marriage, she bears three boys. They live in Ithaca, New York, a small lakeside college town. She is a clean, efficient housewife.

Peter wins a three-year fellowship to Columbia University in New York City. His salary is doubled with no teaching obligations, and his only responsibility is to do research with a man who is a leader in his field. He asks Beatrice if she wants to go. Although she knows that she has to go, she dreads losing her peaceful, clean life in Ithaca. They rent their home in Ithaca to a German couple who are scientists.

Others call the apartment in New York City a jewel, but Beatrice does not like it. The apartment is old and looks unclean to her, so she bleaches the floors and makes repairs. Her husband takes their sons to various activities on weekends while she goes to the New York museums.

A slovenly professor, on medical leave from Columbia, lives in the apartment below theirs. He complains that when her sons were playing ball, they made too much noise and caused a chunk of plaster to fall down from the ceiling, hitting him in his bed. She promises that she will make the boys stop.

When Beatrice tells her sons that they have to stop playing ball indoors, they become angry. After making them supper, she develops a severe headache and goes to bed. Before she goes to sleep, her neighbor across the hall calls to tell her that she should ignore the downstairs neighbor, whose apartment is cavelike, dirty, and smelly. When she tries to go back to sleep, she becomes obsessed with the fact that a dirty apartment is right below her clean one. She also imagines that her breathing and that of the downstairs neighbor are following the same rhythm. She stays in her bed for several days and cuts herself off completely from her family.

The downstairs neighbor returns and confronts Peter, complaining that the boys are still making too much noise. Peter defends his sons, shouting that they are entitled to play in the afternoon. He closes the door in the man's face. Later Peter calls the neighbors together to have the downstairs neighbor evicted. They have a meeting in Peter and Beatrice's apartment. During the meeting, Beatrice, after several days of deep depression and sleep in her bedroom, dresses and slips, unseen, downstairs to the neighbor's apartment. She warns the neighbor that her husband and the others are trying to get him evicted. She looks around and wants to tell him that his filthy place is wonderful and beautiful, like her childhood home. She falls asleep on his lounge chair. He shakes her awake and makes her leave. She returns to her apartment upstairs.

### Themes and Meanings

The themes explored in Mary Gordon's novels—self-sacrifice, the limitations of love, and the dangers inherent in ordinary life—are evident in "City Life." Self-sacrifice is apparent in Beatrice's actions and the story's complex male-female relationships. Beatrice escapes the horror of her squalid childhood by learning from her school teachers how to better herself. She carefully plans her life, working and attending classes. As a full-time student, she lives on yogurt made from powdered milk, eats half-rotten vegetables she buys at a discount, and purchases day-old bread. She buys her clothes from the Salvation Army and lives in a tiny room near campus.

When Peter meets Beatrice, he admires the brilliant white of her shirt collar, her overall cleanliness, and the refinement of her hands. He also sees clarity, simplicity, and thrift, which appeal to his mathematical mind. When he learns that she is three years older than him, he believes her explanation that she had to work before attending college because her parents had tragically died. Beatrice also knows that Peter likes her lack of encumbrances: With Beatrice as his wife, he has no in-laws.

Beatrice's parents' lifestyle is contrasted with that of Peter and Beatrice. Her parents are alcoholics, and her mother spends most of her time sleeping off a hangover or drinking to get one. Quite often, Beatrice's supper consists of the only food in the house, cheese spread mixed with pimentos on crackers. However, Peter and Beatrice have an immaculate home, and their relationship with each other and their children is amicable. Also, Beatrice keeps her family well fed.

Another theme is love's limitations. Beatrice plays the role of a dutiful marital partner to express her appreciation to Peter for providing her with a life of clean linen, bright rooms, and matched dishes. She accepts his ardor as if it were a violent and fascinating storm. She bears children and is effective in her roles as wife and mother.

Like other works by Gordon, this story exhibits the dangers in ordinary life that are rooted in self-deception and self-discovery. Even though Beatrice tries to deceive Peter regarding her origins, she is unable to escape from her past. After she is married and has children, she tries to locate her parents and is shocked to find that they have disappeared without a trace. The incident with the disgusting neighbor triggers her desire to seek her lost childhood. She feels remorse for having left home and guilt that she has a pleasant life when her parents live in poverty.

*Style and Technique*

The moral earnestness of Gordon's style makes her writing similar to that of Doris Lessing. Gordon's style has also been said to resemble the graceful language of Flannery O'Connor. Her deep, moving, and intelligent insights focus on ordinary themes such as debilitating alcoholism, slovenly housekeeping, and fragile relationships. Her omniscient narrator offers insight into the motivations of her characters.

Gordon uses similar characters, settings, and situations in many of her stories and novels. For example, Columbia University, Peter's employer in "City Life," also figured in her novel *The Company of Women* (1980). In her third novel, *Men and Angels* (1985), Gordon created a complex story regarding how the carefully ordered life of a woman named Anne is disrupted when her professor husband travels to Europe for a year on a fellowship. So, too, was Beatrice's life disrupted when her husband was offered a high-paying fellowship at Columbia. Just like the protagonist Beatrice, Anne is exposed to otherwise hidden dangers related to everyday living.

Gordon uses repetitive language to create the rhythm that flows throughout her stories and her novels as well as precise dialogue to add to the development of the characters. The chronological plot of "City Life" contains many details and descriptions. The author's descriptive skill allows the reader to develop a familiarity with the story's characters that surpasses ordinary fictional characterization. For example, the detailed description of Beatrice's temporary breakdown makes it almost possible for the reader to hear the breathing patterns of the slovenly downstairs apartment neighbor orchestrated with Beatrice's breathing in her bed.

Finally, the danger that Beatrice experiences is part of Gordon's literary emphasis. Her danger is not physical harm from someone else but psychological damage directly related to her childhood environment. Her exposure to an unloving, unwholesome household caused lasting damage. The means of escape Beatrice has used is not to forget about her horrible past but to learn to accept what has been and go forward with her life rather than dwelling in the past.

*Annette M. Magid*

# CITY OF BOYS

*Author:* Beth Nugent
*Type of plot:* Psychological, impressionistic
*Time of plot:* The 1980's
*Locale:* New York City
*First published:* 1985

> *Principal characters:*
> THE NARRATOR, a young woman from Ohio
> AN OLDER WOMAN, her lesbian lover
> TITO, the older woman's live-in male companion
> A YOUNG MAN who is briefly the narrator's lover

*The Story*

"City of Boys" is told in the first person through the ramblings of a young woman who lives on the Upper West Side of Manhattan, the central borough of New York City. The story begins with the two principal female characters in bed together, the older one admonishing the younger to avoid boys because they will only take advantage of her. After this relatively straightforward opening, the story rambles back and forth, but two general narrative streams emerge. The first stream, which dominates the work, is the home life and conversations among the two women and Tito, the older woman's live-in companion. The second stream of narrative involves the young woman's obsession with boys.

The narrator is from Fairborn, Ohio, the first "city of boys" mentioned. She has come to New York for an unspecified reason, perhaps to get away from her mother, who kept insisting that she grow up and get married. On the street, the narrator meets an older woman who is never named or described, but the fact that the narrator refers to her as "her mother" many times suggests that she is considerably older. The older woman takes the narrator back to her apartment. There she meets Tito, who clearly wants to have a physical relationship with her, but who is kept at bay by the older woman.

Tito is the older woman's live-in lover, but he is also a married man, with a wife in Queens, one of the outlying boroughs of New York. Not much more is revealed about him, but his presence suggests that the older woman, like the narrator, has sexual feelings for men as well as women. Tito leaves, saying that he is tired of seeing two "dikes" making love all the time. Before doing so, he tells the narrator that her lover was once married and is using her alimony to pay the rent.

Almost all the action in this section of the story takes place in a tiny apartment. The apartment is in a poor neighborhood, dominated by Puerto Ricans, though it is never made clear whether the older woman is of that background. There is a brief trip to Staten Island, a ferry ride from Manhattan, but Staten Island proves to be no different.

In between descriptions of the action taking place, there is a great deal of discussion of the narrator's thoughts and feelings about the situation she is in and the circumstances that led her to that situation. Much of this discussion has to do with her uncertain feelings about boys in general, and one in particular.

New York, like Fairborn, is a "city of boys," and the narrator is constantly trying to learn about them. She approaches a car full of boys, all somewhat younger than she is, and asks for a ride uptown. She picks out one young man, who she calls "my boy." They ride up to the boys' "clubhouse," which turns out to be a filthy, roach-laden apartment. At the clubhouse, the boys use various types of drugs. The narrator asks "my boy" to take her out for some air. The boy insists that he has to take a drug first. He injects some unspecified narcotic into his arm and then suggests a car ride. The girl and her boy drive up to Inwood Hill Park, at the northern tip of Manhattan, where they are completely alone. They have a brief moment of sex, which the narrator describes as just what she wanted; short and to the point. The boy then drives off, leaving the narrator to find her own way home.

The story ends with the two lesbian lovers in bed, as it began. The narrator tries to elicit some feeling from the older woman by saying she is a "marked woman" because she has had sex with a boy. The older woman shows no reaction at all.

## Themes and Meanings

"City of Boys" is marked by a continuing sense of despair. The narrator states over and over that nothing ever changes, that all is fated to continue in exactly the same way as it always has. However, at the same time, she repeatedly states that "rent control will not last forever in New York," the implication being that sooner or later she will lose her home and her lover.

There is not a single pleasant setting in the entire story. The apartment in which the principal relationship takes place has roaches, rats, and other vermin. The clubhouse is even more rundown. Even Inwood Hill, which in reality is a beautiful stretch of woods, one of the few examples of relatively untouched nature in Manhattan, is used merely as a setting for sex.

The young narrator is clearly uncertain about her own sexual urges. She is obsessed with boys, but all the while describes her female lover as the only person in the world who matters. The sexual acts are never described explicitly, but one is given the impression that they are never really satisfying. It also appears that no relationships can ever be truly permanent.

The characters are never really happy or pleasant to others. The older woman tries to dominate the younger one, and this seems more important to her than any real sense of love. It is clear that she has had other sexual relationships, male and female, and that the present one is neither the first nor the last. The boy the narrator picks out as her own is a drug addict, whose life is likely to be short and meaningless.

Significantly, the only character in the story who has a name is Tito, and even he leads a double life. The reader never learns anything about his wife out in Queens or how he manages to keep up any relationship with her, if indeed he does.

The twin themes of this story are that nothing ever changes and that nothing is permanent. These two ideas are not, as they may appear, contradictory. Physical situations change because there is no point in having them continue as they were and because the characters, or at least the narrator, are striving to make changes in their lives. However, the most important part of life, the feelings of the people who live it, are fixed and unchangeable.

"City of Boys" is far from a happy story. It ends, as it began, with two women in bed, and the reader is left with the impression that this scene will go on, largely unchanged, forever.

*Style and Technique*

"City of Boys" is told in the first person, present tense, as are all the stories in the collection of which it is a part, *City of Boys: Stories* (1992). There are no paragraph indentations and no quotation marks. When the stream of consciousness of the narrator changes, this is indicated merely by a double space between lines.

The result of this type of narration is that the reader seems to be reading the mind of the narrator, experiencing only her thoughts, her impressions, and her memories. This technique is heightened by the fact that almost none of the characters are given names, and none are described physically.

First-person narrative often gives the reader a sense of realism, but this is not quite true here. Although the events described are quite realistic, there is a sense of a dream-like quality to the narrator's musings. The events are not told in chronological order. There seems to be no outside world, and the settings are described in a minimal way. The apartment is tiny and infested by vermin, but the reader does not know what it contains besides the bed. The description of the clubhouse is similarly limited.

New York City functions only as the setting for the narrator's thoughts. The setting is used to magnify the sense of despair; any unpleasant area of any city would do as well. Also, the characters have no function outside their relationship to the narrator. They are never shown when they are out of her presence, and what sort of lives they really lead remains unknown.

*Marc Goldstein*

# CLARISA

*Author:* Isabel Allende (1942-    )
*Type of plot:* Fantasy
*Time of plot:* Unspecified; possibly the 1980's
*Locale:* A city somewhere in South America
*First published:* 1989 (English translation, 1991)

> *Principal characters:*
> CLARISA, a poor, saintly woman known for her charity
> EVA LUNA, her friend, the narrator
> THE JUDGE, her aged, reclusive husband
> DON DIEGO CIENFUEGOS, a congressman, national hero, and
> longtime friend of Clarisa's

## The Story

Eva Luna tells the life story of her old friend Clarisa, who died of amazement when the pope arrived for a visit and was met in the street by homosexuals dressed as nuns. (The reference is likely to one of John Paul II's visits to South America in the early 1980's.) The bizarre old woman, who is well into her eighties, is widely considered to be a saint but from performing humble and improbable miracles such as curing hangovers and minor illnesses.

Eva traces the story of Clarisa's life from her unhappy marriage to a greedy and vulgar provincial judge who is still alive and would be about a hundred years old. Traces of Clarisa's aristocratic upbringing show in her talent as a classical pianist, but after the birth of their two retarded children, her husband closed himself up in a malodorous room, where he has lived in silence for more than forty years. Clarisa was forced to sell their possessions and take up the sewing of rag dolls and baking—of wedding cakes, ironically—to keep the family together. Although her ancestral home is dilapidated, she manages to hold onto it.

Clarisa deals admirably with her children's abnormality, considering them pure souls immune to evil and treating them with great affection. She believes that God operates by a doctrine of compensation, and her faith is rewarded when she gives birth to two healthy sons who are kind and good and who help with their retarded brother and sister until they die in an accident involving a gas leak.

Throughout her life, Clarisa practices charitable acts despite her poverty. In one episode, she talks an armed robber into accepting her money as a gift so that he will not commit a sin, and then insists that he join her for tea. Her special talent, however, is in getting funds from the wealthy by working at cross purposes. For example, she convinces the influential politician Don Diego Cienfuegos to donate a refrigerator to the Teresian Sisters even though he is a socialist, arguing that the sisters provide free meals for communists and other children of the working poor who make up the congressman's constituency. She and Cienfuegos subsequently become lifelong friends.

After the homosexuals disguised as nuns disrupt the papal visit to protest the pope's stands on divorce, abortion, and other issues, Clarisa tells Eva that she has seen too much, and she predicts her imminent death. Eva notes that her old friend has developed two bumps on her shoulders, "as if her pair of great angel wings were about to erupt." As her last days approach, Clarisa eats only flowers and honey. To her deathbed come all the people to whom she has shown charity throughout the years, including the robber (now a professional thief who steals from the rich, and is not, as the reader might anticipate, reformed), a madame named "La Señora," and Don Diego Cienfuegos.

The dying Clarisa attempts to make amends with her repulsive husband to no avail and tells Eva that she feels she has sinned in some way. When Eva recognizes the similarity between Clarisa's two healthy sons and Don Diego—now a national hero—she assumes that that is her friend's grave sin. Clarisa insists that it was not a sin, "just a little boost to help God balance the scales of destiny." Clarisa dies without suffering, not from cancer, as the doctors diagnose, and not of saintliness, as the people believe, but, Eva says, of astonishment that goes back to the pope's visit.

*Themes and Meanings*

Isabel Allende presents in her stories, and in three of her four novels, a world in which the corrupt and powerful—who are generally male, macho, and brutal—are defeated by the innocent and powerless—who are generally female, maternal, and virtuous. It could be argued that through her fiction Allende, the niece of Chilean Marxist president Salvador Allende, who was assassinated in 1973, seeks to correct the abuses traditionally associated with life and politics in Latin American society. Whereas justice often seems to occur only randomly in real life, it is almost always the outcome in Allende's fiction.

Despite her own misfortunes, Clarisa remains compassionate and loving. She is affectionate with her difficult retarded children, and her kindness is transmitted to her normal sons. Her acts of charity bring her deserved popularity and renown, and she dies peacefully. Her wretched husband, however, who becomes a recluse because he cannot bear the disillusionment of having sired two retarded children, is doomed to a life of self-imposed, monkish isolation, although Clarisa does continue to feed and care for him. We are not invited to sympathize with his plight, because he is introduced as a man whom she marries simply because he was the first person to ask her and because he is associated with avarice and vulgarity. In short, the good are rewarded and the evil are punished. Clarisa's simple and sensible view of justice is also implicit in her theory of compensation, that God balances advantages and disadvantages in life.

In "Clarisa," as elsewhere in Allende's fiction, the oppressed classes are superior to the ruling class, both in humanity and in spirituality. Clarisa is saintlike in her simple and active piety. What distinguishes her charitable acts is her boundless understanding of human weaknesses. This understanding, ironically, is the source of her power.

## Style and Technique

Allende has been influenced by the Magical Realists, whose work has dominated Latin American writing since Jorge Luis Borges began to make his mark in the 1950's. These writers are concerned with the representation of the miraculous within the real, so their work usually is realistic but with some elements of fantasy. With writers such as Luisa Valenzuela and Gabriel García Márquez, fantasy tends to dominate, but Allende maintains a light touch. For instance, Eva Luna notes that her friendship with Clarisa has lasted to this day and that her old friend's death has only put a slight crimp in their communication. She also mentions that Clarisa has bumps on her shoulders that seem to be the beginnings of angel's wings. Allende does not emphasize such fantasy elements, however, and most of the story is grounded in credible reality.

On the other hand, the reader's credibility is almost always strained. In "Clarisa," the reader is asked to accept the crazed husband living forty years in isolation and the protagonist living in a rundown house where the walls "sweat a greenish mist." Such details are sufficient to keep the reader alert to whatever comes next; the reader is also encouraged to be open-minded. Allende also promotes an atmosphere of unreality by neglecting to situate her stories in any particular city or country, although it is usually apparent that the setting is somewhere in South America. The reader may suppose any given story is set in Peru, where Allende was born, or in Chile, where she grew up, or in Venezuela, where she lived for a number of years until moving to northern California, or elsewhere on the South American continent.

An epigraph at the front of *Cuentos de Eva Luna* (1990; *The Stories of Eva Luna*, 1991), the book in which "Clarisa" appears, concerns Scheherazade and the famous *One Thousand and One Nights*. These exotic tales of adventure and romance, known sometimes simply as *The Arabian Nights*, were translated into French early in the eighteenth century and into English in the early 1840's. In her novel *Eva Luna* (1987; English translation, 1988), and in these stories, Allende presents Eva as a sort of natural storyteller with a magical gift of sorts, a modern-day Scheherazade whose stories reestablish justice in the world, often by employing ironic reversals. The implication would seem to be that in a corrupt or violent world, one must work counter to expectation if one hopes to succeed. For example, in "Clarisa" the judge turns out to be unjust in the way he treats his children, and Don Diego succeeds in politics despite, not because of, being incorruptible.

*Ron McFarland*

# CLAY

*Author:* James Joyce (1882-1941)
*Type of plot:* Symbolist
*Time of plot:* About 1900
*Locale:* Dublin, Ireland
*First published:* 1914

> *Principal characters:*
> MARIA, the protagonist, a middle-aged spinster, a kitchen helper
> in a Dublin laundry
> JOE DONNELLY, her former nursling

*The Story*

Halloween (October 31) is the Celtic New Year's Eve and Feast of the Dead, Christianized as the Feasts of the Blessed Virgin and All Saints (November 1) and All Souls (November 2). In Irish folk custom, it is a night of remembrance of dead ancestors and anticipation of the future through various fortune-telling games. This Halloween story, "Clay," is about Maria, a middle-aged spinster, who works in the kitchen of a laundry established for the reform of prostitutes. Readers follow Maria from the routine of her job there, as she makes her way across the city of Dublin to the seasonal festivities at the home of her former nursling, Joe Donnelly. In these few scenes, James Joyce draws a complex character portrait that, by means of its symbolic devices, conveys much of Maria's past, present, and future.

The story unfolds by means of the contrasts between the narrator's view of Maria and her own emotionally limited self-awareness. The story develops in three scenes: at the laundry, on the journey across the city, and at the Halloween party. In the first, readers observe Maria's prim, fussy personality as she prepares the women's tea while privately anticipating her reunion with Joe and Mrs. Donnelly and their family. She suffers many slights in this institution, set apart by temperament and experience from the inmates, and by her Catholic piety from its Protestant management. On this particular occasion, the search for the wedding band hidden in the traditional Halloween cake causes some pointed disquiet for Maria. Indeed, her private chagrin at her single state is a recurring embarrassment throughout the evening.

As she travels northward across Dublin, stopping off at the city center to purchase her gifts, she is again reminded of her isolation: first by the irritation of the girl in the cake shop and again by the polite attentions of the gentleman in the tram. She is so flustered at this that she evidently leaves the rather expensive cake behind her.

At the Donnelly household she is greeted dutifully and with mixed emotions. She irritates the children by interrupting their party and by suggesting that they stole the lost cake intended for their parents. Joe and Mrs. Donnelly make her welcome, though, and she is soon relaxed enough to raise a question about Alphy, Joe's estranged brother. This again disrupts the festive atmosphere, only restored by the traditional fortune-telling games. When the children's fortunes are told (the prayer book, signifying the religious life; the water, emigration; and the ring, marriage, respectively), Maria—oddly enough, as an adult—is invited to play. When her lot turns out to be clay (signifying the fortune of death), however, the rules are changed and she gets the consolation of religion. The evening concludes with Maria's song, "I Dreamt I Dwelt" (from Michael William Balfe's opera *The Bohemian Girl*, 1843), but she sings the first verse twice, forgetting or censoring the references to lovers and knights of the second verse. When she is finished, the story focuses on Joe's response: His eyes fill with tears motivated by a mixture of drunken nostalgia and guilt.

## Themes and Meanings

This story can be viewed as an astute study of a psychologically repressed personality. The setting implies frames of reference encompassing the social, religious, cultural, and political circumstances of that repression.

First, Maria's character is marked by persistent self-deception: To herself, she is tidy, pious, proper, and nice; to others, she is well-meaning, dull, sometimes vindictive, and pitiable. She is dutiful, generous, and punctilious, yet her officiousness and tactlessness cause offense and resentment in others. It is clear, too, that she feels that life has betrayed her, that she has never found a husband and probably never will. She consoles herself with attention to the duties of her job and religion while retaining some small connection with the Donnellys, whose Halloween party is the nearest to family life she will know. However, even there, her resentments break out, and the pathos of that revelation is barely restrained.

These conflicts in Maria's character are developed by means of several sets of contrasts in the story, the most notable of which is that between images of the Blessed Virgin Mary and a witch, or Celtic cailleach (old hag). These images (for example, Maria as a quasi-virgin and mother, versus the recurring representation of her profile) correspond to the positive image Maria has of herself, and the less flattering one suggested by the concealed narrator. These correspondences reflect, in turn, the historical Christianization of what was originally the Celtic Feast of the Dead, as conveyed in the contrast between the religious and fortune-telling rituals in the story. Thus, although Maria consciously regards herself in the light of the Christian promise, her story takes place among shadows cast by a darker past.

In these contexts, then, Maria can be considered as a type of her race, or as an allegorical representation of Mother Ireland. She is a typical Dubliner, in Joyce's view, in that she is paralyzed by circumstances beyond her control or awareness (her appearance, her apparent ejection from the Donnelly household, for example), while not examining too critically what lies behind the flattery and patronization of her employers, fellow workers, and personal friends. As a victim of division of the household, feeling herself a stranger in her own home, observing outsiders in control, and appealing, in vain, for a liberating hero, she is a version of the ancient symbolic representation of Mother Ireland dominated by imperial England.

*Style and Technique*

"Clay" is told in language very close to Maria's own: The sentences are simple, the vocabulary limited and repetitive, and the tone naïve, even prissy. Note the repeated use of the words "nice" and "right," for example. This tone is finely managed. At first reading, it seems naïve and objective. Closer observation, however, shows it to be a complex interweaving of controlled irony, sentiment, and cool understatement. The narrator describes the various sides of Maria's character by means of subtle innuendo, suggestive images and symbols, delicate restraint or even silence. Consider here the repeated description of Maria's profile, the references to witchcraft sprinkled throughout the narrative, and the pointed suppression of the title in the body of the story. The story is very expressive on these terms but gains in power if attention is paid to its historical, cultural, and religious allusions.

Joyce's personal background and education made him deeply aware of the tragic history of Ireland, including the destruction of its ancient Celtic civilization. He was alert to elements from this national past surviving into the modern age in the language, songs, and folklore of the ordinary people. He was also thoroughly conversant with the teachings, history, and rituals of the Catholic Church. A reader sensitive to these various influences will derive a more complex pleasure from "Clay," because it is situated at precisely that time in the Celtic calendar when the normal laws of nature are suspended, when past and future are indistinguishable, and when the dead pay a visit on their living relatives. The Christianization of these traditions, Ireland's subsequent conquest by the English, and the inertia that Joyce observed in the Dublin of his time are all recurring themes in Joyce's fiction. In this particular case, he is able to exploit the rich fictional possibilities afforded by a Halloween story about a poor, pious, disappointed spinster whose profile is like Ireland's battered western coastline. "Clay" is scrupulously accurate in respect to all "objective" details while at the same time resonating with echoes from ancient and popular culture. Joyce's integration of these realistic, psychological, and symbolic themes is masterful.

*Coilin Owens*

# A CLEAN, WELL-LIGHTED PLACE

*Author:* Ernest Hemingway (1899-1961)
*Type of plot:* Naturalistic
*Time of plot:* The 1930's
*Locale:* Spain
*First published:* 1933

>*Principal characters:*
>AN OLDER WAITER and
>A YOUNGER WAITER, workers in a Spanish café
>AN OLD MAN, their customer

## The Story

Two waiters in a Spanish café are waiting late one night for their last customer, an old man, to leave. As they wait, they talk about the old man's recent suicide attempt. The younger waiter is impatient to leave and tells the deaf old man he wishes the suicide attempt had been successful. The young waiter has a wife waiting in bed for him and is unsympathetic when the older waiter says that the old man once also had a wife. The old man finally leaves when the younger waiter refuses to serve him further.

The older waiter argues that they should have allowed their customer to stay, that being in the café is not the same as drinking at home. He explains that he is also one of those "who like to stay late at the café. . . . With all those who do not want to go to bed. With all those who need a light for the night." He is reluctant to close because there may be someone who needs the café. When the young waiter says there are bodegas open all night, the other points out that the bright atmosphere of the café makes it different.

After the younger waiter goes home, the older one asks himself why he needs a clean, pleasant, quiet, well-lighted place. The answer is that he requires some such semblance of order because of "a nothing that he knew too well." He begins a mocking prayer: "Our nada who art in nada, nada be thy name thy kingdom nada thy will be nada in nada as it is in nada." He then finds himself at a bodega that is a poor substitute for a clean, well-lighted café. He goes home to lie awake until daylight may finally bring him some sleep: "After all, he said to himself, it is probably only insomnia. Many must have it."

## Themes and Meanings

One of Ernest Hemingway's shortest stories, "A Clean, Well-Lighted Place" has been the subject of considerable critical analysis, much of it focusing on the significance of nada, or nothingness. This concept of nada is clearly central to Hemingway's worldview; characters obsessed by death, by the apparent meaninglessness of life, appear throughout his fiction. In a century in which religion, politics, and various philosophical stances have failed for so many, modern life has devolved into spiritual emptiness and moral anarchy. Nada in "A Clean, Well-Lighted Place" becomes a metaphor for this modern chaos; the older waiter's nothing represents an absence of light—including that word's associations with reason and belief—of order, of meaning.

What is important for a Hemingway character, however, is how to respond to this seemingly meaningless universe. Hemingway dramatizes this dilemma through contrasting the two waiters; as the older one explains, "We are of two different kinds." The young waiter is selfish and cynical, lacking in empathy, inexperienced at life without realizing it. "I have confidence. I am all confidence," he tells the older waiter. He is like many young people who think that they and their world are as they should be and will always be the same. The older waiter responds ironically, "You have youth, confidence, and a job. . . . You have everything." This "everything" will last only until experience, as it must, teaches the young waiter about life's disappointments, about the chaos that youthful confidence now allows him to ignore.

The older waiter is one of the initiated, one who understands the true nature of the world, who clearly sees the distinction between cafés and bodegas, between day and night, between values as they should be and harsh reality. He represents the so-called Hemingway code, which can be seen as a humanistic, as opposed to theological, effort to create a dimension of meaning. The Hemingway code character recognizes the seeming futility of man's headlong rush toward death and, instead of despairing, attempts to create what meanings or values he can, as with the hero's "separate peace" in *A Farewell to Arms* (1929). Thus, the older waiter wants to keep the café open because someone like the old man, like the waiter himself—someone bruised by the dark, disordered world—may need it.

The café, rather than nada, becomes the most important symbol in the story because it represents a kind of hope, pathetic though it may be. The old man's despair at home leads him to try to hang himself; in the café he can drink his brandy with dignity. The older waiter recognizes this dignity: "This old man is clean. He drinks without spilling. Even now, drunk." (The young waiter spills the brandy he pours for the old man.) The cafe is a place where those without the innocence of youth, the illusions of belief, can pass the time with dignity. It is a refuge from meaninglessness—but only a refuge, not an escape. The café must eventually close; all must go home. The older waiter finds the bodega to which he wanders "very bright and pleasant," but the bar is unpolished. It is a temporary substitute for the café just as the café is a temporary respite from the chaos of the dark world outside.

"A Clean, Well-Lighted Place" dramatizes modern man's quest for dignity amid the destruction of the old values. The individual needs to escape his responsibilities while realizing that this escape is but momentary. The individual's responsibility to himself is to find a clean, well-lighted place or create one of his own. The ironic paradox of the story is that meaning can be created only through an awareness of its absence.

*Style and Technique*

"A Clean, Well-Lighted Place" is one of the best examples of Hemingway's distinctive style: objective point of view; short, active declarative sentences; frequent repetition of key words; heavy reliance on dialogue in which the characters speak in short, clipped sentences or fragments, an impressionistic representation of everyday speech: "This is a clean and pleasant café. It is well lighted. The light is very good and also, now, there are shadows of the leaves."

In *A Moveable Feast* (1964), Hemingway identifies one of the key elements of his technique as recognizing that what is left out of a story is just as important as what is included, as when Nick Adams's recent return from the chaos of war is not directly mentioned in "Big Two-Hearted River" (1925). This approach can be seen in "A Clean, Well-Lighted Place" in which there is no overt reference to the disappointments the young waiter will certainly experience, the nights he will not be so eager to run home to his loving wife, there is no explanation of why the old man attempts suicide, no evidence of what has specifically taught the older waiter about nada. Considerable dramatic tension, as well as universality, is created by revealing so little about the characters and the time and place.

A corollary to this technique is that everything in the story must be there for a reason. A brief reference early in the story to a soldier and girl, apparently a prostitute, passing by the café is significant to illustrate the younger waiter's concern only with the practical, the immediate: "He had better get off the street now. The guard will get him." The older waiter's view is more worldly: "What does it matter if he gets what he's after?" As the couple pass, "The street light shone on the brass number on his collar." By ignoring the rules, the soldier has captured a moment in the light. Ironically, he is similar to the young waiter so restless to join his wife in bed. Such economic, perfectly controlled storytelling is the epitome of Hemingway's style at its best.

*Michael Adams*

# THE CLIFF

*Author:* Charles Baxter (1947-      )
*Type of plot:* Fable
*Time of plot:* The 1970's
*Locale:* The California coast
*First published:* 1984

> *Principal characters:*
> THE OLD MAN, the teacher of the spells
> THE BOY, his fifteen-year-old protégé

## The Story

A young boy is being driven to a cliff at an unspecified location on the California coastline. The driver, a cantankerous old man, interrogates the boy en route, suspicious of his experience with women, how well he has memorized the old man's instructions, his moral, spiritual, and emotional purity, and his impatience to get started with the initiation into what the old man calls "the spells." Noting the old man's incessant coughing and smoking, his occasional hits from the wine bottle stashed under his seat, and his irritability in general, the boy wonders aloud about the old man's purity, whether or not he still believes in the spells. Outraged by the boy's temerity, the old man reminds him that his body has been pure. More important, he tells the boy that he, the old man, is the spells. Besides, he adds, "nobody is ever pure twice."

When they arrive at the cliff, the old man orders the boy to remove his shoes and sweatshirt, and to make a circle in the dirt with his feet. The boy reminds the old man that there is no dirt, but the old man insists he follow his orders. So the boy traces an invisible circle around his body and then speaks to the horizon, using the words the old man has given him. The old man hands him one end of a rope, takes another swig of wine, and then lets out the slack as the boy jumps down the slope of the cliff.

At this point the boy takes it into his mind to "swoop toward the cliffs." The ambiguity of the phrase—is he imagining flight while rapelling down a cliff or he is actually flying?—is maintained as he soars and dips above the old man. Even as he does so, he begins to realize that this kind of flying is not for him. He wants to "fly low, near the ground, in the cities, speeding in smooth arcs between the buildings, late at night." The boy grins down at the old man, who has "forgotten the dirty purposes of flight."

## Themes and Meanings

Charles Baxter's story is yet another rendition of the age-old conflict between the generations. It concerns the meaning of tradition, what gets passed on to the next generation. This story suggests that tradition is never received in the pure form of its transmission. Those of the next generation will always alter or transform the tradition in some way, reworking in order to make it their own, to satisfy their own needs and desires.

From the beginning of the story until the moment the boy takes off, the old man is a grouch, suspicious of the young boy's worthiness. He wheezes, coughs, smokes, and swigs wine even as he preaches the virtues of faith, hope, charity, and love and insists on moral and physical chastity for the initiate. Baxter provides a clue to the source of this wanton self-destructiveness when, responding to the boy's query if he still believes in the spells, the old man insists, "I am the spells." Despite the sop to ritual and the sacred—summarized in the boy's drawing an invisible circle around himself, removing his shoes as though he is on holy ground, removing his sweatshirt to expose his unsullied heart—the old man knows that the only spells are those that he himself wills. Perhaps when he was young some older man taught him to believe in something outside himself, something just beyond the horizon of human knowledge. Now an older man, no longer innocent, no longer pure, he knows that the only spells are those he himself imagines.

The bitterness of this knowledge also inflates the old man. Having the secret of the spells that the young boy desires gives him power over the boy. However, he knows this knowledge of the spells, once revealed, will release the boy from his power. Hence the old man's sour demeanor, his ejaculations of platitudes—faith, hope, love, and charity—that he regards as a sham. At the same time, the old man understands that the knowledge of the spells must be passed on if it is not to be lost forever with his death. In the character of the old man, Baxter paints a picture of paternal resentment. This resentment is directed at the boy, but its source is the mortality of the old man. The old man knows and resents the fact that his mortality demands the passing on of knowledge.

However, something happens when the man sees the boy soar above him; he begins laughing and, for once, is no longer coughing. It is as though the boy's flight momentarily revitalizes the old man, taking him back to his innocence and ignorance when all was possibility, when the future beyond the horizon could still be imagined, before all knowledge. The boy knows this, knows that his flight has pleased the old man, has made him pure again, if only momentarily, if only under the hallucinogenic power of the imagination. This flight does not, however, satisfy the young boy. He wants something else, wants to be somewhere else: to soar, not to fly low; to enjoy not the salty exuberance of the ocean, but the stagnant air of the city. In this moment of joy and communion between the old and young, the young boy and the old man are already going their separate ways.

## Style and Technique

This story has all the requisite features of the fable or parable. It is very short, even by short-story standards, a mere three-and-a-half pages. The subsequent compressed plot—an old man and boy drive to a cliff from which the boy leaps into the sky and begins flying—lends to the story an aphoristic universality. This universality is reinforced by the general treatment of the setting and characters. Readers never learn the name of the cliff or the names of the characters. As a story about a cliff, an old man, and a boy, it takes on mystical, even transcendental depth, precisely because nothing is named or tied to a specific place or time. Finally, the magical climax of the story places it beyond the realm of the ordinary and everyday. This is a story that has something transcendental to say, like all fables.

One literary device that Baxter employs here is allusion. "The Cliff" rewrites the Daedalus and Icarus myth, this time in Icarus's favor. Rather than viewing flight merely from the point of view of tradition—flight as a sign of liberation—Baxter also portrays flight here as the youthful dream of an old man who, because he is no longer young, wants a young boy to follow in his wake so that he, the old man, might live vicariously through the young boy. Seeing the boy flying above him, the old man is suddenly young again. He loses his cough and again finds joy in the simple things of nature: "'The sun!' the old man shouted. 'The ocean! The land! That's how to do it!' And he laughed suddenly, his cough all gone. 'The sky!' he said at last." All the traditional images of freedom—the sea, the cliff (from which one must leap into transcendence), nature in general—are the jealously guarded terrain of an embittered old man. For the young boy, however, it is the city, the girls in their apartments, the musty air of urban squalor, that coaxes. When one reads that the young boy wants to "fly low . . . speeding in smooth arcs between the buildings," one can imagine that what this boy really wants to do is precisely what the old man cannot imagine doing: Drive a car fast through the streets. The car is here the symbol for the new generation, the post-Romantic world of urban life. For the old man, the car is a motor vehicle that has one purpose: to take him out of the city and into the country. For the boy, in a car, one can fly low, girlwatch. This is what it means to fly in this modern-day fable.

*Tyrone Williams*

# THE CLOSING DOWN OF SUMMER

*Author:* Alistair MacLeod (1936-      )
*Type of plot:* Regional, impressionistic
*Time of plot:* The 1970's
*Locale:* Cape Breton, Nova Scotia
*First published:* 1976

*Principal character:*

AN UNNAMED, AGING MINER from Cape Breton, Nova Scotia

*The Story*

"The Closing Down of Summer" is a first-person reminiscence of a veteran miner and crew foreman who contemplates the profound changes that have occurred in his profession and his life, relating the changes to larger cultural developments in the world.

The story opens in late August of an unusually warm summer in Cape Breton, home to the narrator and his crew mates, where they have been enjoying a brief holiday respite between assignments. Telegrams from the mining company head office in Toronto have been urgently summoning them to return and prepare for their next job, which will be in South Africa.

The men are staying together at a remote beach in Cape Breton, between their recent visits with their families and their return to the mines. Stretched out on the beach, the narrator looks at the others and notes the evidence on their bodies of the dangers of their work. Deep scars, missing fingers, and deformities of limbs testify to its hazards for these big, sturdy men.

The narrator knows that soon they will have to get in their big cars and drive to Toronto, but for a brief period, he determines to allow them all to enjoy the healing power of the sun. Thinking about the coming road trip, he affirms an ancient ritual: When they arrive in Toronto they will find small sprigs of spruce stuck in the grillwork of their cars, and they will take those sprigs with them to South Africa much as their Highland ancestors took similar talismans to the battlefields of the world where they fought for foreign kings.

Another ancient ritual to be reenacted is their visit, before they leave, to the community graveyard. There they will pray and share memories of fathers and brothers, close family and friends, many of whom met violent deaths in mines around the world. Specifically, the narrator remembers his brother's horrible death, and the difficulties the family faced in bringing the body home and burying it in the family plot.

These rituals underscore their ties to a heroic past and to their community, their brotherhood as miners, and the dangers of their profession. In contrast the miner thinks about the life of his wife and their children. His wife now has a house full of modern conveniences and is well adapted to the contemporary world of sleek efficiency, security, and popular entertainment. She is insulated from the dirt and violence of the mining shacks and shafts in which he spends most of his life. Their children are insulated as well, having become white collar professionals who will not die young in foreign mines.

The miner is happy about this, yet there is also sadness because the widening rift between his world and theirs makes meaningful communication almost impossible. This sense of loss and separation is compounded by his growing deafness, another consequence of the drills and high explosives used in mining.

The rift between the contemporary world and that of the miner with the consequent loss of communication is evident in other ways as well. He and his crew, for example, are part of a miners' chorus, singing the old Gaelic songs of their ancestors. These songs, which speak directly and powerfully to the emotions of the narrator and his crew, are now curiosities and historical artifacts to others, who never had or have lost the language and the cultural heritage necessary to respond to their meaning. He wants true speech, though; he wants to communicate, particularly to his family. He wants to tell them of his life—of the dangers, the skill, the heroism, the pride, and the value—but he feels its impossibility.

Days have passed. The summer is drawing to a close. The narrator realizes that the time has come to move on. As they set off for Toronto, the narrator remembers a fifteenth century Scottish lyric he once read, and thinks of himself as the knight in that lyric, on his final journey toward death.

*Themes and Meanings*

"The Closing Down of Summer" explores the challenges to meaningful human communication, the loss of local cultures in an increasingly standardized world, and the poignancy of one's awareness of mortality.

At the beginning of the story, the narrator states that telephone calls and telegrams from the head office in Toronto have been left unanswered, introducing an important theme relating to human communication. In this case, the lack of communication is deliberate and temporary. In the case of the narrator's growing deafness, the inability to communicate is caused by aging and physical injury. However, throughout the story, the impediments to genuine communication are formidable and sometimes seem almost insurmountable.

The narrator, his crew, and those in the profession have a fund of common experience that enables them to communicate effectively and significantly with each other. However, the difference between their everyday world and that of their families makes genuine communication with even loved ones extremely difficult, if not impossible. When working abroad, the postcards that they send home are entirely superficial in their breezy news and standard inquiries. In their brief sojourns at home, they experience the same inability to connect meaningfully with those who should be closest to them.

The miners in the chorus sing songs in a language and from a culture that fewer and fewer know, and so their songs—meaningful to them—are merely melodic curiosities to the majority of listeners, from younger members of the community to visiting tourists. At one point, the narrator remembers Zulus he has seen dancing in Africa and recognizes that his lack of knowledge of their culture made him a mere spectator of their art, unable to understand or share its meaning with the dancers.

A related theme of the story is the loss of vital local cultures in an increasingly standardized, global world. Cape Breton, for example, is seeing its Gaelic heritage, its local customs, and its economic base of mining and fishing eroded, even destroyed by the forces of modernization. Local cultures are either dying out or being artificially preserved and displayed as a product for tourism.

Finally, "The Closing Down of Summer" is a meditation on mortality. Several dimensions of the story reinforce the sense of an ending to an individual life and even to various ways of life. The ending of summer, the coming journey west toward the setting sun, and the memory of dead family members and friends convey the theme effectively. In addition, the narrator presents his recollections of life and death in the far corners of the world, where once-vital cultures are losing ground to modernization and standardization.

Most poignantly, everything whispers to the narrator that he, too, is coming to the end of his days—the waning of summer, his physical deterioration and increasing isolation from current ways of living, and his deepening nostalgia for the past. Perhaps the most complete expression of this awareness is the lyric poem at the end, powerfully combining a valedictory mood with a sense of heroism in the confrontation with death, a sense of the human spirit as, if not triumphant, at least unbowed.

### Style and Technique

"The Closing Down of Summer" is an extended interior monologue in which the narrator alternately looks at and thinks about the scene before him, anticipating the journey ahead for him and his crew, or reminisces about his past, his family, and his way of life. The reader's sense of intimacy with and confidence in an exceptionally experienced, sensitive, and even heroic spirit accounts for much of the story's power and effectiveness.

At the beginning, the narrator says that the summer has been unusually warm, so much so that the gardens have died, the wells are drying up, and even the trout in the streams are sluggish and dying. The scene is sharply rendered and has a symbolic value as well, prefiguring the fate of the narrator and of his way of life—slowing down, decaying, and tending toward death. The poetic sensibility that is evident from the first scene manifests itself throughout the story, in the cadence of the language, the vividness of the imagery, and the repeated references to lyrics, songs, and dance.

The story's actual time frame is only a few days, beginning with the scene on the beach during the hottest days of August, and ending not long after, with the weather changed, the crew leaving, and the narrator looking back on the sand where they have rested and prepared for the future. As he looks back, he notices that the sea has erased all trace of them, another effective image of transience and insubstantiality. Moreover, the brevity of the actual time elapsed combined with the extensive reach of the narrator's memory is an effective technique for conveying a sense of the speed at which the present becomes the past.

In the space of those few days, the narrator digs deeply into his experience for its meaning and significance. There is a sense of urgency about all this, given his increasing age and the knowledge of the risks he faces. There is also a sense that he is mining his experience for its ultimate meaning and significance, an effort that has dangers comparable to those he faces in the mines of the world, digging for its resources. He fears the search for truth and the sense of inevitable death it brings, but he continues bravely to the end.

*Michael J. Larsen*

# CLOUD, CASTLE, LAKE

*Author:* Vladimir Nabokov (1899-1977)
*Type of plot:* Fable
*Time of plot:* 1936 or 1937
*Locale:* Berlin and surrounding countryside
*First published:* "Oblako, ozero, bashnya," 1937 (English translation, 1941)

*Principal characters:*
VASILI IVANOVICH, a Russian emigre
THE NARRATOR, who wrote the story
GERMAN MEMBERS OF A TOUR GROUP
THE TOUR LEADER
SCHRAMM, a "stimulator" from the Bureau of Pleasantrips

## The Story

Vasili Ivanovich, a mild-mannered Russian emigre living in Berlin, wins a pleasure trip at a charity ball. Although Vasili is reluctant to travel anywhere, he finally decides to go when he discovers that getting out of the trip would involve cutting through all sorts of red tape in the bureaucracy. The tour group gathered at the railway station consists of four women and four men, each a kind of double of the other. The group leader is assisted by a sinister man called Schramm, from the Bureau of Pleasantrips. After their train departs, it soon becomes obvious that Vasili Ivanovich is the odd man out. When he attempts to read Russian lyrical poetry or observe the beauties of nature, his German companions interrupt him and force him to join them in singing uplifting songs or playing games. At first their teasing is good-natured; later, as nightfall approaches, it turns malevolent.

The group disembarks from the train and begins hiking through the countryside, eventually arriving at a blue lake with an old black castle on its far side and a beautiful cloud hanging over it. The insensitive Germans ignore the view, but Vasili is enthralled by its beauty. He sneaks away from the group, follows the shore, and comes to an inn. After the innkeeper shows him a room for rent, with a view of the cloud, castle, and lake, Vasili decides to take the room for the rest of his life. He runs joyfully down to the meadow to inform his companions. The collective of pleasure trippers, however, refuses to accept what they see as a betrayal of their common venture. Infuriated, they seize Vasili and drag him, "as in a hideous fairy tale," down a forest road to the train. On the return journey they torture him, using a corkscrew and a homemade knout. On his arrival back in Berlin, Vasili goes to see the narrator, his employer. He tells the story of what happened and begs to be released from his position and from humanity. The narrator graciously lets him go.

## Themes and Meanings

As in two of Vladimir Nabokov's novels, *Priglashenie na kazn'* (1935-1936 serial,

1938; *Invitation to a Beheading*, 1959) and *Bend Sinister* (1947), the main theme here is collectivist tyranny. The story illustrates how an imaginative, sensitive individual is forced to conform to the vulgar Philistinism of the unimaginative collective. Although the word "Nazi" is never mentioned, the story is obviously a condemnation of the Nazi regime under which Nabokov himself lived for a time in Berlin. It also is an implicit condemnation of collectivist oppression in the Soviet Union and of a widespread human inclination to stifle creative eccentricity.

"Cloud, Castle, Lake" may also be an allegory of life, which is a sometimes unpleasant "pleasure trip" through time toward inevitable death. Before his departure, Vasili has a dim vision of some perfect, timeless world full of happiness. That world seems attainable when he comes on "the lake with its cloud and its castle, in a motionless and perfect correlation of happiness." Here, so he senses, he can stop time, abandon the "pleasure trip" of life, and enter into the realm of motionless serenity. As he is soon horrified to discover, however, one is not allowed to abandon the journey. Furthermore, nothing really is motionless; even beautiful nature is constantly changing. The ideal of static serenity, for which Vasili yearns, does not exist on earth.

A strange twist in the final paragraph illustrates why Nabokov's works cannot be read as realistic fiction. The disillusioned Vasili visits his maker, the writer, and asks to resign from humankind. Although he has just learned that life does not accept such resignations, the writer grants him that release without demur. Note that in the first line of the story the narrator terms Vasili "one of my representatives." Throughout the world of his fiction, Nabokov uses the words "representative" and "agent" to refer to imaginary personages or alter egos that he creates to perform any number of functions in his works. In addition to serving as the protagonist of this story, Vasili Ivanovich appears to work for his creator as a collector of fine detail from nature, to be used by the writer in his fiction. See, for example, the passage in which "his precious, experienced eyes noted what was necessary," followed by a lovely description of a dry needle hanging in a fir grove. Furthermore, in many of his works Nabokov, or the narrator who writes in his name, plays the role of benevolent god of the fiction, mercifully releasing tormented characters. Each of the two novels that have the closest affinities with "Cloud, Castle, Lake" (*Invitation to a Beheading* and *Bend Sinister*) ends with a similar sort of release. It is as if the writer were saying, "Yes, in real life there is no escape from time and human cruelty, but since I am inventing all of this, I can let poor Vasili go." What happens, however, to a fictional character after he is released from his role as a human being? The disintegration of his personality amounts to an escape resembling death. Is the writer who "releases" Vasili really so benevolent after all? Complex philosophical questions are raised when Nabokov openly treats his characters as fictive rather than pretending that they are real human beings.

*Style and Technique*

The story's most obvious message, a condemnation of collectivist tyranny, is subtly convincing because the author distances himself from the brutality rather than blatantly condemning it. He describes it in matter-of-fact tones and even tempers it with humor. One cannot help laughing when Vasili loses the nonsensical game on the train and is forced to eat a cigarette butt as punishment. The genuine horror of his situation is epitomized by the black humor in the description of how he is beaten: "The post-office clerk, who had been to Russia, fashioned a knout out of a stick and a belt, and began to use it with devilish dexterity. Atta boy! . . . All had a wonderful time." Here the irony is obvious. When used in descriptions of brutal events, humor intensifies the shock effect on the reader and makes the horror even more palpable.

Descriptions of nature also play an important stylistic role throughout the story, contrasting the beauty of human beings' surroundings with the beastliness of their lives. In this tale about human inhumanity, it is significant that only the beautiful nature Vasili loves seems to have any sympathy for him in his plight.

The overriding theme of most of Nabokov's works is the artistic process itself, and "Cloud, Castle, Lake" is no exception. The narrator of the story is a central character, and the most interesting stylistic features involve the way he insinuates himself into the action as he tells it. The reader is shocked (or should be) from the story's beginning, when he learns that the narrator is not even sure of his character's name: "I cannot remember his name at the moment. I think it was Vasili Ivanovich." Later, the narrator blends with his character ("We both, Vasili Ivanovich and I, have always been impressed by the anonymity of all parts of a landscape"), and thenceforth descriptions of nature suggest the enthusiasms of the writer as well as those of the character. Three times, exuberant lyrical passages end with the words "my love," obviously the narrator's words, not Vasili's. To whom do they refer? Probably to the muse of the writer, the great love of his life, his art. The most exalted of these invocations of the muse ("my love! My obedient one!") comes amid the description of the harmonious beauty of the cloud, castle, and lake.

These subtleties of style suggest that the story may involve the narrator's search for ideal beauty and serenity as much as Vasili's. Unlike his character, however, the writer is attempting to transcend mundane vulgarity by creating a lyrical world in beautiful words. He yearns to merge with his muse: "if one could stop the train and go thither, forever, to you, my love." When he describes the castle as "arising from dactyl to dactyl," the meter of the passage is dactylic, as is the meter of the original Russian title: "Oblako, ozero, bashnya." This use of metrical terminology and meter implies that the story is a castle built of poetry, epitomizing the joy that a writer takes in creativity.

In the end, the narrator may think that his art has transformed a "hideous fairy tale" into a thing of beauty, but does the fanciful edifice he has built in his mind really provide the transcendence of vicious reality that Vasili sought at the inn on the lake? Is the joy that the artist takes in his creation even somehow reprehensible in the light of the tale's context of horrible human suffering? In a word, is the ideal of art simply another illusion, a sophistry? These are the questions that Nabokov raises in nearly all of his works. They are not easily answered.

*Robert L. Bowie*

# CLOUD COVER CARIBBEAN

*Author:* Ana Lydia Vega (1946-      )
*Type of plot:* Regional, satire
*Time of plot:* The 1970's
*Locale:* The open sea off the coast of Florida
*First published:* "Encancaranublado," 1982 (English translation, 1989)

> Principal characters:
> ANTENOR, a Haitian
> DIOGENES, a Dominican
> CARMELO, a Cuban

*The Story*

"Cloud Cover Caribbean" is told by a third-person omniscient narrator. It is September, hurricane season in the Caribbean, and Antenor has been on the open sea in a makeshift vessel for two days. He has not seen anything or anyone since he left his home island of Haiti. He unexpectedly hears Spanish being spoken and helps a shipwrecked man from the Dominican Republic aboard his little boat, which nearly tips over with the additional weight. Antenor cautiously shares the water from his canteen with the newcomer. Though Antenor speaks French, and Diogenes, the Dominican, speaks Spanish, they share an amiable conversation anyway. Neither can understand the other completely, but they pass the time by telling each other what they are leaving behind and what they are seeking.

Suddenly they hear shouts and see a curly-haired Cuban bobbing among the waves. Though Diogenes and Antenor hesitate to take yet another passenger on the little skiff (there is only one canteen of water to share), they are unable to resist his cries for help, and they pull the Cuban aboard. Once again the boat nearly capsizes. Carmelo, the Cuban, and Diogenes, the Dominican, both speak Spanish and soon marginalize the French-speaking Haitian, who sits on the only box in the boat, resenting "the monopoly the language of Cervantes was enjoying in a vessel . . . sailing under the Haitian flag."

Carmelo smells tobacco and rum and quickly deduces that Antenor must be guarding his provisions in the box he sits on so determinedly. He and Diogenes push Antenor roughly, almost knocking him into the sea, and wrest the box from him. They attack Antenor's carefully collected and safeguarded provisions with vigor, devouring his cassava bread and corn, chewing his tobacco, and drinking up his rum. Nevertheless, the alliance between Carmelo and Diogenes weakens as each makes offensive remarks about the other's homeland. Diogenes nostalgically recalls the prostitution during the Fulgencio Batista era, before the Cuban Revolution of 1959; Carmelo suggests that Santo Domingo, the capital of the Dominican Republic, is in such disarray that the effects of a recent hurricane will go unnoticed. In a moment of frustration, Diogenes reaches for the water canteen, which rolls to Antenor's feet. Rather than let Diogenes have it, Antenor throws the canteen into the sea. Carmelo intervenes only to warn them not to capsize the boat, but it is too late. The boat capsizes, and the three would-be immigrants together shout for help. Some time later, they are rescued by an American boat, and the blond, blue-eyed, English-speaking captain sends them below to be cared for by the Puerto Rican crew members, whose Spanish is a welcome sound to the Cuban and Dominican and even to the Haitian. Just as the three refugees begin to smile, happy to be alive and to have found the "promised land" of America, one of the Puerto Ricans growls to the three newcomers that they will have to work hard for anything they get, because "a gringo don't give nothing away. Not to his own mother."

*Themes and Meanings*

Most of Ana Lydia Vega's work centers on her home island of Puerto Rico. "Cloud Cover Caribbean" continues the Caribbean theme but extends it to other islands. Haiti and the Dominican Republic are the two countries on a single island just northwest of Puerto Rico; Cuba is a much larger island northwest of Haiti, just eighty miles from the southernmost point of Key West, Florida.

For each of these would-be immigrants to Florida, the United States is the promised land. Like many refugees before them, they risk their lives on a fragile boat with inadequate supplies in hopes of making a new life. Antenor, the Haitian, puts his skiff to sea. Diogenes, the Dominican, has suffered a shipwreck and is rescued by Antenor. As he is pulled aboard, Diogenes tells Antenor, "Thanks, brother." The narrator reports that each of the men spoke his own language, French or Spanish, but nonetheless communicated the same message, that he was leaving little behind, only suffering, death, and oppression by the church, the military, and even other civilians. Thus "they established an international brotherhood of hunger, a solidarity of dreams." However, no sooner have they established this "brotherhood" than they rescue the Cuban, Carmelo. Allegiances soon shift to a new bond between the two Spanish speakers. Carmelo explains that he is leaving Cuba to escape the constant, day-and-night work at home, and Diogenes complains that in Santo Domingo, there is no work to be had. Carmelo had to cut cane all day long, and Diogenes could not find work because workers were brought in from Haiti.

Diogenes and Carmelo forge a quick alliance against Antenor, steal his food and drink, and then discuss with some contentment their plans for life in the United States. Carmelo hopes to set up a "dating" business in Miami, managing prostitutes. Such businesses are banned in Cuba, complains Carmelo. Diogenes jokes that in the Dominican Republic they have so many prostitutes they export them. Carmelo responds by commenting that Cuban women think of themselves as equal to men and do not want to work the streets. Diogenes counters that Cuban women "used to put out with the best of them." Carmelo's remark reflects the change in Cuban society since the revolution in 1959 when Castro overthrew the dictatorship of Batista. Under Batista, corruption and prostitution flourished in Cuba. Carmelo, somewhat insulted by Diogenes's nostalgic view of the Batista regime, counters with a comment that Santo Domingo does not look any worse after the hurricane hit than it did before.

The alliance among these three refugees dissolves as a result of the historical and political differences that divide them and soon threaten their very survival, as anger leads to a struggle and the three end up in the water together. When they are rescued by an American ship, a fourth Caribbean people enter the story—the Puerto Ricans who work on the ship. However, though the Puerto Ricans share the Spanish language with Carmelo and Diogenes and Antenor seems to recall hearing Spanish in his "tenderest childhood," once again "brotherhood" is impossible in the face of the need to compete for survival under harsh circumstances.

*Style and Technique*

In this brief story, Vega creates a semi-comical microcosm of the historical and contemporaneous context of several Caribbean islands and peoples. Though the dialogue itself is revealing, the omniscient narrator makes the reader aware of each character's thoughts, and much of the story's content and meaning is revealed through those thoughts. Thus the reader discovers that Antenor, the Haitian, is fleeing "famine, the macoutes' war-cries, the fear, the drought." The Tontons Macoutes were death squads employed by the dictatorships of Papa and Baby Doc Duvalier to terrorize and control the Haitian populace. When the Spanish speakers band together against him to seize his food stores, Antenor attempts to avoid understanding their commands to move off the box he is guarding, thinking "our undisputed world illiteracy rate might pay off here." When Antenor later throws the canteen of water into the sea rather than share it with a "Dominican cur," he thinks "that's so you'll remember we invaded you three times." "Trujillo was right," shouts Diogenes the Dominican, referring to the massacre of thousands of Haitians by Rafael Trujillo, dictator of the Dominican Republic. The history of dictatorship, oppression, and in the case of Cuba, communist revolution, are all referenced in the dialogue and thoughts of the characters of these island nations, and events on the makeshift boat reveal the ongoing political tensions among the three countries.

Vega raises the issue of race as well. Haitians are typically black, and Dominicans, Cubans, and Puerto Ricans may be black but are more commonly mixed race. The Spanish speakers repeatedly refer to and denigrate the Haitian's race, which reinforces the irony of their rescue. The captain of the American vessel is an "Aryan, Apollo-like seadog . . . [with] golden locks and the bluest of eyes" who lumps all three refugees together as "niggers" whom the "spiks" (Puerto Ricans) should assist.

Vega also creates an ironic comic tone through the use of high-flown language. Antenor's box of food is "the very Ark of the Covenant" whose contents are "the fabled Horn of Plenty." The narrator in effect enters the story, referring to the refugees as "our heroic emigrés" and denying responsibility for the story: "Don't ask me how in the hell they kept the sharks at bay." "Cloud Cover Caribbean" treats a potentially tragic theme in a comedic way.

*Linda Ledford-Miller*

# COACH

*Author:* Mary Robison (1949-    )
*Type of plot:* Domestic realism
*Time of plot:* The 1970's
*Locale:* Pennsylvania
*First published:* 1981

> *Principal characters:*
> HARRY NOONAN, the Coach
> SHERRY, his wife
> DAPHNE, their daughter
> TOBY, a college news reporter

## The Story

Harry Noonan dries breakfast dishes as he waits for a college reporter to arrive for an interview. He has been hired to coach the freshman football team. His wife, Sherry, asks him to rent a studio for her, where she can do her painting. Their daughter, Daphne, is looking in the refrigerator for something to eat. She wants to stay for the interview, but Coach says no. He remembers a fall night seven years earlier when he set Daphne on a football field during the half-time ceremonies; she was dressed in a football uniform with the number "½" on her back. Now, Daphne asks him for help with her algebra. He declines, so she asks her mother, who says forget it.

After the reporter, Toby, arrives, he asks only a few questions and takes no notes. He then engages Daphne in conversation. Afterward, Daphne remarks that Toby was nice and Coach tells her that she would be wasting her time on him—like "trying to light a fire with a wet match." When the newspaper interview appears the next day in the *Rooter*, it is full of inaccurate information, making Coach furious. Trying to console him, Sherry says that Daphne liked it.

Coach takes Daphne out for ice cream in order to explain why he is renting an apartment for Sherry. He denies Daphne's suspicion they are separating and tells her about Sherry's five-year plan for self-development. Coach is distracted from the conversation when one of his new players drives up with his parents. Upset that he cannot remember the boy's name—Bobby Stark—Coach mockingly chastises him for eating ice cream, aware that Bobby's parents and other people are grinning.

When Coach begins his football practices, he learns from Bobby that he has a good chance of coaching the varsity team next year. When he goes home, excited with this news, he is disappointed to find no one there. Sherry has left a note saying she is at "her place" and Daphne is with "Toby K. someplace, fooling around." Coach grabs a beer. While he showers, Daphne comes home. Hearing sounds, Coach goes to the bedroom, expecting to find Sherry, but is surprised to find Daphne dancing and posing in front of the mirror. When he mocks her, doing "the Daphne," she is embarrassed.

Coach begins telling her his good news, but she only says "let me out, please."

Back in the kitchen, Coach drinks more beer and begins constructing a "dream team" roster of former players. Daphne comes downstairs, wearing a team shirt with *Go* on the front, *Griffins* on the back. Pretending to be Daphne, Coach apologizes to himself for her being rude to him upstairs. Conciliating him, she asks Coach about the prospects of his team this year. He offers her a beer. Sherry comes in with a few groceries. Daphne grabs the Oreo cookies. Sherry asks for a beer and says that she cannot paint. Coach reassures her, but she adds: "An artist? The wife of a coach?"

*Themes and Meanings*

"No one at home"—so begins the next-to-final scene of "Coach." The phrase expresses Mary Robison's concern about the disintegration of the American family. There is no true intimacy between Coach and his wife. Just as he is obsessed with his coaching career, she wants only her "room apart." Neglected by both, Daphne must look out for herself. Significantly, she is searching for food in the refrigerator when she appears in the story. This signifies her need for emotional and intellectual nourishment as well. Her parents are unconcerned about her schoolwork, although she is taking makeup courses, and both refuse to help with her algebra.

A fifteen-year-old adolescent, Daphne is becoming interested in boys. When Toby mildly flirts with her, she rolls her chin seductively on her shoulder. Oblivious to her need for parental guidance, Coach and Sherry are glad when she is off with Toby, out of their way. Coach's insensitivity to Daphne's feelings are revealed at the Dairy Frost, where he is more upset that he cannot remember Bobby's name than he is concerned about Daphne's apprehension that her parents are separating. His insensitivity is also demonstrated when he makes fun of her dancing before the mirror.

Rather than encourage the development of Daphne's individual identity, Coach, with the complicity of Sherry, uses Daphne to support his own ego. He probably wanted a son instead of a daughter, a boy such as Bobby Stark. Failing this, he turns Daphne into his personal cheerleader. The charm bracelet that her parents put together for her has a miniature football and a megaphone on it. Daphne, however, is starting to imitate her parents by looking out for number one. She has stopped wearing the charm bracelet and serving food at Sunday dinners honoring Coach's best players.

Robison sees far-reaching implications in the ways that parents such as Coach and Sherry treat their children. Coach's attempts to dominate Daphne and his and Sherry's failure to provide for her needs parallel the development of industrialism at the expense of nature. This is suggested by the fact that Coach teaches history courses at the college on European Industrial Development and the Atlantic World. In high school he taught World History and Problems of Democracy. Coach takes his teaching job no more seriously than he does his role as Daphne's father. When Coach describes one of his courses as a refresher course "in nature," Toby corrects him: "or out of nature."

In finding a parallel between Daphne and nature Robison expresses her own concern for the future of civilization. The greatest problem of democracy, she implies, is the disintegration of the family. Her story asks what the United States—what the world—will be like in the future without healthy, well-adjusted, well-informed citizens.

## Style and Technique

"Coach" is written in a realistic style, with an emphasis on dialogue, which is ironic, as the characters communicate with each other only superficially. The point of view is third-person, limited omniscient, as Robison enters only the mind of Coach. This is also ironic, because there is very little in Coach's head. Most important, however, is Robison's use of Greek myth and patterns of imagery. She alludes to the myth of Daphne and Apollo in the name Daphne. In mythology, Apollo, the sun god, is charmed by Daphne's beauty and pursues her. About to be overtaken, she prays for help and metamorphoses into a laurel tree, which becomes the favorite of Apollo. Robison links Coach to Apollo by using words and images that associate him with the sun. His last name, Noonan, contains the word noon, implying the sun. References are made to the sun porch of Coach's house; the colors of his new team are maroon and gold; he tells Daphne to "be on the beam"; and his influence on her is implied when she takes "sun on her back, adding to her tan." Something akin to emotional sunburn is suggested when Coach embarrasses Daphne in the mirror scene: "You are beet red," he says. Robison puns on beet, pronounced like beat, which means both punished and defeated.

Like Apollo, Coach causes Daphne to metamorphose into a tree. A travesty of this event occurs in Coach's memory of the eight-year-old Daphne on the football field wearing a player's jersey and helmet. "Lost in the getup," she is transformed into "a small pile of equipment." Toward the end of the story, Coach succeeds in transforming Daphne into a tree, but not as he would wish. She escapes from him, as Daphne did from Apollo, and becomes dead to his demands for unconditional adoration. He yells at her: "Hey! Why am I yelling at wood, here?" The tree is dead.

Robison extends the significance of Daphne's transformation into a tree with a series of nature images: "green water . . . sliced by a power boat," "frog in a blender," "lime-eaten grass." In each case, nature is violated by machines and other products of modern civilization. Robison uses further nature images to relate her meaning to evolution. References are made to "warm salt-water," the origin of life; an insect, "a plastic ladybug"; an amphibian, the frog; a reptile, "a green family with scales"; and a mammal, "it's monkey time."

Robison also alludes to the evolution of civilized man. The Daphne and Apollo myth invokes ancient Greece and the beginning of Western civilization, and the subject matter of Coach's courses includes both European and American history. Robison questions the direction of evolution. By using animal images to describe Bobby, referring to his "rump and haunches," as well as Coach, who "trotted for the sidelines," Robison suggests that human beings are regressing on the evolutionary ladder. Sherry jokingly refers to their family as "having scales." In their survival-of-the-fittest lifestyle, they are becoming reptilian.

*James Green*

# THE COAL SHOVELLER

*Author:* Keith Fort
*Type of plot:* Antistory
*Time of plot:* The 1960's
*Locale:* Washington, D.C.
*First published:* 1969

> *Principal characters:*
> THE NARRATOR, an author and professor
> MICHAEL, his alter ego
> MARGARET, Michael's wife
> AMELIA, Michael's small daughter
> REGINALD COWPERSMITH, another alter ego
> AN AFRICAN AMERICAN COAL SHOVELLER

*The Story*

A writer tries to create a short story while looking through his window at an African American man shoveling coal into a basement across the street. He experiments with various stylistic approaches and characters but repeatedly gives up. After his first abortive attempt, he writes: "To ask words to make fiction into photographic realism is to demand a performance which they are totally incapable of giving."

He begins a personal story. His six-year-old daughter enters his study and breaks his concentration, so he takes her outside into the snow. He is only imagining this scenario, however, as he is actually still writing. Once again he stops. He now is beginning to sound like James Joyce in "The Dead" (1914)—a story that ends with a typical Joycean epiphany. He writes: "I am inclined to agree with those who say that literature (no matter how negative the theme) which reinforces the habit of extracting ideas from reality panders to the self-interest of the middle class."

Still determined to persevere, the narrator next begins a story involving an old woman telling her grandson about Washington, D.C., of the past. Now his sentences sound like the convoluted, hypnotic prose of William Faulkner. He does not like to imitate but candidly admits: "I wish I could honestly see the fall of the Old South as tragic in the way that Faulkner did."

Increasingly frustrated, the narrator indulges in self-recrimination, blaming himself for being emotionally bankrupt, nihilistic, arrogant, and narrow-minded. He now decides to try writing a visceral, action-packed story and invents a young white coal shoveller named Reginald Cowpersmith, who uses his status as a building employee to get into a young woman's apartment in order to rape her. After getting well into a convincing yarn, he breaks off and exclaims: "God, but I hate bastards who write stories like that."

Finally, he tries to write a satirical vignette in which an anonymous writer befriends the black coal shoveller in a bar frequented by middle-class whites vaguely associated with the arts. He wants to expose the hypocrisy of white liberal intellectuals by introducing a real lower-class black into their midst. His imaginary coal shoveller gets along well with his imaginary white liberals but fails to understand his creator's complaints, such as his complaint that "art has been dehumanized so that no man can honestly write on anything but the problem of writing." The mystified but compassionate coal shoveller quite reasonably asks his creator why he keeps trying to write if he finds it so frustrating. The writer replies, "in my business it's publish or . . . ," stopping before saying "perish." Instead, he releases a smokescreen of hyperintellectual verbiage. He obviously covets his privileged position as an intellectual and professor even though he questions the value of any literature that people like himself produce.

Like its predecessors, his new story fizzles out and the narrator finds himself back at his window, watching the man shoveling coal. He states that he does not want to turn on the light because it will prevent him from seeing out the window but that he cannot continue writing because it is now too dark.

### Themes and Meanings

"The Coal Shoveller" is an important work in which Keith Fort has found the ideal form for expressing the problems of many aspiring writers. Although dissatisfied with the old styles—especially realism and naturalism—they cannot find new styles that will liberate them to express themselves. The main theme throughout this story concerns the difficulty of being honest. Its narrator admires many great writers of the past and appreciates that they were great because they wrote what they passionately believed. He wishes to emulate them but without imitating them. As a modern man, however, he finds it difficult to know in what he should believe. Traditional religion has been undermined by science, and socialism has been discredited by its practitioners in Russia, China, and elsewhere.

The narrator's abortive attempts to concoct a story based on a man shoveling coal are efforts to discover what he himself truly believes. His mind is full of ideas, but he does not know whether he really believes any of them. His indictment of certain anti-intellectual writers suggests that he would agree with William Butler Yeats's assessment of the modern condition in "The Second Coming" (1921): "The best lack all conviction while the worst are full of passionate intensity."

It might be argued that the theme of "The Coal Shoveller" is the difficulty of finding a theme, because a theme represents what a writer believes. It is appropriate to such an experimental story that its theme and meaning should be the search for theme and meaning. One thing in which the author does believe is the truth. He cannot force himself to regard the coal shoveller as either a victim or a hero. Such attitudes can lead into stylistic dead ends and ideological traps.

Fort rejects one style after another because he feels that although they might have been appropriate for authors such as Alain Robbe-Grillet, James Joyce, Henry James, William Faulkner, Jack Kerouac, J. P. Donleavy, and Henry Miller, they are false for him. He does not mention Ernest Hemingway, who was one of the most influential writers of the twentieth century, but he would certainly subscribe to Hemingway's dictum that a good writer's most essential gift is a built-in, shockproof bunk detector, the "writer's radar" that all great writers have. The author does not know what he believes in, but he knows what he does not believe in, and that knowledge serves as his radar.

It may be more difficult to be creative in modern times because people have become too educated, too intellectual, and too sophisticated. The problem that many aspiring writers have in creating fiction is related to problems that others have in trying to read fiction. Many readers, because of the glut of media information that they absorb, have become too intellectual and too jaded to believe in fiction. People are increasingly asking why they should be concerned about the problems of people who do not even exist.

It is understandable that short story writers should wonder whether they have anything meaningful to communicate when their labor is largely a labor of love. Short fiction might become obsolete without the patronage of literary journals subsidized by academic institutions. It is not unusual for writers—like the narrator of "The Coal Shoveller"—to be professors, and for them to wonder whether they are writers who teach, or teachers who write. If writers persist despite guilt, frustration, and self-doubt—as the author and his alter egos do in "The Coal Shoveller"—they may create new forms of fiction more suited to alienated, agnostic modern times. Writers such as Fort are creating forms that often seem like bizarre amalgamations of fact and fantasy. The problem of the writer—like many other problems—may prove to be an opportunity in disguise.

## Style and Technique

Although an experimental work classified as an antistory, "The Coal Shoveller" has important elements in common with conventional stories. In order to interest the reader, any story must be dramatic. Drama is provided by conflicting motives, which have been categorized as "humankind against humankind," "humankind against nature," and "humankind against itself." "The Coal Shoveller" falls into the last category. Its narrator is strongly motivated to write a story but finds, after a number of false starts, that he cannot do so. His strong motivation to persevere is what keeps the reader wanting to learn whether he ever succeeds.

William Shakespeare's *Hamlet, Prince of Denmark* (c. 1600-1601) is a classic example of "man against himself." Fort's protagonist resembles Prince Hamlet in being intelligent: He has too much education, he has read too many books, he has too much imagination, and he thinks too much. He is his own worst enemy. If dramatic conflict usually involves a protagonist pitted against an antagonist, then the narrator of "The Coal Shoveller" can be seen as both protagonist and antagonist.

"The Coal Shoveller" is a combination story, essay, and journal entry. The reader forms the impression that the narrator is in the habit of writing in this manner. He writes about his thoughts, observations, and problems, including problems in trying to find something worth writing about. Occasionally he comes across the germ of an idea that he can develop into a full-fledged story.

On the occasion that is chronicled in "The Coal Shoveller," the narrator is not necessarily defeated in his attempt to write a short story. What he is going through is his own personal method of working, his way of jump-starting his creativity. He may not be able to expect a successful outcome every time that he uses this technique, but he is better off writing about writing—or writing about writing about writing—than he would be simply staring at a blank sheet of paper. It would be a mistake to regard him as a failure because he has not succeeded in writing a story about a man shoveling coal. He has produced germs of several stories that might one day blossom into finished works.

*Bill Delaney*

# THE COLLECTOR OF TREASURES

*Author:* Bessie Head (Bessie Amelia Emery, 1937-1986)
*Type of plot:* Vignette
*Time of plot:* 1966-1975
*Locale:* The villages of Puleng and Gaborone, in Botswana
*First published:* 1977

> *Principal characters:*
> DIKELEDI MOKOPI, the protagonist, who murders her husband
> GARESEGO, her husband, the antagonist, an administrative clerk
> BANABOTHE, their eldest son
> PAUL THEBOLO, the principal of the Puleng primary school
> KENALEPE, the wife of Paul Thebolo and Dikeledi's first genuine
> friend

*The Story*

Bessie Head's vignette of a village woman abandoned and abused by her husband begins *in medias res*. In the first of the story's four sections, Dikeledi is on her way to prison in Gaborone, the country's new capital city, from her village, Puleng. She gazes indifferently at the passing landscape of the bush as she rides in the police truck. As a result of the long day's lonely journey and her emotional turmoil, she finally collapses, "oblivious to everything but her pain." On her arrival at the prison that night, she is stirred to consciousness by the police, who dutifully record her crime, "manslaughter," and her life sentence. As Dikeledi is led to her barren cell, the wardress remarks sarcastically that she will be the fifth woman currently in the prison to have been sentenced for the same offense, murdering her husband, and notes that the crime is "becoming the fashion these days." Having been locked up, Dikeledi is left to her own silence in the dark cell.

On rising early the next morning, the other four women—Kebonye, Otsetswe, Galeboe, and Monwana—introduce themselves. Kebonye asks Dikeledi why her parents have named her tears, and she replies that it was after her mother, who died when Dikeledi was six years old, her father having died in the year of her birth. In the ensuing conversation, Dikeledi expresses little sorrow for her crime, which was murder by castration. As the women begin their work in the prison, they observe that Dikeledi's "hands of strange power" are especially skillful with sewing, knitting, and weaving. She has, in fact, reared her three children largely through her own efforts, because her husband abandoned her after four years of marriage.

After the day passes in intimate disclosure among the five women, the third-person, omniscient narrator describes Dikeledi's newfound friendships as "gold amidst the ash, deep loves that had joined her heart to the hearts of others." In this "phase three of a life that had been ashen in its loneliness and unhappiness," Dikeledi accepts the tender compassion possible in friendship: "She was the collector of such treasures."

Having established the protagonist's complexity of character, yet withholding the comprehension of it from the reader, the narrator begins the second section with a digression on the "two kinds of men in the society." With cultural background analyzing the evolution of the type of man who bears no responsibility for his family or for his community, Garesego is introduced as the model of the man who is "a broken wreck with no inner resources at all." For Garesego, national independence has brought a two-hundred-percent increase in salary that permits him to engage "in a dizzy kind of death dance of wild destruction and dissipation." He leaves his wife and three sons in favor of drinking and prostitutes. Ironically, he does so in the same year, 1966, of Botswana's independence.

Against Garesego, the narrator sets the second type of man, modeled by Paul Thebolo. He devotes himself entirely to his family's stability and to the community's well-being. Not only is he principal of the primary school, but also he is the epitome of the caring neighbor. Further, he is an example of leadership, moderating discussions of politics and assisting the villagers whenever they require his skills in literacy. His inner resources give him "the power to create himself anew."

Dikeledi meets Paul when he arrives in Puleng to build his house. She, renowned for her ability to thatch a roof, offers to assist in setting up the household. Not long after, his wife, Kenalepe Thebolo, arrives; the two women develop an intimate, enduring friendship. Because of the Thebolos's reputation, Dikeledi's dressmaking business begins to boom. Throughout the next eight years, the friendship deepens. By virtue of her craft skills, Dikeledi becomes nearly self-sufficient. Kenalepe even offers to "loan" her husband to Dikeledi in order to share the joy of sexuality, which she has renounced, never having experienced sexual pleasure with Garesego. Dikeledi refuses Kenalepe's offer, but when Kenalepe is hospitalized after a miscarriage, Dikeledi cares for her children and household.

As Dikeledi cleans the kitchen hut one night while Paul is visiting his wife, he returns to find her hard at work, and they share a moment of intimacy, one that does not rest on a sexual perception of each other: "It was too beautiful to be love." Such an affirmation that a man can possess goodness yields one more "nugget of gold" for Dikeledi. This second phase of her life has led to a sense of hope and joy in her independence and friendship.

During the developing intimacy with Kenalepe and Paul, Dikeledi confides much of her past. In reply to Kenalepe's question of why she married Garesego in the first place, Dikeledi explains that, having been orphaned at six, she was reared by an uncle, who regarded her as a servant; even her cousins thought of her as their servant. She was forced to leave school early, and she was never included or loved as a member of the family. When Garesego proposed through her uncle, Dikeledi married him to escape the bondage of her uncle's family. While this first phase of Dikeledi's life continued, she tolerated Garesego's irresponsibility, drunkenness, and unfaithfulness, nurturing a fragile pride based on his claim to prefer her for her traditional values and an uncertain hope for love within a family of her own. Garesego, however, regarded traditional women as primarily servants; thus, he abandoned her and the children altogether as soon as his post-independence promotion made it financially feasible.

Dikeledi's crisis comes when she learns that her eldest son, Banabothe, has been accepted for secondary school. Remembering the disruption in her own education and having witnessed Banabothe's dedication to his studies, she is distraught to learn that she has not saved enough money to pay all of Banabothe's fees and still pay the primary school fees for her two younger sons. Out of a desperate refusal to interrupt the education of one son, Dikeledi decides to seek Garesego's help to pay the fees for all of them; they are his sons, too. When she approaches him as he leaves his office, she is shocked not so much at his hesitation as at his accusation that she is the mistress of Paul, who, Garesego argues, should bear the cost of the fees. Paul, later hearing of the slander against himself, confronts Garesego; after an exchange of insults, Paul punches Garesego, giving him cause for further slander. He tells the villagers that his "wife's lover" did it. They in turn spread the gossip about the man who many consider "too good to be true," but they also criticize Garesego for failing in his duty to Banabothe.

To save face with the village and to provoke Dikeledi, Garesego sends a note to her, announcing that he will return home and requesting that she prepare a meal and a bath for him. Despite his stated intention for a reconciliation, Dikeledi knows that he is coming home to demand sex in exchange for even considering the partial payment of the fees; she agrees to the visit, and she begins her extensive preparations—including the sharpening of "a large kitchen knife used to cut meat." When Garesego arrives that evening, he responds to her with callous indifference and ignores his children, further convincing Dikeledi of the righteousness of her plan.

After drinking beer and feasting, Garesego believes that he has won his claim to his wife over Paul, because he does not see him next door. He dismisses Dikeledi's request about the fees without a firm commitment. While she bathes him, he drifts naked into a smug, self-satisfied sleep. Dikeledi leaves him, kisses her children goodnight, and, in a detached trance, unconsciously attempts to wake him with the noise of her cleanup. When he sleeps on, "lost to the world," she kneels by the bed, removes the knife from where she had hidden it, and castrates him in a single stroke. Garesego's bellowing as he bleeds to death brings Banabothe, who is sent to summon the police, and Kenalepe, who flees in terror. Paul, too, arrives and, after staring dumbfoundedly at Dikeledi, promises to rear and to educate her sons.

*Themes and Meanings*

Head's brutal, despairing tragedy of contemporary village life in post-independent Africa grounds itself clearly in the historical and cultural background of the story. Aware of a non-African audience, she offers at once a scathing condemnation of masculine dominance and an affirming challenge to local leadership. The three phases of

Dikeledi's life parallel Head's analysis of the evolution of Bamangwato society. In tracing the three periods of moral decay, she notes that although traditional laws may have provided discipline for society as a whole, they failed to acknowledge the individual's needs; further, traditional society doubly compounded the error for women, regarding them as inferior to the male. In the second period, colonialism, migratory labor patterns to South African mines further eroded traditional family life. Men were forced to be absent from their families for long periods of time in order to earn enough to pay the British poll tax. With men demeaned by their racially inferior status under colonialism, the third period, independence, presented the challenge for a new order of family life, but both men and women, suffering from legacies of simplistic traditional custom and of colonial degradation, had little more than their own inner stamina to draw on in shaping that necessarily new order.

In *Serowe: Village of the Rain-Wind* (1981), Head describes two additional factors in the story's central theme: "the complete breakdown of family life." Head claims that "of every one hundred children born in Serowe, three on the average are legitimate." This widespread anonymity and, subsequently, irresponsibility of fathers results from erosion in traditional customs of polygamy and *bogadi*, "the bride price or the offering of a gift of cattle by a man to his wife's family at the time of marriage." Without polygamy, women are no longer assured a husband (provider); without *bogadi*, there is no guarantee of legitimacy for her children.

Head, however, does not advocate a return to these practices, charging that polygamy promoted "jealousy and strife" while *bogadi* had "undertones of a sale-bargain" in which "women were merely a marketable commodity." Rather, she argues through her fiction, the inner resources necessary to reverse the family's collapse are the treasures of compassion.

"The Collector of Treasures," then, provides a study in the origins of post-independent family misery and contrasts two divergent responses to the family's collapse. The Mokopi marriage models the plunge into an ever-increasing despair, while the Thebolo marriage provides the creative challenge. Garesego's moral decay, not exclusively of his own making, is obvious; Paul's ability to act out of integrity and dignity in order to shape self-respect in the village family is equally obvious. The story is, in fact, a polemical challenge to the new African male: He must act with traditional respect for the community but do so in the modern context of individuality that confronts him.

### Style and Technique

Blending polemic, history, and anthropology without compromising aesthetic merit tests the skill of any writer. Head's achievement is that she can address African readers while informing her audience abroad. Although origins of eroding family life in this story are specific to Botswana, the threat of materialistic moral decay to modern families is universal. By beginning her story with Dikeledi's affirmation of love and intimacy, she involves her readers in a complex character, yet the detached narrative voice withholds judgment of the character for her crime. As one questions Dikeledi's motives, the narrative flashback unfolds not only her background but also the complexity of Kenalepe, Garesego, and Paul, who all sustain the developing characterization and provide parallels and contrasts. Simple, direct imagery plays an important part in the story, from the title motif of fellow feeling as a kind of "treasure" to the animal images used to describe Garesego. Although Head employs dialogue sparingly, she does so effectively. Her characters speak openly and directly to one another, embodying the intimacy achieved first among the prisoners and later in the friendship between Dikeledi and Kenalepe; the authenticity of human compassion and its power to create new stability in the family and community are thus affirmed. Ironically, Dikeledi creates a new order of stability that excludes the very society that sentenced her; symbolically, she finds her deepest freedom in prison.

*Michael Loudon*

# COLOR ME REAL

*Author:* J. California Cooper (1931-    )
*Type of plot:* Character study
*Time of plot:* The 1980's
*Locale:* Rural South, New York, Chicago
*First published:* 1984

> *Principal characters:*
>      ERA, a light-skinned African American woman who lives as a
>          white person
>      MINNA, her mother, seduced by her white employer
>      HER BIOLOGICAL FATHER
>      GEORGE, her childhood protector and eventual mate
>      HER WHITE HUSBAND
>      REGGIE, her black husband

*The Story*

In "Color Me Real," a third-person narrator relates how Minna, a thirteen-year-old African American girl in a small southern town, is seduced by her white employer and bears him two children, Era and her brother. Because he will not pay her the money he owes her and still insists on sex, Minna uses herbs and roots to make a potion that blinds him and eventually makes him impotent. Despite the way she has been treated, she tends the man until he dies. As the children grow older, she works in a schoolhouse so that they can get an education.

The story's focus shifts from Minna to her daughter, Era, who at age seventeen, rejects her childhood protector, George, and leaves for New York with four hundred dollars of her father's money. To get ahead more quickly, the light-skinned young woman chooses to live as a white person. She attends secretarial school and secures a job at a brokerage firm. She marries one of the firm's clients and is happy until she finds him in bed with a black woman. When she tells him that she also is black, he beats her and divorces her.

Era returns home, meets George again, has an argument with her brother at her mother's wedding to Arthur, and leaves for Chicago a short time later. While working for a black political candidate, she meets Reggie, a black lawyer, who believes that she is white. At a party at which the guests consist mostly of black men married to white women, the conversation turns to the inferiority of black women, and Reggie declares that he will tell his son not to marry a black woman. Era confronts Reggie, verbally attacks the black men for criticizing black women, and reminds him that she never told him she was white. Embarrassed, Reggie beats and rapes her after the guests leave.

When Era again returns home, she encounters George, who is working in his garden. They verbally spar with one another, she urging him to get married, and he reminding her that marriage has not benefitted her. In the course of the conversation, he declares, "I'm gonna marry the woman I love. I don't love them women I fool with." When she presses him about who these women are, he says that he goes up the highway to get sex. Other conversations follow, and Era begins to realize that he is "deeper" than she thought and that she is not as "deep" as she thought. He forces her to realize that she helped her husbands see what they wanted to see and that she was too concerned with appearances and too little with her feelings. George finally admits that he has always loved her, but because he is afraid of another big heartache, he will do nothing about his love. Resorting to coyness, she avoids George, thinking that he will come running to her. When he does not but instead pays two visits up the highway, she thinks she is angry, but she is really jealous.

George's question "How you FEELING, Ms. Era?" makes Era think about her life and reality. She wears "new cute shorts outfits" to work in her yard, and George spends a lot of time in his garden. In response to his question as to whether she is going to paint the house, Era replies "If I FEEL like it!" Although George leaves, apparently for another trip up the road, he quickly returns and meets her in the yard. After a discussion about love and feeling, they embrace, and at that point, the omniscient narrator returns to inform readers that their love lasted until death parted them and that they had many beautiful brown children.

*Themes and Meanings*

Like many of J. California Cooper's stories, "Color Me Real" is rooted in a small rural community and concerns a poor young black woman who seeks affection and respect from the men in her life. Although Era may suffer, she does retain her courage, determination, and sense of humor. "Color Me Real" is also about self-discovery and race. Not wanting to experience the same kind of exploitation her mother endured, Era "chose to pass for white because it would make her way easier." During her first marriage, Era wrongly reasons that her white husband, who confesses his addiction to black women, will not mind that she, too, is black.

Although she does not attempt to establish herself as a white woman when she moves to Chicago, she knows that Reggie, her black lawyer husband, thinks that she is his white trophy wife. It is when Reggie and his friends criticize black women that Era gains some insight into racial issues and identifies herself as one of the "sisters." She tells Reggie, "What makes us so disgusted with you, is that you have to stand on our shoulders, tear us down, make us look like nothing, to make yourself big enough to do what you want to do." These words are similar to the comments she earlier made to her brother, who beat his black girlfriend at their mother's wedding: "You tryin to pass for a man!" Era wants to love someone "real" and has her mother's marriage to Arthur as a model, but it is not until the end of the story that she can see reality. The narrator twice mentions that Era does not "see" George, who is the real man.

Eventually, Era recognizes that he is "deeper" than she had thought, but thinking without feeling is not enough. It was thinking and logic that made her prefer to be "colored" white rather than real. George accurately describes her problem: "Era, you ain't always sposed to see what you doing, you sposed to feel it! Seem like all you did was for the look of things." When Era and George do get together, they meet "half-way," "in the middle of the road," suggesting that each has moved away from an earlier position: she, from an unwillingness to feel; he, from fear of commitment and heartbreak. At the end of the story, Era is "neither white nor black," but is instead a real woman, "his woman."

### Style and Technique

Although the narrator refers to herself as "I" when she directly addresses the reader, the story is really a third-person narration that shifts from omniscient to limited and back to omniscient. The story seems to be told by a woman talking intimately with friends, almost gossiping, about people she knows. At times the narrator speculates about what a character thinks (the white seducer may have been blinded by his power), editorializes (Minna sold her body to her seducer because her family was starving), and shifts from anecdotes to detailed conversations.

Because Era's first husband is essentially a type, he is unnamed, as are the white seducer and Era's brother; names are reserved for women and significant black men. The incident with the first husband is intended to make an obvious point about racism, so there are few details; but the story of the second husband is more developed because the narrator needs to have Era voice the narrator's thoughts about the way black men treat black women.

To preserve the informal, vernacular style, Cooper's characters speak with appropriate dialects, and she uses frank descriptions (the white seducer "rode her all morning"). "Color Me Real" is a cautionary tale about the dangers of not knowing one's identity, not understanding the importance of feeling, and not understanding that "reality" is emotional rather than physical.

"Color Me Real" may not seem like a standard short story in terms of its plot or characterization, but it does use traditional literary devices. Seeing and feeling are recurring motifs, and the garden is used symbolically. The only man who gardens is George, who makes flowers bloom. Working together in the garden brings Era and George closer together and makes Era bloom. The fertility in the garden contrasts with the sterility Era finds in New York and Chicago; Cooper juxtaposes the positive values of the country and the negative values of the city. Era and George have beautiful brown (not black or white) children, live on the "brown earth" and work in their garden, which almost acquires edenic status. Their most important "crop" consists of "love and a peace of mind."

*Thomas L. Erskine*

# COLOR OF DARKNESS

*Author:* James Purdy (1923-     )
*Type of plot:* Psychological
*Time of plot:* 1956
*Locale:* United States
*First published:* 1957

> *Principal characters:*
> THE FATHER, twenty-eight years old, a success
> BAXTER, his young son
> MRS. ZILKE, a housekeeper, past middle age

*The Story*

The father in "Color of Darkness" is disconcerted because he cannot remember the color of his wife's eyes. She left him and their son, Baxter, some years back, and her features have almost entirely slipped from his memory. Eager for his father's attention, the child stays as close to him as possible and attempts to draw him into conversation. The father's work requires that he be absent most of the time; even when at home, however, he seems to be psychologically absent. The housekeeper, Mrs. Zilke, is not an adequate replacement for Baxter's mother; indeed, she is more a mother figure for the father than for his son. To the father, Mrs. Zilke appears as a repository of wisdom, as someone secure in her relationship to the world about her, as someone for whom the world was "round, firm, and perfectly illuminated," as it was not for him. His world is as amorphous, unstable, and hazy as the pipe smoke that swirls around his head. His inability to remember the color of his wife's eyes reflects not only his lack of connection with her but also his inability to achieve any vital emotional connection with anybody. He soon realizes that he cannot remember the color of Baxter's eyes, either.

When Mrs. Zilke tells the father that Baxter is lonely, he confides to Mrs. Zilke that he does not know children, that he does not know what they know, so he does not know how to talk to them. She reassures him that because he is a success at work, it is not necessary that he worry about anything else. In effect, Mrs. Zilke mouths the platitudes of society that endorse the public life at the expense of the private or personal life. As a token of his appreciation of her support, he invites her to join him in a glass of brandy. This symbol of communal understanding fails, however, as she does not drink. When he closes his eyes, he realizes that he does not remember the color of her eyes, either.

One night, the father becomes uncomfortable when he discovers that Baxter sometimes sleeps with a stuffed crocodile; consequently, he readily agrees when Mrs. Zilke suggests that Baxter needs a dog. Baxter does not take to the puppy; he especially does not want to sleep with it, for he needs a father, not a dog. Baxter has become to the father like "a gift someone has awarded him," rather than as someone intimately connected with his own being. In addition, "as the gift increased in value and liability, his own relation to it was more and more ambiguous and obscure."

Baxter tries to find a connection between himself and his father by asking him whether he had a dog when he was young, but the father's responses are, as usual, vacuous. In response to his father's absentmindedness, the boy begins to retreat into himself, declaring that he does not want anything. Noticing that Baxter has something in his mouth, Mrs. Zilke and the father demand to know what it is. For the first time Baxter allows himself to feel resentment toward them, and defiantly lies about the object and refuses to spit it out. When the father touches Baxter in his attempt to remove the object, Baxter declares that he hates him and swears at him. The object the father forces from his son's mouth turns out to be the wedding ring the father took off his finger the previous night for the first time since his marriage. As they stare at the ring, Baxter sharply kicks his father in the groin, and runs upstairs, calling him an obscenity connected to his conception. The story ends with the father refusing Mrs. Zilke's offer of help as he writhes on the floor in pain.

*Themes and Meanings*

The primary theme of "Color of Darkness" is the central theme of James Purdy's work: the pain that comes to human beings through their failure to bridge the gaps between individuals, a failure deriving from man's tendency to transform his existential experience into abstractions. The information that Baxter is lonely leads to the father's generalization that commitment to work precludes any commitment to people. All the generalizing discussion between the father and Mrs. Zilke results in this abstracting of experience. The father's concern about what Baxter knows becomes the abstraction that children know everything. Mrs. Zilke's comment about the bouquet of the brandy leads to his assertion that she knows everything. This tendency to generalize creates a barrier between the self and the immediate. Baxter complains that his father is always thinking about something other than the immediate or looking as if he "didn't know anything." The inability to remember the color of people's eyes reveals his inability to know the particular or the specific.

This failure to know specifics translates into failure to commit himself to people or to empathize with anyone, even his son. He knows intellectually that Baxter is lonely, he even feels guilty about not fulfilling Baxter's need for a closer emotional relationship with a father, but all he is able to do in response is to buy him a dog.

Baxter reacts to the pain that comes from his father's abstractedness in two ways: He inflicts pain on his father by kicking him and he retreats into abstraction himself. The kick is Baxter's last attempt to make his presence real to his father. Baxter has learned that to be aware is to be aware of pain; the father, writhing in pain on the floor, is at last sharing Baxter's world. In refusing the puppy, Baxter generalizes that he does not want anything. His father's use of the word "son" makes Baxter feel nauseous; the obscenity he calls his father reduces the father to an abstraction, just as the father's use of "son" has made Baxter feel that he is merely an abstraction.

*Style and Technique*

Purdy achieves much of the intensity of his story through the contrast between the inertness of the generalizations spoken by the characters and the vitality of his symbols. The abstract assertions of both Mrs. Zilke and the father are the deadest of social cliches, meaningless abstractions: "You know everything," "As long as a parent is living, any parent, a child has something." Every conversation degenerates into such meaningless, trite, vague nonstatements with the repetition of highly abstract nouns such as "something," "everything," "thing," or equally vaporous verbs such as "know" or "seems." Such generalizing vitiates all of their perceptions.

The images, on the other hand, accrue meaning or significance as Purdy either directly associates them with characteristics of his characters or takes images with strong traditional meanings and gives them deliberate twists. The pipe smoke of the father and the cigarette smoke of Mrs. Zilke, which are examples of the first use of symbols, represent the amorphous deadness of their thoughts and feelings expressed in the equally dead words that issue from their mouths. As the smoke obscures their faces, so their words obscure reality by acting as a screen between themselves and their feelings as well as the world about them. The image of the title is symbolic in the same way. The color of darkness is a noncolor or the most abstract of colors. It represents the opposite of the particular blue of Baxter's eyes, which stand for phenomenological specifics. The color of darkness, then, is the color of abstraction.

As the phrase "color of darkness" contains within itself its own negation, so many of Purdy's major images have their traditional meanings reversed by the context of the story. The symbolic significance of the brandy, which traditionally would serve to suggest sharing, is reversed. The adults discuss the look, the smell, and the taste of it, sharing their experience of it, but as usual, the discussion becomes generalized in the extreme. Finally, Mrs. Zilke does not drink it. There is no real bond among these people; the bond of abstraction can be no more real than the color of darkness. The dog bought to replace the crocodile wets on the floor, bites Baxter, and leads to Baxter's attack on his father. In like manner, the wedding ring, a traditional symbol of the communion between people, becomes a symbol of the absence of any communion. These images of the denial of communion culminate in that of the father crying in pain after refusing Mrs. Zilke's offer of help: an image that expresses the theme of the story in uniting the specific with the abstract. Baxter's kick has penetrated the father's shell of abstraction, making him feel the pain of being alive.

*William J. McDonald*

# COME OUT THE WILDERNESS

*Author:* James Baldwin (1924-1987)
*Type of plot:* Psychological
*Time of plot:* About 1960
*Locale:* New York City
*First published:* 1958

*Principal characters:*
> RUTH BOWMAN, a twenty-six-year-old African American
> secretary for an insurance company
> PAUL, her white lover, an aspiring painter
> MR. DAVIS, an African American executive at her insurance
> company

## The Story

Ruth Bowman, a young African American woman, begins her day by talking with and making love to her white lover, Paul. She feels desperately dependent on his affection, but also senses that he is slipping away. After she gets to her job as a secretary for an insurance company, she tries not to worry about Paul but fails. Her grim day is relieved when Mr. Davis, an African American executive who is about to be promoted, offers to make her his personal secretary. At noon a chance encounter leads to Ruth's lunching with Davis. It is the beginning of a friendship that Ruth wants to welcome, but which she resists out of distrust and feelings of unworthiness. Her despair returns when Paul fails to return home that night as he has promised, and she is left alone, worrying.

Ruth wants to marry and raise children, but Paul seems to assume they will never marry. Ruth loves him, and he treats her kindly and seems to be concerned for her welfare; however, she also hates him, especially when she detects his unconscious condescension toward her gender and race. As she grows more sure that she is losing him, her reflections become more bitter. Although she wants to believe that love will release her from guilt and terror, loving Paul imprisons her in guilt. She also feels imprisoned in silence; she cannot tell Paul what she really thinks, thus calling him to account for his failures, because then he certainly will leave her sooner, as no marriage promise holds him.

Ruth's deepest and most pervasive source of suffering is undeserved guilt. Although she knows that her feelings are unfair, she cannot escape the conviction that she deserves to suffer and is unworthy of love and happiness. She ran away from home after her older brother caught her with a boyfriend in the barn. Although she had not yet done anything worthy of blame, everyone assumed that she had and that what she wanted must be evil. Her brother called her "black and dirty," linking her sexual desires with evil, family betrayal, and skin color. She has since spent her life trying to escape these labels and undo these connections. So far, however, she has failed and all of her relations with men seem to be poisoned.

The story ends as she walks briskly through the crowded New York streets, trying to hide from herself and others the fact that she does not know where she is going.

## Themes and Meanings

The old Negro spiritual from which this story takes its title celebrates the joy and release felt by one who accepts belief in Jesus and thereby finds a way out of the wilderness of sin. James Baldwin's complex narrative explores several ways in which Ruth Bowman is lost in a wilderness. The story takes place mainly on three levels of Ruth's consciousness: She moves through a workday that opens a new opportunity for her; she broods over her failing relationship with her lover, Paul; and she struggles to come to terms with the events that drove her from her rural southern home at the age of seventeen. On each level, Ruth feels conflicting wishes and fears.

Rich in implications about race and gender in the modern United States, the story can also be examined through the concepts of master and slave. Ruth ends her day drinking in random bars and sees a young white man who seems as lost as she is. She connects him with Paul and with all the white "boys" she has known: "The sons of the masters were roaming the world, looking for arms to hold them. And the arms that might have held them—could not forgive."

The main offense that Ruth cannot forgive is being forced into slave consciousness by a white male master. Although her white lovers acknowledge that slavery ended a century earlier, they unconsciously treat her as a slave, eliciting her protest, "I'm not the black girl you can just sleep with when you want to and kick about as you please!" These men are probably blind to their offense because they treat her as men have treated women for ages—the way that Ruth's brother and father treated her when she was found in the barn. She is property of the men in her family, and she is expected to serve and obey. She is aware that Paul's expectation that she will patiently await his unexplained late arrival at home and then prepare his meal reflects the way all men treat "their" women, but she cannot keep from reading racism into his behavior.

Both black and a woman, Ruth is doubly the slave, daily experiencing, even at the hands of those who should most care for her, reminders not only that she does not belong to herself but that her treatment has a racial history. Ruth's slave consciousness means that she cannot avoid reading racial exploitation into what may be "merely" gender exploitation. Because she feels powerless as an immoral woman living with a man to whom she is not married, she cannot force Paul or any other man to hear her story and give her justice. Seeing double, she is doubly torn, wanting to love a man freely and without guilt and to begin a family, and yet unable to see any man, black or white, simply and freely. Also, she is doubly bound, trapped in such labels as "Negro" and "Fallen Woman" that she feels she cannot discuss without exploding everything she depends on, just as she can never speak the truth at her office. Unable to change her experience or her perceptions, she is lost in a wilderness, unable to forgive or to love or accept love at face value.

*Style and Technique*

Baldwin layers this story in several ways. At her job, Ruth finds the possibility for a better life opening up as she and Davis benefit from the integration of African Americans into better jobs. Davis's promotion promises to improve Ruth's own life, and their friendship suggests the possibility of a more fulfilling love relationship. Beneath this layer of bright prospects, however, is Ruth's brooding over her failing love relationship, and beneath that is another layer of fundamental guilt and terror over her family's betrayal of her innocence.

Baldwin moves the reader back and forth through these layers, always coming back to Ruth's fundamental problem—her family's failure to love her. Throughout the story, events in Ruth's day return her to thoughts of Paul, and then to thoughts about how she came to be as lost as she is. As Baldwin brings these three layers of experience into focus, words and events take on increasingly rich meanings. Each rereading of the story leads to new discoveries of the depth of Ruth's experiences, until the reader feels resonances that are only suggested. For example, in their morning conversation, Paul says it is time to paint a portrait of her, which she silently reads as a sign that he considers their relationship over. Paul's joke that he could sell her for a thousand dollars hurts her because it makes her remember how her female ancestors were bought and sold for sexual use. On the level that Paul understands, they are merely joking together, but for her this conversation calls up her fear of losing Paul, her sense of being sexually dirty, and her racial history of sexual exploitation and terror.

Sometimes Baldwin's layering gives complex meanings to even simple sentences. During a telephone conversation, for example, Paul tells Ruth, "It sure would be nice to unload some of my stuff on somebody." He is speaking only of his hope of selling paintings, but Ruth sees other meanings in his sentence. He is, she believes, deceiving her about his plans and so unloading stuff on her. He has been using her as a sort of servant, unloading his work on her. He plans, she believes, to use sexual persuasion with a gallery owner's daughter in order to get a show of his work, unloading on the daughter. In every meaning that she sees and he does not, his unloading involves exploitation. The better one knows Ruth's story, the more sentences and events become double and triple in their meanings, and the more fully one sees how Ruth is trapped spiritually and psychologically in the web of her history. That history is characterized by betrayals both in Ruth's personal experience and in the more general experiences of racial and gender relations in the United States.

*Terry Heller*

# THE COMEDIAN

*Author:* John L'Heureux (1934-    )
*Type of plot:* Magical Realism
*Time of plot:* The 1980's
*Locale:* San Francisco
*First published:* 1984

> *Principal characters:*
> CORINNE, a thirty-eight-year-old stand-up comedian
> RUSS, her husband, a construction worker

*The Story*

Corinne and her husband Russ are surprised that she has become pregnant and are a bit nonplussed by her condition. At thirty-eight years of age, Corinne thinks she is a little old to be having her first child; the timing is especially awkward because her career as a stand-up comedian seems to be about to take off. Her gynecologist agrees with her and suggests that she consider having an abortion. Over the next few months, this question dominates Corinne's life.

Before long, however, the baby enters Corinne's internal conversation: The baby, she thinks, has begun singing. Sometimes the songs are Broadway show tunes, sometimes operatic arias. Although mystified and unable to explain the strange phenomenon, Corinne has trouble denying that it is really happening.

Three months into her pregnancy, Corinne begins to get bookings at comedy clubs, and it seems to her that the baby sings even more exuberantly just before her performances. She goes over well at one club but is not renewed because, the club's owner says, her humor is all mental stuff: It lacks guts or feeling. She is not surprised. Almost everyone in California smiles a lot, she thinks, but few seem to laugh much.

After Corinne tells Russ about the baby's singing, he tries to be understanding but concludes that the strange phenomenon is a sign that the pregnancy is overstraining his wife. He suggests that an abortion would probably be best. When she tells her gynecologist about the singing, he laughs and assumes that it is one of her typical jokes. When Russ presses her on the question of the singing, Corinne reluctantly admits that it is all in her imagination. The baby immediately stops singing.

When amniocentesis indicates that Corinne's baby will probably be deformed, Corinne decides on an abortion. During her initial pre-abortion examination, however, she finds herself sinking into darkness. She only manages to pull herself out of it when she shouts that she wants the baby after all.

Suddenly, Corinne's humor shows real feeling, and she begins receiving job offers from all the major clubs, whose audiences totally identify with her and her pregnancy. She has never been the sort of comedian to make fun of the way she looked or ridicule other people. Instead, she finds humorous things with which others can identify and still feel respected. Corinne now finds herself praying for her deformed baby, who sings all the time.

The prospective mother's sight is becoming overly sensitive to light, which seems increasingly to surround her. Soon the time comes for her delivery, and she drifts into a semiconscious state. She seems delirious, saying "please" and "thank you" constantly. The singing becomes more intense, the light brighter and brighter until she enters completely into the light.

## Themes and Meanings

A former Jesuit priest, John L'Heureux often centers his stories around moments in ordinary lives in which something extraordinary—something possibly spiritually charged—takes place. This is one such story, an account of a crisis in the life of a woman who decides to have a few laughs before it is too late.

Corinne is unusual only in her fascination with getting on the stage as a stand-up comic. The first complication that the pregnancy causes is her increasing self-consciousness, her awareness that she is, in fact, different from the other people around her. Her body is changing shape and, unless she has an abortion, there is no avoiding the fact that she no longer blends into the crowd. She must stand on her own two feet and make choices of her own.

Corinne's growing sense of self causes further problems in her burgeoning career as she recognizes that she hates the jokes that other comedians find so funny, because they demean their audiences and themselves. The pregnancy changes Corinne's sense of what is important in life; she suddenly becomes serious.

In the process of Corinne's growing sense of individual identity and responsibility, her senses come alive, almost painfully so. Her eyes become overly sensitive to light, as if she is seeing the world around her for the first time and finds there is a great deal that is painful to look at. Even more significant, perhaps, is her increasingly acute sense of hearing. She is the only one who can hear the baby's singing. It may be that this is a sign of mental problems, as her husband suspects, but since the beginning of pregnancy, Corinne has consciously developed her ability to listen. She listens more closely to her husband than ever before, and discerns that he is as alone in life as she now recognizes herself to be. Mostly she listens to her interior, hearing not only the baby but also her own spirit that she has ignored for so long.

The result of these heightened senses is that Corinne now feels more than she used to, and empathizes with Russ, her baby, and her audience. Her comedy becomes the human comedy, sensitive and gently optimistic, which is why her lounge act becomes so successful.

## Style and Technique

The writing in this story is simple and unembellished, rendering the characterization completely believable and familiar. L'Heureux cleverly lulls the reader into a recognition of his imagined protagonist, and then shocks us with the central plot twist: the singing fetus. The matter-of-fact manner in which the event is described is reminiscent of the magical realism of South American fiction, which combines the totally inexplicable with the utterly mundane. In both cases, the effect is to delight the reader with the possibility of something wonderful and unexpected breaking in on the humdrum world.

"The Comedian" also might be compared to the work of Flannery O'Connor, a Georgia writer who uses eccentric rural characters to embody the startling religious truths of Roman Catholicism. L'Heureux's characters here are certainly not eccentric, but the central crisis they face can be compared to that which faced Mary and Joseph in the New Testament. Corinne is undergoing a mysterious pregnancy that was totally unexpected. Her husband is a laborer, like Joseph, who wishes to support his wife in her decisions even though he thinks there might be something wrong with her. The child is apparently going to be unlike other children, but Corinne, like Mary, decides to go through with the delivery and take the consequences.

L'Heureux's technique is to leave the ending of the story mysterious and ambiguous, forcing readers to draw their own conclusions. Some might conclude that Corinne dies on the delivery table, and that the light that she sees is something like the tunnel described by some who have returned from near-death experiences. More plausible, however, is that the birth is a totally transformative experience for her, an occasion for her to see all of reality in new terms, as if bathed in bold light. This is often the experience for mothers, particularly in their first delivery. In terms of the implicit biblical allusion to Mary, who "treasured all these things in her heart" as Jesus grew up, this would mean that for the reader the story is ending, but for Corinne it is just beginning. As in Mary's famous prayer, the Magnificat, Corinne accepts what will be and what is.

The reader is left to decide whether Corinne has encountered something mysterious, or has simply lost her mind. L'Heureux's decision to quietly pass along the protagonist's dilemma to his readers explains the story's early suggestion that comedy saves people not from truth but from despair: They are left mystified, but possibly hopeful. Comparing Corinne at the beginning of the story with the protagonist at the end shows a transformation from a rather shallow middle-aged woman to one who addresses an unnamed reality and offers thanks.

On a more secular plane, L'Heureux's conclusion quickly alludes to the famous ending of James Joyce's *Ulysses* (1922), in which Leopold Bloom's life-affirming wife gets the final word, which is "yes" to all of life, including its complications, deformities, jokes, and questions.

*John C. Hawley*

# COMFORT

*Author:* David Michael Kaplan (1946-    )
*Type of plot:* Domestic realism
*Time of plot:* The late twentieth century
*Locale:* Saratoga, New York
*First published:* 1986

*Principal characters:*
LAURIE, a Skidmore College graduate
MICHAELA, her friend and roommate
TED BREMMER, her mother's current boyfriend

### The Story

Laurie and Michaela have been friends since their senior year at Skidmore College. Because neither girl has definite plans, they have rented an apartment in Saratoga together while holding down nondescript jobs.

One spring evening about a year out of college, they are rocking themselves in wicker chairs at home facing tall bay windows, open to admit the warm breeze. They are waiting for Laurie's mother's current boyfriend, Ted Bremmer, to arrive for dinner. Laurie's mother, who lives in New York City, works for a business firm. She has asked the girls to give the presumably middle-aged man a little tender loving care while he is in Saratoga to direct a television spot for the Saratoga Performing Arts Center.

While killing time, the two girls talk of Laurie's mother, whose affairs Michaela has always followed with interest. In Laurie's opinion, her mother has not been very discriminating in her choice of boyfriends, but she has been with Ted for almost a year, longer than with some of the other "jerks." Although she allows that her mother feels comfortable with Ted, she distrusts him. She explains that the previous summer, Ted ogled her while the three of them were at the shore. Michaela, grinning mischievously, suggests that Laurie test him by attempting to seduce him. When Laurie objects, Michaela volunteers to try it herself. Laurie has always compared herself unfavorably with Michaela, whose control over things, grace and ease, "a sensuality that offered refuge yet promised nothing," she admires. She reluctantly acquiesces to Michaela's suggestion.

Ted appears belatedly with excuses and a bottle of good wine. At first, he lavishes his attention on Laurie rather than on Michaela, who he is meeting for the first time. He talks disparagingly about his work but nevertheless appreciates the role of television spots in paying for programming. As the conversation proceeds, Laurie becomes more critical and Michaela more appreciative of these television commercials. Laurie ventures that the world might be better off without the propaganda. Observing Laurie's critical mind-set, Michaela observes that she sounds like something left over from the 1960's.

While they talk of other things, more wine is being consumed all around, following the hard drinks that the two girls drank while waiting for Ted to appear. Eventually, all three move to the kitchen to prepare the salad, the pasta, even baste the bread—a deviation from the girls' normal dinner routine of heating of frozen foods and throwing salads together with whatever vegetables are wilting in the refrigerator. While Ted steps out to his car to pick up pills for the hay fever that has bothered him all evening, Michaela tells Laurie that she thinks he is nice and good-looking, and that she likes him. Laurie is more judgmental, characterizing him as smooth and slick.

Laurie's mostly repressed hostility to Michaela mounts. She silently resents Michaela's tendency to think of their place as if it were her house, with her as the hostess and Laurie herself as merely another visitor. Because of the drinks, Laurie is becoming light-headed and fantasizes that she is a young child and that Ted and Michaela are her parents.

Ted is both cynical and funny in his comments. He talks about trained cats who refuse to perform on cue and about not finding a talking seal for an art director for whom he once worked. He confesses that at times he does not know why a grown man does these things. Meanwhile, Laurie's anger keeps mounting. At one point Michaela follows her and asks pointedly what is wrong with her.

Back in the front room, they talk about Greek islands that Ted and Michaela both happen to know. In order to arouse Ted, Michaela spins a story about a sexual event, allegedly part dream, part fact, that involves a boy about twelve years old and includes a bit about her sleeping naked on a beach in Crete. Laurie, feeling increasingly left out and embarrassed, tries to change the mood and derail Michaela's increasing obvious play for Ted by suggesting they telephone her mother and all talk to her. When Ted rejects the idea, Laurie goes to her room and falls asleep. When she awakens in the middle of the night, she discovers that Ted is in her friend's room.

The next morning, Laurie wakes up again with a hangover. Michaela is still asleep but now alone. Laurie cleans up the front room and the kitchen, then calls Ted at his motel. When he answers, she lets out an expletive and hangs up.

Michaela eventually gets up and admits to the seduction, breaking the promise of silence that she made to Ted. Laurie becomes even more disconsolate and swears that she will kill Michaela if her mother ever finds out. Michaela replies, "But at least we know, don't we? That's sort of a comfort, isn't it?"

### Themes and Meanings

In "Comfort" and several other stories, David Michael Kaplan deals with people emotionally or physically estranged from their parents, but he does not always offer a resolution to the strange relationships and the unbridgeable distances between the characters he creates. This story is no exception. Its suspense flows from not knowing whether Laurie and Michaela will continue to be friends after the story ends. Laurie is seized with a strong sense of betrayal by her friend, but she emerges from the experience more emotionally mature than her roommate.

It also is not evident whether Laurie's mother, given the pledges of silence made separately among the threesome, will ever learn of her lover's seduction by Michaela. In this story, as in others by Kaplan, the mother is unimportant. Here, she does not make even a cameo appearance. More important, the chasm between daughter and mother must have grown, considering Laurie's critical mind-set of her lifestyle and now of her latest boyfriend as well.

## Style and Technique

Kaplan focuses on sudden moments of recognition in the lives of ordinary people. He looks at how such flashes of discovery, such revelations, may alter, for better or worse, the relationship of his protagonists to those with whom they are deeply bound—in "Comfort," Laurie's roommate and her own mother.

The story of Laurie's casual acquiescence to her friend's suggestion that she seduce her mother's lover to prove whether or not he is a jerk like the woman's previous boyfriends is psychologically devastating to Laurie. The story is told from her perspective because she is the one who quickly matures emotionally. Unlikely as such a story may seem, it does not stretch the reader's credulity beyond measure. The girls' obviously liberated lifestyles and attitudes mixed with Michaela's inclination toward mischief, as shown by her fabricating the story about a beach in Crete, help to keep the story line in character.

Despite his economy of words, the author does not profile cartoon characters. When Michaela wakes up the morning after her seduction, Laurie, although feeling an acute sense of betrayal, is still solicitous about her roommate's having fresh coffee, and she is apologetic because there is no milk in the house. The reader senses, however, that even Laurie's not-too-literal threat to kill Michaela if her mother ever finds out about the seduction can barely conceal the emotional storm brewing in her psyche. Accordingly, the use of the word "comfort" in the story's last sentence could not be more ironic. For it is the continuing sense of discomfort—a tension that is not released—that makes the story arresting for the reader long after the last word is read.

*Peter B. Heller*

# COMING, APHRODITE

*Author:* Willa Cather (1873-1947)
*Type of plot:* Psychological
*Time of plot:* The early twentieth century
*Locale:* New York City
*First published:* 1920

> *Principal characters:*
> DON HEDGER, a young artist
> CAESAR III, his dog
> EDEN BOWER, an aspiring singer

*The Story*

Don Hedger, a talented young painter who lives in a dingy top-floor apartment in Washington Square, leads a solitary life of dedication to his art. His only close companion is his dog, Caesar, a fierce English bulldog whose character mirrors that of his owner in many ways, and who also is the self-appointed protector of Hedger's privacy. Although he is far from rich, Hedger is successful by his own standards; indeed, when, as has happened on several occasions previously, he is on the verge of commercial success, he deliberately refuses to pursue this success.

Into this ascetic way of life comes Eden Bower, who moves into the apartment next to Hedger's. Eden, a beautiful and ambitious young girl from the West, plans to study singing in Paris. Hedger hears her singing but soon forgets about her, as he forgets everything when absorbed in his painting. When they do meet, however, he is overwhelmed by her beauty. Some time later, as Hedger is rummaging through his closet, he discovers a knothole in the wall that allows him to see into Eden's apartment. In the middle of a sun-drenched room, Eden stands naked, engaged in a series of gymnastic exercises. Hedger watches, enthralled. The richly suggestive imagery evokes a sense of Eden's beauty and energy, and appears to confer on her the status of a divine being. Hedger views her with the eyes of an artist, but as he continues to gaze raptly at the shower of golden sun pouring in through the windows after Eden has finished her exercises, the echoes of the story of Zeus impregnating Danae in a shower of gold not only add to the mythological overtones but also give a strong sexual suggestiveness to the entire scene.

Hedger becomes obsessed by Eden and is no longer able to paint. The two become friends, and one day she agrees to accompany him on an expedition to Coney Island, where they observe a friend of Don executing the daring feat of ascending in a balloon. Eden is so enthralled by this sight that, unknown to Don, she arranges to go up in the balloon herself. Furious at Eden for taking such a foolish risk, Don is moved against his will by the beautiful sight as she descends from the sky like a "slowly falling silver star."

Eden's daring has charged the air with sexual excitement for both of them, and over dinner that evening Hedger tells her an ancient Aztec story called "The Forty Lovers of the Queen." This queen has been dedicated to the gods from early childhood, and taught the mysteries of rainmaking. Her chief qualities are her voracious sexuality and her miraculous ability to bring fertility to the land. This power endures until she tries to save the life of one of her lovers, thus violating the unspoken law that such lovers must die after having sexual relations with her. She is put to death and a drought follows. This extraordinary and powerful myth has clear symbolic connections with the story of Eden and Don. The woman, like Eden, is seen as having divine powers; her sexuality has a primeval quality that transcends the personal. That night, Eden and Don become lovers. As they embrace for the first time, they are "two figures, one white and one dark, and nothing whatever distinguishable about them but that they were male and female."

Inevitably, the relationship breaks down when Eden tries to help Don get ahead. She enlists the assistance of Burton Ives, a successful artist whose department-store conception of art Hedger loathes. Desperately hurt by the revelation that Eden has no understanding of his idea of art, Hedger takes a train to Long Beach and stays away for several days. He returns, however, because Eden "was older than art," but she has left for Paris with the Chicago millionaire who is financing her studies. Thus, Hedger is left, saddened and lonely, in the knowledge that the rest of his life will be spent in solitary dedication to his painting.

Twenty years pass, and Eden returns from Paris, where she has become a famous opera singer. "Coming, Aphrodite," the legend that announces her name in lights at the opera house, refers both to the opera in which she will perform and, once again, to her association with the goddess of love. Curious to know what has become of Don Hedger, she asks an art dealer of her acquaintance about him. She learns that he enjoys a considerable reputation but has never become commercially successful. The story concludes with an image of her face, hard and settled in the glow of an ugly orange light. The contrast with Hedger is clear. Eden has succeeded in getting everything she wants, and has led a very exciting life in conventional terms. Moreover, when she sings, she has the capacity to become the divine Aphrodite, in the eyes of her audience at least. However, as Willa Cather has commented earlier, Hedger "has had more tempestuous adventures sitting in his dark studio than she would have in all the capitals of Europe." Eden's art as well as her life are empty by comparison with Hedger's.

## Themes and Meanings

Through the two central characters of this story, Cather asks the question of what it means to be an artist, and she examines the dangers that lie in wait for those who have chosen to follow this path. Both Don Hedger and Eden Bower are artist figures, but whereas Hedger understands the real nature of art and remains true to his ideals, Eden, although gifted, chooses commercial success and does not understand that there can be a difference between being a good artist and achieving material success. The title of the collection in which the story first appeared, *Youth and the Bright Medusa*

(1920), indicates Cather's continuing obsession with this theme. Although the indifference of society can harm the artist, the bright Medusa of success can also lure him to his downfall. Hedger realizes that in order to achieve success by his own definition, he must remain always open to new ideas and always ready to discard what is old or outworn, even though it may be what the public wants.

Cather also explores the artist's encounter with elemental beauty and sexuality in the form of a woman. The mythological resonance of the story of the Aztec queen, with its emphasis on a primitive sexuality stripped of all the superficialities of civilization, lends power and dignity to the love affair between the young couple. However, solitude must be the way for Hedger in the end: The true artist must place his art above everything else. Although it is Eden who literally leaves Hedger behind, in her zeal to get ahead, the implication is that the permanency of human relationships is not permitted to the artist. Unlike the Aztec queen who tries to save her lover and dies, bringing about drought, Hedger remains alone but also remains an artist.

*Style and Technique*

There are a number of recurrent image patterns in the story that underline its themes and meanings. Romantic images of light and beauty are associated with Eden. The sun, the moon, and the stars are all connected with her, and her apartment is airy and full of light. Hedger, by contrast, is seen in terms of images of darkness. His apartment is dark and dingy and his desperate attempts to clean it up after he has met Eden are to no avail. He is also seen as living in a kind of fish tank, suggestive of the artist's necessary isolation from the more active pursuits of life. Animal images add to this idea of isolation: Hedger is compared to a wolf and also to his dog Caesar.

The mythic dimension of the story is another significant aspect of Cather's technique. As a kind of modern-day Venus, Eden Bower takes on an allegorical dimension, yet there are many ambiguities in this view of her. On one level, she transcends the triviality of her own individual nature and is certainly viewed with sympathy and even admiration by Cather. Similarly, Cather can mock Hedger because of his lack of interest in worldly things. However, Hedger remains the type of the true artist, while Eden, possessing both artistic talent and a powerful, almost superhuman, beauty that connects her to the world of myth, is perhaps not really an artist at all by Cather's definition.

*Anne Thompson Lee*

# COMMUNIST

*Author:* Richard Ford (1944-    )
*Type of plot:* Realism
*Time of plot:* 1961
*Locale:* Near Great Falls, Montana
*First published:* 1985

> *Principal characters:*
> LES, the narrator
> AILEEN, his mother
> GLEN BAXTER, Aileen's boyfriend

*The Story*

Les, the forty-one-year-old narrator, looks back to 1961, when he was sixteen and still living with his mother in a house left by his late father. His mother, Aileen, was a part-time waitress in the nearby town of Great Falls, where she met Glen Baxter, a self-proclaimed labor organizer and communist who had seen a side of the world that Les could then only imagine. A transplanted Westerner, Baxter was a drifter who "stayed out of work winters and in the bars drinking with women like my mother, who had work and some money"—a common way of life in Montana. All of this is merely the backdrop. The real story that Les wants to tell happened in November of that year: a single day that he would forever remember as a turning point, his rite of passage into awareness, when life as he knew it would never again be the same.

Although two months pass during which Aileen does not see Glen Baxter, she is not pleased when he shows up from out of nowhere and wants to take Les hunting for snow geese. Unlike his mother, Les is pleased by Baxter's sudden reappearance and he enthusiastically accepts Baxter's invitation. Aileen strongly disapproves of senseless bloodletting—as well as the attempt at male bonding between her son and the man who has deserted her. Eventually, however, Baxter and Les prevail and Aileen rides with them into the Montana prairieland that appears to lack any sign of wildlife.

Baxter, however, knows that the snow geese are there, and he finds thousands of them stretched out across a low-lying lake away from the road. Baxter proves to be experienced as both a hunter and a guide. Les recalls the moment when the birds break off into flight, and thinks to himself that this is something he will never see again and will never forget. Unfortunately, that one memorable moment is quickly dwarfed by another.

Aileen reappears, her spirit temporarily lifted by the magical sight of the snow geese rising up into the big blue Montana sky. It is clear that Aileen is impressed both by the geese and by Baxter's grace and expertise with a shotgun. For one moment, at least, it seems as if all is well. Then Les makes the mistake of pointing out to his mother a wounded goose that is "swimming in circles on the water." Aileen insists that they should wade out in the lake to put the bird out of its misery, but Baxter disagrees. He tells Aileen that she does not understand the world, that one small mistake does not really matter much in the grand scheme of things. Then he settles the issue by firing four shots into the goose. When he turns around, Aileen is gone. Just like that, Les says, looking back on these sad and distant events, "A light can go out in the heart."

Later that night, after Baxter has left to lead whatever life he is destined to live, Les and Aileen share a tender moment together as geese pass by invisibly in the darkness overhead. For the first time, they see each other as they really are: not just mother and son, but two grown people who in a year's time will be like strangers passing silently in the night.

*Themes and Meanings*

"Communist" dramatizes a single sweeping moment in the life of a family as the ties that bind them together begin to unravel before their eyes. It is a theme that Richard Ford has explored in two other stories in his collection *Rock Springs* (1987)—in "Great Falls" and "Optimists"—and in his novel *Wildlife* (1990). These stories, like "Communist," have adult male first-person narrators who have struggled to transcend the often hard and unforgiving circumstances of their lives. Their events revolve around the themes of adultery and violence, of life and love not working out as they have dreamed. In "Communist," nothing—not even the snow geese—mates for life. Unforeseen events and people intrude, often assuring that nothing will ever be the same again. "Sixteen is young," Les muses in the closing lines, "but it can also be a grown man." He is prematurely forced to come of age, "pushed out into the world, into the real life." Les's voice is not, however, tinged with bitterness or even regret. Telling what has happened helps him to understand the complex reasons behind the seemingly harsh behavior of the few people who have entered his emotional landscape and helped to shape his character. Les is thereby able to reconcile himself with the hard cold fact that often people do not really know those whom they love the most—that they are estranged from them and left to face the world alone. Like many of Ford's characters, Les is a victim of having "too much awareness too early in life." However, it is his very sense of awareness that gives him the resilience to go on living; the strength to stride forward, and to live independently—even if it means going at it alone.

*Style and Technique*

Ford has been criticized for giving his characters too much insight, too much room to muse and find meaning in those moments that remain memorable through their lives. Critics of his fiction claim that the men who typically populate his stories are a luckless breed of Westerners who should not possess the lyrical impulses that drive his stories. They argue that the author imposes his own voice on his narrators, and that men such as Les—who come from broken homes and marginalized backgrounds—could not possibly be as sensitive and articulate as Ford depicts them. It is true that

Ford usually gives his characters dialogue that means something—words weighted with dramatic implication. Ford defends his method of meaning-filled conversation, however, by explaining that he is not trying to write dialogue that "is actual to life. I'm trying to write dialogue that refers to life." He adds that he does not think readers need to read stories merely "to have life rehashed. Stories should point toward what's important in life, and our utterances always mean something." Ford jeopardizes credibility when his characters step outside the boundaries of their emotional landscapes and go beyond the expectations of the reader; however, the risk is rewarded with an intimacy that would not exist if Ford refused to let his narrators speak. When Les reflects "I don't know what makes people do what they do, or call themselves what they call themselves, only that you have to live someone's life to be the expert," the simple wisdom of his words seems to be merited by the experience that he has lived through. He is forty-one years old at the time of his telling, looking back at a time when he was sixteen. He has had twenty-five years to think about the events of that November day. It is not at all surprising that he has learned a few hard lessons.

*Peter Markus*

# IL CONDE

*Author:* Joseph Conrad (Jósef Teodor Konrad Nałęcz Korzeniowski, 1857-1924)
*Type of plot:* Psychological
*Time of plot:* The early 1900's
*Locale:* Naples, Italy
*First published:* 1908

> *Principal characters:*
> IL CONDE (THE COUNT), the protagonist, an urbane European
> aristocrat
> THE NARRATOR, his cultured acquaintance

*The Story*

Set in Naples, Italy, early in the 1900's, "Il Conde" is a tale told by an anonymous narrator about his brief companionship with a northern European aristocrat whom he knows only as the Count. Like the narrator himself, the Count emerges as a man of the world and a person distinguished by cultivated tastes, impeccable manners, and fastidious sensibilities.

The narrator meets the Count while both are viewing art works in Naples's National Museum. After discovering that they both are guests in the same quietly refined Neapolitan hotel, they spend three evenings enjoying pleasant meals together. During their conversations, the narrator learns that three years earlier the Count left northern Europe in order to seek relief from a dangerous rheumatic disease by living in small hotels and villas on the warm Gulf of Naples. A middle-aged widower who is virtually exiled by his affliction, the Count returns home during the summers to visit a married daughter in her Bohemian castle; it is the only hiatus in his pleasant, tastefully subdued, and orderly life. To leave the south for longer periods, he believes, would mean forfeiting his life to his disease.

Called away from Naples to attend a sick friend, the narrator returns ten days later to find the Count shaken and dispirited, although he is not prone to unbalanced emotions. The Count reveals the cause of his distress. After seeing the narrator to his train, the Count walked through a park toward a villa where a public concert was in progress. On reaching a secluded spot, however, he was accosted by a young knife-wielding Neapolitan who demanded his wallet, watch, and rings. The Count had prudently left most of his money safely locked in the hotel, and the watch he wore chanced to be a cheap substitute for a valuable one that was being cleaned. He bravely refused to part with his rings, however, which were gifts from his father and his wife. After closing his eyes, expecting to be stabbed by his outraged assailant, the Count opened them to find that the thief had departed.

Upset and hungry, the Count immediately sought out a café in which to regain his equanimity, only to recognize the mugger among the crowd. When the Count asked a café peddler if he knew the mugger, the peddler identified him as a respectable university student, adding that he was also a leader in the Camorra—a secret criminal organization dedicated to ridding Naples of the taint of aristocracy. As the Count paid the peddler with a forgotten gold piece undiscovered by the mugger, the mugger saw the transaction, cursed the Count for holding out on him, and snarled that he was not through with him yet.

Thoroughly cowed and convinced that he is a marked man, the Count bids farewell to Naples and to the narrator. As the Count's deluxe train pulls away from the station, the narrator recognizes that the aristocrat's return to the cold north is a form of suicide.

## Themes and Meanings

Many literary scholars, and indeed early reviewers, regard "Il Conde" as the best example of Joseph Conrad's short fiction. Conrad wrote it as one of a group of six short stories—the so-called "Set of Six"—that he published early for popular consumption when he needed money badly. He proudly declared that the story had taken him only ten days to write after he decided to elaborate on an event that occurred in the life of Count Zygmunt Zzembek, whom he had met on Capri. Although the "Set of Six" stories are separate, they gain unity as critiques of then current political tendencies within Europe's class structure. At one level, to be sure, each story explores individual integrity, honor, glory, romance, and bravery. However, more important, each also embodies political observations on European class warfare.

Scholars have noted that "Il Conde" intimates the decline and eventual demise of the aristocracy with which Conrad identified himself. Obviously, Conrad's Count delineates both the admirable qualities and the flaws typical of his class. The Count is a polylingual cosmopolite; he is cultured and sensitive—an unostentatious and emotionally disciplined man devoted to living a balanced and moderate life of quiet comforts nourished by select tastes. Until he feels the Neapolitan's knife on his belly, he seems unaware of the social discontents that might imperil him, of the dark forces through which previously he had moved without disturbance.

That the dark young Neapolitan leaves the Count physically unharmed is irrelevant to the Count's reaction. The assault fractured the Count's sensibilities and irrevocably cracked his aristocratic perception of living within a shell of civilities and privilege that he had thought rendered him inviolable. Already forced by his rheumatic disease to live in warm climates, the Count moved south to prolong his life. In abandoning Naples and southern Europe, he consciously consigns himself to death. Conrad's message is clear: Europe's aristocracies were themselves debilitated by their own diseased estate, victimized, as it were, by their adaptations to secure lives and bourgeois comforts. By the opening of the twentieth century, their safe range had become tightly constricted, and they were psychologically too fragile in spirit to stave off the violent, sinister forces seething about them.

"Il Conde" underscored Conrad's perception that his own age contrasted sharply with the "heroic" spirit of the early nineteenth century Napoleonic Era—a period that deeply interested him. Instead of savoring the charms of living dangerous lives, instead of being motivated by strong beliefs, by personal honor, or by personal integrity, Conrad thought that men of his own era (such as the Count) were more apt to be motivated to seek secure, comfortable, and unheroic lives, or to act less from conviction than from boredom, like the villainous young men of Naples.

*Style and Technique*

Conrad relates the Count's story through an anonymous first-person narrator. In having an episode in the life of a nameless aristocrat recounted by an equally nameless narrator, Conrad signals his intention to explore social and political forces and their symbols, rather than to create distinctive characters. The narrator speaks for Conrad himself, very much the civilized man, conscious of aristocratic virtues but also aware of the aristocracy's wasting, ineffectual condition.

Although the narrator maintains a charitable detachment as the Count's "pathetic tale" unfolds, he fills the story with ironic commentary and contrasts. By wandering back and forth through a darkened park, for example, the Count almost tempts the mugger, whom in fact he had passed several times and acknowledged once. Conrad adds another ironic touch by having the concert band play the aristocracy's traditional harmonious music, reaching its blaring *fortissimo* as the mugger pushes his knife against the Count. Likewise, Conrad repeatedly stresses the darkness of "sunny" Naples, emphasizing its sinister dimensions. As Conrad well knew, many Italians once viewed Naples and southern Italy as a land of thieves and as a dark "Africa." Again, both the narrator and the Count refer constantly to the dark young Neapolitans with bandit-like mustachios, deep, dark eyes, and curled lips, ensuring that readers are aware that the Count could scarcely have placed himself in a more dangerous environment.

By stopping short of overt and bloody violence, Conrad all the more skillfully establishes an ambiance of menace. Given the Count's sensibilities, it is the threat of violence more than violence itself that intimidates him and sends him packing—in, as the narrator ironically records, a suicidal journey on Europe's most luxurious train. Superb author that he was, Conrad was not above giving an ironic twist to the old Italian adage "*Vedi Napoli, et poi mori!*" ("See Naples and die!"). The Count, as the narrator tells us, would have regarded the phrase as excessively patriotic, but Conrad helps tie his story together by having the Count obey it.

*Clifton K. Yearley*

# CONDOLENCE VISIT

*Author:* Rohinton Mistry (1952-    )
*Type of plot:* Psychological
*Time of plot:* The 1980's
*Locale:* Bombay, India
*First published:* 1984

> *Principal characters:*
> DAULAT MIRZA, an elderly widow
> MINOCHER MIRZA, her dead husband
> NAJAMAI, her neighbor, a nosy, garrulous woman
> MOTI, her second cousin
> A YOUNG MAN
> A PERIPATETIC VENDOR

## The Story

Told from a limited omniscient point of view, "Condolence Visit" focuses mostly on the inward consciousness of Daulat Mirza, a Parsi widow, and reflects her attitude of quiet defiance in the observance of the social customs and beliefs of her traditional community. Rohinton Mistry uses the flashback technique to fuse the present action with the widow's intermittent remembrance of the past.

The story begins in the morning in the flat of Daulat Mirza, who lives in a Bombay apartment building known as Ferozsha Baag. She is the widow of Minocher Mirza, a prominent member of the Parsi community, who passed away ten days earlier. Because all the funeral ceremonies have been performed, she is worried that, according to Parsi customs, her community members will start pouring into her flat to offer their condolences. She dreads the thought of being asked about her husband's illness.

To avoid answering questions, she wishes she had a tape recorder in which to record all the painful details about Minocher's illness so that the visitors could play, rewind, or fast forward the machine according to what part they were interested in. She even thinks of leaving her flat for a few weeks to escape the inevitable visits, but she is afraid of gossip. As she is lost in her thought process, she is startled by the doorbell. The remaining story covers the visits of four outsiders—a neighbor, a relative, a vendor, and a young man—punctuated with Daulat's continual remembrance of the past.

The first visitor is Najamai, her nosy neighbor and a self-proclaimed authority on "Religious Rituals and the Widowed Woman." The moment she walks in, she reminds Daulat of the start of the condolence visit season. Then she happens to see Minocher's *pugree* (ceremonial turban), which Daulat had brought out into the living room to show it to a young man who had expressed interest in buying it for his wedding. She warns Daulat not to move the *pugree* from its original place because it will make Minocher's soul unhappy. As she is about to leave, she sees the lamp burning near

Minocher's bed. She admonishes Daulat to put out the lamp immediately so as not to confuse Minocher's soul on its way to the Next World.

Daulat's stream of thought reveals that she will keep the lamp burning as long as she needs. The lamp's constant flame reminds her of Minocher's unflinching love. As she replenishes the lamp with oil, her memories of Minocher flash back. Several incidents come back to her in a new light, and she begins to smile in her sorrow. Then she begins to empty the drawers containing Minocher's clothing and other articles so that she can deliver them to the old people's home. As she empties the steel cupboard, each garment brings back happy memories of her forty years of marriage with her childhood sweetheart.

The second visitor is a peripatetic vendor from whom Daulat buys a bottle of oil for the lamp. The third visit is paid by her cousin Moti and her two grandsons. After a superficial expression of sympathy, Moti starts telling an inopportune funny story she had read in the paper. Daulat is relieved that at least for the time being her cousin has drifted from "the prescribed condolence visit questioning." Meanwhile, Najamai comes back on some pretext, and she is invited to share Moti's story.

The final visit is paid by a young man who has come to inspect Minocher's *pugree*. Both Najamai and Moti resent Daulat's decision to let the young man try the *pugree*. As the *pugree* fits him perfectly, Daulat offers it to him free, asking him to take good care of it for her Minocher's sake.

In the last scene, Daulat goes back to her room, stands before the lamp for a while looking intently into the flame, and then she places a saucer so that it covers the glass completely, just as Minocher's face was covered at his death. As the lamp goes out, Daulat is left alone in darkness thinking that she has definitely won the first round.

*Themes and Meanings*

Thematically, "Condolence Visit" questions the relevance of traditional customs in modern society. By juxtaposing the intense human feelings of a Parsi widow against the prescribed conventions of her community, Mistry develops an ironic perspective on blind adherence to tradition. Because the story focuses primarily on the thoughts and perceptions of the female protagonist, it reveals her attitude of quiet rebellion against social customs and beliefs as she attempts to reaffirm the claims of life over death.

As the story demonstrates, Daulat Mirza publicly observes all the funeral ceremonies and death rituals sanctioned by the Parsi community. For example, following the instructions of *dustoorji*, the Parsi priest, she keeps a four-day vigil at the Towers of Silence where supposedly the vultures come and consume the body. She also keeps a small oil lamp burning day and night at the head of Minocher's bed at home to welcome his soul. To observe *dusmoo*, the tenth day ceremony after the funeral, she offers prescribed prayers at the fire temple. Finally, she prepares herself mentally for the impending condolence visits, though she is fully aware of their perfunctory nature.

Despite her public observance of these social conventions, she does not allow them to strangle her heart's needs and human values. She therefore keeps the oil lamp burning beyond the prescribed period without caring about the belief that Minocher's soul would be confused between here and the Next World. One sentence in the story clearly reveals her heart-felt need beneath the veneer of public observance. When Najamai explains to her the implications of keeping the lamp burning beyond four days, the story reads: "Nothing can confuse my Minocher, thought Daulat, he will go where he has to go. Aloud she said, 'Yes, I'll put it out right away.'"

The most crucial step in her rebellion involves actively rejecting an accepted custom and violating a norm. This is evidenced by her twofold decision to give away her dead husband's enshrined *pugree* to a young man who needs it for his wedding and to carry his clothing and other effects right away to the old people's home for distribution, without waiting for the prescribed period. She knows in her heart that her husband would have wanted her to do so. In both these acts, she breaks the cycle of restrictive tradition in order to reaffirm human values and the needs of the living.

*Style and Technique*

Mistry's style in "Condolence Visit" is concise and subtle, laced with irony and flashes of wit and humor. He uses a number of Parsi words and allusions to add local color to the story and to give it a peculiar atmosphere of a closed community that is struggling to hold on to its traditional rituals, language, food, and dress.

The plot of the story deals with the events of a single day from morning to evening in the life of its female protagonist. The events include both contemporaneous happenings and past incidents. Mistry employs the flashback technique to interrupt the temporal flow of the narrative to introduce earlier incidents recaptured through the protagonist's memory. Consequently, the narrative moves back and forth in time, contributing to the loose and episodic structure of the plot. The apparent lack of compactness in the plot is to some extent compensated by Mistry's adherence to the unities of time and place. The interplay of linear time and memory in the protagonist's consciousness provides psychological coherence to the plot.

Mistry employs time and memory as structural devices to build his story. He uses clock time as well as the psychological view of time as continuous flow in an individual's consciousness to indicate respectively the temporal and the spatial movement of the story. To suggest this time pattern, he carefully places a few signposts of recurrent symbols, such as the watch, the music, and the lamp flame. Daulat's looking at her watch every time a visitor comes indicates the immediacy, the "presentness" of temporal action. Each time she thinks of music or looks at the lamp flame, her mind is transported back to the past, flooding her consciousness with memories.

Mistry's skillful manipulation of a limited omniscient point of view allows him to bring the reader directly into Daulat's inner consciousness, where the past is continually impinging on the present and reasserting itself through the mechanism of memory. Mistry uses memory not only as a structural device but also as a therapeutic device to heal the interior life of the female protagonist.

*Chaman L. Sahni*

# THE CONJURER MADE OFF WITH THE DISH

*Author:* Naguib Mahfouz (1911-      )
*Type of plot:* Domestic realism, existential
*Time of plot:* The 1960's
*Locale:* Cairo, Egypt
*First published:* "Al-Hawi khataf al-tabaq," 1969 (English translation, 1978)

> *Principal characters:*
> A YOUNG BOY, who is sent on an errand
> HIS MOTHER, who scolds him
> A CONJURER, who strikes him
> A BEAN SHOP OWNER, who roughs him up

*The Story*

"The Conjurer Made Off with the Dish" is a subtle metaphor told in first-person narration about the loss of a young Egyptian boy's innocence and his need for parental protection. One morning the boy is sent out by his mother to buy a piaster's worth of beans for breakfast. There follows an account of all the things that happen to the boy as he tries to complete this seemingly simple errand. However, even after several visits to the neighborhood bean seller, his mission is unsuccessful.

The first time the boy is sent out to buy the beans, he does not know or has forgotten whether the beans need anything on them and, if they do, whether it should be oil or cooking butter. On returning better informed to the store the second time, he is still unable to specify which kind of oil he needs—linseed, vegetable, or olive. On his third visit, following a scolding by his mother, the boy is unable to find the coin that she had given him to pay for the beans. After his increasingly irate mother gives him another piaster, threatening to recoup it from his money box and to break his head if he returns empty-handed, the boy is diverted from his destination by a conjurer's show. He is attracted by the man's sleight of hand involving rabbits, eggs, snakes, and ropes. However, the conjurer, incensed by the boy's refusal to pay after watching the performance, hits him on the back. On reaching the bean seller's store, the boy realizes that he no longer has his mother's dish to carry the beans. He retraces his steps, suspecting the conjurer of having made off with the dish. However, when he confronts the man, he is threatened with further bodily harm and escapes, weeping in frustration.

He happens on dozens of children watching a performance. Fascinated, the boy parts with his coin to see the show. It depicts a gallant knight engaging and killing a ghoul, thereby winning the love of a beautiful lady. The boy, forgetting about dishes, piasters, and beans, is transported into this heroic world. He reenacts aloud the climactic scene. A young girl who had stood next to him at the show and who now overhears his declamation, agrees to sit down with him on the steps by an ancient wall. However, soon she must rush off to perform an errand for her mother—fetching the local midwife—but agrees to return later. Thereupon the boy remembers his own mother and hurries home—minus the piaster, the dish, and the beans—crying aloud at the prospect of punishment. However, his mother is not home. So the boy takes another coin, this time from his own savings, and another dish from the kitchen. He has to rouse the bean seller who by now is sound asleep outside the store. The incensed man roughs up the boy, who, energized by the knight's action at the show, hurls the dish at the man's head and runs for his life.

Fearing retribution at home, the boy decides on a final fling with his piaster, but neither the conjurer nor the show operator are around. He returns to the ancient stairway, hoping to find the girl, but instead, he hears the whispers of a couple below. Their whispers remind him of his encounter with the girl. Their conversation is followed by an amorous episode but it ends with a violent confrontation about money that the man, seemingly a tramp, demands from the woman, who appears to be a Gypsy. It looks as if the man is about to strangle his companion. The boy, until then unnoticed, screams and escapes in terror. When he finally stops running, out of breath, he notices that he is in an unfamiliar place. By now dusk is falling, and he wonders whether he will find his home.

### Themes and Meanings

Naguib Mahfouz wrote "The Conjurer Made Off with the Dish" in the fall of 1967, when he and most other Egyptians felt traumatized by Israel's quick defeat of his country in the Six-Day War. In it and the other stories that appeared in *The Time and the Place and Other Stories* (1991), he seems to be questioning the meaning of events and life in general. Unlike Mahfouz's earlier works set in ancient Egypt or his novels depicting the Egyptian social milieu, his later writings, like this story, have realistic, symbolic, and existential themes.

The underlying theme of "The Conjurer Made Off with the Dish" is that the world and the events in it cannot always be understood from a rational viewpoint, that pure reason is not a sufficient guide to explain everything that happens in this highly unpredictable world in which the anxiety of the human condition is a constant. However, despite all the frustrations and anxieties that civilization has created and fostered, inexplicably and even unjustifiably, there remains a glimmer of hope in the happiness that people seize for themselves where they can. For the individual's initial reaction to these frustrations and anxieties is to look for some kind of consolation or release.

Thus, when the boy fails to complete the simple errand of bringing home a few pennies' worth of beans, he is either threatened with or actually experiences physical retribution from his mother, the conjurer, and the bean seller, even though he eventually shows up with everything he needs for the purchase. If the boy had not run, probably the tramp would also have beaten him up for eavesdropping and witnessing the violent scene.

The happiness that the boy finds and that partially redeems the unfortunate events of the day springs from his discovery and later recollection of his romantic interest in the story. However, even this is ultimately frustrated because the girl does not reappear. At the end of the day, his anxiety over returning home to a possibly wrathful mother is overshadowed by the fear that he has lost his way in the descending gloom.

The few pages of text provide a living picture of the lower class in Egyptian urban society. Mahfouz describes everyday activities such as taking a dish to the bean seller to buy and carry home the brown broad beans that are the staple of the masses and depicts commonplace sights and people such as the conjurer and show, the architectural relics of ages past, and the ubiquitous beggars on the sidewalk.

When all is said and done, "The Conjurer Made Off with the Dish" may leave the reader wondering what the story really means, for here as in Mahfouz's other works, the question of the meaning of life—if any—is complex and ambivalent. Although the story contains a hint of sexual attraction and even love, it also includes violence and frustration. Mahfouz may wish to suggest that people should accept life as a series of discrete events, some painful and others pleasurable, and not be concerned about any ultimate truths or grand design.

## Style and Technique

In "The Conjurer Made Off with the Dish," as in some of Mahfouz's well-known novels, a slice of Cairo life is packaged in a picaresque style—a young boy discovers life as he proceeds through places, experiences, and human contacts. The story is strongly existentialist, possibly suggesting the influence of the likes of Franz Kafka or Albert Camus on the Egyptian author. At its more symbolic level, the story is about the young boy subconsciously attempting to define the sense of existence in an essentially meaningless, even absurd, universe.

The few touches that Mahfouz uses to add local color introduce the reader to another culture, a simpler way of life in which people go about with dishes fetching beans. The references that the author uses will be highly familiar to his readers because they are evident in all large-city neighborhoods. Accordingly, although the major protagonist is concerned with such immediate and seemingly down-to-earth issues as satisfying his mother, keeping out of harm's way, and reliving the feelings that had welled up in him after viewing the show about romantic gallantry and later encountering the young girl, a tension is created in the reader's mind about the human condition at a deeper level of analysis.

Unlike Mahfouz's earlier stories, this one contains more dialogue, interspersed with occasional narrative, in a unilinear form. This new trend has led to some of Mahfouz's other stories being converted into one-act plays.

*Peter B. Heller*

# CONSOLATION

*Author:* Giovanni Verga (1840-1922)
*Type of plot:* Social realism
*Time of plot:* About 1880
*Locale:* Milan, Italy
*First published:* "Conforti," 1883 (English translation, 1958)

> *Principal characters:*
> ARLIA, the protagonist, a hairdresser
> MANICA, her husband, a barber
> FATHER CALOGERO, her uncle, a parish rector
> FORTUNATA, the daughter of Arlia and Manica
> ANGIOLINO, Fortunata's brother
> SILVIO LIOTTI, Fortunata's lover and, later, her husband
> A FORTUNETELLER

*The Story*

A healthy young couple, a barber named Manica and a hairdresser named Arlia, marry, in spite of the misgivings of Arlia's uncle, Father Calogero, who knows that tuberculosis runs in their family. He had become a parish priest, thereby keeping moderately healthy and avoiding many of the troubles that beset the urban poor.

Each year, Arlia becomes pregnant, affecting adversely her work; Manica, too, is unsuccessful financially as a barber. Child after child dies of tuberculosis; the costs of medicine, special broths and food, and burial expenses offset any economic gains of the working couple.

One of the boys is named Angiolino; he is bitter at having been born, when facing death. Arlia seeks help for the child from the Church, through prayer and a mass, though Manica is cynical. Finally Arlia has recourse to a woman who tells fortunes from the whites of eggs. She has been told that a countess who had wanted to have her hair cut because of unhappiness in love had found consolation from the fortuneteller. The fortuneteller tells Arlia that she will be happy, but that she will have troubles first. Her uncle believes that the prophecy is a satanic fraud, but Arlia's despair is overcome temporarily by the hope that Angiolino will recover. The child grows worse, however, and Father Calogero offers to pay for his funeral. Still, Arlia persists in her faith in the prophecy and pities Manica for his lack of belief. Her hope is finally dashed by the death of the boy. Filled with despair, she wonders what the fortuneteller's promise could have meant.

The suffering causes Manica to turn to drink; Arlia persists in her trust in the prophecy. A daughter, Fortunata, is the only child who survives. The family's economic situation becomes worse, debts pile up, and customers desert Arlia and Manica. Arlia seeks reassurance from her daughter that the prophecy of the fortuneteller will come true, but Fortunata is interested in a young man, a clerk named Silvio Liotti.

When questioned by her mother, Fortunata says that she does not want to die like her brothers; the neighbors and the girl's father warn the mother to be careful about her daughter's relationship with Silvio. Finally, Fortunata confesses to her mother that she has been seduced by Silvio.

Through an intermediary to Father Calogero, Silvio learns that Manica cannot afford a dowry for his daughter; thus, any marriage seems impossible. Fortunata begins to show signs of developing tuberculosis, as well as a tendency toward suicide, so that Arlia fears that she will lose her daughter also and that Manica will learn about Fortunata's affair. Arlia finds solace in the prophecy and turns to gambling, buying lottery tickets each week, as a key to financial success, and to her daughter's health and happiness. One day, Manica, looking for money with which to pay for liquor at the tavern, finds some of the lottery tickets and becomes angry. Arlia explains that they must allow good luck to come to them. He demands money from her and later returns drunk from the tavern.

Fortunata, however, finds no consolation. Arlia continues to be certain of their future happiness; they invite Father Calogero to a fine meal at their home on Christmas Day. He becomes touched by their problems and arranges for a dowry for Fortunata, making possible her marriage to Silvio.

The marriage does not work out well; Silvio spends the dowry and beats Fortunata. Each year, as her mother had before her, she gives birth to a child. Her children are healthy and have huge appetites, putting a strain on family finances. Arlia is forced to continue to work in her old age, running errands for shopkeepers. Manica, too, continues to work each Saturday at his trade, spending the remainder of the week at home or in the tavern. Arlia now spends the lottery-ticket money for brandy, deriving a measure of consolation from her secret drinking.

*Themes and Meanings*

"Consolation" is the English translation of the Italian title, which literally means "comforts." A key to the meaning of the story is immediately provided in the opening words, which announce the prophecy of the fortuneteller that Arlia will be happy after passing through hardships and troubles. The theme of the story is how this illusory hope permits a poor woman, representative of Milan's urban poor, to survive and to find partial, temporary consolation amid the suffering.

Father Calogero expresses well the situation facing Arlia and her family and, by extension, all the urban poor: "The world is full of troubles. It's best to keep away from it." This formula for surviving in a hostile world seems to work well for Calogero, who has "purposely become a priest so that he wouldn't have to listen to the troubles of the world." He has managed "to put a little fat on himself," as well as having the money to pay for little Angiolino's funeral and Fortunata's dowry.

The other characters seem to be facing a life that seems to contain nothing more than hunger, fatigue, illness, and early death. Whatever progress is made is eaten up by the ills of life. The children, before dying, "gobbled up the small profit of the year," the son-in-law Silvio "ate up his wife's dowry." Even Fortunata's healthy babies eat "like horses," bringing more trouble to their overworked grandparents.

The answering refrain to Calogero's formula for survival comes from the fortune-teller: "You will be happy, but first you'll have troubles," or, as Arlia interprets it, "We have to leave the door open to luck." Arlia, until the end, believes and hopes for the best. Her heart, which was "black with bitterness," becomes "like a burning lamp," filled with hope. When hope fails, each character finds his own form of consolation: Fortunata (her name, ironically, means "happy") chooses love; Manica uses drink; Arlia, because she holds more tenaciously to her hopes, tries magic, the Church, gambling, and, finally, drink.

Ultimately, however, there is only death, evoked by the window from which Fortunata thinks of jumping: "See that window, Mamma? . . . See how high it is?" The "terror of that window," and thus of death, drives the characters to work, to scheme, to hope, but in the end they all must face it: Manica's nose is "pressed against the clouded window" of his shop; Fortunata confesses to her dishonor "in front of the open window"; and at the end, with only the consolation of brandy, Arlia sits "before the window thinking of nothing, looking out at the wet, dripping roofs." Her heart, once lit by hope, is warmed only by drink.

*Style and Technique*

Giovanni Verga's name is associated with verismo, or Verism, in which the prime purpose of the writer is to present the truth, without avoidance of unpleasant or depressing aspects of life, and at the same time with no attempt at moralizing or other subjective interference. In "Consolation," Verga paints a bleak picture of the lives of the poor.

One device that helps him do this is "free indirect discourse," wherein a character's attitude, thoughts, or words are expressed indirectly, as if part of the author's commentary. For example, when the lottery ticket is first bought, Arlia's motivation is suggested by the following statement: "The blessed souls of her children would take care of it from above." Again, when Arlia's husband takes to drinking, "she" (actually the narrator) thinks: "Now that all the troubles had fallen on her shoulders, happiness would come. That's the way it often is with the poor!" Although it is the narrator's voice here, referring to Arlia in the third person, it is only Arlia's perceptions—her deluded hopes—that the narrator relates. The ironic contrast between Arlia's view and Verga's probable skepticism (happiness never comes to the poor in this story) thereby emphasizes the theme: the futility of hope in a hopeless world.

In addition to free indirect discourse, Verga makes prodigious use of eye and sight imagery to point up the contrast between the characters' perception of their situation and the dark reality: The reader is constantly presented with images of the characters' eyes—consumptive "mother-of-pearl eyes," "eyes circled black," eyes fixed on other characters or "fixed on a point that only she could see." Similarly, the big barbershop that Arlia's husband envisions owning at the story's beginning, "with perfumes in the window," stands in contrast to the poor, empty facility where he "waited for customers all day long, his nose against the clouded window."

Perhaps the most telling device used in this story, however, is the contrast established between the fortuneteller and Father Calogero, the priest: Each is representative of a force that influences or controls the human condition—chance and God—yet neither can offer a solution to the poverty and disease the characters suffer. The fortuneteller offers hope without truth—mere self-delusion; the priest rightly denounces the deception but can offer nothing but the cold fact of death in its place. In such a world of false hope versus unmitigated suffering, the characters end by choosing the meager *conforti* of the title.

*Edgar C. Knowlton, Jr.*

# A CONVERSATION WITH MY FATHER

*Author:* Grace Paley (1922-     )
*Type of plot:* Metafiction
*Time of plot:* About 1971
*Locale:* New York City
*First published:* 1971

> *Principal characters:*
> THE DAUGHTER, the narrator
> HER FATHER, a bedridden old man
> A MOTHER,
> A SON, and
> A YOUNG WOMAN, the daughter's fictional characters

*The Story*

One evening, the narrator's eighty-six-year-old father lies in bed in his New York home. Unable to walk, he suffers from a heart condition after having lived a rich life as a doctor and an artist. He appears near death, for he has pills at hand and breathes oxygen from a bedside tank. He has not lost his intelligence, interest in art, or concern for his daughter, however. In what might be the speech of one knowing that he is near death, he confronts his daughter about the kind of short stories that she writes. He wishes that she would write "simple" stories like the old masters of the form: the Frenchman Guy de Maupassant and the Russian Anton Chekhov. He reminds her that she once wrote stories like that.

Although the narrator does not remember writing any such stories, she wants to please her father, so she quickly writes a very short story about what has been happening to a woman and her son who are their real neighbors. Her story is odd but simple, perhaps the sort that her father will like:

> A mother and her son live happily in the city. After the son becomes a drug addict, the mother becomes an addict in order to maintain their closeness. The son then gives up drugs, becomes disgusted with his mother, and goes away, leaving her alone and without hope.

The narrator's father does not like the story, finding it too spare. Classic short story writers, he maintains, would humanize the story with descriptions. After the daughter obligingly adds perfunctory details about such things as hairstyles, the father is still not satisfied because his daughter does not take her characters seriously.

When their conversation turns to how the daughter writes her own stories, they discuss what happens when she stumbles on a good character—one to be taken seriously. It takes time to devise an appropriate ending to such a story, but the father asks her to take the time. After an interval, the daughter writes a much longer version of her story. It is now full of evocative detail and bizarre complications, but its action remains essentially the same. The most important change concerns the son, who now edits a periodical that advocates drug use.

Even this version does not satisfy the writer's father, though he seems to approve of its definite and tragic ending. The daughter protests, however, that her ending is not so final as her father assumes, explaining that after the story ends, the mother goes on to have a satisfying career helping others. Again the father objects, arguing that such a hopeful ending is bad art because it evades life's ultimate tragedy—death. The conversation ends when the father asks his daughter when she will face such facts.

## Themes and Meanings

Grace Paley's story deals with the conflicts between generations, specifically those between an elderly parent and an adult child. Although the father is old and sick, he is sufficiently alert to ask searching and intelligent questions. The narrator is clearly her father's daughter for she shares his quickness of mind. She seems devoted to him as she sits by what may be his deathbed, but she does not humor him. She does not hide the fact that she is younger and stronger than he. Even though she changes the story that she writes at his request, she concedes nothing in their argument.

Though their argument is often playful, it is significant. One of Paley's themes is the difference between the stories told by masters of the past and those present-day authors feel they must tell. The father prefers the old-fashioned kind because they progress to definite endings that evoke the tragic nature of life. The daughter's stories (and presumably "A Conversation with My Father" itself) are not like that. They are witty—sometimes grimly hilarious—and their endings are not necessarily final. Their open-ended nature evokes not the climactic catharsis of tragedy, but a sense of the flatness and minor pathos of everyday life. Paley suggests that the stories that satisfied readers during the father's modern era are not so satisfying to writers and readers of the postmodern present.

The argument between the father and his daughter in this story is about what stories should be like. For this reason, it is an example of metafiction: fiction about fiction. The contrasts that metafiction makes between its main stories and the stories within it help to make readers conscious of the differences between fiction and real life. In the narrator's exuberance, readers sense how much joy a writer may derive from inventing details and actions. Paley's story may also suggest the differences between the kinds of fiction that women and men write. Some critics argue that women's stories tend to be less climactic and more open-ended than those written by men.

No matter how theoretical "A Conversation with My Father" becomes, it remains a human story. Like its themes, its characters develop gradually. At the end, the reader senses that the father's preferences in fiction mirror his own preoccupation with the approach of his own death. When he tells his daughter to face the facts of tragedy and death within her stories, he also implies that she must face it in her own life. The contrast between the characters can be seen as one between a man about to die and his grown daughter who is not near death, who is not ready for total closure in fiction or in her own life. In her insisting that her story is not closed, we also see how much she is moved by pity for other people and how much she wishes to see new life (not death) in their future. Perhaps the contrast can be read as one between the prophetic wisdom of age and the evasions of comparative youth. In any case, Paley's "A Conversation with My Father" implies that it is a story of its times, for its conclusion does not neatly summarize its themes but leaves open the question about what the daughter has learned.

*Style and Technique*

"A Conversation with My Father" is related in the first person by the daughter. By briefly describing her father's past life, present situation, and a few of his actions, and most importantly by recording what he says to her, she builds up a good sense of his character. As is usual in first-person narratives, the narrator's own character and ultimate opinions are more difficult to discern. Unlike many first-person narrators, this one is never confessional. Aspects of her style help reveal her: She tells her story efficiently and economically; she enjoys telling stories and is good at weaving facts from real life together with details of her own invention; her words are incisive, as when she describes her father's mind as flooded with "brainy light." Many readers will find her story full of a grim but effervescent humor.

The work's most obvious device is the story-within-a-story. In this case, there are two versions (and written versions at that) of the same general story, and both contrast markedly with the main story. This device enables Paley to illustrate the differences between the endings of her own stories and the types of endings that her father prefers. It also presents a contrast in styles. The stories-within-stories have a strange tone: a factual, abrupt, and plodding style tells of absurd happenings. By contrast, the main story at all times reveals the serious intelligence and emotional depth of characters whose lives are not at all silly.

Paley constructs her story artfully. At first one meets a demanding but understandable old man who says that he likes "simple" stories and a daughter who seems to toy with him by writing precisely the kind of story that he hates. Only gradually does one understand that what really matters to the old man is not merely a kind of plot, but an attitude toward the tragic nature of life. Even though the daughter will not back down in their intellectual tug-of-war, her playfulness is gradually shown to mask her real love and admiration for her father and her understanding of his situation. By the end of the story, the reader senses that, although her kind of story (that is, this story itself) allows no neat resolution, its open-ended future may include her understanding of what her father has tried to tell her.

*George Soule*

# THE CONVERSION OF THE JEWS

*Author:* Philip Roth (1933-      )
*Type of plot:* Coming of age
*Time of plot:* The 1950's
*Locale:* An American city
*First published:* 1958

### Principal characters:

OSCAR (OZZIE) FREEDMAN, a thirteen-year-old Jewish student
MRS. FREEDMAN, his widowed mother
ITZIE LIEBERMAN, his friend and classmate
RABBI MARVIN BINDER, a thirty-year-old Hebrew teacher
YAKOV BLOTNIK, a seventy-one-year-old synagogue custodian

## The Story

Ozzie Freedman has been attending a synagogue Hebrew school in preparation for his Bar Mitzvah confirmation. He is a bright student, but entirely too inquisitive for the comfort of his teacher, Rabbi Marvin Binder. Binder is irritated by Ozzie's inability to accept traditional doctrinal answers to fundamental religious questions, and he has summoned Mrs. Freedman three times to discuss her son's disruptive influence on his class.

During the Wednesday afternoon class prior to their third scheduled meeting, tensions between Ozzie and Binder precipitate a crisis. Earlier, Ozzie resisted Binder's facile dismissal of Christian claims for the divinity of Jesus. He was also dissatisfied with Binder's explanation for an airplane crash and for why Jews were particularly grieved over the number of Jews on board. Now they clash over the issue of God's omnipotence.

During the free discussion period, none of the boys volunteers any comments or questions. Binder, however, sensing that Ozzie has something on his mind, goads him into speaking. Ozzie wants to know why, if God can do absolutely anything, it was not possible for Him to have arranged a virgin birth for Jesus. His insistence that Binder does not know what he is talking about provokes an uproar in the class and an angry reaction from the rabbi.

When Binder slaps him, Ozzie runs up onto the roof of the synagogue. The fire department is summoned, and Ozzie soon finds himself looking down at a growing crowd of spectators. Binder first demands and then pleads that Ozzie come down from the roof, but Ozzie's fellow students cheer his stand against the rabbi and urge him to jump. Ozzie's mother, arriving for her appointment with Binder, becomes part of his audience.

Stimulated by this unexpected turn of events, Ozzie exerts his power over the assembled crowd. He declares that he will jump off the building unless everyone—

Binder, his mother, the students, the firefighters, even pious old Yakov Blotnik the synagogue's custodian—kneels before him on the ground. Then he demands that Binder and all the others acknowledge vocally that they believe "God can make a child without intercourse." Finally, after exacting a promise that no one will ever be punished because of God, Ozzie descends—by jumping into the yellow net held up by the kneeling firefighters below.

### Themes and Meanings

"The Conversion of the Jews" is the story of the coming-of-age of a boy on the brink of manhood as defined by the Jewish ritual of Bar Mitzvah. Set in a modern American city where Jews are a tolerated minority, it raises questions about the continuing vitality of Jewish culture and about the coherence of a Jewish community within a pluralistic society. In Ozzie's refusal to accept traditional dogma, it also takes a critical look at strategies to justify the ways of God to young men.

As befits his last name, Freedman, Ozzie is not tied to historical explanations for fundamental questions that he is confronting for the first time. Alone of all his classmates, Ozzie dares to challenge the authority of the rabbi, whose name, Binder, suggests his own fealty to tradition. Binder, a tall, handsome, and imposing man, is a sort of surrogate father to Ozzie, whose deceased father is commemorated by the ceremonial sabbath candles his mother lights each Friday at sunset. Ozzie is intoxicated by the sense of power he feels his defiant, independent stance can exert over the others. He sees himself as a lone champion of truth battling the obscurantist forces of tribal superstition. He is also asserting his own personal dignity against a condescending elder who is merely patronizing toward the young man's quest for explanations.

When he climbs up onto the roof alone, Ozzie realizes that he has passed a turning point in his life and that there is no possibility of reversal. His mother begs him to come back, not to become a martyr. Though they do not understand the term, his classmates invert the request, urging him indeed to be a "Martin." Caught in this dramatic situation, Ozzie feels too committed to retreat from the principles that suddenly seem more important to him than life. His dedication to the ideals of free thought provides him with the moral force to perform, symbolically, a task that is proverbially impossible: convert the Jews. When he finally jumps off the roof, into the safety net provided by the community, it is as if Ozzie the child has died and Ozzie the man is born.

The transformation of this bold adolescent is explicitly related to a sexual theme: the possibility that Mary conceived Jesus without having had intercourse. The very euphemism "to have intercourse" is somewhat shocking and titillating to the boys when they hear it employed by their rabbi. Binder would just as soon not discuss the subject at all, but when Ozzie refuses to accept Binder's dismissal of Jesus as merely historical, the teacher is forced to deal directly with that feature of the Christian story that most troubles the boys: Mary's sexuality. The thirteen-year-old's curiosity over the mysteries of religion also suggests a burgeoning interest in sex.

The Gentile firefighters are bemused by and impatient with the entire confrontation. They do not understand Jewish separatism any more than the Jewish boy on the roof does. Ozzie can find no reason why his mother is most distressed about eight of the fifty-eight casualties in a plane crash, simply because they were Jews. For him, Jewish tradition is represented by grotesque, incoherent old Blotnik and the tyranny of a Hebrew school that attempts to inculcate by rote ideas that do not accord with reason. Written in the 1950's, when American Jewish literature was emerging as a major and respected force, "The Conversion of the Jews" helped establish Philip Roth as a peer of Saul Bellow and Bernard Malamud, yet it also marked his alienation from an ethnic tradition that he was often to satirize as having grown complacent and obtuse. His assimilated Jews cling to meaningless vestiges of ancient allegiances and values.

*Style and Technique*

A brief conversation between Ozzie and his friend Itzie, who has missed a previous class, helps to establish the background of Ozzie's conflict with Binder. Then, five short paragraphs describing the Freedman household on a Friday evening provide useful information on Ozzie's family background. The remainder of the story concentrates on the crucial Wednesday afternoon on which Ozzie challenges the rabbi. With considerable narrative economy, Roth depicts a compelling battle of wills.

Much of "The Conversion of the Jews" is presented as the dialogue of the principal characters. Most of the rest conveys important information through detached, third-person assertions. Simply by stating, for example, that class discussion time is often devoted to Hank Greenberg, a baseball star who was Jewish, Roth makes a telling point about the tenuousness of Jewish identity in a secular, tolerant society. Rarely does the author intrude with his own commentary. The effect of organizing the material so that it shows rather than tells is to provide a paradigm of the resistance to authority that Ozzie represents; readers cannot rely on a privileged voice for perspective but must arrive at their own conclusions.

As Ozzie is the focus of the reader's perceptions, one tends to be sympathetic to his aspirations and frustrations. The motivations of Binder are not nearly as well developed as are those of his defiant student. Because of the detached mode of narration, Ozzie's fundamental theological questions are made to seem highly pertinent, impossible to dismiss from the perspective of an impatient adult. However, posed in the vernacular of a self-righteous thirteen-year-old, they are also simplistic and naïve. Roth maintains an ambivalent attitude toward the conflicts between faith and reason and between tradition and the individual talent he depicts. He relates, without commentary, how the young man in effect accomplishes what he sets out to do. However, the story's final sentence recounts Ozzie's return to earth, albeit with an aura, only partially ironic, of the sacred—"into the center of the yellow net that glowed in the evening's edge like an overgrown halo."

*Steven G. Kellman*

# THE CONVICT

*Author:* James Lee Burke (1936-     )
*Type of plot:* Social realism, regional
*Time of plot:* About 1945
*Locale:* Louisiana
*First published:* 1985

> *Principal characters:*
> AVERY BROUSSARD, the narrator
> WILL BROUSSARD, his father
> MARGARET BROUSSARD, his mother
> THE CONVICT, an African American escaped criminal

*The Story*

"The Convict" describes an encounter with an escaped African American prisoner from the point of view of a young white boy. The events of three days make an indelible impact on young Avery Broussard as he observes how his mother and father and the community act and react.

The story begins in the small town of New Iberia, Louisiana, where Avery is with his father and several other men in a hotel bar. Will Broussard, his father, is a respected member of the community, but when he mentions the possibility of racial integration in the schools, it is clear none of the other men share his view. After they leave and pick up Avery's mother from a book club meeting, Avery asks his father why he drinks with the men as they always end up arguing. His mother, Margaret, says that Will should not provoke them.

At a roadblock they are told that two dangerous convicts, one of whom is an African American, have escaped from an Angola prison truck and are in the area. Margaret becomes increasingly anxious, and when they hear the door on their tractor shed banging, she does not want her husband to go outside in the rain. When her husband returns, Margaret tells him that she has heard on the radio that one of the escapees is a murderer. About 3:00 A.M., they hear the door bang again. Avery watches his father go out, then come back and take some towels and a lunch pail back to the shed.

Margaret stays in her room that morning, clearly upset with her husband. Will suggests that his son go to a picture show, but instead Avery pokes around an old houseboat left stranded on the shore years before. He sees a bloodied black man huddled on the floor, the chains of his broken handcuffs nailed to a beam of wood. Before Avery can say anything, his father yanks him away.

Margaret insists that they call the sheriff. Will promises that the man will be gone that night and that he is no threat to them. The rest of the day they do not speak to each other. That evening, Avery watches his father take a sack to the old houseboat and hears him tell the man to take the provisions and get out of the area. The next day Margaret goes to her sister's house.

When night comes, Avery sees a light in the trees and knows the convict is back. Will and Avery find him carrying a knife and no longer wearing his prison uniform. He says he came back because there are too many men looking for him. He admits he was in prison for murder and needs a place to hide. Will makes Avery go back to the house, and soon Avery hears a shotgun blast. He assumes his father has shot the convict, but Will says he just shot to scare him away and that he will have to call the sheriff now.

Later Avery and his parents stand on the front lawn with the sheriff and watch four deputies put the convict in a squad car. Will says that he had helped the man the night before. The sheriff says no one would believe that. Margaret is relieved that the sheriff is not going to tell what really happened and fixes a fine meal for her husband and son. The story ends with Avery thinking that at the time he did not understand why his parents acted as they did, he only felt grateful that the strife was at least temporarily over.

*Themes and Meanings*

The overriding focus of the story is racial discrimination. Set in the American South toward the end of World War II, it conveys the prejudice the white people have against people of color and its effects on both races. It is also a story about being idealistic or realistic. The men at the bar are scornful and upset when Will brings up the need for a change in the relationship of the races. The bartender sends the African American shoeshine man on an errand so he cannot hear any talk about integration. Avery feels he has made a mistake asking his father why he talks to these men because his mother immediately takes the stance that Will should not bring up such topics and mutters that Will is always supporting black people.

Margaret Broussard would have every right to be concerned about escaped convicts near her home, but it seems clear that it is the color of the man in the tractor shed that most disturbs her. She disagrees with her husband, then withdraws into silence and absence. Avery is caught in the middle. He finds it hard to understand why his father would give food to a man and tell him to escape to another state when the man does not even say thank you. Avery often plays with an African American boy about his age, but he senses forces much larger than himself at work in this tense situation.

After the convict returns the second night, Avery is relieved when Will says he fired the shotgun only to try to scare the man into leaving. However, at this point Will has decided that he must telephone the sheriff.

The reason for Will's decision is not stated, but this night's confrontation suggests Will has realized that working toward a good cause is not the same as mindlessly making assumptions about individuals. The convict had been suspicious and belligerent toward him the first night, claiming Will must be helping him only because he himself has something to hide from the law. This time, he says he was in prison for murder and refuses to tell how he acquired the new clothes and the knife. He threatens Will, saying Will already broke the law by helping him and that he is not going to leave. Will's position has been shattered; his automatic defense of an entire race has been in its own way as misguided as the extreme racial stereotyping by the men in the bar.

By pretending that no one would believe Will harbored the fugitive and then later reported him, the sheriff tries to protect the family's reputation and avoid controversy in the community. Margaret gratefully accepts the sheriff's invitation to come visit his wife, which indicates his intent to return the situation to normalcy.

Will, like his name, has the will and the strength of character to treat the battered convict as a fellow human being who needs help, but the convict makes hostile and unfulfillable demands. Margaret and the sheriff leave Will little choice; they conceal his acts of compassion so the community can keep up its pretense that the two races have nothing in common and that white supremacy remains intact.

## Style and Technique

James Lee Burke chooses the narrative point of view in the story well: that of a boy largely innocent of the racial prejudice that dominates his world but of an age to begin to see how it affects everyone's lives. Avery relates the events of the plot in present tense, luring the reader into the suspense and confusion as the events unfold. He has a keen eye for detail as he describes people, food, and his surroundings. He gives the dialogues between characters, revealing them dramatically rather than through summarization.

Another literary device Burke uses is to have Avery reveal his own thoughts and mixed feelings about the situation, particularly the conflict between his parents. Avery knows he should not go looking for the convict, but he is curious and even sees himself as protective of his father. However, when the convict is recaptured, Avery is little boy enough to be distracted and won over by the dinner his mother prepares and to be glad his father carries him to bed. He says he does not know or even care what his father meant when he spoke of "battered innocence."

However, at the very end of the story the narrative time frame changes. Avery says that it was only years later that he understood that "it is our collective helplessness, the frailty and imperfection of our vision that ennobles us and saves us from ourselves." The rich and lyrical prose style here is that of a reflective adult, one who has learned that regardless of whether an individual always manages to act compassionately toward others or is always wise in choosing to help, it is that vision, or goal to be compassionate, that is humanity's greatest quality.

*Lois A. Marchino*

# COOKING LESSON

*Author:* Rosario Castellanos (1925-1974)
*Type of plot:* Domestic realism
*Time of plot:* The 1960's
*Locale:* Mexico
*First published:* "Lección de cocina," 1971 (English translation, 1988)

*Principal character:*
THE NARRATOR, a young Mexican housewife

*The Story*

A recently married Mexican woman explains that because she does not know how to cook, she must resort to a cookbook for guidance. Her frustration grows as she skims through recipes too difficult for novices to follow. Feeling dishonest in wearing an apron that suggests an expertise that is generally assumed to be second nature to women, the narrator finally decides to defrost and prepare a roast. While thus occupied, her mind wanders back and forth between her culinary task and the changes that have occurred in her life since she met her husband. Remarks that she makes, such as, "The meat hasn't stopped existing. It has undergone a series of metamorphoses," apply to both her cooking and her life—both of which have undergone major transformations. Meanwhile, her resentment toward other household matters surfaces.

Despite her supervision, the roast eventually burns, leaving her to contemplate two possible ways in which to deal with the problem. As a woman who has been socialized to be a wife who embodies perfection, she can air out the kitchen, toss out the burned roast to hide the evidence of her failure, and await her husband coquettishly dressed to go out for dinner. Her other option is to accept responsibility for the fiasco and risk shattering her husband's image of her. The story ends with her weighing the satisfaction of showing her true self against the ensuing consequences of not using traditional feminine wiles.

*Themes and Meanings*

The questioning of gender roles, especially women's, is a principal theme of Rosario Castellanos's "Cooking Lesson." Its opening sentence indicates the space that culture assigns to females: the kitchen. Lacking cooking skills, the narrator resentfully comments: "My place is here. I've been here from the beginning of time." She embodies generations of women who have been socialized for domesticity.

As the story progresses, the young woman's resentment toward other household matters surfaces, suggesting that her struggle with making dinner is merely a catalyst in questioning the cultural forces that give women the roles that trap them in the home, stripping them of self-identity. These views are presented through the anonymous character's interior monologue. Significantly voiceless and nameless, this woman

represents countless married women who silently suffer the loss of their independence, identity, and self-esteem. Castellanos's irony lends relief to the tale of profound disillusionment with marriage.

In a traditionally patriarchal society, such as that depicted in this story, public fo-
rums are reserved for men, while married women are relegated to the private realm of
the home. For the narrator, marriage means giving up the independence that she enjoyed while single. Her allusions to schooling and job skills suggest that she was previously gainfully employed. Quite literally, she sacrifices her engagement with the
outside world at the altar.

As a devalued worker, the housewife recognizes the selflessness that marriage requires of women. Adopting her husband's name is the first step in assuming his identity and losing her own: "I lost my old name and I still can't get used to the new one."
She feels nameless because her own identity is subsumed in her husband's. His infidelity further accentuates her loss of self.

The patriarchal double standard in sexual matters that condones premarital and ex-
tramarital sex for males, while condemning females for the same behaviors, is also a
point of bitterness for the narrator. The culture allows a husband to exercise his sexual
prowess as a male prerogative; however, the ideal wife is one who "believes the evening executive meeting, the business trips and the arrival of unexpected clients . . .
[even] when she catches a whiff of French perfume (different from the one she uses)
on her husband's shirts." Significantly, the description of the kitchen that opens the
story alludes to the ideal female image. Such words as "shining white," "spotless-
ness," "pulchritude," and "halo" suggest the purity that is prized in women.

Given that virginity and the ability to cook are valued traits in females, it is not surprising that food and sexuality, as essential drives, are integral components of the
story. The narrator finds contradictions in both cooking and sexuality. Some incongruities in cooking are "slimness and gluttony, pleasing appearance and economy,
speed, and succulence." The wife believes that sexual innocence before marriage becomes clumsiness, and inexperience becomes frigidity. The husband, annoyed by her
modesty, behaves as if after the wedding she should immediately erase all the inhibitions that she has internalized during her years of patriarchal socialization.

Analogies may be drawn between the young woman as a cook and the roast. For example, the narrator comments that when her husband discovered she was a virgin, she
felt "like the last dinosaur." When the meat that she is cooking turns out unusually
tough, she remarks that "it must be mammoth." Her mishap with cooking oil evokes a
parallel with the roast, which is now "spitting and spattering and burning me. That's
how I'm going to fry in those narrow hells, through my fault, through my fault,
through my most grievous fault." This last example suggests a prayer in the Roman
Catholic Mass in which the confession of sin includes articulating *mia culpa* ("through
my fault") three times while pounding the chest.

Sin and guilt are key elements in Roman Catholic religious indoctrination that influences sexual behavior, especially among women. Because the narrator does not
feel that she is appreciated as a wife or is desired as a woman, she begins to fantasize

about dressing up, leaving the house, and encountering male admirers on the street. It takes the smoke from the burning roast to bring her back to reality. As is apparent, the previous reference to burning in hell alludes to her adulterous carnal desire and its punishment.

Elsewhere in the story, the wife associates fire and blisters with sacrifice and the body. The redness of the uncooked meat reminds her of the color of the sunburned backs that she and her husband got during their honeymoon in Acapulco. Although making physical love became agonizing for her, she did not breathe a word of complaint while her sunburned back ached under the weight of her husband—just as the Aztec emperor Cuauhtémoc remained silent while being tortured by the Spaniards over a bed of scorching coals. Recalling Cuauhtémoc's fate, the housewife feels imprisoned and a mute object of sacrifice.

"Cooking Lesson" is about women's struggle for subjectivity and autonomy. This concern is best illustrated by the narrator's self-reflection: "I'm myself. But who am I? Your wife, of course. And that title suffices to distinguish me from past memories or future projects. I bear an owner's brand, a property tag."

*Style and Technique*

"Cooking Lesson" uses interior monologue to portray a housewife's silent indictment of gender roles as representative of the general voicelessness of women in Mexican society. The monologue suggests that those in a subordinate role are not free to speak their minds.

Irony is used throughout the story to address and debunk cultural conventions. While mocking her role, the wife suggests the burden social dictates place on women: "For example, choosing the menu. How could one carry out such an arduous task without the cooperation of society—of all history?" The narrator, who obviously resents her role, describes herself as a "self-sacrificing little Mexican wife, born like a dove to the nest." She sarcastically denounces both male sexual competence and female pleasure: "The classic moan. Myths. Myths." Deriding the notion that a woman is an incomplete being without a man, she says that she has undergone "a profound metamorphosis." Previously, she "didn't know and now I know; I didn't feel and now I feel; I wasn't and now I am." Because society at large considers that a female's greatest accomplishment is securing a husband, the narrator ridicules the gratefulness implicitly elicited from brides saved from spinsterhood.

By consistently alternating the wife's train of thought between two frustrating experiences (marriage and cooking), Castellanos juxtaposes the focus to suggest the analogy of wife to meat. Furthermore, the use of flashbacks to depict a change in consciousness suggests the wife's daydreaming state while cooking. The lack of transition between past and present in the narration can be as abrupt as "I . . . The meat," thus exemplifying the wife's blurring of identity, a subject turned object.

*Gisela Norat*

# COUNTERPARTS

*Author:* James Joyce (1882-1941)
*Type of plot:* Symbolist
*Time of plot:* About 1900
*Locale:* Dublin
*First published:* 1914

> *Principal characters:*
> FARRINGTON, a middle-aged scrivener
> MR. ALLEYNE, a lawyer, Farrington's boss

*The Story*

The action of "Counterparts," one of James Joyce's *Dubliners* stories, occurs during a February afternoon and evening in the life of a lawyer's scrivener in Dublin. Farrington, the heavyset protagonist, is frustrated by his demeaning, monotonous job of copying legal documents. Mr. Alleyne, his boss, chastises him for taking an extended lunch hour, and rather than complete the work in hand, Farrington slips away from his desk to a nearby pub for a quick mid-afternoon drink.

Unable to finish the task before closing time, he turns it in two documents short while attempting to conceal his negligence. This time he is reprimanded by Mr. Alleyne for the compounded dereliction before his fellow clerks and an attractive, wealthy client. Faced with this public humiliation and affected by the combination of alcohol and suppressed rage, he blunders into an impertinent and accidentally witty answer, which sinks him in deeper trouble: He may now lose his job.

To drown these accumulated anxieties, when his workday is over he pawns his watch and spends the proceeds boozing with his pals. His embellished retelling of the confrontation with Mr. Alleyne earns for him their temporary admiration. As the evening progresses, however, and as they move from bar to bar, he pays for almost all the alcohol consumed in his honor, feels snubbed by a passing actress, and is defeated in Indian wrestling by an English vaudeville acrobat. He feels abused, cheated, and betrayed. When he finally arrives late that night at his cold, dark home to find his wife away at church, he turns in violent exasperation on his own son as the most convenient victim of his accumulated anger.

*Themes and Meanings*

Farrington is Joyce's most brutal creation. Evidently devoid of redeeming social or personal qualities, he does not appear to be respected by anyone. His relationships at work and home are marked by threats, evasion, and fear. His leads a life of desperate routine, never realizing an ennobling or liberating moment. Instead, he escapes into the temporary and insincere refuge of his drinking friends. The mood of the story suggests that their fates are very much like his: Their evening together does not lead to enlightenment or solidarity; rather, it is the occasion of mutual exploitation. Thus, when Farrington at the end of the story realizes his abandonment, his sadistic response amounts to an implicit admission of self-hatred. The design of the story, however, suggests that Farrington is not really a free agent and is not fully responsible for his actions.

"Counterparts" is Joyce's portrait of alienated labor. Farrington has little or no control over his own life, and his work is utterly mechanical and repetitious. His employers clearly belong to a higher social class—as various details, such as the hats and the accents, attest—and they deal imperiously with their employees, as shown by the two dramatic encounters in the first part of the story. Farrington's work, moreover, is the mind-numbing transcription of legal documents that mean nothing to him. He is kept to this treadmill by sheer intimidation, but the reader sees his mind and feelings constantly wandering to more pleasurable arenas and fixing on thoughts of vengeance. Whatever human feelings he possesses are perverted by the endless round of repression, repetition, and recrimination.

"Counterparts" traces the chain reaction of violence as it spreads, partially fulfilled, frustrated, reversed, and finally displaced, to an innocent and defenseless victim. The story illustrates how relationships based on power and control perpetuate and reproduce themselves, as brutality and bitterness pass from one level of authority to the next and from generation to generation. Farrington responds to his employer's abuse by repeating his offense, provoking even heavier censure. His several attempted escapes from humiliation in the office are encouraged by the appearance of success: in the bravado of the smart answer to Mr. Alleyne, its subsequent improvements, the extra shilling yielded on the watch at Terry Kelly's, and even the chastisement of his child at home. However, Farrington must also face the reality of accumulating defeats: the apology to Mr. Alleyne, the "hornet's nest" his office will henceforth be, the defeat in Indian wrestling, the extra shilling now owed to the pawnbroker, and the browbeating that awaits him when his wife gets home.

As each victory has a corresponding defeat forward or backward in time, so has each character and relationship in the story its own counterpart, horizontal or vertical in the power structure. From this study of a very plain citizen, the reader is invited to infer something of the quality of the network of relationships in the larger society. It can be observed, for example, that, saving his infamous retort, Farrington's self-expression derives its substance and style from his boss: He copies Mr. Alleyne's documents, mimics his accent, bullies his underlings, and unconsciously imitates his rhetoric. Further, the mechanical imagery ("ring," "shoot," "vibrate," "manikin"), the click of Miss Parker's machine, and the silent supervision of the clock all conspire to chill the atmosphere and formalize the relationships at Crosbie & Alleyne's.

*Style and Technique*

The various dictionary meanings of the word "counterpart" hold the key to the symbolic technique of this story, which proceeds by means of a complex set of corresponding, reduplicative, and complementary elements. Each character in the social scale has his or her counterpart: from Crosbie and Alleyne to Charlie and Tom ("twin" in Aramaic). Ultimately, in one sense or another, all are counterparts of Farrington: his fellow office-workers, his drinking cronies, and his wife (horizontally); Alleyne, Weathers, and Tom (vertically). In addition, each of these latter counterparts is associated with a woman, a different shade of red, and a distinguishing accent. Thus, they are all counterparts of one another. This pattern of correspondences and repetitions embraces the "rounds system" of buying drinks, Farrington's imitation of Weathers's taste for Appollinaris (a relatively expensive English mineral water), Farrington's and Higgins's retelling of the retort, and O'Halloran's corresponding experiences at Callan's of Fownes Street. This structural and symbolic pattern enlarges Farrington's very ordinary experiences and suggests, among other things, that they are self-perpetuating: The paralysis is contagious. Farrington is scarcely aware of the design of the events that determine his life. This perspective is cleverly suggested, for example, in that every character has a double letter in his or her name, and that Farrington has only a fleeting awareness of the repeated *b*'s in one of the documents he is required to copy.

Farrington's employment as a legal scrivener suggests another structural pattern: The story makes use of some forty legal terms ("counterpart," "consignor," "trial," "fair," and so on) and is designed according to the consecutive, formal stages in a legal action. The import of this symbolic structure is to cast Farrington as the victim of an unfair trial, and the function of this theme is best understood in conjunction with Farrington's allegorical representation of Irish manhood.

The reader may observe that he is almost exclusively referred to as "the man" in the first and third scenes, while, in the bar scenes, he is called almost exclusively by his surname. This contrast of alienation and acceptance is clearly thematic. However, if one considers that Joyce's naming of Farrington owes something to the Irish word for "man" (*fear,* pronounced as the English "far"), that he is called on "to uphold the national honour" against the Englishman Weathers, and that in the course of the story he is seen as failing every test of manhood (as servant, sexual object, athlete, father), a larger conclusion presents itself: that the story has a theme related to political justice—and indeed it does.

Farrington is a figure of brutalized Irish manhood, the victim of the colonial legal establishment, abetted by a succession of publicans and pawnbrokers. These figures form a collective symbol of British-capitalist interests preying on the energies of native Ireland while at the same time criminalizing their victims. Here in "Counterparts," as in all the *Dubliners* stories, Joyce interweaves a scrupulous attention to realistic detail and multiple symbolic patterns. The result is a complex theme that, like Farrington's chance witticism, gives the dull human drama of his characters an unexpected moment.

*Coilin Owens*

# COUNTING MONTHS

*Author:* David Leavitt (1961-    )
*Type of plot:* Psychological
*Time of plot:* 1980
*Locale:* An unnamed California suburb
*First published:* 1984

> *Principal characters:*
> ANNA HARRINGTON, a recently divorced mother with cancer
> JOAN LENSKY, her nosy acquaintance
> GREG LAURANS, the disturbed son of a friend

*The Story*

Six months before the story opens, Anna Harrington was told that she had six months to live. Now, sitting in the oncology department waiting room, she is suddenly overcome by the realization that she was supposed to be dead by now. Instead of elation, she feels only dread, for she does not interpret the fact that she is not dead as a reprieve but as a stay of execution. When her doctor praises her for keeping up an active life, she suddenly realizes what a lie she is living.

The doctor's optimism only depresses her as she leaves the hospital and drives to a supermarket. It is Christmas, and she marvels at sights and sounds that she never expected to live to see, but she feels no joy. The more she tries to forget her condition, the more obsessed with it she becomes. She is overwhelmed by the irony of the fact that she is living in a body that is killing itself from within.

Back home, she is plunged into the familiar domestic routine of dealing with three energetic young children who have no idea of what she is going through. At odd moments, the horror seizes her, then recedes as family demands intervene. Recently divorced, she has the added burden of being a single parent. Tonight she is supposed to take her children to a party at the Lauranses, Jewish friends whose son Greg is a born-again Christian who is displaying signs of bizarre behavior. Soon after the Harringtons arrive at the Lauranses, Anna settles a dispute between her son Ernest and a boy who he says broke his thermos bottle. The fact that Ernest is not telling the whole truth bothers her, especially when she remembers that she will probably not be around much longer to guide her son.

Two things happen at the party to aggravate Anna's fragile emotional condition. First, she is accosted by Joan Lensky, a woman who pretends to be a concerned friend but who is really a busybody. Joan seems to live for nothing but comparing other people's sorrows with her own. She presses Anna for details of her condition and seems to enjoy speaking graphically of radiation therapy, chemotherapy, and hair loss. She even goes so far as to suggest that Anna consult an organization that arranges things before people die to ensure that everything will be properly taken care of afterward.

Anna is no sooner rescued from Joan's morbid prying than she is confronted by a group of retarded children whom Greg Laurans has brought from the state hospital to sing Christmas carols. One of the girls is a dwarf with a deformed head and large, alert eyes set unnaturally low beneath a broad forehead. When the children sing, they have such trouble pronouncing even the simplest words that their singing becomes grotesque. Anna sees their performance as a deliberate cruelty to all concerned and tries to comfort Greg's distraught mother.

Shortly thereafter, Ernest announces to his mother that his brother, Roy, is in the bedroom with some boys smoking pot. Instead of recoiling in horror, Anna merely tells Ernest not to be a tattletale, as if nothing else can now happen that could possibly upset her. Just as she says this, she spies the dwarf girl looking up at her. The girl is holding a glass of water in her tiny, fat hand, and on her face is an expression that Anna thinks could indicate either extreme stupidity or great knowledge. As the story ends, the dwarf girl is staring at Anna, unblinking, as if Anna herself "were a curiosity—or a comrade in sorrow."

## Themes and Meanings

Being stricken in the midst of life with cancer is a theme in much of David Leavitt's fiction. At an age when most people have not yet even grasped the idea of mortality, Leavitt was probing the minds and hearts of cancer patients with uncanny authority. He is most concerned with the way cancer both unites and separates people. He uses cancer as a metaphor for the inescapable loneliness of life. Although disease can help one to sympathize with others similarly afflicted, Leavitt presents it as a reminder that everyone must pass alone through the valley of the shadow of death. His characters take no comfort in knowing that others may be suffering, for it means nothing to them. Only their own suffering is real, and thus their cancer becomes the ultimate reality. Although it heightens the awareness of life around them, it also intensifies their loneliness.

Leavitt does not portray this loneliness as a cause for sadness or self-pity. People such as Anna Harrington do not envy the healthy or resent the well, nor do they view life at such a distance that it becomes meaningless and absurd. Although their disease focuses their attention on themselves, it does not make them selfish or spiteful, but neither does it make them philosophical. In this respect, Leavitt's is a fresh view and a fresh voice. Unlike the characters of Anton Chekhov or Thomas Mann, who are either in love with their disease or angry with God for allowing it, Leavitt's characters have a dignity and courage that suggest, if anything, that the sentence of death summons forth something mysterious and fine, something essentially human that is not the result but the source of spirituality. In this respect, Leavitt is closer to Leo Tolstoy and Albert Camus, who see the acceptance of death as the first step toward wisdom. To them, death defines life and gives it its meaning.

Anna shrinks intuitively from Joan Lensky, because the latter's obsession with disease and death is really a form of denial. Her fussing about hair loss and funeral arrangements is her way of evading reality, not confronting it. Anna is drawn to the dwarf girl because this poor deformed creature is a visible manifestation of the disease that is invisibly disfiguring Anna herself. The girl can only be what she is. It does not matter whether she is stupid or wise. She exists without shame in an utterly private world, and she ventures forth into the social world heedless of whether or not she belongs there. For who belongs anywhere? This is what Anna finally realizes when their eyes lock, and they see each other as both curiosities and comrades in sorrow.

*Style and Technique*

Leavitt writes short stories that are economical, suspenseful, and satisfying but still left open-ended. He respects the purpose of the short story, which is to direct all its elements toward a moment of eye-opening awareness, of sudden realization, with a minimum of incidental material and the good sense not to drive the point into the ground.

The economy of this story is illustrated by its series of set pieces: scenes in a waiting room, in a car, at the supermarket, at home, at a party. In quick succession, Leavitt provides glimpses of a frightened woman fighting a losing battle with cancer against a backdrop of banal suburban life. The narrative moves swiftly from Anna's sudden memory of the six-month deadline, to her being inexorably drawn into the hectic life of family and social obligations, and finally to her chilling encounter with the dwarf girl.

Suspense is created from the beginning when it is revealed that Anna has cancer and is apparently living on borrowed time. As she gazes into an aquarium in the oncology waiting room, she sees herself floating in time, emotionally isolated from those who are closest to her. The question raised is not just how long she will live, but how she will live out the time that is left to her. Leavitt quickly moves through the rest of Anna's day, as she gets her children to the party, settles the feud between Ernest and Kevin, puts up with Joan Lensky, and finally comes face to face with the dwarf girl.

Leavitt is particularly good at incident: Anna's reactions to the bustle in the supermarket; her sitting at the traffic light, counting the seconds (as she has counted the months) until it changes, while superstitiously basing her chances for recovery on the accuracy of her guess; the particulars of the children's possessions and games; Joan Lensky always in black; Dr. Sanchez's hairy hands; her husband's running away to Italy with a law student; and, finally, the bizarre image of the dwarf girl, "owl eyes in a huge head," staring Anna down.

Leavitt also knows when to stop. The moment that Anna and the dwarf girl look deeply into each other's eyes, the reader knows that a bond between two human beings has been formed. It is not a bond based on the mutual deception and false optimism that Anna has received from the doctors. It is a bond based on the full acceptance of who they are—and of each other. To Leavitt, the two are inseparable.

*Thomas Whissen*

# A COUNTRY DOCTOR

*Author:* Franz Kafka (1883-1924)
*Type of plot:* Fable
*Time of plot:* The late nineteenth or early twentieth century
*Locale:* Possibly rural Bohemia
*First published:* "Ein Landarzt," 1919 (English translation, 1940)

> *Principal characters:*
> A COUNTRY DOCTOR, the narrator and protagonist
> A YOUNG BOY, his patient
> ROSA, his maid

## *The Story*

On a snowy night, a country doctor desperately seeks a way to reach a very sick patient in a village some fifty miles away. His own horse died from overexertion the night before, and Rosa, his servant girl, has found no other horse in the village for his carriage. While absentmindedly searching his barnyard, he accidentally knocks open the door to an unused pigsty, only to find there two powerfully built horses and a groom. He instructs Rosa to help the groom hitch the horses to his carriage, but the groom attacks her as soon as she gets near him. The doctor climbs into the carriage but is reluctant to leave when the groom says that he plans to stay behind with Rosa, which causes her to run screaming into the house. The doctor protests in vain, as the horses whisk him away and arrive seemingly instantaneously at the patient's door.

The parents and sister of the patient rush out to greet the doctor and practically carry him into the poorly ventilated room of the sick boy. The boy, thin but without a fever, whispers to the doctor that he wants to die. At a loss as to what to do, the doctor aimlessly takes out his instruments and curses the miraculous assistance that has been provided him. He suddenly remembers Rosa, toward whom he has never paid much attention but whose fate now troubles him.

The horses manage to open a window in order to observe the sick boy. One neighs loudly when the doctor approaches the bed. As an underpaid employee of the district in which he works, the doctor believes that he is taken advantage of by his impoverished clientele. He convinces himself that the boy is not sick after all and prepares to leave but is interrupted by the disappointed parents. Their intervention brings him to admit that the boy might be sick after all, and when he approaches the bed a second time, both horses neigh loudly in approval.

The doctor discovers that the boy is indeed very sick. There is a hand-sized wound on his right hip, pink (*rosa*, in German), with many shadings and containing worms the size of his fingers. Although the family is overjoyed to see the doctor's activity, he thinks to himself that there is no possible way to save the boy. These people always "demand the impossible from the doctor," he thinks; "they've lost their old faith; the minister sits at home and pulls apart his vestments, one after another; and the doctor is supposed to do everything with his delicate surgical hand."

As a school choir sings, "If you undress him, he will heal," the family and the recently arrived village elders undress the doctor, place him in the bed next to the boy's wound, and then leave the room. When the boy tells the doctor that he has very little confidence in him, the doctor tries to excuse his shortcomings and tells the boy that his wound is not so uncommon—many people, he claims, sacrifice their sides to two strokes of a mattock in the forest. Although sensing that the doctor is deceiving him, the boy does not question him further.

The horses have faithfully remained at the window. The doctor gathers up his clothes and instruments. Thinking that the return trip will be as swift as the arrival, the doctor hastily hitches the horses to his wagon and commands them to take him home but slowly, "like old men," they plod through the snowy wasteland. Behind him the doctor hears another song of the schoolchildren: "Rejoice, you patients, the doctor has been laid in bed for you."

Never will he arrive home, the doctor complains to himself; he has lost his practice, a successor is robbing him, the groom rages in his house, and Rosa has been sacrificed. "Naked, exposed to the frost of the most unhappy of times, I, an old man, drive around with an earthly wagon and unearthly horses. . . . Deceived! Deceived! There can be no making amends for having once followed the false ringing of my night bell."

## Themes and Meanings

One of the richest and most suggestive of Franz Kafka's texts, "A Country Doctor" depicts the tragic self-deception of an individual faced with his own loss of faith in his profession. The doctor readily blames other factors—the conditions of his employment, his patients, the decline of religious belief—for his failure to carry out his responsibilities, principally, to heal those in need. Once he fails to perform his duties as a healer, his life loses all sense of purpose and meaning.

The doctor's existential crisis is partly of his own making and partly the result of his extreme social isolation. He has neglected Rosa for years, says that it is very difficult to reach a mutual understanding with his patients, and feels tormented by the allegedly false ringing of his night bell. Although there does seem to be a breakdown in a viable social community—the doctor is an official of a political district and thus part of a bureaucratic system at some remove from the people (illustrated in the text by the distance that he must travel this particular night)—the strong subjective bias of his report of his relationships to other people puts into question his whole understanding of who he is and what he does. The reader needs to approach the doctor's own assessment of his situation with skepticism and ask what is the reality behind his self-pitying failure to heal, or even begin to treat, the boy's horrible wound.

## Style and Technique

Despite his failure to heal, the doctor tells his story in a remarkably poetic and convincing way. So convincing is it, in fact, that the reader is likely at first to be fully taken in by the doctor's account. The doctor begins innocently enough by saying, "I was in a dilemma," namely, that he lacked a horse to take him to the distant patient. A change in the doctor's story first becomes noticeable when he breaks into the present tense at the point when he tells of the groom's attack on Rosa. He continues to use the historical present until he says that the patient accepted his story about the origin of the wound and fell silent. This change in tense sets off the story's long middle section, in which the doctor's self-pitying complaints, hesitations, and doubts about his profession predominate.

The reader must keep in mind that the doctor relates the details of his final sickbed visit in a state of utter despair, as he is driven in a seemingly endless winter night by a pair of horses over which he has absolutely no control. The desperateness of his situation, however, does not become clear until the last paragraph of his story. At first the doctor's detached narration draws the reader's sympathies and blocks any skeptical response to what is being told. As the account unfolds, there are more and more indications that the doctor's consciousness is clouded by his own fears and anxieties—his sudden concern for Rosa, his paranoia about the miraculous assistance of the horses, who seem at the disposal of higher forces, his need to justify to himself his failure to act. Thus, the most fantastic elements of the story—the horses' speed during the initial journey, the terrible beauty of the boy's wound, and the undressing of the doctor—reflect the unreality of the doctor's distorted consciousness rather than a fantastic reality that might have confronted him. The artistic skill with which the doctor turns his failure to cope with the realities of his work into a brilliantly seductive narrative suggests that his real calling is as a storyteller and not as a healer.

*Peter West Nutting*

# A COUNTRY GIRL

*Author:* Mary Hood (1946-    )
*Type of plot:* Social realism
*Time of plot:* The mid-twentieth century
*Locale:* Rydal, a rural Florida community
*First published:* 1984

*Principal characters:*
ELIZABETH INGLISH, a country girl
MAY INGLISH, her mother
UNCLE BILLY, her uncle
UNCLE CLEVELAND INGLISH, a senior family member
PAUL MONTGOMERY, a reporter
JOHNNY CALHOUN, a forty-year-old family friend

*The Story*

A pair of Florida tourists stops in the small rural community of Rydal to enjoy the scenery. The man takes photographs while his wife paints a picture, which she gives to a barefoot young country girl named Elizabeth, who sings and plays a guitar. In return, Elizabeth sings a song for the tourists, who view her as a bit of local color—a part of the scenery. As the couple leaves the town, the man says "Country Girl," as he thinks of the caption for his slide.

Paul Montgomery, a reporter for a Sunday magazine, comes to Rydal to write an article on the life and works of a local writer named Corra Harris, who has been dead for several years. He arrives as members of the Inglish family gather for their annual reunion. Women busily prepare the food that they will serve on paper plates placed on picnic tables resting on sawhorses and covered with sheets.

Elizabeth is making potato salad when Montgomery appears in the kitchen looking for Cleveland Inglish, whom he wants to interview because the man once worked for Harris. Because Cleveland is not there, Elizabeth offers to show him Harris's writing studio. She leads him down a path thick with blackberry brambles and blueberries, past gardens blooming with geraniums, Shasta daisies, and hollyhocks. With everyone else gone fishing, the studio is locked, but Elizabeth and Montgomery look at Harris's workroom through the windows. As they look at stacks of yellow paper and a dry ink well, Elizabeth thinks the place is sad because it looks as though its objects are waiting for their owner to return. When Montgomery asks her if she has read any of Harris's books, she replies, "After sixteen they caint make you."

Back at the Inglish family gathering, Elizabeth introduces Montgomery to her Uncle Cleveland, who invites him to stay for the meal. Montgomery listens to the conversation but does not learn much about Harris. As he leaves for his motel, he promises to return with his camera and questions about Harris.

More members of the family arrive—aunts, uncles, cousins, and children, as well as dogs—and they take their customary stations around a beech tree and engage in small talk. Johnny Calhoun, a forty-year-old yarn manufacturer, arrives and is invited to join the party, although he is not a family member. He is a handsome man who enjoys the ladies. When Jeff's wife, Patty, runs to welcome him with a kiss, Johnny and everyone else laughs.

Elizabeth stands near a group of children, hoping to avoid being asked to sing. From the time she was young she has vowed that she will "never love but one man." So far she has not fallen for anyone but feels that her family is watching her to see if she has made a fool of herself yet. After slipping away from the group, she walks to a tree, where she lies down. Johnny follows her and gives her a present, a small music box. He is paying attention to her now just as he has done to a different girl each summer. As Elizabeth listens to the music box, she asks herself, "Johnny?" She then smokes a cigarette, waits, and decides, "Johnny."

Montgomery also leaves the main group and sets off with his camera to take pictures and look for Elizabeth. He is startled to find Johnny and Elizabeth lying together under the tree. Johnny nonchalantly says that they will return to the picnic, as Montgomery clutches his camera to his pounding chest and jogs off. Back at the reunion, only Patty, Jeff's wife, seems to notice that Elizabeth and Johnny are missing.

Several weeks after Montgomery's article on Harris is published, more tourists begin stopping in Rydal looking for her gravesite. The story ends with the image of Elizabeth sitting on the porch, guitar in hand, absorbed in reverie. Some strangers think she is blind, others think she is a fool.

*Themes and Meanings*

The third-person omniscient narrator observes the landscape and people of this small southern town without participating in the action or passing judgments. The narrator merely records the scenery, dialogue, and actions. Paul Montgomery, with his reporter's eye, camera, and notebook also watches and records the actions of the people. He is a guest at the reunion, an outsider who stands on the sidelines and observes the rituals, conversations, and relationships. He appears to be interested in Elizabeth but does not communicate that interest to her. The narrator says that "there wasn't a decade between, just the wide world." Montgomery thus remains isolated from the group.

Elizabeth also seems lonely and isolated. A dreamy, restless young girl who waits for something to happen, she has told her family that she will love only one man but does not have anyone in particular in mind. The older women wait to see if she will be true to her word or make a fool of herself. When Johnny Calhoun singles her out for his attention, she decides, without much thought, that he is the one for her, and gives herself to him. Later she realizes that she has indeed been a fool for succumbing too easily to Johnny's charms. In fact, there is no purpose to her decision. Unable to communicate her feelings, she simply drifts into the situation with no real commitment. She has moved out of the circle of childhood into the world of mature women but does not understand her own motives in allowing Johnny to seduce her.

The story is full of ritual. The family prepares for the reunion in the same way that they have for years. Each person has his own place in the family order and acts accordingly. The women prepare the food. They go about the ordinary business of their lives. Horace swaps lies with the men at the barber shop, Uncle Cleveland goes fishing. Uncle Billy is "out in the corn, potting crows." Elizabeth is part of this community, part of its customs and rituals, and has passed from childhood to womanhood in the same way as countless other women.

*Style and Technique*

In Mary Hood's story the people and landscape blend together to create a picture of the rural community. It is full of local color, descriptions of country ways and customs. Almost every paragraph contains such regional expressions as "she sent him round to the front door like company" or "the lights were on like a funeral was happening." Characters become part of the setting as they perform ordinary little acts such as polishing "a little twig smooth as a chicken bone." Adding to the flavor of country life, the characters' speech is marked by grammatically incorrect expressions such as "that don't differ." Characters exchange bits of country wisdom as they go about their daily tasks. One character observes that "old folks don't wear out their shoes." Elizabeth says of one farmer, "God never gave him quittin' sense." When Montgomery asks Elizabeth if she thinks he looks old, she replies "You're you. Just yourself. Born in God's time and going to last till you're done."

Hood describes scenes in realistic detail. She portrays a domestic scene with such images as "the tap-tap-tap of May flouring the cake pans." She shows us watermelons on chipped ice in a galvanized tub and a landscape filled with verbena, mint, lavender, geraniums, Shasta daisies, and hollyhocks. She captures the sounds of country life: crickets and June bugs, the slam of screen doors, the pop-pop-pop of Uncle Billy's gun as he shoots at the "laughing crows." The local customs, regional expressions, rituals, sights, and sounds of this community provide the key elements of this story.

*Judith Barton Williamson*

# THE COUNTRY HUSBAND

*Author:* John Cheever (1912-1982)
*Type of plot:* Domestic realism
*Time of plot:* The early 1950's
*Locale:* Shady Hill, a fictional suburb of New York City
*First published:* 1954

> *Principal characters:*
> FRANCIS WEED, a businessperson and father of four
> JULIA, his wife
> ANNE MURCHISON, their teenage baby-sitter
> CLAYTON THOMAS, Anne's fiancé

## The Story

"The Country Husband" recounts Francis Weed's brief rebellion against the mundane norms of his prosperous, dull community. Francis and Julia Weed have long been at the center of social life in Shady Hill, experiencing the conventional joys of suburban marriage and child rearing. Events conspire to jog Francis out of complacency and make him question his satisfaction with life.

The first of these events is a plane crash. Returning from a trip to Minneapolis, Francis and his fellow travelers experience an emergency landing in a field outside Philadelphia. They are shepherded to a nearby barn, and Francis takes a train to New York that arrives in time for him to catch his normal commuter train to Shady Hill. Naturally shaken by this occurrence, Francis is dismayed to discover that no one at home seems able to understand his brush with death. He arrived home on time, he looked fine—all his family went on with their normal routine. In fact, his children are more quarrelsome than usual, and Francis irritably compares his home to a battlefield, sending his wife upstairs in tears.

The next day, Francis is again disconcerted when he recognizes the new French maid at a neighbor's dinner party. After some pondering, he realizes where he has seen her before: At the end of World War II, he had witnessed her public humiliation by the people of her town in Normandy. She had been accused of living with a German officer during the occupation of France. As punishment, her head had been shaved and she had been made to stand naked before the townspeople. This memory overwhelms Francis, all the more because he does not feel able to share it with anyone, not even his wife. This experience, combined with the trauma of the plane crash, has made Francis suddenly aware of mortality, of danger, of passion, and his senses are heightened. Something is bound to happen.

That something comes, rather anticlimactically, in the form of Anne Murchison, the baby-sitter who is waiting for Francis to drive her home when the Weeds return from the neighbors' party. Anne strikes Francis as impossibly beautiful—"he experienced in his consciousness that moment when music breaks glass, and felt a pang of recognition as strange, deep, and wonderful as anything in his life." For the next several days, lustful fantasies about Anne fill his waking thoughts and his dreams. He buys a bracelet for her and carries it in his pocket, awaiting the right moment to give it to her and take her in his arms. Although terms such as "statutory rape" enter his thoughts, he nevertheless imagines sneaking off with her to a lovers' lane.

Francis's obsession with Anne has two immediate consequences. On the one hand, it heightens his enjoyment of physical reality. He is thrilled when he sights the first frost of autumn; the view of an express train hurtling down the platform excites him with "the miraculous physicalness of everything." On the other hand, Francis's passion makes him dangerously cavalier about the social proprieties on which a town such as Shady Hill depends. Accosted on the train platform by a boring chatterbox, Francis explicitly insults her. Later his wife reminds him that this woman is the town's social arbiter and might prevent their daughter's invitation to the important dances. This reminder precipitates a dreary, tearful fight in which Julia accuses Francis of leaving his dirty clothes on the floor to torment her.

The next morning, Francis again escapes this domestic banality by imagining that he sees Anne on the morning train. He chases after her only to discover that he has been mistaken—the woman he has followed is much older than Anne. Later that day, however, he realizes the folly of his obsession. He receives a call asking him to recommend for a job a college boy, Clayton Thomas, who visited the Weeds the night before. During the visit, Clayton—a rather earnest and immature young man—announced his engagement to Anne Murchison. To his own horror, Francis finds himself telling his caller that he cannot recommend Clayton Thomas, that in fact the boy is a thief. Recoiling at what he has done, Francis telephones a psychiatrist.

The story ends with a view of Francis building a coffee table in the cellar of his house: The psychiatrist has recommended woodworking as therapy. He is absorbed in "the holy smell of new wood"; for the moment, at least, his crisis seems to have been resolved in a straightforward way. Life is back to normal.

### Themes and Meanings

It would be possible to read "The Country Husband" as an ironic commentary on what has come to be known as a "mid-life crisis," in which a man approaching middle age suddenly becomes infatuated with a much younger woman. Although John Cheever gently satirizes the particular form that Francis Weed's crisis takes, however, he treats more seriously Francis's realization that he and his friends have stopped paying attention to the meaning of life. This realization is most explicit in the moments following his recognition of the French maid: "The people in the Farquarsons' living room seemed united in their tacit claim that there had been no past, no war—that there was no danger or trouble in the world."

One theme of the story, then, is suggested by the question: How can life be meaningful in the absence of the sharp awareness brought on by crises such as death and war? Cheever suggests several answers. First, a consciousness of the past—of possible "danger or trouble"—is important to maintain. Francis has never had a good memory; as Cheever says: "It was not his limitation at all to be unable to escape the past; it was perhaps his limitation that he had escaped it so successfully." The thoughtful person, Cheever suggests, maintains a balance between the ordinary surface of daily life and an awareness that the extraordinary has happened in the past, and will happen again, for better or worse.

Second, the story suggests that in the absence of the extraordinary, individuals can heighten their perception of life by concentrating on the small pleasures of physical life (as Francis is encouraged to do first by his love for Anne and later by his psychiatrist). The beauty of architectural detail, the smell of ink rising from the morning paper, a random glimpse of a beautiful woman on a train—all these common moments can seem like revelations to the heightened awareness. What is more, occasional flights of fancy may be good for the soul. One of the last images in the story shows Francis's youngest son, Toby, struggling out of his cowboy outfit and putting on his "space suit" with a "magic cape." As he "flies the short distance to the floor," Toby proves that people have the resources within them to escape the ordinary, if only for a moment at a time.

## Style and Technique

Consistent with the story's theme that even the mundane world contains much that is worthy of notice, Cheever's writing is rich in detail; for example, in his careful description of the Weeds' preparation for their yearly Christmas photograph. Moreover, the pattern of classical allusions that recur in the story emphasizes the reality of history, and in fact the lingering presence of the past in the modern world.

The classical allusions are diverse. The Weeds' living room is said to be "divided like Gaul into three parts." A neighbor says of his wife, "She makes me feel like Hannibal crossing the Alps." Francis notes on Fifth Avenue the statue of Atlas bearing the globe on his shoulders, and his love for Anne, it is suggested, may result from some "capriciousness of Venus and Eros." The beautiful woman glimpsed on the train becomes "Venus combing and combing her hair." The classical allusions are capped by the fact that the neighbors' retriever—"black as coal, with a long, alert, intelligent, rakehell face"—is called Jupiter. Although these allusions are used with an ironic tone, their cumulative pattern is enough to suggest that the distant classical world can still provide an enriching presence in the modern world. To see one's neighbors, their living rooms and their pets, as analogues to the heroes and gods of classical antiquity endows them all with a certain dignity, even if tempered by gentle irony. At the end of the story, as Francis works happily in the basement, Jupiter comes prancing through the garden, and the evening suddenly seems "a night where kings in golden suits ride elephants over the mountains." Romance and beauty can be found in the modern world, even in Shady Hill.

*Diane M. Ross*

# A COUNTRY LOVE STORY

*Author:* Jean Stafford (1915-1979)
*Type of plot:* Domestic realism
*Time of plot:* About 1950
*Locale:* Rural New England
*First published:* 1950

> *Principal characters:*
> MAY, a housewife, nearly thirty years old
> DANIEL, her husband, a college professor, nearly fifty years old
> DR. TELLENBACH, Daniel's Swiss physician

## The Story

"A Country Love Story" focuses on a couple, May and her much older husband, Daniel—a college professor recuperating from an illness (presumably tuberculosis)—and their relationship set against the rural isolation of an old house in the country, to which they have just moved to aid in Daniel's convalescence.

Though the story begins with emphasis on May's and Daniel's failure to follow through on their plan to remove an antique sleigh that stands in the yard (a symbol of both erosion and hope that resurfaces throughout the story), on their increasing silence as winter comes on, and on May's original lack of enthusiasm for the seeming exile from Boston, these negatives are balanced by the couple's love for the country house, their regained intimacy ("it was like a second honeymoon"), and their mutual pleasure in reading, gardening, and repairing the new home. The crucial change occurs with the arrival of autumn, when Daniel withdraws to his historical research and May finds that she has nothing to fill her days; her complaints elicit from Daniel a heretofore unrecognized tendency toward passive-aggressive behavior. He puts May on the defensive and keeps her there by means of his self-pity, his preoccupation with blame, and his condescending to her as childish.

May does not seem to understand the sources or implications of his changes: His year in the sanitarium Dr. Tellenbach describes as "like living with an exacting mistress," an image that hints at Daniel's suspicion that May had an affair during their separation. It also does not occur to her that the year's illness has made mortality very clear and personal to her husband and that he now resents her for her youthfulness and health. All this is disguised as repeated attacks on her mental state. May does seem to understand subconsciously, however, for she creates a lover where none existed before and through the winter concentrates on bringing him more and more to life, until finally he sits in the sleigh, a pale young man from an earlier era, a kind of romantic and antique image of Daniel himself.

In the final scene, Daniel unwittingly but appropriately superimposes himself on the image of the lover in May's dream, bringing May back to the unpleasant reality and the shock of admitting that he is "old" and "ill" and now very much dependent on her, that the imaginary lover is gone forever, and that she is "like an orphan in solitary confinement." There is not the smallest spark to brighten this last morning.

### Themes and Meanings

The double irony of Jean Stafford's title—May's love for Daniel ends, and her imagined adulterous love also disappears—hints at the deceptive nature of her story. The surface of May and Daniel's domestic life in their country home shows only a steady decline into mutual distrust and almost total silence; though there are brief quarrels, there are no truly dramatic events. Stafford creates here a kind of gothic configuration: The female protagonist is trapped in the dark house with an enemy, while her rescuer-lover appears just outside. That the ogre is May's once-adored husband and that the lover is only an imaginary expression of her desire for revenge and her wish to escape make for further irony, as does the presence of the derelict sleigh as a romantic symbol, but all of it is entirely without humor.

Stafford's title suggests that some of the story's meanings cohere around notions of the pastoral, specifically as a place of simplicity and calm that will somehow engender the same qualities in those who venture there. Early in the story, Dr. Tellenbach makes clear his belief that life in Boston will, with its "strain," "pandemonium," "excitements," and "intrigues," hinder Daniel's recovery, and that the purity and solitude of country life will further it. Behind his belief lies the assumption that self-absorption and "little talk" are beneficial, and that complexity of any sort is to be avoided. The narrative demonstrates the fallacies of these positions, hinting that the condition of married love is a social one and needs the stimulation of a society outside.

On the other hand, the presence of individuals outside but very close to a marriage creates the threat of triangles, and there are several in this story. The most destructive third person is Dr. Tellenbach: He speaks to May in a "courtly" way but is "authoritative" and treats her like a child; his mention of Daniel's mistress-disease furthers the triangle theme. May herself is bothered by what she perceives to be a greater intimacy between the doctor and her husband than she enjoys herself. Daniel, for his part, creates but does not name the imaginary-lover motif, and by rejecting May verbally and presumably sexually as well he sets in motion a strange sort of gestation in her: she "felt a certain stirring of life in her solitude," and "nursed" her injury, "hugged it," and feared that others sensed the "incubus of her sins." The result, her lover-in-the-sleigh, completes the series of triangles, and though the implied betrayal does not destroy the marriage, this lover's presence signifies that the marriage has already failed, just as his disappearance signals that May has no alternatives to comfort her.

Another, related theme is May's initiation into an awareness of her sensuous needs and her ability to desire revenge. At the beginning of the story, her eagerness to please the men and to stifle her objections makes her essentially passive. Daniel's abuse gradually forces her rebellion, and her breaking out takes the form of a rejection of the retentive influence of the Swiss doctor in Boston. Not coincidentally, she discovers on Christmas Day both her "weighty but unviolent dislike" for Daniel and her connecting the sleigh with her attraction to the "passionate, sweating, running life" of the animals that once pulled it. This transformation changes the significance of the sleigh: It becomes the setting for her desire. Thus, her decision not to go to the scent-filled barn for firewood at the story's end hints that she understands desire now.

*Style and Technique*

Typical of Stafford's work, this story does not call attention to its stylistic features; nevertheless, it shows meticulous care in its strategies. The story's purpose, to reveal May's growing consciousness of despair, is well served by the unobtrusive voice and the restriction of the third-person narrative to May's own consciousness. There is much that May does not recognize in the early part of the story, but by refusing to reserve the highest consciousness for her narrator, Stafford avoids condescending to May, allows her to retain full stature, and emphasizes her gradually maturing vision. The persona who tells the story implies a sympathy exclusively for May but does so only in arranging events: Daniel speaks his intolerance and retreats to his study. The narrative voice itself is unfailingly objective, following realism's assumption that the events, told completely, will interpret themselves.

The arrangement of events and placement of images shows Stafford at her masterful best. For example, descriptions of the earlier years of the marriage emphasize their intellectual sharing. Daniel's refusal to converse with May about his research or his year in the sanitarium reveals his inability to speak of what actually preoccupies him: jealousy and suspicion. The story's imagery, however, implies in other ways that May has never wished to be unfaithful: May's dream of canoeing with her lover in a meadow of water lilies parallels exactly an earlier scene wherein she rowed with Daniel and first noticed changes in him; the lover himself, as mentioned above, is physically like Daniel, only younger. Similarly, Stafford handles the adultery theme with reference not to human beings but to animals: During Daniel's exile, May takes refuge from her guilty sexual longings by "imitating the cats," sleeping. This initiates the series of images connecting the barn and its passionate animals with the sleigh and May's desires, all of which culminates in the cold final scene's "lion foot" unlit stove and the blacksmith's cat that climbs into the sleigh. These elements allow Stafford to develop themes never explicitly named by the characters, and to show the developing of May's psyche as she responds to Daniel's accusations though never consciously understanding them. The technique allows May to retain not only essential innocence but also a truly human complexity.

Finally, there is in both the setting (the claustrophobia of the old house, the ghostly horses and lover, the lone woman) and the action (especially Daniel's mysterious and vaguely threatening behavior) more than a small hint of the gothic horror story. By means of a quiet irony, Stafford manages to create a rescue scene in Daniel's kisses and brusque supplication and at the same time to leave her protagonist more trapped than ever. By technique, she reveals that initiation is not always hopeful.

*Kerry Ahearn*

# THE COUNTRY OF THE BLIND

*Author:* H. G. Wells (1866-1946)
*Type of plot:* Fable
*Time of plot:* The early 1900's
*Locale:* An imaginary valley in Ecuador
*First published:* 1904

*Principal characters:*
NÚÑEZ, a Colombian mountaineer
YACOB, an old blind man
MEDINA-SAROTE, Yacob's daughter

*The Story*

Long years ago, a valley in Ecuador's Andes was accessible to all. Then came a great landslide that cut the valley off from the outside world. An early settler who chanced to be outside the valley when the earthquake occurred was never able to return. Before he died, he described the place whence he came. A place where it never rained or snowed, it was a virtual utopia until a strange disease rendered everyone blind. Because people then considered sin to be the cause of disease, the settler was chosen to leave the valley to find priests to build a shrine that would buy holy help from the blindness. The mountain moved, however, so the settler could never return.

Lost to civilization, the valley was forgotten by the outside world and the disease ran its course. After fifteen generations had passed, the ways of the blind became the custom and culture. It then chances that a young man inadvertently enters the valley.

The stranger named Núñez is a mountaineer who has seen the world. While guiding a party of climbers, he falls from a mountain during the night. Although he tumbles more than a thousand feet, he survives. The next morning he climbs further downward until he finds himself among meadows dotted with flocks of llamas. He sees a cluster of strange windowless stone huts and remarks to himself that the builder "must have been as blind as a bat."

After shouting to three man who cannot tell where he is, Núñez realizes that he must be in the legendary Country of the Blind. He advances toward the men with the confidence of a sighted man thinking of the old proverb: In the country of the blind, the one-eyed man is king. He tells the men that he comes from Bogota in a country where people can see. Sensing that Núñez is not like them, the men hold him fast and examine him with their hands. As they perceive the malformation of his eyes, Núñez assures them that he can see. Because Núñez appears to be speaking nonsense words, such as "sight" and "see," they decide he is a wildman and give him the name of "Bogota."

When Núñez is taken before the elders, who have long since abandoned belief that the people of the valley ever had sight, he realizes that what he perceives as a miraculous gift is deemed as a flaw by those around him. He cannot even make the people understand that they are blind. After failing to impress them with his superior ability, Núñez considers using force; however, as a civilized person he cannot strike a blind man.

One day, Núñez walks on grass that is in a protected area and he refuses to get back on the path. The villagers drive him outside of the city walls. After two days without food and shelter, he returns and attempts to come to terms with his captors. Claiming that he now is wiser, he repents of all he has done. The blind people regard his rebellion as a mark of general idiocy; they whip him and give him the simplest and heaviest work to do. Seeing no alternative, Núñez acquiesces.

Núñez's adoptive family is that of old Yacob. Yacob's youngest daughter is Medina-Sarote, who is little esteemed in the world of the blind because her closed eyelids are not sunken as those of the other blind people. Finding her attractive, Núñez tells her about his ability to see and she appears to understand. Eventually Yacob understands that Núñez wishes to marry Medina-Sarote. Although no other village man wants to marry Medina-Sarote, there is opposition. Her sisters oppose it on the grounds that it discredits them, Yacob on the grounds that Núñez is an idiot, and the young men on the grounds that it will corrupt the race. Medina-Sarote is inconsolable, so Yacob goes to the elders to ask for advice. One of them who is a great doctor and philosopher believes that Núñez is better than when he first arrived and that he can be cured. The cure is to make Núñez just like everybody else—blind. "Thank Heaven for science," Yacob states.

The choice belongs to Núñez. He has believed that Medina-Sarote understands the meaning of sight, but he soon realizes that she does not. She urges him to subject himself to the surgery that will remove his eyes, but he elects not to do so. At first he intends to simply retreat to a place of solitude, but he instead leaves the city and begins to climb out of the valley, satisfied merely to escape from the valley in which he had thought he would become the king.

*Themes and Meanings*

"The Country of the Blind" aptly reflects H. G. Wells's criticism of both human limitations and possibilities. It illustrates his belief in the gradual advancement of humanity through evolution and scientific innovation in which the ideas of liberated individuals intrude on a conformistic society. Núñez, figuratively, is the person of imagination in revolt against his social environment. He is the person who sees among those who do not see. As a symbol of an open mind among conformists, he is the opposite of the author's perception of the average, admirable citizen. The average citizen to Wells is a person dominated by the everyday routine of obtaining the physical necessities of life. This citizen is a person of prejudice, convention, habit, and imitation. All of this deprives the person of spiritual appetite, of a thirst for knowledge. It is this characterization of the blind men that gives the story its profoundly pessimistic outlook.

The symbolic meaning of the story hinges on the fact that the gift of sight symbolizes the human mind. Sight is a human being's reason; it creates the urge to think and search for truth. To live in blindness or darkness means to live in ignorance. Núñez's fate is meant to reflect the fate of the bearer of the light of truth. He offers spiritual light that has literally fallen from heaven in an attempt to enlighten the darkened minds of humankind. The blind men, however, do not acknowledge his mission nor do they accept it or honor his insight. Instead, they try to draw him into their darkness, even to blind him. The instrument for this is woman, with her power over the senses, and whom Núñez at first believes has an understanding of the spirit. Thus, as in many of Wells's other works, the idea that the demands of sexual love and society are dangers to the free spirit of humankind is an integral part of the story.

At the end of the story, it is obvious by Núñez's escape to where he came from originally that the spirit no longer has a place in the world. Humankind does not want intelligence, the guidance of the wise, nor anyone to know more than anyone else. Ignorance is bliss, and ignorance will be defended by the multitude through force. Wells explained, "It is always about life being altered that I write, or about people developing schemes for altering life."

*Style and Technique*

Though the story is not typical of Wells's work, its narrative movement is as forceful and as well controlled as his earlier writings, and it is often classified among his finest achievements in short fiction. The story itself resembles a novella in that the topic is an extraordinary event; the setting and the plot are inherently connected; it has a turning point; it has a central symbol; and it has an obvious moral. The story is set as a leitmotif: the title is mentioned in the first sentence and then repeated several times. Thus, setting and story are a unified whole. In this way, its meaning is stressed and brought constantly to the forefront of the reader's mind.

Wells uses apparently trivial items of action and commonplace information to give an almost believable format to a fantastic story. For example, the setting is presented in the manner of an objective report: exacting geographical locations, details of the catastrophic event, and pseudoscientific language. The free play of imagination within this format of realistic fiction is typical of Wells's ability to invert life, to turn it inside out.

*Lela Phillips*

# THE COUNT'S WIFE

*Author:* Dino Buzzati (Dino Buzzati Traverso, 1906-1972)
*Type of plot:* Fantasy
*Time of plot:* The 1970's
*Locale:* The home and estate of the protagonist
*First published:* "La moglie con le ali," 1971 (English translation, 1983)

*Principal characters:*
COUNT GIORIO VENANZI, the protagonist, a wealthy farm owner
LUCINA, his wife
HIS MOTHER
DON FRANCESCO, the family chaplain
MASSIMO LAURETTA, the best friend of the Count and Lucina

## The Story

Giorgio Venanzi, a thirty-eight-year-old count and squire of a province, is caressing the back of his wife, Lucina, when he feels a small protuberance on her left shoulder blade. Alarmed, Giorgio inspects the lump carefully with two magnifying glasses, which reveal only that the lump is covered with a fine down.

The next morning, Giorgio examines his wife's back again and finds another lump matching the first, at the apex of her right shoulder blade. The lumps are significantly wider now and contain minuscule soft, white feathers. His wife seems to be growing wings. Giorgio's anxiety has turned to depression; the monstrous growths suggest to him witchcraft rather than miracle.

Giorgio's depression cannot be attributed to concern for his wife but rather to a fearful reaction to the unknown. University-educated in agriculture, vigorous, and apparently active, he is nevertheless conventional to a fault, unimaginative, poorly cultured, and painfully jealous. His wife, eighteen years old, delicately small and beautiful, married him not out of love but to please her parents, who wanted her to marry someone of their own noble class. Lucina lives a fairly restricted life, mainly because of her husband's jealousy, but she does not complain, having grown accustomed to Giorgio, who is, after all, greatly enamored of her.

Giorgio questions Lucina about her recent activities, suspecting the work of gypsies, then insists that Lucina see no doctors. He leaves the house, mainly not to be looking at her back the whole day. He is still obsessed, however, with his wife's monstrosity. For his beautiful wife to sprout wings and become a spectacle is horrible enough, but the threat of scandal, the threat that his dignified family may be subject to ridicule, troubles him even more.

When Giorgio returns home, his worst fears are materialized: The two protuberances have taken the unmistakable form of wings, similar to those on angels in churches. Lucina, to Giorgio's irritation, is undisturbed and apparently enjoying herself, even laughing through these changes in her.

Giorgio consults his mother, who is equally horrified—reminding Giorgio that she never liked the marriage—and she recommends their talking with Don Francesco, the family chaplain. At first incredulous, the good-humored old priest views the wings of Lucina, who reveals them by unzipping the two vertical zippers she has put on the back of a cotton dress she has made. Don Francesco decides that the wings are either the work of the devil, in which case they are merely illusory, or a gift of God, in which case they are genuine, and functional, wings. To determine which is the case, Lucina must soon attempt flying. Against his wishes, Giorgio agrees to a test flight.

Accordingly, one night Giorgio, Lucina, Giorgio's mother, and Don Francesco drive out to a clearing in a remote forest of Giorgio's holdings, and Lucina attempts a flight. It is not long before the wings, which are now more than three meters across when fully spread, lift the light, frail body of Lucina, who is immediately intoxicated with exhilaration, feeling more happy and beautiful than ever before. Don Francesco, moved by the flight as well as by Lucina's beauty, declares that the wings are a divine investiture. Lucina is an angel. Though Don Francesco argues that Lucina must not be locked up in secrecy, believing she has some divine mission, perhaps as "a sort of new messiah, of the female sex," Giorgio insists on keeping her change a secret. He curses the possibilities of "gross headlines . . . interviews . . . every kind of annoyance."

Giorgio is convinced that his wife will accept her imprisonment at home, but she grows increasingly restless, unable to accept this fate: "less than twenty years old . . . chained in her house without being able to . . . look out the window." She takes advantage of the dense October fog by taking clandestine flights from her garden, which bring her "a blissful delirium."

One afternoon, Lucina's confidence betrays her, and she is seen flying by Massimo Lauretta, a brilliant young man who is best friend to her and her husband. She must speak to him while still in flight so that he will not mistake her for a bird and shoot her. At sight of Lucina alighting before him, Massimo kneels and begins praying the "Hail Mary." Both of them nervous and excited—Massimo by Lucina's angelic beauty and Lucina by the delirium of flight and, perhaps, the wonderful freedom to be with someone—they have a brief, tender exchange. Massimo offers to take her into a cabin, out of the cold, and Lucina declines, fearful of being seen by the gamekeeper within. Then:

They stood a little while watching one another puzzled. Then Lucina said:
"I'm cold, I told you. At least hold me."
Although the young man was still trembling, he didn't need to be told twice.

In the next scene of the story, Giorgio is returning home to find his wife, wingless, calmly sewing in the parlor. Giorgio is confused, shocked, and relieved. Some months later, Giorgio explains to Lucina, "God really loves you. . . . You were able to meet the Devil at the right moment." He has overcome his jealousy and possessiveness for the relief of having his wife normal again, safely returned to a conventional existence with him.

*Themes and Meanings*

"The Count's Wife" dramatizes one of Dino Buzzati's characteristic interests, humankind's preoccupation with fear, particularly of the unknown or anything that transcends understanding. In this story, it is the protagonist who is preoccupied, and his fear is of the monstrous, inexplicable deformity of his wife. Buzzati has created here a man without imagination, who is easily challenged by anything outside the conventions of his household and village. His own life is routine and unimaginative. He has married a beautiful young woman of nobility, apparently because of his great attraction to her ("he regarded her as the most fascinating woman in the town"), and he keeps her fairly isolated from the rest of the world while he occupies himself with tending his farms and pursuing the peasant girls. He is, in other words, in control of his world. He thus becomes an ideal target for fear and ironic reversal. His wife's wings threaten to wrest him from his privileged position of control by exposing his family to unwanted attention and subjecting his name to scandal. It is one of the protagonist's weaknesses that he can imagine no result of his wife's being appointed by God other than the ruin of his own quiet, conventionally respectable life. He and his wife are both victimized by this weakness. If Buzzati enjoyed depicting man as mainly fearful in face of things unexplainable, he has here made his point especially clear by portraying a man whose small-mindedness is easily transcended.

*Style and Technique*

Many qualities of this tale are reminiscent of fables. It is simply and directly told in the third person, lacking in ornament and almost devoid of explanation. It is almost purely narrative, moving action quickly and keeping dialogue spare. The opening lines, "One night Count Giorgio Venanzi, a thirty-eight-year-old landowner and squire of his province . . . " echo many qualities of fables: the nonspecific time reference "One night" (echoic of "Once upon a time"), the title of the protagonist, and the medieval sounding "squire of his province." It is a story in which one might be prepared to find winged angels and possible allegorical suggestions. The angelically pure wife falling, as a result of the influence of her husband's spiritual blindness, does invite an allegorical reading (purity loses to the evil of ignorance or self-centeredness).

Irony is the dominating literary device of the story. The plot leads step by step to the bitterly humorous, final irony: The formerly jealous, possessive husband is relieved to know that his wife has been adulterous, for by meeting the devil she returned their life to normal. This irony is made more striking by Buzzati's careful preparation for it. The husband's jealousy is depicted more and more intensely as his protectiveness becomes a mania. At the same time, his horror at the possibility of his wife's bringing shame to his name and personal ruin to him also crescendos so that at the end these two emotions are nearly indistinguishable. The concluding irony is the focal point, or target, of the story, resolving these two tensions simultaneously.

*Dennis C. Chowenhill*

# THE COUP DE GRÂCE

*Author:* Ambrose Bierce (1842-1914?)
*Type of plot:* Horror
*Time of plot:* 1862
*Locale:* An American Civil War battlefield
*First published:* 1891

> *Principal characters:*
> CAPTAIN DOWNING MADWELL, the protagonist, a Union Army
> officer
> SERGEANT CAFFAL HALCROW, his wounded friend
> MAJOR CREEDE HALCROW, Caffal's brother and the superior
> officer of Madwell, whom he hates

## The Story

Major Creede Halcrow is the commanding officer of a Union Army infantry regiment from Massachusetts that is in combat during the Civil War. Captain Downing Madwell commands one of Halcrow's companies. Sergeant Caffal Halcrow, the major's brother, is an enlisted man in Madwell's company. When Madwell was a second lieutenant in the regiment, Caffal was such a close friend that he joined as an enlisted man in order to be with him. Although the two men had each risen in rank, it was hard to maintain their friendship because military protocol created a "deep and wide" gulf between them.

One day as the regiment is on outpost duty a mile ahead of its main unit, it is attacked in a forest but holds its ground. Major Halcrow approaches Captain Madwell and orders him to take his company forward to hold the head of a ravine until the company is recalled. Halcrow offensively suggests that if Madwell is apprehensive, he may order his first lieutenant to go into the dangerous area instead. Just as sarcastically, Madwell agrees to take command personally and expresses the hope that the major will go along—preferably on horseback—so as to present a "conspicuous" target. He adds, "I have long held the opinion that it would be better if you were dead." A half an hour after their ordered advance, Madwell and his company are driven back with a third of their men dead or dying. The rest of the regiment has been forced back several miles. With his company scattered through the forest, Madwell finds himself alone until he comes on Sergeant Halcrow, who has been horribly wounded.

Madwell examines his friend, finds his abdomen torn open with part of his intestine exposed and evidence that wild swine have been gnawing on him as well. The doomed man is in unbearable pain and cannot speak, but with his eyes he silently pleads for "the blessed release, the rite of uttermost compassion, the *coup de grâce.*" Madwell's tears fall on his friend's agonized face. As Madwell walks by himself for a moment, he sees wild pigs racing out of sight. Then he sees a horse with a shell-smashed leg.

Without a thought, he dispatches the wounded creature with a revolver shot. The dead beast soon has "a look of profound peace and rest." Returning, Madwell puts his revolver to his friend's forehead and pulls the trigger. Nothing happens. He has used his last cartridge on the horse. He then draws his sword and resolutely pushes its point through Caffal's heart and deeply into the ground beneath. Just as the dying man tries instinctively to withdraw the weapon with his hand, three men approach. Two are stretcher bearers. The third is Major Halcrow.

*Themes and Meanings*

First published as "A Coward" in 1889, "The Coup de Grâce" is one of the most bitter tales by the celebrated horror-story writer Ambrose Bierce. Bierce was a Union Army infantry and topographical officer during the Civil War. Between 1861 and 1865, he saw action in major battles at Shiloh, Murfreesboro, Stone River, Chickamauga, Chattanooga, and elsewhere. After receiving a severe head wound at Kennesaw Mountain in June, 1864, he recovered in time to participate in part of General William Tecumseh Sherman's Georgia campaign. Bierce often saw hideous, useless, and indiscriminate carnage, and the memories of it colored his life and literary production ever after. A graphic example is "What I Saw of Shiloh," a reminiscence that he wrote in 1881, long after the war. In his characteristic prose, he describes a "variously hurt" soldier, details his ghastly head wound, and closes with this statement: "One of my men . . . asked if he should put his bayonet through him. Inexpressibly shocked by the cold-blooded proposal, I told him I thought not; it was unusual, and too many were looking." This memory was surely an inspiration for "The Coup de Grâce."

War was not merely the central experience of Bierce's life; it became his metaphor for life itself—whether in wartime or in times of so-called peace. In Bierce's view, life is a meaningless struggle against incomprehensible forces. Because it is futile to understand such imponderables, we should not bother trying. What we can do, however, is be aware of life's grotesque ironies, not grow too disappointed when things turn out badly, and try to laugh, though perhaps with considerable bitterness and scorn.

It is darkly instructive to trace the complexly knotted motives of the three central characters in "The Coup de Grâce" and those of Bierce himself in writing it. Caffal Halcrow enlists to be near his friend Downing Madwell but is rigidly separated from him by rank and is eventually killed by him. Major Creede Halcrow orders Madwell into an action that causes his brother to be fatally wounded. Madwell finishes off his friend with his sword, which Caffal instinctively grabs—with the ironic result that the merciful action looks like murder. Presumably, the relief trio has come to aid but witnesses a killing. Looking more deeply into the story, we can wonder whether Major Halcrow should objectively be relieved that his brother's agony has ended. Could the wounded man possibly have been saved if he had not also been stabbed? It is certain that the major ordered the captain into risky combat hoping that he would be killed. When the story ends, is Major Halcrow fiendishly delighted that his enemy is in his clutches, even when he considers the circumstances? Deep down, does he figure that if only his own brother died, his enemy would at least be deprived of the sort of friendship that he himself can never know?

In "The Coup de Grâce," Bierce surely seeks to dramatize the folly of human planning. Everything turns out wrong here. Madwell and Caffal, friends who are separated by the military code, fight bravely, perhaps hoping for at least a surly commendation. Instead, they end up in misery—short for one, prolonged for the other—and this because fate sees to it that Madwell's major observes his self-sacrificing act of mercy to his friend. For Bierce, the story is no less than a blood-curdling parable illustrative of the human condition.

*Style and Technique*

Of the many authors who wrote about the Civil War, Bierce was probably the most intensely involved; he saw the most horrific action and was influenced the most pervasively. His literary style, which was a function of these experiences, combines irony, incongruous diction, and photographic detachment.

It is ironic (that is, when one is led to expect something but is surprised by an opposite outcome) that two friends in the same military unit cannot remain close because one is an officer and the other is not. It is ironic that when a major orders his personal enemy into danger, his own brother dies. It is ironic that a man who mercifully kills a friend is likely to be court-martialed and ordered shot by the dead man's brother. Madwell will later have occasion to ponder the irony of his expressed hope for his enemy's demise.

Bierce's language is deliberately unsuited to the drama that he narrates. For example, after the murderous battle, the burial squad is said to be "tidying up." When Madwell first finds his injured friend and gently touches his face, we read that "it screamed." Just after Madwell shoots the horse, it "grin[s]" before it dies. Bierce describes the battlefield tree trunks at twilight as "a tender gray." Nature, as well as Bierce, seems contemptuous of the human condition.

As Bierce has his protagonist approach the hungry swine, his description resembles that of a movie script: "On the crest of a low, thinly wooded hill . . . several dark objects moving about among the fallen men—a herd of swine." He focuses on one: "Its forefeet . . . upon a human body, its head . . . depressed and invisible"; seen closer, "the bristly ridge of its chine . . . black against the red west."

It remains to praise the crisp structure of "The Coup de Grâce," which is presented in three distinct parts. First, Bierce describes the scene after the gory battle—the general confusion, then specific rows of corpses, and finally Madwell's return to the forest where he finds his friend. Second, a summary flashback sketches the background of his three central characters. Finally, Madwell undertakes well-intentioned actions—with unexpected and hideous consequences. Characteristically, Bierce breaks off his bitter tale abruptly, leaving the reader to speculate on the probable consequences.

*Robert L. Gale*

# THE COURTING OF SISTER WISBY

*Author:* Sarah Orne Jewett (1849-1909)
*Type of plot:* Regional, frame story
*Time of plot:* The late nineteenth century
*Locale:* A New England village
*First published:* 1887

> *Principal characters:*
> A WALKING WOMAN, the unnamed narrator
> MRS. GOODSOE, his storytelling friend
> MRS. JERRY FOSS, a widow whose three children have died
> JIM HERON, an Irish fiddler
> ELIZA WISBY, a well-to-do townswoman
> SILAS BRIMBLECOM, a back-country farmer turned deacon
> PHEBE BRIMBLECOM, his daughter

*The Story*

While walking one August day in a sunny pasture, the female narrator encounters Mrs. Goodsoe, her old friend, gathering a medicinal herb called mullein. They sit, eat some peaches the narrator has brought along, and chat. Mrs. Goodsoe needs little prompting as she reminisces garrulously. First, she mentions Mrs. Peck, a widow who had two daughters. One of them was forsaken by a "rovin'" boyfriend; the other married Jim Heron, the first Irishman ever seen in the region. Remembering Heron reminds Mrs. Goodsoe of Mrs. Jerry Foss, a hard-scrabble widow whose three children suddenly died of scarlet fever in a single horrifying week. She fell into a stony anguish until Heron was summoned. He played magically soothing music on his fiddle, and charmed the distraught mother into tears, a gentle sleep.

The narrator uproots some goldthread, a bitter herb that Mrs. Goodsoe recalls Eliza Wisby savored so often that it "puckered her disposition." Mrs. Goodsoe proceeds to tell Eliza Wisby's story. It seems that Silas Brimblecom, a back-country farmer, was easily persuaded by an itinerant preacher to leave his wife in favor of an evidently beckoning "spirit bride." Angelic enough but no housekeeper, this creature soon died. Silas returned to his flesh-and-blood wife, a forgiving homebody. Then she died. He joined the recently established Christian Baptist church, was promoted to country deacon, and came to town to attend a church assembly scheduled to last four days. As a joke, some townspeople sent him to Sister Wisby to ask her for room and board. Though well enough off and standoffish too, Eliza surprisingly accepted Silas, soon "bawled and talked" alongside him during their church meetings, and actually "went a-courtin' o' him." This led to a trial marriage in November, much to the neighbors' annoyance. The two planned to make their relationship official in the springtime. However, they did not, and Eliza ejected him in April. Cruel neighbors, mainly boys, guffawed at his retreat. Because Eliza had boarded Silas free, she decided to call him back and have him repay her by doing some garden chores. Not only did they get married, but in time Eliza welcomed Silas's pleasant daughter Phebe into their household. Silas took to drink. Eliza cared for him conscientiously but trusted him with nothing and willed most of her property to Phebe. Mrs. Goodsoe and the narrator finish their tasty peaches and, at the older woman's suggestion, plant the pits in the pasture ground where they have been talking. She says that the pits will become trees in due time and, moreover, that she would like to be buried right there herself.

## Themes and Meanings

The twofold purpose of Sarah Orne Jewett's best stories, of which "The Courting of Sister Wisby" is one, is to depict in graphic, ironic, frequently humorous detail the harsh but usually spine- and soul-strengthening conditions that challenged late nineteenth century New Englanders, particularly those living in rural, coastal Maine, and to reveal the endurance, and ultimate dominance, of often mistreated women in old New England's cramping physical and social environment.

The relationship of the narrator and Mrs. Goodsoe is thematically significant. The younger woman begins by saying she felt tempted to go for a stroll into the pasture. Enticed to venture farther, into higher land, she is drawn by "an invisible messenger" to a spot where she encounters Mrs. Goodsoe, who immediately says that all morning she has been thinking "these twenty times" of the younger woman. The two are attuned in an extrasensory way. Mrs. Goodsoe explains that she doubtless inherited her mother's Scotch-Irish family's "second sight" and ability to foretell events. However, even while lecturing the narrator on herbs with the indulgence of an expert to a neophyte, she is modest enough to praise her own mother's superior herbal lore, much of which, she sadly adds, died with her.

The narrator combines courtesy, deference, and determination; she prompts Mrs. Goodsoe not to stray by seemingly extraneous chatter from what becomes the main topic, which is Eliza and Silas. Clearly, not all of Jewett's women are bracing inspirations. We learn that Mrs. Foss never appreciated her Celtic husband's musical wizardry. Silas's "spirit wife" was a husband stealer and is ridiculed as a poor housekeeper. Also, Eliza is initially motivated by sexual frustration only partially overcoming her ingrained stinginess. Mrs. Goodsoe, eager to right the balances, does say that Eliza was habitually kind when neighbors fell sick.

Jewett's characters endure and prevail only when they come to terms with harsh reality. When Mrs. Peck's daughter was abandoned, she failed to accept her setback but instead went "into screechin' fits"; however, others, like Mrs. Foss, renew their resilience. Still others, like Eliza, make a virtue of necessity; she ministers to alcoholic Silas and bequeaths Phebe money to smooth that young woman's future. Jewett's best characters rely little on attending noisy church services. Mrs. Goodsoe digresses to excoriate a minister who once got himself foolishly all "wound up for a funeral prayer." Better, Jewett says, it is to commune with Mother Nature. In fact, Mrs. Goodsoe, who says that she is a behavioral Christian, figures to look, "when my time comes," right up through her planned-for grave site, in the old pasture cemetery near the trees she hopes will grow from the peach pits, and to see pleasant weather and sweet ferns. This sturdy woman prefigures Jewett's finest fictional character, Almira Todd, heroine of her finest work, *The Country of the Pointed Firs* (1896). Both are herbalists, have survived hardships, love nature, and have found their place in it.

*Style and Technique*

In "The Courting of Sister Wisby," Jewetts employs the formula of a first-person narrator repeating a story told by another. Mrs. Goodsoe, the central narrator, is a born storyteller—with seemingly total recall of events. Her speech patterns combine directness, pathos, and rural humor, and include folksy grammar mangling. Mrs. Goodsoe's gossip about one neighbor after another is reminiscent of dialogue in regional humorists from Mark Twain to William Faulkner. Its apparent wandering aimlessness conceals a solid structural unity. Her first tale concerns the natural goodness of Jim Heron. He materialized out of the dark forest to play restorative music. His last name echoes the title of Jewett's most popular short story, "The White Heron" (1886). The name Goodsoe is deliberately close to "good soul." By contrast, Brimblecom's exploitative quack religiosity is vilified, together with Eliza Wisby's hardly different failings. The two "lovers," if they may be so designated, survive for a time, and Eliza becomes humble and generous. Silas, the dependent male spouse, earns the nickname "Brimfull" pinned on him by critical neighbors.

By contrast, Mother Nature is brimful of gifts for those who love and respect her. Aspects of the landscape—sloping fields, nearby evergreens, vines, fences, wind off the coast, pennyroyal and a half dozen other named herbs, dangerous swamps, and berries—all harmonize as in an impressionistic painting to offer this message: Human nature and Mother Natue are, or should be, akin. When the narrator sees some berries, they "twinkled at me like beads." Later, when she fondly studies Mrs. Goodsoe's face, it appears as dried as "her mullein leaves" but also features "twinkling eyes." Relishing her peach, the old woman generalizes that "anything taste[s] twice better out-o'-doors." Unifying the story are contrapuntal contrasts: youth and age, conceit and generosity, mocking and loving, and new-fangled things versus the old ways. The narrator and Mrs. Goodsoe debate the difference between the cramped, narrow, but cooperative lives the oldsters remember, and the more expansive but less sociable behavior of youngsters, what with the advent of the telegraph and the railroad. Mrs. Goodsoe agrees that these two innovations have resulted in wider communication and travel, to be sure, but also the weakening of local considerations. She opines that now, if neighbors hear "a niece's child is ailin' the other side o' Massachusetts," they drop their immediate responsibilities and "off they jiggit in the [railroad] cars." She reckons that "Massachusetts has got to look after itself." More than remnants of such isolationist politics may be found in the United States today.

*Robert L. Gale*

# THE COUSINS

*Author:* Elizabeth Spencer (1921-　　)
*Type of plot:* Psychological
*Time of plot:* The 1950's and 1980's
*Locale:* Martinsville, Alabama, and Italy
*First published:* 1985

>*Principal characters:*
>ELLA MASON, the narrator and protagonist
>ERIC MASON, her cousin, whom she loved
>BEN, another cousin, now a professor
>JAMIE and
>MAYFRED, other cousins
>DONALD BAILEY

## The Story

Ella Mason, a twice married woman in her early fifties, recalls a European trip that she and four cousins made thirty years earlier. The five of them—Ella Mason, Eric, Ben, Jamie, and Mayfred—are members of the "three leading families" of Martinsville, Alabama, who were, the narrator confesses, somewhat "snobbish" about their social position in the small town. They are all descended from a famous Confederate general. Ella, whose mother was a Mason, has the same great-grandfather as Eric.

On a visit to New York, Ella Mason has lunch with her cousin Ben, who surprises her by remarking that he has always felt that in some way it is her fault that "we lost Eric"—an allusion to the fact that their cousin has lived for many years in Florence, Italy. Stunned, "as though the point of a cold dagger had reached a vital spot," Ella determines to return to Italy, which she has not visited in thirty years, to see Eric and solve the riddle of his exile.

In Florence, Ella is surprised to find her cousin aged and stooped, no longer the handsome young law student whom she loved thirty years before. After dinner at a restaurant, the cousins sit on the terrace outside Eric's apartment, reminiscing about their early years and the trip that they once made with their other cousins.

Full of optimism and *joie de vivre* shortly after World War II, the cousins are in many ways alike but also different, each in his or her own way. Ben, a graduate student, intensely devoted to literature and especially the work of Edgar Allan Poe, becomes a father figure to the group, while Eric, then twenty-five, has just completed final exams in law school. The young Jamie is hungry for experience, to see all the museums and churches and to gamble at the casinos. Mayfred, a beautiful distant cousin of the group, shows up in New York where they are to board the ship, accompanied by Donald Bailey, whom she has just secretly married. Ella, a college student at the University of Alabama and the narrator, is still treated as a younger sister by Ben and Eric during the trip.

The visit to England, Italy, and France draws them together into an even tighter bond than their youth has done, enlightening them to much they had been denied in their provincial world. Although most of their time is spent in Italy, they also journey to Monte Carlo so that Jamie can gamble in the casino, where he wins a considerable amount of money before Mayfred insists that he leave. Mayfred's husband Donald becomes ill and returns to America; shortly thereafter Mayfred receives word that he must have an operation, so she returns home as well, leaving a lovesick Jamie to grieve.

During the trip, Ella is attracted to both Ben and Eric but gradually her devotion focuses on Eric, and while the others are away in Rome, the two of them carry on a brief but passionate affair, which ends when Eric determines that they should rejoin their cousins. (Thirty years later Ella is still attempting to discover why things did not work out between them, attached as they were to each other.)

When the group must return to America, they are sad, for the trip has been, as Ella later recalls, a "Renaissance" for all of them. Subsequently their lives diverge into their own distinctive paths. Ella marries, has two sons, and, when her husband dies, marries again, then divorces. Ben marries a Connecticut heiress and becomes a professor. Jamie, much influenced by the Italian experience, converts to Roman Catholicism, marries a Catholic girl, and rears a large family. Mayfred, after divorcing Donald, becomes a New York fashion designer and marries several more times. Eric, having failed his law exams, moves to Italy where he remains, marries, and works for an export business. He, like Ella, is now widowed.

Thirty years after that eventful trip, Ella and Eric recall the events of the past and ponder their significance. Ella has come to Italy to discover what happened between her and Eric and why Eric has chosen to live as an expatriate, but she finds no simple answers to any of her complex questions. "You and I," Eric asks her as they sit in the darkness, looking out over Florence, "we never worked it out did we?" Her response is "I never knew if you really wanted to. I did, God knows." He replies that while she was always on the move, his life had become static after failing his law exams; he could move, "but not with much conviction," so he left her to lead her own life.

The story ends with them talking in the dark, knowing that "midnight struck long ago." Most of their lives are now behind them, and answers to the puzzles of those lives are not readily available.

*Themes and Meanings*

Elizabeth Spencer is a southern author, born in Mississippi, who has lived much of her life in Italy and Canada. The influences of all these places and their interaction are evident in her fiction. Like many southern writers, she has an acute sense of place, and she is fascinated by the southern character, whose nuances she keenly perceives. Like Henry James, she became intrigued during her Italian sojourn with the interrelationship between Americans and Europe, an interest "The Cousins" clearly reflects. The visit abroad is a maturation process for these young people, who are well educated and well read but essentially provincial until their encounter with the ancient, artistic, religious, and social wonders of the Old World.

Clearly one of the predominant themes of the story is the inability of human beings to understand one another in any but the most limited sense, even though they have been reared together in the same background, with the same antecedents and influences. This lack of communication leaves them puzzled by the full implications of their actions; however, the sensitive characters in "The Cousins" have clearly grown emotionally and spiritually as a result of their experiences. Thus the European journey and its aftermath have not been lost on them, and their lives are more fulfilled from having known one another and having gone together through the events that occurred in their early maturity.

## Style and Technique

Spencer's story achieves much of its effect through the contrast of Ella and Eric as they are in their fifties with how they were thirty years earlier. This retrospective method allows for a reflection on the part of the middle-aged characters on what happened to them in their youth and in the intervening years. Because this is a first-person narrative, with all the events seen through the eyes of Ella Mason, the reader can only guess at the true feelings of the other characters that the narrator interprets for us. Henry James argued that one essential element for a good story or novel is a "fine central intelligence," on whose judgment the reader can rely; in Ella, Spencer has created just such a figure. Her tone and the depth of her reflection on events and characters convince us that she is a reliable reporter of what has happened and what its significance may be.

Spencer is one of the most skillful of modern American short-story writers, and one of her strongest points is her ability to create credible characters with whom readers can empathize. Although her most perceptive portrayals are usually women, her male characters are often equally convincing. She has a feeling for the subtle interrelationships among people that often go undetected by any but the most sensitive observers. Ella, the "fine central intelligence" in "The Cousins," comes as close as anyone can to understanding the implications of the events that occurred three decades before.

*W. Kenneth Holditch*

# COWBOYS ARE MY WEAKNESS

*Author:* Pam Houston (1962-    )
*Type of plot:* Psychological, regional
*Time of plot:* The early 1990's
*Locale:* Montana
*First published:* 1987

> *Principal characters:*
> THE NARRATOR, a single woman about thirty years old
> HOMER, her current boyfriend, a naturalist
> MONTE, a cowboy on the ranch at which she and Homer are
>     staying
> DAVID, the owner of the ranch

*The Story*

An unnamed female narrator begins her story with a description of her romanticized picture of an ideal relationship, in which a woman has just kissed her bearded husband good-bye on their ranch. The narrator wishes she could paint the picture to see if she is the woman in the painting.

She has moved west from New Jersey and now lives in Colorado. She has always been attracted to cowboys and is involved with an emotionally distant wildlife specialist named Homer. Every year, Homer spends five weeks studying a herd of deer on a ranch in Montana, and this year the narrator goes with him, primarily because she knows if she does not, some other woman will. She was once madly in love with Homer, but by the time they arrive at the ranch, her passion for him is evaporating.

Homer spends all the daylight hours at his observation post, seldom moving, and if the narrator goes with him, she is not allowed to move or talk except when he does. Homer's contract to study the deer is up the week before Thanksgiving, and the narrator is excited about being home to prepare a holiday feast because her family always traveled over the holidays. Homer thinks her plans are childish and decides to stay another week at the ranch.

The narrator becomes friendly with the ranch owner, David, a poet and vegetarian who practices sustainable organic ranching and will not hire ranch hands who smoke cigarettes. She realizes that David is the type of man to whom she should be attracted but never is. When she and David share tea and take walks on the ranch, he tells her about the woman that Homer had an affair with the previous year and how devastated the woman was when Homer ignored her calls and letters after he left.

One afternoon, Homer and the narrator engage in unprotected sex, and she begins to consider the consequences. Because Homer has always been careful about birth control, the narrator begins to imagine that he has done this deliberately because he wants to settle down and raise a family with her. However, Homer coldly makes it clear that he does not intend to have a child with her, prompting her to observe that one of her problems in relationships with men is inventing thoughts for them that they do not have.

The next day the narrator meets Monte, a cowboy on the ranch. Monte observes her struggling to help Homer weigh a deer that had been killed and asks her to go to the Stockgrowers' Ball with him that night. At first she declines because she has agreed to cook dinner for Homer and David, but after Homer scoffs at Monte's invitation, she reconsiders. She borrows clothes for the dance and rides there with two of Monte's friends, who tell her how wonderful Monte is and how he suffered after his wife left him.

At the dance, Monte presents the narrator with a corsage of pink roses. The flowers clash badly with her orange blouse, but she is so delighted that she blushes. After dinner and speeches, the dancing starts, and Monte and the narrator dance together beautifully until 3 A.M. She begins to fantasize that she could settle in Montana with Monte. On the drive home, they have little to talk about but their horses; however, she is busy planning how to respond when he asks her to go to bed with him. When they arrive at their adjoining cabins, however, he says only that he would like to kiss her if he did not have a mouthful of chewing tobacco.

The narrator decides to go home for Thanksgiving without Homer. When she is getting ready to leave, Homer announces that he wants to marry her and treats her with unusual attention and kindness. However, she no longer cares. As she is driving off, Monte gallops up on a chestnut horse to say good-bye and ask her to write him and come back to visit. As she drives through Wyoming, listening to country songs in which all the women are victims, she realizes that life on a ranch in Montana will not be her happy ending.

## Themes and Meanings

"Cowboys Are My Weakness," like many of the tales in Houston's short-story collection of the same name, concerns the problems many women face in finding and sustaining relationships and the tendency of some women to be attracted consistently to unsuitable men. The narrator, as the author was at the time of the story's publication, is a single woman living in the West. Since moving from her east coast home ten years earlier, the narrator has had several boyfriends, many tall and bearded like the man in her fantasy painting. Like many single women in the late twentieth century, the narrator is conflicted about her goals: She says she wants to settle down and be a rancher's wife, but she has remained involved with the clearly unavailable Homer for more than a year. She becomes immediately infatuated with the ranchhand Monte, even though she realizes that she and he have virtually nothing in common. In David, she recognizes a man who embodies the values she claims to be seeking, but she keeps him at a distance emotionally, although it is clear that he would reciprocate any interest she showed.

The story's narrator, typical of most of Houston's heroines, is both an independent woman of the 1990's and a vulnerable, needy person. The story is an excellent and well-known representation of the genre of stories told by and about single women who want to have it all but end up getting none of the things they say they want, except their freedom. Houston's stories differ from most such stories in that her locale is the rural West, rather than the more common urban environment, and her narrator is an active, adventurous, outdoor woman, unconcerned with style and glamour.

The picture in her mind that opens the story is referred to several times throughout the story. Other references indicate that the narrator is more interested in fantasizing about a solid relationship than working to create one. At one point, she says that despite her years of education, she has a "made-for-TV mentality" that she cannot get past in her relationships.

*Style and Technique*

The plot is linear, with most events presented chronologically. Houston uses small but significant details and well-chosen metaphors to create vivid pictures of the people and landscape of Montana. The narrator shares her situation with wry humor, behind which she may hide her vulnerability from herself but not from her reader.

Use of an unnamed narrator serves two somewhat contradictory purposes: First, telling the story in first person enables the author to speak to her reader in a chatty, conversational tone, much as a woman might share the story of her current relationship with a girlfriend, which gives the story a personal feeling. Second, it allows the author to hide information about her narrator, a device that emphasizes the narrator's abdication of power in her life but also creates distance between narrator and reader.

Unlike the narrator, each of the men in the story—even Monte's friends, who appear only briefly—is named, although only Monte is described physically. Little information is given about the narrator: The reader can guess that she is fairly short, but only because Monte is described as being much taller than she. Each of the other characters' jobs is specified, but there is no information about what the narrator does with her life other than go on field trips with Homer, obsess about Homer when she is not invited to go with him, and daydream about a fantasy relationship.

*Irene Struthers Rush*

# CRAZY SUNDAY

*Author:* F. Scott Fitzgerald (1896-1940)
*Type of plot:* Social realism
*Time of plot:* 1931
*Locale:* Hollywood
*First published:* 1932

*Principal characters:*

JOEL COLES, a motion-picture scriptwriter new to Hollywood, the son of a once-successful actress

MILES CALMAN, a famed motion-picture director for whom Joel has written

STELLA CALMAN, the motion-picture star Stella Walker and wife to Miles Calman

*The Story*

Joel Coles, a twenty-eight-year-old screenwriter, son of a once-successful stage actress, has spent his childhood between New York and London, trying to separate the real from the unreal. For six months he has been in Hollywood writing scenes and sequences for films as a continuity writer. He is invited to a Sunday cocktail party at the home of the Miles Calmans, a mansion in Beverly Hills "built for great emotional moments." Miles Calman is the most significant director at the studio; his wife is the star Stella Walker, whom Miles has created ("brought that little gamin alive and made her a sort of masterpiece"). Joel sees the invitation as evidence that he is getting somewhere in his career, as well as an opportunity to mix with the important people of the industry.

Though he resolves not to drink at the party—Miles Calman is "audibly tired of rummies"—Joel breaks his vow. As a result, he performs for the crowd a tasteless impersonation of a crass independent producer, Dave Silverstein, burlesquing the man's cultural limitations. Tempted to show off for the attentive Stella Calman, Joel seizes on this routine, which has been well received at other parties. The result is disastrous: The feeling of the audience is expressed by the booing from an actor, the Great Lover of filmdom. "It was the resentment of the professional toward the amateur, of the community toward the stranger, the thumbs-down of the clan."

The next day, back at the studio lot, abashed and alarmed, Joel writes an apology to Miles but receives the following day a letter of praise from Stella and an invitation to her sister's Sunday buffet supper.

At the buffet, Joel learns of the Calmans' troubles—Miles's affair with actress Eva Goebel, his jealousy of Stella, his trials with his psychoanalyst, his mother fixation and its linking of sex with dependency. Joel is informed of this by the Calmans themselves, mostly Stella, back at the Calmans' house. It is obvious by now that Joel is falling in love with Stella and that Stella is using Joel to spur Miles's jealousy so that his attraction to Eva will be neutralized. The Pygmalion story of Miles and Stella—the creation that he brought to life with the marriage—is in peril, both Miles and Stella feeling they might lose the dream: he as artist/fairy godmother, she as Pygmalion/Cinderella. Eva is Stella's best friend; Joel is considered by Miles a friend and confidant.

Monday, at the studio, Joel is invited by Stella to escort her to the Perry's Saturday dinner and theater party, for Miles is flying to the football game at South Bend.

On Wednesday Joel asks Miles about the flight to the football game and about the party, finding that Miles is indecisive because of his jealousy and guilt: He might stay, he thinks, and escort Stella safely to the party. Reassured when Joel says that he is not even planning to go to the party, Miles asks him to go, for he likes Joel. The problem, says Miles, is that he has trained Stella to like the men he likes.

Miles flies east to attend the game and sends Stella telegrams from there, yet she insists that he could have had the telegrams sent falsely and could be observing what she does. What she has done is to take Joel into her house and seduce him, or anyway, to invite his seduction of her. This occurs just before midnight, but the result is that Joel becomes aware that she still loves Miles, a fact she admits. Just past midnight, on the third Sunday of the story, a phone call informs Stella of Miles's death in an airplane crash.

With the news of Miles's death, which Stella refuses to accept, Stella's attitude toward Joel changes, from the distancing that accompanied and followed their lovemaking to begging him to stay the night with her and to make love to her. Joel realizes that Stella is trying to keep Miles alive by sustaining a situation and a problem in which he played an important part; she will play the role of the unfaithful wife that Miles's jealousy created, for she has found her existence in the roles Miles molded for her, and, in fact, has believed her very being to be a creation of his genius.

Joel will not give in to her, this time, under the circumstances. He takes charge, insists on and calls a doctor, and requests her friends to come to Stella's side. Is this an act showing that Joel has taken control of his life, or is it a tribute to the memory of Miles Calman and his creative genius? Joel will not stay with Stella, but he will be back if she needs him.

*Themes and Meanings*

"Crazy Sunday" is a story about the interrelationship of illusions and reality (or make-believe and actuality), of the difficulty people have separating them, and of the confusion of identity that results. Because the story's characters work in a profession that creates and markets illusions, the problem of personal identity is heightened and the thin line between acting and being is blurred. On Sundays, when they are not making films, they are thrown into the challenge of coping with the world of actuality. Because it is psychologically frustrating for them to contend with real problems of fidelity, jealousy, illness, and death, they tend to extend their work week and to find faith in the profession itself, to live in the office of creation. Their weekend lives are staged at parties in theater-like mansions. However, they are vulnerable: Miles is marked for death, Joel has a problem with alcohol, and Stella verges on hysteria with her insecurity.

Miles tries to turn his artistic creation, Stella Walker, into his real-life wife, but he cannot cope with that step in her transformation. Stella, with Miles's death and the loss of her creator-director, believes she cannot manage and pleads for Joel's support. Joel does not accept the real plea for help from Stella, for he still sees her as the little gamin whom Miles turned into a star.

Another theme in "Crazy Sunday" is the coexistence of the characters' glamour and emotional instability—Miles's psychological confusion and weariness of mind and body, Stella's insecurity amounting to complete dependence, Joel's drinking and naïveté. This dark side is also evidenced in the coarse makeup of the film extras and the rummies who write the film scripts. The fact is that these are necessary accompaniments to the dream world they produce for the public and in which they themselves are caught.

### Style and Technique

The point of view of "Crazy Sunday" is that of a limited omniscient, or selected omniscient, narrator. Everything is seen as Joel sees it or could see it; thus, dramatic irony is provided by the contrast between Joel's perception of events and the deeper understanding afforded to the reader. When Joel makes a fool of himself at the Calman's party, he is conscious of his error, but when, at the end of the story, he makes a much more serious mistake, abandoning Stella, only the reader grasps the significance of Joel's action. Joel himself has lost the ability to distinguish between reality and fantasy, and thus he fails to see the reality of Stella's suffering.

This is a dramatic story with cinematic effects. There is a five-part structure, with three strong Sunday scenes separated by interims at the studio. The interims set up the logical business of the Sunday scenes. Each Sunday shows the humiliation of a different main character, first of Joel at the Calman's party, then of Miles being attacked for his adultery, and finally of Stella's collapse with grief at the news of Miles's death. In each scene, Joel's love for Stella progresses a step further, a commitment from which he later retreats.

The fully dramatized Sunday scenes (which include the Saturday of the Perrys' party, extending to the tragic early hours of Sunday) are visually oriented. Readers are constantly being directed to appearances, shapes, colors, positions. Moreover, the characters are always looking, seeing, noticing. In the world of "Crazy Sunday," only appearances count.

As usual with good F. Scott Fitzgerald stories, there is crisp, concise observation: "an Italian-colored sweater," "a dress like ice-water, made in a thousand pale-blue pieces, with icicles trickling at the throat," "under the pure grain of light hair." The descriptive language works well with the theme of glamorous make-believe threatened by reality.

*William E. Morris*

784

# THE CREATURE

*Author:* Edna O'Brien (1930-    )
*Type of plot:* Psychological
*Time of plot:* The twentieth century
*Locale:* A village in western Ireland
*First published:* 1974

> *Principal characters:*
> THE CREATURE, an Irish widow
> HER GROWN SON
> HER SON'S WIFE
> THE NARRATOR, a substitute teacher

## The Story

The story is narrated by a young woman getting over an unhappy love affair, who has come to a village in western Ireland as a substitute teacher. Fascinated with a widow whom everyone calls the "Creature," she seeks to befriend the woman. During visits to the Creature's house, the narrator is invariably served "a glass of rhubarb wine and sometimes a slice of porter cake" and hears the tales of the woman's meager, sorrow-filled life. During these visits, she learns that the Creature has been long separated from her only son and nearest living child. The Creature tells her how the son, after a long absence, returned and married a woman to whom the Creature had great hopes of becoming close. She secretly hoped that her daughter-in-law would pare her corns after the two women became intimate friends.

It happened, however, that the daughter-in-law is a selfish and ill-tempered woman who becomes increasingly intractable as she begins to have children of her own. Finally, she goads the son into betraying his mother. Through the eyes of the narrator, the reader sees the Creature as a loving, self-effacing mother whose daughter has emigrated to Canada and whose surly, pessimistic son has a wife who persuades him to take over the small family farm. The son convinces his mother that the farm should be deeded to him. It had been the sole home of the Creature and her own mother, another widow, who helped rear the Creature's children until she herself died. The townspeople dub the mother the "Creature" in part because they are repelled by her acquiescence in letting the son drive her from her home.

After leaving the farm, taking with her few belongings but among them an heirloom tapestry depicting ships at sea, the Creature sets up house in town, where the narrator learns that the Creature's greatest hope is for a joyful reunion with her son. After learning this, the narrator, motivated in part by her own loneliness and guilt, attempts to effect this reunion by going to the farm and convincing the son to visit his mother. On the eventful day, the narrator calls on the Creature and learns that when the son came, he accepted none of his mother's hospitality and left her feeling more forlorn than ever. The story ends with the narrator realizing that the Creature has been surviving on the hope that she and her son would reconcile. With all hope gone, the Creature is near despair, and the narrator, whose plans have failed, "wished that I had never punished myself by applying to be a sub in that stagnant, godforsaken little place."

### Themes and Meanings

The story's most pervasive theme concerns irrevocable, perhaps inherited, loss. From the Creature's loss of her father, to the loss of her husband, mother, and children, the story records a "tradition" of loss that is symbolized in the heirloom tapestry of ships perpetually at sea and in perpetual threat of destruction. The narrator, who is herself trying to recover from a love affair, becomes a player in this drama of loss—loss of family, innocence, and hope.

Attendant on this theme of loss is the role that landscape plays in the story. The story takes place in a remote part of western Ireland (the same region that James Joyce uses in his great story of loss, "The Dead"), where the narrator's unquestioning referral to the woman known simply as "The Creature," along with the town's godforsakenness, suggests that all the characters somehow assume the semblance of grotesqueness that marks their surroundings.

The theme of grotesqueness also pervades the story, from its very first line ("She was always referred to as the Creature . . . ") to its ending with its grotesque description of the town and its landscape. Every character in the story, including the narrator, is a victim of a social, emotional, moral, and psychological blight. Perhaps one aspect of this theme of grotesqueness is that Ireland—western Ireland in particular—is especially prone to spawn damaged, ill-begotten, and "blighted" individuals. Certainly the last line of the story suggests that, from the narrator's point of view, place plays an important role in situating this sorrowful drama.

Despite the story's insistent themes of loss, grotesqueness, and place, it also reveals the underlying themes: Where there is loss there may also be gain; where there is ugliness, there can also be beauty. Though the story ends on a remorseful note, the narrator does a superb job of revealing to the reader the poignancy of human feeling. Referring to the Creature only in subhuman terms serves to heighten the great beauty of her unconditional love for her son and her warm acceptance of the narrator. Although the brutality of the Irish landscape coincides with the meagerness of life there, by choosing her details wisely and selectively, Edna O'Brien depicts a scene in which redemption, although not achieved, remains a possibility so long as hope can be sustained. Meaning within the story emerges not out of resolution but out of struggle and the final failure, which is tempered by intention.

### Style and Technique

O'Brien's use of a first-person narrator to relate her story has advantages as well as limitations. As an educated and articulate woman, her narrator can articulate the pain of those who suffer mutely. However, this narrator also has special limitations as an observing consciousness. Not even she can penetrate the mystery of the Creature's full identity; she thus ends her narrative by still calling the woman for whom she feels such compassion "The Creature." Although this suggests that the woman possesses no true human identity, it simultaneously suggests that identity rests on more than names, labels, or reputations. Instead, the Creature's identity is captured and made alive for the reader by the narrator's greater attendance to the qualities of her character.

The use of a first-person narrator makes the reader always aware that the story is told through a limited point of view. However, this use of a first-person narrator also contributes to the authenticity of the story largely because the narrator is not simply telling a story from her own life; as an outsider reporting on the lives of others, she can achieve an objectivity that the principal characters do not possess.

O'Brien's story is short and she selects her details tellingly, giving the reader only as much information as is necessary for them to enter into the drama and feel compassion for the Creature and the narrator. For example, the narrator catalogs the personal possessions that the Creature carries with her—her clothing, her Aladdin lamp, and the tapestry—just as sparely as the life that the possessions detail. However, the selection of these details is accurate and revealing enough to create, within the story's small scope, a realism of the highest degree. At all times, the reader is made to feel that the locale, the people, and the motivations of the characters are true to the life that is lived in that "blighted" region of Ireland.

As an outsider, the narrator, despite her compassion for the Creature, does not redefine the identities of the characters as fixed for them by their surroundings. Though she comes to know the Creature better perhaps than anyone else, she nevertheless continues to call her the "Creature." Her consistent use of this pre-established identity of the main character allows her to remain apart from the factors that determine the characters' lives. By having the narrator fail in her attempt to reunite the mother and son, O'Brien reinforces her own refusal to view the story in sentimental terms. This results in ambiguity, which heightens the drama of an otherwise merely pitiful story. Ambiguity is evidenced by the fact that though the story is titled "The Creature," the reader always senses that the story is at least equally about the narrator and her own sense of loss, despair, and futility. Ultimately, the reader wonders who "The Creature" really is: the lonely mother or the narrator herself?

*Susan M. Rochette-Crawley*

# CRIERS AND KIBITZERS, KIBITZERS AND CRIERS

*Author:* Stanley Elkin (1930-1995)
*Type of plot:* Domestic realism, psychological
*Time of plot:* The 1950's
*Locale:* A street of small stores
*First published:* 1962

*Principal characters:*
> JAKE GREENSPAHN, an aging store owner
> HAROLD, his deceased son
> FRANK, his produce man and assistant manager
> HAROLD, his porter, an aging African American man
> AN IRISH POLICE OFFICER
> MARGOLIS, a television store owner
> MRS. FRIMKIN, a customer

## The Story

Jake Greenspahn returns to work in his small supermarket saddened and disillusioned by the death of his now idealized son, Harold. The story, told in third person in prose infected by Jake's vision and vocabulary, tracks his thoughts from a rejection of the seamy world to awareness that all mortals, including his Harold, are flawed. As participants in the imperfect processes of life, people must accept imperfections.

Jake, feeling bloated, his belly pressed against the steering wheel of his car, begins his day of disillusionment as he pulls in next to a parking meter. The Irish police officer, who accepts a bribe of two dollars a week to put nickels into parking meters for people who work in the neighborhood, is already giving out tickets. The police officer, aware that Jake's son, Harold, has died, expresses sympathy. He has sent Jake a condolence card, but his good intentions have been thwarted by the tasteless pink heaven depicted on the card and his thoughtless choice of a card bearing the Christian symbol of a cross for a person who is Jewish. When the police officer offers an inadequate excuse for missing the funeral, Jake ironically responds, "Maybe next time." The police officer refuses this week's two dollars from Jake, but Jake is not impressed.

His attitude darkened by his loss of Harold, who was just twenty-three when he died, Jake approaches his small supermarket. Violating Jewish law, which specifies a pine coffin, Jake had Harold buried in a metal casket that the mortician assured him would preserve the body. Still, Jake is intent on following another Jewish law by offering prayers in his son's memory at the synagogue for a year. He encounters Margolis, who owns the television store on the block. Margolis, bemoaning the decline in business during Jake's absence, clumsily tries to be sympathetic. Unimpressed, Jake sourly reviews the state of his supermarket. Frank, his able produce man and assistant manager, attributes the reduced profit during Jake's absence to repercussions from a strike in West Virginia, but Jake suspects that his employees are stealing from him.

The African American porter is late, and Howard, Jake's married butcher, and Shirley, the cashier, who has brazenly hung one of her brassieres on Jake's work pants, appear to be lovers. On top of it all, Jake is constipated.

As the workday proceeds, an old woman buys two cans of the on-sale coffee, returning several times and making the same purchase to get around the two-can limit. Siggie, the cheese salesperson, escapes when Jake tries to confront him about the bad cheese he has been delivering. Able to go to lunch because Frank has cramps and does not feel like eating, Jake sits with other store owners but is disturbed when he sees Harold and Shirley having lunch together. The thoughtlessness of his colleagues, including Margolis, who tease their fellow store owner Traub for not picking up any checks, annoys Jake. Traub has three daughters and a son to take care of. Everyone is either a crier or a kibitzer, Jake decides, a complainer or a tease and braggart like Margolis, who boasts about his trick of turning window shoppers into buyers. Jake, who owns the property on which his store and others are located, considers selling.

Still constipated, Jake endures Howard's disrespectful treatment of an old man who buys liver, hoping to sustain his strength. Jake is vexed when Frank shakes down—for ten dollars—a woman who tried to steal a can of salmon. When Jake upbraids Frank, he counters that Jake's son Harold filched five dollars from the cash register and was never punished. Angered by this assault on his dead son's character, Jake fires Frank, only to realize that he cannot do without him, and then apologizes.

The African American porter, also named Harold, finally arrives and overhears the argument. Jake is ready to upbraid old Harold for being late, but Harold explains that he was visiting young Harold's grave. Moreover old Harold has dreamt twice that Frank, not young Harold, was supposed to die, and assures Jake that if he wishes Frank dead, Frank will die. When dreams repeat themselves, they come true.

Jake dismisses the idea, but it further disturbs him. His annoyance turns to rage when Mrs. Frimkin, a doctor's wife who has been saccharinely sympathetic, undertakes to buy a shopping cart full of expensive items but damages a ten-cent loaf of bread in the hope of getting it at a reduced price. Frank tries to reason with Jake, pointing out that the rest of her order more than offsets the pennies lost, but Jake chases Mrs. Frimkin out of the store. He then rushes off himself to pray for his dead son.

That night, Jake Greenspahn dreams of himself, encouraged by the rabbi, trying to pray for young Harold. The rabbi encourages him to imagine his son and then pray, but Jake's efforts are disturbed by thoughts of his disillusioning day. His final vision is of young Harold, with his hand in the till, being caught by Frank.

### Themes and Meanings

Everything in "Criers and Kibitzers, Kibitzers and Criers" is tainted, marked by contradictions. People are sympathetic and self-seeking. The Irish police officer means well, but he shakes people down for two dollars and change a week. Margolis wants to be helpful, but he cheats customers. Jake's employees and customers both sustain him and rip him off. The taint hits even young Harold.

Jake's loss has depressed him and turned his vision dark, saturnine. According to primitive medicine, the cure for black moods is defecating, the elimination of black bile, but Jake is constipated. His wife, acquaintances, and employees tell him he has to let go, move on with life, but with his son dead and with no grandchildren, literally Jake is lost; he cannot relinquish his sense of loss.

At best, life entails compromises, but Jake's life is utterly compromised. Mortally wounded, he can compromise no more. He cannot countenance police, employees, colleagues, or customers who, though generally helpful, cheat in small ways. He wants everything to be wholly what it should be, but even poor Traub, whose very name means trouble, is silently an object of envy because he has living offspring.

Stanley Elkin, a product of the school of understated potently symbolic fiction, speaks to the issues of human fallibility and what it takes to survive in a mortal world. There are links that are intentionally left open in the story, even as life itself contains unresolved possibilities. Will Frank's cramp develop into an illness that kills him, as old Harold seems to sense? How did young Harold die? Was the note in Harold's handwriting actually a suicide note or was it only, as Greenspahn suspects, an unfilled order? In either case, Harold never filled the order mortal existence puts in at people's births, to carry the human species forward to the next generation. The only certainties Elkin embodies in this story are human imperfection and the fact of death.

## Style and Technique

Elkin writes in the everyday language of average people about the mundane experiences of common folks. In this story, he peppers his prose with the Yiddish expressions that would be natural to an aging Jewish store owner like his protagonist, Jake Greenspahn. Both the style and the quality of thought expressed in this third-person narrative are those of the store owner; this is the way Jake sees things in his present state, and this is how he thinks about them. However, under the surface of the seemingly mundane words and activities lies the symbolic poetry of great fiction. For example, the foreign spelling of the second syllable of the protagonist's name, Greenspahn, allows it, as pronounced, to mean both "span" and "spawn." Humans have a limited span of time in this green world. They spawn offspring, but like all other mortals, they eventually die. When they die before their parents, the biological reason for parenting disappears, especially if they die before producing offspring of their own.

The airtight metal coffin in which young Harold's body is enclosed will preserve a corpse, not Jake's living son. Moreover, for Jews, the act of preserving corpses is sacrilegious. It violates the millennia-old Jewish belief that mortal flesh must be returned to the earth, while spirit returns to the divinity. Therefore, even as Jake Greenspahn sees people morally compromised all around him, he himself is morally compromised with respect to his treatment of his dead son's body. The Kaddish, the prayer for the dead, which Greenspahn plans to say for his fallen son, honors a tradition that has been violated by the young man's coffin. Jake is already prevented from contributing to the physical survival of his people, and his failure compromises him spiritually.

*Albert Wachtel*

# A CRITICAL INTRODUCTION TO *THE BEST OF S. J. PERELMAN* BY SIDNEY NAMLEREP

*Author:* S. J. Perelman (1904-1979)
*Type of plot:* Parody
*Time of plot:* 1944
*Locale:* New York
*First published:* 1947

> *Principal characters:*
> SIDNEY NAMLEREP, a literary critic
> S. J. PERELMAN, a prominent American humorist

## The Story

S. J. Perelman uses Sidney Namlerep to comment on his style and subjects and to make fun of himself and any possible detractors in this "Critical Introduction" to *The Best of S. J. Perelman* (1947), a collection of forty-nine stories from four previous volumes. Namlerep (Perelman spelled backward) writes from 1626 Broadway (Perelman's office address) this "consideration" of a humorist who "certainly deserves the same consideration one accords old ladies on streetcars, babies traveling unescorted on planes, and the feebleminded generally."

Many of Perelman's stories begin as essays only to develop elaborate plots, but in "A Critical Introduction to *The Best of S. J. Perelman* by Sidney Namlerep," his narrator is concerned solely with attacking, while ostensibly explaining, the writer's supposed talent, his physique, and his sanity. All three defects are conjoined by the critic's claim that Perelman's "entire output over the past two decades has been achieved without benefit of brain."

Namlerep questions the writer's morality and his insistence on using arcane language. The two complaints merge when Namlerep analyzes a lengthy passage from a story entitled "Scenario," which ridicules the clichés of melodrama: "It is all very well to condone Perelman on the ground that he wrote the foregoing after extended servitude in Hollywood, but what if such passages were to fall into the hands of children? Particularly children who did not know the meaning of words like 'patchouli'?"

Namlerep also accuses his subject of being a phony. References to a Tattersall vest and the Cesarewitch Sweepstakes in "Kitchen Bouquet" imply that the writer is "an habitue of the tracks." However, the ever-diligent critic uncovers the truth. Twenty-four years previously Perelman borrowed a Tattersall vest to wear to a tea dance at his university, and ten years later he overheard two elderly jockeys discussing the Cesarewitch. "It was therefore inevitable," Namlerep concludes, "that, since Perelman suffers from what psychologists euphemistically term total recall, he should have dredged up these references when the opportunity arose."

The critic predicts a "disastrous future" for his subject because "the two most dominant themes" in his work are those involving women and money: "Obvious infantilism of this sort can be forgiven a gifted writer; in one so patently devoid of talent as Perelman, his continual absorption with the fleshpots indicates the need for speedy therapy." Namlerep suggests he "betake himself to that good five-cent psychiatrist he is forever prating about."

## Themes and Meanings

In "A Critical Introduction to *The Best of S. J. Perelman* by Sidney Namlerep," Perelman lampoons both introductions to books and literary criticism. He ridicules the pomposity of Namlerep by having him accuse Perelman himself of that and similar literary sins. Namlerep's ego, humorlessness, literal-mindedness, and vindictiveness represent both the narrowness and the excesses of literary criticism at its worst. Perelman's tongue-in-cheek presentation of Namlerep's inability to separate the man from the writer, his obsession with puerile psychological insights, and his almost religious fervor for the omnipotence of modern psychiatry show that such critics are not to be taken seriously.

Namlerep indicates both the triviality and the pedantry of his method when he supports his money-and-women theory by counting "thirty-seven direct allusions to the former and twenty-four to the latter." Most enjoyable of all is how blissfully unaware Namlerep is that he evinces all of Perelman's supposed weaknesses and superfluities in his own writing. Such an approach by Perelman is particularly appropriate because he is a practitioner of what his friend and colleague Robert Benchley called the "dementia praecox" school of humor.

In passing, Perelman comments on some of his usual subjects involving what passes for normality in twentieth century America. For example, Namlerep wonders how his subject "contrives to fulfil the ordinary obligations of everyday life—to get to his office, philander with his secretary, bedevil his wife, and terrorize his children."

## Style and Technique

All the elements that have made Perelman not only one of the best American humorists but also one of the most distinctive literary stylists are on display here. He has the largest working vocabulary of any American writer, rivaled only by Vladimir Nabokov, and, with boyish glee, he works the most uncommon words into his narrative: "bayaderes," "equinoctial," "lubricity," "midden," "palliate," "yokefellow," "zeugma." He also employs more familiar words in unusual senses: "blinked" to mean ignored.

Perelman's main subject is language, and he finds as much pleasure in the vernacular as in the esoteric. He glories in such clichés as "cheek by jowl" and "grain of sense." Even the occasional slang term such as "moola" slips in. The slang, clichés, and elevated language are not that amusing in themselves but rather in the masterful way that Perelman juxtaposes them. He is a literary vaudevillian, constantly juggling the sophisticated and the sophomoric.

Non sequiturs and plain silliness abound in "A Critical Introduction to *The Best of S. J. Perelman* by Sidney Namlerep." Mysteries of science include not only the common cold but also mixed bathing, and Namlerep describes the anger of the aroused author: "At the least suspicion of an affront, Perelman, who has the pride of a Spanish grandee, has been known to whip out his sword-cane and hide in the nearest closet."

Central to Perelman's style is hyperbole: "With fiendish nonchalance and a complete lack of reverence for good form, he plucks words out of context, ravishes them, and makes off whistling as his victims sob brokenly into the bolster." Namlerep charges that "what Flaubert did to the French bourgeois in *Bouvard and Pecuchet*, what Pizarro did to the Incas, what Jack Dempsey did to Paolino Uzcudun, S. J. Perelman has done to American belles-lettres." The latter example also illustrates the humorist's penchant for allusions, for the incongruous grouping of the famous and infamous, for the bizarre name.

"A Critical Introduction to *The Best of S. J. Perelman* by Sidney Namlerep" is a virtual catalog of this slapstick linguist's stylistic devices. It ends appropriately with the last of a long series of puns: "A plague on all his grouses!" Perelman epitomizes the joy of lexicology.

*Michael Adams*

# CRITIQUE DE LA VIE QUOTIDIENNE

*Author:* Donald Barthelme (1931-1989)
*Type of plot:* Domestic realism
*Time of plot:* Probably the 1970's
*Locale:* Probably New York City
*First published:* 1972

> *Principal characters:*
> THE NARRATOR, who is separated from his wife
> WANDA, his wife
> THE CHILD, their son

## The Story

This "critique of daily life" records the disintegration of the marriage of a young urban couple. The narrator, given to excessive drinking, retrospectively sketches a series of domestic clashes that highlight the nature of the conflicts between him and his wife, Wanda, and their unnamed child.

The narrator and his wife quarrel, sometimes violently and finally almost lethally, about various domestic matters, among them their child's behavior, a game of chess, the narrator's stinginess, and his abandonment of her. The father's relationship with the child is marked by his irritation with the child's requests, by his exasperation with the child's behavior, and by his fury at the child's inferences about his character.

In the final section, a separation has taken place, and the wife is visiting the narrator's bachelor quarters. A round of friendly toasts to each other quickly degenerates into mutual recriminations, and Wanda pulls a large pistol from her bosom and fires at her husband. She misses and instead shatters the bottle of liquor on the mantel. The concluding scene shows the wife in Nanterre, France, studying Marxist sociology while the husband is at home, content with his favorite brand of scotch: "And I, I have my J&B. The J&B company keeps manufacturing it, case after case, year in and year out, and there is, I am told, no immediate danger of a dearth."

## Themes and Meanings

Like many other stories by Donald Barthelme, "Critique de la Vie Quotidienne" is about failed relationships. The narrator, probably in his thirties, is thoroughly disenchanted with domestic life. He attributes his drinking to his boring evenings at home: "Our evenings lacked promise. The world in the evening seems fraught with the absence of promise, if you are a married man. There is nothing to do but go home and drink your nine drinks and forget about it."

The narrator scorns Wanda's attachment to *Elle*, the French magazine for women, to which she turns for trendy advice on food, fashions, interior decorating, and entertainment. Wanda herself is discontented. A French major in college, she now has little to do except "take care of a child and look out of the window." Sex is also a problem; Wanda withholds her sexual favors if the narrator does not behave properly, and he is inclined to visit a prostitute after fights with his wife. After the separation, Wanda charges the narrator with other failings, including stinginess when he hid the charge card or refused to pay to have her overbite corrected. Once he also forced Wanda to don a chauffeur's cap, drive him to the Argentine embassy, and wait outside with other chauffeurs while he chatted with the ambassador.

The narrator's relationship with the child is marked by deep hostility. The child, who significantly is never called by his first name, angers his father by asking for a horse. Also, the father remembers an unpleasant incident when the child, sleeping with them in a narrow hotel bed, urinated on the sheets. The father is aggravated, as well, by the child's constant, pervasive, and unpleasant singing, augmented by the television set and the transistor radio. The narrator does record one moment of a happy father-son relationship when he fixed the seat on the child's bicycle (after his wife had berated him for buying a cheap bicycle in the first place), but this is one of only two transitory interludes in a generally unhappy relationship.

Part of the hostility between them is rooted in the child's discerning understanding of his father's failing and fears. A discussion with his father about the life masks for a school project exposes the father's dread of death and his regret of the course that his life has taken. The discussion ends in a "certain amount of physical abuse" of the child by the father. The father's anxiety about getting old, which the son uncovers, is revealed as well in the final confrontation with the wife, when her attempt at murder is directly precipitated by his untactful remarks about signs of aging in her face.

"Critique de la Vie Quotidienne," as the title suggests, is an analysis of daily life. The narrator, bored with his domesticity, in conflict with his wife and child, and bedeviled by his own mortality, seeks relief in alcohol, which in turn exacerbates his relationships with his family and leads to eventual alienation and an attempt on his life. In a larger context, Barthelme is examining the prevalence of failed relationships in modern American society. At one point the narrator tells Wanda, "There has been a sixty percent increase in single-person households in the last ten years, according to the Bureau of the Census." She, however, fails to be consoled by his subsequent statement that they are part of a trend.

Barthelme's fiction in general shows a remarkable awareness of the surfaces of contemporary American life. He has a keen satiric eye for faddish brand names and trends and an accurate parodist's ear for clichés and fashionable phrases. "Critique de la Vie Quotidienne" reflects the ambience of a post-baccalaureate crowd of an urban center on the East Coast, probably New York City (the mention of a brownstone apartment and the *Times* is evidence for this), which is the location for some of his stories, many of which appeared, appropriately enough, in *The New Yorker* magazine. The narrator reads the *Journal of Sensory Deprivation*, a publication, probably fictional, whose subject matter was in style at the time of the story. However, it is Wanda who is most afflicted by the desire to be au courant. On the advice of *Elle*, she cultivates "the schoolgirl look." She dotes on pictures of restored mills in Brittany, and she comes to resemble, says the narrator, Anna Karina, an actress about whom the magazine has run innumerable pieces. Her choice of wines, sauces, and flatware all reflect a sharp concern with products and brands favored by a chic group. Her trip to France to study Marxist sociology with Henri Lefevre, the author of a book also titled *Critique de la Vie Quotidienne*, indicates her fashionably leftist tendencies. In France, Wanda also makes sure that her son does not suffer from a conventional education. She enrolls him in an experimental school conducted "in accord with the best Piagetian principles."

*Style and Technique*

Unlike many stories by Barthelme in which he ignores or distorts traditional techniques of fiction, "Critique de la Vie Quotidienne" is a readable and conventionally coherent story with clear plot and characterization. The self-revelation of the first-person narrator-protagonist is of particular interest. Although he is telling an essentially sad tale of domestic abuse, neglect, alcoholism, and separation, his manner of telling his story—detached, wry, and self-excusing—enhances the reader's perception of the irony. Although the narrator reveals his own flaws, he fails to criticize himself or to feel guilty for his role in the dissolution of his family.

Another distinctive aspect of the narration is the humor. The narrator tells his story by employing devices that Barthelme's narrators have used in many other stories, such as repetition. On learning about the child's making of life masks as a school project, the narrator says: "I cursed the school then, in my mind. It was not the first time I had cursed the school, in my mind." The story also displays the odd turns of phrase and unexpected juxtapositions that are part of Barthelme's distinctive style.

The most enjoyable aspect of the narration, however, is the narrator's antic and whimsical recording of events. Beneath the surface of the serious conversation between father and son about life masks lies a vein of intensely comic repartee. After a fight with his wife, the narrator decides to visit a prostitute but cannot because he has only three dollars, and the bordello will not accept his credit card. When the narrator forces Wanda to act like a chauffeur on his visit to the Argentine ambassador (an improbable social call in the context of the story), he explains to his wife, who wants to be included, "You know no Spanish." When Wanda attempts to murder her husband, she "withdrew from her bosom an extremely large horse pistol," a ludicrous action considering the disparity between the size of the weapon and its place of concealment.

The pistol also emerges as a key symbol. When Wanda's aim wavers, and she hits a bottle of J&B scotch instead, it is clear that Wanda, herself a little drunk, has inadvertently taken action against her principal enemy—alcohol. Their marriage is beset by many problems—the child and their mutual discontent with each other and with the patterns of their daily life—and it could be argued that the narrator's alcoholism is a symptom as well as a cause of their difficulties, but it is, in the story, the most prominent, tangible, and immediate source of the failure of the relationship.

*Walter Herrscher*

# THE CROCODILE

*Author:* Fyodor Dostoevski (1821-1881)
*Type of plot:* Parody
*Time of plot:* 1865
*Locale:* St. Petersburg, Russia
*First published:* "Neobyknovennoe sobytie: Ili, Passazh v passazhe," 1865 (English translation, 1895)

*Principal characters:*
IVAN MATVEITCH, a Russian bureaucrat
ELENA IVANOVNA, his wife
SEMYON SEMYONITCH, their friend and the narrator of the story
THE CROCODILE
THE GERMAN, the owner of the crocodile
TIMOFEY SEMYONITCH, an elderly Russian bureaucrat

*The Story*

The story opens on January 13, 1865. The narrator, Semyon Semyonitch, and his married friends, Elena Ivanovna and Ivan Matveitch, go to St. Petersburg's arcade to see a crocodile that is on display. The arcade is a popular spot in St. Petersburg for public exhibitions and lectures. Semyonitch and Matveitch are distantly related and both work in the same government department. Because Matveitch is scheduled to go to Western Europe for intellectual advancement and has no official duties for the day, he can join his wife and friend on the excursion to the arcade. He thinks that it will be valuable to see the crocodile because, before he visits Europe, it is well to acquaint himself "with its indigenous inhabitants."

The crocodile is housed in a large tin tank with only two inches of water, located inside a shop that also exhibits cockatoos and monkeys. Disappointed to find that the crocodile is not active because of the cold Russian climate, the visitors wonder if the animal is even alive. Its German owner uses a stick to prod the crocodile. Showing no fear, Matveitch moves forward and tickles the crocodile's nose with his glove at the same moment that Elena Ivanovna and Semyonitch turn their attention to the monkeys. In an instant, Matveitch is swallowed by the crocodile. His wife screams when she sees her husband in the jaws of the great beast, which swallows him, legs first, as a terrified audience looks on. After disappearing inside the crocodile, Matveitch's head pops out of its mouth, causing his glasses to fall off and land at the bottom of the tank.

Although horrified, Semyonitch finds the tragedy absurdly comical and cannot help but laugh. The German owner and his mother are outraged by what has happened; however, they are concerned not about the fate of Ivan Matveitch but with the safety of thei2r crocodile. The German thinks it is only just that he be compensated for any damages to his property. Elena Ivanovna shouts for the crocodile to be cut open, using the Russian word *vsporot*, for "cut." The crowd, however, think that she is using the Russian word *vysporot*, for "flog." Because flogging is no longer tolerated in Russia, she is informed that it would be cruel to flog the crocodile. To everyone's amazement, Matveitch speaks from inside the belly of the crocodile. The German now realizes that he can charge higher fees to view his property. Because the animal is much more valuable than before, he declares that he will only part with it if he is paid thousands of Russian rubles. Matveitch advises his wife to apply directly to the superintendent's office because, without the assistance of the police, the German will never see reason.

Although seemingly unhurt, Matveitch is saddened that he will miss his trip to Western Europe because the German is asking such an exorbitant price for his crocodile. Semyonitch agrees to go see the respected bureaucrat Timofey Semyonitch and ask his advice concerning this peculiar situation. He leaves the arcade with Elena Ivanovna, who feels "something like a widow."

Timofey Semyonitch sees no justification for interceding in this matter because he believes that private property is more important than Matveitch's life. The elderly bureaucrat rambles on about the need for Russia's communal land to be sold to foreign investors and suggests that Matveitch's fate may encourage other crocodiles to be brought into Russia. To him, the accumulation of capital is of primary importance. Semyon Semyonitch returns to the arcade without a solution to his friend's problem. There he finds that the crocodile's owner is overjoyed at the prospect of making a fortune because the public will flock to see a man living inside a crocodile. Semyonitch is surprised to learn that Matveitch now wants to preach great thoughts from the belly of the crocodile, and he is not sure what to make of his friend's pronouncements. Elena Ivanovna concludes that it may be necessary to divorce her husband.

The story concludes with wild descriptions of the incident that appear in Russian newspapers. There is no resolution to Matveitch's predicament. (It is known that Fyodor Dostoevski intended to finish this story, but he never got around to it.)

*Themes and Meanings*

Although Dostoevski never finished "The Crocodile," it nevertheless stands as one of the most powerful indictments against humankind's inhumanity to humankind. His narrator, Semyonitch, seems to be the only person truly concerned with Matveitch's welfare. Even the victim's wife decides that divorce would be best for her. The German owner of the crocodile and his mother are concerned only with protecting their investment. The German realizes that he can make huge profits by selling tickets to people anxious to see a man living inside a crocodile. Even the victim agrees that the "principles of economics" should rule the day. Dostoevski is thus making the point that when capitalist doctrines dominate human behavior, all notions of common decency among people will cease to exist.

During the 1860's in Russia, such prominent intellectuals as Dmitry Ivanovich Pisarev and Varfolomei Aleksandrovich Zaitsev argued that Russia should look to Western Europe for its economic model. Regarding rapid industrialization as a paramount goal, Pisarev theorized that the perfect individual to thrive in a capitalist society would be a "superman" type not constrained by the bounds of good and evil. The prospect of combining capitalism and nihilism in Russia worried Dostoevski, who feared that Russian virtues would be trampled. These theorists had little or no faith in the potential of the Russian people.

Dostoevski expresses his distrust for both the political left and right in "The Crocodile." Although the bureaucrat Matveitch is described as being politically "progressive" and is the victim of the story, he still agrees that economic interests should prevail over even his own safety. It can be argued that "The Crocodile" foreshadows the linkage that Dostoevski forcefully developed between nihilism and capitalism in his 1866 novel *Prestupleniye i nakazaniye* (*Crime and Punishment*, 1886). Many of his short stories touch on the issues that he more fully developed in his mature novels. In *Zapiski iz podpolya* (1864; *Notes from the Underground*, 1913), for example, he touches on the idea of social theorists attempting to mold a perfect society without taking into consideration the rights of the individual. Dostoevski is noted for juxtaposing the individual against a bureaucracy, the city against the countryside, and religious faith versus atheism. Even unfinished, "The Crocodile" stands as a merciless portrait of where an amoral approach to life might lead.

*Style and Technique*

In 1864, Dostoevski and his brother Mikhail began publishing the journal *Epokha*, in which "The Crocodile" appeared in February, 1865. With the death of his brother and mounting financial problems, Dostoevski was forced to cease publication of *Epokha* in March, 1865. The Russian subtitle of the story can be translated as "Or, Mauled in the Mall." It should be clear from the use of such a grotesque yet playful subtitle that the story that follows will have a strong satirical edge to it. As in Nikolai Gogol's 1836 story "The Nose," in which "a most extraordinary thing happened in St. Petersburg," Dostoevski presents a bizarre event in a matter-of-fact manner. In Gogol's story, a Russian barber discovers a human nose in a loaf of bread. In "The Crocodile," a Russian bureaucrat is not only swallowed by a crocodile but he lives through the experience, and the belly of the animal becomes his new residence. Both stories savage Russia's government bureaucracy. Dostoevski parodies the radical theorists of the 1860's not only through the swallowed bureaucrat Matveitch but especially through the elderly and venerated bureaucrat Timofey Semyonitch—a buffoon who pontificates about foreign investment in Russia. As wild and absurd as the situation is for Matveitch, it is only the narrator who is concerned with his friend's safety. The "principles of economics" must rule the day. Dostoevski also includes parodies of newspaper articles about the event at the end of the story. Their various slants and exaggerations add to the uneasy feeling with which the reader is left.

Dostoevski left documents that make it clear that he hoped to resolve "The Crocodile." Although he left the story incomplete, it stands as an important precursor of what was to follow creatively for the author.

*Jeffry Jensen*

# CROSSING INTO POLAND

*Author:* Isaac Babel (1894-1940)
*Type of plot:* Impressionistic
*Time of plot:* 1920
*Locale:* Poland
*First published:* "Perekhod cherez Zbruch," 1924 (English translation, 1929)

> *Principal characters:*
> THE NARRATOR, the protagonist, an unnamed officer in the
>     Russian cavalry
> A JEWISH WOMAN, unnamed, in whose house the narrator is
>     billeted
> HER FATHER, who was killed in the recent fighting

## The Story

To appreciate fully this very short story, apparently no more than a sketch, one must understand its context. Most significant is its position as the first of thirty-five related stories originally collected under the title *Konarmiia* (1926; *Red Cavalry,* 1929). The stories all deal with the Russian campaign against Poland—from July through September, 1920—undertaken by General Semyon Budyonny's First Cavalry. The author, a Jew from Odessa who rejected Judaism to become a communist, participated in this campaign (which was unsuccessful) as a propaganda officer and a war correspondent.

The narrator of the various *Red Cavalry* stories is apparently the same person throughout and autobiographical in essential features. Consequently, although little information is given about the narrator of the initial story, one learns from later stories that he is Jewish.

"Crossing into Poland" begins with a note that Novograd-Volynsk was taken at dawn. Now the rearguard is marching on the highroad from Brest to Warsaw, crossing into Poland over the twisting torrents of the River Zbruch.

The largely peaceful and brightly colored sights of nature—fields, flowers, streams, the sun, and finally the moon—are described as a prose poem often employing striking, disturbing, and contradictory imagery. Late at night, the narrator reaches Novograd and is billeted in a house where Jews live. He describes them as "scraggy-necked" and living in filth. He angrily orders the young pregnant woman of the house to clean up the mess.

Eventually he lies down on the floor, on a ragged feather bed, next to one of the Jews, who is lying huddled to the wall with his head covered up, evidently asleep. The narrator soon sleeps but then is awakened from a nightmare by the pregnant woman, who tells him that he has been crying out. Suddenly he sees that the old man, next to whom he has been lying, is dead: "His throat had been torn out and his face cleft in two; in his beard blue blood was clotted like a lump of lead." The woman laments the loss of her father, killed by Poles that day—and the narrator is shocked to silence as the story abruptly ends.

### Themes and Meanings

In "Crossing into Poland" one may note at least three of the important themes to be developed in full detail throughout *Red Cavalry*. The first of these is disapproval of war—conveyed in this story through disturbing imagery and the gruesome description of a victim of war. One might conclude that the author is in fact a pacifist but that he declines to voice that view explicitly on the grounds that subtlety and understatement will have a greater effect on the reader.

However, the author also must have felt some ambivalence toward the Polish campaign, as a communist and as a supporter of the Russian Revolution. Hence, there may be discerned in the stories a tentative (perhaps merely ironic) effort to seek justification for the sacrificial victims of the war. (Note that the old man may be seen specifically as a sacrifice because his throat has been cut, as in Jewish ritual slaughter of animals.) This second theme in "Crossing into Poland" occurs as little more than a suggestion, as the narrator, in describing the mess spread out over the floor of the Jews' house, refers to the "fragments of the occult crockery the Jews use only once a year, at Eastertime." This one reference to "Eastertime" (in Russian, "Passover" is also indicated, as the word for Easter and Passover is the same, Paskha) implicitly evokes the sacrifice of Jesus, with whom the old man, in retrospect, becomes tentatively associated. (One may think of him as a sheep or lamb offered to God.) Because this implicit comparison is in no way resolved, one is left with two ironic possibilities, depending on one's religious convictions: Either the old man may somehow benefit humankind as Jesus did, through his sacrificial death, or there is no such benefit at all, and the old man died in vain, as did Jesus.

It is important that the old man is presented as an exceptionally good person. He submits to death voluntarily (as the narrator learns from his daughter), pleading with the Poles, "Kill me in the yard so that my daughter shan't see me die." The daughter asks the narrator at the end: "I should wish to know where in the whole world you could find another father like my father?" An implicit comparison with Jesus is not unjustified. Meanwhile, the reader may believe in any case that Isaac Babel's story—as a kind of redemption through art—accords transcendent dignity to the sacrifice of the unknown Jew. There is even a hint at resurrection in the daughter's pregnancy.

A third major theme deals with anti-Semitism—rampant among the Russian cossack troops as well as among the Poles. In this story, the reader is invited to share in the apparent anti-Semitism of the presumably Russian cavalry officer as he describes the Jews skipping about (to his orders) "monkey-fashion, like Japs in a circus act." (It is their faintheartedness and passivity that seem to him especially objectionable.) However, suddenly Babel brings the narrator—and the reader (originally a Russian reader)—face to face with the mutilated corpse and the weeping woman. The only decent emotion at this point is shame for having forgotten that all people are one under

God. The fact that the narrator is himself Jewish (a fact deducible only in the later stories, but which does not prevent the reader from rereading "Crossing into Poland") merely adds poignancy to Babel's basic theme: A Jew also may experience the shame of anti-Semitism. In addition, one may suppose that the narrator must see himself, forever a Jew despite his atheism—and all other suffering Jews—in the sacrificed old man.

## Style and Technique

Despite what at times appears to be stark realism in his works, Babel's literary art is often more concerned with style than content. Usually, however, one may perceive some basic relationship between the two, as in the following images from the opening section of "Crossing into Poland": "the highroad . . . built by Nicholas I upon the bones of peasants"; "the orange sun rolled down the sky like a lopped-off head"; and "into the cool of evening dripped the smell of yesterday's blood." This imagery found early in the story is given an especially ominous character as it is contrasted, in the same opening paragraph, to bright visions of peace and serenity: "on the horizon virginal buckwheat rose like the wall of a distant monastery"; "the . . . peaceful stream . . . wound weary arms through a wilderness of hops"; and "On the waves rested a majestic moon."

However, after all in the house have gone to sleep, and "faint-hearted poverty" has "closed in" over the narrator's bed on the floor, the reader is confounded by the following elaborately poetic line: "Only the moon, clasping in her blue hands her round, bright, carefree face, wandered like a vagrant outside the window." At this point, the narrator is already being assailed by a nightmare in which "the Brigade Commander's head" is pierced by bullets, and "both his eyes" drop to the ground. It is no doubt true that the clasped face of the moon and the commander's pierced head anticipate the wounds of the old man, but the imagery seems excessive (why the "bright, carefree" face?) and enigmatic (why the eyes dropping to the ground?). However, the overall impressionistic effect is very satisfactory, even if somewhat puzzling. This highly colored style, characteristic not only of the early Babel but also of other Russian writers of the 1920's, has been referred to as "ornamentalism."

Babel's ornamentalism usually yields to meaning, or at least to some significant insight, perhaps not fully resolved but disturbing and unforgettable. Such is the case, at the end of "Crossing into Poland," with the sudden and shocking revelation of the dead man by his grieving yet angry daughter. The reader is not told what the narrator is thinking as the story ends but nevertheless knows the narrator's thoughts exactly, because the reader becomes him through Babel's astonishing "epiphany," or "showing forth," in which all the elements of the story seem to have coalesced. The literary epiphany, a conception brought into use by James Joyce, is one of Babel's most effective stylistic devices.

*Donald M. Fiene*

# CRUEL AND BARBAROUS TREATMENT

*Author:* Mary McCarthy (1912-1989)
*Type of plot:* Psychological
*Time of plot:* The mid-twentieth century
*Locale:* New York City
*First published:* 1939

>*Principal characters:*
>THE YOUNG WOMAN, an unnamed woman soon to be divorced
>BILL, her husband
>THE YOUNG MAN, her paramour

*The Story*

In this, Mary McCarthy's first published story, the initial two sentences summarize the whole. The remainder of the narrative details the careful, ritualized process by which the protagonist makes her way from a clandestine affair to public disclosure and impending divorce. McCarthy's satiric view of bourgeois society is never sharper than in this study of how a bored woman transforms her life from a series of "time-killers, matters of routine" to one of "perilous and dramatic adventures," merely by ending her marriage in three steps. This is a story wherein the third-person narrative voice is orchestrated with a care matched only by the protagonist's own arrangement of events.

The young wife loves groups of three: the love triangle that she has brought into being, the three-times-a-week minimum for social outings during which she can "tremble . . . on the exquisite edge of self-betrayal," and above all the three-part sequence into which she organizes her drama of marital disintegration and from each of which she squeezes all the excitement she can before moving on to the next.

First, during the period of secrecy, the "subterranean courtship," there is the Public Appearances routine. Its main advantages come from its "outlawry," which tends to force the illicit lovers into an especially strong dependency and which gives the young woman intense feelings of superiority. This latter derives from her feeling that she has "bested" her husband and can feel good about her restraint in not gloating over the victory. Then too, she can feel superior to the callow Young Man, whose "imperfections" seem so clear under the pressure of his having to attend parties and act as if they were her "private theatricals." In this triangle she has power: "She was undoubtedly queen bee."

The second "preordained stage," made necessary when the possibilities of the first are "exhausted," the young woman calls the Announcement. It, too, has special characteristics that provide not only emotional stimulation but also feelings of superiority. To make the Announcement rids the lovers of the "morally distasteful" secrecy, and, more important, it allows her to satisfy her curiosity about What People Would Say.

What good is a secret if it is never revealed? It is not only revealed to a wider and wider circle of friends but also finally used to discover How Her Husband Would Take It (and to discover the full strength of his love by putting it "face to face with its own annihilation," and thus putting it into "the category of completed experiences"). Once again, the young wife's genius for arranging stage performances shows itself in the public conference á trois, and her instincts for the ritualistic reveal themselves in her arranging "the confession in the restaurant and the absolution in the Park."

The final, Post-Announcement phase proves to be the shortest and least satisfying of the three: There is no triangle; there are only the "dull moments . . . she spent alone with the Young Man." For a person who finds pleasure in the flux of instability and manipulation, some method of breaking the stasis of pairing must be found. The young woman does not perceive the situation in these terms, however, and concludes that she is the "victim" of unconscious forces, "a sort of hypnotic trance." In the throes of a depression that is neither "dramatic" nor "pleasurable," she takes refuge in this vague sense of fate, wondering if it might be that she is "designed for the role of femme fatale," to be "a bad risk," to enjoy the "glamour" of the title Young Divorcee.

Just when her options seem to be gone, when she remembers the old fear of spinsterhood, when she realizes there is "no signpost to guide her"—just when, in other words, the story seems about to deliver something as artistically vulgar as poetic justice—she rallies and finds new improvisations, saving both herself and the narrative from a final triteness and exhaustion.

## Themes and Meanings

The social and psychological themes of "Cruel and Barbarous Treatment" become clear after a moment's reflection: the superficiality of social friendships, the difficulty of understanding another human being, the battle of the sexes, and what Edgar Allan Poe once termed "the imp of the perverse," one's desire to throw over what in rational terms is in one's best interest for something more intense and passionate, though risky and destructive. The young woman, while manipulative and dishonest, is nevertheless a very attractive character because of her energy, inventiveness, and ability to play her game with great dexterity. Though condemnations of her behavior spring to mind, nothing in the narrative itself announces or invites them. McCarthy's satire here is not of the heavy, moralistic sort. The husband, after all, does quite well without her, his social life so busy that he does not have time to see her off on the train to Reno. The wife has more than sufficient resources. Only the Young Man will be hurt, and his problems are never significant in the story except as comedy.

McCarthy herself referred to the story's main concern as "the quest for the self," which is also the unifying theme for the collection of short stories *The Company She Keeps* (1942), in which the story appeared as the first in a connected sequence about a woman who attempts to create a sense of who she is by means of dramatic and often scandalous actions. The cleverness of this protagonist in "Cruel and Barbarous Treatment," as in many of the other stories, is not to be seen as defining a self but rather as a nervous indication that no identity has been found. The great insight into human character here is of the comic: People are unable to learn from their mistakes, and this fixity is the basis for the comedy that keeps the story from sinking into the didactic. What defines the protagonist is the need for excitement, the need to feel superior, and the essential triteness that this "quest" demands. Thus, the cliched phrases that name the ritual phases of her progress are capitalized (Woman With A Secret, and so forth), and thus near the end of the story, she shows the essentially unimaginative quality of the quest when she takes refuge in the self-delusion and silly fatalism of such lines as, "If the Man [to replace her husband] did not exist, the Moment would create him." However, she is, above all, consistent, as the comic stasis requires. McCarthy in her essay "Characters in Fiction" describes her desire "to be as exact as possible about the essence of a person," nicely underlining the idea of a static conception of character.

*Style and Technique*

McCarthy describes this story as a "stylization." The voice itself in this third-person-limited narrative stays for the most part very close to the vocabulary and mental forms of the character being described. The sequence of events, the capitalized divisions of the ritual, the mental improvisations within the tightly closed divisions, the carefully balanced parallels of a sentence such as "the deception was prolonged where it had been ephemeral, necessary where it had been frivolous, conspiratorial where it had been lonely," all describe a mind that loves, not free spaces but securely fenced ones. All this evidence of symmetry and control supports the idea that this woman is not interested in wild abandon, or even passion but rather in power (and in a very small arena).

This explains McCarthy's technique of condescension, for the reader is always made aware that there is a world bustling about outside this self-absorbed mind, that there is a great irony in the direct quotation marks as the protagonist announces to her silly Young Man that she should have been "a diplomat's wife or an international spy." In irony, the highest consciousness must be reserved for the implied author, and McCarthy here has taken it. The protagonist, clever rather than imaginative, is not "superior" as she believes herself to be, and the authorial consciousness shows this, in the protagonist's fear of what others will think of her lover once he is revealed, in her jealousy at her husband's warm reception by their mutual friends, and in her self-delusion concerning fate near the end of the story. The character's lack of self-knowledge reveals her inferiority to the consciousness that controls the story itself.

The protagonist is in the best sense a "flat" character, or to repeat McCarthy's own term, an "essence." Thus there is no development of awareness, or other evidence of change. The story is frankly analytic, depending on explanation of a fixed principle of character. The surprises result not from revelations of hidden recesses but from the virtuoso variations on the single theme: How much excitement, how much plot, can the young woman create for herself using such limited resources? All these variations reflect on the satiric mind behind the story's conception.

*Kerry Ahearn*

# THE CRUISE OF *THE BREADWINNER*

*Author:* H. E. Bates (1905-1974)
*Type of plot:* War
*Time of plot:* World War II
*Locale:* On the ocean off the coast of England
*First published:* 1946

> *Principal characters:*
> GREGSON, a large, heavyset man in his sixties, skipper of *The Breadwinner*
> JIMMY, the engineer of *The Breadwinner*
> SNOWY, about seventeen, the cook and chore boy on *The Breadwinner*
> KARL MESSNER, a German pilot
> AN UNNAMED RAF PILOT

## The Story

*The Breadwinner* is a small rickety fishing boat that has been pressed into service by the exigencies of war to patrol the coast of England, complete with an unreliable engine and an ancient Lewis gun mounted on the stern. On the day of the story, everything is as usual: Gregson, the skipper, is impatient for Snowy, the cook, to bring his cup of tea; Jimmy, the engineer, is fretting over the balky engine; Snowy is in the tiny galley reluctantly making tea and wishing that something exciting would happen. Snowy becomes more interested when a squadron of Hurricane fighter planes leaves the coast looking for German aircraft. As always on these occasions, he thinks bitterly of the binoculars the skipper has been promising him for weeks. The routine of the day is suddenly interrupted by the noise of gunfire well out in the channel, and Snowy's keen ears detect the sound of German Messerschmitt fighter planes.

For some time, the boat cruises uneventfully in the direction of the gunfire, until Snowy detects the sound of a whistle. Excitedly, the crew rushes toward a speck in the distance, which proves to be a downed Royal Air Force (RAF) pilot in a dinghy. The pilot is unhurt and in good spirits, full of praise for the German pilot whose plane he believes he has shot down. From him they also learn that his was not the battle they had heard earlier, so they head farther out to sea in case there are more pilots to be rescued. Sent to the galley to peel potatoes, Snowy is sullenly and bitterly angry at being away from the excitement and the glamour of the pilot. Moments later, Jimmy announces that another pilot has been sighted, a wounded German. As the English pilot brings him toward the boat, Snowy sees around the German's neck a leather binoculars case. War seems to him now wonderful and romantic.

A few minutes later, while Snowy is in the galley making tea for the pilots, he hears the deafening roar of a plane and a burst of cannon fire. Rushing on deck, he sees to his horror that Jimmy has been killed and the two pilots wounded. Gregson is too angry at the enemy to attend to the German, but the RAF man insists that he be treated decently. As Gregson nurses the Englishman, Snowy hopes the German will try to escape so Gregson can kill him and he can claim the binoculars. When rain begins falling, Gregson and Snowy move the wounded men to the cabin below. Snowy attempts to take Jimmy's place as engineer but discovers that gunfire has damaged the motor beyond repair. Gregson rigs a sail, but they must hurry as bad weather is brewing. Below, Snowy tries to administer first aid to the wounded German, whose name is Karl Messner, but the man is badly wounded. Snowy also tries to talk to the RAF pilot, a hero in his eyes, but the pilot downplays his actions and seems more concerned for Messner's welfare than his own. As they sail for home, first Messner dies, then the Englishman.

As *The Breadwinner* nears shore just ahead of the advancing storm, Gregson's face bears a look Snowy has not seen before. Suddenly the skipper bursts into an angry, cursing denunciation, "Why don't they let our lives alone? God damn and blast them—all of them, all of them, all the bastards, all over the world!" Snowy, clutching the binoculars, sees the older man's face wet with tears and feels grateful to be alive amid the horrors of war.

*Themes and Meanings*

As is so often the case in H. E. Bates's fiction, the theme of this story is a young man's fall from innocence. In this instance, Snowy's innocence is his belief that war is a romantic adventure, especially for fighter pilots. Like most adolescents, he sees his own life as dull and commonplace, and his almost childish desire for a pair of binoculars signifies his longing for something just beyond his reach. One by one, Snowy's illusions are stripped away, first by the sight of Jimmy's mangled body lying inert in a pool of blood, then by the strange camaraderie of the two pilots, and finally by Gregson's outburst against the nameless and faceless "them" who inflict war on ordinary, decent people. Snowy is left at the end of the story clinging halfheartedly to the binoculars, now a symbol of his former illusions, stunned into the realization that modern war is only organized, mechanized horror.

*Style and Technique*

In the early days of World War II, Bates was commissioned to write a series of stories under the pseudonym "Flying Officer X" to publicize the quiet heroism of the Battle of Britain pilots. By the end of the war, however, he had seen enough of war's destruction, and this story is indicative of his new perception. The "Flying Officer X" stories were not entirely romantic, but in "The Cruise of *The Breadwinner*," Bates employs his most grimly realistic manner to the subject of war and its dehumanization. Like his earlier stories, "The Ox" and "The Mill," this one is marked by Bates's unrelenting starkness of vision and style. In clear, pictorial prose, Bates describes the laughably fragile boat, the ineffectual Lewis gun, the devastation wrought by the strafing German airplane, and the lingering, painful deaths of the two young pilots, who might, except for the accidents of war, have become friends. In direct contrast to the passages of destruction and death are the descriptions of the characters. Gregson is first depicted as tough and confident, but his jingoistic patriotism, like Snowy's innocence, melts into common human caring because of the pilots' deaths. The two young pilots, only a few years older than Snowy, are presented as willing but tragic participants in a war they did not cause. Brooding over the events of the story is indifferent nature, which first provides a "good day" for flying, then a storm that threatens the lives of them all. In short, Bates employs his most incisive, vivid style to describe his characters and their sufferings, depicting all of them as victims of forces beyond their control.

*Dean Baldwin*

# THE CURSE

*Author:* Andre Dubus (1936-1999)
*Type of plot:* Domestic realism
*Time of plot:* The 1980's
*Locale:* A small town in Massachusetts
*First published:* 1988

> *Principal characters:*
> MITCHELL HAYES, a middle-aged bartender
> SUSAN, his wife
> BOB, The bar's manager
> BAR PATRONS

## The Story

Mitchell Hayes, a forty-nine-year-old bartender at a small-town, working-class bar, feels old, exhausted, and depressed one night. He is alone in the bar with its manager, Bob, after closing time. The police have just left, after taking Mitchell's statement about a rape that occurred in the bar that night.

Earlier that night, five men had arrived on motorcycles near closing time and ordered beers. The men were loud and edgy, and Mitchell thought they had been using drugs. The stepfather of a teenage boy and girl, Mitchell fears and hates drugs. A young woman came into the bar to buy cigarettes and asked Mitchell for change. The five men intercepted her before she could get to the cigarette machine and raped her on the floor, despite Mitchell's presence. After the rape, Mitchell went to the sobbing woman and handed her clothes to her, then called 911 and Bob. Mitchell wished he could comfort the young woman, but she kept crying. He knew both of the police officers who responded to his call and had gone to high school with one of them, Smitty. After the woman was taken away on a stretcher, Mitchell told Smitty that he could have stopped the assault, but Smitty said that was the job of the police, and if Mitchell had intervened, he would probably be in the hospital along with the girl.

When Mitchell gets home, his wife, Susan, awakens and comes into the dining room, where he is smoking and drinking a beer. He tells her what has happened, and she agrees with Smitty that he could not have prevented it. However, Mitchell is sure that if he had intervened and ended up in the hospital, she still would have said he did the right thing. Susan, who has been a caregiver for elderly persons, soothes her husband until he falls asleep.

In the morning, Mitchell is awakened as usual by the sounds of his family getting ready for their jobs. On ordinary mornings, he quickly falls back to sleep, but today he gets up and joins them at the breakfast table. Joyce and Marty, his stepchildren, wonder why he is up so early. He tells them of the incident at the bar, adding that when he went to call the police, one of the men stopped him. He thinks he should have attacked the man with a bottle, but Marty says that Mitchell would have put himself in danger and would not have been able to overcome five drugged, violent men. Susan says that the men were caught and proudly says that Mitchell will be a good witness at the trial.

That night, Mitchell is back at work. The regular customers are all there, and Mitchell observes that none of the women fear the men there, even the young men who ride motorcycles. Mitchell also notices that not even the women treat him as if he had been an uncaring coward. He feels shamed that many people act as if he had been a victim himself.

Reggie, a regular customer, has had too much to drink, as he sometimes does. When Reggie asks for another shot of whisky and a beer, Mitchell tells him it is time to switch to coffee, adding that he does not want to hear that Reggie has died. Reggie does not argue, and when he goes home, he leaves a sixteen-dollar tip for Mitchell. As Mitchell presses the money into his overflowing tip jar, he sees the woman being raped, and hears the men cheering and the woman screaming, then hears her sobs melt into the sound of the ambulance siren fading into the night. From behind him, he feels "her pain and terror and grief, then her curse upon him. The curse moved into his back and spread down and up his spine, into his stomach and legs and arms and shoulders until he quivered with it. He wished he were alone so he could kneel to receive it."

*Themes and Meanings*

Andre Dubus often peoples his stories with working-class characters and crafts plots that show how a random act can transform an ordinary life forever. Mitchell is a plainspoken man who had given up on finding love and a family until he married Susan, a divorced woman with two children. They do not have a great deal of money, but they have become a happy, functioning family. After witnessing a rape in the bar where he works and feeling there was nothing he could do to stop it, Mitchell's joy in living is shattered. He feels he had an ethical responsibility to the victim but at the same time did not want to put himself in danger of being beaten up by the five men, which would have brought grief to his family.

The dilemma Dubus presents haunts the reader, who is led to ponder the moral questions, What would I do if I saw a crime being committed, but I were outnumbered and unarmed? How could I live with myself if I stood by and watched? The question is as relevant in a small-town bar in the United States as it was in the days of Nazi leader Adolf Hitler in Germany.

Dubus gets into Mitchell's soul, showing in a few paragraphs how his suffering is increased, rather than alleviated, by the compassion that people show him. Even the understanding of his wife and stepchildren does not comfort him. In fact, Susan's total acceptance of his actions leaves him unable to share with her his deeper feelings of guilt and inadequacy. The reader feels that Mitchell believes that he can only be redeemed if he is punished for his "sin," but the loss of peace in his heart is the biggest punishment he could receive.

Dubus also confronts the culture of violence common in the United States. Mitchell is immediately uncomfortable with the five rowdy strangers who come into the bar, primarily because he thinks they have been using drugs. When he realizes the men are about to rape the young woman and goes to call the police, it takes just a shove from one of the men to stop him. Fear of what such men would do to him is enough to immobilize him.

*Style and Technique*

Dubus was a great admirer of the Russian writer Anton Chekhov and emulated his style of realism in his short stories rather than adopting the postmodernist and minimalist styles that were typical of many short stories of the late twentieth century. Dubus's style allows him here to create a compelling story, in which the reader can identify with the protagonist, in slightly over six pages. Using the limited omniscient point of view, he offers an intense look at the tortured man's soul over a period of less than twenty-four hours. Other than a short passage in which Mitchell tells Joyce and Marty about the rape, there is almost no dialogue; the third-person narrator describes what Mitchell sees and feels.

The title of the work can be seen as having a double meaning in that it relates to both the curse that Mitchell feels he will bear forever for his failure to protect the woman and the blood that the woman presumably lost from the assault. "The curse" is an old term for the menstrual cycle; after the men left and Mitchell goes to the woman and hands her her clothes, "She lay the clothes across her breasts and what Mitchell thought of now as her wound." The image of her wounded, bleeding genitals calls to mind the blood associated with the monthly "curse."

In Dubus's narration of what novelist Henry James referred to as "the detached incident," the author vividly sketches a picture from which readers learn a great deal about the characters through their responses to incidents. The protagonist, Mitchell, is presented in the most detail; however, readers can also learn as much about his wife and stepchildren through their responses to Mitchell as through what the narrator says about them. Dubus never actually describes the rape or the woman's condition, only her shame and crying; nevertheless, Mitchell's reactions tell the reader the emotional truth about the rape.

*Irene Struthers Rush*

# CUSTOMS OF THE COUNTRY

*Author:* Madison Smartt Bell (1957-    )
*Type of plot:* Domestic realism
*Time of plot:* The 1980's
*Locale:* Western Virginia
*First published:* 1988

> *Principal characters:*
> A YOUNG WOMAN, the narrator
> DAVEY, her son
> PATRICK, her son's father
> SUSAN, her neighbor, an abused woman

## The Story

"Customs of the Country" is narrated by a woman whose attempts to recover custody of her son lead her to settle temporarily in the rural Virginia countryside near Roanoke. The woman does what she believes to be all the right things to convince authorities of her fitness as a mother, hoping that the child will be removed from foster care and returned to her. She rents a small apartment in a cluster-housing development, where through the thin walls, she is able to hear her neighbors quarreling. Occasionally, she hears a man beating a woman, but she does nothing to stop him. Instead, she goes about fixing up her apartment with furniture and decorations so that authorities will judge it a fit place to raise her son, Davey.

To prove that she can care for Davey financially, the woman takes a job as a waitress at a truck stop near Interstate 81. The proprietor, Tim, and a coworker, Prissy, sympathize with her and assist her in her efforts to work through the social services system to secure a hearing before a magistrate. That process is complicated, however, and the woman meets one roadblock after another; even the attorney she hires to help her cannot seem to get social services personnel to cooperate. During the time the woman is working to gain back her son, she tries to befriend her neighbor Susan, who is abused by the man with whom she lives. The narrator's efforts are rebuffed, however, and she soon abandons attempts to be sociable.

The woman achieves some small success when she is granted the opportunity to visit with her son. In relating the story of her son's birth and childhood, the woman reveals that Davey's father, Patrick, is in jail, having been arrested for drug possession and sale. The woman herself had been addicted to drugs, relying on Patrick to support her habit. Patrick's arrest had occurred at a time when she was particularly dependent on drugs; the irritating behavior of her small son sent her into a frenzy, and she tossed the child against a wall, breaking his leg. Although she quickly realized what she had done and sought treatment for the boy, social workers at the hospital recognized the symptoms of abuse and managed to have Davey taken from her.

Although the woman has a good relationship with her son, it becomes clear to her that his foster parents, the Bakers, are providing him a good home and that they want to keep him. Nevertheless, she continues to plead her case with social workers. Finally, however, when she is given a chance to talk to her son's case worker, she realizes her efforts are hopeless. The woman does not even wish to visit the apartment to see where Davey might be living.

Disappointed and disillusioned, the woman returns home and packs her belongings. While she is packing, she hears the man next door beating Susan again. Something inside the narrator snaps; she takes a large skillet and goes to her neighbor's and hits the man across the face. As he crumples to the floor, she invites Susan to come away with her. Instead of doing so, however, Susan stoops to care for the man. Disgusted, the narrator rushes out to her car and drives away.

### Themes and Meanings

In "Customs of the Country," Madison Smart Bell exposes readers to the lower stratum of southern society, choosing as his narrator a woman of limited financial means who has been caught up in a life of petty crime and drug abuse. By creating such a narrator, Bell gives readers new insight into a universal commonplace in American society, a mother's love for her child.

Despite her hard life, the narrator is able to evoke sympathy from readers who can see that she is struggling to re-establish a relationship with a child whom she had lost through her own abusive behavior toward him. The narrator's description of her time with her son is a poignant reminder of the way the maternal instinct drives women to make significant sacrifices for their children.

One might also assume that the story is an indictment of the social welfare system that separates a mother from her child and makes reunification of the family exceedingly difficult. From the narrator's point of view, the bureaucrats who determine the fate of her child seem to have no understanding of how deeply she cares for Davey. What becomes apparent to astute readers, however, is that the case workers are acting in the child's best interest because the narrator is actually unfit to raise Davey. As the narrator herself makes clear, when she is with her son she behaves more like an older sibling than a parent; they are like two children playing together. Even if it is not clear to her, it is clear to readers that the Bakers will provide the stability Davey needs.

No matter how appealing she becomes as she tells the story of her hard life, one cannot overlook the fact that the narrator is still suffering from the effects of abusive behavior and that her ability to relate to her child depends on her ability to control her own emotional outbursts. Her decision at the end of the story to assist her neighbor to escape from an abusive relationship by resorting to physical violence suggests that she has not yet learned how to behave in a manner expected of one responsible for raising children.

The dominant theme of "Customs of the Country" is actually the lasting effects of abusive behavior. Nearly every character in the story suffers in some way from abuse, either as perpetrator or victim. The men are principally abusers and suffer retributive justice either from the authorities or from the vigilante efforts of the narrator. The women suffer as victims: The narrator becomes dependent on the drugs provided to her by the father of her child and her neighbor Susan from physical beatings at the hands of her partner. The ending of the story shows that nothing is resolved: Susan chooses to stay with the man who is abusing her, and the narrator runs away from the situation, giving up hope of ever proving her fitness as a mother.

*Style and Technique*

Bell relies on the technique of first-person narration to create a sense of irony throughout this story. Because the narrator does not understand fully the role she has played in creating the situation in which she now finds herself, Bell arouses tension that causes readers to question the reliability of the narrator's view of her situation. Although the woman's direct address to readers at first generates sympathy, readers come to realize that she is really not yet ready to resume responsibility for raising her child. The narrator has a strong sense of justice, but her means of achieving it are not socially acceptable. Her decision to resort to violence when she does not get her way affirms to readers that, while likable in many ways, she should not succeed in her quest to regain her child if the boy is to be given a chance to grow up normally.

The story's title, "Customs of the Country," alludes to *The Custom of the Country*, a 1913 novel by Edith Wharton, an early twentieth century writer who explored the dark underside of fashionable life in New York City. The contrasts between the high society of Park Avenue and rural Virginia may seem at first too drastic for meaningful comparison. The irony that Bell wishes readers to see, however, is that Wharton's heroine, who possesses all the advantages of high society, rejects her son because he is detrimental to her attempts at social climbing. By contrast, Bell's uneducated drug addict from rural Virginia cares deeply for her son, and although readers may see the wisdom in the state's decision not to return him to her custody, there is a deep sense of sympathy for her, even if she does not know how to express her love appropriately.

*Laurence W. Mazzeno*

# THE CYCLISTS' RAID

*Author:* Frank Rooney (1913-      )
*Type of plot:* Realism
*Time of plot:* The late 1940's
*Locale:* Central California
*First published:* 1951

*Principal characters:*
> JOEL BLEEKER, a widowed hotel owner
> CATHY BLEEKER, his seventeen-year-old daughter
> BRET TIMMONS, Cathy's boyfriend, a drugstore owner
> FRANCIS LASALLE, co-owner of a hardware store
> GAR SIMPSON, the leader of the Angelenos, a motorcycle gang
> AN UNNAMED ANGELENO, who is different from the others

*The Story*

The tranquillity of a small town in California's San Joaquin Valley is shattered toward sunset one day when the Angelenos, a band of motorcyclists from Los Angeles, arrive unannounced, planning to spend the night and part of the next day.

Joel Bleeker, a lieutenant colonel during World War II, has returned from overseas to this peaceful haven, where he operates one of the town's two hotels. Bleeker's wife died two years earlier, her neck broken when she was thrown from a horse. Bleeker now lives a quiet and methodical existence, managing a small hotel with the help of his seventeen-year-old daughter, Cathy. Each day at precisely the same time, he checks his old redwood clock in the lobby against the railroad watch that he wears on a chain and keeps in his pocket.

On the day of the story, when Bleeker hears a noise that he mistakes for aircraft engines, he moves the hands of his redwood clock ahead a minute and a half before investigating the commotion. On the veranda of the hotel, Cathy sits with Francis LaSalle and Bret Timmons, local businessmen. Suddenly, the noise becomes so great that no one can be heard above the din. A column of red motorcycles invades the hotel like an army column bent on taking a town. It is led by a man on a white motorcycle, Gar Simpson, unctuously polite and powerfully commanding.

Simpson addresses Bleeker by name, asking whether his motorcyclists might use the hotel's facilities, for which he offers to pay. He also asks whether Bleeker's dining room can feed twenty of the men; the rest will eat elsewhere. The bikers ogle Cathy, thereby unnerving her father, who agrees to feed part of the contingent and allows them the use of the downstairs washroom. Bleeker tells Cathy to work in the kitchen that night instead of serving in the dining room.

The bikers resemble visitors from outer space. Dressed alike, they perform with great precision, obey their "general," who understands his men well, and never remove the green motorcycle goggles that make them look like bug-eyed aliens. As their drinking continues, they sing loudly and begin to race their motorcycles along the town's main street. They also begin to damage Bleeker's hotel, but Simpson promises to pay reparations.

Assured that Cathy is safely ensconced in her bedroom, Bleeker walks down the street to Cunningham's Bar, where one biker, about twenty-five, stands out from the rest. He sits alone drinking Coca-Cola. Bleeker joins him, but the din is too great for sustained conversation. Nevertheless, he learns that beer makes this biker sick, as do many of his fellow bikers' activities. This biker is the only one who removes his goggles.

Before long, the other bikers are out of control. Bleeker returns to his hotel, where he checks on Cathy. He escorts back to the lobby an Angeleno whom he finds on the second floor trying to enter rooms. Someone has struck Francis LaSalle, who is now sprawled uninjured on the floor. Gar Simpson approaches Bleeker, takes out a wallet, and puts money in front of him to cover the damage the bikers have done to his hotel.

Two motorcycles zoom through the lobby door; one of them roars through the lobby, striking Cathy at the foot of the stairs, injuring her badly. A doctor is summoned. After he administers first aid and has her taken to his office, she dies.

Grief-stricken, Bleeker returns to his hotel, where the boy with whom he spoke earlier appears, suffering pangs of guilt over what has happened. Bleeker observes him closely. Townspeople begin to beat the biker, knocking him down and stamping him maniacally. Bleeker, too, finds himself pummeling the boy's body, but soon he is on the ground, cradling the boy's head on his lap, trying to protect him from the others.

The story ends with Bleeker standing on his hotel veranda, physically and emotionally numb. He turns to go into the hotel, knowing that there is time for him to make his peace with the dead but that now he must make his peace with the living, represented by the boy.

## Themes and Meanings

Two major elements pervade this tightly structured and closely observed tale, which became the basis for the 1954 Marlon Brando film *The Wild One*. The theme of death is strong within the story. It is introduced first by the generalized suggestion of death that people connect with World War II, from whose European combat Joel Bleeker has returned physically unscathed to resume his existence in rural California. His postwar life there has been tranquil, marred only by the death of his wife two years earlier.

Bleeker has apparently learned to live with his loss. He adores his daughter, who, like her mother, is feisty, humorous, and caring. Bleeker has laid to rest his memories of war and its horrors. On the day of the story, however, all his painful memories are evoked instantly, first by the high-decibel approach of the motorcyclists—his first thought that they are airplanes must trigger his memories of enemy bombers—and, after the source of the noise is finally identified, by the military precision with which the motorcycle columns approach his hotel.

Clearly, Gar Simpson is "general" of the rowdy gang, whose members he understands remarkably well. He knows that, as commander, he can best maintain control over his men by allowing them the freedom that results eventually in massive destruction and, finally, death. Simpson is meticulously polite and, within his own boundaries, responsible. The Angelenos, all but one of whom are exactly like the others, follow him with a loyalty bordering on blindness—which is suggested by their wearing goggles at all times.

Nowhere does Frank Rooney suggest that the maverick motorcyclist who returns to the hotel after Cathy's death is the one who killed her. It is, in fact, impossible to tell one identically clad motorcyclist from another. This biker returns as an act of expiation, by which act he assumes the collective guilt of his fellow Angelenos.

Underlying the entire story is the rampant sexuality of a male group deprived of a normal sexual outlet. Their libidinous glances at Cathy early in the story reveal their sexual desperation, as does the maverick motorcyclist's telling Bleeker that the bikers are looking for women. Given the overall context of the story, sexual repression helps explain their violence and violence in general, including war. However, as the maverick motorcyclist deviates from his group, so does Joel Bleeker—who is himself seemingly deprived of conventional sexual outlet—differ from those who practice violence as a means of dealing with their urges.

*Style and Technique*

In "The Cyclists' Raid," Rooney demonstrates his clear, crisp style. A master of detail, he creates with precise words and penetrating observation of physical details the story's landscape. His major characters come to life through the details that the reader quickly learns about them. Joel Bleeker—who was successful enough as a leader to become a lieutenant colonel—is methodical and controlled, checking the clock in his lobby at the same time daily against his more accurate railroad watch. No unusual occurrence, even the noisy approach of the motorcyclists, deters him from this established ritual.

Rooney demonstrates that Bleeker has laid to rest two major ghosts. First he has escaped from the dangers of World War II. He has also survived and moved beyond the loss of a wife who was precious to him. His love and concern for his daughter have been heightened by his wife's death.

Gar Simpson possesses the same sort of leadership ability that Bleeker does but to a greater degree. Rooney consistently portrays him as methodical and meticulous. He knows the names of the hotels in the town as well as the names of their owners. He has planned the trip with the precision of a military operation.

Rooney's introduction of the maverick motorcyclist is particularly cogent. It lends itself to the eventual denouement of the story. In his budding individuality, this sympathetic character shows courage and provides readers with hope. That the townspeople turn on him in giving vent to their outrage about Cathy's death is understandable. Bleeker's protection of the pummeled boy, however, reflects a dimension in his personality that, despite surface similarities, makes him inherently different from Gar Simpson.

*R. Baird Shuman*

# DADDY WAS A NUMBER RUNNER

*Author:* Louise Meriwether (1923-    )
*Type of plot:* Coming of age
*Time of plot:* Summer, 1934
*Locale:* Harlem, New York City
*First published:* 1967

> *Principal characters:*
> FRANCIE, the bright eleven-year-old narrator
> JAMES, her father
> JESSIE, her mother
> SUKIE MACEO, her best friend

## The Story

The story opens during a school lunch break, with eleven-year-old Francie collecting number slips for her father; it ends with her father released from jail after being arrested by the police trying to show some power in this mob-controlled neighborhood. Between those two incidents, readers are granted a detailed and revealing look into the naturalistic world of one family's struggles to survive, and a prepubescent girl's struggle for her own identity.

The major details of the story circle around the numbers racket that permeates the community. Everyone plays and everyone dreams of the big win that will get them out of this world. When Francie's number 514—a number based on her dream of a catfish—pays off $215, the family eats well for about a week, but as Francie notes, they soon are back to fried cabbage and ham hocks just as if the big hit had never happened.

Francie's journey toward adulthood is given in terms of this numbers game. Although only eleven years of age, she is responsible enough to collect the number slips and take them home to hide in a buffet drawer. When the police raid her railroad flat after the big win, they do not find the receipts they need for an arrest, but they take Daddy off anyway, charged with assault and battery for protecting Francie. She takes the numbers downstairs to Frenchy, the local agent for Big Dutch, and tells him that her father has been arrested. In this crisis, Francie demonstrates her resourcefulness and intelligence.

The rest of Francie's family has similar struggles in the story. After losing his job as a house painter, her father tries to help the family by playing the piano at parties over the weekend, but he does not make much money this way. Francie's two brothers may be cutting school to hang out with the Ebony Dukes, the local gang. Jessie, her mother, goes off as a domestic day worker for Mrs. Schwartz, and at the end of the story reveals that she has gone to the relief agency and applied for assistance. Daddy is hurt that she has done this but, as she tells her husband, his pride will not feed the children.

Besides incidents concerning family and the numbers racket, the story circles around Francie's friend Sukie. They are best friends, but Sukie fights with Francie whenever the pressures of her own life—her father a drunk, her sister a prostitute— get to her. By the end of the story, the incidents of Francie's life have made her as tough, and, instead of running away from Sukie, she seeks her out to fight. She has become the aggressor, and she beats up Sukie. The fight signals Francie's development into a tougher, more capable adolescent.

*Themes and Meanings*

Louise Meriwether's story works on two distinct levels, the social and the psychological. Its social themes revolve around what it is like to grow up black in New York during the Depression, and the story relates that condition in a broad array of details. Meriwether reveals the socioeconomic conditions—the couch in the living room where Francie sleeps, infested by bed bugs; the educational—Francie's school, P.S. 136, "the baddest girls' school in the world"; and the cultural—the numbers racket, music, food, and so on. Depression-era Harlem life is shown in all its difficulties and violence, with few pleasures. It is a complex and accurate portrait: The Ebony Dukes jump the Jewish boys who attend the synagogue around the corner, but Francie's dining room furniture is a gift from the Jewish plumber downstairs. Meriwether's is no simplistic portrait of urban life and strife.

More significant than the social meaning of the story is the psychological, and this is far more subtle, for the eleven-year-old narrator does not always understand the significance of her own life. Like her slightly older fictional cousin, Huck Finn— likewise a first-person narrator of his own adventures—Francie relates incidents that readers must interpret. She wonders what makes her friend Sukie so mean, for example—but Meriwether gives readers all the evidence they need to make the analysis of Sukie's behavior themselves. Francie cannot articulate the pressures of her own life, let alone recognize them in her friends. She is suspended in that limbo between childhood and adulthood that is not yet adolescence. She still reads fairy tales from the library on her fire escape, and her dreams, such as the fish dream that gives her the winning numbers, aid the family. On the other hand, she witnesses the violence of Depression Harlem, as shown in a reference to mugging any white man caught alone there after sunset, and its poverty, highlighted by her mother searching half an hour for a dime she thought she had lost but that Francie had stolen. She loves her father, who is trying to get her to grow up to be a lady, and still trusts him, wondering why her mother could not. She has not yet learned all the lessons life has taught her mother.

The story provides clues that Francie will successfully navigate her way out of childhood to adulthood, in spite of the numerous dangers in her world. She is, in fact, halfway there. She is already resourceful and responsible for her family, and at the end of the story, after beating up Sukie, turns her face away from home and wanders aimlessly down Fifth Avenue. Her future will be away from this world. When a mob crowds around her and Sukie, she says, "I was suffocating. I pushed against the black, shoving mass until I was free of them. There was something evil in their sweating black faces, and that something was in me also." She must flee this world in order to attain her own healthy identity, even if it means wandering aimlessly at first. Readers can only hope for Francie's future.

The story was written in the Watts Writers Workshop, which screenwriter and novelist Budd Shulberg started after the Los Angeles riots of 1965. Three years later, Louise Meriwether published a novel based on the story. Although the novel brings in many more significant details, sexual and violent, it does not change the basic thrust of the original short story. In both, readers witness a young girl coming of age against the myriad difficulties of urban Depression life.

*Style and Technique*

Meriwether's fictional technique has two distinguishing characteristics. The more apparent is Francie's first-person narration, which is realistic and clever and hardly ever calls attention to itself. From her opening encounter with her neighbor Mrs. Mackey ("Lord, I thought, don't let Mrs. Mackey stand here with her big, black self telling me about her dreams"), through her description of her father's hurt pride and anger at welfare, to her final blasphemy ("Goddamn them all to hell"), Francie's narration comes by way of the authentic voice of a preadolescent girl struggling against the odds of survival in this all-too-real world. Much of the story's power comes from the uninflected but absolutely honest character revealed through that voice.

The broader characteristic of Meriwether's story is its naturalistic style. In detail as in language, the author reveals the ways in which these characters are trapped, not only by socioeconomic factors but by the psychological as well. Naturalism works best in a style that is flat and uninterpretative, which is why Francie's first-person narrative voice works so well. From the vomit-green kitchen walls inside her apartment to the violence of Harlem outside, "Daddy Was a Number Runner" is steeped in the naturalistic tradition of writers such as Richard Wright, James Baldwin, and Paule Marshall.

*David Peck*

# DADDY WOLF

*Author:* James Purdy (1923-        )
*Type of plot:* Character study
*Time of plot:* The 1950's
*Locale:* New York City
*First published:* 1961

*Principal character:*
BENNY, a Korean War veteran

*The Story*

James Purdy's concerns about the vanquished in American society reach full cry in this monologue by a veteran of the Korean War. Speaking from a phone booth, apparently in the hallway of the rat-infested tenement in which he lives, Benny addresses someone who appears to be waiting to use the phone. He asks the person to be patient a little bit longer because he is attempting to get the operator to reconnect him with a woman with whom he has been talking. From his position in the phone booth, he also can see into his flat, the door of which has been left open.

The reader is in the position of the person waiting to use the phone: He or she must listen to Benny's litany, must hear about Benny's wife, who has given up trying to cope with life on the ragged edge of poverty and who has taken herself and their son out of the city. Economic hardships are a commonplace of Benny's existence, and he now works for little pay in a company that makes mittens. So hard-pressed has he been that his only food is a bowl of Cream of Wheat leavened with some brown sugar. In fact, he is about to be displaced in his linoleum-floored apartment by a mama rat and her baby, which emerge periodically from the holes in the floor.

Before his wife left him, she had gotten in the habit of calling someone named Daddy Wolf at a number described as the Trouble Phone number. She would talk to Daddy Wolf about her problems, and he would unfailingly offer the same remedies: Stand by your man, go to church, and read uplifting books whenever sexual desire troubles you. Daddy Wolf was for ladies only, however, and Benny, desperate in his need for his own trouble phone, has picked a number at random from the phone book and has been pouring out his woes to a female voice that responds only occasionally with "I see."

Ground down by a system that offers platitudinous prerecorded messages, Benny and Mabel, the absent wife, represent the urban poor in the United States, victims of a system that they have had no part in creating and that they cannot control. Mabel, the reader learns indirectly, had to resort to prostitution to get money to provide food for the family. A report she heard about the increase of venereal disease in the city provided additional impetus for her flight. Daddy Wolf cannot save her, and in his own desperate search for someone to listen, to care, Benny pleads with the operator at the story's end to help him because his is an emergency phone call.

## Themes and Meanings

The "quiet desperation" about which Henry David Thoreau wrote in describing the lives of the masses of people breaks out in the open in this tale of frustration and loneliness. The American dream of coming to the big city and there achieving the success that the system argues is due each hardworking person eludes Benny, who has served in the Korean War and returned unscathed to make a life for himself and his family. Trouble phones, crisis lines, and dial-a-prayer services are what pass for human compassion, for understanding. Mechanical and electronic instruments become the only means by which desperate people may attempt to make contact with those they believe could help them. Tenements, low-paying jobs, and unfulfilled promises are the legacies that Benny inherits from those who have gone before.

Benny is almost childlike in his recounting of the troubles that he has experienced; his frustration and anger come more and more to the surface as the story progresses, and by its end he is literally shouting at the operator, demanding and at the same time pleading that someone listen to him. However, the trouble phone spins out its never-changing message: Be good; if you are good, God will love you.

## Style and Technique

Because this is a dramatic monologue, Purdy uses several devices to involve the reader directly in the experience. Benny uses direct address as the story opens: "You aren't the first man to ask me what I'm doing so long in the phone booth with the door to my flat open and all." The reader is immediately involved in the situation and recognizes, almost at once, that he or she will be involved in what is about to happen, as a passerby is sometimes engaged by a stranger seeking alms of some kind. Like the monologuists who became staples of radio and television programs, Benny talks to the reader and to the unseen operator who may or may not be on the other end of the line. His voice is ceaseless; he hardly pauses for breath. Purdy lets the reader listen at first and then by the simple expedient of increasing the tone of desperation in Benny's voice, forces the reader, almost against his will, to listen as the broken pieces of Benny's life are spread out before him as on the linoleum floor of his flat. When the reader hears the anguish and discovers the pathos of Benny's situation, he is no longer in such a hurry to use the phone because he knows that it is indeed an emergency call that Benny is attempting to place.

*Dale H. Ross*

# DAMBALLAH

*Author:* John Edgar Wideman (1941-    )
*Type of plot:* Psychological
*Time of plot:* The 1800's
*Locale:* A cane plantation somewhere in the Deep South
*First published:* 1981

> *Principal characters:*
> ORION (RYAN), an intractable slave, alienated from both blacks
>     and whites and intent on preserving his African language and
>     rituals
> AN UNNAMED SLAVE BOY, who is fascinated by Orion's strange
>     habits
> AUNT LISSY, one of Orion's detractors, the black cook in charge
>     of children too young to work in the fields
> MASTER, Orion's white owner who has grown intolerant of
>     Orion's defiance

*The Story*

Orion is the name of a brawny giant in Greek mythology, a slayer of all beasts, who became a constellation. In this story, his namesake is a physically beaten, emaciated African disavowed by all on the plantation except one slave boy; accordingly, his proud name has been truncated to "Ryan." The boy, contemptuous of his vapid chores and the animal stories often repeated to him, is eager to take his place alongside the field hands and to learn the subtleties of male conversation. Restless, he alternately laments both "the nothing always there to think of" in his mind and the bombardment of orders from others on him, "so crowded and noisy lots of time don't hear his own voice." For this reason, Ryan, who maintains serenity while obstinately speaking "heathen talk," abstaining from American food, and meditating in the river, poses an irresistible attraction.

Despite a beating from Aunt Lissy, the black doyenne of Mistress's kitchen and the supervisor of the slave children, the boy follows Ryan every spare moment, hiding behind trees. He even memorizes a word that he has heard the man shout in his direction: "Damballah." Though the boy does not know that this refers to a powerful god in the African pantheon, the word's very sound engenders equilibrium in him. He senses that Damballah will permeate something latent and beneficent inside himself, like a sudden gleam "you knew all the time . . . was there" appearing in a tarnished spoon when he polishes Mistress's silver.

The boy suspects that Ryan, aware of his spying, longs to communicate with him, yet before the two can meet directly, Master loses his patience with the recalcitrant man. Frustrated and irate, Master requests a full refund for Ryan in a letter to the unscrupulous trader who sold him. Then at last Ryan does something powerful, worthy of the legendary Greek hunter but for him, a slave, unthinkable and fatal. He strikes an overseer from his horse with bone-breaking effect, incurring a punishment of death: Master and the other overseers torture and decapitate him. Not even death can stop Ryan from contacting the boy, however, and through Damballah's intercession Ryan transmits to the child the native stories that he had yearned to preserve. When his spirit finally departs, the boy tosses the severed head into the waters where the dead man used to stand.

### Themes and Meanings

As John Edgar Wideman indicates in an epigraph to the collection of short stories commencing with "Damballah," the paternal sky deity of this name—"himself unchanged by life, and . . . at once the ancient past and the assurance of the future"—embodies the concepts of unity and history. Ryan's invocation to this god, then, belies how he and other slaves are scattered in strange lands, severed from their families, tribes, and cultures. In addition to this physical displacement, Wideman suggests how, brainwashed to view the gods of "wild African niggers" as inauthentic, the plantation-born blacks are estranged from real powers such as Damballah and in turn have embraced the bogus Christianity taught them by whites.

Aunt Lissy, for example, is appalled when Ryan shouts Damballah's name during a black preacher's sermon on "Sweet Jesus the Son of God." Her horror at what he has done reflects the typical longtime slave's attitude that anyone, black or white, who is not a Christian is hedonistic, savage, and insane. However, she is the crazy one for accepting a Christianity that condones rather than condemns her enslavers' harsh treatments.

In fact, in his behavior Master himself is unchristian. He justifies as "my Christianizing project" his bondage of blacks, of which Ryan's in particular culminates with a murder by "ax and tongs, branding iron and other tools" wielded by several able-bodied whites. Though Master brags, "I concern myself with the spiritual as well as the temporal needs of my slaves," he actually is preoccupied with neither. He fornicates with slave women at random despite the full cognizance of his anguished wife, and he worries about his slaves' market values instead of providing them with properly sized clothes and undergarments. To these hypocrisies neither God nor Christ, as if nonexistent, replies.

On the other hand, when Orion alerts Damballah in the spirit world, power emanates. This response undercuts the religion of the slaves' owners even more because as part of his ritual Ryan ironically traces a cross, a symbol associated with the triumph and might of Christianity. During one such rite "over the cross the air seemed to shimmer like it does above a flame or like it does when the sun so hot you can see waves of heat rising off the fields." Similarly, the boy has heard that the crossed cuts on a whipped slave have attracted vengeful spirits who "had everything in they hands, even the white folks." Thus, stressing the impotence of the Christian Father and Son, only spirits and gods connected to the slaves are active and responsive.

*Style and Technique*

Wideman's deft shifts in point of view convincingly dramatize the alienation of slaves from owners and of both groups from Ryan. However, whether the boy finally hears Damballah's instructions and the murdered slave's stories or merely has grown simpleminded is a question that the author resolves through other techniques.

First, Wideman suggests a soul-link between boy and man by describing their physical features and actions in related terms. Both Ryan and the child resemble tall, gangly, aquatic birds, specifically storks or cranes, for example. Similarly, just as the story opens with Ryan absently bathing and peering into the shallows, so the boy himself spends much of his day dreamily studying his image, "like his face reflected in the river," in Mistress's flatware. Thus, to the careful reader, this child's communication with the dead old man is merely an extension of a bond that always existed between them.

Also, because of references to versions of the Greek Orion myths sprinkled throughout this story, Ryan comes across as not a pitiful slave but an extraordinarily gifted spirit. Three elements prominent in "Damballah"—eyes, water, and a bull— play key parts in the ancient tales as well. The Greek Orion, blinded by an angry king, regained his sight by looking directly into the rising sun. Interestingly, black Ryan watches the morning sun illuminate the river, and the boy is struck by the penetrating quality of the man's "hooded eyes." Further echoing a variant of the Hellenic tales, wherein the appearance and disappearance of Orion's constellation signal impending rain (the word "Orion" itself means "he who makes water"), the enslaved Ryan senses a storm brewing, a harbinger of his death. Finally, although a bull is associated with the classical Orion's birth—his desperate father sacrificed one so the gods would grant his wish for a child—in "Damballah" a sound like a bull's scream comes from the barn on the night of Ryan's death. The graying slave's thin body and distant air hence cloak a majestic soul searching for someone worthy of his gifts, recalling the Greek gods and goddesses who visited so many mortals, including Orion's own parents, disguised as poor, ragged old couples. Because Ryan shares the legacy of a demigod, it is believable that he can maintain a mystic rapport with the boy even after death.

Indeed, one particular thread from the Orion myths woven through "Damballah" serves to do more than legitimize the boy's talks with a corpse. His eyes put out by his lover's furious father, Orion impressed Cedalion, a young blacksmith's apprentice, into service as his guide. Clearly in a similar fashion the slave youth, drawn magnetically to the outcast, directs Ryan at the end of the story. Whereas Cedalion conducted Orion toward the sun and sight, the boy sees Ryan's spirit home to the light of freedom: "Orion talked and he listened and couldn't stop listening till he saw Orion's eyes rise up through the back of the severed skull and lips rise up through the skull and the wings of the ghost measure out the rhythm of one last word."

*Barbara A. McCaskill*

# DANCING AFTER HOURS

*Author:* Andre Dubus (1936-1999)
*Type of plot:* Domestic realism
*Time of plot:* The 1990's
*Locale:* A beachfront bar in Massachusetts
*First published:* 1996

*Principal characters:*
EMILY, a bartender
JEFF, the bar manager
DREW, a quadriplegic
ALVIN, Drew's personal attendant
RITA, another bartender
KAY, a waitress

## The Story

Forty-year-old Emily has never thought she was pretty, which has affected her relationships with people, especially men. She had been a high school teacher, but the students' apathy made her feel so isolated and useless that she quit teaching to work nights as a bartender. One day, two men, one of whom is in a wheelchair, come into the bar where she works. At first Emily is apprehensive, worrying that the disabled man will be hard to talk to and she will have to entertain him through her long shift. Her discomfort embarrasses her because she prides herself on making her customers feel comfortable and at home. As soon as Drew and his assistant Alvin enter, Rita, who has just finished her shift, joins them, and Kay takes their orders. Emily believes that Kay is falling in love with Rita and is distressed, not because they are both women, but because she feels that love affairs are doomed to cause pain and she does not want to deal with that every night at work.

Emily, who has never lived with a man and has not had an intimate relationship in two years, leads a solitary, structured life. She reads late into the night, escaping temporarily from the sadness caused by her fear that she will never have children. Jeff, the bar manager, is recently divorced, and Emily knows he is interested in her. She truly likes Jeff, who is kind, intelligent, and attractive, but is afraid of becoming involved with him. Eventually he asks her to lunch, but she agrees so stiffly that he knows she does not really want to go.

Watching Drew and Alvin, Jeff tells Emily that he had a good friend who was crippled by a land mine in Vietnam. Jeff used to take him fishing, lifting him and his chair on to the boat. Hearing Jeff talk and watching the gregarious Drew, Emily feels that her soul has atrophied without her having noticed it. She realizes she does not fear pain as much as she is tired of it, and wonders if this means she has lost hope. She thinks that if she has no hope she cannot love with her whole heart, so she will never find someone who can love her with his whole heart.

A recording of saxophonist Roland Kirk is playing in the bar, and Emily remembers seeing him play in a small nightclub when she was young. Kirk, who was blind, had the percussionist lead him through the audience, swaying, playing his sax, and hugging people near him, including Emily. She remembers how alive she felt, and how when Kirk slowed the music down to a soft, loving melody, she felt that everything good was possible. Her memory causes her to cry; Jeff sees her and admits that he denies such feelings, then ends up crying in funny films.

Emily thinks about what Alvin must have to do to take care of a quadriplegic and wonders how Drew handles living without privacy. The two men stay on with Jeff, Emily, Rita, and Kay after the bar closes. Drew tells them that he recently went skydiving, strapped to another diver, although he was warned that the wind that day made it more dangerous for him. Both of his already paralyzed legs were broken when he landed, but he did not regret the experience. He still craves adventure, despite having been paralyzed when he was twenty-one years old by diving into a wave.

Jeff asks Emily to dance, and Rita dances with Alvin. Emily is concerned when she sees Kay holding Drew's hands and swaying to the music as though dancing with him, but later Drew says he and his wife used to dance like that. Emily is astonished that he got married after he was paralyzed; however, the marriage ended after Drew learned that his wife was pregnant with a friend's child. Soon, Kay and Rita are dancing and singing along to Frank Sinatra. As dawn nears, Kay invites everyone to her house to continue dancing, but Drew and Alvin are tired and leave for their motel, promising to return on Monday and go fishing with Jeff.

Rita follows Kay home, and Emily tells Jeff she wants to go fishing with him and their new friends on Monday. When he agrees, she suggests that they get together for lunch that day, after they have both gotten some sleep, and Jeff says he will call her at one o'clock and give her directions to his house.

*Themes and Meanings*

After a freak accident in 1986, Andre Dubus was confined to a wheelchair for the last thirteen years of his life. The collection of stories *Dancing After Hours* (1996), from which the story of the same name is taken, was his first work of fiction after the accident. During the intervening decade, he produced one book of essays, many on the subject of disability. Several of the stories in *Dancing After Hours* feature characters with disabilities similar to his.

Although many authors would have made the wheelchair-using Drew the object of most of the reader's sympathy, Dubus shows that Drew has come to grips more fully with his problems than some of the others have. Emily is more attractive than she thinks she is, but her experiences with romance have left her sad and fearful of seeking love. Seeing how Drew, who has used a wheelchair for years, still seeks joy and adventure helps her to open her heart to the possibilities around her. She is able to appreciate Jeff's kind heart when he speaks of his disabled friend and to look affectionately on the possible romance between Kay and Rita, rather than focus on how she might be inconvenienced if they become involved in a relationship.

Although Drew is the catalyst for the changes in the story's protagonist, his situation is seen only through Emily's eyes. Even with this limited view, however, the author gives his readers an authentic look at the quotidian routines of a quadriplegic. First, Emily worries about how she will be able to interact with a disabled person and is relieved to find that Drew is lively and engaging; then she ponders the personal care he requires from his attendant; eventually, she talks to Alvin about what is involved in caring for Drew; finally, she asks Drew about his marriage and sex life.

## Style and Technique

Dubus began publishing fiction in the 1960's, but his work never followed the late twentieth century trend toward minimalism and postmodernism. Dubus's literary hero was Anton Chekhov, and his writing shares the same devotion to realism. Some critics have called him old-fashioned, and others consider his style timeless.

In "Dancing After Hours," Dubus uses a limited omniscient narrator to tell the story from Emily's point of view. Always a careful observer of human nature, Dubus creates and presents characters in such a way that readers are drawn to care about their fate. The main characters, each with his or her own demons with which to contend, slowly coalesce into a group, finding a moment of communal joy in the pleasant bar. Dubus has been noted for his facility in presenting the thoughts and emotions of his female protagonists authentically, and this story is an excellent example of that ability.

The whole story takes place in a few hours, yet the author provides insight into the lives and backgrounds of six well-realized characters. The setting, a bar in a small town in Massachusetts, is a common setting in Dubus's fiction. Dubus is a master of painting vivid pictures from small details. Here, for example, by referring throughout the story to well-known jazz musicians playing on the bar's sound system, he establishes the scene as an upscale bar without stating it explicitly.

*Irene Struthers Rush*

# DANTE AND THE LOBSTER

*Author:* Samuel Beckett (1906-1989)
*Type of plot:* Farce
*Time of plot:* The late 1920's
*Locale:* Dublin, Ireland
*First published:* 1932

### Principal characters:

BELCQUA SHUAH, the protagonist, a student and idler
SIGNORINA ADRIANA OTTOLENGHI, Belacqua's Italian teacher

## The Story

As the story begins, Belacqua Shuah, the protagonist, is reading canto 2 of Dante's *Paradiso* and having difficulty understanding it. At noon, he lays his task aside and considers his schedule for the day, consisting of lunch, picking up a lobster for his aunt, and his Italian lesson. The preparations for his lunch are strange. First, he toasts bread, which must be blackened through and through to suit him. He succeeds in achieving the desired glassy texture, but he burns his wall in the process. He then applies a thick paste of Savora, salt, and cayenne, wraps the "burnt offering" in paper, and goes out to buy cheese. Nothing would do but "a good green stenching rotten lump of Gorgonzola cheese." Warning the grocer that if he does not come up with rottener cheese in the future, he will take his business elsewhere, Belacqua, with his now completed Gorgonzola sandwich in hand, heads for the public bar for his daily two pints of stout, looking forward to his lesson with his Italian teacher, Signorina Adriana Ottolenghi, whom he idolizes.

Belacqua then goes to school, lunch having been "a notable success," far better than he had anticipated. The "pale soapy piece of cheese" had proved strong, and the toast had had the texture of glass: "His teeth and jaws had been in heaven, splinters of vanquished toast spraying forth at each gnash." His mouth still burning and aching from his lunch, he then goes to pick up the lobster, which he believes to be freshly killed, and proceeds to his Italian lesson. While he is with the signorina, a cat attacks his parcel, which has been left out in the hall, but the French instructress rescues the lobster before any harm is done. The lesson continues. When it is over, Belacqua takes the lobster to his aunt's house, where he is horrified to learn that the lobster is not yet dead and will have to be boiled alive. He comforts himself that at least it will be a quick death. The last line of the story is, "It is not."

## Themes and Meanings

Belacqua Shuah, the prototype for many of Samuel Beckett's fictional heroes, makes his presence felt initially, in this the opening story of the author's first book of fiction, by means of a failure. He is unable to understand a passage from canto 2 of

Dante's *Paradiso*. The story ends with another failure, Belacqua's misunderstanding of how a lobster is cooked. In the afternoon between these two incidents, typical scenes from what must be regarded as Belacqua's ordinary life are presented.

In contrast to the stupefaction that accompanies his failures, the demeanor to which Belacqua's afternoon activities give rise is intense, aggressive, fastidious, and perfectionist. By means of this contrast, the story satirically places activity above thought. Belacqua's round of time-killing appointments serves to distract him from the abyss of unknowing into which his mind, in its ignorance, can lead him. The vehemence and relish of Belacqua's encounters with the everyday are astutely and economically dramatized as overstatements. The air of triumph with which Belacqua concludes his business with the story's various, almost invariably anonymous tradesmen is misplaced and, in any case, ephemeral. The sense of completeness that attends these transactions is spurious, given that they occur between the twin inscrutabilities of Dante and the lobster. Thus, the story can be seen as a comedy of misperceptions and absurdly inflated responses, framed by what the mind cannot grasp (the passage from Dante) and by what it grasps so well that it cannot bear to contemplate (the fact that, to be cooked, lobsters must be boiled alive).

Dante and the lobster are extremes, in the presence of whose reality Belacqua becomes virtually speechless. As though to distract himself from the ineluctability of such extremes, Belacqua creates an extreme of his own, the story's celebrated Gorgonzola sandwich. The production of this concoction, which it is pleasant to imagine Belacqua uniquely capable of consuming, is a splendid comic set piece. In a way that Beckett's later work perfects, however, the sandwich ritual's excruciating humor has a directly conceptual, but obliquely narrational, bearing on the more distressing components of the story's framework. The tears that the preposterously spiced sandwich bring to Belacqua's eyes are tears of consummation. His mouth palpitates in the aftermath of the self-inflicted culinary assault, but his mind rejoices in the completeness that he has perpetrated. ("The lunch had been a noticeable success, it would abide as a standard in his mind.") Idea transcends experience, as is borne out by Belacqua's laughable tendency to idealize his Italian teacher, Signorina Adriana Ottolenghi.

It is the signorina, however, in a brief outburst of impatience and anxiety, who returns Belacqua to an awareness of immutability and a recognition of the unalterable nature of things. By this outburst and, earlier, by her questioning the desirability of translating Dante, the signorina, in effect, prepares Belacqua for the lobster's death. The preparation is, however, cerebral only; it does not prevent Belacqua from being shocked when his aunt (another of the story's anonymous characters) is about to carry out the crustacean's execution. In this instance, as in the opening case of the *Paradiso* passage, experience defies idea. Whatever cannot be understood, whatever retains its unamenable integrity, obtains to a different plane of reality than the repetitious features of the everyday—drinking porter, making sandwiches, and attending lessons (for the most part; Belacqua is a creature of habit). It may be that Belacqua's engrossing fidelity to a familiar daily round (hinted at by the circular shape of the bread for his sandwich) leads him to assume that the world is his oyster. His comically exaggerated sense of his own importance may be a dramatization of this assumption. However, together, Dante and the lobster undermine such posturing.

In addition to being, by virtue of his idleness, related to a character of the same name in Dante's *The Divine Comedy*, Belacqua is a member of a long line of Irish fictional students. All these characters are notable for the varying degrees to which their makeup combines intensity, subjectivity, and vanity. As in the case of the line's most illustrious members (James Joyce's Stephen Dedalus immediately comes to mind), the challenge that Belacqua must face concerns the mind, its range and efficiency. The contrast in "Dante and the Lobster" between what can be effectively undertaken or satisfactorily experienced and what cannot may be considered as a differentiation between the mind as a mechanism (responding to urges and appetites) and the mind as an organism (susceptible to evolution). Despite its philosophical inclinations, however, "Dante and the Lobster" should not be thought of as a philosophical argument.

On the contrary, Beckett impartially gives both conceptions of the mind equal attention. Belacqua embodies both but controls neither. He is a space where both models of mind come randomly into play. Beckett seems to do no more than establish the space and invoke the play. The two kinds of mind are permitted, or even perhaps encouraged, to collide with and override each other. The fact that one version of mind is being attended to at a given juncture in the story does not mean that its opposite (though it is also possible to say, its counterpart) is totally in abeyance. The story is so committed to a sense of duality that it may be suggesting that its two models of mind share a mutuality as well as an antagonism. Dante and the lobster, in different ways, produce a common effect. However, as Belacqua's flounderings reveal, it is possible, because of the ineluctable nature of time, to inhabit only one of the terms of the duality at once. Thus, the interplay between experience and idea succeeds in both substantiating and undermining its own conceptual structure.

*Style and Technique*

Much of the conceptual dimension of "Dante and the Lobster" is borne out by the story's stylistic variety. Beckett's later stylistic virtuosity may be seen in embryo here. The story's preoccupation with disruption, discontinuity, interruption, and reversal is given its primary salience in the author's language. Veering from the mandarin to the demonic, from the platitudinous to the rarefied, from the language of Dublin to the language of Dante, Beckett provides a telling form of dramatic validation for Belacqua's experiences of finality and indeterminacy. The oscillations of style occur unpredictably, devoid of a sense of pattern or overall objective. Their reality, like that of everything else in the story, is ratified by Belacqua's failure to rise above them.

Supplementing the story's plethora of styles is an equally wide and unpredictable range of literary allusions. In addition to Dante, a greater influence on Beckett—James Joyce—subtly pervades the story. A reader gains an interesting perspective on Belacqua through noting his fear (mentioned on two different occasions) of "some brisk tattler . . . bouncing in now with a big idea or petition"; fear, that is, of a confrontation dramatized in Joyce's *A Portrait of the Artist as a Young Man* (1916). Similarly, it is amusing to compare the fitful Belacqua's lunchtime with that of steady Leopold Bloom in *Ulysses* (1922): Bloom lunches on Gorgonzola and burgundy. Besides cryptic references to Joyce's works, "Dante and the Lobster" directly invokes *Hamlet, Prince of Denmark* (c. 1600-1601), the Bible, and a number of nineteenth century Italian authors. However, none of these references provides anything like an explanation or a rationale for Belacqua's many frames of mind. On the contrary, in context, the allusions seem inappropriate. Their effect, indeed, is to reinforce the sense of arbitrariness provided by the story's potpourri of styles.

The ultimate expression of the story's use of arbitrariness occurs toward the end: "Belacqua drew near to the house of his aunt. Let us call it Winter, that dusk may fall now and a moon rise." Here Beckett dispenses with and satirizes fiction's conventional pretense to consistency and uniformity. Because such criteria of credibility are repudiated by Belacqua's behavior throughout the story, and by the stylistic variety that communicates that behavior, Beckett's artistic deviation here hardly seems extravagant. Moreover, no sooner has the arbitrariness of invention been introduced than Beckett goes on to sketch an effective, twilight, urban pastoral. Invention may be arbitrary, but it is also final. By locating the juxtaposition of that antithesis in the story's technique, Beckett bestows aesthetic substance on, and thereby legitimates, the interplay of opposites, contradictions, and antinomies that are discernible in the conceptual underpinnings of "Dante and the Lobster."

*George O'Brien*

# DARE'S GIFT

*Author:* Ellen Glasgow (1873-1945)
*Type of plot:* Ghost story, frame story, fantasy
*Time of plot:* The early twentieth century
*Locale:* Virginia
*First published:* 1925

*Principal characters:*
THE NARRATOR, a Washington corporate lawyer
MILDRED, his wife
PELHAM LAKEBY, an elderly country doctor
LUCY DARE, a former resident of the house during the Civil War

*The Story*

The narrator asks himself if he is sure that the event of the previous year really happened, for he thinks "the whole episode, seen in clear perspective, is obviously incredible." He knows that haunted houses are merely hallucinations, neurotic symptoms, or optical illusions because the supernatural has been banished in the modern scientific age. However, he must admit that for once in his life as a corporation lawyer in Washington, D.C., the impossible really happened.

The story begins with the narrator's desire to find a place in the country for his wife, Mildred, who has suffered a nervous breakdown. On a fishing trip, he discovers what seems to be the perfect place, Dare's Gift, a vacant house on the James River near Richmond, Virginia. Although the narrator's wife likes the house, saying that it affects her like a "magic spell" and that entering it is like stepping into "another world," she does not seem to be herself after moving into the house. The narrator knows that her mind is unhinged when he discovers that she has written a letter to expose an illegal transaction made by his law firm that he told her about in confidence.

When Pelham Lakeby, an elderly local doctor, is brought in to examine Mildred, he strongly urges the narrator to get her away from the house as soon as possible. He tells the narrator some of his theories about old houses with memories. When the narrator asks if the house is haunted, the doctor says it is "saturated with a thought. It is haunted by treachery." The doctor argues that although an act dies, the idea is immortal. He describes an event that took place fifty years earlier.

The doctor tells the story of Lucy Dare, who lived in the house during the last years of the Civil War. He says that to understand the story, the narrator must remember that the South was dominated by an idea, a dream that commanded the noblest devotion and the most complete self-sacrifice: the Confederacy. Lucy became intoxicated by this idea, believing in it much like a religion.

Lucy broke her engagement at the start of the war because her fiancé sided with the North. During the war, her former fiancé escaped from a Confederate prison and asked to hide in her house. When Confederate soldiers came searching for him, they said that if he got away, he would give the North information that would mean the end of the Southern idea, so Lucy surrendered her former fiancé, and the Confederate soldiers shot him. The doctor says that Lucy, still alive in a nursing home, has forgotten the incident, but that the house has remembered; it was the influence of the house that has made the narrator's wife betray his confidence.

## Themes and Meanings

"Dare's Gift" is a classic example of the turn-of-the-twentieth-century American supernatural mystery story, with many of that genre's themes and conventions clearly highlighted. It is similar to Charlotte Glaspell's "The Yellow Wallpaper," one of the most famous treatments of the theme of a woman taken to a country home after suffering a nervous breakdown and then being emotionally affected by some supernatural or psychological event there. Similar stories of an invisible presence, with a quasi-scientific explanation, were also written during the late nineteenth century by Guy de Maupassant and Ambrose Bierce.

Another thematic convention of the story is to have the story-within-the-story told by an old doctor, for old men since biblical times have seen visions and a doctor can provide a quasi-scientific explanation for the strange effect of the house. When the narrator asks if the house is haunted, the doctor says it is "saturated with a thought . . . haunted by treachery." Although an act ends, the doctor argues, the idea of the act is immortal. The treacherous event that has affected the lawyer's wife took place fifty years earlier, but the thought of it still lives and inhabits the cracks, crevices, and masonry of the house. The doctor theorizes that the multiple impressions and thoughts that have taken place in the house in the past perhaps have created a current of thought, a mental atmosphere with a powerful force of suggestion. Nervous natures, such as that of the lawyer's wife, yield to the influence readily but recover quickly once removed from that influence.

In the central thematic passage in the story, the doctor says he came to play a part in the story by accident, if there is such a thing as accident in this world. "That has always seemed to me the supreme fact of life," he tells the lawyer, "the one truth overshadowing all others—the truth that we know nothing. We nibble at the edges of the mystery, and the great Reality—the Incomprehensible—is still untouched, undiscovered."

The story of Lucy Dare is a story of the conflict between personal loyalties and loyalty to an idea. Lucy, a stranger to the soul of the South, becomes obsessed by the idea of the Confederacy and, having no physical outlet for her obsession, makes an extreme emotional response. The doctor says that the thoughts in Lucy's mind when she chose to betray her fiancé left an "ineffaceable impression on the things that surrounded her." In fact, the doctor argues, because of the extremity and horror of her action, she created an unseen environment more real, because it is more spiritual, than the physical house itself. As is true in many stories in this genre, the spiritual elements are judged to be more powerful than those of the physical world.

*Style and Technique*

The structure of "Dare's Gift" is typical of the nineteenth century supernatural mystery story genre. The first half focuses on the present inexplicable behavior of the wife and her rational husband's puzzlement. The second half focuses on the quasi-scientific explanation for an occurrence that formerly would have been considered supernatural. What the doctor provides as a scientific explanation for ghosts is the spiritual residue of a past powerful event; such events, he reasons, never really die but remain as a kind of invisible atmosphere that can "infect" the susceptible.

The narrator, a man of reason himself, tells the story in a rational, straightforward, realistic fashion, with no suggestion that the events, no matter how incredible, take place within the realm of the supernatural. The doctor, the conventional man of science, tells his story in much the same way. However, the doctor is old enough and wise enough to know that neither superstition nor science can explain everything. He has a great deal of respect for what he calls the "Incomprehensible." Thus, the style of the doctor's story is not only scientific but also metaphysical.

"Dare's Gift" is a hybrid, somewhere between the early nineteenth century supernatural tale common before Edgar Allan Poe and the twentieth century psychological story that arose after Maupassant. It begins with an inexplicable phenomenon, raises the ambiguity about whether the event really happened, focuses on an obsessed character choosing an idea over individual concerns, sets up a story-within-a-story told by a wise old doctor that provides a quasi-scientific, metaphysical explanation, and portrays the listener as a puzzled man of reason caught in the middle between the old supernatural and the new scientific explanation for what the doctor calls the great mystery of the incredible.

At the end of the story, the old doctor theorizes about the difference between a single powerful experience and the series of ordinary experiences that make up a life. He says that Lucy drained the whole of experience in an instant, leaving nothing except the "empty and withered husks of the hours." She now remembers nothing about the betrayal because she felt too much during the act to ever feel again. "After all," the doctor says, "It is the high moments that make a life, and the flat ones that fill the years."

*Charles E. May*

# THE DARING YOUNG MAN ON THE FLYING TRAPEZE

*Author:* William Saroyan (1908-1981)
*Type of plot:* Character study
*Time of plot:* The 1930's
*Locale:* San Francisco
*First published:* 1934

Principal characters:
THE WRITER
THE LADY AT THE EMPLOYMENT AGENCY

*The Story*

"The Daring Young Man on the Flying Trapeze" is divided into two short, titled parts. The first and shortest (only three paragraphs long), called "Sleep," describes the dream images and thoughts of a young San Francisco writer before he awakens on the last day of his life. His sleeping mind is flooded with a series of unconnected impressions, including cities (Rome, Paris, Jerusalem), writers (Gustave Flaubert, Fyodor Dostoevski), political figures (Joseph Stalin and Adolf Hitler), animals (a reptile and a panther), and purely imaginary scenes ("the magnified flower twice the size of the universe").

The writer's sleep is ended in the second and longest section of the story, "Wakefulness." He is poor, having only one tie and drinking only coffee for breakfast. He reminds himself that in the unconscious world of sleep, from which a welter of images has just been presented, all human experiences are unified. In that death in life, one can experience eternity.

The real world that the writer inhabits is quite a different matter. The streets are cold and grim, and he walks noisily, as if to affirm himself in the face of an uncaring world. The lyrics of the popular song "The Daring Young Man on the Flying Trapeze" float through his mind and, throughout the story, he associates himself with the circus acrobat who so skillfully performs feats of daring. His amazing feat is merely to get through the day.

The writer finds a penny in the gutter, and realizing that he can buy almost nothing with it, fantasizes about what he would do if he had money; he would buy a car, visit prostitutes, but most important, buy food. He is reduced to meals of bread, coffee, and cigarettes, and now he has no more bread. There is no work for him at all, much less work for a writer. From a hill he looks at the city and thinks of it as a place from which he is denied admittance. He lives in a society in which the work he does is not respected. He plans to write *An Application for Permission to Live*. He thinks of the possibility of visiting a Salvation Army kitchen, but he decides instead to live his own life, and play out the part that he has chosen for himself. Once again he thinks of himself as the daring young man on the flying trapeze, but now he also considers that the landing place of the trapeze artist may be God or eternity, the eternity he glimpsed in sleep.

He continues his walk through the city, passing restaurants that he dares not look into, enters a building, and visits an employment agency. When asked what he can do, he says he can write, and the clerk expresses no interest in this skill, asking further if the writer can type. There is no work even for a typist. He visits another employment agency with the same result, and department stores also have no jobs available. He visits the YMCA to obtain paper and ink to write his *An Application for Permission to Live* but begins to feel faint from hunger and must go to a park to drink a quart of water and revive himself. He sees an old man feeding pigeons and almost asks him for some of the crumbs this man is tossing on the ground. The writer goes to the library near the park and reads but again feels faint and has to drink water to recover.

The writer leaves the park and walks back to his room, thinking to go back to sleep, as there is nothing else left to do. Back in his room, he prepares coffee without milk or sugar, both of which he has run out of and for which there is no more money. He had stolen paper from the YMCA and hoped to finish his *An Application for Permission to Live,* but the act of writing is too difficult for him. He looks at the penny he found and wonders if he could get more pennies and thereby obtain enough money to go on living, but he inventories all the items that he has already sold and realizes that there is nothing left to sell. He has sold his clothes, his watch, and his books. None of these losses troubles him except that of the books, which he wishes he still had.

The writer looks at the details on the penny and considers its simple beauty. Now utterly weak, he falls on his bed, expecting to do the only thing left to do, sleep, but in fact the only thing left for him to do is die. His last conscious thought is that he should have given the penny to a child, who might have been able to buy many things with it. As he dies, he joins the unity that he had seen in sleep that morning. Like the trapeze artist, he makes a graceful exit, not from an acrobatic apparatus but from his body. Now that he is dead he becomes "dreamless, unalive, perfect."

### Themes and Meanings

During the Great Depression of the 1930's, when "The Daring Young Man on the Flying Trapeze" first appeared, many people were out of work and hungry, so the story had a strong impact for its initial audience as an account of daily life during hard times. However, William Saroyan does much more with his material than provide a naturalistic view of a day in the life of one oppressed man. Saroyan takes a phrase, "starving artist," which has become a cliché and almost a joke, and gives it new power by taking the reader not only into the life but also into the mind of a writer who is literally starving to death. The death of this man is doubly tragic, for as well as being a fellow human being, he is a person who is able to transform the apparently meaningless flow of circumstance, order it, and give it a meaning that might help others to understand their lives and thereby endure them. In a society primarily concerned with survival, however, art seems an extravagance. Depression-era America, or perhaps any society, does not recognize the role of the artist as a seer and healer. Throughout his last day, the writer sees details that no one else observes and of which he continues to try to make sense. His last conscious act is to look closely at the coin he has found and marvel at its beauty. He wants to bring his sense of joy and wonder to others, but the world does not respect his function, and he no longer has the energy to write. This tragedy is brought to focus in the only scene in the story in which the writer exchanges words with another person. When he tells the lady at the employment agency that he is a writer, she ignores this statement and asks him if he can type. There is no work for his mind, only for his hands. Finally, the writer finishes the task of assimilating all the myriad details he has been trying to capture and organize, not by explaining them but by joining them in death.

## Style and Technique

"The Daring Young Man on the Flying Trapeze" brought instant fame to Saroyan, establishing him as an important talent, not only because of its timely subject and timeless conclusions about the life of an artist but also because of its arresting style and view of the subject. The story combines a stream-of-consciousness account of the interior monologue of the artist with a detailed, realistic view of the outside world he inhabits, thus uniting two of the major technical approaches of modern literature. The bizarre images that tumble through the writer's mind as he sleeps both accurately reflect the strange world of the dream and alert the reader that this story is something different, something that will demand full attention. The enigmatic dream images also involve the reader in the story by giving him a glimpse of what the writer's life is like: The writer's dream is as bewildering to the reader as are the details that the writer encounters as he walks through the streets of the city, and as the writer must take up the hard work of organizing the details of everyday existence, so must the reader work to piece together the elements of the story. Little by little, the reader must infer that the writer is dying in part from integrity, because he refuses to be anything less than an artist, a role with dignity, in a society that does not respect that dignity. Because this bitter truth is inferred by the reader, its impact is more stunning than if it had been directly stated by the author.

Ironically, the psychological style and bleak viewpoint of this story, which made Saroyan a celebrity, are not at all typical of his work. Saroyan preferred direct, open, declarative statements and affirmed the positive value of human experience in spite of tragedy, qualities that are seen in such stories as "The Summer of the Beautiful White Horse."

*James Baird*

# DARK AVENUES

*Author:* Ivan Bunin (1870-1953)
*Type of plot:* Sketch
*Time of plot:* The late nineteenth century
*Locale:* Russia's Tula district
*First published:* "Tyomnyye allei," 1943 (English translation, 1949)

*Principal characters:*
NIKOLAI ALEXEYEVICH, an elderly army officer
NADEZHDA, his former lover, the owner of a roadside lodge

*The Story*

On a cold autumn day, a mud-spattered carriage stops at a small roadside inn. The elderly yet handsome officer who alights is evidently glad to enter a warm, tidy room after his chilly, damp ride. He locates the innkeeper, an attractive woman who resembles a Gypsy, and engages her in conversation. When he compliments her on her establishment's cleanliness, she says that she knows how to keep things orderly because she grew up around nobility. She then astonishes him by calling him by his name—Nikolai Alexeyevich. As he looks at the woman more closely, he realizes that she is a woman whom he passionately loved some thirty years earlier, when she was eighteen and he was about thirty.

Their conversation begins innocuously. Nikolai tells Nadezhda that he lost touch with her after their affair ended, and he learned that her masters had released her. When he asks her whether she has ever married, she says no. He wonders why not, because she was so beautiful. She again answers simply that she was not able to marry. Disconcerted by her reply, Nikolai asks her what she means. This time, her response carries an implicit reproach: "What is there to explain? Surely you remember how much I loved you." Nikolai seems to be stung by this and tries to minimize the seriousness of her words by saying that everything passes: love, youth—everything. Nadezhda does not retreat, however. She agrees that youth passes but says that love is another matter.

As their dialogue continues, it becomes clear that Nikolai heartlessly abandoned Nadezhda, leaving her so distraught that she more than once considered suicide. She asks him to recall how he once read poetry to her. When he asks her to recall how beautiful and passionate she once was, she tells him that it was to him that she yielded all of her passion and her beauty, and that no one can forget such an experience. He again tries to downplay the seriousness of what she is saying by reiterating that "everything passes, everything is forgotten." Unwilling to let him get away with such an easy platitude, Nadezhda counters that although everything may pass, not everything is forgotten.

Perhaps feeling trapped by Nadezhda's responses, Nikolai asks her to leave, adding that he hopes God has forgiven him as, he assumes, Nadezhda has. Nadezhda rebuffs his attempt to dismiss the past, however, and says that she has never forgiven him. Just as there was nothing dearer than him in her life when she was with him, she has had nothing dearer since then. Overcome by the steadfastness and depth of Nadezhda's emotion, Nikolai confesses that he himself has never found any greater happiness in his own life. The woman whom he married abandoned him even more cruelly than he had abandoned Nadezhda; his son, on whom he pinned all his hopes, turned out to be a scoundrel without heart, honor, or consciousness. Nikolai finally admits that in losing Nadezhda, he lost the most valuable thing he ever had in his life. After she kisses his hand, he kisses hers and leaves the inn in agitation.

Back in his carriage, Nikolai ponders the encounter he has just undergone. Struggling with the feelings that the meeting has aroused, he is ashamed of his final declaration to Nadezhda but then feels ashamed of this very shame. He acknowledges that his affair with Nadezhda gave him the finest minutes of his life but then tries to cast off this vision of the past. What might have happened, had he not abandoned Nadezhda years ago, he wonders. Might she have become his wife, the mistress of his St. Petersburg home, the mother of his children? The thought seems so incredible that he merely closes his eyes and shakes his head.

### Themes and Meanings

"Dark Avenues" (which has also been published as "Dark Paths") is not only the name of Ivan Alexeyevich Bunin's sketch but also the title of a collection of stories that he published in 1943. He did not make his decision casually. The sketch explores several themes that were especially important to Bunin toward the end of his career. His late writings tend to concentrate on depicting the intensity of romantic passion and its brevity as a lived experience, while simultaneously revealing how powerfully passion can affect the human soul. "Dark Avenues" exemplifies how a passionate encounter, even a brief one, can leave an indelible imprint on the human heart.

This sketch depicts a brief but moving encounter between two people from vastly different social classes who meet after many years of separation. Bunin's reserved and understated approach to this encounter offers an effective counterpoint to the intense feelings that the meeting itself releases. The dialogue between the former lovers, Nikolai and Nadezhda, forms the heart of his story. Although the words that they exchange are simple, they contain a powerful reservoir of emotion.

The sketch also touches on other themes that play prominent roles in Bunin's writings. During the last decade of the nineteenth century, Bunin began relentlessly exposing how the inexorable passage of time affects human affairs, both on a personal level and on the level of human civilization itself. Later, as an émigré writer living in France after the Bolshevik Revolution of 1917, Bunin himself acutely felt the irreparable loss of things that he had cherished. Faced with the inevitable dissolution and decay of human achievements, he looked to memory and to art as ways to preserve the best moments of human existence. The importance of memory in "Dark Avenues" is

underscored by the story's repetitions of such phrases as "Do you recall . . . " and "I remember . . . " As the story unfolds, Nadezhda's undying remembrance of youthful
love eventually penetrates her former lover's attempted detachment, briefly bringing
the characters together in a silent homage to the power and intensity of their shared
passion. Life may go on, but the experience of profound love can never truly be erased
from human memory.

*Style and Technique*

Bunin's sketch displays all the stylistic features that characterize the last part of his
career. Deceptively simple in form, "Dark Avenues" reveals his penchant for paring
away all that is superfluous in narrative exposition. A worthy successor to the art of
Anton Chekhov, Bunin relies on carefully crafted descriptions to convey palpable
moods or emotional conditions. For example, the sketch opens with a description of a
cold autumn day in which elements of dirt and darkness prevail. This chilling external
world through which the careworn Nikolai Alexeyevich travels contrasts sharply with
the clean, tidy, and warm interior world of Nadezhda's lodgings. For a brief moment,
Nikolai Alexeyevich comes in from the cold and is warmed by the ardor that Nadezhda carries within her. The sketch ends with Nikolai resuming his seemingly
directionless travels. The narrator notes that the sun is setting as Nikolai departs. The
image of a bleak autumn day drawing to a close provides a marvelous evocation of the
condition of Nikolai's very existence.

Bunin's sensitivity to nuances of language is evident in other ways as well. The fundamental disparity in the social status of Nikolai and Nadezhda is conveyed through
the forms of the personal pronouns with which they address each other. Nikolai addresses Nadezhda with the singular form of the pronoun "you" (*ty*), although she uses
the pronoun's more formal plural form (*vy*). Her use of the more formal form indicates
that she acknowledges Nikolai as socially superior to her, but the reader understands
that in matters of the heart, it is she who is morally superior to him. "Dark Avenues"
provides eloquent testimony of Bunin's own appreciation of the power of language to
communicate on several levels, and the sketch stands out as a gem of his final years.

*Julian W. Connolly*

# THE DARK CITY

*Author:* Conrad Aiken (1889-1973)
*Type of plot:* Psychological
*Time of plot:* The early twentieth century
*Locale:* The suburbs of a large city
*First published:* 1922

> *Principal characters:*
> ANDREW, the protagonist, a business executive
> HILDA, his wife
> MARTHA,
> MARJORIE and
> TOM, their children

## The Story

This slice-of-life account focuses on a commuter husband, involving only those events that occur between late afternoon and bedtime. The story begins on the commuter train that carries Andrew from the city to the suburbs, where he works in his garden, plays with his children, eats, takes a post-dinner stroll, plays chess with Hilda, his wife, and then prepares for bed. Aiken, however, does not restrict himself to the external plot, which is prosaic in its typicality, but instead includes his protagonist's inner life, which indicates that Andrew has, at best, a tenuous grip on his sanity.

In the first part of the story, Aiken presents Andrew as an executive who attempts to put the "staggering load of business detail" behind him as he "devours" the evening newspaper on the train. When he reaches his station, he begins his walk home and thinks about "news amusing enough to be reported to Hilda." He sees his children playing, and after engaging them in light banter about how much he is needed in his garden, he jokes with his children and wife about having lost the flannel trousers that are apparently part of the "uniform" he wears as he readies himself for the gardening ritual.

Gardening is a welcome respite for Andrew, for whom the "order" is a welcome change from business. With his children, particularly Martha, Andrew has a series of ritualized games in which the actors have clearly assigned roles: The children hide his hoe, he declares himself a slave to the children and to the garden, the children and he personify the plants, and the children and he regard caterpillars as enemies and carefully circumvent the toad, "obese, sage, and wrinkled like a Chinese god." If the garden affords Andrew with the chance to play with his children, it also provides him with the opportunity to drift off into a world of his own, where he can meditate about the meaning of his activity and of his existence. For example, the transplanting of strawberry plants becomes, for him, an analogue to "resurrecting" them and giving them "life" through, presumably, his role as a godlike creator.

At dinner Andrew shares his philosophizing with his family, which is more concerned with "beany" bread pudding and with unripe strawberries. In mock exasperation, he wonders why he and Hilda married and paraphrases William Wordsworth's "London, 1802," suggesting that their powers have been "wasted" by "feeding and spanking." After dinner he strolls on the lawn, and in the gathering darkness he sees, apparently not for the first time, the "dark city, the city not inhabited by mortals." Despite the city's "immense, sinister, and black" appearance, he does not seem upset by his vision.

When Andrew reenters the house, he wakens Hilda, who says that she has been dreaming about Bluebeard. He assures her that he is instead intent on the upcoming chess game, which he soon wins. When Hilda asks him about the "dark city," he gives her an elaborate description of not only the city but also the "maggots of perhaps the size of human children" that inhabit the city. Hilda understandably suggests that he is "going mad," to which he laughingly responds that he is "gone" and that his "brain is maggoty." They then close up the house for the night.

*Themes and Meanings*

In "The Dark City" Aiken depicts two "dark cities," the one in which Andrew toils and from which he attempts to escape, and the one that exists within his tortured mind. Aiken is not concerned with the literal city, which he dismisses in a phrase: "the staggering load of business detail, under which he had struggled all day in the office." Andrew "instantly" forgets this city (or believes that he does) as he reads the newspaper as "prelude" to "his greatest pleasure in life," which comes with the dusk at home in his garden or with his family. The suburbs, with their suggestion of rural innocence, initially seem to offer Andrew a conventional refuge from the grind of the job and the city, but Aiken suggests that in this Edenic garden paradise there is also a darker, more corrupt reality: "at the core so vile a secret."

When he first describes Andrew's dark city, Aiken clearly indicates that it is a bleak vision: "the dark city, the city submerged under the infinite sea, the city not inhabited by mortals." There is no entrance to the city with "immense, sinister, and black walls," walls that are as "old and cold as the moon." When Andrew describes the city to Hilda, however, he embellishes that description with unsavory details about the various inhabitants of the city:

> Its people are maggots—maggots of perhaps the size of human children. . . . What horrible feast is it that nightly they celebrate there in silence? On what carrion do they feed? It is the universe that they devour; and they build above it, as they devour it, their dark city like a hollow tomb.

Andrew's additions are significant because they suggest an identification between the maggots and children (and, by extension, the family) and because the real world, including Andrew, is seen as dead.

Clearly Andrew has ambivalent but strong feelings about himself and his family.

Andrew's "greatest pleasure in life came always at dusk," and after gardening he has, "for a moment, an extraordinary satisfying sense of space." (This "moment" is, however, transient, and Aiken suggests that Andrew will lose his "space"—another writer might have used "peace" instead—and will be hemmed in again.) However, dusk also brings his dark vision, at once repulsive and fascinating, and his half-joking remark about his madness. In fact, Andrew typically relies on humor to escape or conceal his true feelings. He jokes, "Spare your neurotic father," and his Wordsworth parody about "wasting" his "powers" because "our kids are too much with us" may reveal his other, darker view of his children. Even his attitude toward Hilda is suspect. If Hilda notices his neurotic, compulsive behavior and senses the hostility that motivates it, then her remark about dreaming of Bluebeard, the wife murderer, is grimly appropriate.

When Hilda mentions that he resembles Bluebeard, Andrew typically laughs it off and then comments enigmatically, ostensibly about the chess game, that "queens die young and fair." The reader senses that beneath the clever banter and the superficial camaraderie there is an undercurrent of hostility and suspicion.

Andrew's behavior oscillates between compulsive haste and meditative calm. Until he reaches the garden, he rushes, hurries, and runs; in the garden, however, he is in "profound meditation" before the order of the rows. Through his "methodical" hoeing with the rising and falling hoe-blade, he is "hypnotized" with his thoughts in a "rhythm." As he "resurrects" the strawberries, the gardening becomes a religious ritual. He "enshrines" a flame, and the cloud of smoke seems like "incense." Then, after Martha's comic interruption, he comments, "O Lord, Lord, what a circus we are."

Andrew's wry observation is indicative of his plight, for he is aware of both the potential, represented by "pilgrims who struggle upwards in the darkness for pure love of beauty," and the reality, represented by the feasting maggots that also work in darkness. Despite the hylas that sing of "peace," Andrew lives in a world of corruption, decay, and death, and his own destruction is suggested by his comment about his "maggoty" brain. Although Andrew and Hilda avoid any further discussion of madness, they live in a volatile situation, one in which murder and suicide are a distinct possibility—and the reader is reminded that Aiken himself saw his father kill his mother and then take his own life.

### Style and Technique

Aiken uses the third-person point of view in "The Dark City" and uses Andrew as the "central intelligence" through whom the events are screened. That literary device enables readers to understand Andrew thoroughly, for readers share his thoughts through the stream-of-consciousness technique. To indicate Andrew's delicate balancing act, Aiken also distances himself from his protagonist and under the guise of objective description reveals the contradictions within Andrew. For example, reading a newspaper should relax Andrew, thereby allowing him to escape from the bustle of the city, but Aiken's diction implies that even a sedentary activity involves repressed aggression for Andrew.

Aiken has Andrew "devour" with "rapacious eyes" the newspaper, and the activity "consumes" time—the imagery would be more appropriate in financial situations in the city. In his refuge at home, replies become "missiles," a metaphor readers may regard as part of Andrew's "comic rage," but that "rage" is not altogether "comic." Even the setting sun assumes destructive force: "The red sun . . . was gashing itself cruelly on a black pine tree." When he returns from his evening walk, Andrew says, "He had no watch, and his trousers grew like grass," an enigmatic and apparently innocuous comment, but in its allusion to the watch, the object of earlier musings, and to the lost trousers, the comment serves to tie up loose ends for Andrew, who needs to retain his "grip" in a situation that is steadily deteriorating. In a very real sense, Aiken's protagonist is a symbol for modern man.

*Thomas L. Erskine*

# THE DARLING

*Author:* Anton Chekhov (1860-1904)
*Type of plot:* Parody
*Time of plot:* The 1880's
*Locale:* A provincial town near Moscow
*First published:* "Dushechka," 1899 (English translation, 1915)

### Principal characters:

OLENKA PLEMYANNIKOVA, the protagonist, a village housewife
IVAN KUKIN, her first husband, a local entrepreneur
VASILY ANDREICH PUSTOVALOV, her second husband, manager of
the local lumberyard
VLADIMIR PLATONICH SMIRNIN, her lover, a veterinarian
SASHA SMIRNIN, the son of the veterinarian, a ten-year-old
student

### The Story

Olenka Plemyannikova is a lonely spinster who is constantly in love with someone or other. She finds it difficult to live without loving someone; she turns pale, loses weight, and is unable to form opinions of her own. When the reader encounters her at the beginning of the story, she has been infatuated with her French teacher, loved her father dearly, and is now ready for marriage. She is young, healthy, and well liked by all, men and women, young and old.

Ivan Kukin, the manager of the local theater and amusement park, lives by Olenka and converses with her regularly. He constantly complains about the indifference of the ignorant public to good theater, the rain and poor weather that keep people from the outdoor amusement park, his financial worries, and life in general. Olenka feels sorry for the hapless Kukin and gradually falls in love with him. They marry, and Olenka begins to help him in his business affairs. Because she has no opinions of her own, she merely repeats whatever her husband says about the public's relation to good theater and she faithfully echoes his other complaints. She states her feeling that the theater is the most important thing in the world and necessary for all people. Optimistic Olenka prospers in her new life and radiates health while her incurably pessimistic husband continues to complain.

During Lent, Kukin goes to Moscow to book acts for his summer repertoire at the theater. Olenka is beside herself without her husband; she is unable to sleep and compares herself to a hen in the henhouse without a rooster. Kukin dies unexpectedly in Moscow; Olenka returns from his funeral and enters a period of deep mourning, sobbing so loudly that her neighbors can hear her grief.

Three months later, Olenka walks home from church with Vasily Andreich Pustovalov, and a friendship blooms. At loose ends without someone to love, Olenka now fills a void in her life as the courtship progresses. Olenka and Pustovalov marry and the dutiful wife begins to assist her husband in his duties as manager of the local lumberyard. Her conversation is now filled with references to lumber, lumber prices, and the difficulties of managing the yard. Lumber now replaces the theater as the most important and necessary thing in the world. In fact, her previous opinions concerning the exalted nature of the theater are completely reversed, because her new husband, a very stolid businessperson, has no use for the theater and views it as a trivial amusement for people of no serious interests. When her husband is away on trips to buy lumber, Olenka becomes bored and restless; she cannot live without her husband, just as she was unable to be apart from her first husband, Kukin. Olenka and Pustovalov lead a very respectable and sedate life for six years, until Pustovalov dies suddenly after catching a cold. Once again Olenka plunges into deep mourning.

A military veterinarian, Vladimir Platonich Smirnin, has rented a room from Olenka, and soon the two become fast friends. Friends and neighbors become aware of the closeness of the relationship when Olenka begins to repeat the opinions of the veterinarian concerning animal health and veterinary inspections in the town for domestic animals. Marriage in this case is an impossibility, however, as the doctor has an estranged wife and child living elsewhere. When the veterinarian is transferred to a distant town, Olenka's life is changed once again; although no death has occurred, she has been deprived of the source of her opinions. Her physical appearance worsens, she becomes listless, and even her house begins to fall apart, reflecting a general degeneration. The author of the story makes it very clear, however, that her greatest loss is the inability to have opinions and consequently to have conversations with her neighbors.

A few years later the veterinarian, now a civilian, returns with his wife, with whom he has reconciled, and his child to settle down in the small provincial town. At Olenka's invitation, the family moves into her house, and she herself moves into the small outbuilding that Smirnin formerly occupied. The wife soon leaves the family, Smirnin himself is often absent on business, and Olenka becomes the de facto mother of the child. She now springs into life, for she has discovered a new purpose, a new person to love. She begins to repeat the opinions of the ten-year-old student as if they were on the same level as those of the male adults whom she loved. She complains to neighbors about the amount of homework the students are receiving, the difficulties of the academic program in the classical high school that little Sasha is attending, and she sympathizes with the sleepy boy when he has to get up in the morning. Olenka's demeanor changes and her old radiance and vivaciousness return. The story ends as Olenka lovingly listens to the boy talking in his sleep.

*Themes and Meanings*

Anton Chekhov, considered by most students of Russian literature to be the foremost Russian writer of short stories, often uses exaggeration to point out a human foible. Olenka's total inability to think, speak, and form opinions of her own is rarely, if ever, met in this world, but there is a kernel of truth in this caricature. Chekhov wishes to poke fun at people who rely on others to form opinions instead of forming their own, people who prefer to follow the crowd rather than question and probe. In a number of stories, the author uses the same technique with different types of examples to make the same point—too many people are prisoners of conformity and prefer to eschew critical thinking. Olenka's complete lack of self-worth is evident as she goes through life repeating the opinions of other people, even a ten-year-old schoolboy.

The theme of love is also present in this story. The reader can find a pattern in Chekhov's stories that concern love, a pattern that may reflect the skeptical and world-weary author's own feelings about the subject. Love rarely works out to the satisfaction of the parties involved. Love is usually illusory. Either the love is not reciprocated, or two people who love each other are not aware of the other's love through a lack of communication, or two people marry and become unhappy. In this story love seems to be successful, but fate intervenes to remove the two husbands and one lover. Olenka does not live happily ever after with a husband but is forced to transfer her enormous capacity for love to a child. Although the reader leaves Olenka at the end of the story in a very happy and contented state, it is also clear that the child will grow up and go his own way, once again leaving Olenka alone and probably very unhappy.

## Style and Technique

Unlike many other well-known Russian authors, such as Leo Tolstoy and Fyodor Dostoevski, Chekhov is famed for an economy of words and a sparing use of detail. Almost every word is important and is used to convey a single impression of a person or situation. Chekhov portrays Olenka in three very different romantic situations with the identical result; the reader cannot fail to grasp the point. The fourth situation occurs when the time for romantic love has passed, yet the love for the boy, Sasha, produces the same result: complete adoption of the opinions of the person loved. In the limited space of the short story the various characters are well-defined, demonstrating the ability of the author to impart much information in a very small space.

*Philip Maloney*

# THE DAUGHTERS OF THE LATE COLONEL

*Author:* Katherine Mansfield (Katherine Mansfield Beauchamp, 1888-1923)
*Type of plot:* Psychological
*Time of plot:* The early twentieth century
*Locale:* England
*First published:* 1921

> *Principal characters:*
> JOSEPHINE "JUG" PINNER, the older daughter of Colonel Pinner
> CONSTANTIA "CON" PINNER, her sister
> KATE, the insolent young maid

*The Story*

"The Daughters of the Late Colonel" is an account of the activities and thoughts of two spinster sisters during the week after the death of their dictatorial father. Although the sisters think of themselves as having been extraordinarily busy that week, it is obvious that most of their efforts have been psychological. They have agonized over the one necessary decision—to bury their father—and they have accomplished that, not without misgivings. However, they are still unable to assert themselves, even in the most mundane areas of life.

The story is divided into twelve sections. In each section, Mansfield concentrates on one area of the sisters' preoccupations, penetrating the mind of one sister or the other, or of both, alternately, reproducing their churning thoughts. Most of the sections take place on the Saturday that marks a week after his death; there are flashbacks, however, to the death, to the funeral, and to an earlier visit by a grandson.

Although the prime tyrant of the sisters' lives was their father, the incidents related in the story show their fear of Kate, the bad-tempered young maid, of Nurse Andrews, and of public opinion. In the first section, they worry about the propriety of wearing colored dressing gowns and slippers during the mourning period, when Kate or the postman might see them. In the second section, they cannot summon up the courage to ask Kate for more jam or to restrain Nurse Andrews from gobbling up their butter. Later, although they have proved to themselves that Kate snoops in their bureau, and although they are the victims of her consistent impertinence, they cannot summon up the resolution to dismiss her.

If Constantia and Josephine Pinner are unable to confront people, they are even more emotionally crippled by the possibilities of demands on them for action. When the vicar of Saint John's, Mr. Farolles, offers to bring Communion to them at their home, it is the possibilities that frighten them. What if Kate came in? What if the bell rang? What would they do? It is easiest to reject any new situation, rather than dealing with their fears of decision.

Naturally, the sisters are preoccupied with the death of their father; they find it difficult to believe that he is really dead and not somewhere waiting to criticize them. In the third section, they are haunted by the deathbed scene, particularly by the fact that he opened only one eye before he died. Accustomed as they are to assuming that everything their father did was significant, generally involving blame for them, the sisters cannot dismiss that single-eyed glare. In fact, they torment themselves with thoughts of his reappearing to scold them for burying him and to go into a fury about the expense of the funeral. A third worry involves disposing of the Colonel's clothes. Two days after the funeral, Constantia and Josephine attempt to go through his possessions. Merely opening the door to his room without knocking takes almost more courage than they possess. Even Josephine, who seems to be the braver sister, cannot open the chest of drawers. Typically, the decision that Constantia makes, and which she considers one of the boldest of her life, is a denial of action: She locks up the wardrobe and thereby postpones real action. To Constantia and Josephine, however, it is like locking up their father.

Sections 7 through 9 have to do with two relatives, their brother Benny Pinner and their nephew Cyril Pinner. Evidently, both men have escaped the Colonel's domination, Benny by going to a distant part of the British Empire and Cyril by spending his time in London. Josephine and Constantia must decide which of the men should have the Colonel's gold watch. Constantia's imagination sends the watch by runner to Benny, but then she begins to worry about its getting there safely. Deciding to deliver it to Cyril instead, the sisters remember his last visit, when they sacrificed to buy him treats for tea, which he refused, and when Cyril unwillingly saw his deaf, irascible grandfather and escaped by inventing an appointment. Remembering only a problem about time, the sisters are certain that Cyril needs a watch.

After two sections in which the sisters admit Kate's imperfections but cannot resolve to dismiss her, there is a long section containing a brief flicker of hope for Constantia and Josephine. When they hear the barrel organ, they realize that they are free to hear the music as often as they like. Their father is truly dead. The sun comes into the room, and both sisters begin to speak about the future. However, the sentences are never finished. Again, the thought that might have led to action is stifled, and as a cloud covers the sun, both the sisters say that they have forgotten what they began to say.

## Themes and Meanings

Like many of the stories of Katherine Mansfield and of her major influence, Anton Chekhov, "The Daughters of the Late Colonel" deals with the theme of captivity. Josephine and Constantia have been imprisoned in a world with two objectives: to avoid displeasing a testy old father and to stay out of his way. Their lives, then, have been directed toward negatives rather than toward positives. Over the years, they have become imprisoned not only in their father's house but also in their own passivity. The causes of their condition are touched on in the story: their mother's death, their father's habit of command and unconcern for their social life, and their own timidity. After his death, the sisters are still imprisoned by their habitual responses of fear and obedience, which make decisions impossible for them.

However, throughout the story there are impulses toward freedom. The very fact that the imaginations of the sisters are not dead, that they can summon forth the runner moving toward Benny, that they can respond to the sunshine and the barrel organ, that Constantia has yearned in the moonlight and by the sea, suggests that they may be able to escape from their prison, now that their father is dead and they are still alive.

The final section, however, makes it clear that there will be no escape. The sisters cannot even confess their impulses to each other. When they repress their impulses to speak of the future, the sun is symbolically covered by a cloud, and it is clear that captivity has conquered.

*Style and Technique*

Because Mansfield's stories are primarily psychological, point of view is particularly important. In her journals, Mansfield makes it clear that she sees her characters from the inside out, that she assumes their identities as an actor assumes a role, while at the same time making the reader aware of the authorial judgments on them. "The Daughters of the Late Colonel" is especially complex in point of view because there are two protagonists, and Mansfield alternates between them, except for a brief passage where she penetrates the mind of Cyril. However, sometimes she treats the two sisters as a single entity, as in the first paragraph. In one of the most interesting passages, in the seventh section of the story, she gives their imaginations the same subject, the runner on his way to Benny with the watch, but then she reveals the divergent images in their minds. At the end of the story, the single point of view is thematic. If one of the sisters could have contemplated a future, there might have been hope for both; their very unanimity dooms them.

In a story such as "The Daughters of the Late Colonel," in which there is almost no real action, slight events become symbolic, but the symbolism is used in various ways. Actions may be symbolic: The fact that Kate hands the sisters an empty jam pot indicates her domination of them; the fact that Nurse Andrews questions the taste of the marmalade shows her contempt for her former employers. Sometimes Mansfield uses symbols to indicate an authorial comment, as when the cloud blots out the brief sunlight at the end of the story. Often, however, the symbols are used to reveal the characters' feelings. In their father's white room, the sisters feel cold, thinking of death. Throughout the story they see images of freedom, such as the flapping tassel of the blind, the sunlight on the photographs, the moon, and the sea. The Buddha suggests to Constantia the unknown in life, which she will never experience. At times there is even an identification with pitiable, vulnerable creatures, such as the mice that Constantia fears will find no food or the sparrows whose crying outside the window becomes a crying inside Josephine's heart. Finally, a symbol may be used ironically. To Constantia and Josephine, the locking of their father's wardrobe seems like a triumph, a real defiance of the tyrannical old man; actually, it is an admission that they cannot lock out his memory by dealing with it. Thus, the final imprisonment is theirs.

*Rosemary M. Canfield Reisman*

# DAWN OF REMEMBERED SPRING

*Author:* Jesse Stuart (1907-1984)
*Type of plot:* Psychological
*Time of plot:* The 1930's
*Locale:* Rural Kentucky
*First published:* 1942

> *Principal characters:*
> SHAN, a rural adolescent, the narrator
> MOM, Shan's mother

*The Story*

Left to his own devices for the day, Shan decides to seek revenge on snakes for the bite received by his friend Roy Deer, whose family Shan's mother visits to pay a condolence call. Given his freedom, the boy states, "I would like to be a man now. . . . I'd love to plow the mules, run a farm, and kill snakes." Much of the action of the remainder of the story involves Shan's playing at being a man, a common adolescent fantasy. He breaks a club from the wild plum thicket close to his home and wades the creek to search for water moccasins to kill.

His knowledge of his prey is rich beyond his years, attesting his experience with nature. For example, he plans his strategy for slaughter by relying on the knowledge that it is impossible for the water moccasins to bite him while their heads are beneath the water. Too, the snakes will raise their heads above the surface if the water is muddy, a fact that he turns to his advantage by stirring up the bottom frequently. Though he experiences fear concerning the danger of his hunt, not once does the boy exhibit any pity or compassion for his victims. One of their kind has bitten his friend without cause, and Shan takes on himself the duty of wreaking revenge on the whole race of poisonous serpents. Stealth and knowledge serve him well, and by the end of the afternoon he has killed fifty-three water moccasins. On his way home, after leaving the creek, Shan comes on two other poisonous snakes, copperheads.

These two snakes are wrapped around each other and pay no attention to him. The boy believes that the copperheads are fighting, and he plans to kill them too if they fail to kill each other. From a passing neighbor he learns the truth: "It's snakes in love!" Uncle Alf Skinner tells him. The neighbor quickly fetches his wife to see the spectacle; soon a small crowd assembles to witness the event. Shan's mother returns and joins the group and, because of the danger he was in, she is angry with Shan for going on his unescorted hunt.

Before he is sent away by his mother, Shan notices the changed expressions of the adults who remain to witness the mating of the copperheads. Their smiles puzzle him and he observes that "their faces were made over new." The boy persists in his notion that the snakes are fighting, and the crowd finds his innocence amusing. In the end, as he leaves, he is baffled by the laughter of the adults. He cannot quite figure out how the grown-ups in a rural community plagued by poisonous serpents can smile and laugh at such a sight, and their laughter seems to follow and haunt him as he walks home alone.

## Themes and Meanings

"Dawn of Remembered Spring" is a complex story of fear, hate, and love. On the surface, it appears to be nothing more than a boy's boast about the number of snakes he has killed, but although Shan's action on the snake hunt takes up much of the space of the story, the title shows that the focus of the tale is really not on its simple plot.

What is the reader to make of the title? None of the story takes place at the hour of dawn, neither Shan nor his mother seems to dwell on remembering anything, and even if the story takes place during springtime (though this is not at all certain) very little is made of the importance of the season to the action of the story. Because a literal interpretation of the title is so unproductive, investigating it figuratively may prove more profitable.

The dawn that Jesse Stuart seems to have in mind is more in the sense of beginnings and awakenings than an actual hour of the day—much in the manner in which Henry David Thoreau uses the idea of dawn in *Walden* (1854). The remembrance of the title suggests that the story is a recollection by an adult of an incident from his youth, and what is remembered is his spring, the period of his adult awakening, an emergence from the chrysalis of adolescence into the lush, green atmosphere of sex and love. For the narrator, this was a very important period in his life, a time when he made a discovery that influenced him deeply. Though Shan seems to discover nothing from the incidents related in the story while it is actually taking place, the narrator, through the selection of the title, gives readers a strong clue to the meaning of the narrative.

Shan's action, his snake hunt, is in one sense an act of bravery and manhood. With his strength and intelligence, he seeks to rid the world of an ancient evil. His story, like almost all boasts, relates his acts of heroism, as do heroic stories from both the Anglo-Saxon and Greek precursors of modern fiction. In "Dawn of Remembered Spring," however, it is not the heroism itself that teaches the hero what he needs to know to further his existence. Instead, it is the unimportance of his actions in comparison to something else that furnishes him with a new value that allows him to progress into maturity. In effect, he has discovered (though not during the actual time related during the story) that courage and cunning by themselves are not the sole admission price into the cherished state of maturity. It is at this point that the story diverges from its ancestor, the heroic narrative, and it is at this point also that Shan finds out that his society places higher values on love and the creative urge than it places on simple acts of heroism. His mother is on the whole displeased by his undertaking, and the neighbors who assemble to watch the courting of the copperheads are not at all impressed by his hunt.

"Dawn of Remembered Spring" is a coming-of-age story, a pattern that Stuart had used earlier in his better-known narrative "Split Cherry Tree." However, whereas

"Split Cherry Tree" exhibits the pattern in its complete form, with the young man reaching a new level of maturity, "Dawn of Remembered Spring" uses only the beginning and middle elements of the coming-of-age form. Stuart's decision to forgo the narrator's realization of the importance of love and procreation over heroism complicates the story. Although Stuart's decision invariably makes the tale more true to life, it nevertheless makes the story's meanings and themes more obscure.

## Style and Technique

In the creation of his character Shan, Stuart uses psychological realism to elevate this coming-of-age story above its ancestor, the heroic boast. The narrator's inability to speak of what he has learned from watching the faces of his neighbors and hearing their laughter is much more true to life than anything Shan might have thought to say about what he has witnessed. Shan resists the lesson he has learned at the end of his day of snake killing: that love is more powerful, more compelling, more appealing to humankind than hate, revenge, and death. The boy is really not quite as puzzled as he seems; he simply refuses to believe what his elders tell him about what the snakes are doing, but in his heart he knows that they are right. Stuart's delicate handling of this matter raises Shan above the level of the stereotypical youngster, giving his central character the depth and dimension necessary to make a story of this complexity and delicacy believable.

A further example of Stuart's psychological realism occurs in the beginning and middle portions of the story. Shan repeats three times that a snake bit his friend, but none will bite him. The reader knows full well that the boy is in danger, and this is one of the main reasons that he or she continues to read further—to find out whether Shan will actually escape harm. Through repetition, the author both shows his main character's fear and endows him with a very human characteristic, the ability to hold a belief in spite of what one really knows to be the case. This complex structuring of character easily eludes the careless reader, but for those who read Stuart's story deeply, such craftsmanship serves both as preparation for the ending and as a guide to the understanding of human ways of thought.

*Charles Hackenberry*

# THE DAY STALIN DIED

*Author:* Doris Lessing (1919-        )
*Type of plot:* Coming of age
*Time of plot:* March 5, 1953
*Locale:* London
*First published:* 1957

> *Principal characters:*
> THE NARRATOR, a writer
> JESSIE, her cousin
> EMMA, Jessie's mother, the narrator's aunt
> JEAN, a Communist Party associate of the narrator
> BEATRICE, an old friend of the narrator from South Africa
> THE HOST, the manager of a photography studio
> JACKIE SMITH, his friend and assistant

*The Story*

The day begins badly. The narrator receives a letter from Aunt Emma in Bournemouth, reminding her of a promise to take her cousin Jessie to have her picture taken that afternoon. Aunt Emma, Jessie's mother, wants the photos because she intends to show them to a television producer who visits his older brother in the boardinghouse where she and her daughter live. Aunt Emma hopes that Jessie will prove sufficiently photogenic to induce the producer to whisk her off to London to be a television star. Jessie is a broad-shouldered girl of about twenty-five who looks eighteen.

The narrator, forgetting all about the promise, has made other plans, which she is now obliged to cancel. She quickly tries to call off a date that she made with an American screenwriter named Bill. Bill, it seems, had some trouble with the House Committee on Un-American Activities, was black-listed, and could not find work in the United States. He is also having difficulty getting a permit to live in Great Britain. The narrator is trying to help him find a secretary and has gotten in touch with an old friend from South Africa, Beatrice, who is out of a job. The date was arranged to introduce the two. The narrator believes that these friends will get along because both have been involved in left-wing causes. (As she subsequently discovers, they prove not at all compatible.) It takes the narrator an hour to get in touch with Bill, only to discover that he has forgotten about the appointment. She then sends Beatrice a telegram because Beatrice has no phone.

Having freed the afternoon for Jessie, the narrator starts to get some work done in what is left of the morning. She has just begun when she is interrupted by a call from one of her Communist Party comrades, who says that she wants to see the narrator at lunchtime. The caller, Jean, is the narrator's self-appointed "guide or mentor towards a correct political viewpoint." Jean is the daughter of a bishop and has worked unquestioningly for the party for the past thirty years. Having divorced her husband when he became a member of the Labour Party following the Nazi-Soviet Pact, she now lives alone in a sitting room with a portrait of Joseph Stalin over her bed. Jean is disturbed about a remark that the narrator made the week before at a party meeting, that "a certain amount of dirty work must be going on in the Soviet Union." Jean arrives, bringing her sandwiches with her in a brown paper bag, and berates the narrator for flippancy. She tells her of the necessity of "unremitting vigilance on the part of the working class." She says that the only way that an intellectual with the narrator's background can gain a correct, working-class point of view is to work harder in the party to attain "a really sound working-class attitude." Jean recommends reading the verbatim transcript of the purge trials of the 1930's as an antidote to a vacillating attitude toward Soviet justice.

Jean's visit leaves the narrator, "for one reason or another," depressed. However, there is not much time to brood; no sooner has Jean left than a call comes from Cousin Jessie, who asks if the narrator can meet her in twenty minutes outside a dress shop, as she has decided to buy new clothes in which to be photographed. The narrator therefore quits work for the day and takes a cab to her rendezvous.

Jessie is waiting outside the dress shop when the narrator arrives; she is already wearing her new dress, but it does not seem any different from the clothes she usually wears. Jessie, almost by way of greeting, announces, somewhat aggressively, that her mother, Aunt Emma, is coming to the photography studio with them. Aunt Emma then emerges from a corner tearoom, and the three of them set off to take a bus to the studio. Between Aunt Emma and Cousin Jessie there is a constant tension, which sends off "currents of angry electricity into the air around them." Aunt Emma's bulldog eyes are "nearly always fixed in disappointment on her daughter." Whatever their divisions, however, mother and daughter share a mutual detestation of the lower classes, with which they carry on incessant guerrilla warfare. This form of entertainment, the narrator explains, is conditioned by their extremely dreary lives. Their conversation on the bus therefore is a constant running battle against the lower classes and each other.

They get off the bus; the entrance to the studio is not far away. As the three women hurry down the street, their heads under Aunt Emma's umbrella to protect them against the cold, drizzling rain, the narrator notices the announcement on a newsstand bulletin board that Stalin is dying. She stops and buys a paper but has only a brief moment to exchange words with the vendor, as Aunt Emma is obviously annoyed at being held up. Aunt Emma has more important things on her mind: "What do you think, would it have been better if Jessie had bought a nice pretty afternoon dress?" The studio is on the second floor. The stairs have a plush carpet and striped gold-and-mauve wallpaper; upstairs is a white, gray, and gold drawing room with a small crystal chandelier, the prisms of which tinkle from the reverberations of Igor Stravinsky's *The Rite of Spring*. The studio is run by two very effeminate men, one of whom, the host, is a disturbingly outspoken racist.

The highly charged atmosphere makes all three women ill at ease, especially Jessie.

"You don't look relaxed," the host tells her gently. "It's really no use at all, you know, unless you are really relaxed all over." To break the ice, the host suggests "a nice cup of tea" so that "our vibrations might become just a little more harmonious." Aunt Emma tries to steer the conversation in another direction and blurts out that Stalin is dying, or "so they would have us believe." The subject of the great man's demise produces only more trivialities. The host comments that he does not know much about politics but that "Uncle Joe and Roosevelt were absolutely my pin up boys" during the war, "But absolutely!" All this chitchat does nothing to calm Jessie's nerves. She now demands that they get "this damned business over with." The host happily agrees and asks for what use the photos are intended: dust jackets, publicity, or "just for your lucky friends?" Cousin Jessie answers that she does not know and does not care. Aunt Emma insists, "I would like you to catch her expression. It's just that little look of hers." Jessie clenches her fists at her mother. The narrator suggests that she and Aunt Emma absent themselves for a while, and Jessie goes into another room to be photographed.

Aunt Emma starts to ask about all the exciting things that the narrator has been doing that day. The only incident that the narrator thinks might be of interest to her aunt is that she had lunch with the daughter of a bishop. The conversation is interrupted by the reemergence of Cousin Jessie, who is more distraught than ever. She says that she is simply not in the mood and then has the whole session called off. Aunt Emma has never been more ashamed. Jessie could not care less. The three women leave the studio. The narrator leaves behind the newspaper that she has just bought. They say good-bye outside. Aunt Emma and Jessie get into a cab; the narrator gets on a bus.

When the narrator returns home, she receives a phone call from Beatrice, who says that she received the telegram and then says that Stalin is dying. The narrator says that she knows and tries to change the subject. Beatrice's call is followed by one from comrade Jean, who announces that Stalin is dead. Jean is crying and says that it is obvious that he was murdered by capitalist agents. The narrator remarks that it is not unusual for death to come naturally to people who are seventy-three. Jean tells her that they will have to pledge themselves "to be worthy of him." The narrator replies mechanically, "Yes, I suppose we will."

*Themes and Meanings*

The narrator is an author, a writer of short stories, who cannot work on the day that Stalin dies because of constant interruptions by members of her family and by her associates in the Communist Party. Such impositions on her time are apparently commonplace and are a constant source of tension and depression. The narrator finds it impossible to say no.

However, the frustration goes deeper. The narrator finds it difficult to reconcile her involvement with the communist movement and various other left-wing activities with the independence of judgment and spirit necessary to practice her craft. A party hack, such as Jean, has a special commitment to trivializing the author's talent, reducing it to the level of the class struggle. With obvious delight, she says condescendingly that intellectuals such as the narrator are under "greater pressure from the forces of capitalist corruption than any other type of party cadre." Clearly, no middle ground can exist between orthodox communism and a free spirit. There is no possibility of compromise. Jean is in effect saying that one cannot have it both ways, although the narrator apparently believes that it is possible.

On this conflict between independence of mind and the quest for political-social identity is built a pedestrian story. The motives that prompted the narrator to join the Communist Party are not stated directly, but it seems certain that these motives, ostensibly idealistic, have something to do with a strong impulse to belong and to serve: those traditionally feminine characteristics that condition her to respond to any request, no matter how trivial. It becomes clear, for example, that her presence at the photography studio is completely unnecessary.

The death of Stalin is symbolic. It dramatizes an important change in the author's life, a change that has been a long time in coming. The news of the communist leader's death is disturbing at first because he is so closely linked to the past from which the narrator has derived stability and identity. She is annoyed when the reactions of other people are so superficial and trivial. By the end of her wasted day, however, it is clear that the defection from Stalinism and the adjustment to a new relationship with people has been well established.

## Style and Technique

Much of Doris Lessing's work is autobiographical. Although the narrator is unidentified in this story, her attitudes presumably mirror the author's own. Like the narrator, Lessing was at one time associated with the Communist Party and subsequently broke her ties with it. Her disaffection probably did not occur as she describes it in this story, but some of the issues she raises and the conflicts she relates no doubt figured in her decision. Stalin's death is the occasion for the parting of the ways, not the cause of it.

Lessing is particularly effective in revealing character through dialogue and in describing the way people speak. Jessie, for example, "always speaks in short, breathless, battling sentences, as from an unassuageably inner integrity which she doesn't expect anyone else to understand." Another technique of Lessing is to relate her main character's values through that character's reactions to the comments of others, including those she hears by eavesdropping on the conversations of strangers. In the bus, a middle-aged couple are arguing about fish, "all those little fishes," says the man. "We explode all these bombs at them, and we're not going to be forgiven for that, are we, we're not to be forgiven for blowing up the poor little fishes." The narrator says, "I had known that the afternoon was bound to get out of control at some point; but this conversation upset me." The reaction masterfully reveals an intellect troubled by surroundings from which it had previously drawn support.

*Wm. Laird Kleine-Ahlbrandt*

# THE DAY THE FLOWERS CAME

*Author:* David Madden (1933-   )
*Type of plot:* Psychological
*Time of plot:* The 1960's
*Locale:* Rolling Hills Homes, an upper-middle-class subdivision in an unnamed city
*First published:* 1968

### Principal characters:

JAY D. "J. D." HINDLE, the protagonist, second vice president of an insurance company

CAROLYN HINDLE, his wife, mother of his children, Ronnie and Ellen

BILL HENDERSON, his friend, known for his practical jokes

### The Story

After a night of solitary, heavy drinking, the protagonist, J. D. Hindle, wakes up on the couch in the living room of his house in a subdivision called Rolling Hills Homes. He has trouble getting his bearings. There are two glasses next to the empty bottle of Jack Daniel's on the coffee table, but J. D. remembers being alone. He seems to have fallen asleep reading *True* magazine. The voices of a man and woman on television, actors in a situation comedy, at first seem to be talking to him. The sunlight coming through the window hurts his eyes, and J. D. pulls the drapes to darken the room. The doorbell is ringing, and it takes him a few moments to remember that it is Labor Day and that his wife, Carolyn, and children, Ronnie and Ellen, are away in Florida. When he answers the door, he finds a delivery man from a florist with a basket of roses and a printed card that reads, "My deepest sympathy."

This opening situation is charged with implications that the unfolding of the story's plot confirms. Although J. D. convinces the man from the florist's shop, at least initially, that "there's been no death in this family," the deliveries of flowers continue. There are visits from neighbors and friends bearing food and expressing sympathy, for they have seen a newspaper account of the deaths of Carolyn Hindle and her children in Daytona Beach. Their deaths were caused by Hurricane Gloria. J. D. telephones the Breakers Hotel and Mr. Garrett, the local newspaper editor. A telegram sent from Florida that morning, obviously delayed by the weather, lets him cling to the belief that his wife and children are alive. He even accuses his friend Bill Henderson of engineering the whole affair as an elaborate practical joke.

J. D.'s unwillingness to accept the truth, implied by the details of the opening situation, arises from more than normal shock at the news of an accident. As the story develops, other details reveal that J. D.'s marriage was in trouble, and that this is the reason Carolyn took the children and left for Daytona Beach. As he stumbles around the house between telephone calls and trips to the door to receive deliveries of flowers, J. D. reveals his unfamiliarity with his home. He does not know how to operate the kitchen stove, where to find razor blades in the bathroom, or where his clean clothes are kept. Carolyn has always had things ready for him. In this house, their fourth since they were married, he is virtually a stranger. "As second vice-president, perhaps he spent more time away now, more time in the air. Coming home was more and more like an astronaut's re-entry problem."

J. D.'s isolation from his family becomes permanent with the deaths of Carolyn, Ronnie, and Ellen. Acceptance of this fact comes hard. When Mr. Garrett calls back, reporting that the Associated Press confirms all three deaths, J. D. turns on his friend Bill Henderson, who has suggested that J. D. is responsible for the fact that Carolyn and the children were in Florida. Still denying reality, J. D. tells Mrs. Merrill, the PTA president, that Carolyn and the children will be home soon: "They're having a wonderful time in Florida." He also loses control at a call from Gold Seal Portrait Studios, which is trying to sell him a package deal on family photographs; he throws the flowers that have been delivered all over the front lawn; he attempts to break the doorbell with his fist. Finally, he turns off the electric current to stop the chimes, now ringing continuously, and collects the flowers on the lawn before stretching out on the living room carpet for a nap.

Rather than obliterating the facts that he wants to avoid, this period of sleep reconciles J. D. to the deaths of Carolyn and the children. The climax of the story occurs when he recalls something his wife said on the way to the airport the day before. Trying to explain her need to go away, Carolyn told him, "Something is happening to me. I'm dying, very, very slowly; do you understand that, Jay? Our life. It's the way we live, somehow the way we live." He had not understood her words at the time. His feeling then was relief at the prospect of being alone in the house for a few days. Turning on the electric power again, thereby reactivating the doorbell, J. D. goes to the door of his home and looks at the houses in the darkened subdivision spread below him. He looks up at the moon, but he cannot see the face of the man in it. Continuing to look at the heavens, however, he sees the faces of Carolyn, Ronnie, and Ellen in the stars. At this moment, in September, "snow began to fall, as though the stars had disintegrated into flakes."

*Themes and Meanings*

In the imagery of that star-filled sky, David Madden objectifies J. D.'s realization that his wife and children are dead and that he is fundamentally alone in the universe. This isolation, with its overtones of existential philosophy, is different from the unself-conscious isolation J. D. had experienced in the last few years of his marriage to Carolyn. Like his wife, J. D. is dying inside, and the cause of the problem is the way he has chosen to live his life. Having put career before marriage and material measures of success before emotional ones, J. D. embraces the middle-class success ethic that Madden indicts in the story. It is ironically appropriate that "The Day the Flowers Came" takes place on Labor Day.

In one sense, the story is about J. D.'s death and not the deaths of his wife and children. When he picks up the flowers he has hurled all over the front lawn, he "took them into the house and laid them in his leather easy chair." The nap he takes on the carpet puts him at a level below that of the flowers. When he awakens, therefore, J. D. rises metaphorically from the grave. He contemplates the darkened exterior world from inside his home, now fully lighted, and sees with real intensity the full moral and psychological dimensions of his situation. This final episode reverses the lighting system of the opening of the story, when J. D. closed out the light of day and resisted facing the truth in a darkened house.

The cold, wet whiteness of the snow with which the story ends reveals J. D.'s capacity to feel grief for the deaths of Carolyn, Ronnie, and Ellen. Paradoxically, he is closer to them at this moment than at any other point in the story. The tension between J. D.'s sense of isolation and his newfound capacity to feel close to his family defines the ending of Madden's story.

*Style and Technique*

Madden's style in "The Day the Flowers Came" is straightforward, even colloquial in places. He uses a limited third-person point of view to get inside J. D.'s mind and to show how J. D. sees his own situation, but much of the story is rendered in dialogue between J. D. and his various visitors. The narrator does not comment on J. D.'s thoughts and actions. Their meaning emerges from the juxtaposition of events and from the implications that arise from Madden's handling of them.

Aside from the use of light and darkness to underscore J. D.'s changed perspective of himself, the chief images are the doorbell chimes and the flowers referred to in the title. The chimes have the single function of calling J. D. to his door to confront a reality he does not begin to accept until the end of the story. The flowers serve a dual function. They are the literal expression of the sympathy of J. D.'s friends and neighbors, and they are also symbols of life's impermanence. The day the flowers come is a turning point. It is the day on which J. D. is first able to see life clearly and to recognize his place in the universe.

*Robert C. Petersen*

# THE DAY THEY TOOK MY UNCLE

*Author:* Lionel G. García (1935-      )
*Type of plot:* Domestic realism
*Time of plot:* The 1940's
*Locale:* A small Texas town
*First published:* 1992

> *Principal characters:*
> THE BOY, the narrator of the story
> MERCÉ, his uncle, a local madman
> HIS PARENTS
> THE SHERIFF, who takes away the uncle

## The Story

The narrator recalls a moment during his childhood in Texas when he and his young girlfriend played under the house, and she gave him his first look at female genitalia. He then remembers his uncle, a man he recalls as "insane, crazy." The uncle's madness manifested itself in bouts in which he would yank his earlobes violently and curse at people obscenely while remarking on imaginary scandalous events of their past. The narrator particularly remembers the moment when his uncle called the town mayor "a sonofabitch and a son of a whore, plus a bastard" and then accused the mayor's wife of being unfaithful by taking up with the mayor's cousin.

As the uncle's favorite relative, the boy often saw his disquieting episodes. In addition to being mad, the uncle also had a drinking problem. According to the boy's grandmother, the uncle's madness began when he drank the remains of a bottle of beer "that had been laced with a special potion, a potion so powerful it would cause insanity." At the local bar, which was the uncle's favorite hangout, the townsmen enjoyed watching his episodes, hooting and hollering as he paced back and forth screaming his insults. Unable afterward to recall what he had done, he quickly became gentle and docile. The man's behavior naturally embarrassed the boy and his sister—who lost her first suitor because of his lunacy and because the young man "would never call on a girl who had heard so many curse words in her young life."

The narrator reflects on the joys of small-town life, when things were simple. Even when his uncle died, there was no need to learn the cause. In a small town, people die: That is all one needs to know. While the uncle was alive, he had only one set of tasks to perform each day: milking the cow in the morning, taking her out to pasture, bringing her back before sunset, and milking her once more before putting her up for the night. When he had maniacal episodes or got drunk, however, he would forget his responsibility, leaving the boy and his father to search for the cow, which the uncle never left in the same pasture twice.

One day the uncle cursed the mayor one time too many and the town leaders—

including the local priest and sheriff—decided it was time to put him away in a mental institution in Galveston. Selected to perform this task, the sheriff arrived at the house at the same moment at which the narrative begins—with the boy under the house with his girlfriend.

From this hidden vantage point the boy sees and hears everything. The sheriff doubts the boy's mother when she says that the uncle is not home. After searching the house, the sheriff turns his attention to the toolshed. As he approaches it, the boy's mother and grandmother plead for the uncle, who they know is hiding there. The sheriff keeps his hand on his revolver, expecting the uncle to become violent when he is discovered, but after hunting with his uncle many times and never bagging anything, the boy knows that his uncle is incapable of hurting any living creature.

The sheriff enters the toolshed and causes a great commotion as he searches it. From under the house, the boy knows that his uncle planned to hide there, but then he detects the faint smell of stale beer: His uncle is now under the house also. As the uncle confesses his fear of being sent away, he enters another maniacal episode, crawls out from beneath the house, and begins tugging his earlobes violently and loudly cursing about the sexual antics of the priest and the nuns who live across the street.

The sheriff tackles the uncle and handcuffs him. As the madman gets into the sheriff's car, his relatives tell him to behave himself in the hospital so that he can return soon. When the car pulls away, the boy's father chases it calling to the uncle to tell him where the cow is pasturing.

A year later, the uncle returns home. Although he is not cured, he carries a card stating that he is "not a menace to society."

*Themes and Meanings*

A bittersweet coming-of-age story, "The Day They Took My Uncle" explores the theme of awakening, both socially and, to a lesser degree, sexually. Most important, Lionel G. García's narrator learns that family loyalty transcends everything. Despite the uncle's recurring bouts of madness and alcoholism, the family never considers ostracizing him. On the contrary, there is considerable tolerance for his erratic behavior. The boy's father, for example, does not become angry with his brother. When reproaching Mercé, the boy's father "would scold him lightly and in a very gentle way." Except for the narrator's sister, all the family members stand by Mercé.

By contrast, the characters in positions of power in the town exercise great control over the uncle's life. It is not until the mayor, the sheriff, and the priest band together that Mercé is taken away as a simple nuisance. Although the uncle has never acted violently, they treat him as a dangerous criminal. In the end, the boy feels incapable of helping his uncle avoid capture because he realizes that there is "no escaping the law." Although the family bond is strong, the need to conform to societal norms and not challenge those in power ultimately overrides all else. Nevertheless, the uncle enjoys a minor victory in the end when he returns home with psychiatric proof that he does not pose a menace to society.

*Style and Technique*

Told in the first person, the story has a confessional style. It begins with the narrator sharing his first sexual experience with the reader, then proceeds quickly to explain the strange case of madness that existed in his family.

Although a tale of an insane and alcoholic relative might easily be a sad one, the author tells it with humor, and this becomes his favorite device. His description of the uncle's maniacal episodes turns comical when he quotes the insults that his uncle hurls at other townspeople. The mayor and his frail old wife are the madman's favorite targets, followed by the priest and three nuns from the Sisters of Charity—the very characters least likely to commit the scandalous deeds of which they are accused.

The most comical figure, however, is the cow, which García endows with human qualities. At night, after the uncle has forgotten to pick her up, the boy and his father search for her, and they eventually find her waiting patiently, although a bit confused. Whenever the uncle has a fit as he leads the cow somewhere, she "would stop, look at him stoically, as if she knew this was the cross she had been given to bear." After the uncle is taken to Galveston, the narrator's mother and grandmother cry each time that they see the cow. Never knowing what it is about herself that brings tears to their eyes, the poor animal looks "inquiringly from one side of herself to the other, as if looking for some clue." The humor that García employs in the telling of this story is without a doubt the main factor that allows one to describe it as bittersweet.

*Silvio Sirias*

# THE DAYDREAMS OF A DRUNK WOMAN

*Author:* Clarice Lispector (1925-1977)
*Type of plot:* Coming of age
*Time of plot:* The 1950's
*Locale:* Brazil
*First published:* "Devaneio e embriaguez duma rapariga," 1960 (English translation, 1972)

> *Principal characters:*
> MARIA QUITERA, the narrator, a dissatisfied Brazilian housewife
> HER HUSBAND, a businessperson

*The Story*

Maria Quitera is a housewife on the edge. She is looking for her place in the world; not finding it, she is searching for someone to blame. The story begins on a Thursday afternoon just before her husband returns from work. Maria is in a tipsy mood, acting childish and as if she is drunk. She is talking and singing to herself, brushing her hair, admiring herself in the mirror, flitting from one mood and subject to another. Her children are away, and her husband is soon to be out of town on business. She prepares herself by sleeping.

The story falls loosely into two sections: the first being Maria's "day off," and the second, the Saturday night dinner. On her day off, when her children are away and her husband is to spend the day in the city on business, Maria fleetingly feels the freedom and consequent fear of not having a particular role to play for the day. When her husband comes in to kiss her farewell, she realizes that she does not even know what he has had for breakfast—the preparation of which is doubtless one of her daily rituals. She realizes that she need not get his meals nor check his suit for lint. However, if not these things, what then should she do? Her answer is to snap at her husband and spend the next thirty-six hours or so in a dizzying, whirling sleep, effectively avoiding the self-defining task of asserting her will on the day. When Maria finally does get up late on Saturday morning, she is clearly happy to find the everyday routine restored as she goes about her chores and errands.

The Saturday night at the fancy restaurant, where Maria accompanies her husband to dine with a wealthy businessperson, plays out this same scenario but more elaborately. Now drinking wine, Maria actually is tipsy, playing with her altered perceptions and self-awareness. On the outside she is socializing in the role of the loyal, if slightly shallow, wife. She feels alienated from that role, however, and is instead becoming hypersensitive to her own sense of self, as if that self were a secret. "But the words that a woman uttered when drunk were like being pregnant—mere words on her lips which had nothing to do with the secret core that seemed like pregnancy." She plays a bit with this duality, relishing it, as she remembers that she is a woman of culture, a woman who has traveled, who has an artistic sensibility. Wanting to pursue this identity, she becomes more and more drunk, reasoning that she has after all acquired a certain position in life, which affords her protection from the social world. It is this very realization that brings her back into "reality." Her position is nothing if not the adjunct to her successful husband, whom she was just silently mocking. In an instant the "position" that saved her from misfortune has become a cloud that shadows her self into obscurity.

Maria's response to this sense of annihilation is again vehemently to defend her role as model wife and mother, as she jealously and hatefully criticizes another woman who has caught her eye at the restaurant. Though not wanting to do so, she still plays by the rules of the superficial, fluctuating from self-righteous disdain and indignation to humility and shame at going out to dinner without a hat like that which the slim socialite is wearing.

While recovering at home from her indulgent night, her hidden self makes one last stab at emerging and taking hold. The physical sensations of such a state of heightened awareness, however, become unbearable for Maria. Accordingly, she recites a series of Christian and domestic platitudes, as she resigns herself to a defeated state in subjugation to her "real world" position—cleaning house and being pretty and plump—at the side of her husband.

## Themes and Meanings

"The Daydreams of a Drunk Woman" is fundamentally the story of a woman whose realization of self puts her at odds with the people and social structures that surround her. The issue of self-identity versus social alienation is a theme that dominates Clarice Lispector's work. The very first image of the story—that of Maria's trembling reflection in the mirror as the trolley cars go by—sets up the symbolic yet undeniable theme of a wavering sense of self. This is reinforced a few lines later when Maria catches the reflection of the intersected breasts of several women as she studies herself in the mirror.

Maria's drunken daydreams explore the duality of self while depicting the inherent alienation of a frustrated human existence. The seeming opposites of sober and drunk, awake and asleep, practical and reckless, physical and psychological, happy and sad, love and hate, are all conflated as Maria carries on her social functions while delving separately into her individual thoughts and perceptions. In so doing, she becomes acutely aware of her solitude and isolation within a supposedly collective, cohesive humanity. She recognizes concurrently both the freedom that isolation brings as well as the meaninglessness it connotes for the individual. This contradictory state of mind proves to be unbearable and unmanageable.

The personal discovery of the truth about one's own private human condition and how one deals with that truth is what Lispector brings to light. Maria's ambivalence about taking responsibility for her private condition keeps her fluctuating between bored resignation toward her own fate, animated disapproval of others for their apparent superficiality, mental self-flagellation for her inability to stay within the confines of her social position, and awestruck wonder at what her senses can perceive in this intense world. The recognition of her nothingness, and the nothingness of those around her, brings about fear, which manifests itself as petty jealousy and self-righteousness. This is clearly an act of both self-assertion and escape from the primordial fear of being without boundaries or meaning, ultimately dispensable and always alone.

The parallels between the author and her character are obvious, despite differences in their circumstances. Lispector, a well-educated wife of a diplomat, was successful as a writer and journalist in her own right. Maria is also apparently educated but without a goal, a career, or a life of her own separate from her husband's. The degree to which the author identifies with Maria's difficult struggle of carving out a niche for herself and finding fulfillment as a woman in a man's world is so complete, however, as to seem wholly autobiographical. She projects her own psychological reality onto the character of Maria, allowing the reader a glimpse into her private dreamworld.

*Style and Technique*

Lispector is internationally known for her lyrical style of writing, which blurs the line between prose and poetry. This lyricism is in large part a result of the subject matter with which she deals. Her stories are primarily interior monologues, probing their characters' psychic reality. The conflict of one of her stories is always within the mind of the main character, exploring the way people, things, and events in the physical world effect unexpected and seemingly unrelated reactions in the individual's psyche. The character's changing psychic perspective dominates both the style and structure of the narrative, as the author's focus tightens around the effects of situations, rather than the situations themselves. This structurally inventive style was considered at least unconventional, if not radically groundbreaking, in 1944 when Lispector's first novel was published.

The lyricism of Lispector's prose is found not just in the rhythm of its sentence structure but also in the way the actual words used move seamlessly between real-world and the other-worldly realm. Again, this is reflected in the nature of her subject matter, flowing between the practical, social quotidian and the dreamlike inner reality of self. For language to have meaning one must be able to relate to it; in order to relate, the gap between self and other must be bridged. Lispector is skilled at transforming the nonlinear inner reality of her characters into a linear expression that retains its meaning.

As in Lispector's other stories, "The Daydreams of a Drunk Woman" is structured around an epiphany. The first half of the story, in which Maria moves in and out of consciousness, toying with different constructions of her self, can be viewed as a slow build toward the epiphanal moment in the restaurant when she realizes that the freedom afforded her by her position as wife is also her shackle keeping her from exploring her true self. The ambiguous ending is also typical of Lispector, leaving the reader to wonder whether Maria will again resign herself with a sigh, or free herself with a boisterous laughing shout.

*Leslie Maile Pendleton*

# DE MORTUIS

*Author:* John Collier (1901-1980)
*Type of plot:* Horror
*Time of plot:* The mid-twentieth century
*Locale:* Upstate New York
*First published:* 1951

> *Principal characters:*
> DR. RANKIN, a fifty-year-old small-town physician
> IRENE RANKIN, his wife, a younger woman with a bad reputation
> BUD and
> BUCK, his fishing companions

## The Story

As mild-mannered Dr. Rankin puts the finishing touches to a patch of wet cement on his cellar floor, he is startled by sounds, signaling the entrance of Bud and Buck, who call out, "Hi, Doc! They're biting!" Not wanting to be disturbed, he remains silent, but his friends figure out where he is and come down the stairs.

When the friends ask Rankin about the wet cement patch, he explains that he has repaired a spot where water has been seeping in from an underground spring. Bud—the realtor who sold him the property—refuses to believe that such a spring exists, and both men are skeptical about Rankin's explanation that his wife, Irene, is visiting friends. After asking several more questions, they announce that he has buried his wife's body under the cement. When Rankin reacts indignantly to this suggestion, his friends reassure him that they are on his side and will help cover up his murder. After telling him that they do not blame him for wanting to kill Irene, they reveal everything they know about her character, calling her "the town floozy." Both men admit to having had sexual relations with her themselves, but they hasten to assure Rankin that these incidents occurred before he married her.

All these revelations shock the unworldly Rankin, who has doted on his young wife. His love for her turns to hatred as he learns about her moral depravity and realizes how he has been deceived by her beauty and surface innocence. He concludes that she never loved him, that she married him only for financial security, and that she has been making a fool of him since the moment that they met. Rankin honestly believes the story that he has told Buck and Bud about his wife's visiting old friends named Slater in Watertown; however, his friends assure him that no such people exist. Rankin now believes that Irene has lied to him in order to meet a secret lover.

As Bud and Buck leave, they promise never to breathe a word about the supposed murder. They will swear that they saw Irene riding out of town with a man in a roadster—a story that everyone in town will believe because of Irene's reputation.

While Rankin is still in the cellar, his young wife unexpectedly returns. She has missed her train and asks him to drive her to another station where she can still make connections. He asks her if she met anyone coming back. She tells him that she has not met a soul, leaving Rankin as the only person who knows that she is still in town.

At the end of the story, the doctor asks Irene to come downstairs so that he can show her a problem that has developed with the patch of cement he has been working on. It is clear that he intends to murder her and put her under the cement floor, now that Buck and Bud have provided him with an airtight alibi.

*Themes and Meanings*

In his cynicism about human affairs in general and about modern marriage in particular, John Collier has been compared to such authors as W. Somerset Maugham, Noël Coward, Oscar Wilde, and the vitriolic American journalist Ambrose Bierce. He has also been compared frequently to Edgar Allan Poe. Poe, however, did not possess Collier's ability to make his readers laugh, although he tried rather desperately to do so in some of his less successful stories.

Twice married himself, Collier often wrote disparagingly about marital relationships. His *His Monkey Wife: Or, Married to a Chimp* (1930) is about a man married to a chimpanzee. One of his most bitterly cynical short stories about marriage is "The Chaser," in which an old merchant who deals in magic potions advises a passionate young suitor to plan ahead for the time when he will get tired of the woman he adores and will want to rid himself of her cloying presence with a fatal dose of poison. "De Mortuis" is another of Collier's cynical stories dealing with the complications of modern marriage.

Collier's attitude toward marriage reflects modern realities. During the twentieth century the United States divorce rate soared until sociologists predicted that a marriage had little better than a fifty-fifty chance of success. Such statistics suggest there may be many husbands and wives who hate each other but remain married because of finances, children, religion, or other considerations. Collier was not only cynical about marriage, he was cynical about human nature in general. He dramatizes this theme in "De Mortuis" in the ease with which the gentle Dr. Rankin is about to become a cold-blooded murderer and the casual way in which his two buddies become his co-conspirators. It is difficult to find likable or entirely innocent characters in Collier's stories. Those who start out innocent generally do not remain so for long.

The thesis of "De Mortuis" is similar to that of "The Chaser." Both stories suggest that love can easily turn into hatred and that people who have romantic or idealistic notions about other human beings are bound to become disillusioned unless they are stupid. Like many of Collier's stories, "De Mortuis" suggests that it is impossible for one truly to know another human being, that we are all born strangers who live and die alone. What saves Collier's short stories from being overwhelmingly depressing is their quirky, sophisticated humor. This sugarcoating of Collier's bitter pills of worldly wisdom keeps the reader from taking his cynical outlook too seriously.

*Style and Technique*

"De Mortuis" belongs to a specialized mystery subgenre often called "the body in the basement story." It also belongs to the larger subgenre of "perfect crime" stories. In typical stories of this type, a man murders a relative, buries the body somewhere inside his home, and congratulates himself that he has gotten away with the perfect crime. Then, because of some fatal mistake, the murderer is caught and punished. Poe, the American genius who created many modern literary genres, was responsible for the popularity of both body-in-the-basement and perfect-crime stories. Examples of Poe's contributions are "The Tell-Tale Heart" and "The Cask of Amontillado."

What makes Collier's "De Mortuis" so effective is its ironic twists, its departure from the norm. In order to appreciate Collier's story, the reader must be familiar with stories of the conventional pattern, such as those of Poe and his imitators. Collier plays with fictional conventions in a manner that is hypermodern. Writing in the earlier decades of the twentieth century, he presaged some of the experimental innovations of much later writers. Collier is a sophisticated modern writer addressing sophisticated modern readers of magazines such as *The New Yorker*. "De Mortuis" almost completely reverses traditional mystery story conventions, betraying the reader's expectations: Because no body has actually been buried in the basement, it appears that the perfect crime really will be committed.

There are other reversals in "De Mortuis" as well. In typical perfect-crime stories, cunning murderers are proud of their ability to plan their crime and fool the police. In sharp contrast, Dr. Rankin is such a simple soul that he is completely unaware of what is well known to everybody else in his community. In a typical body-in-the-basement story, the murderer tries to get rid of someone he hates. If he murders his wife—as is often the case in such stories—she is likely to be old, unattractive, shrewish, demanding, and a "ball and chain." By contrast, the doctor's wife is beautiful and sexy, and he is deeply in love with her until he learns the truth.

Collier is a master storyteller; the unity of time and setting that he creates in "De Mortuis" is admirable. He ranges over many years and suggests the existence of a whole town without departing from the immediate present or from a single spot in the doctor's cellar. Another way in which Collier displays his craftsmanship is in orchestrating his characters. For example, the youthful, scatterbrained Irene makes Rankin seem old and stodgy by comparison, and his quiet, thoughtful manner highlights her hedonism and extroversion. Collier keeps his story dramatic through having Buck and Bud reveal Irene's scandalous past. A less skillful writer might have had Rankin find a letter or some other incriminating clue. Buck and Bud make the situation more immediate, bringing it "on stage" and adding dramatic tension by their initial suspicions and ultimate complicity.

Collier's short stories are invariably humorous in an ironic or bizarre manner. There is much humor in "De Mortuis," including the paradox that the doctor idolizes the town floozy, the fact that everyone knows about her behavior except him, and the fact that Bud and Buck assume that he has buried his wife's body in the cellar.

*Bill Delaney*

# THE DEAD

*Author:* James Joyce (1882-1941)
*Type of plot:* Naturalistic
*Time of plot:* 1904
*Locale:* Dublin, Ireland
*First published:* 1914

*Principal characters:*

GABRIEL CONROY, a university-educated teacher and journalist
who considers himself a writer and sophisticate

GRETTA CONROY, his wife, a country girl from the west of Ireland

KATE MORKAN, his aunt, who is old and feeble and who gives
piano lessons for beginners

JULIA MORKAN, Kate's sister, an organist and the mainstay of the
family

MARY JANE, the only niece of the Morkan sisters; she lives with
them and teaches piano

MOLLY IVORS, Gabriel's friend and colleague, a teacher dedicated
to the ideals of Irish nationalism and the Gaelic League

LILY, the caretaker's daughter, who works as the Morkan
housemaid

FREDDY MALINS, a forty-year-old houseguest, given to drink

MR. BROWNE, another socially awkward houseguest, an expert on
opera singers of years past

MRS. MALINS, Freddy's mother, who is visiting Dublin from
Glasgow, where she lives with her daughter

BARTELL D'ARCY, a well-known, second-rate tenor "full of
conceit"

MICHAEL FUREY, a Galway boy who died at the age of seventeen
but whose memory dominates Gretta Conroy's consciousness

*The Story*

This story begins one way and ends another. The shifting nature of the story is balanced by the shifting perception of the protagonist, Gabriel Conroy, a teacher who wants to be considered a writer, though his writing seems to be confined to journalism. The opening exposition suggests that the story mainly will concern a social event, "the Misses Morkan's annual dance," held during the Christmas season, at which the Morkans' favorite nephew, Gabriel, and his wife, Gretta, are significant guests because Gabriel serves as master of ceremonies. The impact of the story, however, comes much later, after Gabriel has left the party and is confronted with new information about his wife and her past.

The cast of characters at the Morkan house is large and representative of many Irish stereotypes: the Morkan sisters, Kate and Julia, who are musically inclined spinsters; their musical niece, Mary Jane; and other assorted characters, ranging from Miss Molly Ivors, the Irish nationalist, to Freddy Malins, whose sobriety is a matter of continuing concern. On his arrival, however, Gabriel is defined as the focal character, a man who is a little too proud of his education and sophistication, foolishly smug and superior, but aware nevertheless of his social awkwardness. Gabriel is expected to perform as an after-dinner speaker and is condescending in his assessment of his audience. Gabriel is destined, however, to learn a lesson in humility before the story is over.

Gabriel Conroy is bored by his country, his relatives, and his colleagues and their provincial ways. Molly Ivors criticizes him for his lack of interest in Irish politics, for writing for *The Daily Express* (the slant is "West Briton" rather than properly Irish, she asserts), and for his preference for traveling to France and Belgium rather than to the native Aran Islands, a focal point for Irish nationalism. In response to these charges, Gabriel embarrasses himself by telling her that he is "sick" of his own country. Molly Ivors is so upset by his bluntness that she leaves the dance before dinner is served. Gabriel knows that he is responsible for her "abrupt departure." Joyce provides ample evidence that Gabriel is insensitive and cannot control his rudeness. In his own way he is a social misfit, offending people without intending to offend them.

Gabriel gets through his hypocritical after-dinner address without apparently offending anyone, extolling the virtues of traditional "warmhearted courteous Irish hospitality," flattering "the Three Graces of the Dublin musical world," Kate, Julia, and Mary Jane, and then toasting them. As the party is breaking up, Gabriel notices his wife, standing on the stairs, listening in rapt attention as Bartell D'Arcy, accompanied by Miss O'Callaghan at the piano, sings a traditional Irish air, "The Lass of Aughrim." Gabriel romanticizes the moment and imagines his wife to be the subject of a painting that he would entitle "Distant Music." His blood is warmed by her shining eyes and the color in her cheeks.

Gabriel remembers the intimate moments of their courtship, and the spark of romance kindled in him by Gretta begins to flame. He then takes his wife to a hotel, feeling "that they had escaped from their lives and duties, escaped from home and friends and run away together with wild and radiant hearts to a new adventure." Little does he know. The problem is that Gabriel does not understand his wife's emotional state, for hearing "The Lass of Aughrim" has reminded her of a boy she had known and loved in Galway, Michael Furey, who, at the age of seventeen, died of a broken heart when Gretta left Galway to come to Dublin.

Learning of the dead Michael Furey causes Gabriel to reassess his relationship with his wife, his own petty vanity, and his self-image. The result is frustration and disappointment. He is forced to realize that his wife experienced a deeply felt romantic loss that had nothing at all to do with him. Gabriel aspires to be a writer, but he has failed to know and understand the person with whom he is most intimate. This is the subjective epiphany that provides the ironic reversal that Joyce uses to conclude the story. Gabriel is finally forced to realize that he has "never felt like that himself towards any women," that he himself is incomplete and unfulfilled; his illusions about himself are destroyed; the truth he discovers is painful.

*Themes and Meanings*

"The Dead" is the most obviously autobiographical story in the *Dubliners* (1914) collection in that Joyce offers through the character of Gabriel Conroy a speculation concerning the sort of person Joyce himself might have become had he chosen to build a career for himself in Ireland. Gabriel is a vain and frustrated man who can find no genuine joy or pleasure in a nation that can look only to its past and constantly cherish, as Gabriel proclaims in his after-dinner speech, "the memory of those dead and gone great ones." Can a nation so obsessed with its past look forward to a promising future?

"The Dead," then, offers the reverse image of Joyce's optimistic (though also ironic) reflection of himself posed by Stephen Dedalus in *A Portrait of the Artist as a Young Man* (1916), an untested but confident artist who leaves his family and his country to escape the environmental ties that would surely impede his artistic development. Joyce was working on "The Dead" at the same time he was transforming his fragmentary *Stephen Hero* (1944) into the more carefully controlled narrative that was to become his *A Portrait of the Artist as a Young Man*. No doubt his mind was playing on two extreme alternatives during this period following the most important decision he had made in his life to that point. "The Dead" can be seen as Joyce's portrait of the failed artist as an older man (though not necessarily a wiser one).

There can be no doubt that the source of this story is autobiographical. Richard Ellmann devotes chapter 15 of his biography *James Joyce* (1959) to the genesis of "The Dead." As a young girl in Galway in 1903, Joyce's wife, Nora Barnacle, had been courted by Michael ("Sonny") Bodkin, who suffered from tuberculosis. When Nora decided to leave Galway for Dublin, Sonny Bodkin left his sickbed in rainy weather to bid her farewell and to sing to her. After Nora arrived in Dublin, she heard that the boy had died. Knowledge of this courtship nettled Joyce, a jealous man by nature. The courtship letter that Gabriel quotes in the story is nearly a verbatim transcription of a letter that Joyce wrote to his wife, Nora, in 1904.

Ellmann offers an impressive list of biographical detail to support his point further. Every year, the Joyce family would gather for a Christmas party at No. 15 Usher's Island, where the writer's great aunts lived—Mrs. Lyons, Mrs. Callanan, and her daughter, Mary Ellen. According to Stanislaus Joyce, the writer's brother, their father would perform the annual ritual of carving the goose, as Gabriel does in the story, and would address the dinner guests in the same florid style that Gabriel affects after dinner.

Like Gabriel, Joyce wrote book reviews for *The Daily Express*. Gabriel shares Joyce's own disdain for west country provinciality and for the Gaelic League, represented by Miss Molly Ivors in the story. He shares Joyce's frustration over having to compete with a dead man, idealized in his wife's romantic memory, for his wife's love and affection (though one suspects that this dilemma, heightened in actuality by the writer's jealousy, was exaggerated in the story so that the futility of the dilemma would be more effectively dramatized).

Gabriel's ego is bruised and his cultured self-image of superiority undercut when he learns that Michael Furey was employed by the "gasworks," forcing on him the realization that there is no necessary connection between a man's employment and his sensitivity. The man of learning may not in all respects be superior to the man of feeling.

The major themes of the story, then, are jealousy and intellectual pride, both major sins in Roman Catholic theology, and both of these sins attach to the character of Gabriel, who is as callow and unfeeling, as insecure and insensitive in his own way as Stephen Dedalus seems to be in Joyce's *A Portrait of the Artist as a Young Man*. The theme of escape is understated in the story but insinuates itself into the basic fabric of Gabriel's character. Gabriel's frustration is shaped and exacerbated by his career decision to remain in Dublin and work there. His interests obviously tend elsewhere—toward England and the Continent. However, the story suggests that he can still learn important lessons through the intelligent exploration of native Irish culture and that he has been out of touch with the natural virtue and goodness that Michael Furey represents to his wife and with the instinctual understanding that makes his wife superior to him. Gabriel learns an existential moral lesson through his revelation and humiliation.

As a young man, Joyce scorned the provincial limitations of Dublin and the enthusiasm of the Irish nationalists for native culture and folkways. As an older and more mature writer, Joyce continued to draw on those elements, dominant in his memory and imagination, for the rest of his creative life. Joyce never really lost touch with the fact that he was Irish and Catholic by birth and background. Although the stories of *Dubliners* all document the spiritual impoverishment of Irish life, and "The Dead" is no exception in that regard, Gabriel is stunted in his human potential mainly because of his arrogant rejection of the culture in which he has chosen to live. His character shaped by frustration, rancor, and disappointment, this teacher still has much to learn about his country, his family, and himself.

## Style and Technique

"The Dead," Joyce's capstone story for his *Dubliners* collection, represents the most complex application of his device of the epiphany, defined by Stephen Dedalus in *A Portrait of the Artist as a Young Man* as a moment of revelation in which a new perception of reality is suddenly achieved, illuminating "the soul of the commonest object" or the "whatness of a thing." These naturalistic narratives involve realistic characters trapped by their environment, but the revelation is symbolic and, in the case of "The Dead," imagistic, as demonstrated by the snow that is constantly falling.

Joyce structures "The Dead" so as to offer twin epiphanies that are internal and external, subjective and objective, specific and general. The subjective epiphany is Gabriel's new insight into his wife's past, which places his own significance in their relationship into a new light. The objective epiphany, grasped by the reader, is Joyce's revelation about the nature and quality of life in Ireland.

The wonderful achievement of this story is the way in which Joyce raises the stylistic device of the epiphany to a complex symbolic level, and the way in which the subjective epiphany (Gabriel's perception that his wife has loved another man, idealized and immortalized in her memory) combines with the objective epiphany, the reader's realization that the Dublin of Joyce's imagination is a city of the dead, its citizens dwelling in the past and held captive by the memory of those who had gone before them. The snow that is "general all over Ireland" suggests that the whole country is gripped by the cold hand of death. Joyce creates the chilling impression that the dead are more vital and interesting than the living who carry on with their dull routines. The most for which any Irishman can hope, Joyce seems to suggest, is to be immortalized by death, thereby establishing a hold on the living.

The atmosphere of the story also shifts from the external to the internal. Outside, winter, the season of death, is symbolized by the snow. Contrasted to the cold, sterile exterior setting is the interior setting of the Christmas gathering, suggesting warmth, hospitality, and human companionship, but this celebration is dominated by the "distant music" of ancient voices, such as that of Aunt Julia, who was in her prime as a singer thirty years before. The celebration is set, moreover, in a household ruled by two sterile old women.

The symbolism of the story is multiplaned and complex. Gretta has been wooed by two angels—Gabriel, the archangel who will awaken the dead on the final day, and the more militant Michael, whose last name, "Furey," suggests a natural, west country passion that the educated and more intellectual Gabriel lacks. The "journey westward" mentioned in the final paragraph perhaps alludes to a literal journey, with Gabriel granting his wife's desire to return to visit Galway, but there are also traditional symbolic associations between traveling westward and man's natural progression toward death.

Certainly the most complex symbol the story has to offer, however, is the unifying metaphor of the snow, representing isolation and coldness. The disclosure of Gretta's secret gives Gabriel a new insight into her character and his own, but this is a moment of personal insight for the character, when he realizes another man has kindled in his wife a memory of poetry and romance. The epiphany for the reader is that the dead have a hold over the living, and that snow-covered Dublin is a city of the dead.

The story's dramatic impact depends on the ironic reversal of Gabriel's new perception of his wife and, consequently, of himself. Dramatic irony also comes into play as Gabriel reveals himself to the reader through his thoughts, words, and actions. The subjective epiphany is one of self-realization for Gabriel. His newfound self-knowledge puts him in communion with the living and the dead.

The very length of the story, as well as its placement, is indicative of its importance to Joyce. In "The Dead," as well as in *A Portrait of the Artist as a Young Man*, Joyce demonstrated that he had mastered the technique of ironic distance. Simply put, "The Dead" represents the finest achievement of Joyce's early naturalistic fiction, offering an exquisitely structured sustained experiment in extended symbolism and effective irony.

*James M. Welsh*

# THE DEAD MAN

*Author:* Horacio Quiroga (1878-1937)
*Type of plot:* Social realism
*Time of plot:* The early twentieth century
*Locale:* Paraná Valley near Misiones, Argentina
*First published:* "El hombre muerto," 1920 (English translation, 1987)

*Principal character:*

THE MAN, the anonymous protagonist, a banana farmer

## The Story

An unnamed farmer is working in his banana plantation as usual, clearing space with his machete. Satisfied with his progress, he decides to rest before finishing. As he usually does, he plans to cross a barbed wire fence and stretch out on the nearby grass. This time, however, things go terribly wrong. He accidentally trips and falls, landing on the ground. He is in the position he intended but notices that his machete is in a strange position: half of it protrudes from his shirt, under his waist. Trying to look around, he realizes that the other half of the machete has pierced his abdomen.

Incredibly but inexorably, he calmly assesses the situation and concludes that his life has come to an end. He sees that he is so badly wounded that he is now dying; to all intents and purposes he is really already a dead man, as there can be no remedy. He thinks about his life, as he drifts in and out of consciousness. Nevertheless, it is hard for him to accept such a sudden and senseless end. He knows that death is inevitable, but he thought that he would have a normal lifespan, that he would have time to prepare for death. He had expected a full life, with its share of hopes, dreams and problems. Instead, he is suddenly dying—simply because of an accident, a moment of petty carelessness. He realizes that nothing around him has changed, that his surroundings have not reacted to what for him is a cataclysmic event. He resists the horrible thought. Nothing has changed—his own banana plantation is the same. He knows it well, after working on it for so many years.

The midday calm approaches. He sees the distant red roof of his house and the nearby woods. Although he cannot turn to look, he knows that in other directions lie the road to the new port and the Paraná Valley. Everything is the same as always—the sun, the air, the trees. He thinks that he will change the fence. It cannot be possible that he will be dead. It is supposed to be a regular, normal day. He can even see his horse sniffing at the barbed wire.

Suddenly, he hears whistling. He cannot see in that direction but knows that it is the youth who passes by every morning at eleven-thirty, crossing the bridge on horseback, going to the new port, always whistling. He does not call out for help, thinking perhaps that it is useless or that he is too weak to be heard.

The farmer knows the distances in every direction because he measured them himself when he put up the fence. It is still his natural place, his normal surroundings—with the grass, the anthills, the silence. Nothing has changed. Only he is different. He realizes that he can no longer relate to his fields or his family. He has been abruptly yet naturally torn away from the life he had known. Within two minutes of the accident, he truly is dying.

Although he becomes very tired, he resists the transcendence of the moment. Everything is so normal; it seems impossible to him that he has had such an accident, especially because he is so experienced a worker. He even thinks about getting a better machete. He is just so tired from his labors that he needs a short rest.

As he looks at the things that he has planted, he ponders everything that is normal around him—grass, trees, sun, air, his sweaty and cautious horse—and insists to himself that he is merely exhausted, that he is only resting. A few more minutes have probably passed. He knows that his family will come at a quarter to twelve to get him for lunch. He always hears his younger child before the others, calling out for papa. He imagines that he hears the sound now. It seems like a nightmare that all this has happened on such a trivial and typical day. He remembers other days when he felt so tired, returning home from a hard morning in the fields.

He thinks that he can use his mind to leave his body now, if he wishes; he can look down at himself, resting in the grass, amidst his usual surroundings. He is just so tired.

His cautious horse sees him lying there. The animal wants to go around him and the fence, for better grazing, but that is normally forbidden. The horse hears the voices of the family, approaching now. Because the man does not stir, the horse grows calm and finally decides to move, passing by the body of its owner stretched out, just a shape on the grass. The man is finally, fully, and eternally at rest.

*Themes and Meanings*

Born in Uruguay, author Horacio Quiroga often used neighboring Argentina as the setting for his stories. During his own lifetime, he had experienced several family tragedies through accidental shootings and suicides. He was familiar with the dangers of the rugged jungle life in parts of South America. There was a constant threat of sudden, unexpected menace; people were often in the face of an unrelenting and inhospitable natural world, beset by wild animals, insects, disease, accident, and madness. Death could come at any time. This story is a fine example of that recurring theme.

"El hombre muerto" ("The Dead Man") first appeared in the daily *La Nación* in 1920; six years later it was published in the collection *Los desterrados* (1926), which was translated by J. David Danielson and Elsa Gambarini as *The Exiles, and Other Stories* in 1987. "The Dead Man" has been included in many Spanish and English anthologies and is considered one of Quiroga's best stories.

The themes of danger and sudden death are found in many of Quiroga's stories. Concerning "The Dead Man," the reader knows the outcome almost from the very beginning. The protagonist's gradual awareness of his own condition is presented in such a powerful, compelling manner, however, that the reader's interest is maintained. There is a fatalistic, inexorable progression toward death. The end is inescapable, although it may come so suddenly and unexpectedly that the effect is stunning: A single momentary act of carelessness, an accidental lapse in concentration can lead to fatal, ultimate consequences, for anyone, at any time.

In a struggle to tame the wilderness, human beings may think that progress has been made. However, nature may erupt suddenly and violently, causing untold destruction. Likewise, in the course of an ordinary day, a man may die accidentally. Nature does not change or react to that particular person's individual tragedy, at least if the story is told by a realistic rather than a romantic writer.

*Style and Technique*

A realist in style, despite receiving early training in the modernist school, Quiroga is preoccupied with the human situation and state of mind, death, and suicide. He describes his ideas on literary theory in his brief "Manual of the Perfect Short Story Writer" (1925), in which he praises such predecessors as Edgar Allan Poe, Guy de Maupassant, Rudyard Kipling, and Anton Chekhov. In this essay, he stresses the importance of originality, dedication, control, brevity, and precision in writing. Some repetition can heighten effect.

These elements can all be found in "The Dead Man," with its creation of atmosphere through controlled emotional intensity. The structure is tight and precise; the tone is direct, natural, and matter-of-fact. Subtle changes in the man's condition are suggested or implied. Although he knows he is dying, he momentarily lapses into planning for future work on his farm. There is irony in the fact that he is suddenly facing death on an otherwise ordinary day. The reader has the dying man's perspective of events throughout the piece, until the shift in the last paragraph. By then, the protagonist has become "The Dead Man"—and his horse, now less cautious, finally reacts by moving.

Elements of adventure, horror, mystery, and psychological and social realism often appear in Quiroga's stories. "The Dead Man" stresses the latter two aspects with considerable skill. Although his reputation was strong earlier in the twentieth century, Quiroga's fame was eclipsed by that of later writers, notably that of Jorge Luis Borges. There has been renewed interest in Quiroga's writing, however, and in the influence he had on recent authors. He is widely respected as a master craftsman who created memorable stories that linger in the reader's consciousness.

*Margaret V. Ekstrom*

# DEAD MEN'S PATH

*Author:* Chinua Achebe (1930-    )
*Type of plot:* Social realism
*Time of plot:* 1949
*Locale:* An Igbo village in southeastern Nigeria
*First published:* 1953

*Principal characters:*
MICHAEL OBI, the protagonist, a zealous and idealistic young mission-trained headmaster
NANCY OBI, his wife, a shallow woman given to outward appearances and equally infected with a shallow idealism
THE VILLAGE PRIEST, an old man of very few words

## The Story

Michael Obi's ambition is fulfilled when, at age twenty-six, he is appointed to whip into shape an unprogressive secondary school. Energetic, young, and idealistic as he is, Obi hopes to clean up the educational mission field and speed up its Christianizing mission. Already outspoken in his denigration of "the narrow views" and ways of "superannuated people in the teaching field," he expects to make a good job of this grand opportunity and show people how a school should be run. He plans to institute modern methods and demand high standards of teaching, while his wife, Nancy—who looks forward to being the admired wife of the headmaster—plants her "dream gardens" of beautiful hibiscus and allamanda hedges. With Nancy doing her gardening part, they will together lift Ndume School from its backward ways to a place of European-inspired beauty in which school regulations will replace the Ndume village community's traditional beliefs.

So Obi dreams and plans until one evening when he discovers a village woman cutting across the school gardens on a footpath that links the village shrine with the cemetery. Scandalized by her blatant trespassing, Obi orders the sacred ancestral footpath fenced off with barbed wire, much to the consternation of the villagers. The local priest then tries to remind Obi of the path's historical and spiritual significance as the sacred link between the villagers, their dead ancestors, and the yet unborn. Obi flippantly derides the priest's explanation as the very kind of superstition that the school is intended to eradicate because "dead men do not require footpaths." Two days later the hedge surrounding the school, its flower beds, and one of its buildings lie trampled and in ruins—the result of the villagers' attempt to propitiate the ancestors whom Obi's fence has insulted. After his supervisor issues a report on this incident, Obi is dismissed.

## Themes and Meanings

Written early during Chinua Achebe's undergraduate days at Nigeria's University of Ibadan and published in *The University Herald* in 1953, "Dead Men's Path" is one of his earliest published short stories. Later collected in *Girls at War, and Other Stories* (1972), the story contains the germ of what became the major theme of his first three novels: the collision of Christianity and African traditional culture. He most closely explores the theme of culture collision and the tension and estrangement of mission-trained converts from traditional community life in his novels *Things Fall Apart* (1958), *No Longer at Ease* (1960), and *Arrow of God* (1964).

Layered in irony, the essence of "Dead Men's Path" is expressed in the last part of the priest's admonition to Obi: "What I always say is: let the hawk perch and let the eagle perch." Although Obi is fully aware of the cultural code of deference to age and status, he persists in his arrogance because of his newly acquired power and ignores the culture-specific code of existence—the world of dualities that permits two very different things to stand side by side.

To the priest of Ani, the footpath represents continuity; it is the village's lifeline: "Our dead relatives depart by it and our ancestors visit us by it. But most importantly, it is the path of children coming in to be born." To Obi, however, it merely epitomizes what he regards as the backwardness that he has sworn to eradicate through his "modern methods" program. The priest's argument is simple: Two cultures can coexist, their differences notwithstanding, because there are no absolutes in the village's traditional thinking. The priest's view contrasts with the absolutism inherent in the worldview of Obi's newly embraced alien religion. For this reason, the priest's brief reminder of the village's spiritual history and the need to resolve conflicts through dialogue are lost on Obi.

Carrying his modernization mission to an extreme, Obi denounces the villagers' traditional culture as nothing but pagan ideas that he will teach their children to deride and which he will eradicate through his modern methods program. Similarly, he condemns the views of his older, less educated, and allegedly unimpassioned colleagues as embarrassingly archaic, backward, and worthy of contempt and condemnation. To the priest's conciliatory offer to end the dispute by simply reopening the path, Obi offers the absolutism of his "modern methods" manifesto, in which paradoxes do not exist, let alone conciliation to and negotiation with old and so-called "superannuated" village ways. The essence of the lesson, reiterated to him by the old priest, as if he needed such a reminder, Obi haughtily waves off.

Extremism and absolutism militate against balance, the balance that allows, indeed provides, space enough for both the hawk and the eagle to perch. On this point tradition is inflexible. Idealism is one thing, extremism another, and excess yet another. The idealism that comes from youthful energy and enthusiasm that lifts Obi to "pivotal teacher" status and headmastership at twenty-six is admirable. Neither the priest nor the villagers begrudge him his personal achievement. Nor is the village upset about the school's encroaching on their ancestral footpath until Obi erects his ill-conceived barbed wire fence. Beautiful gardens and hedges—the tangibles of Obi's modernization crusade—may also coexist and even coextend spatially with ancestral footpaths and thoroughfares. When burdensome detours infringe on the "perching"

880                                                        *Masterplots II*

rights that connect an entire village's spiritual life, however, the ancestors themselves must take up the war cry against such extremism born of "misguided zeal." It is at this point that the forces of tradition take on a conservative stance.

Ironically, the same energy and enthusiasm that raise Obi to the height of his career are also responsible for his stoop-shoulderedness and frailty, his premature aging, and his eventual tragic fall. His white supervisor's negative report on the "tribal-war situation developing between the school and the village" exposes the superficiality of Obi's idealism. The once acclaimed "pivotal teacher" is then laid low by his own "misguided zeal." The moral seems clear to all (the white supervisor included) except Obi. The philosophy of "balance" prevails.

*Style and Technique*

In prose that is at once leisurely and stately, Achebe blends the credulity of a folktale with an impartiality that is achieved more by allusion and implication rather than by explicit explanation. He uses irony and paradox to portray the contradictions arising from the moral dilemma faced by mission-trained converts whose estrangement from community life delineates the tragic conflict between the binary worldview of Christianity and the simple live-and-let-live duality of Igbo traditional worldview. The forces of the story lie in its condensed brevity and the suggestiveness illustrated by the old priest's pithy style. Unlike Obi's openly derisive mockery of the villagers' traditional beliefs, the priest's decorous but unceremonious style of confrontation and conflict resolution does not question the validity of the Christian religion that Obi represents. Choice of style notwithstanding, it is clear from the exchange between both men that neither side is supported or privileged. However, the symbolic force of the priest's habit of emphatically tapping his stout walking-stick on the floor each time that he makes a fresh point is all too suggestive of the power of the unspoken to which Obi's misguided zeal blinds him.

Rather than explain the showdown between the priest and the young headmaster, Achebe cleverly uses dialogue to contrast Obi's warped mental attitude with the old priest's poise and his economy of words. The patience and wisdom of age are pitted against the restless energy and glib-tongued arrogance of unseasoned youth. Through deliberate impudence and mockery Obi seeks to unbalance the equilibrium of the village that the old priest's wisdom and poise embody. As though the barbed wire fence is not insult enough, Obi's arrogance pushes him beyond cultural bounds when he orders the priest to construct a path that will skirt the school premises, as if he is taking on the village ancestors personally. Obi seals his own doom when he glibly says, "I don't suppose the ancestors will find the little detour too burdensome." The priest's portentous reply, "I have no more words to say," sets the stage for the final irony of the story: the tragic fall of the new headmaster.

*Pamela J. Olubunmi Smith*

# A DEAL IN WHEAT

*Author:* Frank Norris (1870-1902)
*Type of plot:* Naturalistic
*Time of plot:* About 1900
*Locale:* Kansas and Chicago
*First published:* 1902

*Principal characters:*

SAM LEWISTON, a Kansas rancher who loses his land during a bear market in wheat and moves to Chicago to find work

EMMA LEWISTON, his wife

MR. TRUSLOW, a wealthy speculator and "great bear" in wheat who never directly appears in the story but to whom characters constantly refer

MR. HORNUNG, a wealthy speculator who leads the bull market in wheat

HORNUNG'S BROKER, a critic of Truslow who wants the bulls to destroy the "great bear"

## The Story

The price of wheat is the thread holding together this episodic short story. As Sam Lewiston hitches up the buckboard, he and his wife, Emma, anxiously wonder if wheat is still selling for sixty-six cents a bushel. Like so many Kansas farmers, they face economic disaster if the price does not rise. Regardless of the market, Sam must sell his wheat today, and if the bears still rule in Chicago, he and Emma will lose the land they love. Both sense that their worst fears are about to be realized. Looking out across the prairie and into an uncertain future, Emma reminds Sam of his brother Joe's offer of work in Chicago. Sam resists the idea of giving up, but as he kisses Emma good-bye and rides off to town, the reader knows that hope is all but gone.

On entering the office of Bridges & Co., Grain Dealers, Sam gets the bad news from Bridges himself. Wheat is at sixty-two cents. "It's Truslow and the bear clique that stick the knife into us," laments Bridges, who is powerless to help his farmer friends. Sam Lewiston is ruined, and so are many of his neighbors. It costs them a dollar a bushel to raise the wheat, and few, certainly not Sam, can afford to store it any longer. Dazed by this sad turn of events, Sam goes home to Emma. "We'll go to Chicago," he tells her. "We're cleaned out!"

The second episode takes place some months later when Mr. Hornung and the bulls have driven wheat up to $1.10 per bushel. The bears, led by the once dominant Truslow, are on the run. Indeed, the scene opens with Hornung agreeing to sell a hundred thousand bushels of wheat to Truslow, working out the deal with Mr. Gates, one of the great bear's minions. Hornung wonders if he has done the right thing. Truslow has paid dearly for the wheat, which he apparently had to have in order to cover overseas commitments, but Hornung's broker warns that the bulls should have taken full advantage of the great bear's distress to destroy him. Only then would the bull market be safe.

The third episode shifts ahead several days to the frenetic pit of the Chicago Board of Trade. The bulls still hold the corner in wheat, with Hornung setting the price at $1.50. Suddenly, one of the bears, a new man named Kennedy, begins selling wheat in thousand-bushel lots, and the bulls cannot figure where Kennedy is getting it. Had Hornung not held firm and kept buying at $1.50, the market might have broken, and that would have given the bears their chance to drive the price down. Who was behind the raid? Truslow is the prime suspect, but for weeks he had made no move, and rumor had it that he was in Wisconsin, bass fishing at Lake Geneva.

The fourth episode solves the mystery. Cyrus Ryder, a detective, tells Hornung and his broker that he dressed as a hobo and rode the Belt Line around Chicago looking for the source of Kennedy's wheat. Truslow, who owns the Belt Line, was shipping the very grain he had bought from Hornung out of Chicago and back to his elevator as though it were new wheat fresh from Kansas. Truslow had been trying to break the bull market by selling back to Hornung at considerable profit the very wheat he had purchased from the latter and pledged to ship abroad. The broker is incensed at Truslow's chicanery, but Hornung laughs it off as a brilliant ploy and plans to recoup his losses and outmaneuver Truslow by raising the price of wheat to two dollars.

The fifth episode begins in a breadline behind a South Side bakery. It is cold and drizzling and almost 1:00 A.M. Dozens of hungry men have been there for hours waiting for the usual handout of day-old bread. One of them is Sam Lewiston. He has left Emma in Topeka and gone ahead to work for brother Joe. The reader learns that Joe's hat factory has failed, in part because of the repeal of tariff duties on cheap imports, and Sam has found little work since. The breadline is a godsend to him and others like him who are out of work and have nowhere else to go and nothing else to eat. Sam looks into the bewildered faces of the men standing with him and is consoled by the knowledge that the bread will keep them from starving. He likes to think of the breadline as a small platform that for now keeps those on it safely above the dark and threatening waters of complete despair swirling below. Suddenly, the bakery door opens and someone tacks up a sign. Groans are heard, and Sam and others push forward to read that because wheat is two dollars a bushel, the bakery will not be distributing free bread. The platform is gone, the price of wheat has ravaged him once again, and Sam walks away stunned by the loss, a hapless victim of a capricious fate.

However, even as he wanders aimlessly, Sam's fortunes are changing. The reader is told that Sam finds a job the next day cleaning the streets. He works hard, sends for Emma, and gets promoted first to shift-boss, then to deputy inspector, and finally to inspector. Sam sees things more clearly after that night. Learning from the papers of Truslow's scheme against Hornung, he recognizes that he and countless others are powerless victims in the battle between the Bear and the Bull. The speculators carelessly ruin both farmers and workingmen and gamble with the nourishment of nations. Only they—the powerful bears and bulls—remain prosperous and unassailable. It is a chilling insight but one based on painful experience, and the reader is left with the impression that understanding this harsh reality somehow helps Sam Lewiston survive.

## Themes and Meanings

"A Deal in Wheat" clearly reflects the influence of naturalism and its leading European practitioner, Émile Zola. Some critics call Frank Norris the first naturalistic American writer; others hotly disagree, citing his devotion to and identification with Romantics such as Rudyard Kipling. In fact, Norris combined elements of both Romanticism and naturalism in much of his writing. Perhaps the purest naturalistic piece he ever wrote, "A Deal in Wheat" sets forth in coldly analytical terms several themes that he first introduced in *The Octopus* (1901) and would develop further in *The Pit* (1903). As in the two novels, the overriding theme in this short story is that of economic struggle against almost irresistible forces. "A Deal in Wheat" is especially important because it marks a significant shift in Norris's thinking away from the optimistic determinism of *The Octopus* and *The Pit*. The story ends on something of a positive note, but it is dominated by a sense of pessimistic determinism.

Sam and Emma Lewiston are representative types. Good and wholesome, hardworking, they lose their Kansas ranch because of the rivalry between the bears and the bulls in Chicago. There is absolutely nothing they can do; they are victimized by circumstances well beyond their control. As for the speculators, they are battling not for survival but for wealth, and their economic warfare takes on a rationale of its own; it is a contest of wits. The injustice of it all is an underlying theme basic to much naturalistic writing. The speculators, however, are not vicious men; they are simply the haves in an amoral system that compels the haves to exploit the have-nots.

The story is bleakly depressing, yet in the very capriciousness of human existence, there shines a glimmer of hope. As he is about to sink into complete despair, Sam Lewiston finds a job and makes the most of it. The good man wins out in the end, but it is not so much because of who he is or what he has done. Inscrutable Fate, for reasons of her own, has smiled on him. Sam understands this, and that is Norris's final point.

## Style and Technique

Norris was much more committed to the method of Zola than to the latter's philosophy; he found in naturalism the tools to probe humankind and the natural world and to convey the "truth" of what he discovered to the reader. Hence, Norris tells his story coldly and concisely, giving it much the quality of a documentary drawn directly from life. The realism is enhanced by pertinent details that add to the mood of impending doom or increasing despair. The descriptions of Sam hitching the wagon and of Emma twisting her apron around her arms, for example, accentuate the commitment and concerns of two desperate people. Tying everything together is the wheat itself. An artful paradox is at the very heart of the story: Low wheat causes Sam to lose the ranch; high wheat almost takes his life.

The five episodes of the story progressively emphasize the helplessness of Sam the farmer and worker on the one hand and the power of the speculators on the other. Truslow's deception and Hornung's response to it bring matters to a head. These events serve to emphasize the speculators' fundamental lack of concern for anything but their own pursuit of wealth. Sam's reappearance in the last scene serves as an interesting contrast and makes clear the impact on ordinary people of the games the speculators play. Although Norris cared little for the short-story form, he achieved in this work a remarkable unity of character and purpose that was sadly lacking in his novels. "A Deal in Wheat" represents the momentary triumph of naturalism over Romanticism in the writing of a man who was strongly influenced by both.

*Ronald W. Howard*

# DEATH AND THE CHILD

*Author:* Stephen Crane (1871-1900)
*Type of plot:* Symbolist
*Time of plot:* The Greco-Turkish wars
*Locale:* Greece
*First published:* 1898

> *Principal characters:*
> PEZA, a young correspondent whose father was Greek
> THE LIEUTENANT
> THE CHILD

## The Story

A university-educated correspondent named Peza arrives on the scene of a mass exodus of peasants who flee an approaching battle between Greek patriots and Turkish invaders. Although assigned to cover the event for an Italian paper, Peza identifies with the Greek people because his father was a Greek. Moved by the sights of war, he wishes to become immediately involved in fighting rather than in merely observing. His adventure, however, carries him through a moral process that changes his feelings about the war and himself.

Divided into seven sections, each of which focuses on a crucial event in Peza's transformation, the story begins by establishing the pattern of the events into which Peza is drawn. It opens with the great human torrent that sweeps down the mountainside away from the threatening booms of artillery. Moving counter to this wave of refugees, Peza walks up the mountain. Overcome by pity and awe at the sight of such misery, Peza is inspired to join the fight. A young lieutenant returning to the front agrees to become Peza's guide into the war. The contrast between these two characters foreshadows the difficulty Peza will have in his attempt to become involved in the war's action. Although young like Peza, the lieutenant has already experienced battle and knows it is not the romantic adventure that Peza imagines it to be; he finds Peza's fervent patriotism and heroic innocence at once amusing and contemptible.

The second section of the story, although not directly concerned with Peza, introduces the child whose image will bring about Peza's ultimate transformation. The child has been left behind by his parents in their rush to escape. He plays tranquilly at his homesite on a mountain overlooking the plain on which the fighting rages. Though the lines of battle are moving imperceptibly closer, the boy shows only minimal interest in such distant action. It is too childish an affair for one who, like himself, is "dealing with sticks" in a pretend-game of sheepherding. Unlike Peza, who is caught up in causes—in ideals and abstractions—the child's involvement in his play is direct, immediate, and concrete.

Sections 3 through 6 follow Peza as he further engages the experience of war. At the beginning of section 3, he is struck by the war's failure to erase the "commonness" of familiar objects. The "immovable poppies," images of nature's endurance in the midst of human upheaval, also impress him. Seeing that the torrent of peasants has now become a stream of fatigued and wounded soldiers, Peza discovers that "pity ha[s] a numerical limit"; he is no longer moved by the sight of the wounded, but instead his vision becomes "focused upon his own chance." At this moment, the lieutenant parts company with Peza, leaving him alone and unguided to "wander helplessly toward death." Unable to see the troops for the trees, Peza moves blindly forward. When a shell shatters a nearby tree, he perceives the previously "immovable" natural world now "astounded," "bewildered," and "amazed" at its own vulnerability. He realizes that he is in this spot not primarily because of his conscious decision or noble ideals, but "because at a previous time a certain man [the lieutenant] had smiled."

As section 4 opens, Peza inflates his influence on the war, personifying it as a "barbaric deity" that he must "surprise" so as not to give it pretext for further vengeance. His arrival at a company of peasant soldiers, however, inspires no extraordinary act. The soldiers ignore him, while he imagines them as dumb puppets ignorantly carrying out the superior will of great men. Approaching a captain of the battery, Peza reasserts his desire to fight, but the officer and soldiers only want from him political news of the war. In the midst of their civilized conversation, shells fly overhead and far beyond their position. Peza is elated that the shells "kill no one" and that "war ha[s] turned out to be such a gentle business." It is as though he were "having coffee in the smoking room of some embassy where reverberate the names of nations," rather than the guns of battle.

Sections 5 and 6 take Peza into the front lines of battle where his romantic notions are shattered and where death becomes an actuality. As he climbs toward the high infantry position, he encounters a soldier whose jaw is half blown away. Running from this "spectre," he happens on a squadron positioned in trenches. From this vantage, Peza sees for the first time the Turkish battalions as they move steadily against the Greek lines. Fearing that they will "take the position," Peza runs again, this time into the rifle pits near the front. Here, he announces to an officer his desire to fight for the fatherland. When the officer instructs him to take a gun and ammunition from a corpse, however, Peza shrinks back. A soldier performs the task for him and, donning the bandolier, Peza feels himself strangled by death and drawn into its "mystic chamber." Terrified, he bolts for the rear, hardly noticed by the soldiers who continue to fight.

At the beginning of section 7, the child reappears. Weary of his game and hungry, he realizes that he is alone. The battle, now obviously closer, captures his attention for the first time, and he weeps at its incomprehensible mystery. Distracted by a nearby noise, the child sees a man covered with dust and blood—Peza—drag himself over the crest of the hill and fall to the ground panting. The child approaches him, looks into his eye, and asks a simple question: "Are you a man?" The question strikes at the heart of Peza's dilemma, his attempt to define himself in relation to the war. As he gazes up into the child's face, however, he sees a power beyond the personal—he sees "the primitive courage, the sovereign child, the brother of the mountains, the sky, and the sea, and he knew that the definition of his misery could be written on a wee grass-blade."

## Themes and Meanings

Throughout the story, there is an emphasis on eyes and vision. When Peza first appears, he "look[s] at everything," specifically the fleeing peasants, "with . . . pitying glances." His protestations of patriotism to the lieutenant are described as the overflow of emotion "which heretofore had been expressed only in the flash of eyes." At every step along his journey, his eyes are assaulted with the sights of war. He often imagines eyes gazing at him, most horrifyingly when the "two liquid-like eyes" of a corpse seem to stare into him. When he encounters the child, he "roll[s] his eye glassily" toward him and "gaze[s] up into his face." Compelled again and again to open his eyes to the immediate facts of the world, Peza undergoes a literal visual awakening through which his vision is successively cleansed of his mind's romantic and theoretical attitude toward war and life.

In the first phase of this visual evolution, Peza is struck by the disturbing sight of the refugees as they course wildly down the mountain. This image arouses his physical emotions, the feeling of pity and consanguinity that culminates in his patriotic vision of the war. As he ventures farther and the images of jaded soldiers replace those of the miserable peasants, he experiences an aesthetic perception. The soldiers' oversaturation with the tragedy and ferocity of war he compares with a visit to a picture gallery where his mind had become so glutted with "all the strength of Argus-eyed art" that he had come away feeling "a great hollow quiet." When, at the battery position, he is besieged by questions concerning the politics of the war, Peza's vision becomes further abstracted from its immediate dangers. Not until the soldier with the broken jaw appears does Peza's intellectual perspective radically fail him. Rapt by the "mystic gaze" of this specter, Peza begins to feel the immediacy of death that climactically consumes him when the corpse looks at him with liquid eyes, and he runs.

Peza's mystical vision culminates in the imaginative vision of the child. Throughout his "grand venture," it is the image of death that Peza has been seeking; the gradual stripping away of the intellectual scales from his eyes reveals not death, the grand abstraction, however, but life, in the concrete image of the child, as the source of his moral transformation. When he comes to see the child "as some powerful symbol," it is not merely as a figure of suffering humanity and thus as an intellectualized reflection of his personal misery. Rather, Peza sees the child's unanalyzable union—his brotherhood—with the profound forces of nature—the sky, the sea, the mountains—so that the child's image bears within it the entire potential of the visible creation. It is the child's emergence, out of the war, as an imaginative event—a "symbol" of new possibilities—that takes Peza beyond the need to define himself and man through death and opens him to the greater venture of life.

## Style and Technique

In keeping with Peza's evolution beyond the tragic self, Stephen Crane employs a self-effacing style. The "author" as an authority over his story becomes submerged within an action whose central interest is the narrative process itself, the visible rendering of change. Consequently, there is no clearly identifiable point of view, no self-conscious first-person narrative or authorial omniscience. The narrator, as inextricably involved in his narrating as the child's image is symbolically united with the elemental powers of nature, becomes simply the shifting visual perspective through which events rise into view, run their course, and issue into new events.

An important instance of the narrative's shifting visual perspective occurs when the child weeps. First, the narrator shows the scene from the child's vantage point: "The child took seat on a stone, and contemplated the fight. He was beginning to be astonished. . . . Lines of flame flashed out here and there. It was mystery." Then, he renders the same moment from the correlative perspective: "If the men struggling on the plain had had time, and greater vision, they could have seen this strange, tiny figure seated on a boulder, surveying them while the tears streamed."

The "symbolic" value of the child, so central in Peza's evolution, originates precisely in this imaginative shift in perspective. Moreover, the author's self-effacing narrative generates the moral equivalent in style of the impersonal natural forces that impel Peza into his venture, that operate within the war, and that illuminate the child's image.

*S. Elaine Marshall*

# DEATH IN JERUSALEM

*Author:* William Trevor (William Trevor Cox, 1928-    )
*Type of plot:* Psychological
*Time of plot:* The 1970's
*Locale:* Tipperary, Ireland, and Jerusalem, Israel
*First published:* 1978

*Principal characters:*

> FRANCIS DALY, a shy thirty-seven-year-old bachelor who lives
> with his mother in a small town in Ireland
> FATHER PAUL, his fifty-one-year-old brother, a sociable priest
> based in San Francisco

### The Story

"Death in Jerusalem" concerns the disintegration of the relationship between two Irish brothers, unlike in all ways, but especially in the ways they regard their mother.

Francis Daly, the younger brother, has always lived at home with his mother in a small town in County Tipperary. He is not unhappy with his uneventful life, which consists of managing a hardware store in the daytime, spending many silent evenings sitting with his mother in the parlor, much praying and churchgoing, and occasionally going on quiet vacations with a few friends. However, for many years, Francis has dreamed of traveling to the Holy Land. One July, when his much respected elder brother, Father Paul, a gregarious Roman Catholic priest from San Francisco, is on his annual visit to see his mother in Tipperary, the brothers decide to meet in Jerusalem the next year for a vacation.

For the next twelve months, Francis spends much time and effort trying to obtain his mother's blessing regarding the trip. He is unsuccessful. She utters not a word about it, but her demeanor indicates her disapproval. From the time he sets out, Francis feels a sense of unease that prevents him from enjoying himself as he had thought he would. A fellow passenger on the flight to Jerusalem, intending to be friendly with advice on sights to see and food to enjoy, intrudes on Francis's privacy. By the time the two brothers meet at their luxurious hotel, Francis is too exhausted to appreciate its splendors and goes to bed early.

Father Paul, on the other hand, is glad to spend several hours more at the bar, sipping whiskey and chatting with some American tourists, until he is interrupted by a summons to the reception desk to receive a telegram. The message shocks him: His mother, back in Ireland, is dead.

Father Paul retires to his own room immediately, says some prayers for his mother's soul, drinks more whiskey, and paces the floor. Eventually he decides what to do: He sends a telegram to Ireland, asking that the funeral be postponed for several days. This will give him and Francis time to do some sightseeing before the flight to Ireland. He also decides to postpone telling his brother that their mother is dead until they reach Galilee, which he believes would be a suitable place for Francis to hear the sad news.

The next day, as the brothers visit landmarks in Bethlehem and Jerusalem that are sacred to Christians, Francis's uneasiness grows. As he is jostled by noisy and frequently irreverent crowds, the holy places seem unreal and disappointing. The din, the activity of buyers and sellers, the sight of prostitutes in doorways, and the overheard comments of a religious skeptic all confirm Francis's sense of incongruity between his interior vision of Jerusalem and what he actually sees.

Father Paul, too, though he enjoys the sights and especially the food and drink Jerusalem provides, occasionally feels uncomfortable because his mother is lying stiff and cold back in Ireland and because he has not yet told Francis that she is dead.

That evening, after a postprandial walk during which he is propositioned by a young woman, Francis finds his brother drinking with some people in the hotel lounge. When they are finally alone, over Francis's protests, Father Paul orders two more whiskeys and, unable to keep his secret any longer, finds relief in telling his brother the bad news.

As soon as Francis takes in what has happened, he begins to pray for his mother's salvation. However, when he realizes that his brother has concealed her death from him for a whole night and a day and that his brother intends that they continue their trip for a few days, go to Galilee, and return to Ireland barely in time for the funeral, he becomes angry. His deference to his elder brother gone, Francis insists on returning to Ireland immediately. Then he bursts into tears. At last, he stops weeping and goes to his room without saying a word to his brother.

Father Paul arranges for their departure the next morning, realizing that this trip to Tipperary to bury his mother will most likely be his last. Then he goes to the bar and drinks whiskey until after midnight when, drunk and disheveled, he staggers off to bed.

*Themes and Meanings*

This story invites readers to try to understand and to feel compassion for two very different people who happen to be brothers but whose relationship with each other is based more on habit and convention than on mutual affection.

At the center of Francis's world is his mother, to whom he is tethered. It is she who determines the slow pace of time and the narrowness and passivity of his experience. Francis accommodates himself to this constricted space by limiting his own activity and ambition. This means that he is left without a sense of perspective about what lies beyond his small town in Tipperary. It also means that his mother's negative spirit controls him. Although Francis thinks her sins few and insignificant, she has done such things as deliberately spoiling her daughter's chance of marrying a man she loved and deliberately alienating her other children.

Francis's trip to Jerusalem is a departure from his mother's influence. However, away from her and without her approval, Francis does not thrive. He is uneasy and unhappy. In the midst of activity and noise but disconnected from what gives meaning to his life, he experiences discomfort, emptiness, and a sense of unreality. He becomes aware that he prefers the Holy Land of his imagination to the real Jerusalem and Bethlehem and that he longs for the time when, safely with his mother, he will be able to savor his own religiosity without the distractions and incongruities of rough and raucous real life.

After Francis learns that his mother is dead, he sees his trip as a mistake and as the cause of her death. He realizes that he is disgusted with everything about his brother Paul, whom he had heretofore adulated. He wants to return to his mother and her world immediately. However, will such a return be possible? It seems not, because both his mother and his illusions are dead.

His mother had exerted enough power over Father Paul to make him fly annually from the United States to Ireland to visit her, although he neither loved nor liked her. For him, her death is a release from an inconvenient obligation. When she dies and especially after Father Paul witnesses Francis's passionate reaction to the news of her death, the mutual tolerance of the two unlike brothers is replaced, even for the genial Father Paul, with mutual hatred. That is the real death in Jerusalem.

*Style and Technique*

"Death in Jerusalem" is a third-person narrative that unfolds in a mostly chronological order. William Trevor uses no startling or unusual devices in telling his story but instead employs conventional techniques in a masterly way. Take, for example, the manner in which the story is framed and the way tension is managed. The first segment of the story, which follows the parting words of the two brothers at the train station when they confirm their intention to meet in Jerusalem the next year, is succeeded by Francis's musings as he walks back to town. These musings provide background information about the two brothers, their different temperaments and situations, their mother, and the rest of the Daly family.

When Francis reaches the town center, a woman's greeting interrupts his train of thought. This interruption permits the narrator to change gears to give an account of the activities of Father Paul in San Francisco and of the concerns and doings in Francis's small town in Tipperary. The narrator then shifts to a more intense degree of perception to let the reader know what goes on in the minds and hearts of Francis Daly and his mother.

The second part of the story, longer and containing more circumstantial detail than the first part, focuses on several scenes in which generalized narrative, conversational exchanges, and telling description move readers through the brothers' tour of the sights of Bethlehem and Jerusalem and through hotel bars and lounges. Here, helped by the narrator's observations, commentary, and occasional entry into the minds and hearts of the two brothers, readers can determine what each man is like from the brothers' reactions to their surroundings and their experiences.

The narrator controls the pace of the account, the importance assigned to its every element, and the increase in tension as the story progresses. Readers might assume at first that the two brothers, although they are different in background, temperament, and outlook, have a good enough relationship with each other. However, when the brothers are in close proximity to each other in Jerusalem, their relationship is revealed as shallow and unsympathetic. Francis, whose nature is both fastidious and provincial, is revolted by his hard-drinking, garrulous brother and horrified by his insensitivity in face of his mother's death. Father Paul, accustomed to act according to more objective standards of practicality, comfort, and self-interest, cannot deal with a situation that has gotten out of his control. In the moment-by-moment encounter near the close of the story, the words exchanged by the two brothers show that hatred has rushed in to fill the vacuum of feeling between them.

*Margaret Duggan*

# DEATH IN MIDSUMMER

*Author:* Yukio Mishima (Kimitake Hiraoka, 1925-1970)
*Type of plot:* Psychological
*Time of plot:* The early 1950's
*Locale:* Tokyo and an inn on the Izu Peninsula
*First published:* "Manatsu no Shi," 1952 (English translation, 1956)

> *Principal characters:*
> Tomoko Ikuta, the focal character, a wife and mother
> Masaru Ikuta, her husband
> Yasue Ikuta, her spinster sister

*The Story*

Staying at an inn near the southern tip of the Izu Peninsula, Tomoko Ikuta escapes the summer heat by taking a nap in her room. She sends her daughter Keiko, age five, and her sons Kiyoo and Katsuo, ages six and three, to play on the beach under the supervision of her sister-in-law Yasue. Proud of the whiteness of her skin, Yasue does not want to tan, so she remains under a beach umbrella and the children play near the edge of the water. Keiko and Kiyoo are caught in an undertow and pulled under the water; Yasue hurries toward them but collapses in the water from a heart attack. People on the beach pull her out and take Katsuo and Yasue's body back to the inn. They do not know that the other two children are missing.

Awakened with the news that Yasue has had a swimming accident, Tomoko hurries to the lawn and finds a man administering artificial respiration to her sister-in-law. She sees Katsuo in the arms of a local fisherman. Four hours pass before the doctor gives up the effort to revive Yasue, and only then does Tomoko find out from her youngest son that the other two children have drowned. It is already after sunset, but young men begin to dive to locate the children's bodies. Tomoko waits until nearly morning before she sends her husband, Masaru, a telegram advising him that Yasue is dead and that Kiyoo and Keiko are missing.

Masaru leaves Tokyo immediately for the inn on the Izu Peninsula. When he arrives, both Tomoko and he play the roles expected of them. Tomoko kneels before her husband and says that the accident was her fault, and Masaru expresses understanding and sympathy. The two bodies are found the next day, and both parents begin to experience the emotions associated with a traumatic loss. Tomoko resents her husband's grief over the death of Yasue, for example, thinking that it somehow diminishes his feelings for his dead children. She masters her feelings and does the conventional thing when Masaru's parents come up from Kanazawa for the funerals. She assumes responsibility for the accident again and apologizes to her husband's father and mother. To her own parents, however, Tomoko complains, "But who should they feel sorriest for? Haven't I just lost two children? There they all are, accusing me." In the days and weeks following the accident, Tomoko struggles with ambivalent feelings. At times she seeks punishment for her guilty sense that by leaving the children under Yasue's control, she is genuinely responsible for their deaths. At other times she seeks sympathy for her loss and seems to nurse her sorrow.

Tomoko also fears that another accident will occur. Masaru had had an accident with the car shortly before she had gone on vacation and will not ride in the car with her husband if Katsuo is going with them. Visiting Tama Cemetery to see the lot Masaru has bought for the burial of his sister and children, Tomoko will not allow Katsuo to drink from a public water fountain. She is afraid of germs and carries boiled water for him to drink. On the way back from the cemetery, Tomoko buys her son a toy from a vendor in the train station, and for a moment, thinking that Kiyoo and Keiko have been left at home, wants to buy something for the other children, too. Despite such occasional tricks of the mind, Tomoko adjusts to her loss but with great difficulty. For a time she keeps herself busy going to plays and concerts; later she takes up sewing. Both activities allow her not to think about the accident.

That winter Tomoko learns that she is pregnant once more, and with this change "forgetfulness came as a natural right." Both Masaru and she feel like spectators, rather than participants, in the events of the summer. The accident comes more and more to seem like something that happened to other people. Tomoko finds it possible to reduce the incident to the clichéd statement that one must watch children constantly at the beach. The past seems to be closed with the birth, the following summer, of a daughter named Momoko; when the new baby is a year old, however, Tomoko expresses the wish to go back to the beach on the Izu Peninsula. She does not want to go alone. As the entire Ikuta family stands on the beach, Masaru sees in Tomoko's face an expression familiar since the accident. She looks out to sea as if she were waiting for something, the implication being that she is waiting for Kiyoo and Keiko to return.

*Themes and Meanings*

The sea is an appropriate image of the timeless reality that Tomoko comes to perceive behind the surface of her comfortable, middle-class life. The essence of that reality is the fact of death's constant threat. Yukio Mishima shows Kiyoo and Keiko, shortly before the accident, aware of the power of death but too young to recognize it. It is significant that Tomoko is asleep when the accident occurs, for she too is innocent about death. Mishima's description of her sleeping form stresses its youthful, girlish quality; unlike Sleeping Beauty, however, she is not awakened to reality by a loving Prince but through the agency of the sea that takes both her children. It is important to Mishima's thematic point that Tomoko not be present during the accident and that Yasue experience death as her surrogate. Tomoko both participates in the children's deaths and is removed from them, and she thereby becomes aware of the universal fact of human mortality.

Initially, Tomoko has no such awareness. She reacts to the accident in purely personal and social terms by worrying about how she can face Masaru and his parents. Her husband has similar reactions: He responds to the telegram from Tomoko by making sure that he is carrying enough money to deal with the expenses of the emergency. He takes on himself the organization of the funeral and arrangements for the burials in Tama Cemetery. For Masaru, the deaths of Kiyoo, Keiko, and Yasue present him with largely practical problems. Mishima concedes that he feels genuine grief but claims that his emotions are more sentimental than Tomoko's and more easily survived. Tomoko's feelings, initially centered on herself as the victim of fate, change over the course of the story. Her understanding of life at the end of "Death in Midsummer" is deeper, and more frightening, than Masaru's.

Despite the emotional growth Mishima attributes to her, Tomoko is not an easy character to like. The treatment of her feelings is too uncompromisingly honest for that. Mishima requires that the reader acknowledge that her self-centered reaction to the deaths of her children is true to human nature.

## Style and Technique

Despite the dramatic intensity of the opening pages of the story, it is Mishima's manipulation of the third-person narrative point of view that gives this story its chief effects. The narrator exhibits unlimited omniscience and both enters into the minds of nearly every character in the story and comments on their thoughts and actions from a position to be identified as the author's viewpoint. The story succeeds or fails to the degree that a reader accepts or rejects the narrator's commentary.

Mishima's use of the narrator is most effective in the handling of the secondary characters in the story. He manages to convey the feelings of the children Kiyoo, Keiko, and Katsuo by combining brief dramatized incidents and deft commentary. He shows the insecurity that causes Yasue to accept the domination of the younger Tomoko, and he makes convincing the vanity that causes her to leave the children alone near the water. Mishima's narrator is less convincing in the characterization of Masaru. Tomoko's husband comes across as a stereotype of the modern Japanese husband. He is more wedded to job than wife, and the affection he seeks from her is as much maternal as conjugal. Masaru is more talked about by the narrator than shown in action. His grief for his dead children may be sentimental, as the narrator claims, but little in his behavior confirms the statement.

Mishima's treatment of Tomoko, like that of Masaru, combines dramatized action, summary of thought, and narrational commentary. Because she is the focal character of the story, there is both more dramatization and more summary of her thoughts than is true of any other character. The narrator succeeds in conveying the complexity of the feelings of a woman who has lost children in an accident and who feels at least partly to blame for their deaths. Nevertheless, Tomoko remains more a type than an individual. She is used by Mishima to make a metaphysical point; her development is a schematic of the ideas about death he seeks to illustrate in the story. As a result, Tomoko seems more a function of the narrator's perception of her than a character genuinely independent of the narrational voice.

*Robert C. Petersen*

# DEATH IN THE WOODS

*Author:* Sherwood Anderson (1876-1941)
*Type of plot:* Psychological
*Time of plot:* Probably the late nineteenth century
*Locale:* Illinois
*First published:* 1926

> *Principal characters:*
> MRS. GRIMES, whose death forms the center of the story
> JAKE GRIMES, her husband
> THE UNNAMED NARRATOR, who remembers the story
> HIS BROTHER, who shares his experience

*The Story*

"Death in the Woods" ostensibly concerns a farm woman, Mrs. Grimes, who, although only in her early forties, seems old and probably demented. She has no first name in the story, and, indeed, very little is known about her at all. The narrator, a man who remembers and re-creates the story's events from his childhood, tries to put together the few things that he actually does know. Through this re-creation, he searches for meaning and for completion. He needs the events to make sense.

"The old woman was nothing special," the narrator remembers. "She was one of the nameless ones that hardly anyone knows, but she got into my thoughts." In her youth, the woman had been a bound girl, practically a slave to a harsh German farmer and his wife. Her job was to feed the stock and to cook for the couple. Her life with them was very unhappy. "She was a young thing then and scared to death," the narrator says. In addition to the demands of her work, she was sometimes the victim of the farmer's sexual advances. One day he had chased her into the barn and torn away the front of her dress before he was stopped by the sound of his wife's returning. In such a situation, the girl looked desperately for any means of escape. Thus, when Jake Grimes, the wastrel son of a failed sawmill owner, offered to marry her, she accepted.

The woman's new life, however, was hardly an improvement over the former. Settled on a new farm, she again became a servant, first to her husband and later to her son. She soon withdrew into silence and routine, a deadly existence in which she was abused by her family and ignored by all others. "They left everything at home for her to manage and she had no money," the narrator says. "She knew no one. No one ever talked to her in town."

The central episode of the old woman's story occurs on a cold winter day. As is her custom, she makes her solitary trek into the village for the meager supplies for which she can barter and the scraps of liver and dog meat that the butcher sometimes gives her out of pity. On her way home, toward the end of day, the snow begins to fall, and by the time she reaches the woods, she is exhausted. Struggling along the forest path, she comes to a clearing and stops there to rest, despite the danger of the cold. Soon she falls asleep and slides quietly toward death.

Accompanying the woman on her journey are a pack of dogs. As the night comes on and the moon rises, these animals undergo a change. "Such nights, cold and clear and with a moon, do things to dogs," the narrator says. "It may be that some old instinct, come down from the time when they were wolves and ranged the woods in packs on winter nights, comes back into them." The scene takes on a magical quality as the dogs begin to run in a circle in the moonlit snow. If the old woman awoke before her death, she would have seen that queer, wonderful sight, or so the narrator imagines. She soon dies, however, and then all rules, all expectations and unspoken agreements between human and beast conclude. The dogs nudge, then tear at the backpack containing the meat. They drag her body into the center of the clearing, and, in doing so, rip away the top of her dress so that she is exposed to the night. Not one of the animals touches her body, however, and she is left undisturbed in the snow.

When the body is found several days later by a rabbit hunter, he is mystified and frightened. In town he tells everyone that he has seen a "beautiful young girl" dead in the snow. A crowd of men led by the town marshal hurry to the site, and with them go the narrator, then a young boy, and his brother. Together they follow the men into the woods. It is again night when they reach the clearing. Standing by the tree under which the woman died, the two boys see the body, now magically transformed by the snow and the moon. "She did not look old, lying there in that light, frozen and still," the narrator remembers. "One of the men turned her over in the snow and I saw everything. My body trembled with some strange mystical feeling and so did my brother's. It might have been the cold."

The town blacksmith respectfully covers the old woman's body with his own coat and carries her gently into town. The next day her body is identified, and she is again soon forgotten, except, that is, by the boy—now the man telling the story. He has listened to his brother recount the events that they have witnessed, but this telling has not seemed sufficient. Facts alone do not adequately explain the mystery of the events. "The whole thing, the story of the old woman's death, was to me as I grew older like music heard from far off. The notes had to be picked up slowly one at a time. Something had to be understood."

Thus, he returns to the story again and again, mystified, compelled to probe at the essence of the woman's life and death. "A thing so complete has its own beauty," he says, and it is that beauty that haunts him.

## Themes and Meanings

The most obvious theme of the story is found in the narrator's emphasis on feeding, on giving of oneself to satisfy others. The old woman's job was always to feed others—the German farmer and his wife, her own husband and son, the animals that surrounded her. "Horses, cows, pigs, dogs, men"; the narrator numbers them off, the men undifferentiated from the beasts in the woman's mind.

One aspect of this "feeding" is sexual in nature. Certainly the farmer's desires for her are basic, brutal, and animal-like. He tears away the top of her dress, paralleling the action by the dogs in the clearing—although, ironically, the dogs treat her with greater respect than do the humans. When she runs off with Jake Grimes, she tells him that the farmer never actually possessed her, but she gives herself to Jake without resistance, at least in the narrator's imaginative reconstruction of the scene. Sex is, for the woman, simply another form of feeding, and she is relieved when, grown bent and wasted by hard work, she is no longer attractive to Jake and no longer has to satisfy him in this way.

In her deathly transformation, however, the woman once again regains her youthful sexuality. She becomes a young girl, untouched and pure. When the body is discovered, and as the young boy and his brother watch, the woman's breasts are revealed. The narrator remembers that he "saw everything" and that his body "trembled with some strange mystical feeling," which he attempts to attribute to the cold. Still, it is clear that at least part of the reaction is sexual. The boy sees and feels an aspect of existence that has heretofore been hidden from him. The weird connection of sex and death is ironic and, no doubt, disturbing, but, as the adult narrator realizes, there is an unknowable quality, a shared "mystical" reality in them both. At this moment, the boy gains awareness. He cannot truly understand what he feels, but his life is forever changed by the experience. He can never return to his own innocence; he can only wonder at the mystery of life and death.

### Style and Technique

As is so often the case in a work by Sherwood Anderson, the means of telling the story can be as compelling as the story itself. Such is the case with "Death in the Woods." Anderson wrote several versions of the tale before he felt that he had come close to telling it adequately, and one of the most obvious narrative devices employed in the story is the narrator's apparent difficulty in saying exactly what he means, in capturing in words the truth of the event. The "story" is simple, but the feelings evoked by it are very complex.

It may be argued, in fact, that the story is concerned more with the narrator than with the old woman whose death serves as inspiration, or catalyst, for the narrator. The unnamed narrator is a grown man looking back to his childhood, and there is considerable ambiguity concerning the actual events that he recounts. At one point he wonders how he could know some of the details that he is relating, and clearly there are many aspects of the story that he could not know. Later he tells the reader that he is drawing on events in his own life to help make sense of, give structure to, and fill the gaps in the old woman's life. For example, he remembers having himself worked on the farm of a German who abused the hired girl. He also had "a half-uncanny, mystical adventure with dogs in an Illinois forest on a clear, moonlit winter night." In addition, he had once stumbled onto the woman's old, run-down farmhouse, inhabited now only by "tall, gaunt" dogs, the kind that he has imagined as accompanying Mrs. Grimes on her journey.

The point is that the narrator is admitting to the reader that he is creating the story in an attempt to make sense of the central event—the discovery of the old woman's body and its magical transformation. He is not satisfied with the way that others have told the story; thus, he adds to it selected events from his own life, from snatches of overheard conversation, and from "small town tales." These he has put together with the actual events of that night, the ones he could factually know, in order to create the larger, more resonant, more universal story of life and death.

Thus, "Death in the Woods" can be seen as an explanation of storytelling: What causes the teller to repeat his tale; in what manner does he draw on fact, fantasy, and personal experience to transform the basic events of the world into the wonder of imaginative creation? Like the old woman's body—become that of a lovely young girl—the story, seen in the mystical light of the moon, transfixes readers with its hidden magic and touches them with its revealed beauty.

*Edwin T. Arnold*

# DEATH IN VENICE

*Author:* Thomas Mann (1875-1955)
*Type of plot:* Character study
*Time of plot:* 1911
*Locale:* Venice
*First published:* "Der Tod in Venedig," 1912 (English translation, 1925)

> *Principal characters:*
> GUSTAVE VON ASCHENBACH, a distinguished German writer with
> an international reputation
> TADZIO, a Polish boy of perfect beauty

## The Story

The opening pages of the novella brilliantly foreshadow the theme of death by cholera in Venice, a city whose history of sensual self-indulgence has led to moral decline and physical collapse. The first of three symbolic messengers of death—a distinctly exotic figure with straw hat, red hair, snub nose, prominent Adam's apple, and glistening white teeth laid bare to the gums—suddenly appears in the Byzantine-style mortuary chapel (a parody of St. Mark's Basilica in Venice) while Gustave von Aschenbach is walking near the North Cemetery in Munich. This disturbing apparition weakens Aschenbach's repressive self-control, stimulates his visionary dream (which represents the source of the Asiatic cholera in the moist swamps of the Ganges delta), and inspires his voyage to Italy.

This thematic prelude and the revealing sketch of Aschenbach's dignified and repressed character establish the intellectual framework, suggest the inevitability of his tragic fate, and lead to a series of encounters with menacing and vaguely theatrical figures. The goat-bearded "circus director" sells Aschenbach a ticket across the northern Adriatic from Pola to Venice and seals their satanic pact with sand that warns of human mortality. Charon, the second messenger of death, conveys Aschenbach, against his will, from the dock to the Lido in a coffinlike gondola and, with a cryptic warning, suddenly vanishes.

When Aschenbach, in the grand hotel, encounters Tadzio's perfect beauty, delightful charm, and expression of pure serenity, he does not see him as an actual boy of fourteen, but as an embodiment of Greek art, transmuted and gilded with mythic significance. The irony of Aschenbach's futile attempt to idealize his pederastic passion is emphasized by the parallel development of his degrading love and of the cholera that insidiously infects the city. Aschenbach, the highly respectable widower with a married daughter, changes from a purely aesthetic admirer of Tadzio's beauty to a man who suddenly realizes that the acute pain he felt during his quite sensible attempt to leave the city (fortuitously prevented by the loss of his trunk) was entirely attributable to his rapturous though unacknowledged feeling for the youth.

Aschenbach's passion is like a crime, and the city's evil secret of the cholera mingles with the one in the depths of his heart. A sanitary inspector greets Aschenbach's ship as it approaches Venice, the lukewarm air of the sirocco breathes on him as he is rowed to the Lido. He smells the stagnant odor of the lagoon when he opens his hotel window, the sickening exhalations of the canals nearly drive him from the city, and the pungent smell of carbolic acid and municipal placards warn him of the dangers of certain intestinal infections. The blustering street musician, the third messenger of death, laconically confides that the oppressive sirocco is not good for the health. Even when the English clerk in Cook's travel agency advises him to leave immediately, he cannot tear himself away from the grip of the pestilence or the spell of his beloved.

Tadzio's poor teeth connect him with the aged and garishly dressed homosexual that Aschenbach has observed on the ship to Venice. This symbol of his anemic disease and human mortality is pleasurable to Aschenbach because it equalizes youth and age, beauty and ugliness, and diminishes Tadzio's godlike power over him. The writer is possessively jealous of the youth's perfect form, and wants him to die at the height of his beauty, before he is ravaged by decay and old age.

Overwhelmed by passion and disgusted by his aging body, Aschenbach submits to the cosmetic attentions of the hotel barber, who transforms him into a grotesque replica of the repulsive old invert on the ship. In the little square where he had once conceived the plan of his abortive flight, he eats the overripe strawberries that infect him with the fatal cholera. The doomed Aschenbach then returns to the hotel to discover that Tadzio is leaving. When he rushes to the beach for a final glimpse of the beautiful boy, he finds that Tadzio's friend Jaschiu is avenging himself for his long weeks of subservience. Jaschiu challenges Tadzio to a fight and presses his face into the sand, symbolizing both degradation of beauty and spiritual forbearance in the face of fate. After witnessing this scene, Aschenbach is "summoned" by Tadzio to his death.

## Themes and Meanings

Thomas Mann makes Aschenbach a homosexual for several reasons. On one level, his inversion is a manifestation of strain and disorder, a release from psychological repression that results in the vulgar and degrading passion of an elderly gentleman for a rather cruel and unworthy boy. Aschenbach abandons his will, conspires with pseudoartists such as the equivocal musician and the cosmetic barber, sadly deludes himself about his relationship with Tadzio, and condemns himself—and probably his beloved—to death.

More important, Aschenbach's homosexual pursuit symbolizes the artist's noble but tragic quest for perfection. Mann's imaginative artist, who paradoxically creates in his work a life that he is unable to live in reality, must maintain a perilous balance of feeling and thought, and cannot surrender to either without losing his capacity to write. In the doomed love of the suspect and antisocial pederast, Mann found the perfect pattern for the artist's desperate struggle to recapture the ideal form of sensual beauty, and to unite passion with thought, grace with wisdom, the real with the ideal. The theme of the novella is the seed of self-destruction inherent in creative genius.

*Style and Technique*

The novella is structured by a series of polarities and contrasts: north-south, age-youth, health-sickness, art-life, reason-instinct, reality-illusion, order-chaos. Once Aschenbach breaks free from his northern restraints, he is unable to establish the proper balance between his Germanic culture, intellect, discipline, and serenity and Italian passion, license, freedom, and decadence.

Mann also uses the structural device of the leitmotif: the repetition of a certain phrase in different contexts, which he associates with a particular theme. His allusions to the composers Richard Wagner and Gustav Mahler, the musicians in the gondola and the street, and Tadzio's name, which sounds like a musical description (adagio means "slowly"), all suggest that art can arouse dangerous emotions. The demonic tempters and messengers of death all have the same physical features and bad teeth; the black gondola, blackened corpses, and snapping black cloth of the camera symbolize death.

Mann's style changes from coolly objective to intensely passionate as Aschenbach moves from a passive to an active lover and is gradually overwhelmed by moral and physical degeneration. Aschenbach first sees Tadzio as would an intellectual connoisseur, changes to a sympathetic and paternal view, realizes that he is staying in Venice for Tadzio's sake, and compares their relationship to that of Socrates and his favorite pupil, Phaedrus. As he approaches death, Aschenbach is overcome by panic, hysterical desire, demonic frenzy, and orgiastic dreams, driven as he is into the bottomless pit of excess and damnation.

*Jeffrey Meyers*

# DEATH OF A HUNTSMAN

*Author:* H. E. Bates (1905-1974)
*Type of plot:* Wit and humor
*Time of plot:* The mid-twentieth century
*Locale:* A rural area outside London
*First published:* 1957

*Principal characters:*
> HARRY BARNFIELD, a middle-aged businessperson
> KATEY, his shrewish wife
> EDNA WHITTINGTON, his old flame
> VALERIE, Edna's nineteen-year-old daughter

### The Story

The story begins with Harry Barnfield shown in his accustomed routine: perpetually late, running to catch his commuter train out of London, short, aging, and vaguely clownish, the butt of good-natured jokes by his fellow commuters. The reader soon sees why he is always late: His rural home, lovely as it is, is hardly the sort of place one would make a special effort to reach, for Harry's wife, Katey, is a more vicious shrew than her namesake, Katherina, in William Shakespeare's *The Taming of the Shrew.*

Rather than try to tame Katey—their marriage has been sour for too long, the reader senses—Harry takes solace in Valerie, a girl he accosts for riding her pony, without permission, across his property. Valerie is everything that Katey is not: young, vivacious, sensitive, and, most of all, caring toward Harry. Harry's fondness for her is hardly lessened when he learns that her mother, Edna, is the same who many years ago initiated him into the joys of sex. Edna, in fact, would very much like to strike up the match again, Katey notwithstanding.

For more than two months Harry and Valerie meet for walks and horseback rides in the woods, but the situation is too volatile to continue forever. The crisis comes at the Hunt Ball, an autumnal rite involving much dancing and drinking. Edna pressures Harry into taking her and, as an afterthought, Valerie. There, Harry and Valerie's feelings for each other become evident even to Edna. Edna tells Valerie to go home. Valerie refuses and dances with and openly kisses Harry before her dangerously calm mother. After the ball, Harry drives mother and daughter home. Harry and Edna have a discussion in the car, during which Edna warns that Valerie will have to be told everything about their past. Enraged, Harry strikes Edna and drives wildly off with her down the twisting lanes, screaming that he will kill her. Edna leaps out, shaken but unharmed. The car crashes, and Harry is killed.

The story ends with Harry's funeral, attended by friends, neighbors, and fellow commuters—but attended by no one who loved him.

*Themes and Meanings*

"Death of a Huntsman" involves its protagonist, Harry Barnfield, in a love triangle; strangely enough, his wife is not one of the three "corners." It is one measure of the sterility and joylessness of his marriage, in fact, that when Harry has an affair with young Valerie Whittington, he hardly considers his wife to be an issue or obstacle. The third corner of the triangle is occupied by Valerie's mother, Edna, an old flame of Harry.

A brief summary of the story's plot may seem to indicate that things would have worked out fine for Harry and Valerie, that true love would have triumphed, had not old Edna insisted on getting in the way. On the contrary, a closer reading indicates that the affair was doomed from the start, doomed by the lovers' very natures.

"Death of a Huntsman" is, in fact, a variation on the ancient *senex amans* pattern of comedy, that is, an old man made foolish by love for a much younger woman. Harry and Valerie's age difference is emphasized throughout. To his fellow commuters, Harry looks a decade older than his forty-three years. Harry is surprised, on the other hand, to learn that Valerie is nearly twenty rather than the fifteen or sixteen that he takes her to be. The difference between fifteen and twenty is greater than only five years: It is—emotionally, for Harry—the difference between having an affair with a young woman and having an affair with a schoolgirl. Indeed, a feeling of things being not quite right pervades the story from the start. H. E. Bates manipulates the reader by favoring dramatization rather than idyllic and serene scenes of love in the woodlands—moments when things go wrong, when doubt enters Harry's mind.

The feeling of unease emanates primarily from Harry. It is he who feels that there is something "disturbing" about Valerie. Exactly what is disturbing he cannot say, but it is associated with Valerie's ridiculously long legs dangling from her pony and her husky, woman's voice appended to a girl's body. Obviously, Harry is disturbed by the age question—is she old enough or too young?—and its thinly disguised sexual implications. The unease only increases as the story progresses, culminating at the Hunt Ball. Harry is afraid that Valerie will go to the ball dressed in her schoolgirl uniform. When she emerges wearing a very mature dress and gloves, however, his discomfort hardly abates but turns into a "turmoil of fright and indecision." Is Valerie a girl or a woman? Harry says that he will dance with her if she does not mind being stepped on—but he had almost said, "If your mother will let you." Valerie pours Harry a glass of sherry, but she herself is not allowed to drink. Most telling of all, at their happiest moment at the ball, Valerie actually reverts to baby talk: "You're the bestest good one," she tells Harry. "The most bestest good one in the world."

That Harry should have "seen" more clearly the consequences of his folly is evident from a "sight pattern"—a motif of images denoting eyes, vision, or the lack thereof—that runs throughout the story and includes not only Harry but Edna, Katey, and Valerie as well. Harry, for example, wears thick glasses that he polishes with "scrupulous short-sightedness." The reader is assured early in the story that Katey does not see Harry very well—because of her drunkenness, overtly, but more fundamentally because she is totally insensitive to his emotional and physical needs. Valerie's eyes, on the other hand, are "too big for her face," like Harry's, connoting a similar straining to see (because of a similar short-sightedness). More telling, at almost every crucial juncture in the story, Harry's glasses fog over, blinding him—an objectification of his being blinded by passion for Valerie. The sight pattern intensifies at the ball, where Edna, with her "ice-gray microscopic" eyes, sees everything all too clearly. At the same time, Harry must continually rub away at the mist fogging his glasses, and Valerie—after declaring Harry to be the "most bestest good one in the world"—finds her eyes "drowned in tears of happiness." The happiness is only momentary. The ugly scene between Harry and Edna in the car ensues, at the climax of which Harry hits Edna with a blow that "partially blinded her" and she counters with one that breaks his glasses. Blinded, he wrecks the car and dies.

All of them were blind all along. None saw clearly enough the realities of the situation until it was too late. Bates reemphasizes the foolishness of the aging man's passion by noting the mourners at his funeral. Many of them were "very bald."

## Style and Technique

The *senex amans* pattern mentioned earlier is generally a comic one; indeed, with merely a few twists of the plot "Death of a Huntsman" could have been comic. Even before the situation begins to sour, however, the reader knows that events are moving toward tragedy, not comedy, because of a rich pattern of foreshadowing—perhaps the most interesting technical feature of this otherwise simple story.

The most obvious example of foreshadowing, one that hardly warrants analysis, is the title. Subtler examples, however, follow. It is the nature of foreshadowing that any one instance taken in isolation might seem insignificant, but repeated instances affect the tone of the story and the reader's expectations. In the first scene of "Death of a Huntsman," for example, Harry's fellow commuters gleefully anticipate Harry's nightly "race with time." No special significance seems implied by the phrase at this point. (Even here, however, the thoughtful reader might ask himself, "Who ever wins, ultimately, the race against time?") When the reader is told a page later that sometimes before Harry arrived "a final door would slam with doom," the implications become much more pointed.

The most obvious example of foreshadowing involves one last fruit of a quince tree, which both Valerie and Harry take as a symbol of their love. At the climax of their happiest moment together, the quince falls with a thud. The idyllic mood is broken. Immediately thereafter, Valerie reminds Harry that tomorrow is the night of the Hunt Ball and that he must dance with her. The scene ends with Valerie humming a tune in anticipation of the dance, but for Harry, "he remembered the sound of the quince dropping into the reeds, the last vanishing phial of the summer's honey, filling his mind like an ominous echo."

In the last brutal exchange between Harry and Edna in the car, "ominous" is turning to "fatal" when, to Harry, Edna's drawn face seems "skeletonized," her mouth "almost cadaverous." Ironically, it is blind, foolish Harry who is about to die.

*Dennis Vannatta*

# DEATH OF A TRAVELING SALESMAN

*Author:* Eudora Welty (1909-2001)
*Type of plot:* Psychological
*Time of plot:* The 1930's
*Locale:* Rural Mississippi
*First published:* 1936

> *Principal characters:*
> R. J. BOWMAN, a traveling salesperson
> SONNY, a country farmer, about thirty years old
> A COUNTRYWOMAN

*The Story*

The crucial action of "Death of a Traveling Salesman" takes place in the mind of the protagonist, a shoe company representative, in the last hours of his life. Feverish and weak, R. J. Bowman has sought shelter in the home of a simple country couple. His initial misperceptions about them eventually give way to a recognition that they possess some vital knowledge about life, knowledge that he has been denied.

Bowman has been a traveling salesperson for fourteen years, living alone in hotels as he drives from one city to the next with his sample case of shoes. As the story begins, he has recently recovered from a serious case of influenza, during which he was cared for by a hotel doctor and a trained nurse. Although he had believed himself to be cured, Bowman finds himself oddly tired and anxious during his first day back at work. By midday, he has lost his accustomed road, and finds to his horror that he has driven his car to the edge of a ravine. He is able to get out before the car topples over. To his surprise, the car does not crash but is caught by a tangle of vine leaves and sinks to the ground unharmed.

As Bowman begins to walk toward the only house in view, he feels his heart beat rapidly and wildly, so much so that he has difficulty thinking or speaking. He feels better after he has entered the house and has been seated in the cool living room. He finds himself uneasy, however, with the taciturn woman of the house. She is a big woman, still and slow-moving; Bowman estimates her age to be about fifty. He is relieved when she refers to Sonny, who will be able to help him pull his car out of the ditch. In fact, Sonny is able to do so with the help of his mule. While Bowman and the woman wait for the powerful young man to complete his task, Bowman feels a surge of unaccustomed emotion. He interprets his pounding heart as a protest against the lack of love in his life, as a plea that his empty heart should be filled with love. Somehow, he imagines, these people know more than he does about the meaning of life. He wonders what secret they shelter.

Prompted both by his fascination with the life of these country people and by his own fatigue, Bowman asks if he may spend the night there. Permitted to do so, he observes more of the habits of his hosts. They obtain their fire by going to a distant neighbor and carrying back a burning stick. They make their own illegal whiskey and bury the jug in the yard. As they sit down to eat dinner, Bowman makes a startling discovery: The woman is not fifty, as he had thought, but young, the same age as Sonny; Sonny is her husband, not her son as he had supposed. Finally, the reasons for her large, shapeless body and ponderous movements becomes clear: She is pregnant. Bowman is stunned to realize that this couple's secret is simply the possession of a fulfilled marriage.

Trying to sleep before the fire later that night, he listens attentively to the many sounds of a country night. As he hears the couple breathing in the next room, he wishes that he could trade places with Sonny and be the father of the baby soon to be born. Something propels him then to leave the house and return to his car. First, however, he empties his billfold and leaves the money under a table lamp. Then, running out to the car, he feels an explosion in his chest; he covers his heart to muffle the loud noise that seems to be coming from within. Bowman has arrived at the moment of his death.

## Themes and Meanings

This quiet story offers an indirect portrait of sickness and health in both a physical and a psychological sense. Weakened by illness, Bowman comes to recognize that his life has never been strong or whole in an emotional sense. He has never before regretted his own failure to settle down and rear a family. Now, just before his death, he learns what he has missed. However, it is difficult to define exactly what quality of the young couple's life Bowman envies. His admiration for their existence goes beyond the simple yearning to have a child, important though that is. Even before he realizes that the woman is pregnant, Bowman is drawn by her composure and by the way she responds to Sonny's every action. For example, he senses her wordless pride while Sonny works to pull the car from the ravine and in the way she points out that Sonny had made the whiskey offered to Bowman. The quiet bond between them contrasts with his own memories of indistinguishable women and faded hotel rooms. As a salesperson, Bowman has developed a line of conversational patter that he uses with his customers. With his hosts, however, he finds it difficult to get beyond the first few words of his usual line. Their silence compels his respect.

The theme of the story depends on the contrast between Bowman's progressively deteriorating health and the young couple's strength and purposefulness. Although Bowman is superficially more sophisticated and knowledgeable than Sonny and his wife, their lives have a meaning his has been denied.

## Style and Technique

"Death of a Traveling Salesman" focuses on the last hours of the protagonist, and the story's style emphasizes the psychological changes of illness. In particular, the imagery used to describe Bowman's thoughts suggests his unconscious recognition of his approaching death. As the last day of his life progresses, his mind fills with images of comfort, rest, and letting go. For example, early in the story, Bowman remembers his grandmother and wishes that "he could fall into the big feather bed that had been in her room." Soon afterward, he notices a cloud that "floated there to one side like the bolster on his grandmother's bed." When his car goes into the ravine, a tangle of grapevines catches it and "rock[s] it like a grotesque child in a dark cradle." All these images indicate Bowman's unconscious readiness for the sleep and shelter he received as a child.

These images of rocking motion and safety carry over even into Bowman's thoughts about his failing heart. When his heart begins to beat erratically, it surges powerfully and then falls "gently, like acrobats into nets" and is "as quiet as ashes falling." Bowman's entire world falls under this gentle spell; even when he drops his bags they seem to "drift in slow bulks gracefully through the air and to cushion themselves on the gray prostrate grass near the doorstep." His former impatience gives way to a calmer demeanor, and he attributes this to his illness, when he learned to submit to the ministrations of the nurse.

The calm and receptive mood that overtakes Bowman, as suggested by the examples of the earlier imagery, makes it possible for him finally to recognize his hosts for what they really are. In his initial quick judgment of the woman, he had wrongly assumed that she was old and tired. He had associated her stillness with fatigue. However, once his own impatience is transcended, he sees that her quiet attitude stems from her pregnancy and her happy marriage.

Ironically, Bowman's perception of the couple's happiness makes him wish to return to his former vigorous life. This desire is ironic, because Bowman's life is, in fact, nearly over. When the moment of his death arrives, the images of comfort give way to harsher images: For example, "his heart began to give off tremendous explosions like a rifle, bang, bang, bang." Earlier in the story, the abruptness of his death had been hinted at by descriptions of his heart leaping "like a little colt invited out of a pen" or his pulse leaping "like a trout in a brook." These images of quick motion contrast with the images of slowness and comfort. Perhaps Bowman's death must be thought of as combining the two poles: Although it comes on him with suddenness, he is ready for the peace it brings.

*Diane M. Ross*

# THE DEATH OF IVAN ILYICH

*Author:* Leo Tolstoy (1828-1910)
*Type of plot:* Domestic realism
*Time of plot:* The 1880's
*Locale:* St. Petersburg and nearby provinces
*First published:* "Smert Ivana Ilicha," 1886 (English translation, 1887)

*Principal characters:*

IVAN ILYICH GOLOVIN, a Russian magistrate
PRASKOVYA FYODOROVNA GOLOVINA, his wife
PIOTR IVANOVICH, Ivan's nearest acquaintance and colleague
VASYA, Ivan's son
GERASIM, Ivan's servant

*The Story*

This story begins with the news of Ivan Ilyich's death reported by his closest acquaintance from law school, Piotr Ivanovich. When his coworkers hear the news, their immediate reaction is one of self-centered concern over their possible promotions and other changes that Ivan's death might bring about in their own lives. Only after these considerations do the dead man's so-called friends think of the tiresome duties of attending the funeral and consoling the widow.

Giving up his usual nap to attend the wake, Piotr, meeting his bridge partner at the widow's house, takes the time to arrange for their regular game that evening after viewing the body. Then Ivan's widow, Praskovya Fyodorovna, escorts him into a room for a private talk, in which she, too, dwells on her own concerns, telling him how much she suffered through Ivan's screaming for the three days before he died. Her main interest in speaking with Piotr, however, is to find out whether and how she might get extra money from the government because of Ivan's death. On hearing his opinion that there is nothing she can do, she loses interest in their conversation, and Piotr takes his leave.

The first of twelve chapters sets Leo Tolstoy's tone, which mixes grotesque humor with the somber reality of death coming to a respected minor functionary—an ordinary death of an ordinary man (the name Ivan Ilyich is as common in Russian as is the name John Smith in English). In describing the family's and friends' reactions to Ivan's death, the narrative concentrates on their obsession with their own lives and petty comforts and their disregard for the deceased.

The next section, chapters 2 through 5, recounts the life and career of Ivan. The second and most successful of three sons of a minor official, he had risen to the position of examining magistrate and married a proper girl as the "right thing" to do. His married life did not, however, meet his expectations: His wife turned unaccountably jealous and ill-humored, and several of his children died. Ivan retreated steadily into his work, becoming progressively more aloof at home.

Finding his only consolation in the dignity and social activities attached to the official world of the magistrate, Ivan suffered a particularly heavy blow when, despite the fact that he was held in high esteem by his colleagues, he was passed over for several prestigious appointments. His ensuing financial difficulties catapulted him into a severe depression, and Ivan resolved to seek a post that would pay him sufficiently and relieve him from a department that had ceased to appreciate his talents.

By chance, a friend was in a position to help him to a new post two stages above his former colleagues. After this promotion, Ivan's relationship with his wife and family improved, and he secured a beautiful new home and had it decorated exactly like the homes of others in similar positions. He gave typical parties to which he invited only those of the proper social position, and cultivated only the proper acquaintances, keeping his real life separate from his official life. Ivan and his family, having achieved middle-class success, were happy: "And everything went on in this way without change, and everything was very nice."

In the process of having the new house decorated, Ivan slipped on a ladder while hanging curtains and injured his side. At first, he made light of the injury, but his illness got worse, and the family discord returned. The doctor's original nebulous diagnosis changed to that of a floating kidney and vermiform appendix. Ivan finally realized it was a matter of life and death. Facing death, he came to hate his wife, and she, pitying herself for having to put up with his bad temper, reciprocated the feeling.

The final section, comprising chapters 6 through 12, recounts Ivan's suffering through his terminal illness and his contemplation of life and death. At first, Ivan accepts the truism that all mortals will die but only as an abstraction not applicable to himself. He thinks of how terrible and stupid it is for him to lose his life for a curtain. He is irked by the deception of others who console him, saying his illness will go away. Only his faithful servant Gerasim comforts him and helps him by holding up his legs. He believes that the only other person to pity and understand him is his son Vasya. His daughter Lisa is annoyed that his illness interferes with her social life.

Ivan alternates between despair and hope and finally no longer leaves the sofa. The only joy he can recall is that from his youth, and he begins to question whether his life might somehow have been wrong. He finally sees clearly that he has lived a life of self-deception, evading the meaning of life and death. He confesses his sins to a priest and takes communion.

Ivan's last three days are spent in agony. He screams as he feels himself thrust into a dark hole. He clings to the belief that his life has been good, and this belief seems to hold him back. At the moment that his son kisses his hand, Ivan falls through and sees the light; he realizes that, though his life has not been what it should have been, it can still be rectified. He pities his wife and the others and loses his fear of death. Then, as he looks for his former fear of death, he finds instead light and joy. His suffering continues for two more hours, and he dies.

## Themes and Meanings

As the title indicates, Leo Tolstoy's story concentrates on the death of a very ordinary middle-class person. The second chapter opens with the sentence, "Ivan Ilyich's life had been most simple and most ordinary and therefore most terrible," which has been called one of the most frightening sentences in all literature. Ivan's life has been lived according to those middle-class values set by his society. Ivan has always done the correct thing to achieve success; while in school, he did things that disgusted him until he noticed that those in good positions did the same things and did not consider them wrong.

In working at his career, he is punctilious, reserved, completely honest; when he has affairs, they are with women of the best society. He marries, not really for love but because this is what society expects him to do. Everything Ivan does is according to what one should do to rise in society; his values are material values, exemplified by his remodeling his house to look exactly like the homes of others in his social position. His relations with people have the semblance of friendliness, but he never develops any close or deep relationships.

It is not until he experiences his fatal illness that Ivan ever questions his values and his life. Even the cause of his illness—a freak accident that occurred as he was hanging curtains—is insignificant. Ivan comes to the realization that his life has been wasted. It is only with his death that he comes to a joyful revelation that, though his life had been wrong, it can still be rectified. He thus dies at peace with himself and with the world.

## Style and Technique

Tolstoy's first draft of this story was written in the first-person point of view with Ivan interpreting the events. Probably because of the importance of the theme of the story, Tolstoy later changed to an omniscient point of view, which more clearly shows the attitudes of the other characters toward Ivan's death. In the opening section, Tolstoy emphasizes the others' lack of concern over their friend's death. In describing Piotr's interview with Praskovya Fyodorovna, he concentrates on the little details of her shawl catching on the end of the table and Piotr's discomfiture in sitting on a pouf with broken springs, showing their distractions from the important event of Ivan's death. He thus prepares the reader for the simple, ordinary, and "most terrible" life that Ivan led, as is described in the second section of the story.

The second section is simply a prelude to the climactic death throes of the third part. Ivan's life is detailed in a straightforward narrative emphasizing his aloofness both with his family and official associates, and, one might say, with his own feelings. All of his attitudes and values seem to come from without, from what society considers the proper thing to do.

Fully half the chapters of the story are devoted to the fatal illness and Ivan's reactions to his family, friends, and doctors, as they all come to the realization that there is nothing they can do for him and that he is fatally ill. Here, too, Tolstoy describes the alternating feelings of hope and despair that Ivan experiences and the exasperation of his acquaintances with his annoying behavior. The doctors' treatments are described as perfunctory after they realize that there is nothing they can do; they prefer not to understand his questions. His daughter, dressed in evening clothes, becomes impatient with his illness and resents that he causes her feelings of guilt as she attends the theater. Praskovya Fyodorovna asks after his health not to learn about it but because it is expected of her. Everyone comes to resent him for reminding them of their own mortality.

In the last section, Tolstoy turns to giving Ivan's reactions to his illness, to describing his feelings and his questioning of the meaning of life and death. In this way, he emphasizes the epiphany that Ivan experiences at the moment of death.

*Roger Geimer*

# DE DAUMIER-SMITH'S BLUE PERIOD

*Author:* J. D. Salinger (1919-    )
*Type of plot:* Psychological
*Time of plot:* 1939
*Locale:* New York City and Montreal, Canada
*First published:* 1952

*Principal characters:*
ROBERT (BOBBY) AGADGANIAN, JR., the narrator's stepfather
DE DAUMIER-SMITH, the narrator and protagonist, an aspiring art
  instructor and aesthete
YOSHOTO, the director of Les Amis De Vieux Maitres
  correspondence art school, the protagonist's employer

*The Story*

The essential plot is a memoir of events recalled by the narrator in the year 1952. The narrator indicates in the initial paragraph that he wants to dedicate the following autobiographical account "to the memory" of his "ribald" stepfather, the late "Bobby" Agadganian, who married his mother after her divorce from his father in 1920.

After the Wall Street crash, Agadganian ceased being a stockbroker and took up a new occupation as agent-appraiser for a group of independent American art galleries. This necessitated, in 1930, a family move to Paris. Thus, the narrator had lived for more than nine years in Paris when he moved back to New York with his stepfather in the spring of 1939.

The cultural and social feelings of dislocation are considerable for this bright, bilingual nineteen-year-old boy as he attempts to come to terms with rude bus conductors, New York crowds, and art instruction at a school that he "loathes." In his spare time, he draws countless self-portraits in oils. The rapport between the narrator and his stepfather begins to deteriorate as they are "both in love with the same deceased woman" and both living in the cramped space of the same New York hotel room.

The narrator, after enduring life with Bobby for ten months in the Ritz Hotel, answers an ad in a Montreal paper for an instructor at a correspondence art school. Bilingual instructors are apparently being hired to coincide with the opening of the June summer session.

"Instantly, feeling almost unsupportably qualified," the young aspirant applies, enclosing examples of both academic and commercial art work ("lean, erect, super-chic couples" in evening clothes and "laughing, high-breasted girls"). He falsifies most of the biographical information in his personal and career resume, pretending to be related to the French painter Honore Daumier and feigning a close friendship with Pablo Picasso. His application accepted, "De Daumier-Smith" prepares to entrain for Montreal and informs Bobby and Bobby's girlfriend at dinner in the hotel dining room. De Daumier-Smith imagines that Bobby's companion is attempting to seduce him; actually she seems intent only on piercing his almost impenetrable egoism.

Self-consciously overdressed (gabardine suit, navy-blue shirt and yellow tie, brown-and-white shoes), De Daumier-Smith arrives in Montreal and is met by school director Yoshoto, whom he describes as "inscrutable." The school itself occupies the second floor of a run-down building in the slums of Montreal.

The rest of De Daumier-Smith's account relates the events of 1939 at the art school, Les Amis Des Vieux Maitres, in the succeeding months.

The narrator chronicles his problems with the director and his wife, Madame Yoshoto, who apparently is the only other instructor. He cannot find an ashtray; he is kept awake by the moaning of the sleeping Yoshotos; he is unaccustomed to the Japanese cooking, which disagrees with him, as does the banality of his duties, which are for the most part merely routine translation.

Finally, he is assigned three students, but two of them appear to be without much talent. Only the third student is promising and inspires De Daumier-Smith to initiate an animated correspondence. His excitement over the work of Sister Irma, a talented nun who lives in a convent near Toronto, prompts him to write to her, suggesting a possible visit. He also writes letters to the others, discouraging them from continuing to pursue a career as artists. Unfortunately, the mother superior writes that Sister Irma can no longer continue the course, and De Daumier-Smith, crushed, goes to a fashionable restaurant for a solitary meal to assuage his depressed thoughts.

Returning toward the school on foot and at twilight, De Daumier-Smith notices a light in the display window of the orthopedic appliances shop on the ground floor. Earlier, he described himself as doomed to live his life as "a visitor in a garden of enamel urinals and bedpans with a sightless wooden dummy deity standing by in a marked-down rupture truss." There is a well-built girl among the surgical hardware, changing the window display. Her confusion at the sight of De Daumier-Smith in his dinner jacket, watching her, causes her to fall as he tries to reach through the glass window to avert her fall. These actions, in turn, trigger a mystical experience, and the narrator is conscious of a brilliant light traveling toward him and the transformation of the surgical display into a field of "shimmering . . . exquisite, twice-blessed enamel flowers."

Liberated by his experience ("a borderline case of genuine mysticism"), De Daumier-Smith walks back to his room, rests, and then writes letters to the students he has dismissed, reinstating them.

In a postscript, De Daumier-Smith reveals that the school survived only a week more and that he joined his father briefly in Rhode Island before returning to art school. In a whimsical final statement, he reveals that he had no further correspondence with Sister Irma but that another student, Bambi Kramer, had later turned her talents to designing her own Christmas cards. ("They'll be something to see, if she hasn't lost her touch.")

### Themes and Meanings

J. D. Salinger's early stories, which appeared first in *The New Yorker* and were later collected under the title *Nine Stories* (1953), all concern children or adolescents. Salinger seems to believe (with William Wordsworth) that the young are the true visionaries of society and that their consciences are untainted and unencumbered with the hypocrisy and evasions that are common to the daily activities of the adult world. Salinger's stories also emphasize the quest for meaning and for an understanding of existence characterized by Zen Buddhism and the approach to satori (oneness with all things, enlightenment, and ultimate acceptance and awareness of self). Salinger's characters are often self-deprecating but nearly always self-analytical as well. They typify a type of behavior, popular following World War II, of disengagement and disaffection, a refusal to participate fully in the adult social apparatus but a less than complete withdrawal from these habits as well. The involved yet uninvolved upper-middle-class teenager of the 1950's can be seen to perfection in the character of Salinger's most famous adolescent, Holden Caulfield, the hero of *The Catcher in the Rye* (1951).

Certain characteristics of De Daumier-Smith's reminiscence are symbolically suggested by the title, which refers to a period in the artistic development of the contemporary painter Pablo Picasso (1881-1973), whose "Blue Period" (1901-1904) was largely concerned with portraits of unhappy outcasts who were impoverished and lonely. Salinger draws a parallel with the unhappiness of his protagonist and his "blue" mood during the period of his late adolescence as chronicled in the story.

The narrator is also a student of Buddhism, a fact revealed on his first day in Montreal, when the Yoshotos claim to be Presbyterians. Thus, the mystical experience that causes De Daumier-Smith to see the surgical appliances in the store window transformed into brilliant, enamel-like flowers has been foreshadowed in the earlier text.

The cause of De Daumier-Smith's epiphany is the bond that the young artist feels with the nun, his student. The picture of "Christ being carried to the sepulchre" touches him (especially the woman signaling in the foreground to the viewer). He seeks a kindred spirit, and he acknowledges that Sister Irma is "greatly talented." He reaches out in his correspondence to place himself "entirely at [her] disposal." Sister Irma, or the presentiment of her presence, breaks the spell of the narrator's isolation and hypocrisy. Suddenly he sees himself as a Pierre Abelard, the romantic lover of Heloise, whose affair also ended in a famous correspondence and a tragic separation.

Later, De Daumier-Smith experiences at least partial enlightenment and true self-knowledge when the window of surgical appliances formerly presided over by a "dummy-deity" becomes a garden of light and color, no longer representative of emptiness in a mechanical, unfeeling world but rather of the power of empathy. Thus, finally the narrator realizes that "everybody is a nun" in his search for meaning and his capacity for understanding, even love. All petty distinctions are swept away, and even the untalented Bambi Kramer is forgiven as De Daumier-Smith attains Buddha-like acceptance and awareness.

## Style and Technique

The method of narration is typical of Salinger's ironic tone. In another story, Salinger uses the phrase "the wise child." His stories are frequently concerned with intelligent, even brilliant, young people who point out some lesson to their elders, many of whom do not profit from the experience. De Daumier-Smith never reveals his legal name, but he reveals much else through his articulate comments, his mature vocabulary, and his sensitive observation of those around him.

De Daumier-Smith, the narrator, uses phrases such as "feeling almost unsupportably qualified" to describe himself at one point. However, a few paragraphs later, he says that he used "all my spare time plus some that didn't quite belong to me," indicating a certain insecurity. Salinger's adolescent tends to "reiterate earlier lies" while reinforcing the dramatic irony of his situation as the plot develops. The reader is aware of the narrator's inadequacies as a result of the narrator's totally candid revelations about himself while presenting an opaque facade to the rest of the world—his "armor." The narrative is mainly chronological in its relation of the events of several months in 1939. Slight shifts or gaps in this sequence are indicated by double spaces between paragraphs.

The irony of the hero's situation is constantly underlined by the author with the use of words whose connotations are unmistakable and frequently amusing. A "highly unendowed-looking building" describes De Daumier Smith's first view of his art academy. The "Harvard Senior" represents De Daumier-Smith's stepfather in his relation to the narrator, who is "a Cambridge Newsboy." Salinger also uses anticlimax ("Her eyes sparkled with depravity") for comic effect.

Thus, the tone of the story is lightly ironic and combines a self-deprecating narrative with the more serious aspects of character development and theme. As with many of Salinger's short stories and in spite of the considerable length of the narrative, the falling action is minimal and consists of a short epilogue of only two short paragraphs.

*F. A. Couch, Jr.*

# DÉDÉ

*Author:* Mavis Gallant (1922-     )
*Type of plot:* Character study
*Time of plot:* The 1990's
*Locale:* Paris
*First published:* 1993

> *Principal characters:*
> AMEDÉE (Dédé's full name), a young man
> M. BROUET, his brother-in-law, a magistrate
> MME. BROUET, his older sister
> PASCAL BROUET, his nephew

## The Story

At the story's opening and ending Dédé's nephew Pascal is fourteen years old, but the main part of the story takes place one Sunday afternoon when Pascal is nine years old. Dédé is living with the Brouets, supposedly studying for a civil service examination to qualify him for employment with the railroad. Dédé's exact age is never given, but he is most likely twenty or so. It is revealed that Dédé had caused various kinds of trouble at home in Colmar and his mother no longer knew how to handle him, so she sent him to Paris to live with his doting sister.

On that memorable Sunday afternoon in the early fall, the Brouets had invited the Turbins and the Chevallier-Crochets for lunch in their garden. Pascal and Dédé were also present. The reason behind the gathering was to introduce Dédé to the Turbin's daughter Brigitte, for Mme. Brouet had decided that her wayward brother needed a woman friend. Her plans were foiled when Brigitte was called away on an emergency and could not attend the luncheon. The day had not started well; a fire of undetermined origin had broken out in Dédé's room that morning. It is revealed that when Dédé was living with his mother in Colmar, he caused two other fires, although they were believed to have been accidental.

The luncheon, in a typical French manner, lasts all afternoon, and the spirited account of its near catastrophes evolves into gentle social satire. First hornets attack the melon, then the inept maid delays the next course, and finally everyone argues over eating the dessert. Meanwhile, the conversation becomes more and more desultory, its topics ranging from corruption in French politics to the advantages and disadvantages of foreign travel. People tell stories that everyone has heard many times before. At intervals, Dédé interrupts with non sequiturs, and his sister hushes him or tries to change the subject.

When the guests finally leave around five o'clock, Dédé announces that he has received a degree in the mail but has lost the letter. Even though Dédé has been studying haphazardly for only a month, M. Brouet, anxious to be rid of his troublesome brother-in-law, does not question the absurdity of Dédé's claim. Instead, he suggests that it is time for Dédé to go home now that he has finished his course. Dédé agrees, and late that night, M. Brouet takes him to the railway station.

The narrative returns to Pascal at age fourteen. Dédé had vanished from their lives since that fateful evening after the luncheon. The Brouets know that Dédé returned to Paris a year earlier and is working part time with a television polling service, but he has not called on them. Now almost as tall as Dédé, Pascal finds his father looking at him "as if he were suddenly setting a value on the kind of man he might become. It was a steady look, neither hot nor cold." Although it is not stated, Pascal must have wondered if his father feared the existence of another Dédé in the family.

### Themes and Meanings

Mavis Gallant's outstanding strength as a writer lies in her ability to develop character. Most often her central characters, such as Dédé, are exiled and isolated from traditional society. The narrative never fully reveals Dédé as an individual. Instead he is developed through the other characters' reactions to him. The Brouets and their luncheon guests all thrive on their conventionality and their secure place in society. In contrast, Dédé is neither conventional or secure but an outsider. When Pascal was nine, he accepted his peculiar uncle, but at age fourteen, it appears that he is rejecting Dédé as he enters into proper society.

This preoccupation with the outsider comes in large part from Gallant's own life. Born in Montreal of Scottish heritage, she grew up in Canada and was educated there and in the United States. For several years, she worked as a newspaper reporter in Montreal and at the same time began writing fiction. At age twenty-eight, she left Canada and settled in Paris, where she lives while maintaining her links to Canada. Bridging cultures herself, she has frequently focused on those who find themselves adrift in a world that is unfamiliar both physically and emotionally.

Dédé does not suffer from the kind of alienation afflicting people transplanted into another culture. Still, his disconnection with his environment remains as acute as that experienced by those literally separated from their homelands. The narrative reveals that Dédé is drawing plans for an extraordinary apartment in which the inhabitant could spend a lifetime without having to leave. In stark contrast to his dream, Dédé moves through a society both familiar and foreign to him. He is altogether unprepared for a career and unable even to communicate logically, but he is expected to lead the kind of conventional life that the Brouets do. Most likely he will not adjust, for the story's inconclusive ending hints that Dédé will continue to drift aimlessly, perhaps even to set a few more fires.

### Style and Technique

A third-person narrative, "Dédé" is told from the point of view of Pascal, the Brouets' son. Although the character Dédé lends his name to the title, his role is minor in the development of the narrative. However, the action revolves around Dédé even as he remains in the background. Such an inverted technique is typical of Gallant's subtle approach to fiction. Although Gallant's strong point is character development, all other aspects of her urbane and polished fiction are admirable as well, each one enlarging her primary focus on character.

The language used in the story remains simple, direct, and economical. At times it verges on the elliptical but never turns purposefully vague. Gallant is a singular writer in that she captures French society and mores so well while writing in English. Although she is fluent in French, she writes only in English, considering it an anchor for an understanding of the world about her. In addition to writing about the French, Gallant also records the lives of Canadians both at home and abroad. Whether they are about French or Canadian subjects, her stories always offer flawless accounts of human behavior.

On the surface, Gallant's stories appear to be constructed in a random manner. Sometimes the most significant details emerge at unexpected turns in the narrative. The shifts in time from past to present also give the impression that this story is simply unfolding on its own with no overall design. However, this apparently simple structure actually is notably complex. Through this technique, Gallant manages in each piece of fiction to open up a world that is intact and marked by reality.

The selected details woven into the action lend all of Gallant's fiction its distinctive texture. For example, the luncheon scene in "Dédé" reveals not only Dédé's social ineptitude and the tedium of the guests but also provides a description of French cuisine. Each course is described, beginning with the ill-fated melon attacked by hornets, moving on to the partridges on a bed of shredded cabbage—unfortunately a little cold because it was delayed by the inefficient maid—then to the salad, finally to the caramelized plum tart served with heavy cream. Such minute details on food, on décor, on clothing, on characters' physical oddities, and on their speech habits abound and are always fully integrated into the narrative structure. No detail, however trivial it might appear, can be called extraneous.

Gallant also handles dialogue skillfully. To a degree, she uses it as her main tool in character development. Many of her short stories, such as "Dédé," contain several characters. However, there is never a problem identifying them, even though they are often not described physically. Instead, what they say and how they say it distinguishes each person.

*Robert Ross*

# DEER WOMAN

*Author:* Paula Gunn Allen (1939-     )
*Type of plot:* Magical Realism
*Time of plot:* The mid- to late twentieth century
*Locale:* An Indian reservation near Anadarko, Oklahoma
*First published:* 1991

*Principal characters:*
RAY, a young Native American man
JACKIE, his friend
LINDA, an attractive traditional deer woman
JUNELLA, her equally attractive friend
THE OLD MAN, the deer women's uncle

*The Story*

Two beautiful deer women, Linda and Junella, arrive at a "stomp dance"—a traditional Sioux ceremony that is conducted with certain modifications on an Oklahoma reservation. The dance ground is ringed by a motley assortment of Cadillacs and pickup trucks, whose headlights provide illumination. Two "'skins," Ray and Jackie, arrive at the dance hoping to "snag," that is, to score with, women. Pretending to want to go to the nearby town of Anadarko, the women accept a lift from the men, who cannot believe their good luck, and pile into Ray's pickup.

As the women climb into the truck, Ray thinks that he sees their feet look like deer hooves. After the women ask to stop by a river in order to refresh themselves, they lead the men up a path to their "old house," where their ancient Uncle Thunder is sitting. "I see you've snagged two strong men," the old man says, punning on the term "snag" and commenting sarcastically on the word "strong." Leading the men by their hands, the women then take them to a second ceremonial site—a field where a baseball game is being played.

In the midst of the game, the deer women vanish, leaving Ray and Jackie to search for them futilely. Ray awakens from a deep sleep to find himself lying by a river at midday. Jackie is nowhere to be found, but Junella is beside him. She tells him that "Jackie is staying there," and gives him Jackie's wristwatch as proof. Ray then becomes dizzy. He takes a step toward the woman, but the rock on which she has been sitting is empty.

Fifteen months later Jackie's fate is revealed: A sudden move to Seattle with Linda, the birth of a child, alcoholism, and a premature death for revealing things that he learned inside a mountain that he was not supposed to tell.

The story concludes with an ambiguous image of Ray rushing to catch a subway in San Francisco. On his way to a meeting, he is firmly entrenched in the modern wristwatch world.

## Themes and Meanings

The implied moral of Paula Gunn Allen's story is that the fates suffered by Ray and Jackie are the consequences of their sexist, derogatory, and nontraditional attitudes toward Native American women. There is an instructive, retributive quality underlying the inversion of gender mistreatment. Firmly rooted in the didactic, allegorical, and oral Native American storytelling tradition, the story is meant to teach a lesson, to model an ideal for comportment in general, and particularly behavior between the sexes.

Jackie's slide into alcoholism and premature death can be viewed as his punishment for viewing women as sexual objects and for his dim-witted passivity. Ray notices the women's deerlike feet, but Jackie does not. Ray asks pertinent questions about the women's identity, but Jackie merely shrugs silently. Ray inquires about where they have been taken, but Jackie lapses into an almost catatonic passivity. Of the two men, Jackie is the more overtly sexist: "Well, I used to say I'd walk a mile for a camel . . . but I didn't say anything about snags."

Doubling the male victims allows Allen to prosecute her attack on un-Indian male behavior (Jackie), while simultaneously offering Ray some hope. The latter is evinced by Ray's awakening to the realities of the situation ("maybe those old guys know something, eh?"), his perception of the underlying reasons for Jackie's death (for telling "what he wasn't supposed to tell"), and the fact that he is allowed to return to the world, perhaps wiser for his experience. The story's ambiguous offering of punishment and hope is mirrored in the unforgettable look that Ray gives—"a look that was somehow wounded and yet with a kind of wild hope mixed in."

"Deer Woman" is thus not only an attack on un-Indian male attitudes and actions, but a celebration of the universal power of femininity—particularly Native American womanhood. Women are presented as strong, assertive, and mysterious corrective influences on errant Native American masculinity. Women are both seductresses and guides; indeed, the deer women present themselves as seductresses in order to mask their role as guides to reaffirmation of traditional Native American values. "Deer Woman" is thus a tribute to the lasting relevance of the beliefs practiced by Allen's ancestors. Linda and Junella are the womanly watchdogs of transgressive Indian behavior whom Old Man Thunder dispatches in order to render justice, teach lessons, and give potentially redeemable offenders a second chance to live in accordance with the traditional ways of what Black Elk called "the good Red road." The deer women function as a kind of moral compass governing behavior in general, and behavior between the sexes in particular—a compass aligned not with true north but with true Native American virtues.

## Style and Technique

The thematic content of "Deer Woman" is effectively reinforced by Allen's style, which consists of a variety of elements including sensory detail, sardonic irony, metaphor, foreshadowing, and symbolism. The opening passage affords evidence of her use of effective sensory detail to create a sense of realism and give her setting a feeling of immediacy: "The slowly turning fan inside felt cool"; "They drove for some distance . . . bumping across cattle guards." Her successful appeal to the senses creates an almost Faulknerian sense of place.

One of the finest features of the tale is its grim irony, as the would-be victimizers become victims of their own lust. Perhaps the most striking example of sardonic irony occurs when Ray wryly observes that this "is the only time I've heard of Little Red Riding Hood leading the wolves to Grandma's." In this, the story reinscribes the powerful Lakota Sioux myth of Buffalo Woman, who first brought the sacred pipe to the people of the Northern Plains, and exerted a similarly fatal allure on a young 'skin, whose lust she exploited to bring about his ruin. Allen writes in this same ancient, didactic, oral tradition, using myth to model good and bad Native American behavior, as the vehicle for constructing and disseminating a collective Indian ethos.

At times Allen weds sensory detail to alliteration and metaphor, thereby enhancing the verisimilitude of her writing. For example, she describes the day as "sultry and searing as summer days in Oklahoma get, hot as a sweat lodge." "Deer Woman" is also encoded with symbols that in turn are deeply embedded in the Indian psyche. Whether deployed consciously or unconsciously, they work to underscore the themes of the tale. For instance, in the Native American mythic landscape the river is a traditional symbol of closeness to the source of life, of being in touch with oneself. Thus, the deer women's immersion in the current may be read as a symbol of their intimacy with the everlasting ways of the "traditionals." Their association with the river is reinforced through simile, for "their long hair flowed like black rivers." Likewise, the return of Ray and Jackie to the river, under the guidance of the deer women, may be viewed as a return to the imperishable ways of their ancestors.

Though not a complete list of the elements that make up Allen's style and technique, these examples demonstrate her command of writing and particularly her mastery of the Native American storytelling craft in which she is firmly rooted. At the same time, however, she is breaking new ground in an effort to construct a Native American feminine subjectivity that both situates itself in the conflicted past and orients itself toward an empowered future.

*Stephen G. Brown*

# THE DEFEATED

*Author:* Nadine Gordimer (1923-       )
*Type of plot:* Social realism
*Time of plot:* The 1920's to 1940's
*Locale:* Cape Town, South Africa
*First published:* 1952

### Principal characters:

THE NARRATOR, a student in South Africa and daughter of
 Scottish immigrants who are mine owners
MIRIAM SAIYETOVITZ, her friend, the daughter of Jewish
 immigrant shopkeepers
MR. AND MRS. SAIYETOVITZ, Miriam's parents

*The Story*

As the narrator recalls her student years in Cape Town, South Africa, near which her parents owned a mine, she remembers her long friendship with her schoolmate Miriam Saiyetovitz and Miriam's parents, who owned a concession store.

Against her mother's initial objections, the narrator finds herself drawn into the exotic world of the concession stores where Africans shop. She is enticed by the sights, smells, sounds, and activities of the shopkeepers and the Africans. Though she is careful to keep her physical distance, because she is repulsed by some of the customs, sights, and smells that accompany this busy merchant world, she experiences an excitement and abundance of life that is seemingly missing from her own.

One day, as she visits the shops, she recognizes a schoolmate among the faces in a crowd and befriends Miriam Saiyetovitz (whose name the narrator initially terms "ugly"). The narrator's description of Miriam's mother makes it clear that she is befriending the daughter of a Jewish immigrant family, whose socioeconomic status falls far below that of her own family. Miriam's parents are hardworking, however, and try to give their daughter everything they can. The narrator is impressed that her newfound friend can retrieve a lemonade from the kitchen inside the shop whenever she desires. She also notes that although Miriam does not physically distance herself from the Africans, she seems not to notice them either, talking only of school and how the future will unfold for the two girls. In fact, Miriam appears unaffected by her surroundings in general.

Miriam is invited to the narrator's house for a birthday party but appears to think no more of it than of the concession stores. When Miriam tells her mother about the party, Mrs. Saiyetovitz, in her eagerness to reciprocate, invites the narrator to a party for Miriam that is to be held at their newly built house on the outskirts of town. On the day of the party, however, Miriam takes all of her friends to town instead of her house, to the disappointment of her parents. Her parents rationalize Miriam's actions, believing that she knows better than they do "what is nice and what is right" by virtue of her education. The narrator is eventually introduced into the interior of the store and notes Mr. Saiyetovitz's "hangdog gentleness" toward the two schoolmates, in contrast to his "strange blasts of power" when dealing with the Africans. She learns, too, that Mr. Saiyetovitz's name was changed, from Yanka to John, on his arrival in Cape Town.

The narrator and Miriam continue their friendship through their matriculation year, then decide to continue on to the university. Unlike the Saiyetovitzes, the narrator's parents need not worry about the money to fund an education. The narrator notices that although Miriam's parents own a newly built house, they still spend most of their time at the store. One day, as the narrator and Miriam ride the bus to town in order to purchase a new winter coat with money provided by Miriam's father, Miriam ironically declares her preference for the narrator's father, because he is educated and not a merchant.

During the years at the university, Miriam becomes a "lady," soft, bored, and conforming to whatever environment in which she finds herself. She socializes with young successful Jewish students and vacations in Johannesburg, while the narrator goes home to the mining town. After they become teachers, the two friends part ways. Some years later, the narrator hears that Miriam has married a doctor. One day, while back in Cape Town, the narrator is reminded of the days spent at the concession store, and visits the old shop to inquire after Mr. and Mrs. Saiyetovitz. She finds Miriam's parents, "older, sadder," and waiting "as animals wait in a cage; for nothing." The couple tell her about Miriam's success. She has married a doctor, had a son, and lives in a beautiful home in Johannesburg.

The source of the Saiyetovitzes' pride is also the source of their pain and defeat. They rarely see their daughter and have never been invited to her home. The story ends with a picture of Mr. Saiyetovitz lashing out against an African customer in the back room. The narrator realizes, sadly, how in spite of their own suffering, the Saiyetovitzes are "defeated, and without understanding in their defeat."

*Themes and Meanings*

Nadine Gordimer's "The Defeated" reveals the strong class system of South Africa in the mid-twentieth century—a system based on the exploitation of the labor of others by the ruling class. The most obvious underclass is made up of Africans who work in the mine owned by the narrator's parents. The narrator describes the unhealthy skin color and symptoms of tuberculosis among the mineworkers without naming the disease or its connection to work in the mine. She also fails to connect her own family's prosperity and leisure with the privations suffered by the mineworkers. The second class introduced is the Jewish immigrant class, represented by the Saiyetovitzes. They, too, are "defeated" in their labor, because they work so hard among the very underclass that they, too, seek to rise above.

Gordimer distinguishes among the various sources of affluence and subsistence among the South Africans in Cape Town. The narrator's parents gain wealth through their education and commercial astuteness, while others, belonging to the merchant class, rely on "instinctive peasant craftiness." Still others, such as Mr. Saiyetovitz, lack "craftiness" and so are relegated to "hard . . . dirty work" for which there is little payoff. In every case, affluence ultimately depends on the sweat and blood of someone, though the relationship remains hidden to most people.

Gordimer makes a strong statement about the nature and consequences of the class system in South Africa through the character of Mr. Saiyetovitz. An immigrant forced to change his name and therefore his identity, he must labor just as the even "lowlier" Africans must in order to provide for his family. However, he treats those "below" him as he is treated by those "above" him. Miriam, even more than the narrator's parents and the narrator herself, demonstrates how the labor of others is taken for granted by those who benefit from it. She, too, refuses to recognize the source of her affluence.

## Style and Technique

Gordimer is known for her treatment of complex social and political issues, and "The Defeated" is no exception. At the same time, the story is simply told, enjoyable for its abundance of descriptive detail, and without overt judgment or moralizing. Gordimer effectively employs irony and contrast in her story. She sets up a strong socioeconomic contrast in the backgrounds of the narrator and Miriam. The narrator lives in a quiet, easily afforded home, while Miriam lives in a store, where she witnesses her parents' daily struggle for survival. In this way, Gordimer sets up the expectation that Miriam will be more appreciative of her gains because her parents must work day and night to fund her education. Another expectation is that Mr. Saiyetovitz will empathize with others who share his plight. All of these expectations, when they are foiled, make Gordimer's portrayal of the class system even more powerful and frightening than could be conveyed by her vivid descriptions alone.

Another feature of Gordimer's style that makes the story so powerful is that the narrator, in effect, reports on the action instead of interpreting it. The evidence laid out before the reader during the course of the narrative becomes almost overwhelming by the end of the story. The narrator's reporting leads the reader through a series of predictions and disappointments about predictions about the action and characters. This process builds tension in the reader, as well as suspense, causing the final picture of the Saiyetovitzes to appear all the more anguished. Perhaps it is Gordimer's aim that the reader undergo some of the tension experienced by the South African "defeated."

*Jennifer Vinsky*

# DEFENDER OF THE FAITH

*Author:* Philip Roth (1933-      )
*Type of plot:* Social realism
*Time of plot:* May, 1945, to August, 1945
*Locale:* Camp Crowder, Missouri
*First published:* 1959

*Principal characters:*

SERGEANT NATHAN MARX, the top sergeant of a basic training
  company at Camp Crowder, Missouri
CAPTAIN PAUL BARRETT, the company commander
PRIVATE SHELDON GROSSBART,
PRIVATE LARRY FISHBEIN, and
PRIVATE MICKEY HALPERN, trainees

*The Story*

Sergeant Nathan Marx, a veteran of combat in the European theater, is rotated back to the United States and assigned as top sergeant to a training company in Camp Crowder, Missouri. He soon becomes acquainted with a trainee, Sheldon Grossbart, who appeals to their common Jewish heritage as the rationale for granting him and the two Jewish fellow-draftees whom he dominates, Fishbein and Halpern, a succession of special favors. Grossbart cunningly uses their shared roots in the New York Jewish community to exploit Marx's humaneness, generosity, and sense of fairness. Their relationship is characterized by deviousness and self-serving opportunism on Grossbart's part, while Marx changes from open vulnerability to wariness to righteous indignation at Grossbart's increasingly outrageous conduct.

The first episode revealing their conflict occurs when Grossbart wants Marx's permission to attend Jewish services Friday night yet does not wish to give Gentile recruits the impression that he is ducking the customary "G.I. Party," or barracks cleaning. He insists, "this is a matter of religion, sir," deliberately using the salutation reserved for officers despite Marx's continuing reminder to address him as "Sergeant." At the synagogue Marx observes, from a back-row seat, Grossbart and Fishbein playfully pouring the contents of the sacramental wine to and from each other's cups, while their prayer books remain closed—until they notice his presence.

Army food becomes an issue for intrigue. Although Grossbart has a lusty appetite for it, he composes a letter for his father to sign and send to his congressman, complaining that his son is forced to eat nonkosher meals that Orthodox Judaism forbids. After Marx has been forced to explain Jewish tradition to his irate captain, Captain Barrett contrasts Grossbart's "goldbricking" to Marx's valor under fire: "Do you hear him [Marx] peeping about the food? Do you?" Formidably flexible, Grossbart writes another letter for his father's signature, addressed to the general who is the post commander, praising Marx as being "in part responsible for Sheldon's changing his mind about the dietary laws" and calling the sergeant "a credit to the U.S. Army and the Jewish people."

For a time, Grossbart eschews scrambling for special privileges. Then he confronts Marx with a request for a weekend pass to celebrate Passover with St. Louis relatives. At first Marx is firm: "No passes during basic, Grossbart." Grossbart, however, weeps and wears down Marx's defenses. After Marx has issued weekend passes not only to Grossbart but also to Fishbein and Halpern, he muses to himself, "Who was I to have been feeling so grudging, so tight-hearted? After all, I wasn't being asked to move the world." Marx soon discovers, however, that Grossbart and his friends never did attend the Passover dinner—they enjoyed a Chinese meal instead. Brazenly, Grossbart even presents Marx with an egg roll as a souvenir of the occasion.

The egg roll proves the last straw for Marx's tolerance. He now becomes Grossbart's enraged enemy. When he discovers that Grossbart is the only company recruit who will be assigned to a safe, stateside station at Fort Monmouth, New Jersey, and all the others are to be shipped to the Pacific combat zone, he smells connivance and goes into counteraction. This time, he pulls strings of his own, phoning the sergeant in charge of cutting orders to ask him for a favor: Marx tells him that a Jewish trainee in his company is burning to see action, having had a brother killed in Europe. Could Sergeant Wright therefore change one Monmouth order to the Pacific? Sergeant Wright can and does.

*Themes and Meanings*

This is a complex, powerfully imagined tale portraying a conflict of loyalties and delineating the difficulty of being a decent and fair-minded person in a world beset with opposing priorities.

For Grossbart, Jewishness has no devotional or ritualistic substance. He is a cleverly conniving barracks lawyer who poses as a defender of the Jewish faith to manipulate Marx and other authority figures into granting him undeserved privileges. He articulates litanies of whining and wheedling, flattery and hypocrisy—all in a consuming desire for special treatment.

Marx's character is deeply layered: He wants to be a good person, a good soldier, and a good Jew—in that order. As a human being, he is at first vulnerable to Grossbart's performance as the victim in danger of having his rights crushed by the dehumanizing institution that the army often is. However, as a soldier, he wants to treat his trainees equitably and humanely, balancing obedience to military regulations with empathy for the loneliness and confusion of young men uprooted from their families in wartime. As a Jew he has a particularly thorny dilemma: how to observe his tradition yet also fulfill his military duties; how to avoid the sentimental claims of Jewish solidarity when they contradict the ethical mandate for justice and equity; how to be strong without bullying; how to be compassionate without showing weakness.

Philip Roth concludes the story with a twist: Grossbart accepts his fate, to be treated no differently from his comrades, and Marx accepts his own fate after "resisting with all my will an impulse to turn and seek pardon for my vindictiveness." Thus, Roth stresses the existential nature of the protagonist's moral anguish: Marx finds training camp a far trickier moral terrain than the battlefield. He discovers that the best—for him, the only possible—way of defending the faith of Jews is to defend the faith of all recruits in the cause of a just community, to watch out not for one individual but "for all of us."

## Style and Technique

Roth's style is brisk, pointed, compact, and morally lucid. He masters with unobtrusive authority the sharply observed details of characteristic gestures, such as Grossbart sitting on the edge of Marx's desk the first time he approaches him, and then, on being ordered to stand on his feet, slipping up to the corner of the desk—"not quite sitting, but not quite standing, either." Then there is Fishbein, "his long yellow face a dying light bulb" while "his eyelids beat a tattoo." Captain Barrett is observed by Marx: "His helmet liner squashed down so far on his head that I couldn't even see his eyes."

Roth's ear is even better than his eye. Grossbart and Marx duel in a vernacular charged with caustic, incisive urban idioms stripped to their starkest rhythms. "I owe nobody nothing," Grossbart shouts in their climactic scene. "I've got the right to watch out for myself." Replies Marx, "For each other we have to learn to watch out, Sheldon."

Ironies pervade the story. The title phrase, "Defender of the Faith," mockingly alludes to a traditional obligation of English monarchs. More directly, it refers to the role of religious champion that Marx finds himself filling, no matter how unintentionally. Not only does Sergeant Marx defend the honor of his own heritage by rejecting Grossbart's advantage mongering, but also he can succeed in restoring the balance of the scales of justice only by using Grossbart's exploitive skills against him. In lying to Sergeant Wright regarding Grossbart's thirst for combat, Marx has to "pull a Grossbart," has to usurp Grossbart's identity as an unprincipled manipulator. For once, Roth indicates, a worthy end does justify unworthy means.

*Gerhard Brand*

# THE DELICATE PREY

*Author:* Paul Bowles (1910-1999)
*Type of plot:* Grotesque
*Time of plot:* The early twentieth century
*Locale:* Mauretania (North Africa)
*First published:* 1950

*Principal characters:*
> Two FILALA TRIBESMEN, merchants and brothers
> DRISS, their young nephew
> A MOUNGARI TRIBESMAN
> ECH CHIBANI, a Filali

## The Story

"The Delicate Prey" is the narrative of a journey through isolated places and hidden terrors. Three Filala tribesmen and leather merchants are about to move their business to a new town. Two are brothers—serious, older men. Driss, their nephew, is a young man interested in the pleasures of love.

To arrive at their destination, Tessalit, as soon as possible, the brothers choose a route through a remote and dangerous region. The area is prey to the marauding Reguibat tribe, known for its ferocity. An insignificant company of three men and their camels, so the brothers argue, offers no temptation to raiders seeking rich caravans. Still, they travel carefully, maintaining close watch at night.

Several days out, the travelers spot a lone figure moving toward them, matching his course with theirs. As the figure approaches, he hails them in friendship. The brothers are relieved to see that he is not dressed as a Reguibat but observe him carefully for any irregularity. Driss is troubled by the man's small eyes that "give out nothing," but is dissuaded from his suspicion by his uncles' reaction. The man identifies himself as a Moungari, a respected tribe from a holy area. The stranger offers his skills as a hunter if allowed to join the group. Skeptical about finding game in these remote regions, the brothers accept him to increase their numbers in the dangerous environment.

One morning the Moungari goes off alone, on foot, to hunt gazelle among the hills. As distant shots are heard, first one brother, then the next, goes off to join the hunt. Driss is left alone, disappointed, to watch the camp. He dozes in the heat but is suddenly awakened. He feels an evil presence about him. Immediately he recognizes the danger he saw in the man's eyes and knows the fate of his uncles. Seeking safety in the open desert, he mounts his camel and sets off blindly. He lets himself be carried along, without purpose, for several hours before he stops and heads for camp. What if he is only foolish and his uncles are cooking the gazelle even now? He cannot bear the thought of the older men's mocking laughter.

As Driss approaches camp, a bullet whizzes by his head. A second catches him in the arm. Before he finds shelter among the rocks and grabs his fallen gun, the Moungari is on him, pinning him down with a rifle. There is a new, peculiar intensity in the man's face that Driss knows only comes from hashish. The man quickly strips the boy, using a razor to cut away his robes, and binds his wrists and hands. Possessed by the excitement of the drug, the Moungari in one stroke severs Driss's sex.

Startled by a camel's grunt, the Moungari wheels about, nervous. He imagines the boy, who can see nothing in his pain, a witness to his fright. There is one last indignity he can inflict on the boy, this time with leisurely pleasure. In the morning, he stifles the boy's moans by severing his head.

Once the body is concealed, the Moungari sets off for Tessalit, where he attempts to sell the Filala merchandise. Filala leather is unmistakable and sold by no other tribe. Ech Chibani, a local Filali, is suspicious, and persuades the French commandant to question the man. As the French leave, the Moungari remains sitting, unaware that he has been tried and sentenced.

Justice, however, is left to the Filala tribe. The tribesmen return, and, above his screams of innocence, they bind the Moungari. They wait calmly for night, drinking tea, before setting out into the desert. They place the Moungari, tightly trussed, into a deep pit and fill it in until only his bald head is visible. There the Moungari waits for day, for the inevitable heat and thirst, and finally for the visions; he will lose hold on reality and his sense of self, and die.

*Themes and Meanings*

In "The Delicate Prey," the harsh surroundings match the harsh realities of tribal jealousies and loyalties on which Paul Bowles bases his stories. The route the brothers take exists, as do each of the tribes with their hostilities toward one another. The loyalty of Ech Chibani to his tribesmen reflects an ancient and efficient mode of justice in which responsibility rests with the family, not with a state. The French do not interfere with traditions centuries old but let the Filala handle what is a family matter.

Another strong tradition is the fundamental sacredness of property. Each man must respect the property of others and the bond of trust crucial to survival in harsh environments. The uncles understand this and comment on the trust the Moungari shows in going off alone. In this case, that sacred trust is used perversely to trick the old men. The Moungari flaunts his villainy, however, and seals his fate by trying to sell property that belongs to others.

Bowles plays with complex relationships between the hunter and the prey. The gazelle is surely a delicate prey. By pursuing this imaginary game, however, the uncles are drawn into the trap prepared by the Moungari. More frightening is Driss's transformation into the delicate prey. Caught by his hunter, he is bound hand and foot. He is brutally dressed by the Moungari as any hunter might dress a carcass. However, the hunter himself cannot escape becoming the prey as the Filala seek revenge. He, like Driss, is trussed and left to his fate in the desert. There is a precarious balance between the hunter and his prey, one that is easily disturbed.

Of all the characters in the story, Driss is the only one depicted in any detail. He is a young man who lives in his dreams and fails to trust his understanding of the world around him. He daydreams of love and the easy favors of the town beauties. As his uncles are being murdered, he is dreaming of the excitement of the hunt and the glory he is missing. He lets himself be readily convinced by his uncles' perceptions about the stranger even though his immediate reaction is distrust. Even when he acknowledges the danger and knows the truth, he lets himself again be persuaded by his imaginings of mocking laughter. For this reluctance to trust his intuition, Driss loses his life.

"The Delicate Prey" reflects Bowles's conviction that human civilization is fragile. Stripped of his superficial civility, man is a cruel animal capable of horrifying brutality. Hashish releases the Moungari's savage nature. No drug is needed for the rest of society. The veneer of modern civilization is thin, and the ancient traditions of blood revenge are strong and easily tapped. With a quick wink, the French commandant breaks that veneer and hands the Moungari over to an ancient justice, gruesome but swift.

## Style and Technique

The story is marked by a muted, direct style that lets the action remain sharply in focus. There is little characterization, and the scenes are drawn with little description. There is a great economy of language as the author focuses on the events and their consequences without commentary. Bowles captures the exotic nature of his setting by using French and Arabic words: *hanoute, hammada, aoudad, mehari, mechoui, quartier reserve*. The author provides no explanations and lets the context of his words supply the meaning.

Bowles carefully weaves the motif of music throughout the work to create relationships between characters and events. Driss often plays a small flute on his watches; he prefers sad songs for the desert, regarding livelier tunes suitable only for the joys of town. He is destined never to hear brighter tunes again. The second uncle goes off to his death singing of "date palms and hidden smiles." As he waits alone at camp, Driss is too restless to play. As he approaches the camp after his flight, he hears singing, too indistinct to be recognized but immediately perceived as that of the Moungari. The last song is reserved for the Moungari. As he loses his mind in the punishing heat of the desert, the dust blows along the ground "into his mouth as he sang."

A smaller motif is that of tea. When the travelers first accept the stranger into their group, they make tea to seal their friendship. The Moungari, who violates this sign of trust and hospitality by his brutal actions, finds himself trapped by the Filala as he makes tea. As he lies trussed in a corner, the avenging tribesmen sit quietly and drink the tea that the Moungari has brewed.

*Joan A. Robertson*

# DELTA AUTUMN

*Author:* William Faulkner (1897-1962)
*Type of plot:* Realism
*Time of plot:* November, 1940
*Locale:* Mississippi
*First published:* 1942

> *Principal characters:*
> ISAAC MCCASLIN, the central consciousness of the story
> ROTH EDMONDS, his kinsman and owner of the plantation he
> relinquished
> THE NEGRESS, Roth's lover and a distant relative

*The Story*

The story is set on the eve of the 1940 presidential election. As Isaac McCaslin and his fellow hunters drive the two hundred miles it takes to get to the wilderness, he reflects on his sixty years of hunting and of how the land has been radically changed by human habitation. His life seems to draw inward as the wilderness itself draws inward in retreat from human progress.

The first half of the story is told almost exclusively from Isaac's point of view. He seems noble, selfless, and magnanimous—even in the face of the fact that his beloved wilderness has been virtually destroyed. The other hunters, especially Roth, are extremely cynical about the present. Roth, who is in a foul temper over an affair that is ending badly, taunts Isaac and tries to get him to say that better men hunted the land in the old days. Isaac, however, is serene in his faith in humankind, that human beings are only a little better than their circumstances usually allow them to be.

Isaac's values have, in fact, isolated him. Although the hunters respect him for his bond with nature, he is as outmoded as the wilderness with which he seems to be coeval. This becomes apparent when he has trouble keeping up with the conversation in which one of the hunters, Legate, taunts Roth about the "doe," the woman he has been seeing during their hunting trips. Roth seems disgusted with the whole human race, not only with Legate's barbs, when he scorns Isaac's romantic view of the congress between men and women as close to God-like. "Then there are some Gods in this world I wouldn't want to touch, and with a damn long stick," he retorts.

The point of Roth's remarks is apparent in the second half of the story. The men have left for the first day's hunting. In the past few years, Isaac has not joined them immediately, and Roth, taking advantage of Isaac's position, asks him to give an envelope to a woman who may visit the camp. Isaac chides Roth for not having the courage to face the woman himself. When she arrives, Isaac is hard with her. In spite of his criticism of Roth, he is sure the woman has been given ample warning. Indeed, she admits Roth has been true to his "code."

As the woman begins to explain about her family, about her mother taking in washing, Isaac suddenly realizes that she is a "nigger." The harshness of the word, especially after his eloquent evocation of the wilderness and of the love between men and women, is shocking. He, in turn, is shocked to learn not only that the woman is a "Negress" but also that she is related to his family.

Suddenly a flood of details about the woman, details he has observed but not registered, make him realize that an unsuspecting Roth has loved a woman who is the descendant of a black woman by whom his grandfather had a son he would not acknowledge. Isaac compounds this family sin by advising the woman to go North, to marry a man of her race. In a frenzy of condemnation, Isaac thinks of "this land which man has deswamped and denuded and derivered in two generations so that white men can own plantations and commute every night to Memphis and black men own plantations and ride in jim crow cars to Chicago to live in millionaires' mansions on Lakeshore Drive." Isaac has preserved for himself a kind of purity in his reverence for the wilderness, and his isolation has kept him from the messiness of affairs such as Roth's, but his noble repudiation of plantation immorality has also led to his misunderstanding the modern world of which Roth, at least, is a part.

To the baby boy the woman has had by Roth, Isaac offers, as a weak reconciling gesture, a hunting horn, the symbol of all the good he has learned in his years in the wilderness. At the very end of the story, hearing that a deer has been killed, Isaac says to himself that it is the very doe, the principle of womanhood that he defended against Roth's bitterness but that he himself has defiled in his confrontation with the "Negress."

## Themes and Meanings

The beautiful writing and themes of "Delta Autumn" remain intact when it is read alone, but the story's larger significance and resonance can be understood only by situating it within the context of *Go Down, Moses* (1942), the novel for which it was written. Like much of the novel, the story centers on the character of Isaac McCaslin, a veteran hunter who reveres the wilderness, deplores the civilization that is destroying it, and refuses to own or to run the plantation that his forebears helped to build with slavery.

Written on the verge of America's entry into World War II, "Delta Autumn" explores in the context of a hunting story a country that has gone through momentous changes in the twentieth century and is uncertain of the extent to which its founders' values remain relevant. Isaac and the hunters debate Roth's fierce attack on the degradation of the times. Dictators will prevail in a country where men sing "God Bless America in bars at midnight" and wear dime-store flags in their lapels, Roth predicts. Unemployment, welfare, and the centralization of government are all deplored and debated.

This complicated political world is juxtaposed against the grandeur and purity of the wilderness. Very appealing images of nature make human corruption even more intolerable. However, the narrator make clear that to hold to a vanishing wilderness is to become caught in the rigidity that Isaac reveals at the end of the story.

In this respect, the "Negress" is a striking figure, for with her northern pronunciation and educated manner she ought to scorn Roth's code and Isaac's antique ethics. Although she does criticize both men, she feels great tenderness for them—after all, they are her kin even if they do not know enough to accept her. She is steadfastly loyal to her love for Roth and will not deny her roots in the very shame that led her father, James Beauchamp, to leave the McCaslin-Edmonds plantation.

The "Negress" is the best evidence in the story that times indeed have changed, changed more than Isaac or Roth have realized. She is the only character in the story to reconcile herself to the past and the present, to Roth's "code" and to her own sense of family and of the love that a man and woman should have for each other. By failing to make the transition to the present, and to see no more than its corrupt aspects, Isaac has rejected his own family, a part of himself.

*Style and Technique*

The language of this story brilliantly captures the realities that divide the characters from one another. In long, nearly hypnotic sentences, the reader is carried by the flow of memory into the past while never losing sight of the present. A single sentence, for example, begins by describing a car and two trucks forming a caravan on a gravel road, "lurching and splashing and sliding among the ruts," and by its very rhythm shifts to the cadence, the "retrograde of his [Isaac's] remembering," so that the road, in his mind, gives over to "the ancient pathway of bear and deer." Such sentences, in other words, mimic the action of Isaac's consciousness, which constantly moves from present to past.

Clipped dialogue and short scenes among the hunters efficiently provide the context in which Isaac's reveries take place, and the final dialogue with the "Negress" shows the consequences of his absenting himself from worldly affairs. This kind of technique forces the reader to reevaluate Roth's harshness and Isaac's seemingly saintly behavior. Each man denies vital parts of himself and of reality. Roth has meant the hunting trip to be his last one, and Isaac has reneged on similar decisions in years past. That both men return to the hunting grounds in spite of knowing that the world of the hunters is now defunct is a sure sign of their inability to come up with a set of values that might bridge past and present.

*Carl Rollyson*

# THE DELUGE AT NORDERNEY

*Author:* Isak Dinesen (Baroness Karen Blixen-Finecke, 1885-1962)
*Type of plot:* Psychological
*Time of plot:* 1835
*Locale:* Norderney, a bath on the west coast of Holstein, a duchy of Denmark
*First published:* 1934

> *Principal characters:*
> CARDINAL HAMILCAR VON SEHESTEDT, a seventy-three-year-old
>   divine
> KASPARSON, his valet or secretary
> MISS MALIN NAT-OG-DAG, a wealthy and aristocratic maiden
>   lady close to sixty years of age
> COUNTESS CALYPSO VON PLATEN HALLERMUND, her sixteen-
>   year-old companion
> JONATHAN MAERSK, a melancholic young man among the
>   survivors at Norderney

## The Story

The storyteller, looking back from the twentieth century, sets her tale before the backdrop of Romantically influenced early nineteenth century European culture. Fashionable society, in search of desolate scenery, moved its resorts to such areas as the wild seacoast of what was then a part of Denmark. In late summer of 1835, a terrible storm churned the sea, causing it to rise and break the dikes. Disastrous flooding ensued.

Cardinal Hamilcar von Sehestedt had been living for the summer in a small cottage near the bath at Norderney; there he was collecting his writings into a book on the Holy Ghost. Of an old and distinguished family, the cardinal was famous throughout Europe for his insight and compassion. He had traveled throughout the world and wielded great influence over all he met; he was credited with the power to work miracles. His only companion in the cottage that summer was Kasparson, his valet or secretary, a former actor who had known various adventures and who spoke several languages and read widely.

During the flood, the cardinal's cottage was destroyed. Kasparson was killed; the cardinal was wounded and wore a bloody bandage around his head during his rescue work. Despite his wound, the cardinal labored steadily all through the day of the flood to rescue survivors. Late in the day, he traveled to the bath to retrieve a group of visitors for whom there had been no room in the earlier boat. As the party returned with him to safety, they passed a castaway farm family unable to escape the rising water; because the boat would not hold the additional load, the group was forced to decide who would remain behind to wait for a returning rescue barge. The cardinal, affirming his safety in God's hands, announced that he would stay. Not to be outdone, the eccen-

tric Miss Malin Nat-og-Dag determined to stay also; her companion, Countess Calypso von Platen Hallermund, would not leave without her. Young Jonathan Maersk
roused himself to action and agreed to stay with them. The four survivors found refuge in the hayloft of a flooded farmhouse and settled in to wait for rescue or death.

The storyteller has set the stage, and the drama begins. Once closed inside the loft,
the four establish the terms of their coexistence. The cardinal asks Miss Malin to act
as hostess and treat the loft as her salon. The company dines on bread; the two older
people drink from a keg of gin.

At this point, the storyteller offers an account of Miss Malin's life. She is and has
long been a somewhat fanatic virgin. Earlier in life, she selected a prince to marry, but
when he died before their wedding, she renounced the idea of marriage. At the age of
fifty she came into a large fortune and then passed into a kind of madness, a condition
in which she remains.

Following this narrative interlude, the action in the loft resumes as the cardinal proposes that each of those present reveal himself to the company by telling his story.
Maersk goes first, calling his tale "The Story of Timon of Assens." His story concerns
his learning that he is the illegitimate son of a nobleman. On learning of his birth, he
became, unwittingly, a man of fashion; everything he did became further proof of his
noble breeding.

As he concludes his tale, Miss Malin realizes that she must have him as a husband
for Calypso. In pursuit of this end, she recounts the girl's story in a fantastic style
more full of glamour and strangeness than Maersk's tale. Calypso was reared by her
misogynistic uncle, the poet Count Seraphina. She decided to unsex herself in order to
fit into the count's environment, but at the moment she prepared to do so, she came to
her senses and escaped to the protection of her godmother, Miss Malin.

At the conclusion of her tale, Miss Malin has the cardinal marry Calypso and
Maersk with a ritual suited to what will be a purely spiritual union. In their present
state in the loft, a state that may end only in death, they have no need of procreation.

Following the ceremony, Miss Malin and the cardinal discuss matters theological
and political. Miss Malin asks the cardinal if he believes in the fall of humankind; he
answers that he believes instead that humankind serves a fallen divinity. Then, to illustrate that there exists something worse than eternal damnation, he offers to contribute to the evening's entertainment by telling a story that he calls "The Wine of the Tetrarch." The story recounts an encounter between the apostle Peter and a troubled
stranger on the first Wednesday after Easter. The stranger, after identifying Peter as
one of Jesus's disciples, tells the apostle a curious story of his recent participation in
the theft of some valuable wine. Caught in the course of his crime, he was arrested, but
now he is free. All wine now tastes bitter to him. He reveals himself to be Barabbas
and claims that his name will be remembered.

After concluding his tale in the early hours before dawn, the cardinal reveals himself to be Kasparson; he struck and killed the cardinal early the previous morning. His
revelation seems to negate the value of all he has said before, but Kasparson reestablishes himself as a figure of dignity, a creator of a great role; he has become the cardi-

nal and appropriated a part of his spirit. Miss Malin sees in him a kindred soul and enters into a sort of "marriage" with him. She offers her lips to him; he kisses her. She lifts the hem of her dress and finds that the water has risen in the loft. They will not be rescued.

### Themes and Meanings

"The Deluge at Norderney" contains a wide variety of Isak Dinesen's characteristic themes. Like the other stories in *Seven Gothic Tales* (1934), this tale deals with characters who create their worlds and their identities through telling stories. In this particular case, Dinesen places her characters in a setting that becomes quite literally a stage, a circle of light in the darkness. She positions the characters carefully and tracks their movements within the confined space as they take turns narrating.

The cardinal, in proposing the tale-telling, furthers the stagecraft by introducing the mask image. In revealing themselves, the characters will "let fall the mask." As he quickly points out, however, masks may reveal more than they conceal; a clever woman at a masquerade, he says, will choose a mask that reveals some quality that her everyday life conceals. The stage is set for each character to be known by his or her mask.

In telling their stories, the characters show their understanding of the world and their place within it. Maersk shows the wit and nobility in his blood. Miss Malin, in narrating Calypso's story, proves that she possesses even greater wit and imagination than the young man. The cardinal's story is a revelation of his true identity and a statement of his understanding of the complexity of his role; he is Barabbas to the cardinal's Christ.

The presentation of their masks brings the cardinal and Miss Malin to a state of self-realization that prepares them to meet the death that comes with the rising water. The two young people, whose stories show them to be appropriately aware of their identities, sleep peacefully in the loft and will die in innocence. By their masks the characters have come to know one another as the reader has come to know each of them. With this resolution, the story concludes.

### Style and Technique

Because "The Deluge at Norderney" unfolds by means of stories told by the characters, each tale must form a building block within the frame of the whole story. Each of the tales within the tale serves as a device, a sort of extended dialogue, which advances the action of the story. The intensity of the tales increases progressively, leading finally to the revelation following the most fantastic tale, "The Wine of the Tetrarch."

The beginning sentence of each tale follows a pause that heightens anticipation of the action to come. Then, with a flourish, the teller begins his tale with a statement that indicates a new development of the story's themes. Maersk begins: "If you had happened to live in Copenhagen, . . . you would have heard of me, for there I was, at a time, much talked about." His is a romantic tale full of barons, ladies, and poets.

"Count Seraphina," Miss Malin begins, "meditated much upon celestial matters." What follows is a fabulously romantic tale containing a mad poet and a dim castle through which the innocent Calypso wanders. The cardinal's tale is different in tone but evokes the greatest mystery of all. He begins: "As, then, upon the first Wednesday after Easter . . . the Apostle Simon, called Peter, was walking down the streets of Jerusalem, . . . deeply absorbed in the thought of the resurrection." In his tale, the cardinal creates a parallel between the stolen and buried wine that Barabbas planned to dig up and drink and the mystical crucifixion and burial of Christ, on whose resurrection Peter meditates.

Each of the tales treats in an increasingly fantastic form the theme of self-knowledge and understanding. As the mysteries deepen, the depth and quality of the tale-teller's understanding grow as well. Maersk realizes that aristocracy is a state of the spirit; Calypso has seen the relation of the physical and the spiritual in her womanhood; the cardinal has penetrated the mystery of the Holy Spirit, a truly great spirit moving among men in strange ways. Following the cardinal's revelation, Dinesen takes her developed themes and weaves them together in the tale's final pages to conclude her story of spiritual unmasking.

*Beverly A. Findley*

# THE DEMON LOVER

*Author:* Elizabeth Bowen (1899-1973)
*Type of plot:* Psychological
*Time of plot:* 1941
*Locale:* London during the blitz
*First published:* 1941

*Principal character:*
KATHLEEN DROVER, a middle-aged wife and mother

*The Story*

A prosaic and dependable woman in her early forties, Kathleen Drover returns to her home in the Kensington area of London one afternoon to retrieve articles for herself and her family, who have taken refuge in the country from the blitz. As she enters the deserted street, a feeling of familiarity and strangeness overwhelms her. The German rockets have taken their toll on the street, on the square in which it is situated, on the house, and, the reader soon learns, on Kathleen herself.

She opens the door of the closed house and is immediately aware of the dead air that greets her. As she makes her way to her bedroom to retrieve the things she has come to fetch, the furniture and the marks on the floors and on the wall remind her of her life between two wars. She soon notices that the humid air outside has given way to rain.

Seeing a letter on the hall table, she is annoyed that it has not been forwarded to her by either the postal service or the caretaker. She notes that the letter has no stamps on it and wonders how it could have made its way there because the caretaker has, ostensibly, been away for several weeks. She goes up the stairs, enters her former bedroom, and reads the letter, which bears that day's date. The brief message, signed K., reminds her of a promise that she made twenty-five years ago when she was engaged to a soldier who later died in World War I. The sender states that he is sure that, even though Kathleen has left London, she will keep the rendezvous. She is frightened not only by the message but also by the mysterious means by which it has found its way to her, by the fact that her every action may have been observed by an unknown person.

As she goes about gathering the items she has come to collect, she is haunted by her memories of the mysterious soldier whom she promised to marry twenty-five years before. She remembers the "unnatural promise" that he exacted from her. Her most vivid remembrance of him, however, is tactile—the feel of the brass button of his uniform against her hand—and she looks to see if the imprint of it is still on her palm. The twenty-five years that have passed since their last meeting dissolve like smoke in her moment of present awareness. She thinks that she cannot remember what her lover did to make her plight so sinister a troth, but as she recovers the emotion that occasioned the promise, she remembers. What she cannot remember is her lover's face.

She recalls that his death caused in her a "dislocation." She remembers that in the last week of his leave, she was not herself. She also remembers her parents' relief that their daughter would not marry the mysterious young man to whom she had engaged herself, and their belief that, after a suitable period of mourning, she would return to normal activity. However, for years no suitors had presented themselves. Much later, when she was in her early thirties, to her parents' and her own surprise, she married William Drover and later bore him two children, the second being a difficult birth.

While making her preparations to leave the house, Kathleen examines and then dismisses the notion of supernatural intervention in her present life. She thinks, however, that she must concern herself with the appointed hour to which the note refers. Having heard the clock strike six, she assumes that she has sufficient time to complete her chores, walk to the taxi ramp at the bottom of the square, find a cab, return to the house for her parcels, and catch her train to the country. As she listens at the top of the staircase, she is disturbed by a draft of dead air that suggests to her that someone is leaving the basement by a door or window. She leaves the house, walks quickly to the cab rank, enters the taxi, and realizes that it has turned back toward the house without her having given directions. She scratches at the glass panel, looks into the driver's eyes for what seems an eternity, and screams as the car speeds into the deserted streets of the city.

*Themes and Meanings*

"The Demon Lover" can be read as a modern retelling of the folk legend and the ballads concerning the return of a lover from the dead to reclaim his earthly bride. As such, the story fulfills the finest demands of the tradition, for K. returns from the dead to exact from Kathleen the promise she made to him twenty-five years earlier. The taxi ride into an Unreal City at the story's end suggests that the lover has found his bride and is holding her to her bargain, to be his in death as in life. However, this is perhaps not the most rewarding meaning of Elizabeth Bowen's story.

In a postscript to *The Demon Lover* (1945), a collection that contains "The Demon Lover" along with other stories that examine the effects of war on those who stay at home, Elizabeth Bowen addresses the central theme of the volume: "life, mechanized by the control of war-time . . . emotionally torn and impoverished by change." In "The Demon Lover" the intensity of an emotion lived in one period of war is revived twenty-five years later by the pressures of another war. The essential meaning of the story can then be interpreted as a nervous collapse brought on by war. Insofar as most novels and stories dealing with war concentrate on the conflict itself, Bowen's view of the effects on civilians of war's devastation is remarkable.

*Style and Technique*

"The Demon Lover," a third-person narrative, achieves its effects by means of the technique of juxtaposition. What appears at first to be a tale of the supernatural becomes in fact an account of a nervous breakdown. The imaginative paralleling of the ghost tale and the case history is achieved primarily through concentration on the details of setting. The boarded-up house, the reluctant lock, the dead air of the hallway, the mysterious letter for whose presence no rational explanation can be made, the mysterious lover from the past, the chiming bells emphasizing the passage of clock time as opposed to emotional time, the betrothed who seems to have no will of her own, and the persistent rain all combine to create a compelling and provocative ambience. Even the claw marks made on the floor by the absent piano assume an eerie significance.

The story also makes use of flashbacks to emphasize the notion that the past, though forgotten, exists in the mind to be recalled by the symbols and images of the present. The girl Kathleen promises in 1916 to marry a soldier who dies in the war. She suffers a psychic "dislocation," the seriousness of which she does not fully comprehend. No suitable young men present themselves for marriage for at least a decade, a comment on the decimation of a generation by the machine of war. Kathleen marries at the age of thirty-two and has two children. She is, furthermore, in her early forties, confronting another change in her life. She is like the cracked teacup mentioned in the story, from which time has evaporated, leaving a residue of memory. There are in Kathleen's psyche, symbolized by the house, "cracks in the structure," and there is nothing that she can do about them.

The letter signed K., her own initial, may be a hallucination, a means of restoring the past to the present. Dependable, prosaic Kathleen Drover, her family's mainstay against time and change, succumbs to the pressures of World War II. The fear of death from the sky, the feeling of desuetude and decay brought to the city by the blitz, and the burdens of responsibility to herself as she was and as she is all combine to catalyze a nervous collapse that manifests itself as the return of a former lover from the dead.

The most compelling sequence in the story, Proustian in the immediacy with which it is rendered, is that in which Kathleen recovers the past as her younger self says good-bye to her doomed young lover in her family's garden. Past emotion overwhelms present inhibitions to fuse into a single overwhelming sensation: Kathleen reexperiences her promise and looks to her palm, feeling again the welt left by the button of her lover's uniform.

*A. A. DeVitis*

# DEMONOLOGY

*Author:* Rick Moody (1961-    )
*Type of plot:* Metafiction, realism
*Time of plot:* The 1990's
*Locale:* Suburban Hackettstown, New Jersey
*First published:* 1996

> *Principal characters:*
> THE NARRATOR, a man remembering his sister
> MEREDITH, his sister

*The Story*

"Demonology" consists of chronologically discontinuous fragments, many of which detail the last two days of Meredith's life; the rest offer apparently random vignettes through which the narrator remembers his sister. The story begins with Meredith taking her children out trick-or-treating on Halloween, and initially, it appears to be a sympathetic portrait of a woman by her loving brother.

Various flashbacks show that Meredith comes from a reasonably well-off family and that she lived an exuberantly hedonistic life as a young woman. Members of both her immediate and extended family (including the unnamed narrator) have had problems with alcohol, but Meredith controlled her drinking, settled down, and become a devoted mother to her son and daughter. Meredith, who works hard at a lackluster job in a photo lab, enjoys amateur photography, and this passion is reflected in the story's disjointed paragraphs, which resemble narrative snapshots. Through these snapshots, Meredith is revealed to be a spirited woman who once sold a camera to the British rock star Pete Townshend of the Who and made a point of telling him she was not a fan of his music.

Her brother, the narrator, does not mention until more than halfway through the story that Meredith has died. He meticulously describes her final moments, though it is evident that he was not present and is imagining what actually occurred. After returning from choir practice and tucking her children into bed, Meredith suffers a seizure, possibly an aneurysm, and collapses in her daughter's bedroom. The remainder of the story describes in considerable detail the physiological changes that took place in Meredith's body after her collapse and her family's immediate response to the emergency and then concludes with the narrator self-consciously deliberating on the story's inadequate narrative and compositional strategies in the face of his sister's death.

*Themes and Meanings*

Although "Demonology" is made up of disjunctive fragments, it is a haunting example of contemporary realism. The narrator ruminates on the problematic nature of time and the shock of death and also presents an acute depiction of suburban America, in particular what it is like to raise young children while working at a dead-end job. The narrator shows his sister Meredith acting within the cultural and economic practices created by late twentieth century capitalism. Her children go out for Halloween dressed as Walt Disney characters.

Meredith's position in the economic order is marginal, and she is alienated in a Marxist sense in that her work is unfulfilling, repetitive, and pays little. Her life pivots around her family and private interests; however, because of her poverty and the demands of motherhood, she is continually exhausted. In many ways, the story is a indictment of a society that promises much to its citizens but distributes wealth in a very unequal manner. The narrator's rage at a social system in which Meredith has no recognized identity apart from her role as parent and consumer is counterbalanced by his insistence that her life was worthy of celebration. In a broad sense, the story implies that art pays attention to individual lives and the particularities of experience, whereas corporate power defaces the individual and reduces human complexity to the banalities expressed in popular animated films.

Facing his loss, the narrator looks hard into the metaphysical abyss that death creates. He finds it impossible to understand not only how the multitudinous incidents that constituted Meredith's life somehow vanished when she died but also how a myriad of potential future moments, desires, and hopes also suddenly disappeared that night. Although the story focuses on the narrator's memories of Meredith, these remembrances are less concerned with static moments than with those that are charged with the mysterious characteristics of temporal change. A minor detail such as the photograph Meredith took of their father and stepmother boating, for example, identifies a specific moment; however, the image also implicitly contains the presumably lengthy passage of time that led to the disintegration of the marriage of their father and mother.

The fact that the story is set around Halloween—and that the narrator refers to Meredith's experiences on previous Halloweens—is significant because the holiday is a recurrent cultural event that is nevertheless pointedly specific. Each Halloween not only is a repetition of those that came before but also forecasts those still to come. However, each Halloween is markedly different from all the rest, a fact underscored by Meredith's death. Further, the holiday itself deals with the boundary between life and death. Rick Moody brings out the dualistic aspect of the festival by juxtaposing its modern American commercialized form with its historical roots in Christian theology and European pagan folklore. The story's philosophical inquiries thus dovetail into its social critique.

*Style and Technique*

The story's title, "Demonology," refers to a demonology, a learned treatise on demons, often associated with the Middle Ages, as well as the narrator's attempts to come to terms with his various personal demons. This division between the arcane and the colloquial is a stylistic device that permeates the story and illustrates post-modernism's tendency to operate in at least two registers simultaneously. The story unobtrusively blends religious diction and terminology with clichés and everyday language. Frequently announcing the discrepancy between his melancholic, often esoteric, erudition and Meredith's less self-conscious immersion in everyday life, the narrator invokes postmodernism's recognition of the limits of discourse and representation.

The narrator wishes to construct a taxonomic description of reality—he wonders what species of shark his nephew's costume was meant to signify. By contrast, Meredith is primarily interested in actively filling her days. Describing how his sister was never good in the morning without a cup of coffee, the narrator repeats the word "never" several times. This is a knowing allusion to the famous speech in William Shakespeare's *King Lear* (c. 1605-1606), in which the bereaved king mourns how his murdered daughter Cordelia will never live again. That Moody incorporates this allusion into a series of sentence fragments further connects this story to postmodernist aesthetic techniques, which often favor the rhetorical mode of parataxis (the placing of phrases one after the other without connecting them) over synthesis.

Parataxis becomes especially crucial toward the story's end. The narrator piles up numerous observations of what happens just before Meredith has her seizure, but he does not link them together in a causal fashion as much as list them through repeated conjunctions. It is as if Moody is deliberately slowing the story down so as not to have to report the fatal seizure. Merging content with form, Moody purposely shows his narrator anguishing over the generic and formal decisions he has made in telling Meredith's story. This extreme self-consciousness, a hallmark of postmodern art, undercuts the narrator's authority and announces his impotence before his subject matter.

Death cannot ultimately be represented; utter loss cannot be mediated through discourse. Moody's use of postmodernist aesthetic strategies, however, does not mean that the story conforms to postmodern theoretical postulates regarding the self. According to postmodernist theory, individuals cannot be removed from the cultural discourses—particularly those pertaining to gender, race, and class—of their moments in history. "Demonology" maintains, however, that this understanding of human subjectivity is overly reductive. Although Meredith's life is constrained by social, historical, and economic forces, the story is adamant that she cannot be so defined.

The story's notable emphasis on photography highlights Meredith's distinct individuality, further distancing the story from the attitudes of mainstay postmodernism. Photography as a mode of representation captures the specific nuances of the photographed subject. Although photographs can be faked or manipulated, ordinary snapshots hold the precise images of actual people as the camera shutter clicks at a singular, unrepeatable moment in time. As fiction, "Demonology" cannot reproduce either photographs of Meredith or those that she took. In making photography a subtext of the story, Moody accentuates that subjective agency cannot be ignored: Meredith posed for photos, but she also took them to document family life.

Finally, however, photography is insufficient for rendering the intricacies of experience. The narrator, pondering his sister falling asleep, worn out after a fatiguing day, recognizes that no camera can capture her unconscious dream life, a situation that is poignantly magnified when one considers a camera's inability to capture the moment of someone's death. By suggesting that there is something crucial to experience that is unique to each individual and cannot be represented and whose loss cannot be circumscribed by the communal, "Demonology" partakes of postmodernist aesthetics and its skepticism regarding discourse. However, the story ultimately moves beyond postmodernism as the dominant cultural paradigm of late twentieth century American culture.

*Michael Trussler*

# A DESCENT INTO THE MAELSTRÖM

*Author:* Edgar Allan Poe (1809-1849)
*Type of plot:* Adventure
*Time of plot:* The early nineteenth century
*Locale:* Northern Norway
*First published:* 1841

*Principal characters:*
THE NARRATOR, a tourist visiting Norway
THE FISHERMAN, a Norwegian who has survived a maelström

*The Story*

A Norwegian fisherman tells a tourist how he was caught during a storm in a maelström three years earlier and how he survived his ordeal. The tourist is the story's narrator, and he speaks as a reporter who has met an interesting character while traveling in Norway. The story opens with the description of their arrival at a fifteen-hundred-foot cliff on Helseggen mountain, from which the pair may observe the maelström to the south. Though the fisherman seems old and weak, he is rather comfortable on this narrow and windy cliff, where the narrator is unwilling to rise from a crawl in order to observe the sea below. The fisherman coaxes the narrator into looking over the edge; the narrator sees and hears the awesome phenomenon of the gigantic whirlpool that forms there at the changing of the tides.

The maelström is incredible, forming a vast hole, roaring and shrieking far more loudly than Niagara Falls, and shaking the mountain from which they watch. Having described the whirlpool, the narrator quotes from other accounts that find its alleged power to destroy ships and ocean life scarcely credible. For his part, the narrator believes the accounts to be conservative. He also discusses accounts of the causes of the maelström, the most likely of which attribute it to tidal currents. However, his own observation makes the most fantastic account the most satisfying to his imagination. To experience the maelström even at a distance is to believe that it is a vast drain through which water passes, to rise again miles away. The narrator's observations and reading, both distant approaches to the maelström, are then enriched by the fisherman's account of his descent into the maelström.

The fisherman tells how he and his two brothers made a practice of fishing near the maelström because the risk of the venture was justified by the richness and the quality of the catch. One day, however, they were caught by a hurricane, which drowned one brother, rendered their ship helpless, and propelled it into the maelström.

Because the center of the storm passed over their ship as it was about to enter the maelström, the whole scene was brightly lit by a full moon, allowing the fisherman to observe the maelström closely. The ship was drawn toward the whirlpool and over its edge. The ship then rode around it as if it were riding water down a drain, except that its forward speed varied, while its speed of descent remained more or less constant. The fisherman concentrated on his unexpected psychological responses to being pulled in and to the descent.

In his first despair, he found much of his terror dissipated. Instead, he reflected on what a magnificent manifestation of God's power he was seeing and on how wonderful an opportunity it was simply to see it. These attitudes restored the self-possession that his remaining brother had lost permanently. The fisherman relates that he was further calmed by the increasing calmness and regularity of the ship's motion in what had seemed to be lawless violence of motion. He felt a curiosity to explore this wonder of nature and began to do so. Despite the brightness of the moon, he was unable to see to the very bottom of the vortex because of a mist engendered there, but he did see "a magnificent rainbow, like that narrow and tottering bridge which Musselmen say is the only pathway between Time and Eternity." Gradually, his observations became cooler and more scientific. Eventually, he noticed that differently shaped objects descend at different speeds. This observation gave him hope that he might survive if he could attach himself to a cylindrical object.

Unable to convince his brother to join him, he lashed himself to a water cask and leaped overboard. This strategy saved his life, while his brother rode the ship down to destruction.

The fisherman says that when he was picked up by his friends and daily companions, they failed to recognize him, for his hair had turned from raven to white in those few hours, and his face, too, had changed beyond recognition. They did not believe his story of having survived the maelström, and he does not expect the narrator to believe it either.

*Themes and Meanings*

"A Descent into the Maelström" appears on the surface to be little more than a realistic tale of adventure, an eyewitness account of a distant natural wonder for Edgar Allan Poe's American readers. Like several of his adventure tales, this one is constructed in such a way as to be indistinguishable from similar nonfictional reports, which regularly appeared in popular journals of the day. Among the aspects of the story that tempt readers to see more than adventure are the unusual description of the maelström, which suggests that it may be a symbol, and certain patterns that are repeated in other Poe tales.

The maelström as experienced by the fisherman is a whirling storm in the water, which has above it a precisely corresponding whirling storm in the air. At the eye of the storm is the brilliant full moon, which lights and glorifies the maelström, offering the fisherman a doubly unique revelation. Not only is he caught in the maelström, but he is also allowed to see it. The storm seems to allow him this unique vision as a gift. At the corresponding eye of the maelström is the mysterious veiling mist, illuminated by a rainbow that, to the fisherman, seems a bridge between time and eternity. The mist marks a literal entrance to eternity insofar as it marks the point at which a person must die, should he reach that point in the maelström. However, as the vision itself offers a revelation, it may also offer a way for the imagination to bridge time and eternity. This arrangement of storm and maelström indicates a fictional purpose beneath the surface of an apparently nonfictional text; it suggests that the scene may be symbolic, pointing to some meaning beyond itself.

The meaning to which it points is difficult to assert confidently. There are patterns of the story in Poe's works that are suggestive but do not lead easily to certainty. Stuart Levine, in *The Short Fiction of Edgar Allan Poe* (1976), has placed this tale with "The Pit and the Pendulum" because it exemplifies the theme of salvation through terror. The fisherman moves through stages of terror, despair, wonder, calm, curiosity, cool observation, discovery, action, and salvation. This pattern, or one like it, appears frequently in Poe's tales of adventure; it is several times placed in the context of a physical journey during which the protagonist approaches a barrier between time and eternity such as the irradiated mist at the bottom of the maelström. One possible meaning suggested by this pattern is that the recognition of the incomprehensible terror and wonder of the physical universe brings the human consciousness ultimately to a kind of heightened reason, in which fundamental truth may be discovered. What truth the fisherman discovers is also difficult to assert with confidence. It may be important to notice how his ease on the windy cliff contrasts with the narrator's terror at the opening of the story. Perhaps the fisherman has learned not to fear death and, as a result, has come to feel at home with the terrific wonders of the physical universe.

*Style and Technique*

The discussion of possible meanings has uncovered the main distinctive elements of Poe's technique in this tale. He creates what appears to be a nonfiction narrative yet places at its center a symmetrical setting of a hurricane over a maelström, which suggests symbolic meaning. The fisherman seems an ordinary man who has had an extraordinary adventure, but ultimately it appears that he may have been granted a kind of revelation, which has changed not only his appearance but also his attitude toward his life and his world.

Critics have taken note of the similarity between this tale and Samuel Taylor Coleridge's *The Rime of the Ancient Mariner* (1798). Each is a framed narrative, the seaman telling his tale to a landsman. In each, there is a similar pattern: The seaman is drawn into a wonderful world in which despair leads to discovery, transformation, and a salvation that may be both physical and spiritual. Perhaps the main difference between Poe's tale and Coleridge's poem is that Poe presents a believable if extraordinary physical world in a journalistic, reportorial fashion. One result is that the meaning of Poe's tale seems to arise from experience of the world rather than from a fantasy designed to illustrate a moral truth.

*Terry Heller*

# THE DESIRE TO BE A MAN

*Author:* Auguste Villiers de l'Isle-Adam (1838-1889)
*Type of plot:* Horror
*Time of plot:* Fall, 1871
*Locale:* Paris and the Brittany coast of France
*First published:* "Le Désir d'être un homme," 1883 (English translation, 1927)

*Principal character:*
ESPRIT CHAUDVAL, an aging actor, specializing in tragic roles

*The Story*

It is midnight in Paris's Grand Boulevard district on a windy Sunday in October, 1871. Because the city is still under martial law, the cafés and restaurants of that quarter are bustling to meet the curfew, ushering out their few remaining patrons and preparing to close their doors. The menacing gaze of two police officers encourages their haste. The surrounding streets are rapidly emptying of coaches and pedestrians for the same reason. Into this scene of hasty departures, there wanders a tall, sad-faced arrival, dressed in the style of the previous century and moving as though he were walking in his sleep. Oblivious to the bustle around him, the man stops before a tall, thin mirror, which decorates the exterior of an elegant café, and examines himself closely. After this solemn inspection, he ceremoniously removes his hat and bows politely to himself in the old-fashioned pre-Revolutionary manner. Now bareheaded, the man can be readily recognized as the illustrious tragedian Esprit Chaudval, whose real name is Lepeinteur, and whom everyone calls Monanteuil.

Seeming shocked, Chaudval continues to stare at himself in the mirror while all around him silence reigns, for everyone else has gone, and he is alone. What has shocked him is that his hair, salt and pepper only yesterday, is now the color of moonlight. In the mirror he has caught a glimpse of himself growing old. This spectacle sets off in the actor a host of memories and reflections about the sad necessity that faces him: to retire from the stage and give up the pleasures of the theatrical life that he has so long relished. He recalls his recent decision to retire to the Brittany lighthouse that his father before him had tended. He has already requested this government appointment, and, in fact, has the letter of appointment in his pocket but has forgotten about it. Chaudval now reminds himself that his fundamental desire in retirement is to be a man! For most of his life, he has portrayed the passions and emotions felt by others but has himself never experienced a real emotion. Real emotion is, after all, what makes one a genuine human being, Chaudval reasons. Because age is forcing him to leave the stage and return to humanity, Chaudval resolves that he must acquire passions, some real human feeling that best suits his nature. Rejecting love, glory, and ambition as no longer in season for him, Chaudval is led by his "dramatic temperament" to choose the emotion that is right for him: remorse. He recalls characters whom he has portrayed on the stage, such as Nero, Macbeth, and Hamlet, who experience remorse—whose remorse takes the form of a conscience haunted by ghosts. He decides he must do something horrifying enough to make him see ghosts as well—something spectacularly atrocious. With excited satisfaction, he hits on the idea of setting a fire.

Pleased with this carefully reasoned solution to the problem of becoming a man, Chaudval suddenly picks up a paving stone, smashes the offending mirror, and dashes off into the night. Shortly thereafter, a major conflagration breaks out in Chaudval's quarter of Paris in which nearly a hundred people die. Chaudval watches the fire from a coach, in which he has placed all of his belongings. In the morning, he leaves for Brittany.

The ruin of a lighthouse, now his home, preoccupies Chaudval at first, and he forgets about his incendiary crime. However, after reading an account of the event in a Paris newspaper, he experiences a surge of joyous triumph and awaits his reward: a conscience wracked by remorse. To his astonishment, nothing happens. He feels no pangs of conscience, no ghosts, no feeling of any kind. In a fever of despair and shame, he suffers a cerebral hemorrhage and, in his death agony, demands that God show him at least one ghost because he has earned it. His prayer unanswered, Chaudval dies without realizing that he himself had become what he was seeking: a ghost.

*Themes and Meanings*

Auguste Villiers de l'Isle-Adam's ironic horror tale is constructed on the well-known psychological observation that actors pay a heavy price for their talent in portraying the characters and emotions of others. Their concentrated efforts to "think" their way into the skin of someone else drain them of any capacity to live a life of their own. According to this view, actors are tragic figures who, by constantly assuming the identity of others, lose their own identity. The classic case is that of the sad clown, laughing on the outside, crying on the inside. In France, at least, this conception originates in an essay of the eighteenth century writer Denis Diderot, who argues that a great actor's performance is a paradox because the portrayal of strong emotion requires an actor to be cold and dispassionate while performing. If the actor actually experiences the emotion, he will lack the disciplined control he needs to project the emotion accurately.

Villiers's tale pushes Diderot's insight to its logical conclusion, suggesting that a lifetime of portraying the emotions of others has left Chaudval unable to experience an emotion of his own. Feeling dehumanized by that fact and desperate to rejoin the human race somehow, Chaudval becomes a grotesque figure, trapped in the paradox of his theatrical mentality and therefore unable to address his problem. The only emotions he knows are those that he has counterfeited. That is why he commits a heinous crime, and the cruel irony that results is that Chaudval is revealed to be an empty shell of a man, a ghost. A sardonic conclusion to which the story inexorably leads the reader is that, in Chaudval, and perhaps in all thespians, the actor has systematically killed the human being in himself. He becomes the victim of his art.

*Style and Technique*

A striking feature of Villiers's story is that it has but one character. Whatever happens in the tale happens to him or is seen through his eyes. When he speaks, it is only to himself. A tale so concentrated in the consciousness of one character would seem to cry out for the technique of the first-person narrative. Nevertheless, Villiers has chosen to provide a third-person narrator, discreet, unobtrusive, apparently objective, but indispensable for characterizing Chaudval for the reader, and for bringing out the narrative's underlying irony. The narrator's effort, with regard to Chaudval, is to demonstrate that his whole manner of being and thinking is infected with the theatrical virus of make-believe. When Chaudval first appears, the description of his quaint clothing and courtly gestures informs us that he is always playing a part. He is never simply himself, because he has no self. When he starts to reason with himself about his plan for retirement, the narrator blandly observes that the old actor "ventured upon a monologue." When Chaudval reads, in a Paris newspaper, that a benefit performance will be given to raise money for the fire's victims, the narrator reports that Chaudval mutters to himself that he ought to have lent his talent to the benefit performance for his victims because it could have been a brilliant farewell appearance for him. Chaudval betrays not the slightest awareness of how absurd and tragic this reaction is. Thus it is the narrator who reveals for the reader the tragic irony of Chaudval's ultimate fate: Long addiction to make-believe defeats his "desire to be a man."

Villiers's impressive skill as a stylist is especially evident in the way he uses his narrator in this tale. Villiers closely controls the choice of words, images, and even sentence rhythms to assure that not only Chaudval's own words, in direct discourse, but also the narrator's account of events, in indirect discourse, are always consonant with the bizarre persona of Chaudval and of his milieu. Villiers's language throughout is mannered, courtly, histrionic when necessary, a bit archaic, and replete with the expressive colloquialisms used by theater people. Villiers knew this Parisian theater milieu at first hand, having been part of it for several years in his early thirties, writing plays, negotiating with theater directors about getting them performed, and living with an actress who was his mistress. Both the theme and the language of "The Desire to Be a Man" are manifestly the product of those years.

*Murray Sachs*

# DÉSIRÉE'S BABY

*Author:* Kate Chopin (1851-1904)
*Type of plot:* Social realism
*Time of plot:* Sometime before the American Civil War
*Locale:* Natchitoches Parish, Louisiana
*First published:* 1892

*Principal characters:*
DÉSIRÉE, the heroine, a beautiful young woman
ARMAND AUBIGNY, her husband, a rich planter and slave-holder
MONSIEUR VALMONDE, her foster father
MADAME VALMONDE, her foster mother

*The Story*

As the story opens, Madame Valmonde is on her way to visit Désirée and her new baby. As she makes the short trip to the nearby plantation, Madame Valmonde thinks back to the time when Désirée was herself an infant. Her husband had found the child lying asleep near a pillar at the entrance to the Valmonde plantation, probably having been left there by a party of Texans who had passed by that day. Childless themselves, the Valmondes adopted Désirée.

Désirée grows into a beautiful woman, and, when she is eighteen years old, Armand Aubigny falls in love with her. When he proposes, Monsieur Valmonde reminds Armand that her parentage and ancestry are unknown, but Armand dismisses all objections. After all, he can give her one of the finest names and lineages in Louisiana.

They soon marry, and at first their life together is happy. Armand, a harsh man toward his slaves, becomes more humane; following the birth of their first child, a son, Armand grows even kinder. Shortly thereafter, however, Armand becomes crueler than ever. He also stays away from home for long periods of time, and when he is at home he shows no affection for Désirée.

One afternoon, as Désirée sits listlessly in her room, she glances at her child lying on the bed. A quadroon slave is fanning the child, and suddenly she is struck by the similarity in their features. As soon as her husband arrives, she asks for an explanation. Armand replies that her suspicions are correct; the child is not white. If the child is not white, Armand continues, then neither is Désirée.

She refuses to believe Armand's accusation and writes to her foster mother to confirm her racial purity. Madame Valmonde responds by inviting Désirée and her baby to return home. She says nothing about Armand's accusation, though, thus tacitly confirming it.

After receiving this letter, Désirée asks her husband what he wants her to do. He wants her to go. She does indeed leave, but instead of returning to the Valmondes, she carries her baby into the swamp and disappears.

Several weeks later Armand builds a bonfire in the backyard to destroy all traces of Désirée and the child. Into the flames go the willow cradle, the baby's expensive layette, and Désirée's silk, satin, and velvet dresses. Finally he gathers up her letters; these, too, he consigns to the blaze. Now only one piece of paper remains in the desk. As Armand prepares to destroy it, he notices that the handwriting is not his wife's. Instead, he discovers that it is a note from his mother to his father. In it he reads, "I thank the good God for having so arranged our lives that our dear Armand will never know that his mother, who adores him, belongs to the race that is cursed with the brand of slavery." Too late, Armand learns the truth.

*Themes and Meanings*

Kate Chopin clearly sympathizes with the plight of people of mixed blood and points out the evils of a slave system that at once creates and condemns miscegenation. Her chief concern, however, is not with the South's "peculiar institution," a topic she rarely treated in her fiction. Rather, she concerns herself with her characters' inner lives.

Certainly these lives confront external constraints. Désirée and Armand live in a world that values racial purity. To be black is to be condemned to a life of subservience; to be white is to inherit mastery. No matter how beautiful or how fair one may be, blood rules. Armand spends much time in the cottage of a slave named La Blanche, whose name suggests her skin color. Still, she is of mixed race, so she is a slave, and the quadroon boy who fans Désirée's baby is probably the son of Armand and La Blanche. The most such a woman can hope for is to be treated well by her master and to be his concubine because she will never be his wife. Among Creoles, who pride themselves not only on their racial purity but also on their French heritage, the proper pedigree is especially important.

The characters' world is also one in which women, like blacks, are second-class citizens. Women have certain fixed roles—daughter, wife, mother. Désirée's world is small, moving between the neighboring plantations of her foster parents and her husband. She passes her days inside, and Armand is free to come and go as he pleases. Once her husband rejects her, Désirée must choose between disgrace and death; despite Madame Valmonde's offer of sanctuary, Désirée would remain an outcast.

Still, "Désirée's Baby" might have ended differently. The code of the outside world impinges on Armand but does not force him to act as he does. When he married Désirée he claimed indifference to her status as a foundling, but he is not, in fact, strong enough to reject the prejudices of the world. Indeed, he stands for those very attitudes that he seems to ignore: He defines himself by his pedigree and by his role as master of his slaves and his wife. Désirée is desirable only so long as she appears to be a valuable possession. Once he believes that she is not "authentic," he loses interest, for he never regards her as a fellow human being with needs of her own. She is there, he believes, to satisfy him; when she no longer does so, he discards her.

In her poem "Because," Chopin writes, "Tis only man/ That does because he can/ And knowing good from ill,/ Chooses because he will." Armand has a choice: He can love Désirée for what she is (or thinks she is) as his father loved his black mother, or he can let his pride overrule that love. Chopin admires the character who defies convention, who is sufficiently strong to reject the false standards of his time and place. Armand's inability to surmount prejudice leads to the tragedy of the story.

## Style and Technique

Chopin has been described as a local colorist, and certainly most of her stories are set in a particular geographical area that she examines socially and physically. Unlike such local colorists as Sarah Orne Jewett and George Washington Cabel, though, Chopin did not write to preserve the past, nor did she focus on the conflict of past and present that characterizes the typical local color story. Further, her work shows no nostalgia for a previous era. Only five of her stories lack a contemporary setting, and "Désirée's Baby" demonstrates no fondness for the antebellum period.

The carefully defined setting is, rather, a laboratory. What happens when one puts certain characters in a particular world? Like a scientist, Chopin observed their reactions and reported her results without obvious emotion. Significantly, she called this story "Désirée's Baby," not "Désirée," as though seeking to deflect sympathy from the central character. Also, the baby is the crucial ingredient in this experiment: Give Armand and Désirée a child of color and then watch how they behave.

They behave badly, each blaming the other. Neither knows the truth, but because Armand is the more powerful, Désirée is disgraced and banished. Chopin does not moralize; she merely reports. That clinical detachment makes the final lines all the more forceful, as the reader grasps the enormity of Armand's mistake.

*Joseph Rosenblum*

# THE DESTRUCTORS

*Author:* Graham Greene (1904-1991)
*Type of plot:* Psychological
*Time of plot:* The early 1950's
*Locale:* London
*First published:* 1954

*Principal characters:*

T. (TREVOR), the leader of a gang of adolescent boys

BLACKIE, the gang leader whom he replaces and makes a lieutenant

MR. THOMAS, an elderly man known to the boys as "Old Misery"

## The Story

Amid the lingering London ruins of the bombing raids of World War II, a gang of adolescent boys pass their summer holidays carrying out various projects of collective mischief. They are the inhabitants of a neighborhood known as Wormsley Common, one of the poorest sections of the city. They meet and play in a communal parking lot, which adjoins a battered but stately eighteenth century house. The house, more than two hundred years old, stands alone, "like a jagged tooth," while its neighbors lie in wartime rubble. Blackie, the hitherto undisputed leader, is indirectly challenged one day by the newest recruit, a boy known as "T." From the time he first joined the group at the beginning of the summer, T. has had little or nothing to say, simply voting "yes" or "no" with the rest of this curiously democratic collection of children.

Now T. intrigues the boys with a plan of diabolic proportions, an enterprise far beyond any that Blackie could conceive. The house that adjoins their parking lot play area, T. has discovered, was built by Christopher Wren, Great Britain's greatest architect. It was Wren who, in the late seventeenth century, designed and built Saint Paul's Cathedral, the most notable of London landmarks. The sole inhabitant of the house is the owner, an elderly and somewhat cranky gentleman named Mr. Thomas, whom the boys call "Old Misery."

T. has developed a curious fixation on the house. He gains entry by the simple device of asking Mr. Thomas if he can see it. Evidently flattered by the child's interest and attention, Mr. Thomas gives him a tour. The house is clearly an architectural and historical wonder, an enduring remnant of a bygone era when such buildings were the careful work of artistic craftsmen. Amid the antique china and eighteenth century paneling, one particular architectural wonder catches T's attention: a two-hundred-year-old staircase like a corkscrew, held up by nothing. He has learned that Mr. Thomas will be away on a long weekend holiday. T. proposes that they surreptitiously enter the house during that time and destroy it. Blackie and the others are at first hesitant but also are intrigued with an action so daring and audacious. The boys undertake their task with quiet enthusiasm, completely under the spell of T's compelling leadership. In the space of a day and a half, they destroy the house with saws, hammers, screwdrivers, and sledgehammers. Nothing is left standing or intact but the four outside walls. Even the unexpected early return of Mr. Thomas does not daunt T., who quickly devises a plan to lure the old man into the outdoor lavatory, where he is locked up for the night.

As a finishing touch, T. and the boys fasten a rope to the supporting struts on the outside of the house and tie the other end to a large truck left in the parking lot for the weekend. The driver arrives early the following morning, starts his truck, and proceeds toward the street. Suddenly there is a long rumbling crash, complete with bricks bouncing in the road ahead. The driver stops his truck and climbs down. The house that once stood with such dignity among the bombed-out ruins has disappeared. Freed from his lavatory prison by the truck driver, who responds to his shouting, Thomas utters a sobbing cry of dismay: "My house . . . where's my house?" The driver surveys the scene of the devastation and laughs. Thomas becomes angry and indignant. "I'm sorry," the driver reassures him, "but I can't help it. There's nothing personal, but you got to admit it's funny."

*Themes and Meanings*

The reader's first impression of "The Destructors" is that the story is a simple chronicle of senseless violence and wanton destruction carried out by thoughtless, unprincipled adolescents. Graham Greene's story, however, is actually a metaphor for class struggle in English society in the decade following World War II. The tension between working-class Britain and the upper-middle-class society that had absorbed all but the last vestiges of the nobility had surfaced dramatically in the years following the previous world war. These years were marked by repeated challenges, both social and political, to the established order of an empire in decline. Old Misery's house somehow survived the battering of a second great war, as did the monarchy and the entrenched class sensibility of British society. The house, however, is considerably weakened, held in place by wooden struts that brace the outside walls. In its fragile state, it needs support, as does the political and social structure that it represents. It cannot stand as it once did, independent with the formidable strength of the British Empire. The interior, although a trove of revered artifacts of civilized European culture, nevertheless represents a tradition that is increasingly meaningless to the lower classes.

The members of the Wormsley Common Gang—who significantly are twelve in number, like the apostles of the New Testament—are forces of change, agents subconsciously representing quiet, methodical revolution. Their demolishing of the house is painfully systematic. The boys work with steady persistence on their enterprise of destruction. They work, paradoxically, with the seriousness of creators. As Greene's narrator asserts, "destruction after all is a form of creation."

T. and his followers represent the extremes of nihilism, the philosophical doctrine that existing institutions—social, political, and economic—must be completely destroyed in order to make way for the new. In the context of nihilism, the destruction of Old Misery's house is both positive and necessary. T., whose nihilism is intrinsic to his distorted personality, makes it clear that he feels no hatred for old Mr. Thomas; like a true nihilist, he feels nothing, rejecting both hate and love as "hooey." For someone with such a dangerously warped sense of mission, T. is also curiously ethical and high-minded. When he shows Blackie the bundles of currency discovered in Old Misery's mattress, Blackie asks if the group is going to share them. "We aren't thieves," T. replies; "Nobody is going to steal anything from this house." He then proceeds to burn them one by one as an act of celebration, presumably a celebration of triumph over the currency that more than any other entity determines the distinctions of social strata in postwar Great Britain. The truck driver, with his reassurance to Mr. Thomas that his laughter is nothing personal, reflects the position of the underclass: utter indifference to the sacrosanct values of tradition and civilized society.

## Style and Technique

Greene's narrator is selectively omniscient. Although the reader is made aware of the internal doubts and anxieties of Blackie, the deposed leader, the inner workings of T's troubled mind remain closed. The narrator is also decidedly neutral and uncensorious in the general treatment of this focal character. To proponents of the tradition represented by the objects T. destroys, this child seems the very essence of evil. Greene, however, offers nothing to suggest anything other than a mysterious amorality that is cold, implacable, and generally inexplicable, although he piques curiosity with oblique references to T's background and mental state. When Old Misery suddenly returns home and threatens the enterprise, T. protests this unforeseen complication "with the fury of the child he had never been." Earlier, T., who generally looks down when he speaks, proposes the destruction of the house to the incredulous boys with "raised eyes, as grey and disturbed as the drab August day."

Prior to T's membership in the gang, its members' preoccupation was with adolescent mischief, such as stealing free rides on public transportation. T., however, is decidedly unchildlike and becomes the instrument that destroys not only the house but the group's collective innocence. The pleasures of their previous childhood preoccupations are forever lost to them. T. has taken them abruptly from innocence to experience, summarily depriving them of a gradual but essential learning process. In this regard, T's actions are presented as more the product of fate than malevolence.

The economy of description in character development is characteristic of Greene's writing. Extensive graphic detail and character background are all but nonexistent, but there is enough to make the reader more than willing to supply the missing dimension.

*Richard Keenan*

# THE DEVIL AND DANIEL WEBSTER

*Author:* Stephen Vincent Benét (1898-1943)
*Type of plot:* Folktale
*Time of plot:* The early nineteenth century
*Locale:* Cross Corners, New Hampshire, and Marshfield, Massachusetts
*First published:* 1937

> *Principal characters:*
> DANIEL WEBSTER, the famous American lawyer, legislator, and
> orator
> JABEZ STONE, a New Hampshire farmer who makes a pact with
> the devil
> MR. SCRATCH, the name the devil carries in the story

*The Story*

"The Devil and Daniel Webster" is narrated as a folktale told in the border country of Vermont, New Hampshire, and Massachusetts, regarding the famous American orator Daniel Webster. Like so many folk legends, this one contains some exaggeration and several important lessons.

Jabez Stone is an unlucky New Hampshire farmer who, in a moment of frustration, sells his soul to the devil. His farm prospers, but when the devil returns near the end of the seven-year contract, Stone sees the soul of his neighbor Miser Stevens in the devil's pocket, and his dread grows. Although the devil grants him a three-year extension on his contract, the time weighs on Jabez Stone and, in desperation, he goes to see Daniel Webster, who was born near Stone's farm but who now lives and practices law in Marshfield, Massachusetts. Webster says that he has not argued such a "mortgage case" in some time, but he agrees to take it. The two return to New Hampshire to await the arrival of the devil, who comes at midnight to claim his property.

The heart of the story is the debate between the devil and Daniel Webster. At the beginning, it looks as if Daniel Webster has met his match. He argues that no American can be pressed into the service of a "foreign prince," but the devil cleverly demonstrates that he has a long American history: "When the first wrong was done to the first Indian, I was there. When the first slaver put out for the Congo, I stood on her deck." Not to be outdone, Webster stands on the Constitution and demands a trial for his client, with an American judge and jury. Mr. Scratch agrees—and calls up a cast of pirates, cutthroats, and turncoats from the darker pages of American history, and the dreaded Judge Hawthorne, who presided at the Salem witch trials.

The trial that night does not go well for Webster, and his opposition nearly tricks him into getting angry and thereby falling into their power: "For it was him they'd come for, not only Jabez Stone." Thus, in his closing argument, Daniel Webster starts off in a low voice "talking about the things that make a country a country, and a man a man." He talks about freedom and slavery and the early days of the republic.

It wasn't a spread-eagle speech, but he made you see it. He admitted all the wrong that had ever been done. But he showed how, out of the wrong and the right, the suffering and the starvations, something new had come. And everybody had played a part in it, even the traitors.

His speech thus redeems, not only Jabez Stone and himself, but the jury of renegades as well.

And his words came back at the end to New Hampshire ground, and the one spot of land that each man loves and clings to. He painted a picture of that, and to each one of that jury he spoke of things long forgotten. For his voice could search the heart, and that was his gift and his strength.

The jury finds for the defendant, and Daniel Webster wins his toughest case.

However, Webster is not done. He forces Mr. Scratch to draw up a document promising never to bother Jabez Stone or his heirs, "nor any other New Hampshireman till doomsday!" The devil tells Webster's fortune and predicts, correctly, that he will never become president (his secret ambition), that his two sons will die in the Civil War, but that the Union will be saved, thanks in part to Daniel Webster's speeches. Finally, Webster boots the devil out the door.

But they say that whenever the devil comes near Marshfield, even now, he gives it a wide berth. And he hasn't been seen in the state of New Hampshire from that day to this. I'm not talking about Massachusetts or Vermont.

## Themes and Meanings

"The Devil and Daniel Webster" was one of three stories that Stephen Vincent Benét wrote in the late 1930's on the subject of the great orator, and it was a story that brought him, on its publication in *The Saturday Evening Post*, almost instant national acclaim. The story tapped America's love for folklore and legend, and, at a dark moment in the Depression when Americans were looking desperately for such handholds, it re-created the story of a genuine American hero. In the process of elevating Webster to a national honor, Benét also wrote a hymn celebrating America's past greatness and future possibility.

Like the legends of earlier American folk heroes (Daniel Boone, Davy Crockett, and so on), Benét's portrait of Webster is based on actual accomplishments but embellished in a number of ways. Webster takes on Jabez Stone's case, even though he has "seventy-five other things to do and the Missouri Compromise to straighten out." All of his feats in the story are prodigious, in fact, but none so great as his eloquence. He is able in his speech to convince twelve of the most desperate villains ever assembled out of American history to free Stone from the devil's hold.

The story is praise not only for Daniel Webster, however, but also for his country, for the two are inextricably intertwined. Webster is, as Jabez Stone says of him, "the Union's stay and New Hampshire's pride!" Webster himself confesses, "I'd go to the Pit itself to save the Union." Webster's victory is won by describing the very qualities—love of country, love of the land, a belief in justice, and a faith in all humankind—that he himself so eloquently represents, and that America stands for.

Daniel Webster is also a "New Hampshireman," and part of the story's poignancy, and not a little of its humor, come from the delineation of Yankee character traits. Some of the poignancy is a pride of region, "For if two New Hampshiremen aren't a match for the devil," Webster boasts, "we might as well give the country back to the Indians." Another part is clearly satirical. Jabez Stone is indentured to the devil only because, having said in anger that he would sell his soul, "being a New Hampshireman, he wouldn't take it back." Yankees reflect the qualities of their flinty soil, and Jabez Stone is no exception: "Hard and mean," as Daniel Webster admits in his summation, Stone is also pious, ill-educated, slow to brag, but quick to grab a profit. ("For any hades we want to raise in this state," Daniel Webster quips, "we can raise ourselves without assistance from strangers.") The humor of the last line of the story—on the difference between New Hampshire and its neighbors—is based on a regional New England pride and friendly rivalry.

The story is connected, thematically, to the Faust legend, which can be traced from works such as Christopher Marlowe's *The Tragedy of Dr. Faustus* (1592) in the sixteenth century and Johann Wolfgang von Goethe's *Faust* (1808-1832; *The Tragedy of Faust*, 1823-1838) in the nineteenth to Thomas Mann's *Doktor Faustus* (1947; *Doctor Faustus*, 1948). In these and similar works, a man makes a pact with the devil for some profit but suffers dire consequences for his act. In the American literary tradition, the story is also linked to treatments of the New England character, from Nathaniel Hawthorne's story "Young Goodman Brown" (1835), through Edith Wharton's novel *Ethan Frome* (1911) and Eugene O'Neill's play *Desire Under the Elms* (1924), to the much later fiction of John Cheever and John Updike.

*Style and Technique*

Most American folktales, from stories about Paul Bunyan and Pecos Bill through the Uncle Remus stories, depend for their effect on a successful merging of matter and manner: The subjects must sound like what they were. Like these earlier stories, "The Devil and Daniel Webster" manages to capture the very flavor of its Yankee subject. The anonymous narrator of the story is clearly a New Englander, and his voice carries a pride of region as well as its accent. Daniel Webster himself is capable of both sharpness and humor: "I never left a jug or a case half finished in my life." When, at the end of the story, he calls the devil a "long-barreled, slab-sided, lantern-jawed, fortune-telling note shaver," Benét is capturing the language of the tall tale out of the oral tradition in American literature.

Benét chooses, however, not to try to recite Webster's speeches verbatim, but, instead, recounts them in his own modulated, poetic prose, and the effect is telling. (Most readers are not conscious, until it is pointed out, that the closing arguments in the trial are given, not by Webster but by his fictional biographer, the narrator of "The Devil and Daniel Webster.") Benét's prose is capable not only of the broad Yankee humor and folk exaggeration of the story but also of the poignant and patriotic sentiments of Webster's last speech:

And he began with the simple things that everybody's known and felt—the freshness of a fine morning when you're young and the taste of food when you're hungry, and the new day that's every day when you're a child. He took them up and he turned them in his hands.

Much of the story's power comes from this prose.

*David Peck*

# THE DEVIL AND TOM WALKER

*Author:* Washington Irving (1783-1859)
*Type of plot:* Regional
*Time of plot:* The eighteenth century
*Locale:* Massachusetts Colony
*First published:* 1824

> *Principal characters:*
> TOM WALKER, a pre-Revolutionary New Englander who sells his
> soul to the devil
> TOM'S WIFE, a shrewish nag
> OLD SCRATCH, the devil

*The Story*

This tale, which was told to the narrator, Geoffrey Crayon, during a peaceful afternoon of fishing, begins with a local legend concerning treasure buried by the notorious pirate Captain Kidd in a swamp not far from Boston. Near this swamp, in 1727, lives a miserly fellow named Tom Walker and his wife, a woman as miserly as he. These two, so greedy that they even try to cheat each other, are constantly fighting, and Tom's face shows the physical marks of their arguments.

One day, cutting through the swamp, Tom comes across the remains of an old Indian fortification and discovers a skull with a tomahawk still buried in it. As Tom kicks at the skull, he hears a voice and looks up to see a black man, "neither negro nor Indian" seated on a stump. The man, wearing a red sash around his body, has a soot-stained face, which makes it appear as if he works in some fiery place. Tom soon recognizes the stranger as the devil, Old Scratch. The devil confirms the story of Kidd's buried treasure and offers it to Tom but only on a certain condition, a condition that the story does not state but that is surely the possession of Tom's soul. Old Scratch proves his identity by leaving the imprint of his finger burned into Tom's forehead.

When Tom tells his wife of the encounter, she greedily urges him to accept the bargain, but to spite her he refuses. Unable to change Tom's mind, she decides to make her own pact with the devil, keeping the profits for herself. After an initial inconclusive meeting with Old Scratch, Tom's wife sets out again for the Indian fort, this time taking with her all the household valuables she can carry. When she does not return for several days, Tom, uneasy for his valuables, goes to find her. After a long afternoon's search, he sees hanging in a tree a bundle tied in his wife's apron. Thinking that he has found the valuables, he opens the apron and discovers only a heart and a liver. Evidently, his wife died attempting to deal with Old Scratch as she had formerly dealt with Tom, for around the tree are tufts of black hair obviously pulled from the devil's head. Although unhappy about the disappearance of his valuables, Tom is consoled by the loss of his wife.

Feeling grateful and with a growing desire to gain Captain Kidd's fortune, Tom seeks to renew his acquaintance with the devil. Old Scratch does not appear for some time, however, and, when he does, he seems reluctant to discuss the treasure. Finally, though, he agrees to relinquish the treasure if it will be used in his service. He first suggests that Tom become a slave trader. Tom balks at sinking that low but agrees to go into business as a moneylender or usurer.

Tom moves to Boston and becomes successful, exacting hard terms and showing no mercy to those in his debt. Growing older, Tom regrets his bargain and searches to find a way out of the pact. He becomes zealous in church attendance, prays loudly and publicly, keeps an open Bible in his home, and always carries a small one with him. He does not, however, give up his harsh business practices.

One hot afternoon, dressed in a white linen cap and silk morning gown, Tom is about to foreclose a mortgage. When the poor victim begs for a delay, reminding Tom of the money he previously made from him, Tom replies, "The devil take me . . . if I have made a farthing!" Immediately, there are three knocks at the door, and standing in the street is Old Scratch and a black horse.

Having left the small Bible in his coat and having covered the large one with the mortgage, Tom is helpless to prevent the devil from placing him on the horse, which gallops off down the streets of Boston. The next day, his house burns to the ground, and Tom never returns. It is said, however, that the swamp and Indian fort are haunted by a spirit on horseback wearing a white cap and morning gown. The story is so well-known, says the narrator, that it is the source of the New England saying, "The Devil and Tom Walker."

## Themes and Meanings

Washington Irving is said to be the first to have used the phrase "the almighty dollar." This tale, found in part 4 (called "The Money Diggers") of *Tales of a Traveller*, comically presents the results of valuing the dollar above all else. Both Tom and his wife care more for possessions than they do for each other. She urges Tom to sell his soul, and he is more concerned for his household treasures than for her. The two live in conflict and misery because of greed and eventually die from greed, she by trying to bully the devil into better terms and he by attempting to squeeze the last bit of profit from an unfortunate client.

The Faust theme, in which the soul is exchanged for knowledge and power, is reduced here to a story of money grubbing. The occupations that are viewed as of special service to the devil—slave-trading and usury—are those that place monetary profit before humanity. (Irving also attacked the slave trade in his *A History of the Life and Voyages of Christopher Columbus*, 1828, and he had personal experience with the humiliation of debt and bankruptcy.)

Tom's turn to religion near the end of the tale is a combination of superstition and hypocrisy. Tom hopes to ward off the devil through the outward trappings of Christianity, but the tale clearly satirizes those who make a public show of devotion while retaining meanness of spirit.

*Style and Technique*

As in other of his tales, Irving here combines a supernatural subject with a matter-of-fact narration. The reader is allowed to suspend disbelief partly through the framing of the tale, which is recounted by the fictional narrator Geoffrey Crayon, who has heard it from an old Cape Cod whaler, who claims to have memorized it from a manuscript written by a neighbor. Thus, the tale is several times removed from its source, with no one to vouch for its authenticity. The phrase "it is said" is used frequently, and once the reader is told that the facts "have become confounded by a variety of historians." Although the tale ends with a claim for its veracity ("The truth of it is not to be doubted"), readers can believe or not as they wish.

The serious and the comic are juxtaposed. Although the selling of one's soul and the inhumane consequences of greed are significant, they become subjects for laughter through Irving's character portrayals and his use of ironic understatement. The characters are one-dimensional, stereotypical figures. Tom's unnamed wife is the typical nag of antifeminist literature. Tom himself is not described in detail and is given such stock traits as greed and hypocrisy. The reader need not be concerned for the fate of either character.

Irving has a keen eye for the ironies and contradictions of human behavior. When Tom becomes wealthy, he ostentatiously equips a grand carriage but has it pulled by starving horses. He builds a large house but leaves it unfurnished out of miserliness. He exacts the harshest business terms on those least able to pay. Throughout the tale, this irony exposes the vanity and meanness of those for whom material possessions become paramount.

*Larry L. Stewart*

# DHARMA

*Author:* Vikram Chandra (1961-     )
*Type of plot:* Ghost story, frame story
*Time of plot:* 1971 and 1991
*Locale:* East Pakistan, Bombay
*First published:* 1994

*Principal characters:*
SUBRAMANIAN, the narrator
MAJOR GENERAL JAGO ANTIA, a retired army officer whose
    family home is haunted
THAPA, Jago Antia's batman
AMIR KHAN, the long-time housekeeper at Jago Antia's home
TODYWALLA, a Bombay real estate agent
THAKKER, an exorcist
SOHRAB ("SOLI"), Jago Antia's dead brother
BURJOR MAMA, Jago Antia's much-loved uncle

*The Story*

Subramanian, a retired officer in the Indian ministry of defense, tells his listeners that he once knew a man who met a ghost and proceeds to relate the whole story.

When Major General Jahangir ("Jago") Antia turns fifty, he begins to suffer phantom pain in his missing leg. Nothing relieves his suffering, and fearing that the pain and distraction will affect his command and cause the deaths of some of his men, he retires and returns to his boyhood home in Bombay. His parents are long dead, but the home is maintained by the faithful housekeeper, Amir Khan, who tells him that the upstairs rooms have been shut up for years and that he will need to sleep in the study. Jago Antia plans to sell the house but promises Amir Khan that he will provide for him.

Soon after he arrives, Jago Antia lies in bed musing about his successful career when he hears a muffled voice crying out. Strapping on his artificial leg, he starts up the stairs and hears the voice, a young voice, call out again, and he senses "a rush of motion on the balcony that ran around the outside of the house." He hears footsteps approaching, and a flash of lightning reveals wet footprints on the hallway's tile floor. The voice cries out again, low and melancholy, and Jago Antia slumps against the banister and slides to the bottom of the stairs.

For three days, the shaken Jago Antia paces the house in distress. His batman, Thapa, rejoins him and is shocked by his old master's appearance. Jago Antia visits the real estate agent Todywalla, who tells him that the house is unmarketable because "There's something in that house." Mustering the determination to spend a night untroubled, Jago Antia beds down in the study but soon hears the ghostly voice and starts up the stairs with the terrified Thapa following. The voice comes close to him and asks with a sob, "Where shall I go?" Jago Antia then backs up so fast that he tumbles over the balcony and falls to the bottom of the stairwell.

At this point the narrative switches to a flashback of Jago Antia parachuting into Sylhet in 1971 during the war in which West Pakistan was brutalizing East Pakistan and the Indian army intervened to stop the flood of Pakistani refugees into East Bengal. The result of the war was the creation of Bangladesh; Sylhet is a city in the tea-growing area of the northeastern part of that country. In the middle of this flashback, Jago Antia drifts into a reverie about a radio familiar to him from his childhood. While leading his paratroopers into fire, Jago Antia steps on a land mine and splinters a leg, and in a heroic moment, he seizes a sword and in four strokes amputates his crushed leg.

After Jago Antia wakes up and recuperates from his fall, he confers with Thakker, a sales manager who moonlights as an exorcist, who tells him that the ghost is powerful and can be banished only by someone from its family who will go upstairs to confront it naked and alone. The narrative then reverts to when Jago Antia was six years old and he and his brother Sohrab ("Soli") were flying a kite given them by their much-idolized uncle, Burjor Mama, an army officer on whose breast pocket is stitched his name, B. MEHTA. The boys are on the apartment building roof, and in a childish struggle over the kite, Jago Antia knocks Soli over and then falls off the roof with him. Soli's body cushions the impact for Jago Antia but Soli dies. Jago Antia's anguish is extreme, and when on his next birthday he is asked what he would like he can reply only, "A uniform." This knowledge enables an understanding of the ending of the story in which the naked Jago Antia discards his artificial leg, mounts the stairway, and confronts the ghost, who is wearing an olive-green uniform with the name J. ANTIA on the pocket. "In the [boy's] eyes he saw his vicious and ravenous strength, his courage and his devotion, his silence and his pain, his whole misshapen and magnificent life, and Jago Antia said, 'Jehangir, Jehangir, you're already at home.'"

*Themes and Meanings*

Most of the fictional Jago Antia's life seems to flow from his childhood experiences with Burjor Mama and Soli. The young Jehangir (the name Jago came later, chosen by the men in his regiment) lived in the shadow of Soli, who won all of their fights and captained the impromptu cricket teams. Moreover, their father said of Soli's cricket play that he had "a lovely style," a phrase that lingers in the adult Jago Antia's memory. Soli's athletic grace was reinforced by their mother when one evening she came in their room with two glasses of milk and *The Illustrated Weekly of India* with an article about the Indian prince Ranjitsinhji, who distinguished himself in England as a cricket player. Ranjitsinhji "was the most beautiful batsman, like a dancer he turned their bouncers to the boundaries with his wrists, he drove with clean elegance, he had good manners, and he said nothing to their insults, and he showed them all he was the best of them all, he was the Prince, he was lovely." Obviously, Soli is meant to be Ranjitsinhji's successor, and Soli keeps the magazine in his private drawer, occasionally allowing Jehangir to look at it.

Given this relationship, it is natural for Jehangir to make a hero of the manly, good-hearted Burjor Mama, whose military career has established him as a figure of glamour in the household. Jago Antia's courage and leadership derive from his need to live up to the image of Burjor Mama that shines in his imagination. The phantom pain that overtakes Jago Antia in 1991 when he turns the crucial age of fifty works its way up from his subconscious doubts about himself and vanishes after the climactic encounter with the ghost of his childhood. When the boy in the olive green uniform asks "Where shall I go?" Jago Antia consoles him by saying, "Jehangir, Jehangir, you're already at home." The story ends with Jago Antia at peace, drinking tea with Amir Khan and Thapa, thinking that "for him it was too late for anything but a kind of solitude, that he would give his body to the fire, that in the implacable hills to the north, among the rocks, he and other men and women, each with histories of their own, would find each other for life and for death." This spiritual surrender embodies the Buddhist doctrine of dharma.

A precedent for the theme of a man encountering his own ghost in his former home exists in Henry James's "The Jolly Corner," in which an elderly man discovers what he might have been had he taken a different course in life.

## Style and Technique

"Dharma" opens with an unnamed narrator in a bar talking with his friend Ramani about a haunted house with which Ramani is familiar. The discussion inspires the elderly Subramanian, a retired civil servant, to tell the story about Jago Antia that follows. This opening suggests a conventional frame structure in the manner of Joseph Conrad, with a loquacious narrator commenting in passing throughout the narrative and wrapping the yarn up at the end with a knowing commentary; but in fact nothing more is heard of Subramanian and the story could have dispensed with him entirely.

The flashbacks fill in necessary background at the right points in the story. Jago Antia's fall from the balcony leads into the parachute drop in Sylhet that defines his courage and tells the grisly story of his losing a leg. In addition, after Thakker tells him he must go upstairs naked and alone, Jago Antia stands at the bottom of the stairs and in his musings recounts his childhood experiences with Burjor Mama, Soli, and his parents. This manipulation of time succeeds in maintaining suspense by not giving away too much too soon. Ramani's story of haunted houses anticipates the tale that Subramanian will tell, and a major example of foreshadowing occurs when Jago Antia during the battle for Sylhet stares at the radio in a tailor's shop and experiences a "flickering vision" of an earlier radio in an earlier room. This earlier radio emerges in the later flashback as one that Soli owned and that Jehangir was forbidden to touch.

The introduction—and abandonment—of Subramanian serves little apparent purpose, but "Dharma" remains continuously engrossing nevertheless.

*Frank Day*

# THE DIAMOND AS BIG AS THE RITZ

*Author:* F. Scott Fitzgerald (1896-1940)
*Type of plot:* Satire
*Time of plot:* About 1920
*Locale:* Montana
*First published:* 1922

> *Principal characters:*
>> JOHN T. UNGER, a student at "the most expensive and the most exclusive boys' preparatory school in the world"
>> PERCY WASHINGTON, his classmate
>> BRADDOCK WASHINGTON, Percy's father, the world's richest man
>> KISMINE WASHINGTON, Percy's sister and John's sweetheart

## The Story

At St. Midas's School, John T. Unger befriends a new boy, Percy Washington, who invites him to spend the summer on the family estate in the Montana Rockies. Percy's boast that his father owns a diamond as big as the Ritz-Carlton Hotel seems preposterous, but on arrival John learns that the Washingtons' family chateau actually does sit atop a five-cubic-mile flawless diamond.

The next morning, Percy sketches the family history for his friend. In 1866, his grandfather Fitz-Norman, a "direct descendant" of George Washington and Lord Baltimore, left the defeated Confederacy accompanied by a group of faithful slaves to start a ranch in the West. The venture failed within a month. Then, while hunting for food, Fitz-Norman noticed a brilliant stone drop from a squirrel's mouth—a perfect diamond worth one hundred thousand dollars. Returning to the site with his employees the following day, Fitz-Norman soon filled his saddlebags with diamonds. When the sale of a few of these gems in New York City loosed a wave of wild rumors, he realized that he would have to operate clandestinely lest the government seize his diamond mine and establish a monopoly to avert financial panic. Accordingly, he poured his gems into two trunks and peddled them to the courts of Europe and Asia. Later, his son Braddock (Percy's father) sealed the mine and devoted himself to protecting the family's incalculable fortune—and its secret.

The more complex of the story's two strands unwinds from this effort at concealment. Fitz-Norman had corrupted the government surveyors and arranged for omission of the estate from official maps; Braddock, resorting to more elaborate measures, created an artificial magnetic field, tinkered with the surveyors' instruments, and altered the area's geographic features. The advent of the airplane, however, has made discovery of the Washington domain inevitable. At the time of John Unger's visit, about two dozen aviators who have been brought down by Washington antiaircraft fire are being kept prisoner in a glass-lined pit; one of this group has recently escaped, however, and soon a squadron of American planes arrives and begins shelling the mountain in preparation for an invasion. Braddock, realizing that only divine intervention can preserve his family's treasure and privilege, tries to bribe God with a diamond so huge that it requires two slaves to lift it. When the bribe is apparently refused and the planes land on the chateau's lawn, Braddock sets off an explosion that reduces the entire mountain to dust.

Anchored in John's role as protagonist, the plot's other strand develops his romance with Percy's sister Kismine. It crosses the story's baseline at only two points: first, when, after falling in love with Kismine, John surmises that the Washingtons cannot risk allowing him to leave their El Dorado alive; and again in the ironic coda, when he learns that Kismine mistook the only rhinestones at the chateau for diamonds while hastily filling her pocket as they fled from the mountain's apocalyptic destruction. However, even though the relationship between the young lovers weaves no web of significant actions, F. Scott Fitzgerald treats it as the central element; whatever the story's resolved meaning may be, its focus is certainly not on Braddock Washington's failure to escape retribution for his hubris; rather, it is on John's recognition that, for some unspecified reason, he has lost his illusions. (In the torrent of philosophizing that serves as conclusion, it is John who pronounces two of Fitzgerald's most quoted sentences: "Everybody's youth is a dream, a form of chemical madness" and "His was a great sin who first invented consciousness.")

## Themes and Meanings

Published near the beginning of his career (Fitzgerald wrote it in either 1921 or, at the very latest, early January, 1922), "The Diamond as Big as the Ritz" shows a constellation of the motifs that would persist throughout the author's career. Despite the fantastic trappings, it tells a radically autobiographical tale. Fitzgerald situates Hades, the Ungers' hometown, on the Mississippi—like his own St. Paul—and devotes the story's initial pages to ridiculing its pretensions. (Even a Chicago beef-princess, the author sneers, would judge the most sophisticated social functions in Hades to be "perhaps a little tacky.") John Unger reflects the self-congratulatory boosterism of his provincial upbringing, and in this respect he is a target of satire. John also, however, evokes sympathy as a young man daunted by an unshakable sense of his unworthiness among the aristocratic rich. The model is unmistakable. In a letter to John O'Hara in 1933, Fitzgerald described himself as having "a two cylinder inferiority complex. So if I were elected King of Scotland tomorrow after graduating from Eton, Magdelene the Guards, with an embryonic history which tied me to the Plantagenets, I would still be a parvenue [*sic*]. I spent my youth in alternately crawling in front of the kitchen maids and insulting the great."

Fitzgerald attributed his problem, in the same letter, to the tensions inherent in being "half black Irish and half old American stock with the usual exaggerated ancestral pretensions" (his paternal forebears included Francis Scott Key, after whom he was named). Precisely this personal conflict constitutes the story's subtext. As midwestern burghers, the Ungers suggest his mother's side of the family: Grandfather Mc-

Quillan rose from poor immigrant to wealthy merchant through the wholesale grocery business in St. Paul. The Washingtons, whose breeding stands in conspicuous contrast to the Ungers' tackiness, clearly represent the Fitzgeralds (an association emphasized by the name Fitz-Norman), and in particular his father, Edward, a gentleman with southern grace characterized by his son as "one of the generation of the colonies and the revolution."

The biographical reference of St. Midas's is still more apparent. Like Basil Lee's search for acceptance in "The Freshest Boy," John Unger's need to adjust to living among social superiors harks back to Fitzgerald's painful entrance into the prep school world. However, a simple identification of the mythical prep school on the outskirts of Boston as a vast exaggeration of the Newman School, the Roman Catholic academy in New Jersey attended by the author, seems not to reach nearly far enough. The story's dreamlike quality calls for psychological analysis, and from this perspective, the significance of St. Midas's relates to its position within the "dream's" structure: midway, in effect, between the Unger and Washington families. Essentially, "The Diamond as Big as the Ritz" traces a boy's transformation into a man. The pivotal moment in that process (which is set in motion by his departure from the "maternal fatuity" of Hades) is the encounter with his alter ego, Percy, at the school appropriately named for King Midas—in a manner of speaking, the "patron saint" of transmutation. As a result of the friendship with his "dream self," John virtually becomes a Washington, emerges as an heir of sorts to the "father" he has presumably wished dead in his fantasies, and confirms the meaning of his passage through adolescence by spending a symbolically nuptial night with Kismine.

That interpretation, however, strikes to the design written on the story's underside; what Fitzgerald presents at the surface seems to obey no corresponding intent. Indeed, he shifts direction so often that one infers that the fable is obedient to no conscious plan at all. Until well past the introductory sections, Fitzgerald makes a target of snobbery, fixing expectations that the plot will somehow produce a complementary moral. By the midpoint, however, the energy of this attack is spent, and snobbery does not affect the combination of events that brings the story to its climax. Nor, for that matter, does John Unger, who is relegated to the role of spectator while Braddock Washington is being defeated by the United States government and rejected by God. Then, in the final section, Fitzgerald not only reestablishes John at the center but also assigns him a closing soliloquy about youth and illusion that has no discernible connection with either society's vanities or the destruction of the Washington empire.

*Style and Technique*

The thematic uncertainty of "The Diamond as Big as the Ritz" is reflected in the story's style as well. Having identified no urgent, shaping idea for what is presumptively an allegory, Fitzgerald allows himself to be seduced into conceits that develop no coherent metaphoric pattern. For example: John rides the last miles of his journey to the Washingtons' celestial estate in a huge automobile made of precious metals; the train has taken him only as far as the village of Fish, populated by twelve "sombre and inexplicable souls who sucked a lean milk from the almost literally bare rock on which a mysterious populatory force had begotten them." "Fish" points to "ichthus," the emblem of Jesus the Savior, the village's dozen inhabitants patently represent the apostles. The meaning seems clear: The magnitude of the Washingtons' opulence sets them beyond the pale of Christian teaching. However, why invent an extravagant metaphor to introduce an idea that will quickly become self-evident on John's arrival at the chateau? Why, having gone to such lengths, subsequently neglect to elaborate the implications of an existence without moral stricture or to link that philosophical issue to any of the several other themes, including the one grandly paraded in the ending? In this instance, as in others, Fitzgerald apparently became infatuated with his own cleverness: Once he had created the image of the twelve men of Fish nursing at the ungenerous breast of St. Peter's church, he could not surrender it, even though it engages no broader purpose.

A similar self-indulgence is manifest in the story's sophomoric humor. The many puns on "Hades" show no wit. For example, Mr. Unger, on saying farewell to his son, assures him that "we'll keep the home fires burning"—and their coy naughtiness is wearing. Still more annoying is the smirky sexual innuendo that stretches from start to finish. Exactly what information the author is pretending to convey in describing Mrs. Unger as famous for "political addresses" delivered "from hot-box to hot-bed" is unclear, but no one can mistake the covert message. The names Fitzgerald produces are in the same vein. The repeated use of the middle initial stresses that John T. Unger is susceptible to being read "John Tonguer." Kismine is plainly "kiss mine," and the imperative in her sister's name, Jasmine, is only slightly less obvious ("jazz" before it came to mean the kind of music played in black brothels, meant "to copulate"). Most egregious of all, Fitzgerald names the personal servant who assists John at his bath Gygsum—one of several variants of "jism," slang for semen.

Finally, however, "The Diamond as Big as the Ritz" is larger than the sum of its deeply flawed parts. Though immature and crudely executed, it displays a profligate talent, a poetic genius that has not yet learned to respect itself or to value the importance of discipline. In conceiving a symbol of wealth so stupendous as to be beyond valuation, Fitzgerald was not imaging a yearning for luxury or power; rather, the diamond reifies the impossible dream of escape from all humiliating restraint. If, at this stage of his development, the expression of that idea is amateurishly clumsy, one nevertheless responds to the energy the idea is generating as it presses outward from the core of the writer's mind. Two years later, Fitzgerald would complete his masterpiece, *The Great Gatsby*. In James Gatz's transformation into Jay Gatsby, the "Platonic conception of himself," one sees the refinement of John Unger's fantasy.

*Frank Gado*

# THE DIAMOND LENS

*Author:* Fitz-James O'Brien (c. 1828-1862)
*Type of plot:* Fantasy
*Time of plot:* The mid-nineteenth century
*Locale:* New York City
*First published:* 1858

>        *Principal characters:*
>            MR. LINLEY, the narrator and protagonist, a man obsessed with
>                the microscopic world
>            JULES SIMON, the possessor of a rare diamond, for which he is
>                murdered by Linley
>            MADAME VULPES, a spirit medium
>            ANIMULA, a beautiful inhabitant of the microscopic world, with
>                whom Linley falls in love

*The Story*

Mr. Linley has had an obsessive fascination with microscopic investigations from the time he was ten years old. Beneath the microscope, he sees a world akin to *Alf layla wa-layla* (fifteenth century; *The Arabian Nights' Entertainments*, 1706-1708) in which the dull veil of ordinary existence that hangs across the world seems to roll away and to lay bare a land of enchantments; like many of the narrators in the stories of Poe, he feels elevated above all other men, seeing the world in a more profound way. However, as is also typical of Poe characters, it is not a scientific thirst that drives the protagonist but rather the pure enjoyment of a poet lost in the enchanted gardens and fantastic foliage of a world of imaginative wonders. The world he seeks is the world of aesthetic, not material, reality.

When the narrator grows up, he has little real interest in anything but his microscopic investigations. Because he has a considerable amount of money, as is often the case in such stories, he sets up a laboratory in New York City and begins to teach himself to become an expert microscopist. Throughout his studies and experiments, however, he feels frustrated by the limitations of his instruments. He imagines depths beyond that which his microscopes can reveal, and he dreams of discovering a perfect lens that will allow him to see what no man has ever seen. After months spent in a futile search for such a lens, quite coincidentally, as again is often the case in such fantasies, a young neighbor drops by and tells him of his visit to Madame Vulpes, a spirit medium who has related to him secrets that only magic could provide. The young man is a Jew, which supplies the stereotype of mysterious occult connections, as well as the stereotype of a peddler with mysterious objects in his possession. Hoping that Madame Vulpes will direct him to the secret of the powerful lens that he desires, the narrator goes to visit her.

In pursuit of his quest, Linley wishes to speak to Leeuwenhoek, the great father of microscopics, who tells him that he must find a diamond of 140 carats and subject it to electromagnetic currents to rearrange its atoms to make a universal and perfect lens. The greatest ironic coincidence in this story that depends on such coincidences is that Jules Simon, the Jewish neighbor, indeed has such a diamond. When the narrator discovers this, he gets Simon drunk, tricks him into revealing where the diamond is, and then kills him to get it, afterward calmly concealing his crime by making it look like a suicide—all of which is typical of a Poe story.

The last section of "The Diamond Lens" introduces the final element of the story and changes it from a fable about the quasi-scientific overreacher to a Romantic parable about the aesthetic ideal. When the narrator finishes constructing the lens, he puts a drop of water under it and discovers a realm of indescribable beauty filled with an atmosphere of magical luminousness. He knows that he has penetrated below the realm of protozoa to a world of supernatural radiance—a forestlike expanse, without a living thing—a beautiful chromatic desert. Then, most fantastic of all, he sees something moving, a female form, a divine revelation of perfect beauty that makes him think of aesthetic realms beyond actual reality. Given the conventions of such fantasies, it is inevitable that Linley fall in love with her, even though he knows that the planet Neptune is not more distant from him than she.

He names this microscopic vision of beauty "Animula" and longs for her with a passion reserved for that which is totally unobtainable; his whole life becomes absorbed by her. Trying to shake off his obsession, he goes to a theatrical presentation by a dancer reputed to be the most beautiful and most graceful woman in the world. However, he can see only how gross and discordant are her movements, how thick are her ankles, how heavy and muscular are her limbs. When he returns to Animula, she seems to be growing ill, and he frantically tries to discover what ails her, mourning as she withers away. Finally, he discovers (in the typical ironic revelation of the Poe/Bierce fantasy) that the water drop in which Animula lives has evaporated; knowing that it is too late to save her, he watches her shrivel up and blacken. The story ends, in typical Poe fashion, with madness.

## Themes and Meanings

"The Diamond Lens," a scientific fantasy, was very popular in the mid-nineteenth century. This work situates author Fitz-James O'Brien somewhere between Edgar Allan Poe and Ambrose Bierce in the development of such imaginative quasi-scientific fantasies, although O'Brien is not as profound in his use of genre as either of those writers. O'Brien wrote a clever and interesting story about moving beyond the realm of external reality into a world of absolute beauty and mad obsession, a theme that certainly places him in the Poe-Bierce tradition, but "The Diamond Lens" never goes beyond the surface gloss of the slick magazine writing of the time.

The basic theme of "The Diamond Lens" begins to reveal itself only in the last quarter of the story, when the protagonist discovers the beautiful creature in the drop of water under the microscope. It is a typical Romantic theme, predominant in the early part of the nineteenth century and sustained in the century's closing decades by the influence of Poe's work on the Aesthetes. "The Diamond Lens" focuses on the difference between the realm of actual, perceptible physical reality and that realm of a more profound reality that is a projection of the human imagination. The issue is the fineness of the perceiving eye, based on the assumption that there is a realm of reality beneath or beyond that of the everyday physical world that partakes of the spiritual and is thus the truest.

The theme is made most clear in the contrast between the figure of Animula and that of an actual female. There is no way that any actual female can compete with the almost spiritual nature of Animula, spiritual because she has a tiny body. The theme is an aesthetic one, in which it is clear that the most human aspiration is to transcend the physical, for the physical is an indication of the grossness of the body itself. The great Romantic ideal is that one responds to a spiritual transcendence of body. The more that body is distanced from the sense of physicality and thus mortality, the more beautiful it is taken to be.

O'Brien inherits this Romantic ideal from Poe's Platonic retreat from body. The problem of this particular story, however, is that it depends too much on the simple trick ending of the evaporation of the drop of water in which the beautiful creature resides. This event has nothing to do with the theme of the beauty of the spiritual; it is simply a convenient way to indicate the impossibility of the narrator's love for absolute beauty. "The Diamond Lens," although it has some of the characteristics of a Romantic fable, is really primarily a trick story appealing to the mid-nineteenth century fascination with trick endings and with scientific fantasies.

*Style and Technique*

The style of "The Diamond Lens" primarily depends on O'Brien's manipulation of the point of view of a narrator who is so obsessed with his own desire and quasi-scientific aims that the entire world of the story centers on his obsession. The technique is a common one with such Romantic writers of the early nineteenth century as E. T. A. Hoffmann, Ludwig Tieck, and Poe. The language of the story suggests a narrator who is less an actual person than he is a convention of point of view itself—a stereotypical representation of the ultimate Romantic dream, here trivialized by a clever craftsman of the short story who knows how to capitalize on a typical short-story theme but who does not manage to elevate that theme and technique beyond popular slick fiction. It was precisely such stories as O'Brien's that gave the short-story genre during the late nineteenth century the unsavory reputation of being little more than a vehicle for facile technique. What marks the difference between O'Brien's story and the most powerful stories of Poe and Bierce is that O'Brien never achieves either the profound sense of the Romantic ideal of these writers or their keen sense of the particular characteristics of the short-story form.

*Charles E. May*

# THE DIARY OF A MADMAN

*Author:* Nikolai Gogol (1809-1852)
*Type of plot:* Psychological
*Time of plot:* The 1830's
*Locale:* St. Petersburg, Russia
*First published:* "Zapiski sumasshedshego," 1835 (English translation, 1945)

*Principal characters:*
>THE NARRATOR, an unhappy clerk who is part of the vast
>    government bureaucracy of mid-nineteenth century Russia
>HIS BOSS, who is also referred to as "The Chief of the Division"
>SOPHIE, the chief's daughter
>MADGIE and
>FIDELE, two dogs who can speak and exchange letters, the
>    madman claims

## The Story

"The Diary of a Madman," told in the first person, purports to be a diary kept by a forty-two-year-old clerk who has a meaningless job in the vast governmental bureaucracy of mid-nineteenth century Russia. His best prospects for advancement are far behind him, and his duties consist of routine tasks such as sharpening his employer's quills or copying information from one departmental form to another. He is unmarried, bored, and treated without kindness or courtesy. "They don't listen to me, they don't hear me, they don't see me," he realizes late in the story. "I cannot bear this suffering."

The daily entries in his journal reveal a man slowly going mad as he comes to understand his own insignificance. The narrator is scorned by his landlady, reprimanded by his boss, and accosted by strangers in the street. The diary shows how he manufactures explanations for these indignities. "There are so many crooks, so many Poles," so many civil servants "who sit on top of one another like dogs." He is quick to blame others for his shabby life. "I see through his indignation. He is envious," he says of one foe who has belittled him. "Perhaps he's noticed the marks of favor bestowed on me. A lot I care what he says of me." Such entries show the clerk using the conventional and commonplace rationalizations to which many people resort to explain away their failures and to evade their own contributions to their unhappiness. "High officers, they get all the best things in this world. You discover a crumb of happiness, you reach out for it and then along comes a high official and snatches it away."

Increasingly, these mild misperceptions cease to be effective. When reality metes out to the clerk more than his commonplace ideas can explain, he starts inventing more fantastic rationalizations, which seem to remove him further from reality. Adding to the pressures are his rare glimpses of Sophie, his boss's daughter. He indulges in obsessive thoughts of love and devotion toward her that are far out of proportion to her occasional and demeaning comments to him. "Holy Fathers, the way she was dressed! Her dress was white, and fluffy, like a swan, and when she looked at me, I swear, it was like the sun." His comments about Sophie reveal a mind gradually losing touch with reality. "Perhaps I am really a general or a count and only seem to be a clerk. . . . There are plenty of instances in history when somebody quite ordinary . . . turns out to be a public figure." As the madman loses himself in this kind of wishful thinking, his personality begins to fragment. One part of him actually starts believing that he occupies a high place on the social ladder. Another part, the part that seems to need feedback from the "real" world, is reduced to a series of occasional hallucinatory experiences that tell him the truths he otherwise could not hear. He thinks that he overhears Sophie's dog, Madgie, talking with another dog. He thinks that he intercepts some of the letters that the two dogs are secretly writing to each other; one reveals that "Sophie can hardly control her laughter when she sees him," and another suggests that Sophie is about to be married.

As the journal entries start to show the fragmentation of the pathetic clerk's mind, the sane part of him concocts "mad" explanations and the mad part of him that reveals "sane" truths grow further apart. In the gap, yet a third personality begins to emerge. "This is a day of great jubilation. Spain has a new king. They've found him. I am the king." As a way of healing the disparity between who he is and who he wants to be, the madman comes to believe that he is the uncrowned king of a Western European country. At work, he takes to signing his forms as "Ferdinand VIII." At the post office, he inquires about the arrival of his royal retinue. To his landlady, he shows off his new royal robes, patched together from pieces of his overcoat. Three-quarters of the way through the story, the clerk has clearly turned into a madman. His pathological behavior finds little understanding from those who know him, and he is committed to an asylum for the insane.

This attempted cure simply multiplies the madman's disjointed personalities. As the king of Spain, he interprets what happens to him as an international conspiracy to keep him from his throne. He even sees the shaved heads of the lunatics in the asylum and thinks that they are Dominican or Capuchin monks. When his old personality returns and he again knows himself as a clerk, he experiences being beaten with sticks, a common "treatment" for the mentally ill in a nineteenth century European asylum. The beatings bring out an even more childish personality fragment. He cries, "Mother, save your wretched son! Let your tears fall on his sick head. See how they torture him!" The story ends with him once again retreating into his "king of Spain" fantasy, that being the psychological mode that seems to bring him the most comfort. The ending leaves the disconcerting suggestion that sometimes it is better to be mad and happy than it is to be sane but miserable.

*Themes and Meanings*

"The Diary of a Madman" is one of Nikolai Gogol's most troubling and complex stories. It works on several different levels at once. On a psychological level, it is a surprisingly accurate account of the onset of a mental pathology, rendered decades before psychosis was carefully studied by European scientists. The story depicts a man growing increasingly psychotic. He misinterprets the information from his surroundings and gives himself an unrealistic, though more tolerable, sense of who he his. These reinterpretations increasingly remove him from the real world, and those around him begin to see him as a threat. They move to institutionalize him, this prescription for a cure accelerating the speed of his journey into insanity.

On a sociological level, though, this story is not so much about insanity as it is about the kind of society that causes it. The madman's job, his acquaintances, and the characters he meets in the streets are so configured that his madness is in itself a "sane" response or adaptation to the social pressures around him. In this sense, the story is a realistic portrayal of a social system that drives at least one of its members crazy. Nineteenth century Russia's emphasis on status, appearance, and bureaucratic rules, Gogol claims, creates an environment that encourages people to be more concerned with their roles than with their real selves: Their egos seem to have less value than the social positions those egos occupy.

Gogol here explores the effects of such a system, hinting that values such as these may tempt many into attending to the wrong things. His remains a portrait of madness, but a madness brought on by a society that in itself is more than a little mad.

*Style and Technique*

Many of Gogol's stories have such a contemporary ring to them that it is easy to forget that they were written a century and a half ago about a culture that had neither the industrial nor the urban attributes that are supposed to account for some of the characteristic themes and styles of modern fiction. Like many of his stories, Gogol's "The Diary of a Madman" studies how individual selves become alienated from the societies that are supposed to support them. This modern-day motif is developed with an equally modernistic approach to narrative style. In this story, Gogol explores alienation by studying its effects on an individual consciousness. Readers are eased into the conflict by being allowed to experience directly the narrator's twisted thoughts. Like many moderns, Gogol avoids the comforts of a realistic plot and a detached, objective narration. Instead, he plunges his readers into a worldview in which the fantasies, projections, and hallucinations of the narrator are treated as if they were as "real" as the setting, the commentary of other characters, or the incidents of the plot.

Gogol, however, is a bit gentler on his readers than many moderns. He eases them into the fantastic and implausible patterns of perception characteristic of his narrator by starting them off with a relatively "sane" speaker who is keeping an apparently "sane" diary. Because Gogol's interest is in showing how sanity can dissolve under societal pressures, his trick is to begin gradually with a more traditional and familiar narrative style and only gradually to introduce the oversensitized, psychotic quirks of his madman. Thus, when the narrator first claims to have overheard the two dogs, Madgie and Fidele, talking, Gogol returns his readers to a saner ground: "As a matter of fact, the world has seen many similar occurrences before." The narrator alludes to the English fish who broke water and "uttered a couple of words" and to the two cows whose stories recently received newspaper coverage for going "into a store and asking for a pound of tea." These early entries in the diary show a normal or familiar reasoning process trying to explain abnormal and unfamiliar data.

Page by page, though, the reader is encouraged to follow the disintegration of the narrator's personality by deciphering progressively more alien words and ideas. Thus, the dating of the journal entries starts familiarly: "December 8" or "November 13." They then progress oddly to: "Year 2000, April 43" or "No date. A day without date." They end with the nonsense of "25th date" or "da 34 te Mnth. Yr. yraurbeF 349." Similarly, the narrator's experiences seem to begin at the familiar "I see no advantage in working in our department. No side benefits whatever"; they progress to the confusing "But today something suddenly became clear to me when I recalled the conversation between the two dogs I'd overheard on Nevsky Avenue." Finally, they end at what seems to be full-blown psychosis: "I hear the twanging of a guitar string through the fog; on one side, the sea, and on the other, Italy." With such progressions Gogol hopes to give his readers a firsthand glimpse of a mind going mad. For early in the nineteenth century, this was an unusually innovative narrative structure.

*Philip Woodard*

# THE DIFFERENCE

*Author:* Ellen Glasgow (1873-1945)
*Type of plot:* Domestic realism
*Time of plot:* About 1920
*Locale:* A large eastern seaboard city
*First published:* 1923

*Principal characters:*

> MARGARET FLEMING, a forty-four-year-old housewife
> GEORGE FLEMING, her forty-five-year-old husband, a
> businessperson and real-estate developer, to whom she has
> been married for twenty years
> ROSE MORRISON, an artist in her early twenties, George's recent
> lover
> DOROTHY CHAMBERS, a housewife, Margaret's best friend from
> girlhood

## The Story

On a Saturday afternoon, Margaret Fleming gazes out at the autumn rains stripping leaves from the trees, as she has every fall for the past twenty years but with quite different feelings. Before she saw them as symbols of loss; now she sees them sweeping away all her illusions. On the hearth of the library study, her husband George's room, lies the fallen letter that has caused this change. It has announced the death of her marriage. Gazing at herself in the mirror, she wonders how he, one year older, could begin a new love, for her an act of desecration. Hearing his step, she retrieves the letter, hiding it in the front of her dress.

They exchange trivial conversation. Looking at him, vital and healthy as always, she is surprised to discover signs of slackness about his mouth that she had not noticed before. She wonders why these appeared only after he loved another, and suspects she does not really know him even after twenty years. However, until now she had believed her marriage nearly perfect. He admires her colorful flower arrangements; she remembers that she has always been pale and muses on how her surface life can look unchanged while she has been struck to the roots of her being. Does Rose Morrison, George's young lover, have the color she lacks?

Before he leaves for business, he asks if she will correct the galleys of a history of law he has been writing. She realizes he could not have done it without her; she has been necessary to his serious life. She agrees, as always. He also asks her to do some routine domestic tasks for him. She wonders whether Rose has done any of these things.

She paces, hearing the rain and falling leaves, and resolves never to give him up. The butler announces Dorothy Chambers, her oldest friend and principal support, yet

Margaret is reluctant to see her, discovering that suffering leads to deception and fearing that Dorothy will detect the difference in her.

Dorothy asks Margaret's help in a charity drive, then mentions that two of their separated acquaintances have reconciled. Margaret is shocked out of her numbness; she cannot understand how the woman agreed because he had claimed to love the other woman. Dorothy cynically dismisses the quality of man's love and states that the woman enjoys the act of forgiveness because of her "spiritual vanity." To her, Margaret, though lovely, knows nothing of life. When Margaret retorts that Dorothy knows little of love, the latter asks whether she means man's love or woman's—for women love ideally, men only sensually. When Margaret still cannot understand why a man would want to live with a woman he has said he does not love, Dorothy points out that marriage involves more than love; it also involves convenience. Margaret bursts out that the woman then ought to give up the man; Dorothy asks her whether she would in a similar situation.

Margaret hesitates, then declares that she would. In making that decision, she experiences a peace beyond pain, grief, and bitterness. Dorothy tells her that she is a fool; George would be a comfort and a source of security even if love were over. Then she leaves.

Margaret takes a moment to plan her actions, then carries out the routine duties George had requested. Then, disdaining to take the car provided by George, she sets out to ride the trolley to the suburban address given in the letter—a villa George has acquired in an unfashionable suburb. Out in the rain, she is overwhelmed with melancholy, feeling utterly deserted; in the streetcar, immersed in isolation, she finds Dorothy's phrase "spiritual vanity" echoing in her ears. Details from the entire twenty-year marriage drift through her mind like dead leaves.

From the suburban station she walks to the villa through piles of sodden leaves that look like graves. The villa itself is nondescript, neglected. A maid answers the bell, informing Margaret that her mistress is out; when Margaret announces that she will wait, she is led to a recently occupied living room. Then Rose enters. Margaret is at first dazzled by her beauty, then sees it only as the flame of burning leaves.

Behind Rose's youth and beauty Margaret senses the assurance of habitual self-gratification. Rose says that she is glad Margaret came, that it hurt her to write the letter but that she believes in always telling the truth. She says that George does not know she wrote; she wanted to spare him, as, of course, Margaret does. Margaret believes she has spent her life sparing him.

Rose offers Margaret a cup of tea or a cigarette, speculating on what Victorian women like Margaret did for solace without cigarettes. Margaret declines, now seeing in Rose all the crude rapacity of youth and also the insolence of an artist. Rose acknowledges this: She has a studio in Greenwich Village but paints in the summers at Ogonquit, where she met George. She knew George was married but also that Margaret did not understand him, as she does. Rejecting Margaret's claim of shared experiences, she asserts that only an artist could understand him. When Margaret asks whether George claimed to be misunderstood, Rose becomes nearly indignant, stating that George would rather suffer silently than make her unhappy. As proof of George's love, Rose offers to show his letters. Then she states that if she were in Margaret's position, she would gladly give him up out of love.

Margaret recoils from this, finding Rose, like youth in general, eager to benefit from the sacrifices of others and realizing that all of her sacrifices have preserved George's youth at her expense. However, she has been trained in sacrifice, and she feels convinced that George must love Rose; otherwise he would not have brought her this much grief. She resolves to concede; as she leaves, Rose assures her that she and George share a superior understanding.

Margaret returns, convinced that George truly loves Rose, that his dilemma must have been devastating, that she has failed to understand him, and that she must sacrifice herself for him. Her love compels her not to stand in his way.

When they meet, she tells him that she has seen Rose Morrison, expecting him to be overcome by remorse. Instead he is blank, merely asking what she knows of Rose. In the face of this apparent denial, she discloses bit by bit her discoveries of that afternoon, ending with the confession that she does not want to stand in his way. Finally he exclaims, "What does it have to do with you?" and denies that he has ever loved Rose. He admits that Rose loves him, after her fashion, but for him it has been only a tawdry affair and he has no intention of leaving Margaret. He rehearses the history of their liaison, begun the previous summer when Margaret was ill, calling it simply a "recreation."

Margaret feels totally compromised, even sensing for a moment that she and Rose were bonded more closely in this experience of female disillusionment than she and George could ever be. She finds herself incapable of responding to George's pleas, mutely caught up in a sense of loss of more than love, for she has ceased to believe in life. As he embraces her, her glance strays through the window to the falling leaves outside.

## Themes and Meanings

The story is intricately plotted, with three climaxes and reversals, all carefully controlled by the focus on Margaret's consciousness. The first phase centers on her discovery of betrayal and infidelity, on the contrast between her placid assumption of routine domestic duties and George's varied outside interests. She is devastated that a twenty-year marriage should expire in an afternoon, but he blandly carries on with business as usual. Her first instinct is to fight for what is hers. This movement comes to a climax in the visit of Dorothy Chambers with her cynical views of the different ways of men and women in love and her suggestion that marriage involves both more and less than love. Margaret rejects that counsel and decides to confront Rose; the implication is that she continues to feel that marriage depends on mutual love.

The second phase involves her exchange with Rose. Here the conflict is partly older woman and experience against younger woman and the intensity of youth, partly domestic housewife against independent career woman. However, more is engaged than that. Both women speak of love as a common, identifiable experience and feeling, almost a supreme law to which both must conform. Margaret realizes that if George loves Rose—and Rose is confident that he does—in the way the women speak of love, then Margaret must give him up. Only for that supreme reason could he have hurt her so much. She resolves to concede.

The third and final phase is her conference with George. Here, once again, things turn out not as she expected. Far from confirming Rose's account of their relationship, George denies its substance, asserting that it was no more significant than a game of golf. Margaret cannot understand this; he seems to be giving words such as "love" a totally different meaning, and this allows him to treat women as adversaries. This attitude desecrates all of them. Small wonder that she now feels life has no meaning; she has discovered that the kind of love that means so much to women is unappreciated by men. This final climax is shattering, because the only alternative it leaves is the cynical opportunism of Dorothy Chambers.

*Style and Technique*

The major stylistic device used by Ellen Glasgow is the symbolism of autumn rain and falling leaves, which take on different nuances throughout the story. They appear prominently at both beginning and end, enclosing the action in an allusive arch of tone and feeling.

At the outset, the leaves are tied into the annual cycle of year: Their falling signifies the necessity of passing, of the old giving way to the new. Thus autumn reminds Margaret that she too is aging, but she accepts it as the price of her memories and values. This time; however, the fall seems final: Her hopes of continuing happiness have been destroyed.

The image of the leaves recurs at critical points throughout. Margaret's beauty is passing like the leaves; her spirit has been stricken like the leaves and is driven by the storm. She is pale of complexion, colorless like the fallen leaves; Rose has the blazing glow of youth. Margaret remembers her engagement in a rose garden; now the petals and leaves of that garden are nothing but withered ashes. Her universe is dying down.

The flame of love in Rose's eyes is likened to the blaze of color in burning leaves. However, her neglected villa is surrounded with heaps of rotting leaves, like grave mounds; George derides her dream that he and Rose had reached a "secret garden of romance" in which he became the "perfect lover." Both women's hopes and fantasies are stricken like leaves before George's selfish brutality. In the end, they have only the leaves.

*James L. Livingston*

# DI GRASSO
## A Tale of Odessa

*Author:* Isaac Babel (1894-1940)
*Type of plot:* Impressionistic
*Time of plot:* 1908
*Locale:* Odessa
*First published:* 1937 (English translation, 1955)

> *Principal characters:*
> THE NARRATOR, the interpreter of the story, presented as the same
>    person as the author
> THE NARRATOR, as a boy of fourteen, the protagonist of an
>    autobiographical recollection
> NICK SCHWARZ, a dealer in theater tickets (a scalper), for whom
>    the boy works in his spare time
> DI GRASSO, a Sicilian actor, the hero of a play performed by an
>    Italian troupe
> MADAM SCHWARZ, Nick's obese wife

### The Story

Because this brief work is a sophisticated commentary on the nature of art as well as "just a story," it is all the more interesting for the reader to know that it is the last work Isaac Babel published in his lifetime, before he fell victim to Stalinist justice. Although the exact circumstances of Babel's arrest in 1939 are not known, it is believed that he was charged with espionage, a patently contrived accusation; he was executed in 1941. The Jewish author, whose collections of stories were often reprinted during his lifetime, was "rehabilitated" after the death of Joseph Stalin—and his stories were reprinted again.

"Di Grasso" ostensibly focuses its attention on the Jewish theatrical world of prewar Odessa (about 1908), where one learns that the narrator as a boy of fourteen has recently "come under the sway" of the "tricky" ticket scalper Nick Schwarz and his "enormous silky handle bars." Without looking further into the relationship between the boy and the older man who is his "boss," the narrator instead describes (entertainingly) almost the entire action of a very bad play being newly performed by a traveling troupe of Italian actors. In this play, a "city slicker" named Giovanni temporarily lures the daughter of a rich peasant away from her betrothed—a poor shepherd played by the Sicilian actor Di Grasso. Di Grasso pleads with the girl to pray to the Virgin Mary—a huge, garish, wooden statue of whom is on the stage—but to no avail. In the last act, when Giovanni has become insufferably arrogant, Di Grasso suddenly soars across the stage, plunges downward onto Giovanni, bites through his throat, and sucks out the gushing blood—as the curtain falls.

Recognizing a hit when he sees one, Schwarz rushes to the box office, where he will wait all night, first in line to buy at dawn as many tickets as he can afford, for resale. The narrator shortly remarks that everyone in Theater Lane has been made happy by the new hit—except himself.

Now an entirely new story line develops. It seems that the lad has taken his father's watch without permission and pawned it to Schwarz—who eventually grows very fond of the big gold turnip. Even after the boy pays off the pledge, Schwarz refuses to give back the watch. The boy is in continual despair, imagining his father's wrath. He suggests that Schwarz and his father have the same character.

Then one night Schwarz and his wife, along with the boy, attend the final performance of the Italian troupe, with Di Grasso playing the shepherd "who is swung aloft by an incomprehensible power." Schwarz's wife, a fat and sentimental woman with "fish-like eyes," is overwhelmed by Di Grasso's great leap of love. She laments her own loveless life and berates her husband as they walk home from the theater with the boy trailing behind. The boy sobs openly, thinking of his father and the watch. Madam Schwarz hears the sobs and angrily forces her husband to return the watch, which he does, but not without giving the lad a vicious pinch.

The Schwarzes walk on, reach the corner, and disappear. The boy is left alone to experience ultimate happiness; he sees the world at night "frozen in silence and ineffably beautiful."

*Themes and Meanings*

At an elementary level of meaning, this story reveals the hidden relationships that may exist between apparently unconnected things and events. The Italian play, with its fantastic Sicilian actor, acts powerfully on the unloved wife of the swindler Nick Schwarz—and the boy and his watch are saved.

The story becomes more interesting when the reader sees that it is precisely the power of art that is significant, rather than merely "a play." Finally, it is not art in general that is at issue but art of great passion. Here, bad art is "transformed" by a passionate actor. Commenting on Di Grasso's acting, the narrator insists that the Sicilian, "with every word and gesture," confirms that there is "more justice in outbursts of noble passion than in all the joyless rules that run the world."

Such an explicit statement, not all that common in Babel, must be taken seriously. One wonders if "joyless rules" might refer to the Soviet Union of the bleak 1930's, and if Nick Schwarz, with his handlebar mustaches, is not intended to be seen as a pitiless Stalin figure. In any case, however, such political overtones are not the central focus of the work.

Passion in life, as in art, is a recurring motif in Babel's writings. Often it is accompanied by violence, as in the present work—which depicts not only the murderous leap of Di Grasso but also the descent of the curtain "full of menace" and the "vicious pinch" exacted by Schwarz. If life is lived fully and passionately, some violence is inevitable.

As art influences or works itself into life (here moving Schwarz's wife to take pity on the boy), so may life be transformed into art. Thus the boy, dizzy with happiness, sees the ordinary world of the city transformed into ineffable beauty. Here reality, art, and transcendent beauty merge in a remarkable vision. The boy's epiphany has the character of a future writer's first glimpse of the world beyond everyday reality (or of the way reality really is if one looks at it right).

## Style and Technique

One of the most interesting aspects of "Di Grasso" is the author's tone, particularly his attitude toward his subject. Throughout the story, the narrator seems affectionately and playfully condescending toward the characters he describes. For example, the reader learns that the Italian actors are bad not from any direct statement by the author (or by Schwarz, who cannot necessarily be trusted when he says "This stuff stinks"), but from such observations as "the shepherd twisted his head this way and that like a startled bird," or he kept "dashing off somewhere, his pants flapping." In general, Babel uses what the Russian Formalist critic Viktor Shklovsky called "defamiliarization" (*ostranenie*) to induce one to see the play as a profane work, though in a humorous light. That one is suddenly asked to see the terrible actor Di Grasso as a genuinely passionate hero is a welcome surprise, even if one realizes also that this perception is rather more symbolic than real. Babel describes the play much as Leo Tolstoy describes grand opera in *War and Peace* (1865-1869).

Babel employs colorful and exotic imagery to depict not only the Italian actors but also the Jews of the bustling seaport of Odessa. Giovanni onstage seems to have been transported to his native land: "Beneath the Sicilian sun the pleats in his waistcoat gleamed." After reporting the success of the play and making his homage to passion, the narrator notes that a "pink and dusty sultriness was injected into Theater Lane." The imagery hints at a sexual passion shortly made explicit in the description of "moneyed Jews with beards parted down the middle" coming to "tap discreetly on the doors of fat women with raven hair and little mustaches, Di Grasso's actresses."

Babel makes the reader understand that this is the profane world—but he declines to judge it and probably even likes it, as he doubtless likes and respects, though condescendingly, a certain wooden stage prop used by the Italian troupe—"a poverty-stricken but brightly painted image of the Holy Virgin." Babel seems to imply even early in the story that this icon is the profane counterpart to some higher and sacred possibility. Only at the close of "Di Grasso," however, does the narrator fully abandon his condescending tone.

When the boy has his transcendent vision, it is described in a wholly serious tone reflecting the author's recognition of its authenticity. All the elements of the story come together at this point, and one sees the transformed buildings "soaring up into the heights, the gas-lit foliage of the boulevard, Pushkin's bronze head touched by the dim gleam of the moon" as a powerful showing forth of the true relationship between art and reality.

*Donald M. Fiene*

# DINNER AT EIGHT

*Author:* Ezekiel Mphahlele (1919-     )
*Type of plot:* Social realism
*Time of plot:* The late 1950's
*Locale:* Johannesburg, South Africa
*First published:* 1961

*Principal characters:*
    MISS PRINGLE, a single white woman, the director of the
      Sheltered Employment Depot
    MZONDI, a black man who works for her at the depot

*The Story*

    The daughter of an upright pastor, Miss Pringle is a self-righteous white South African woman who enjoys having black people hover over her admiringly. Her superficial liberalism has driven her into welfare work, in which she enjoys forcibly befriending helpless and needy Coloureds and Africans. The work fills a void in her otherwise dull life. She heads the Sheltered Employment Depot, a private workshop that trains "incurable cripples" in new trades. Preferring to work with blacks rather than whites because the latter are too independent, Miss Pringle prides herself in her knowledge and understanding of Africans.

    Miss Pringle hides her fondness for Mzondi, a black inmate with a disability, under the guise of trying to help him with a problem that she alone perceives. She repeatedly invites him to dinner at her apartment, but he views her attention suspiciously and loathes her lack of decorum. One Monday morning, he is about to turn down her dinner invitation for the fifth time when the routine arrival of a police officer checking on a burglary report at the Depot changes the course of the day. When Mzondi sees the constable and Miss Pringle chatting and glancing in his direction, he assumes that she knows his secret and that this time her invitation is designed to get him drunk in her apartment so that he will confess his secret—that he has made two hundred pounds from bootlegging—so that she can turn him in to the police.

    Determined to do Miss Pringle in before she does him in, Mzondi finally accepts her invitation. At her apartment building in Johannesburg's white-only Hillbrow neighborhood, she sneaks him up to her fourth-floor flat through a basement elevator designated for "Natives, goods, and hawkers." Although Miss Pringle knows that the police watch her for possible violations of the national Immorality Act because she entertains nonwhite guests, she is unaware that the building's watchman has telephoned the police. She performs her routine check of her apartment window to ensure that the police are not watching. Interpreting this gesture as a signal to the police, Mzondi decides to carry out his plan. After asking her to massage his aching and useless knee, he clubs her on the back of her head with his crutch, crushing her skull. As

Mzondi leaves the building, he gives five pounds to the watchman—who only minutes earlier accepted a five-shilling bribe from a white police officer—promising him more money if he never reveals what he has seen that night.

Physically and mentally exhausted, Mzondi enjoys only a brief escape. Early the next morning, his body is found by a tree, his arms embracing its trunk.

*Themes and Meanings*

Miss Pringle's superiors in the social welfare organization often describe her with such phrases as "a trifle tiresome, but hardworking," "a little overbearing, but conscientious," and "a likeable person, but a queer fish." Her insistence on repeatedly inviting Mzondi to her flat for dinner points to her shallowness and naïveté, particularly because she always reminds him that they will be alone—an uncomfortable fact of which he needs no reminder. Any relationship between a "tiresome," "overbearing," and "queer" white female supervisor and a "crippled," deeply distrusting black male employee in South Africa's former apartheid system is certain to be ill-fated. Nevertheless, the fates of these two tragic figures seem to be intertwined. One person is white and female, the other is black and male; one is sexually frustrated but powerful, the other handicapped and powerless; one is naïvely trusting and repulsive, the other is immovably distrusting yet intriguing. Despite a lopsided body racked and made useless by "ever-tired bones" and "withering flesh," Mzondi bears his physical problems "with irresistible cheek." The puzzlement of Mzondi's "pathetic beautiful lips" and steady but almost expressionless eyes captivate Miss Pringle, turning her desire to befriend Mzondi into a passion that she feels for no other inmates in similar condition or even with the same dismal doctor's report. Her sexual desire for Mzondi is unmistakable, often expressed in overt behavior "whenever she bent over him to show him how to operate the new machine." Mzondi is as aware of her sexual desire as he is of the country's Immorality Act, which once forbade interracial liaisons between blacks and whites. Miss Pringle, like Mzondi, is not only fully aware of this law but also understands its consequences because she herself is under the constant surveillance of "the boys from Hospital Hill police station" who "knew she entertained non-whites" and are only waiting to "clamp down on her and her black partner in the middle of an 'immoral act.'"

Although Mzondi is more troubled by his distrust and dislike of white authority figures than by the indecorousness of Miss Pringle's behavior, his most powerful motivation is to realize his dream of renting a beautiful house and bringing his motherless nine-year-old daughter from Eshowe to live with him. It is because of this dream that fellow prisoners once savagely beat and paralyzed him. He cares nothing for the unhealthy, uncomfortable attention that Miss Pringle directs toward him. He understands that any friendly gestures from whites, no matter how well intentioned, should be distrusted and rebuffed at all cost. Unable to appreciate white liberalism, particularly when it is mixed with obvious sexual overtones, Mzondi has rebuffed Miss Pringle's advances many times, leaving her to reel under the sting of "being snubbed by a helpless cripple . . . who should grab the hand of friendship immediately it's extended."

For all of Miss Pringle's self-proclaimed insights into Africans after working with them for many years, she cannot understand what they need to do in order to survive in a repressive racist society. Fearing that Mzondi will again reject her dinner invitation, she unleashes an angry tirade at him, thus exposing the hypocrisy of her self-deceiving claim to knowledge about black people: "What is the matter with you black people? Trouble with you all is you feel and think you aren't as good as white people, or better. Other people trample on you because you are willing to become doormats." Her naïve view of black response to institutionalized racism makes her liberalism suspect and dangerous. It is suspect because her apparently well-meaning welfare sensibilities are driven by an unconscious paternalism and her own psychological needs. They are dangerous because her sensibilities are masked by unconscious sexual longings. Her "conscious effort to win non-white friends" is unhealthy because it arises not from her "abundant sympathy for the needy"—as her testimonials state—but from her dislike of fellow whites, who are too independent for her.

Ezekiel Mphahlele expresses his preoccupation with the realities of the human condition through explorations of the nature and effect of racial separateness and relationships. Mzondi is tragically destroyed by forces beyond his control, forces that drain him of physical, emotional, and psychological energy and drive him to act disastrously. Summed up, the moral here is: In a repressive, pernicious police state in which human relationships are circumscribed by inhumane laws that encourage subversion, the Mzondis and Miss Pringles are tragic characters caught helplessly in a quagmire of events that they do not understand or control. How else can one make sense of a legal system that sees fit to acquit Mzondi of theft charges because of insufficient evidence, while simultaneously failing to punish the inhumane crime of savagery for which his useless body stands as crying evidence?

*Style and Technique*

A deceptively short story, "Dinner at Eight" illuminates the world and nature of blackness in South Africa. Woven into the story are the depiction of the event of an undeveloped murder and the human condition responsible for Mzondi's misunderstanding and deep-seated mistrust of Miss Pringle's motives. It is precisely this shift between the actual event of the murder itself and the sociopolitical commentary it is intended to illustrate about the frustrations and indignities to which nonwhites were once subjected in South Africa that constitutes the force of the story.

Ambiguity and irony as well as the direct and implicit commentaries that augment the dialogue between Miss Pringle and Mzondi convey the story's sociopolitical message without making the story seem strident or polemical. For example, there is a mystery concerning three thousand pounds in payroll money that has been stolen; details concerning this crime are sufficiently ambiguous to leave one wondering whether it is of any moral importance whether Mzondi has actually stolen and hidden this money. Whether he has stolen three thousand pounds or two hundred pounds, would there be a difference in the degree of paralysis that he suffers?

*Pamela J. Olubunmi Smith*

# DISORDER AND EARLY SORROW

*Author:* Thomas Mann (1875-1955)
*Type of plot:* Domestic realism
*Time of plot:* About 1922
*Locale:* Munich
*First published:* "Unordnung und frühes Leid," 1926 (English translation, 1929)

*Principal characters:*
DR. CORNELIUS, the protagonist, a history professor
FRAU CORNELIUS, his wife
INGRID,
BERT,
ELLIE, and
SNAPPER, their children
MAX HERGESELL, a friend of Ingrid and Bert

## The Story

At midday dinner, all the Cornelius family members are introduced, their personalities quickly sketched, and their relations with one another indicated. Told entirely from the point of view of the professor, the story begins as his two older children, Ingrid and Bert, remind him that they are giving a party that evening. Ingrid assures her father that he will not be disturbed. Somewhat disconcerted by the slight disruption of his orderly routine, the professor nevertheless is determined to be affable in his formal, old-fashioned way. It is clear from the beginning of the story that Dr. Cornelius is dismayed and bewildered by the discrepancies between his values and those of his older children, and by their slang, their practical jokes, their frivolous ambitions, their casual manners. It is also clear, however, that there is affection and good humor among them as well, though tolerance seems to come much more easily to the youngsters.

The case is different with regard to the two younger children, five-year-old Ellie (her father's favorite) and Snapper (four years old and more comfortable with his gentle mother). The professor is able to set aside his natural dignity while he plays with Ellie and Snapper. Today the games are cut short by preparations for the party, so Dr. Cornelius retires to his study, the little ones return to the nursery, and the others go off on various errands. Later, while the professor is resting, the guests begin to arrive.

Slightly nervous, the professor goes down to the dining room and is introduced to several people, including Max Hergesell, who is charming, courteous, and humorous. Ellie and Snapper join the festivities, and Dr. Cornelius, having conversed with several of the guests, returns to his study to work but with his attention distracted by the dancing and singing in the room next door. In due time he goes out for his nightly walk, first pausing for conversation. He observes with a pang how Ellie persists in trying to get Max's attention while he is dancing with a fat young woman.

As he walks, preoccupied with his professional concerns, Dr. Cornelius also thinks about the need to be just toward the younger generation, especially in these chaotic and desolate times. On his return home, he is called to the nursery, where he finds Snapper asleep but Ellie in tears, suffering because she does not understand her sorrow as her father does. It is for Max that Ellie is weeping, and when he appears to say goodnight, Ellie is transfigured with a joy she also does not understand. The father is grateful to the young man for his kindness but also feels embarrassed and hostile. After Max leaves and Ellie falls asleep, Dr. Cornelius sits by her bed thinking of his angelic daughter and of the games they will play again as Max, he thankfully supposes, will fade into a shadow with no more power to grieve and bewilder her.

### Themes and Meanings

The title of the story suggests the primary issues with which Thomas Mann is concerned. From the opening sentence, with its dismal account of the family's frugal meal, Mann presents a detailed picture of postwar Germany as reflected in the experiences of the Cornelius family. The inflation, the shortages and privations, the general lawlessness and laxity—all are indicated in details about the servants and the guests, in conversations among the family members, and especially in the professor's musings. Frau Cornelius must interrupt her preparations for the party to cycle hurriedly into town to buy provisions with money that may lose all value at any moment. The refreshments are extremely simple, many of the guests are not in evening clothes, the dancing is strange and unattractive, the music too loud.

The professor realizes that he is out of place in this postwar world, and he feels hostile toward the present. Thus, he is troubled by his devotion to his little daughter, suspecting that his great love for her is somehow connected with his love for the past and also connected in some way to death.

The second part of the title is related to Ellie's uncontrollable and bewildered sorrow, her childish yearning for the kind young man who danced with her. In her unrestrained anguish, Ellie also appears to partake of the general "disorder" of the times.

### Style and Technique

The principal characteristic of Mann's style in this story is irony. The story about the professor's dedication to the past and his conflicting emotions about the younger generation's ways is told in the present tense; in addition to giving the narrative dramatic immediacy, the use of the present tense highlights the underlying theme. Mann's distinctive use of telling details is particularly evident here; even minor characters such as the good-for-nothing young manservant and the blue-faced nurse spring to life in a few sentences. The professorial protagonist is characteristically thoughtful, serious, courteous, and restrained; his feelings are merely suggested or briefly mentioned, while his thoughts are expressed clearly and forcefully. Thus, Mann avoids bitterness, contempt, or sentimentality. In the end, the effect of this restrained and controlled style is deeply moving.

*Natalie Harper*

# THE DISPLACED PERSON

*Author:* Flannery O'Connor (1925-1964)
*Type of plot:* Psychological
*Time of plot:* After World War II
*Locale:* The rural southern United States
*First published:* 1954

*Principal characters:*
MRS. MCINTYRE, the owner of a farm
MR. AND MRS. SHORTLEY, white farmworkers
MR. GUIZAC, a Polish emigrant who comes to work on Mrs.
McIntyre's farm
FATHER FLYNN, a local priest

*The Story*
The title of this story suggests that it is about one displaced person. In fact, the tale is about several people who are displaced. In one character's words, "Displaced Persons . . . means they ain't where they were born at and there's nowhere for them to go—like if you was run out of here and wouldn't nobody have you." To explore this idea of displacement, Flannery O'Connor divides her story into three parts, emphasizing Mrs. Shortley, then Mrs. McIntyre, and finally the displaced person, or D.P., who connects all the other D.P.'s, Mr. Guizac.

In the first part, the idea of displacement is introduced through the character of Guizac, a Polish émigré who comes to Mrs. McIntyre's farm with his family after escaping from his native country. Mrs. Shortley, a farmworker with her husband on Mrs. McIntyre's farm, views Guizac as a foreigner who does not belong. His name is strange—she pronounces it "Gobblehook"—and he speaks a strange language. Because of her limited vision, she sees Guizac not only as a stereotype but also as a threat, for he endangers both the predictability of their lives and the security of their jobs. Guizac is, after all, far more efficient and skilled than her husband, Chancey. When she overhears Mrs. McIntyre telling the priest that she will be giving the Shortleys notice that they are to be replaced—displaced—by the Guizacs, Mrs. Shortley decides to pack up her family and depart before Mrs. McIntyre has the chance to fire them. Leaving the farm, Mrs. Shortley has her second dramatic inner vision (the first was immediately before she overheard Mrs. McIntyre's conversation). This final, mysterious, personal vision destroys Mrs. Shortley and leaves her family dumbfounded: "They didn't know that she had had a great experience or ever been displaced in the world from all that belonged to her."

The second part of the story focuses on Mrs. McIntyre's vision, which, unlike the ultimately enlarging vision of Mrs. Shortley, is a gradually restricting view of Guizac. When Guizac first arrives and demonstrates his farming skills and efficiency, Mrs.

McIntyre is delighted, believing that Guizac is her "salvation." His redemptive qualities, however, escape her notice when he arranges for one of the black farmworkers to pay for the transportation of Guizac's cousin to the United States. In return for transportation, the cousin would be married to the farmworker. When Mrs. McIntyre learns of this arrangement, her anger overtakes her earlier delight, and she repeats, with new emphasis, her earlier adage: "The devil you know is better than the devil you don't know." She knows the white farmworkers; she knows the black farmworkers; she does not know the ultimate implications of life with the Polish farmworker. Mrs. McIntyre decides that he is "extra," that he does not fit in, that he "upsets the balance." Estranging herself from the Polish D.P., she becomes increasingly displaced, separating herself from her place and her help. She becomes desperate and cooperates in a desperate action.

This action occurs in the third part of the story, after Mr. Shortley returns to the farm and systematically speaks out about Guizac's foreignness. He announces his dislike for foreigners because, in the war, he saw what they were like. As he recalls, "none of them were like us," and, in fact, one man who threw a hand grenade at him "had had little round eye-glasses exactly like Mr. Guizac's." Although Mrs. McIntyre recognizes the problem with that logic because Guizac is a Pole and not a German, the general unwillingness to accept the foreigner persists. Mrs. McIntyre, Mr. Shortley, and the blacks—all fearful that they will be displaced by the D.P.—are united by their desire to rid themselves of this "devil" whom they do not know.

In the final scene of the story, Guizac is killed by a runaway tractor. The death appears to be caused by the machine, but O'Connor suggests another cause: Perhaps Mrs. McIntyre, Mr. Shortley, and the black farmworkers caused the death because they did nothing to stop the machine. Because all of their eyes had "come together in one look that froze them in collusion forever," perhaps the displaced survivors really destroyed the displaced victim.

*Themes and Meanings*

All the characters in this story are displaced and are displacing someone else. Guizac is literally a D.P., but the other characters are also displaced, alienated from one another and from the place where they were born. As Mrs. McIntyre puts it, "Times are changing. . . . Do you know what's happening to this world? It's swelling up. It's getting so full of people that only the smart thrifty energetic ones are going to survive." Gone is the simple world of simple values; replacing it is the complex world of modern war, technology, and the victims of both.

At the end of the story, even "the smart thrifty energetic ones" do not survive, for Mr. Shortley leaves without notice for a new position, the young black farmworker departs, and the old black helper cannot work without company. Mrs. McIntyre becomes bedridden, visited only by the priest who comes not only to teach her the Catholic Church's doctrines but also to feed the peacock, the ultimate reminder of mystery in the midst of ordinariness.

*Style and Technique*

Because O'Connor is interested in the way in which people see, she uses various strategies and images related to the idea of vision. In the opening scene, Mrs. Shortley is blind to the beauty of nature and the peacock and notes the arrival of strangers through her narrow, bigoted vision. This tunnel vision is replaced by another kind of seeing, one so monumental as to be overwhelming, leading her to prophesy and then to succumb to her own prophecy of destruction.

Mrs. McIntyre's vision is pragmatic, not prophetic, for she sees the universe in practical, useful terms. When she comes to see that the Pole is an unfathomable mystery, she decides that he is the devil she does not know, and she is compelled to rid herself of that unknown quantity.

Contrasting with Mrs. McIntyre's pragmatic vision is Father Flynn's spiritual gaze. He sees everything and everyone as a reflection of the divine: The peacock, for example, is not a beautiful creature on the farm; it is a symbol of Christ and a reminder of the Transfiguration. Mrs. McIntyre on her deathbed is not a woman seeking human comfort; she is a potential convert to the Church. In O'Connor's fiction, what one sees is not always what one gets, but what one sees is indeed what one is.

*Marjorie Smelstor*

# THE DISTANCE OF THE MOON

*Author:* Italo Calvino (1923-1985)
*Type of plot:* Fantasy
*Time of plot:* The distant past
*Locale:* A spot on the ocean, near the Zinc Cliffs
*First published:* "La distanza della Luna," 1965 (English translation, 1968)

> *Principal characters:*
> QFWFQ, the narrator, an ageless being and a born storyteller
> THE DEAF ONE, his cousin, who loves the moon
> MRS. VHD VHD, a harpist, who loves the deaf cousin

*The Story*

Old Qfwfq recalls past times when he and his companions rowed out on the sea every month and climbed up to the moon. This was an enchanted time. Only for a short while, somewhere near the beginning of time as humans know it, did the moon orbit close enough to the earth for the group to climb up ladders from their rowboats and reach it.

The first half of the story tells about these moon visits in general, describing vividly the routine: The group would row the boats out to the place where the moon came closest to the earth, some would hold up ladders, and others would scurry up the ladders and grab onto the moon. The purpose of the visits was to gather moon milk, a cream-cheese-like substance composed of such ingredients as "vegetal juices, tadpoles, bitumen, lentils, honey, starch crystals, sturgeon eggs, molds [and] pollens." Because the gravitational pull of the moon was strong, the moon milk had to be hurled off spoons into the sea, where it was collected, and the group had to jump as high as they could to escape the moon's force so that they too would drop back into the sea or be caught by one of the boat's occupants.

The Deaf One, Qfwfq's cousin, loved the moon. Normally a solitary soul, he relished the monthly trips to the moon and was the most enthusiastic and adept at reaching it, retrieving milk, and returning. Qfwfq, who was usually with his cousin on the moon, most relished each return, when he reconnected with safety by grabbing the breasts or hips or silver arms of Mrs. Vhd Vhd, whom he loved. Mrs. Vhd Vhd, however, loved his deaf cousin.

The second half of the story relates the events of one strange night, the last of the moon visits. Most members of the group are unaware that the moon is moving farther away from the earth. On this night, Mrs. Vhd Vhd joins the deaf cousin and other sailors on the moon. Except for Mrs. Vhd Vhd, who seems to have purposely chosen this night to make her first moon visit, it is only after they all reach the moon that they realize how difficult it will be to return. The deaf cousin gets off first, and the other sailors do so only by clinging together to combine their weight against the increasing gravitational pull. Mrs. Vhd Vhd cannot get off, so Qfwfq jumps on the moon to rescue her. They are stuck on the moon for a month.

Captain Vhd Vhd seems pleased to have his wife gone. Mrs. Vhd Vhd pines for the deaf cousin, with whom she had hoped to be stranded on the moon. Qfwfq discovers that his love for Mrs. Vhd Vhd is not as strong as his love of life on earth; he pines for his return. When, a month later, the crew returns to rescue them, Qfwfq shimmies down the long rescue pole as fast as possible. Mrs. Vhd Vhd stays. If she cannot have the deaf cousin, she will become one with the moon, which the deaf cousin truly loves. It is said that Mrs. Vhd Vhd on the moon is what sets dogs—and Qfwfq—to howling at night.

*Themes and Meanings*

Italo Calvino's book *Le cosmicomiche* (1965; *Cosmicomics* 1968), in which "The Distance of the Moon" appears, is a set of evolutionary tales that combine a world of fantasy with the equally fantastic world of science. The stories are all narrated by the ancient yet ageless Qfwfq, a protean creature and expert storyteller who has been around through every stage of evolution. Calvino's simple but very human characters interact with an intriguing, ever-changing cosmos. Their struggles occur on both the human and cosmic planes, but they are all struggles of attraction.

On the human plane, the attraction is that of love, yearning, and jealousy. Only the Deaf One seems without the anguish of human relations, yet his detachment from others is the cruel result of his deafness. He enjoys his life through a sensual relationship with the physical phenomenon that he loves, the moon. Calvino presents the Deaf One's attraction to his physical environment as a reasonable way to respond to life. Mrs. Vhd Vhd yearns for the deaf cousin's love. She is jealous of the moon, and she turns to her harp to abate her desire. In the end, she chooses to become the moon, to make herself a part of the lunar body that the Deaf One now will be able to watch only from afar. Qfwfq himself yearns for Mrs. Vhd Vhd with all the passion of an adolescent, and he is jealous of the Deaf One for winning her love. During his month on the moon with her, he discovers that love, for him, is an earthly passion. Qfwfq's response to his predicament is to look to the future; his desire to return to earth suggests that he is ready to move on to other attractions.

On the cosmic plane, the attraction is gravity, and the conflict is between the shifting gravitational forces of the earth and the moon. The moon visitors learn that their places are small and their efforts ineffective in a powerful universe that changes randomly and unpredictably. The risks that they take seem at first to be minor, worthy of a few fast heartbeats and giggles as they jump and catapult to release themselves from the moon's gravity. Only the difficulty of the skinny child Xlthlx, who had to eat up the mollusks floating in the air to gain enough weight to drop to earth, hints at the potential seriousness of their risks. By their last visit, however, they know that the risks are real and the moon is indifferent to their plight; a month later, when Qfwfq is rescued from a quickly receding moon, it is sheer luck that the assemblage of bamboo poles reaches him.

After this time, the moon sets both Qfwfq and the dogs to howling. Those howls resonate with a yearning for lost love and for comprehending the cosmos. All are still drawn to a moon that serves as a metaphor for those yearnings, and the moon becomes divine.

*Style and Technique*

Calvino begins his fantasy with a scientific-sounding quotation:

> At one time, according to George H. Darwin, the Moon was very close to the Earth. Then the tides gradually pushed her far away: the tides that the Moon herself causes in the Earth's waters, where the earth slowly loses energy.

This quotation sets the tone for a story in which fantasy and science are inextricably linked. He places his story in a long-gone past; his characters may not even be quite human. However, he gives them very human qualities: They love, they are jealous, and Mrs. Vhd Vhd plays the harp. Calvino uses irony to suggest that, despite the power and size of the cosmos that reminds humans of their diminutive stature and importance, it is human love and goodness that give meaning to life in this cosmos.

This message is presented in two ways. The first is through the use of humor and play. Calvino sets the tone by suggesting that, on these nights of moon visits, the companions "fell into a special mood": "gay, but with a touch of suspense, as if inside our skulls, instead of the brain, we felt a fish, floating, attracted by the Moon." His descriptions are given with a straight face but provoke smiles: the "precious muck" that was moon-milk included much refuse, including "fingernails and cartilage, bolts, sea horses, nuts and peduncles, shards of crockery, fishhooks, at times even a comb." It is difficult not to be attracted to characters who would sift out this refuse to claim their precious milk.

The second is through the use of Qfwfq, the narrator. Qfwfq is a first-rate storyteller with an excellent memory of all past life. He tells his story in long sentences packed with sensory detail. He combines these details with wonder, philosophical musing, and a sense of drama. If the Deaf One seems almost unworldly, and the Captain and Mrs. Vhd Vhd seem mundane, Qfwfq affirms the potential of humanity. He has, for the moment at least, both moved beyond his human dilemma and outwitted the cosmos.

*Janine Rider*

# A DISTANT EPISODE

*Author:* Paul Bowles (1910-1999)
*Type of plot:* Psychological
*Time of plot:* The late 1930's
*Locale:* North Africa
*First published:* 1947

*Principal characters:*

THE PROFESSOR, the linguist who becomes the victim of the
Reguibat
THE BUS DRIVER, who transports the Professor to Ain Tadouirt
THE WAITER, who guides the Professor
THE REGUIBAT, the desert nomads

*The Story*

The story begins with a description of the Professor (who is not named) being transported by bus to Ain Tadouirt, a town in eastern Morocco. The Professor had spent three days in the town ten years previously, during which time he had established a friendship with a café keeper named Hassan Ramani. The driver asks the Professor if he is a geologist, and the Professor tells him that he is a linguist "making a survey of variations on Moghrebi" dialects. The Moghrebi are a people who live in a region in Africa north of the Sahara.

When the Professor arrives in the town, he visits the café and is told by the waiter that his friend Hassan Ramani is now "deceased." This same waiter—whose tone of voice is insolent and whose face takes on a look of anger when the Professor inquires about getting camel-udder boxes—agrees, for a price, to take the Professor to the place from which he can "get camel-udder boxes if there are any."

When they arrive at the place, the waiter-guide tells the Professor that he must proceed ahead alone. The Professor pays him fifty francs and dismisses him. Then, after experiencing mingled feelings of fear of what dangers might lie ahead for him on the desolate road and relief that the guide did not play a trick on him, he starts down the path, which leads into what looks like a quarry. As soon as he reaches the bottom, he is attacked by a wild dog, and while the dog is unrelentingly tearing at him, he experiences the sensation of something "cold and metallic . . . pushed brutally against his spine." It is at this point that an echo of a phrase or maxim that the Professor has heard in many shops and marketplaces in town reverberates in his mind: "The Reguiba is a cloud across the face of the sun . . . when the Reguiba appears the righteous man turns away." Who else could these attackers be but the Reguibat, who go about their brutal business quickly, kicking aside the dog and then, with the same vigor, the Professor, all over his body? Semiconscious, the Professor can hear the low, guttural voices of his attackers as they go about emptying his pockets, fiercely pulling and twisting his tongue, doubling him up and dumping him into a sack before slinging him alongside a camel. Later, he is taken out of the sack and is girdled with tin bands around his torso, arms, legs, and face until he is "entirely within a suit of armor." To celebrate the occasion, one of the Reguibat plays his flute and is accompanied by the general merriment of the others.

The Reguibat keep the Professor for one year and consider him their valuable possession. It is a year during which the Professor entertains the Reguibat by performing a senseless hopping routine, making jangling noises with his tin-banded body, doing handsprings, growling, and making obscene gestures "which never failed to elicit delighted shrieks from the women."

Finally, the Professor is taken to a town and sold to one of the villagers, but he suddenly enters "into consciousness again" and will not perform for his new owner. The man, who paid a handsome price for him, becomes infuriated, thinking he has been cheated by the Reguibat. He seeks out and finds one of the Reguibat still abed with one of the village girls and gets his revenge swiftly by nearly decapitating him. Meanwhile, the Professor, left unattended in his new owner's house, begins bellowing as loud as he can, crying out to escape from his captivity. He bangs against the door and when it finally bursts open, he rushes out into the street "bellowing and shaking his arms in the air to make as loud a jangling as possible." People only look at him with curiosity. A French soldier, after observing the Professor's strange behavior, says to himself, "Hey! A holy maniac," and then takes a "potshot at him for good luck" while the figure of the Professor, cavorting beyond the village gate, grows smaller and smaller in the shadow of the "oncoming evening darkness."

*Themes and Meanings*

"A Distant Episode" reflects a tragic circumstance that goes beyond mere ironic reversal. The obvious, uncomplicated irony in the story is that the Professor, the educated, "civilized" observer, goes among the Moroccans to survey the variations of their dialects and, while he is at it, to pick up a camel-udder box or two; instead, the Professor—whose tongue and whole being are brutally violated by the Reguibat—becomes the victim of a cruel twist of circumstances that turn him into the observed species.

After reading this story, a tale of terror alongside which the stories of Edgar Allan Poe and Flannery O'Connor pale in comparison, one is compelled to ask, why must one whose only real flaw seems to be poor judgment suffer such cruel consequences? Although no explicit explanation is offered, Paul Bowles implies that the Professor is guilty of a certain unconscious arrogance, a presumptuousness that is dangerous in a harshly absurd world.

Evidently, the Professor thinks that because he is an educated man and a linguist by profession, he has the right to practice his profession anywhere. This merely wrongheaded thinking results in consequences outrageously humiliating and cruel. However, who ever said that life was fair? Or that justice measures out equally? Or that going to the grocery store to buy a quart of milk merely because it is a routine business is going to guarantee one a safe return home?

Bowles does not give the Professor a proper name because he represents Everyman; he is an Everyman who does not realize that the contingencies of life combined with one's conscious actions will not be denied their due. For every planned conscious intention one conceives, good or bad, there is a Reguiba lurking in the darkness nearby, waiting to become a part of it and metamorphose its victim into doing its will, which indeed will be done if the right combination of circumstances fall into the intruder's favor. Civilization, personified in the Professor, is simply no match for mindless, free-roaming evil, personified in the Reguibat, who move only in the darkness of night and like night itself are collectively "a cloud across the face of the sun."

The desolate landscape where this "distant episode" takes place is an appropriate setting for such a drama. However, Bowles's North African locale can be seen in its larger metaphorical sense as the centerpiece setting for similar, if less cruel, episodes that take place daily all over the world, episodes that go mostly unnoticed. Who knows when, because of one's little misjudgments, the "Reguibat" may not turn up in the desert of one's own life?

*Style and Technique*

How leisurely and urbane the tone of the language is in the opening paragraph of "A Distant Episode." Long, slowly measured sentences, with modifiers practically banging into one another, abound:

> Now facing the flaming sky in the west, and now facing the sharp mountains, the car followed the dusty trail down the canyons into air that began to smell of other things besides the endless ozone of the heights: orange blossoms, pepper, sun-baked excrement, burning olive oil, rotten fruit. He closed his eyes happily and lived for an instant in a purely olfactory world.

Sun-baked excrement and all, reflected in the opening paragraph is the anticipation of romance or adventure, certainly not a sense of imminent danger. The opening paragraph sets the ironic tone of "A Distant Episode," and the unrelenting, crushing weight of it is felt fully by the time the reader gets to the end of the story.

There is a sharp contrast to this leisurely rhythm when, near the end of the story, the Professor begins to feel "the slow sharpening of his consciousness"; the vital action patterns of the sentences give thrust to his sudden, urgent need to find release from his condition: "He felt . . . he attacked . . . he climbed . . . he began to gallop." When nobody pays attention to him except the French soldier "who takes a potshot at him for good luck," one sees the fading image of what was once a civilized man, a cavorting figure growing smaller and smaller, framed in a funereal "great silence out there beyond the gate."

*P. Angelo*

# THE DISTRICT DOCTOR

*Author:* Ivan Turgenev (1818-1883)
*Type of plot:* Vignette
*Time of plot:* The 1840's
*Locale:* Rural Russia
*First published:* "Uezdnyi lekar'," 1848 (English translation, 1855)

> *Principal characters:*
> TRIFON IVANYCH, a lower-middle-class, semi-educated, but
>   conscientious country doctor
> ALEXANDRA ANDREYEVNA, a beautiful young woman
>   unsuccessfully treated by Trifon Ivanych

*The Story*

Here, as in all the stories in *Zapiski okhotnika* (1852; *A Sportsman's Sketches*, 1855), Ivan Turgenev (or his transparently disguised alter ego, the gentleman sportsman on a hunting trip) encounters the protagonist, the "district doctor," in a natural, casual fashion. The weather is bad, the sportsman falls ill, and his only choice of a doctor turns out to be a modest local man, Trifon Ivanych. Grateful for any distraction, the patient listens to the doctor unburden himself of a haunting incident. Turgenev subtly persuades the reader to identify with the fretfully ailing sportsman and to await the unfolding of the doctor's tale with impatience.

However, the doctor, who tells the story in his own words, has difficulty in sticking to his subject. His apologies, self-deprecations, and fussy details not only increase the suspense but also draw the portrait of an earnest but limited fellow, very uncomfortable with the subject matter that he is trying to convey.

One night, in his younger days, the doctor was summoned to an emergency: A young woman is critically ill with fever. The horses and carriage sent for him are pitiful, the roads are impassable, and the house is a long way off. The doctor feels wretched, both at these conditions and at the meager remuneration that undoubtedly awaits him.

At last, in the middle of this terrible night, the doctor arrives. He finds himself deeply moved. The dying girl, Alexandra Andreyevna, is very beautiful; the widowed mother is in despair; the two other sisters are touchingly concerned. They are cultivated people but very poor: This doctor is their only hope for saving her.

The doctor's life thus veers from its course: He is unable to leave the girl's side. He forgets all of his other patients, virtually stops fretting about fees, and moves into her house to devote himself to curing her.

Long before it is over, the doctor knows that her case is hopeless, yet he cannot bear to leave. His feelings are a mixture of professional duty, pity, and fascination. There is a mystery locked inside this dying young woman. On the first night, she began to say, "I will tell you why I don't want to die," but she has not yet come out with her explanation.

The reader endures increasing suspense, in parallel with the doctor's growing despair, as Alexandra only gets worse the harder he tries to cure her. One night, when she realizes that she is probably never going to get well, she confesses to the doctor: "If I can know for certain that I must die . . . then I will tell you all—all!" What is the terrible secret that has been tormenting her? "Do you hear, I love you!" she lets out at last.

The doctor copes with this most ineptly. Alexandra grasps at him with physical passion, and he almost screams aloud. As an act of mercy, he pretends a proposal of marriage, not very convincingly.

Then a note of bitter comedy enters. Having known him only as "doctor" until now, Alexandra wishes to learn the first name of her beloved. Highly cultivated and high-class as she is (at least in his eyes), she finds his resoundingly plebeian name (which even in Russian sounds funny) hard to take: Trifon Ivanych. The "unpleasant" laugh and the French phrase with which this poor but extremely proud young woman reacts to his ridiculous name are not lost on Trifon.

Nor is the falseness of her position, as his pretended "fiancé," lost on Alexandra. By the next morning, she has seriously deteriorated. The final three days include an excruciating charade of asking for her mother's blessing on their union. The girl herself dies unconvinced.

After years of pondering this strange event in his life, the doctor has come to his own understanding of it: "Say what you will, it's hard to die at twenty without having known love; this was what was torturing her; this was why, in despair, she caught at me—do you understand now?"

Having gotten the morbid story off his chest, and now perfectly calm again, the doctor modestly refers to his subsequent marriage to a merchant's daughter: "seven hundred for a dowry" coming out in the same breath.

## Themes and Meanings

In this very early story, Turgenev introduces some well-worn romantic themes: the motif of three sisters, the confession of love as a terrible secret, and the image of Death itself seemingly in love with Beauty. Amid this romantic material, Turgenev sardonically plunks Trifon, the apologetic, snuff-taking, ruble-counting sawbones who shies away from "exalted emotions" (as he understands Alexandra's passion).

Turgenev stays well in the background of this story, in his guise as a sympathetic listener, giving scarcely a clue as to his own interpretation of the events. He does make clear, however, that Trifon is a very limited fellow and a highly imperfect witness. The reader must fill in and make corrections for Trifon, and this gives rise to many possible interpretations. For example, the fate of the extremely proud girl, who has to be at the point of death before she can bring herself to confess her feelings for the too modest doctor, would seem to be the story's chief irony. If one corrects for Trifon's extreme humility and class-consciousness, however, it may well be Trifon who is the victim of an irony of fate. Perhaps Alexandra's appreciation of his devotion to her had awakened a genuine love in her, which was totally lost on him.

The twin themes of the unendurable burden of unspoken love, and the equally excruciating consequences of confessing it, later attain a rich development in all of Turgenev's mature major works. The type of the morbidly proud woman, although generally associated mainly with the works of Fyodor Dostoevski, is here seen to be a part of Turgenev's world as well, even at a very early stage.

## Style and Technique

In "The District Doctor," Turgenev experimented with a narrative technique that was still new in Russian literature at that time and that later (notably in the hands of Nikolai Leskov) became known as *skaz*. In *skaz*, a humble, semi-educated (or even illiterate) narrator relates an incident from his own life, in his own words, with much unconscious irony as well as unconscious self-portraiture.

Though the doctor appears to ramble, Turgenev crafts every word of the doctor's self-revelations carefully. Apart from contributing to the plot, every phrase that the doctor uses gives another clue as to his own background, virtues, blind spots, and lifestyle.

The advantages of the *skaz* technique are its naturalness and the feeling that it gives of real life as lived by real, ordinary people. It thus helps to forestall any tendency toward disbelief on the part of the reader, especially in a tale dealing with inherently sensational subject matter. It provides a particularly fine foil to romantic themes, infusing them with new realism.

*D. G. Nakeeb*

# DOC'S STORY

*Author:* John Edgar Wideman (1941-     )
*Type of plot:* Psychological, frame story
*Time of plot:* The 1970's to 1980's
*Locale:* A neighborhood park in Philadelphia, Pennsylvania
*First published:* 1986

> *Principal characters:*
> A YOUNG MAN, the narrator
> HIS GIRLFRIEND
> THE STORYTELLERS, men who gather at the local basketball court
> DOC, the legendary blind basketball player

*The Story*

"Doc's Story" is really two stories in one, for the narrator's own story is as important as the title story it contains. The narrator, who lost his girlfriend in May, spends the next few months hanging out at a neighborhood park and listening to the African American men who congregate on the basketball court, swapping stories. He needs their stories for his own survival. His favorites somehow bring him alive, and he finds himself laughing and hugging the other listeners. The story that affects him most is the story of Doc, which he hears only three times, but the presence of Doc presides over the basketball court where the storytellers hang out, and his story is at the heart of their lives.

Doc was an athlete at the local university, where he later taught, the core story begins. At some point, his eyes weakened, and then he went blind. His blindness did not lessen his basketball ability, however, and he would come to the court day or night and sink endless free throws between pickup games. On a certain Sunday, however, Doc's ability failed him, and when a young boy named Sky slam-dunked an errant free throw, Doc confronted him. Then, instead of walking away in anger, Doc joined a game and played. It is a legendary tale, the story of a blind man playing basketball and holding his own in the sighted world.

The narrator wonders, at the conclusion of Doc's story, if the tale would have made his girlfriend feel differently about leaving. She would have thought it was folklore or superstition, he thinks. If he had known Doc's story before she left, however, the miracle of a blind man playing basketball, then, maybe. . . . The thought seems to give him something to hold on to.

*Themes and Meanings*

"Doc's Story" is a narrative within a narrative, and the core story concerns the importance of overcoming defeat. The story the narrator listens to is the lesson of how

Doc, defeated by blindness, then defeated again when he lost his ability to shoot free throws, went on to play a basketball game in spite of his disability. It is a story that still resonates in the neighborhood in which Doc once lived and played because current players continue to repeat it.

The narrator uses that story to give himself hope: "*If Doc could do that, then anything's possible*," the narrator imagines himself at the end of the story telling the woman who has left him. "*If a blind man could play basketball, surely we . . .*" He already knows that the woman would think the story fanciful, and yet he hopes, and his hope gives him the strength to go on. Doc's story, the story of overcoming defeat, lives on to inspire others to try again. The further meaning of "Doc's Story," then, is the function of story itself as healing art, the therapeutic value of stories as they connect humans to one another, to their past, to their own inner lives. Certainly the narrator has benefited from hearing "Doc's Story," which is why he repeats it now. John Edgar Wideman implies that stories and storytelling can have these functions and values wherever and whenever they appear.

This power of story has still another, deeper meaning, and particularly for its African American characters. The narrator remembers when he used to tell his white lover black folktales, such as conjure stories and the stories about Africans who could fly, from the period of slavery, and he recalls her skepticism about them. That does not matter now, the author implies, for the narrator believes the story of Doc, and in repeating it here, he is continuing that African American storytelling tradition. "Doc's Story" is part of a long tradition of black legend and folklore that contains these therapeutic and communal powers. The story of the miraculous blind basketball player belongs firmly in that literary tradition. The surface of the narrator's life may be defeat and depression: He has suffered the worst loss he can imagine. In telling "Doc's Story," however, he has found hope for himself at the same time that he has tapped into a centuries-old oral tradition that not only enriches his life but also enhances the life of his community. As in so many of Wideman's fictions, the stories from the past often emerge to inform the present and give it some new purpose.

*Style and Technique*

The structure of "Doc's Story" is a frame story of the narrator's troubles encasing the core story about the blind basketball player. The two stories interact and infuse each other with meaning, sharing their themes of loss and recovery. Equally important is the language of the story. The narrator's style is literary and works perfectly to capture the educated voice of the jilted lover. The opening paragraph of the story, for example, describes the woman's small white hands and what they meant to him; one of the last paragraphs describes their final spring walk together at dusk in Regent Park, where the basketball court is located. The characters Wideman writes about, however, use a powerful black dialect that is bright and musical in its effects. The men who lounge around the court telling one another stories employ a street language that is as colorful as it is ungrammatical, and this language gives a color and texture to "Doc's Story" that it would not otherwise have. Wideman is notable for being able to fuse these two linguistic levels and to make them work as effectively as they do in "Doc's Story," with a rich literary language blending into a vivid street vernacular.

Wideman's language is itself highly figurative, in both his narrator's exposition ("Blind as wood") and in the street language of the other characters (the basketball dropping through the net "clean as new money"). He also uses multiple sensory markers in rendering the events of this short story, not only the central image of sight/blindness (and thus light/dark), but also the sense of touch (as when the narrator describes touching his lover's body in the first paragraph) and the sense of hearing (as in all the stories he listens to that sustain him). Reading Wideman is often an intense and mixed sensory experience.

The language Wideman uses describes a gritty urban world. The setting of many of Wideman's stories and novels is Homewood, a black neighborhood in Pittsburgh, but here he shifts the scene to Philadelphia (where he was himself a standout on the University of Pennsylvania basketball team in the early 1960's), and the two urban worlds are similar. Fine grit hangs in the air above the park, the narrator of "Doc's Story" recalls, in almost every season. One of the stories the players tell on the court is a violent tale of gang wars in North Philadelphia, ending in murder and mayhem. However, Wideman's stories generally focus not only on this social world but on interior life as well—on the thoughts and feelings of characters struggling just to get through life. Action and incident are almost incidental to the interior experiences of characters caught up in them, as here with a narrator trying to overcome painful personal loss. There are sometimes jumps between incidents and ideas in Wideman's stories that are not easy to follow, a narrative mix that readers may find difficult. Also, Wideman does not use quotations marks to denote the words of speakers, which sometimes makes stories difficult to enter, especially for new readers. Wideman's stories are never linear or stationary: The present is embedded in the past, generations overlap and interact, and language can be both literary and improvisational. "Doc's Story" is a good introduction to these multiple worlds of Wideman's fiction.

*David Peck*

# DR. HEIDEGGER'S EXPERIMENT

*Author:* Nathaniel Hawthorne (1804-1864)
*Type of plot:* Satire
*Time of plot:* The early nineteenth century at the latest
*Locale:* A doctor's study, perhaps in New England
*First published:* 1837

*Principal characters:*
DR. HEIDEGGER, an elderly doctor
MR. MEDBOURNE, an avaricious merchant, now poor
COLONEL KILLIGREW, a debauched seeker of pleasures
MR. GASCOIGNE, an unscrupulous politician
CLARA WYCHERLY, a former beauty, now a widow in seclusion
because of scandal

*The Story*

Dr. Heidegger invites to his study four elderly friends to engage in an experiment. Three are men: Mr. Medbourne, Colonel Killigrew, and Mr. Gascoigne; the fourth is a woman, the Widow Clara Wycherly.

The study is a dusty, old-fashioned room replete with a skeleton in the closet, a bust of Hippocrates, books and bookcases, and a portrait of Sylvia Ward, who died fifty-five years before the night of the experiment on the eve of marriage to the doctor after swallowing one of his prescriptions.

The doctor shows his guests a faded rose that she gave him those many years before, and places it in a vase containing liquid from the waters of the region in Florida where the Fountain of Youth is located, sent to him by a friend.

The rose revives and the doctor pours some of the liquid from the vase into four champagne glasses for his friends. They drink and shed their years, showing signs of intoxication. Dr. Heidegger suggests to them that they allow their experience in life to guide them in virtue and wisdom when they gain a second chance at youth. As they drink, their inhibitions vanish. Colonel Killigrew takes interest in the widow's charms and flatters her; Mr. Gascoigne waxes eloquent in periods of a sort dear to politicians; Mr. Medbourne projects a plan to supply the East Indies with ice by means of whales harnessed to icebergs.

Dr. Heidegger does not take part in the rejuvenating experiment; he witnesses their antics with gravity. Young again, they laugh at their quaint clothes, showing contempt for the traits of old age that they have shed. Finally, the widow asks the doctor to dance with her, but he pleads old age and rheumatism. The three other guests seek to join her in dance, and in the ensuing riot, the table with the vase of the Water of Youth and rose overturns. The liquid reaches a dying butterfly, reviving it so that it flies to rest on Dr. Heidegger's white hair. The rose fades; the guests show their age again. The doctor states that he is glad not to have partaken of the liquid; he has learned that this unnatural return to youth was no occasion for satisfaction. His guests, however, undaunted, determine to sally forth in search of the Fountain of Youth in order to drink from it three times a day.

### Themes and Meanings

The title, "Dr. Heidegger's Experiment," gives clues to the story's meaning. A doctor is a man of science, and the story describes an experiment, from which some sort of lesson might be derived. In conjunction with the word "experiment," the title suggests medicine, chemistry, physiology, or physics.

The name Heidegger is Swiss, meaning someone from the fortress Heidegg in the canton of Zurich. The doctor bears the same surname as that of a Swiss contemporary of the composer Handel, John James Heidegger (1659?-1749), manager of the opera house and master of the revels under England's King George II. The other characters also have surnames of distinguished figures from roughly the same era of English history. Most famous is a playwright known for the immorality of his works, William Wycherley (1640?-1716), who left a widow, a woman much younger than he, named Elizabeth. Others include two dramatists, father and son, Thomas Killigrew (1612-1683) and Thomas Killigrew the younger (1657-1719) and another dramatist, Sir William Killigrew (1606-1695); a master of the revels named Charles Killigrew (1655-1725); a poet, George Gascoigne (c. 1539-1577); an alleged conspirator, Sir Thomas Gascoigne (1593?-1686); and an actor and dramatist, Matthew Medbourne (died 1679), translator of Molière. The name of the long-dead lover of the doctor, Sylvia Ward, may suggest that of the quack doctor Joshua Ward (1685-1761), famous for "Ward's remedy," a "drop and pill" intended as a cure-all, which may have killed as many as it cured. Dr. Heidegger's fiancé, appropriately, swallowed one of her lover's prescriptions with fatal results. It was indeed a "Ward's remedy" in this case. It seems more than possible that Nathaniel Hawthorne modeled his characters on these people for their dissoluteness and effect of recalling a bygone age. Most, too, lived well into old age.

The doctor does not partake of the potion himself, but the elderly group undergoes a temporary rejuvenation. They all represent some vice or weakness and, despite the lessons experience should have taught them, remain true to their flawed characters during their return to youth.

For the doctor, who does not strive to combat the effects of Father Time in his own life, the experiment proves that people of shallow, vicious character do not benefit from the passing of the years but persist in pursuing illusory pleasures.

The guests may be considered as allegorical—the widow representing scandalous coquetry, Mr. Medbourne exemplifying mercantile avarice, the colonel embodying self-indulgent lechery, and Mr. Gascoigne epitomizing political corruption. They continue in accordance with their natures throughout the story, paying no attention to Dr. Heidegger's advice to behave with mature wisdom. The precious elixir spills and they lose their fleeting youth but not the desire to seek the unattainable. Hawthorne amusingly teaches a moral lesson and satirizes human shortcomings.

The transient nature of youth and beauty are symbolized by Sylvia's rose, and by the butterfly, which revives in the spilled fluid.

*Style and Technique*

This moral fable is made palatable by Hawthorne's command. If Dr. Heidegger were a paragon of virtue, the lesson might be less beguiling, but his skill as a doctor is insufficient to prevent the spirits of his deceased patients from staring at him whenever he directs his gaze at the fabulous mirror. The mirror suggests the power of illusion, a motif of the tale, as does the untitled book of magic. Hawthorne (or the narrator) has sport by suggesting that some of the doctor's reputation as an eccentric is attributable to the writer's "own veracious self" in the role of "fiction monger."

Hawthorne makes use of the trappings of gothic romance (the cobwebs, dust, bookcases, skeleton in the closet, and fabled mirror) with skill. One startling event, characteristic of the genre, still not outmoded in the author's time, is that when the chambermaid lifts the book of magic in her dusting, the skeleton rattles in the closet and several faces (presumably of the doctor's deceased patients) peep out from the mirror, while the bronze bust of Hippocrates frowns, uttering the command to forbear.

A whimsical humor can be felt in the story. For example, the narrator hints that the doctor and guests "were sometimes thought to be a little beside themselves—as is not infrequently the case with old people when worried either by present troubles or woeful recollections." Here is displayed a mock gravity. Humorous also is Dr. Heidegger's revelation of the location of the Fountain of Youth, undiscovered by the Spanish conquistador, Ponce de Leon. As the doctor says, "The famous Fountain of Youth, if I am rightly informed, is situated in the southern part of the Floridian peninsula, not far from Lake Macaco." The guests, when they set out in their quest for the elixir, will not be much helped by the reference to Lake Macaco; the name itself, applied to a type of lemur, is humorous. In addition, adjectives used to describe the guests, such as "venerable," "respected," and "respectable," gain humor from their inappropriateness, given the questionable nature of the guests' character and behavior.

Hawthorne is mindful of readers filled with skepticism when confronted by a miracle. He holds out alternative explanations for the phenomena depicted. For example, the youthful actions of the three men are attributed to intoxicating elements in the water from the Fountain of Youth, "unless, indeed, their exhilaration of spirits were merely a lightsome dizziness caused by the sudden removal of the weight of years."

*Edgar C. Knowlton, Jr.*

# THE DOCTOR'S SON

*Author:* John O'Hara (1905-1970)
*Type of plot:* Social realism
*Time of plot:* 1918
*Locale:* Lantenengo County, Pennsylvania
*First published:* 1935

*Principal characters:*
> JAMES (JIMMY) MALLOY, the narrator and protagonist, a fifteen-year-old boy
> DOCTOR MIKE MALLOY, his father
> "DOCTOR" MYERS, a medical student
> EDITH EVANS, Jimmy's girl
> ADELE EVANS, Edith's mother
> DAVID EVANS, Edith's father

*The Story*

"The Doctor's Son," a long story in four parts, concerns James (Jimmy) Malloy, a boy who is confronted with the fact that one may be physically grown yet not grown up. Jimmy, the doctor's son of the title, narrates this story about his loss of illusions against the backdrop of the influenza epidemic of 1918. During the epidemic, Doctor Mike Malloy works himself into exhaustion, and "Doctor" Myers, a medical student, is called in to work Malloy's patients until he has recovered. Jimmy, though only fifteen, is commissioned to drive Doctor Myers around the county to see all the flu victims. Their first stop, at the request of Doctor Malloy, is the Evans home in Colieryville, where Jimmy looks forward to seeing Edith Evans, a girl several years his senior. Because the Malloys and Evanses are friends, Jimmy and Doctor Myers are invited for lunch by David Evans, Edith's father. At lunch (which Mr. Evans cannot attend because of business commitments), Doctor Myers is attracted to Adele Evans, though Jimmy notices something unusual only in the glances passed between Edith and her mother.

As they travel to see patients in single-family dwellings and gathered in bars to await the doctor, Jimmy is impressed by the compassion and skill with which Doctor Myers works. He has an unnerving experience, however, when they visit a miner's house in which the husband has died, and one of the children dies while they are there. Although Jimmy is a doctor's son and has been exposed to death, he has always been prepared for it, "if only by the sound of the ambulance bell. This was different." It is his first realization that death can come unexpectedly, and he is shaken by it.

The third part of the story, the shortest of the four, opens with the story's only extended digression, as Jimmy discusses various people who are taking advantage of the flu epidemic to profit in one way or another, whether financially or sexually. This digression foreshadows the affair between Doctor Myers and Adele Evans, which follows when Mrs. Evans asks Doctor Myers to come by on the pretense of examining the maid; Jimmy and Edith are unsuccessful in preventing the liaison.

Soon after this, Mr. Evans interrupts an examination Doctor Myers is performing in a bar and demands to speak to him about his wife. Mr. Evans knows nothing of the affair; he is simply concerned from Doctor Myers's visits that his wife may be sick. The relieved Doctor Myers assures him that she is fine and agrees to reexamine her after finishing with his patient. While he waits, Mr. Evans shares a bottle of whiskey that is being handed around, even though Doctor Myers advises him not to (it has been identified earlier as a means of passing the flu virus).

At the Evanses' house, a call from Doctor Malloy recalls Doctor Myers and Jimmy. Doctor Malloy feels fit enough to resume his practice, and Doctor Myers returns to medical school (asking Jimmy to "say goodbye to the Evanses" for him). Jimmy and his father resume seeing patients around the clock, but the strain of the two working together so closely begins to tell, and Doctor Malloy decides to drive himself on his next rounds after they have a physical confrontation. The following day, Jimmy discovers that Mr. Evans has died of the flu. He buys flowers for Edith, but she refuses to see him, and he soon finds another girl, revealing that Edith really meant little more to him than Mrs. Evans did to Doctor Myers.

*Themes and Meanings*

The primary focus of "The Doctor's Son" is on Jimmy's initiation into adult behavior and his disillusionment on realizing that many of his accepted beliefs are false. Perhaps the most important of Jimmy's realizations is that his father is fallible, despite the fact that he is a doctor. Doctor Malloy has taught Jimmy to show respect for a doctor as he would, for example, show respect for a priest, and this leads Jimmy to believe that doctors occupy a privileged place in society. The debasement of the medical profession that he observes during the story, however, is followed by a loss of respect for his father.

The flu epidemic is the catalyst for Jimmy's education. First, his father's debilitation, surprising to Jimmy in itself, brings Doctor Myers to town. Myers is a capable doctor, despite his lack of training, but his affair with Mrs. Evans causes Jimmy to lose respect for him, and Doctor Myers is not an isolated case; other doctors are also taking advantage of the situation to make sexual conquests or extra money. By the time Doctor Malloy is back on his feet, Jimmy first reveals his disillusionment with the medical profession by omitting a doctor's title in conversation with his father, an oversight that his father immediately corrects. The final, physical confrontation between the two is almost anticlimactic, as Jimmy has already accepted the fact that his father can make mistakes, and he is no longer afraid to stand up to him.

*Style and Technique*

As the title implies, the story centers on the relationship between Doctor Malloy and Jimmy. The two serve as doubles; both have multifaceted and unpredictable natures, emphasized by the variety of names by which they are known (for example, "Mike Malloy," "the dad," "Daddy," and "Poppa" are a few of the names used for Doctor Malloy; "James," "Jim," and "Jimmy" are all used for his son). After his introduction, Doctor Malloy is unseen for most of the story, yet John O'Hara succeeds in keeping him continually in view by having Jimmy compare his father to Doctor Myers, and by having Jimmy and other characters reminisce about him in his absence.

O'Hara was well known for his exacting attention to dialogue and dialect (he believed that if fictional characters did not "talk right," they would not become "real people" for the reader), and "The Doctor's Son" is an excellent example of his use of dialogue to illuminate character. Each of the characters (and there are many, from several different racial and socioeconomic backgrounds) has a distinctive way of speaking; at the same time, although they have individual idiosyncrasies, they often use dialect that links them to larger groups. The natural conversation both gives insight into the characters involved and enhances the sense of reality found in "The Doctor's Son."

*Greg T. Garrett*

# DOE SEASON

*Author:* David Michael Kaplan (1946-        )
*Type of plot:* Fantasy
*Time of plot:* A cold winter
*Locale:* Pennsylvania woods
*First published:* 1985

*Principal characters:*
ANDREA (ANDY), a nine-year-old girl
HER FATHER
CHARLIE, her father's friend
MAC, Charlie's eleven-year-old son

*The Story*

Two men and their children—a nine-year-old girl nicknamed Andy and a boy, Mac, eleven years of age—go on a hunting trip in the Pennsylvania woods. They leave Andy's home at dawn. Mac's father, Charlie, objects to Andy's coming along because of her age and because she will be the only girl in an otherwise all-male hunting party. Her father tries to conciliate Charlie by noting that animals—including deer, he hopes—seem attracted to Andy, and she is adept at handling a gun, although in target practice. Charlie is not reassured. They drive to an isolated location in the woods that Charlie and Mac previously scouted out as a likely deer-feeding ground. Andy arrives in a fairly congealed state, because the heater in Charlie's vehicle is defective. Still, she carries a day pack, although smaller than the three men's backpacks, and is to do more than her share of KP duties.

On the first day of the trip, while the three males lie in wait for game, Andy goes off to collect firewood, and she spots a buck and two does moving away. That night she and Mac share one tent while their fathers use the other. Mac teases Andy by baiting her with sexual and other matters, but the girl holds her own. For his part, Charlie has been ribbing Andy about her tomboyishness. Andy assesses them both as dumb. Her father tries to blunt their attacks by defending his "punkin" and "honeybun" despite her nickname.

The following day, Andy walks by herself some distance away from the resting threesome, in whose company she feels increasingly uncomfortable, after being subjected to a concerted assault by Charlie and Mac about being like a boy. Even Andy's father concedes that her mother voiced a similar opinion—given what Andy is like, they might just as well have had a son.

As Andy wanders off, she spots a doe, then quietly returns to alert the others, who hurry to the spot. When they find the doe still grazing, Andy's father suggests that she is entitled to the kill because she saw the animal first, but Charlie objects vehemently. He fears that Andy will miss. Furthermore, she does not have a hunting license. Andy herself is ambivalent, silently praying that the doe will run away. Because of the direction of the wind, the deer fails to pick up their scent. Finally, at her father's urging and under his direction, Andy takes aim and fires at the deer.

She appears to make a clean shot through the doe's heart, but after the animal collapses on the frozen soil, it raises itself and disappears into the woods before the approaching hunters can discharge a second shot. Charlie resumes his complaints about Andy's involvement in the hunt.

That night, Andy agonizes over the suffering that she must have inflicted on the doe. Sleepless, she steps out of the tent, just as the living-dead doe enters the hunters' camp. The animal helplessly allows the girl to approach closely enough to touch it and palpate the inside of its gaping wound. As Andy cups the doe's beating heart, its warmth nearly sears her hand. She has difficulty extricating it but finally wrenches the hand free. The girl is struck by the horror and beauty of it all. In this dreamlike sequence—which is narrated as real—she dips her hand in the freezing snow to clean it. Even so, it feels weak and withered to her, so she keeps it concealed in her pocket. The following day, as she lags behind the rest of the party, the three men find the dead doe in a clearing in the brush. "Clean shot," Andy's father declares triumphantly. "My little girl," he adds affectionately. Even the obnoxious Charlie and Mac are excited.

As her father begins to eviscerate the animal with his hunting knife, Andy runs away. The three males call after her, just as her mother called her to join her in deeper waters the previous summer at a New Jersey beach. In Andy's mind, the windblown forest that surrounds her is morphing into a threatening sea.

*Themes and Meanings*

David Michael Kaplan introduces two children who, although certainly not typical nine- and eleven-year-olds, are nevertheless believable, and their contrasting reactions to the hunt are striking. The younger Andy, although hoydenlike, successfully fights off Mac's and his father's baiting even as, despite her dislike of the pair, she tries to prove herself a worthy companion. Eventually, she seems to overcome her ambivalence about being a girl and no longer responds to her boyish nickname because it is not her real name.

As in several other stories, Kaplan illustrates, implicitly if not directly, the familiar theme of parent-offspring relationships. He does so not only with reference to the two parent-child pairs on the hunt but also with reference to Andy and her mother. Except for waving them good-bye after the breakfast she prepares on their departure day, the mother does not appear in the story. Indeed, mothers are generally unimportant in Kaplan's tales; they are often dead, gone, or insane.

During the trip, each father shares confidences with his child, trivial secrets to which the mother at home would not be a party. Andy's father offers her otherwise forbidden coffee; Mac's father tells him it is good to get away from the house "and the old lady." The mother becomes a reality to Andy most dramatically in the flashback of the beach episode. On that occasion the woman, gone for a swim, momentarily lost the top of her bathing suit because of the waves and Andy, embarrassed by the event, ran away from her, just as she is now running away from her father and his friends butchering the doe.

In the last analysis, this is a story about how Andy is initiated into the adult world of sexuality and death. At its conclusion, the ambivalent Andy is maturing into the woman, Andrea. The fact that no analogous development occurs in Mac, who is two years her senior, makes her metamorphosis even more striking.

*Style and Technique*

Adding to Kaplan's suspense about the uneasy relationship that he sets up between Andy on one hand, and Charlie and his son on the other, is the touch of the mystical and the supernatural. Kaplan weaves such dreamlike fantasy as Andy's mysterious nocturnal encounter with the doe with everyday experience, and this story follows others in this respect. Although he confesses to inspiration by the likes of John Cheever, Kaplan is also reminiscent of other late twentieth century short-story writers such as Robert Coover, for whom there is no objective reality different from what individuals perceive. Kaplan tries to show how the magical and the ordinary coexist with an indistinct dividing line between them, at least in Andy's mind.

The story is told from Andy's perspective; the reader is allowed to enter her mind and share her thought processes. As her story unfolds, her musings evolve from the more simple and concrete—for example, how vast the woods might be—to the more complex and abstract—for example, the analogy between the sounds of the forest and of the ocean—perhaps symbolizing her changing state.

The atmosphere of the forbidding frozen forest, through which the wind blows through the treetops chilling Andy and reminding her of the sound of the breaking surf of the "inevitable sea," strikes the key in which the action proceeds. Nature is not gentle, and the atmospherics serve as both prologue and epilogue to the brutalizing hunting event symbolizing the girl's initiation into womanhood.

Another stylistic feature is Kaplan's economy of words. He finds it unnecessary to broadly describe Andy's father, Charlie, and Mac, but their language is self-explicit. Talking about Andy, her father observes: "She shoots the .22 real good," to which Charlie responds: "Popgun. And target practice ain't deer hunting." Mac's language and choice of topics are more vulgar and crass. The economy of words, however, does not make the characters two-dimensional.

The pleasure of "Doe Season" does not flow only from the particular twist that Kaplan gives it, or from the supernatural that hovers over the events and makes them seem like dreams or, conversely, makes ordinary events seem like magic. Its enjoyment also comes from the suspense that the author creates by analyzing emotion (which determines whether Andy will shoot the doe or not) and by leading the reader into the drama, step by step, down to the last sentence of the narrative.

*Peter B. Heller*

# DOG DAYS

*Author:* Judy Budnitz (1973-     )
*Type of plot:* Dystopian, didactic
*Time of plot:* The twenty-first century
*Locale:* A small town in the United States
*First published:* 1998

> *Principal characters:*
> LISA, the narrator
> PAT and
> ELIOTT, her teenage brothers
> HER MOTHER
> HOWARD, her father
> MARJORIE, her only friend, who moves away
> PRINCE, a human dressed as a dog

*The Story*

"Dog Days" uses a third-person narrative from the perspective of Lisa, a young woman, to relate the story of a family caught up in an undefined national crisis. Over a single year, the family's standard of living declines drastically; they lack electricity, experience drastic food shortages, and have their neighbors disappear mysteriously. Soon they appear to be the only people remaining in town.

The unifying thread in this chaotic situation is a creature, presumably a human dressed as a dog, that ingratiates himself with members of the family, becoming their constant companion. Lisa's mother scavenges in the trash seeking food for this man/dog who sits up and begs, rolls over, and licks the hands that feed it. Even when the mother cannot find food, the dog, Prince, remains with the family.

Initially, the mother defends the dog; the father eschews it. Lisa's brothers, Pat and Eliott, sell their clothing to buy drugs and retreat into their basement bedroom, from which they exclude Lisa. They do drugs and leaf through old issues of *Playboy* by moonlight because their electricity has failed. They do not go to school because, in April, the schools close. They boys rejoice in the freedom this closure gives them, but soon they become bored and seek jobs. The town, however, is clearing out. No one is hiring. They are left to their pot smoking and prurient reading.

Lisa's father, Howard, goes hunting with his shotgun but finds little to hunt. Lisa never reports that he brings anything home from his hunting expeditions. The family is short of food, but Howard is powerless to do anything to relieve his family's hunger. Ever the realist, he realizes that the dog his wife is nurturing is actually a human dressed as a dog. Because he discourages his wife's ministrations to the dog, she carries most of them out secretly, feeding the creature behind his back. She accepts the man/dog as a dog because that is what it wants to be. She supports its right to be whatever it desires.

The man/dog behaves like a dog. It acts as dogs do—it sits up and begs, rolls over, and barks. It sleeps curled up on the porch. Howard will not permit it to enter the house. It smells and has fleas, some of which cause pink bumps to appear on Lisa's legs, but she does not tell her mother that the man/dog has given her fleas. Her brothers joke that she should not let the dog get too close to her lest it impregnate her.

The family's world is obviously collapsing around it. The town becomes a ghost town, but the family apparently has no notion of why its neighbors have left. The family has no overt warnings to spur it into fleeing. Its members can neither understand nor accept what is happening but seem powerless to prevent it. When the electricity fails, they sit and stare at the dark television screen until finally Howard smashes it.

The story is told in sequential order by months, from February to the following February. In the course of a year, the mother moves from accepting the man/dog as a dog, as it wishes, to denying it is a dog when her husband, desperate for food, hunts it as though it were the animal that he has earlier denied it was. Finally, he shoots the creature for food. The mother cries out, proclaiming that the animal is a man. She has been reduced to feeding her family on salads made from grass that cause Lisa to throw up. Lisa finds a bottle of vitamins. She takes some, and they give her a stomachache.

As the story ends, Howard has shot the man/dog. The father and the boys fall on the dead animal. They snarl, much as dogs snarl. Their situation has reduced them to an animalistic state. "Dog Days," like William Golding's *The Lord of the Flies* (1954), explores what happens to people when the major aspects of civilization disappear.

*Themes and Meanings*

"Dog Days" revolves around two major themes: isolation and alienation. The family on which the story centers is isolated from its neighbors and, apparently, from the government under which it lives. Over a twelve-month period, the society in which the family lives and of which it has presumably been a part is collapsing, yet the family seems oblivious to the implications of each change that takes place in the lives of its members. Judy Budnitz presents a chilling view of what happens when people are apathetic about what is going on around them.

The family in this story is a compact unit. The only outsider, aside from the man/dog that attaches itself to the family, is Lisa's friend, Marjorie, who lives two and a half blocks away. Marjorie never appears directly in the story. Lisa reveals that she has left with her family in June, just before the roads were closed. The closing of the roads becomes the final, crucial step in isolating Lisa's family. Budnitz never names Lisa's family, thereby intensifying the illusion of anonymity, isolation, and alienation that characterizes it.

The members of this family are faceless characters. They are stereotypes. They have no real identities as Budnitz presents them. One has the feeling that if they were cut, they would not bleed. The mother and father do not communicate. Rather, the mother deceives the father in what seems like a classic example of marital compromise. They keep the peace, but they do so only by using deception. Pat and Eliott, Lisa's two brothers, appear to interact, but their interaction is based on the mutual enjoyment they derive from smoking pot and from the sexual stimulation derived from gawking at the pictures in *Playboy*. They isolate themselves in order to engage in their two antisocial pursuits and, by doing so, alienate themselves from the family. They remain shadowy characters, which is precisely the way Budnitz intends to project them.

As neighbors leave the town, going two by two down the road before it is finally closed, Howard is not unaware of what is happening but he is totally unaware of why it is happening. He compares his neighbors to rats leaving a sinking ship, proclaiming that they seem to know something that he does not know. He does not, however, seek out answers to the questions that should be plaguing him. His alienation from his society and his government is growing exponentially, but he is too apathetic to do anything to forestall it.

*Style and Technique*

The most salient element in Budnitz's style is her use of Lisa as a third-person narrator. This device maintains a distance between Budnitz readers and the other characters in the story. Readers learn nothing directly about the mother, father, and two sons. Everything revealed about them is derived through Lisa's accounts. Even Lisa does not emerge as a fully developed character. She is more a mouthpiece than a rounded protagonist.

The man/dog in the story is reminiscent of the beggars who peppered America's countryside during the Great Depression of the 1930's, when hordes of hungry, unemployed men wandered aimlessly about begging for a crust of bread and a cup of water. These men, homeless and hopeless, were not threatening individually, but they reflected a drastic social condition that was extremely threatening to society overall.

Budnitz purposely obscures the causes of the crisis that surrounds Lisa's family. They are unaware of the causes but are painfully aware of the outcomes of this social upheaval. Howard is similar to Joseph K., the hounded protagonist in Franz Kafka's *Der Prozess* (1925; *The Trial*, 1937), who knows that he is in serious trouble but who is never made aware of what his crime might be. Joseph is paralyzed by his heightened state of paranoia. Oddly, he wants only to be accused of something specific from which he can defend himself.

When Budnitz finally brings Lisa's dysfunctional family together, they have stopped talking, communicating instead with snickers, stares, and shrugs. They gather in the living room only because they need to share the body heat that they can produce collectively. The rest of the house is too cold for them to endure. It is in this setting that Pat remarks that in Korea, people eat dogs. This statement sparks Howard into shooting the man/dog as his wife protests that the creature is human.

*R. Baird Shuman*

# DOG STORIES

*Author:* Francine Prose (1947-     )
*Type of plot:* Domestic realism
*Time of plot:* The 1980's
*Locale:* Western Massachusetts
*First published:* 1990

*Principal characters:*
> CHRISTINE, the protagonist, a painter
> JOHN, her new husband, owner of a small construction company
> ROBERT, a carpenter temporarily employed by John and Christine

### The Story

The story opens with dog stories that are being told at a wedding celebration by guests and the bride, because the bride has a bandaged leg and a slight limp from a dog bite. The dog stories relieve some of the tension in the air—caused partially by the bride, Christine's, pregnancy—but they also remind Christine and the groom, John, of another dog story about their old collie, Alexander. They've both sworn off retelling this story, and Christine thinks that this refusal to mention the story to the guests connects her with John more strongly than the ceremony about to take place. This is no ordinary wedding.

Christine and John's wedding takes place outside, on an unseasonably hot July day; Christine wishes they had gotten married in June, but then she remembers that they had not decided to get married until May. They have been living together for about five years, but the pregnancy seems to have driven them to marriage. The ceremony itself is barely seen in the story, and Christine is glad that it all goes by quickly, in a kind of fog.

Stevie, Christine's son from a previous marriage, was abandoned by his father when it was clear that Stevie had a learning disability. John, on the other hand, is very solicitous of Stevie, and it is his sweetness and patience that seem to bind Christine to her new husband. The story shifts directions during the reception: While John helps Stevie fill his plate, Christine notices the carpenter, Robert, walking to the studio John is having built for her as a wedding gift, and she decides to join him.

Now it is revealed that Christine was bitten by the dog while she was looking for a sink to buy for her new studio, but the search for the sink is not as innocuous as it sounds. She wants the sink because she has been talking about it with Robert and she thinks, because of her attraction to Robert, that mentioning that she stopped for the sink would add up to more than it was, to an irrevocable act. She even feels guilty about stopping at the sale for the sink and believes that perhaps she was bitten because her motivation was not pure.

Robert, too, feels some attraction for Christine, but the flirtatious edge his voice has is tempered by the fact that nothing can possibly come of it. Christine thinks that, because she is older and his temporary employer, this flirtation on her wedding day is innocent, but she also thinks his flirtatiousness makes a bolder claim than John's solicitousness. When Christine accepts a marijuana joint from Robert, despite her pregnancy and her social obligations, the reader recognizes her attachment to him, her irrational—and therefore strong—bond with him.

When Annette, her art dealer from New York, enters the barn and smiles at Robert, jealousy, loneliness, and embarrassment overcome Christine. While Christine, Annette, and Robert talk, Robert learns for the first time that Christine is pregnant, and while Christine thinks about her pregnancy, she reveals that she feels that her life is not just closing down, it has always been closed down. Some clamp on passion and recklessness has never been released inside of her, she believes.

At this point, she brings up the story about Alexander, their collie who ran away for love. This story, which Christine earlier admitted bound her with John more than the ceremony of the wedding, is now revealed as a love story, a story of passion. Christine recognizes the lack of passion in her own life, leaves Robert and Annette behind, and returns to her husband and son.

## Themes and Meanings

In her author's note to *The Best American Short Stories, 1991*, in which "Dog Stories" appeared, Francine Prose said she "wanted to write a story about a wedding that was not exactly an expression of joy and hope for the future, but rather of some darker and less sanguine sense of acceptance." "Dog Stories" is darker than a reader might expect from a story taking place at a wedding and the reception following it, because the author focuses on the ambivalence the central character feels and the revelations about her life that she accepts. Christine is not afraid of the undercurrents in her life: She may acknowledge John's kindness, but she is also aware that kindness may not be sufficient to bring passion to a relationship; John may be applauded for his generosity in accepting Stevie as his son, but Christine notes that John also wants extra credit from the friends at the wedding for being so kind.

What makes Christine an attractive character is her self-awareness. She recognizes that the height of summer calls forth her unruly dreams and desires, but she also is aware that desire cannot always be acted on. She accepts, somewhat tepidly, her relationship with John, not because it is her only option, but because marriage and stability will perhaps be the best for her two children. She would prefer that her life did not feel closed down, but she accepts the limitations of her situation and her marriage and goes on. Christine admits that Alexander, their dog, "was more capable of passion than its owners may ever be," and she struggles with the tension between a desire for comfort and a yearning for passionate fulfillment. The story does not offer any large moral or hidden meaning; it simply examines the multiple levels of human desire.

## Style and Technique

In this third-person narrative, readers are privy only to the thoughts of Christine;

her mind is the subject of the story. The other characters come into focus in the story only as Christine looks their way: Stevie is introduced, "meditatively chewing his hand," when Christine scans the lawn to see who has arrived. Annette arrives at the party and is introduced by the narrator as one of the signs of Christine's success. The fictional world revolves around Christine, and everywhere she looks, the reader can feel emotion: Annette produces jealousy in Christine, Robert awakens her desire, and John frightens her at the story's close with his question about their marriage. If Prose had not allowed us this entry into Christine's consciousness, the story would not have the same power.

The story also achieves power by its gradual unfolding. Nearly every page has a new revelation about the central character and her relationships. The reader only gradually learns about her pregnancy, her ambivalent feelings about John, her attraction to Robert and her feelings of guilt, and the significance of the story's title. The story unfolds for the reader in the same way it unfolds for Christine. It is only in a conversation with Annette and Robert that Christine recognizes that her life has always been closed down. She, like many characters in fiction, discovers something about herself at the same time that the readers discover it. She learns about her inhibitions and her tentativeness in relationships only through telling the final dog story about Alexander; the reader reaches the epiphany at the same moment she does.

What distinguishes this story from many other contemporary pieces is the absence of overt sexuality. Neither Annette, Robert, John, nor Christine engages in any sexual acts in the story; there is plenty of attraction and desire in the story, but Prose keeps everyone's clothes on. She manages to create a story with great sexual tension without providing graphic details. Perhaps that is part of the technique of the story: Everything is hinted at and muted in the piece. Christine finds out gradually and almost indirectly how she feels about her life and her loves, and she accepts her limitations with a certain degree of calm reserve. Although Prose uses humor and colloquial exchanges, the power of the story is in what is not said—except inside of Christine's mind—and what is not done.

*Kevin Boyle*

# DOGGED UNDERDOG

*Author:* Irvin S. Cobb (1876-1944)
*Type of plot:* Regional, frame story
*Time of plot:* The nineteenth and early twentieth centuries
*Locale:* Small town modeled on Paducah, Kentucky
*First published:* 1916

*Principal characters:*
JUDGE BILL PRIEST, one of the town elders
CAPTAIN SHELBY WOODWARD, a Confederate veteran
MISS EM GARRETT, a defiant southern woman
CAPTAIN JASPER LAWSON, the oldest and best storyteller
HARVE ALLEN, the town bully
SINGIN' SANDY RIGGS, a small, weak man who challenges Allen
CAPTAIN BRAXTON MONTJOY, a local war hero

## The Story

Judge Priest and his friends are sitting on the judge's porch, talking as usual. Reminiscing about "the Big War," Captain Shelby Woodward tells two contrasting stories that lead the men to discuss courage and cowardice. In the first, Miss Em Garrett defied a Union commander by refusing to surrender her Confederate flag. For four years, she wore it under her dress while she nursed the wounded of both armies, and eventually her courage and her kindness won salutes from the Union soldiers. Then Woodward describes his brigade's futile attempts to delay General Sherman's advance. Most members of his brigade were eventually killed, and Woodward questions their real reason for continuing to fight: Were they brave, or was everyone unwilling to quit for fear of being considered a coward? Judge Priest suggests that the bravest person is someone who would like to run from trouble but faces it instead; Woodward adds that Southern women, who faced difficulties alone, probably were more courageous than the soldiers.

Captain Jasper Lawson then tells a story of frontier days, when disputes were settled by fistfights instead of gunfights. Harve Allen, who was acknowledged to be the toughest and meanest man in town, had badly beaten so many men that everyone, including the constable, was intimidated. One day he claimed to have been offended by Singin' Sandy Riggs, a small man known only for his perpetual humming. The ensuing fight was totally one-sided, and soon Riggs was so badly hurt that bystanders had to help him to his feet. Once he could stand, though, he vowed to return and continue the fight in a month.

In exactly one month, Riggs returned and renewed the fight, only to be badly beaten again. Once more, he vowed to continue the fight in a month. For the next five months, Riggs returned for additional bouts; each time he was badly hurt, and each time he repeated his vow to return. Gradually he won so much sympathy that some townspeople dared ask Allen not to beat him again.

The eighth fight was witnessed by Captain Braxton Montjoy, a local war hero and the only other man with enough courage to confront Allen. Riggs refused Montjoy's help, explaining that he intended to keep returning until he defeated Allen. This determined defiance won respect from Montjoy and perhaps also from Allen, who fought less aggressively than usual. For the first time, Riggs could pick himself up, but again he vowed to return in a month.

One month later, the townspeople were busy cleaning up flood damage, and they did not think about Riggs until he suddenly appeared. At the same time, they realized Allen was fleeing west across the river in a rowboat. Although Riggs remained in the town for the rest of his life, Allen was never seen there again. Lawson raises the question of why Allen fled from someone he had already beaten eight times. Was Allen a coward after all? The story ends with Squire Rufus Buckley's response, which, as usual, is inconclusive.

*Themes and Meanings*

Judge Priest and his friends are the elders of the community, having gained their wisdom from a lifetime of experience, including the Civil War. Irvin S. Cobb, perhaps influenced by the beginnings of World War I in Europe, seems to be using them and their recollections to introduce his response to the recurring questions of courage and cowardice. Judge Priest states the relatively common view that courage is not the absence of fear but the conquering of fear. Captain Woodward takes this definition a step further, implying that overcoming fear involves more than simply acting as though one is not afraid. He suggests that merely continuing to act brave does not really constitute courage, especially when one is part of an organized group. He implies that courage may be most clearly demonstrated by the individual who does more than is expected or demanded. Therefore, he obviously believes Miss Em's solitary defiance requires more courage than the military actions of a brigade of soldiers, even when those soldiers recognize that theirs is a futile sacrifice.

Captain Lawson's story illustrates these Southerners' insistence on the necessary links among persistence, courage, and independence, and Cobb may have intended the attitudes of these old men to reflect the sentimentalized attitude toward the Confederacy popularized in local color stories of the late nineteenth and early twentieth centuries. For instance, Riggs knew his fights with Allen would result in his being beaten, but he refused to give up. After the first beating, for eight months in a row, he returned at one-month intervals to renew the fight. He insisted that he would continue to return as long as he lived and his son would take up the fight, if necessary, after his death. His persistence, or strength of will, won first the sympathy and later the respect of the townspeople. Likewise, when Riggs refused Captain Montjoy's help, insisting that he must challenge Allen alone, he was asserting the independence that Captain Woodward has described as another significant element in courage.

On the other hand, Captain Lawson's question about Allen's cowardice emphasizes the negative side of these correlations among persistence, independence, and courage. Having always defeated his opponents, Allen had never been forced to show persistence, and eventually he was unable to continue this ritualized fight, even though he always won. Moreover, once he realized that he could no longer intimidate the townspeople and that Riggs had earned their respect, he was unwilling to continue the fight. Thus, physical toughness had been defeated by emotional toughness.

Riggs's eventual victory also suggests that the region was adopting a more civilized code of behavior. Allen's boasts and physical exploits echo those of river men described in Old Southwest humor, but his flight west across the Mississippi River hints that the era of brute force was ending. Allen had been able to bully most of the townspeople because they were willing to accept defeat; Riggs succeeded because he was not, and even the local war hero seems to have acknowledged the superiority of Riggs's type of courage.

### Style and Technique

In his lifetime, Cobb was hailed as the successor to Mark Twain. Given Twain's popularity, it seems inevitable that a younger local color writer would be strongly influenced by him. Certainly similarities exist in the subjects and styles of the two writers. Like Twain, Cobb wrote nostalgic stories about a quiet little town on the Mississippi River. Both writers were strongly influenced by the oral tradition and attempted to reproduce the dialect patterns and speech mannerisms characteristic of the region. Both also used talkative old men to tell stories of unusual local residents. Another significant shared influence was frontier humor. For example, Allen's boasts that he is "half horse" and "half alligator" reflect the bragging that river men used to intimidate the people they were preparing to fight; this dialogue echoes the language used by Twain and earlier writers associated with the Old Southwest humor tradition.

Most of Cobb's stories can be classified as local color. Cobb portrays somewhat sketchily drawn characters who can be identified by some eccentricity. The intent is to portray a quaint way of life that is on the verge of disappearing. The result is a nostalgic narrative intended primarily to evoke sympathy for the characters and provide an understanding of their culture.

Local color frequently employs the frame story, and "Dogged Underdog" gains much of its effect from Cobb's use of this technique. The narrator relates stories he heard as a young boy when he accompanied his uncle to a gathering of Judge Priest's friends, but this narrator quickly fades into the background as these old friends begin to tell their stories. Cobb can allow these old men to move from accounts of the past to philosophical discussions about various definitions of courage. Because the reader is twice removed from the action being described, the narrative takes on the quality of myth, as Judge Priest and his friends seem to speak for the Mississippi Valley culture of the early twentieth century.

*Charmaine Allmon Mosby*

# THE DOLL QUEEN

*Author:* Carlos Fuentes (1928-        )
*Type of plot:* Symbolist
*Time of plot:* Probably the mid-twentieth century
*Locale:* Mexico City
*First published:* "La muneca reina," 1964 (English translation, 1978)

>    *Principal characters:*
>        CARLOS, the narrator, a twenty-nine-year-old Mexican
>            professional man
>        AMILAMIA, his childhood playmate
>        AN OLD MAN AND WOMAN, her parents

## The Story

Carlos is a twenty-nine-year-old bachelor, leading a professional life in Mexico City. Although his life is pleasant, he feels that it is missing something, a central attraction. One day, while rearranging dusty, old books, he finds a card with a message written in a childish hand: "Amilamia wil not forget her good friend—come see me here where I draw it." With the message is a small map.

This message starts Carlos to reminisce about the summer that he met and played with Amilamia. She was an exuberant seven-year-old child; he was a fourteen-year-old adolescent trying to forget the approach of boarding school and adult responsibilities. He spent his days in a small, enclosed park, reading romantic fiction about pirates, runaways, and heroes who rescued princesses.

Into this dreamy refuge, Amilamia intruded herself. In his memory, Carlos sees her in constant motion: laughing, running, jumping, singing, and playing. Amilamia drew the self-conscious teenager into her orbit, becoming a point of support for his life, a visible symbol of the tension between childhood and adulthood. Carlos at this time of his life was beginning to find truth in books; Amilamia forced him for a time to participate joyously in life as a child would. Their friendship progressed from his indifferent tolerance to acceptance, and then, suddenly, to rejection.

Their last afternoon together they spent in playing childish games—running, making paper boats, and rolling down the hill in the park. Suddenly repulsed, Carlos angrily pushed Amilamia away and she fell, hurting herself. Ignoring her tears, he settled on his bench and resumed reading. She left, returning the next day only to give him the little card with the message and map and then leave without a word. He slipped the card into his book and forgot about it.

Now, fifteen years later, Carlos finds the map to Amilamia's house and decides to follow it. At first refused admittance, he discovers the name of the house's owner, Señor Valdivia, and gains entry with a lie about Valdivia's authorizing him to inspect the house for tax assessment.

A shabby middle-aged woman, fingering a rosary, admits him. In his mind Carlos pretends that he is a detective encountering clues, although he does not understand them: wheel tracks in the carpet, a comic book smeared with lipstick, a peach with a bite taken out of it, a child's blue-and-white-checked apron drying on the clothesline. He leaves, still mystified about Amilamia's whereabouts.

When he tries to continue his tax-assessor charade later that afternoon, the woman's husband appears and reveals that they know he is lying because the owner, Valdivia, has been dead for four years. Carlos now reveals that he is actually looking up his old playmate. Becoming less hostile but more emotional, the man and his wife repeatedly ask him what Amilamia used to be like, but he cannot satisfy them; he only remembers what she did and how she appeared. The couple lead him to another room where the scent of flowers is overpowering. Opening his eyes, Carlos sees a shrine, a child's coffin surrounded by flowers containing an effigy of Amilamia, a "doll queen who presides over the pomp of the royal chamber of death." Nauseated, he staggers out of the house, the old man's words ringing in his ears: "If you truly loved her, don't come back again."

The matter seems closed, but nearly a year later, Carlos decides to return once more, to give the card to Amilamia's parents. Whistling lightheartedly, he is unprepared for the shock that awaits him when the door opens. There is his Amilamia, alive, adult in years but child-sized and misshapen, sitting in a wheelchair, dressed in a blue-and-white-checkered apron that does not conceal the lump on her chest. Her once-beautiful hair has a frizzy permanent wave, and garish lipstick is smeared on her mouth. Only her beautiful gray eyes are unchanged. In the space of an instant she is welcoming, then fearful but still hopeful, then frightened and desolate. The story ends with the father shouting from inside the house: "Don't you know you're not supposed to answer the door? Get back! Devil's spawn! Do I have to beat you again?" Her frightened hands drop a comic book onto the rain-soaked pavement.

### Themes and Meanings

A major theme in this story, as in much of Carlos Fuentes's work, is to define the Mexican national character. "The Doll Queen" appears in *Agua quemada* (1980; *Burnt Water*, 1980), a collection of his stories set in Mexico City. Fuentes says, "I own an imaginary apartment house in Mexico City . . . [where] you will find the characters of the stories that are now collected here." This imaginary apartment house is like the house in the story that the narrator explores in his search to recapture that past and Amilamia, the symbol of his past. Its dusty, cluttered rooms are like a museum holding forgotten keepsakes. The map he finds thus sends him on a journey, not only through space but also back in time to his lost childhood innocence, in the Eden-like secret garden where they played. Poised for the journey, he wonders which is the true magnet of his life, the garden or the city. The quest for lost innocence and its symbol of the garden is another theme that recurs in Fuentes.

One's innocence is lost in part from suppressing and denying one's past. Carlos, the narrator, is alienated: He is the product of a cosmopolitan education and background.

He has read the best foreign literature, and he lives in a modern urban world of bureaucracy, traffic laws, and paperwork. He is a part of the orderly, rational world of the city. When he visits the house, he distances himself from emotional involvement by pretending to be a tax assessor and then a detective, both symbols of Western rational capitalist society. He is a good observer, scientifically noting details of sound, sight, and smell, but he lacks insight and cannot get involved—the very quality that Amilamia had briefly brought to his life so long ago. He is repulsed by the evidences of the mother's obsolete (to him) religion: her constant fingering of the rosary in her hand, and the room in which the "doll queen" effigy is enshrined. Carlos's alienation has limited him emotionally, as Amilamia is limited physically.

*Style and Technique*

Fuentes is a member of the group of Latin American writers known as Magical Realists, who blur the boundaries between reality and fantasy. He, however, calls his own writing technique "symbolic realism," which conflates other traditional categories: fiction and history, present and past, natural and supernatural. The narrative is fragmented, rather than strictly linear, and the present and past are jumbled together in the story, showing Fuentes's notion of time as cyclical rather than linear.

The narrator is cut off from his own past, which ultimately cuts him off from himself. His cultural allegiance is international, rather than Mexican, as shown by the foreign books he has read; he has embraced rationality and modernity rather than the irrational, mythical elements of his past, represented by Amilamia. He realizes that his life lacks something, but he is unwilling or unable to risk plunging into direct experience, preferring to remain an observer. As with many Fuentes stories, "The Doll Queen" undermines the surface order of the narration, showing the disorder beneath and implying that embracing the disorder is better than leading a sterile life without passion.

The two main characters, Carlos and Amilamia, can be seen as alter egos, two sides of the same person. Carlos is the rational, orderly, European modern ego; Amilamia is the primitive, intuitive, emotional, Indian primitive id. When he rejects her, he actually is rejecting a part of himself. Amilamia is misshapen and grotesque, emblematic of the distortion and destruction caused when one tries to suppress the primal forces within everyone and within everyone's cultural past. Significantly, the narrator's given name is the same as the author's, and the name is mentioned only once, when Amilamia calls it out at the end of the story. Only Amilamia has the power to name him, and he rejects her.

*Myra H. Jones*

# THE DOLL'S HOUSE

*Author:* Katherine Mansfield (Kathleen Mansfield Beauchamp, 1888-1923)
*Type of plot:* Psychological
*Time of plot:* The late nineteenth century
*Locale:* New Zealand
*First published:* 1923

> *Principal characters:*
> ISABEL BURNELL,
> LOTTIE BURNELL, and
> KEZIA BURNELL, daughters in a rich New Zealand family
> BERYL, their aunt
> LIL KELVEY and
> ELSE KELVEY, poor daughters of a washerwoman
> LENA LOGAN, a classmate of the Burnells and Kelveys

*The Story*

One day Isabel, Lottie, and Kezia Burnell are given a beautiful dollhouse by a houseguest. After it is placed in a courtyard so that its paint smell will disperse through the remainder of the summer, the children lift back its entire front wall to examine its contents. Its beauty overwhelms them. Kezia particularly loves a little lamp, filled with oil, that stands in the middle of the dining room table. To her, the lamp is real.

Burning to boast about their new dollhouse to classmates, the girls go to school the next morning. They are permitted to bring other girls home, two by two, to see the dollhouse in the courtyard. As girls surround the Burnells during a school recess, the eldest sister, Isabel, describes the dollhouse. The girls crowd in to get as close as possible, but two girls do not join the ring; they are the little Kelvey girls, who know better than to try to approach the Burnells.

The Burnell girls are not allowed to speak to the Kelveys, whose mother is a washerwoman and whose father is rumored to be in prison. Lil Kelvey, the elder sister, is a "stout, plain child, with big freckles." Her younger sister, Else, follows her everywhere, holding onto her skirt, which she tugs when she wants anything. The Kelvey girls wear "bits" given to their mother by the people for whom she works. Lil wears a dress made from an old tablecloth belonging to the Burnells, and her feathered hat once belonged to the postmistress. Else wears a white dress that looks like an old nightgown. She never smiles and rarely speaks.

The Kelvey sisters hang about around the circle of girls who raptly listen to Isabel Burnell. When Isabel finishes her story, Kezia reminds her that she has forgotten to mention the dollhouse's lamp. Kezia cries out, "The lamp's best of all," but no one listens as Isabel begins choosing who will be first to see the dollhouse. Every girl around Isabel adores her and wants to be her friend.

As the days pass, pairs of girls visit the Burnells' home in order to view the wonderful dollhouse, whose fame soon spreads. Everyone talks about the house in their classes. The Kelveys remain the only girls who have not seen the dollhouse, but they sit as close to the other girls as they dare so they can hear its descriptions. One evening when Kezia asks her mother if the Kelveys may come to see the house, she is told firmly that they cannot.

Eventually, the dollhouse ceases to interest the girls at the school, who now amuse themselves by taunting the Kelveys. At her classmates' urging, Lena Logan goes up to the Kelveys and insults them. The other girls enjoy this so much that they run off, skipping higher and running about faster than they ever have before. After school that afternoon, Kezia Burnell sneaks out of her house in order to avoid her parents' guests. When she spots the Kelvey girls coming up a road, she invites them to come in to see the dollhouse. Lil gasps and says they cannot because they know Kezia is not allowed to talk to them. Lil resists Kezia's insistent invitation until Else tugs at her skirt. Though still doubtful, Lil gives in and follows Kezia to the courtyard. The moment that Kezia opens the dollhouse so the girls can see inside, Kezia's Aunt Beryl enters the courtyard. Having had a bad day, the aunt orders "those little rats of Kelveys" away and scolds Kezia, thereby making herself feel much better.

The Kelvey girls rest in a field on their way home. Lil has taken off her feathered hat. They dreamily look over the hay paddocks across the creek. Else strokes the feather on her sister's hat; smiling her rare smile, she softly says that she has seen "the little lamp."

### Themes and Meanings

The central theme in Katherine Mansfield's story is the cruelty of class distinctions. Mansfield was born in New Zealand when the country was still a British colony in which class distinctions were rigidly maintained. Her best-known short story, "The Garden Party," also deals with this subject.

The reason that the rich Burnell children attend a school along with working-class children such as the Kelveys is that they live in rural New Zealand, where there are no other nearby schools. These same characters also appear in other Mansfield stories, including "Prelude" (1917). There are biographical parallels between the Burnell family and Mansfield's own Beauchamp family, and also between Kezia and the young Kathleen (later Katherine) Mansfield. Mansfield attended a rural New Zealand school in which she encountered class distinctions; according to Antony Alpers, in *Katherine Mansfield: A Biography* (1953), Mansfield modeled her fictional Kelvey girls on Lil and Else McKelvey, the real-life daughters of a washerwoman. It is possible that Mansfield—like Kezia—tried to stand up for these girls in school.

Mansfield uses this theme as a vehicle for a stinging portrait of the cruelty that was directed toward lower-class children. This portrait also contains a more sinister allusion to the pleasure that people, children and adults alike, derive from abusing those less materially fortunate. Not only are the Kelvey sisters shunned by their schoolmates, but even their teacher has a "special voice for them, and a special smile for the other children." When the girls at school tire of the dollhouse, they look for fresh amusement by inciting Lena Logan to abuse the Kelveys verbally, taunting them about their future and their father. This makes the little rich girls "wild with joy." After Aunt Beryl abuses the Kelvey girls, shooing "the little rats" from the dollhouse in the courtyard, she happily hums as she returns to the house, her bad mood dispersed.

"The Doll's House" is a disturbing story of a society in which snobbery and cruelty are regarded as acceptable behavior. It is ultimately redeemed by Kezia's attempt at kindness; however, it is uncharacteristic of Mansfield's stories to end happily.

## Style and Technique

Mansfield aspired to write the perfect short story and her writing was influenced by the Russian writer Anton Chekhov. Like jewels, her stories exhibit many facets and are complex and luminous. She is skillful in deft character portrayal, creating powerful impressions with metaphor, and manipulating reader responses with a few apt words. Her description of Else Kelvey is an example. By frequently calling the girl "Our Else," she enlists the reader's sympathies: "She was a tiny wishbone of a child, with cropped hair and enormous solemn eyes—a little white owl." In her white "nightgown" of a dress, Else is a spectral image, perhaps a sad angel. She seems to be not quite of this world, and nobody has ever seen her smile. It is primarily through Else that readers experience the cruelty of the other children and adults.

Mansfield uses the doll's house itself as a metaphor for the world of the rich upper class and creates a symbolic language surrounding it. The dollhouse opens by swinging its entire front back to reveal a cross section: "Perhaps it is the way God opens houses at dead of night when He is taking a quiet turn with an angel." It is through Else's eyes that the reader sees into this world that normally would remain brutally closed to a poor child. The little amber lamp that Kezia loves comes to represent what is real, or of real value, in an otherwise desolate emotional world. It is apparently the description of the lamp that Else overhears that emboldens her to ask Lil to go see the dollhouse against Lil's better judgment.

The final view of the Kelveys after seeing the dollhouse, resting together on their way home, picks up on the spiritual overtone in the story. Beryl's cruelty is forgotten. The "little lamp" that Else has seen, a symbol for Kezia's kindness and human warmth that defies the inhumane tyranny of class distinction, is a light that shines in the darkness of the life of this child. Something "real" is redeemed as Else smiles her "rare smile" at the end of the story.

*Tina Kane*

# THE DONAGH
## Or, The Horse-Stealers

*Author:* William Carleton (1794-1869)
*Type of plot:* Allegory
*Time of plot:* The early nineteenth century
*Locale:* Rural Ireland
*First published:* 1830

> *Principal characters:*
> ANTHONY MEEHAN, a thief with an evil and cruel character
> ANNE, his young daughter, who is still uncorrupted
> DENIS MEEHAN, his brother and accomplice

*The Story*

The story is set in an isolated Irish village where the community is closely knit, where the people are bound together by shared suspicions and fears, and where absolute evil is recognizable and verifiable. It relates a test of innocence that the whole community undergoes in an effort to identify a gang of horse thieves. The reader knows that the thieves are led by Anthony Meehan, but the tension of the story is created by the suspense of waiting to see if Anthony will succumb to the test.

Anthony Meehan is introduced as an absolutely evil character: violent, secretive, hateful, fearless, and relentlessly hard-hearted even to his own brother. There is a general assumption in the community at Carnmore that he has sold his soul to the devil, and the narrator frequently refers to him as "diabolical" and "Satanic." His characterization and the setting are calculated to intensify this almost supernatural quality of evil, and his only relief from this role is when he loves his young daughter, Anne.

Denis Meehan has been his brother's reluctant accomplice and is vulnerable to the superstition to which Anthony is immune. One night before they set off to steal a valuable horse, Denis reveals that he is afraid because he has found a bad omen in the ashes of the fireplace. When Anthony begins to imagine Denis as "a Judas," he intimidates Denis with threats of violence against Denis's family, and only Anne's appeals for peace calm down her father. Anthony mocks those who are afraid and doubts Denis's loyalty.

Some days later, the gang reassembles to prepare for the public test of innocence. Anyone who stays away is presumed to be guilty. Some of the thieves relieve their conscience by evasive tricks or theological distinctions between the magistrate's Bible and the priest's mass book, but Anthony insists that fears about perjuring themselves are mere superstition. He argues that "religion's all a sham" and "the world's all chance"; God cannot exist if he allows evil to triumph and innocence to be punished. Fearlessly, he urges them to be courageous and recognize that Providence allows all kinds of injustice in nature compared with which their actions are insignificant.

On the following morning, the community is assembled, and there is quiet gossip about the test. The usual oath on the Bible is required of those who are under suspicion. One thief is caught using the thumb-kissing trick, and Denis reluctantly perjures himself under the threatening eye of Anthony. The older brother swears with an air of mockery toward the whole proceedings. At this moment, the priest holds up a box covered with a black cloth, the Donagh, and announces that all must retake the oath on this ancient shrine. The Donagh has been used in extreme cases before, and the common belief is that perjury on this religious object brings on the offender "awful punishment . . . sudden death, madness, paralysis, self-destruction, or the murder of someone dear to them." The priest challenges the guilty to step back and those who want to prove their innocence to come forward. Almost all step back, and soon the two Meehan brothers stand alone, as the tension builds to a climax.

They advance together, but Denis has already made up his mind that he will not swear on the Donagh. Anthony takes the oath and steps aside for Denis, but the younger brother faints. The crowd assumes that he has been struck dead. When he comes to, he calls out, "Save me from that man," and it appears that he is going to turn witness against the gang. Anthony produces a pistol and prepares to shoot him, but Anne rushes forward; the bullet intended for Denis hits her. Her blood bursts onto Anthony as he desperately tries to ask her forgiveness, but all she has time to do is ask his forgiveness for plotting to deceive her father. Grief-stricken, he collapses and dies.

The community sees in these events the confirmation of its belief in the great power of the Donagh, and for many years swearing on it continues to be used as a test of innocence of even greater reliability than swearing on the Bible.

*Themes and Meanings*

The primary motivation of William Carleton's narrator is to illustrate a thesis: Irish peasants are inescapably governed by a superstitious fear that is intertwined with their religious faith but that is so attached to a religious object that the superstition appears pagan. The story has an almost sociological scheme. It tells of the evil one who is punished by what appears to be divine retribution, which is what the villagers expect to happen, and it also shows an evildoer repenting under the fear of that divine retribution. When Anthony Meehan shoots his daughter at the climax of the story, the narrator comments: "Shudderings, tremblings, crossings, and ejaculations marked their conduct and feeling; for though the incident in itself was simply a fatal and uncommon one, yet they considered it supernatural and miraculous." Such a comment is designed to sum up what the narrator has demonstrated about the villagers and also to distance him from those credulous people. The rational explanation of coincidence rather that the superstitious one of divine intervention is favored by the narrator.

However, the narrator's status as commentator is only one element of his role in creating the world of the village, and the power of the story comes from the fact that, like Carleton's contemporaries Edgar Allan Poe and Nathaniel Hawthorne, the writer is more fascinated and involved with the evil character and the atmosphere surrounding that character than his rational self would admit. At first, Anthony Meehan is an almost allegorical figure representing absolute evil in a medieval morality play. His "dark brow" and "Satanic expression" are clichés, and the purely innocent daughter with natural love for her father also belongs in an allegorical conception. Who sees Anthony in this manner? It appears that the narrator is more in sympathy with the villagers' way of thinking and feeling than he realizes. To depict a character in this fashion is to conceive of him outside realistic psychology, as an elemental principle of evil. The setting and descriptive details draw on the villagers' ways of feeling to heighten their sense of life as a drama in which human actions have supernatural origins or consequences.

The narrator deepens the psychological conception of Anthony in the relationship of the brothers. This adds a sense of an abnormal personality, a perversion of natural affection that is not simply "savage" but is truly chilling. The man who had seemed to be possessed of diabolical powers is shown to gain his power over people and his skill as a thief from a cynical and rational cast of mind. He hates the villagers because their superstition weakens their will, and his satisfaction in life is to dominate by physical abuse or by psychological intimidation. Anthony Meehan is definitely a monster but an intelligible one; he is not a village Faust, only a criminal gangleader.

The narrator's sympathies seem to be divided between this psychological portrait of Anthony and the view of the villagers, which is governed by their urge to mythologize and allegorize. The double title of the story reflects Carleton's awareness of this double manner of seeing. Although he may want to expose the superstitious reverence for the Donagh and the depth of fear that it provokes, his feelings are drawn into the telling of the story so that his detachment fades, and the insulated and special reality of that community becomes more prominent than his thesis.

## Style and Technique

This story was written before the modern short story became a form of conscious literary artistry; here, proverbial advice to trust the tale rather than the teller is appropriate. Carleton's purpose early in his writing career was to present the Catholic peasant population in a satiric light. However, by the time that he wrote *Traits and Stories of the Irish Peasantry* (1830, 1833), his sociological and evangelical purposes had been subverted by his talent for re-creating a fictional world that was deeply rooted in his inherited ways of hearing and feeling. The traditional fiction of peasant life tended to romanticize or caricature, and Carleton's fiction has traces of these tendencies, but whatever the outer intention or theme, the heart of this writer's style is in the re-creation of an integrated community. It is in the dialogue, above all, that his intimate knowledge of the feeling and language of the peasants is made concrete. This is a closed world, less definable in historical or psychological terms than in ways of thinking that are timelessly associated with a mythic drama of Good and Evil and with powers that are beyond human comprehension. These universal concerns become real because of Carleton's intimately communicated feeling for the life of the peasants.

*Denis Sampson*

# DON'T CALL ME BY MY RIGHT NAME

*Author:* James Purdy (1923-     )
*Type of plot:* Psychological
*Time of plot:* A mid-twentieth century Halloween evening
*Locale:* An unspecified city
*First published:* 1956

Principal characters:
    LOIS KLEIN, a newly married middle-aged woman
    FRANK KLEIN, her husband

## The Story

Lois Klein decides that although she likes her husband Frank, to whom she has been married for six months, she does not care for his last name. Her maiden name, Lois McBane, by which she was known both professionally and socially, provided her with a sense of identity that she feels she has lost through her marriage. What it is about the name that annoys her she cannot say, but clearly it involves the fact that because she is a large, middle-aged woman, the name "Klein," German for "small," is inappropriate for her appearance. How long this discontent has been developing the reader does not discover, but it comes suddenly to the surface one Halloween while she and her husband are attending "one of those fake long parties where nobody actually knows anybody," at which all the guests except for Lois are men.

Several men, overhearing Lois's insistence that she cannot go on being Mrs. Klein, laugh at her. Having had too much to drink, she tells them that they would not like being "Mrs. Klein" either, a remark they find even more hilarious. When one man comments that Lois does not look much like Mrs. Klein, an obvious reference to her size, she demands to know why not. He inquires if she has not looked in the mirror. His remark is, to her, like "the last of many possible truths she could hear about herself," and she grows more dismayed and confused.

As Lois becomes more insistent that Frank allow her to change her name, he grows progressively more annoyed, and once again refuses to change "*our* name." When Lois insists that she does not understand what he means by "*our* name," he takes the drink from her hand and strikes her twice across the face. The men, bored with the spectacle, have moved to another part of the room, where they still laugh over the contretemps. Lois expresses to her husband the ultimate truth she has faced when she says that she can no longer be Mrs. Klein because she is getting old and fat. Frank refuses to accept her assessment of herself, insisting that his wife could not be old and fat. The argument grows more intense until Lois interjects the surprising remark that she will not bear his children, which leads Frank to knock his wife to the floor. The men circle around the couple, staring at Mrs. Klein sitting on the floor, her skirt pulled up to expose unattractive legs, and her bewildered and angry husband staring down at her. No one offers to help her to her feet, and one man cruelly answers her repeated insistence that she will not be Mrs. Klein by pointing out that it is too late for her to change now and that she is too old to be sitting on the floor.

Lois acknowledges that when she sobers up in the morning, she will regret her decision but insists that she will not go home as Mrs. Klein. After helping his wife to her feet, Frank leaves the party. Lois throws her coat on, not bothering to straighten it, to hurry after him. While she stands outside, children in Halloween costumes pass and one asks, "Is she dressed as anybody?" Frank approaches her from behind a hedge and, when she again asks if he will change his name, knocks her down. After exchanging a few remarks with him, Lois, who has struck her head on the sidewalk, passes out. When two young men who have been working at a nearby delicatessen come by and inquire if they can assist Lois, Frank tells them that she is his wife and she has fallen. One young man observes that Frank does not look like her husband. The other insists that they should call a doctor because Lois is bleeding from the mouth. When Lois rouses, one of the men asks her if she is Mrs. Klein; she replies that she is not. Frank helps her to her feet, the young men leave, and Lois strikes her husband with her purse. He falls back against the wall, and the story ends with the angry Lois calling Frank a cheap son of a bitch and demanding that he summon a taxi.

*Themes and Meanings*

James Purdy, one of the most skillful of modern American fiction writers, is primarily concerned with the enigmas of human relationships. Employing the grotesque, even gothic, but always credible elements that are a hallmark of his writing, he examines the relationship between human beings, often within one family. In "Don't Call Me by My Right Name," he dramatizes the relationship—acutely painful for both characters and readers—between Lois, a discontented middle-aged wife, and her husband, Frank. One of the abiding human dilemmas dramatized by Purdy in story after story is the lack of communication between people, no matter how close they may be in their relationships. The dilemma is here evident in Lois's unwillingness to be called by her husband's name and his inability to understand her objection. It is obvious that Lois yearns for the individuality that was hers before her marriage, when she was a professional woman with name recognition and an identity of her own, an identity as a woman rather than as someone's wife. Her marriage to Frank has deprived her of this treasured identity and her sense of freedom, and the threat of what her husband may expect of a wife—including bearing children—complicates her responses.

The lack of communication, the animosity that exists beneath the surface of many human relationships, is powerfully dramatized in this story. Set among a cast of strangers—all of them men, significant because part of the wife's problem is her unwillingness to surrender her female self to the role of wife—the violent marital encounter takes on an added degree of irony as the unnamed men witness this most personal encounter as if they were watching a circus act or a stage show.

Another thematic element in the story involves the process of aging, embodied in Lois's frank admission that she is too old and too fat to be called "Mrs. Klein" and

Frank's unwillingness to acknowledge that a wife of his is either of these. The expectations of society as to the roles traditionally assigned to husband and wife are underscored by Frank's attitude and by his inability to understand his wife's problem. The ending is ambiguous: Lois, drunk and now injured as a result of her husband's knocking her to the sidewalk, asserts herself not just in word, by calling him a "son of a bitch," but in deed, by striking him with her pocketbook and, apparently, taking control of the situation. The reader is left to wonder about the future of the couple.

## Style and Technique

In this brief, tightly constructed story, Purdy relies heavily on dialogue to create the almost painful tension of the encounter between husband and wife. The dialogue draws its power from its realistic tone and the use of repetition to create an effect related to the use of musical motifs. One distinguishing quality of Purdy's fiction is the conciseness of his language, the use of a few words to speak volumes about convoluted human relationships. The use of the limited omniscient viewpoint enables the reader to enter the consciousness of both Lois and Frank, and thus stresses the degree to which this husband and wife are strangers, each unaware of the other's feelings. The consciousness of the witnesses is also incorporated into the story, again to stress the limitations of human understanding in viewing conversations, arguments, and other encounters between people we do not know. Through the eyes of unnamed observers, one sees Lois, fat, aging, drunk, somewhat ludicrous to outsiders who know nothing of her feelings. One's awareness of her view, however, neutralizes the negative portrayal and humanizes her.

Purdy effectively uses atmosphere in this story to underscore the irony of the story. The time is Halloween, the setting a party at which most of the people do not know each other—in short, a tension-filled gathering. Although the symbolism is limited, the name "Klein" takes on figurative implications through its meaning and Lois's reaction to it, and the costumed children, curious as to what is happening in the adult encounter they observe between husband and wife, represent a grotesque metaphor for lack of human perception. In story after story, Purdy peels back the surface of seemingly ordinary events—in this instance a married couple talking to each other at a party—to reveal the grotesque and horrible truths of human relationships often lurking just beneath the surface of the seemingly ordinary.

*W. Kenneth Holditch*

# THE DOOR

*Author:* E. B. White (1899-1985)
*Type of plot:* Antistory
*Time of plot:* The late 1930's
*Locale:* A modern American city
*First published:* 1939

> *Principal characters:*
> THE UNNAMED PROTAGONIST, apparently a middle-aged urban
>   man
> A FEMALE TOUR GUIDE
> THE PROFESSOR, a behavioral scientist who studies rats

*The Story*

This story unfolds within the claustrophobic confines of one man's mind. Its unnamed male protagonist is apparently taking a tour of a modernistic model house in a large city, led by an unnamed female guide. He feels profoundly alienated from his surroundings but also trapped by them. He cannot tell if his unease derives from being in the city, from the building itself (which has doorways that turn out to be walls and vice versa), or perhaps even from the high-tech names of the objects and substances around him. He is certain of one thing, however: Like a rat that the Professor has taught to jump at a certain card to get its food, he has dutifully jumped through all the right doors—only now the doors no longer work.

He cannot stop thinking about the rats the Professor drove crazy by forcing them to deal with problems beyond their mental capacity. When the Professor changed his cards so that the rats could no longer find their food, the animals confronted an insoluble problem. After several painful stages, the rats went insane and were eventually willing to let anything be done to them. The protagonist feels that he has reached that stage himself, seeing in the reflection of his own eyes the same imploring look that the rats had.

In this washable, synthetic, scientifically tested, perfectly self-contained, inhuman house, he becomes convinced that his own mental torment is deliberate. "They," like the Professor, wait until their subjects are completely trained for a certain door, and then they change it. He recalls the many doors that once seemed to lead to the rewards people are supposed to desire. For himself as a child, the door of religion, of prayers and holy-sounding words, seemed to work, until one day that door would not open, leading to the first painful bewilderment. Other doors followed: science and rationality, professional success, and economic independence. At some point, each door suddenly failed to open to the anticipated reward, inflicting yet another wound.

He feels that going crazy would not be so bad, if only he could stop thinking about how every aspect of his life seems beyond his power to affect it. Even the ground below his feet seems to anticipate his weight and rises to meet his step. His mind wanders at random. Now his thoughts focus on a man in New Jersey, who has inexplicably begun to chop down the trees on his property and take his house apart, brick by brick. Is the man doing all of this because he is faced with an insoluble problem, a joy that has ceased to satisfy and become unbearable?

He concludes that "they" will always change the doors, because that is their job. The logical response would be to accept that fact, but that would mean opting out of the game, which is not permitted, at least not among humans. He remembers an old friend, a poet, who spent his life following "something I cannot name." After all the preliminary stages, jumping at the doors finally killed him.

The most painful door, the protagonist recalls, promised happiness through romantic and sexual love. He wishes he could speak the truth instead of allowing himself to be guided through this peculiar house. He is exhausted from jumping at doors that inevitably produce a painful disappointment. Do the rats, he wonders, have a name for what they are seeking when they jump at their doors? He does. He calls it plexikoid, and it is "unattainable and ugli-proof."

Once again, his thoughts turn to the man in New Jersey, to the endless effort it must cost him to care for his house and trees, and to the desperation that he must now feel to destroy what he had treasured for so long. The protagonist senses that he is far from alone in his alienation and despair. Indeed, he tells himself, any doctor can confirm how many people seek a surgical solution to ease their minds—the solution of removing part of the prefrontal lobe of the brain. The ones with the large prefrontal lobes simply cannot bear any more bumping against another door that will not open.

At last, the protagonist carefully makes his way to a glass door leading out of the model house. It opens at his approach, and he almost hopes to see one of the doors from his past. Instead he sees an escalator that takes him down to street level, where the ground rises to meet his foot.

*Themes and Meanings*

Although E. B. White is usually considered a humorist with a particularly gentle style, he has treated themes as serious as those in "The Door" in several other short stories and essays. Like Trexler, the psychiatric patient in White's "The Second Tree from the Corner" (1947), the protagonist of "The Door" feels alienated from his urban environment, tormented by bizarre thoughts, and fearful, even paranoid, about coping with life. In common with the army officers on the space platform who casually blow up the earth in White's "The Morning of the Day They Did It" (1950), he feels so disconnected from simple physical pleasures and natural beauty that destruction, whether of a house or of human intelligence itself, makes emotional sense to him. Many of the essays in White's collection *One Man's Meat* (1942) stress the pernicious side effects of technological improvements and urban life when such progress comes at the expense of an intuitive understanding of humanity's place in the natural world.

"The Door" is among the bleakest of White's works. Although its protagonist does find a door out of the model house, he still feels helpless to affect his life; the ground still anticipates his foot. By contrast, Trexler achieves a Zen kind of wisdom, as he accepts, at least momentarily, the rightness of wanting something as real but unattainable as "the second tree from the corner, just as it stands." The narrator of "The Morning of the Day They Did It" escapes the total destruction of the earth and winds up among much gentler people on another planet. White himself, despite his love for many aspects of life in New York City, chose to leave the city in 1938 and move to Maine, where he worked a saltwater farm. From there, he wrote about the satisfactions of rural life for his largely urban audience.

For the protagonist of "The Door," however, there is no escape, no door that will work anymore. He can neither transcend his situation, as Trexler does, nor change his life, as White managed to do. In "The Door," White gives literary form to the despair and alienation of modern urban life that had made his personal choice, just one year earlier, a necessity.

*Style and Technique*

White's third-person narration of "The Door" immediately establishes that the story takes place inside the mind of the disturbed protagonist. Its very first sentence sets a pattern, which continues throughout, of using parenthetical phrases, such as "he kept saying," to indicate that these are the thoughts of a man silently talking to himself. The protagonist's claustrophobic feelings about being inside the model house mirror his entrapment within his own mind. The story's nonlinear structure reinforces the idea that his obsessive thoughts spin helplessly around; he cannot choose a straight path and follow it, for he sees a door that will not open at the end of each one. The seemingly random repetition of ideas and phrases produces the same effect. Nearly everything desirable, from the cards that conceal the rats' food to a beautiful woman's dress, is described as having a circle on it.

The story also makes clever use of language itself. The unnamed female guide smoothly offers logically meaningless phrases, such as "maximum openness in a small room," as though these constitute scientific proof of superiority. The rhythms and phrasing become lyrical, even biblical, however, when the protagonist considers the tragic desperation of the man in New Jersey. White scatters high-tech terminology, words such as "flexsan" and "thrutex," throughout the story.

Technology has apparently permeated modern urban consciousness completely, so that the disaffected protagonist winds up choosing the harsh, ugly, synthetic word "plexikoid" to describe his deepest longings. Even in the privacy of his own mind, White implies, a modern person can no longer find any human words to express his heart's desire.

*Susan Wladaver-Morgan*

# THE DOWNWARD PATH TO WISDOM

*Author:* Katherine Anne Porter (1890-1980)
*Type of plot:* Domestic realism
*Time of plot:* The 1940's
*Locale:* A city in the southern United States
*First published:* 1944

> *Principal characters:*
> STEPHEN, a four-year-old boy in an unhappy family
> MAMA, his mother
> PAPA, his father, who is considered "mean" and unsuitable by his wife's family
> GRANDMA, his mother's mother
> MARJORY, a family servant who shows him little affection
> OLD JANET, a servant who works for Grandma
> UNCLE DAVID, Mama's brother, a bully who believes that Stephen needs stronger discipline
> FRANCES, a girl whom Stephen meets at school

*The Story*

Four-year-old Stephen lives in a chaotic household. The story begins as Papa accuses Mama of spoiling the boy, whom she brusquely pushes from their bedroom. Their servant Marjory calls Stephen "dirty" and "mean" like his father. Soon the family quarreling becomes so severe that Stephen is sent to live with his grandmother.

At Grandma's house, Stephen gets to know his Uncle David, a large man who roughhouses with him and teaches him to box. One day, Uncle David brings home a large box of advertising balloons that he and Stephen share in a game to see who can blow up the balloons and burst them the fastest.

When the summer ends, Grandma enrolls Stephen in school, where he is surprised to discover people who are mostly his size. He is delighted to learn that these other children have ordinary names such as "Frances" and "Edward," instead of titles such as "Grandma," "Uncle," and "Mommanpoppa"—the only people he has known during his short life. There he discovers that his name is "Stephen," not "Baby" as his mother calls him, or "Bad Boy" as he is known by the household servants.

At first, Stephen has great fun in school, but he soon becomes embarrassed when other children make fun of his dancing and his clay cat sculpture. He is particularly eager to impress a girl named Frances and is happy when she accepts two of Uncle David's balloons. That same afternoon, he climbs up on a chair to take down the box of balloons that Uncle David has hidden out of reach. After filling his pockets with balloons, he gives them away at school the next day, thereby increasing his popularity.

On Saturday, Frances visits Stephen and the two of them begin blowing up balloons. When Frances grows bored with this game, she suggests that they buy sticks of licorice to make "liquish water." Embarrassed when he realizes that he has already spent all of his money, Stephen fears losing favor with Frances. He sneaks into the pantry to steal sugar, ice, and lemon juice, which he mixes together in a china teapot, trying to make lemonade as adults do. Knowing that they have broken rules, Stephen and Frances carry the teapot to the back of the house, where they hide behind a rosebush to drink the lemonade.

When Grandma's servant Old Janet finds the pantry in disarray, she sends Frances home and tells Stephen's grandmother what the children have done. As she tells her story, Uncle David finds that his box of balloons is almost half empty. He accuses Stephen of a double theft and says that the entire affair is the fault of Stephen's father. Concluding that Stephen is incorrigible, Grandma and Uncle David order his mother to take him home.

When Stephen's mother arrives to collect him, the three adults get into an argument in which each blames the others for Stephen's problems and dredges up accusations of nearly forgotten wrongs. When Stephen leaves the house with his mother, he indicates his reluctance to see his father again. As his mother drives him home, Stephen sings himself to sleep, quietly expressing his hatred for all those around him: "I hate Papa, I hate Mama, I hate Grandma, I hate Uncle David, I hate Old Janet, I hate Marjory, I hate Papa, I hate Mama." Only Frances' name is missing from Stephen's litany of anger. Exhausted, he falls asleep, resting his head on his mother's knee.

### Themes and Meanings

"The Downward Path to Wisdom" is a symbolic story depicting a four-year-old child's fall from grace. At its heart is imagery that suggests paradise and the Garden of Eden. Like Adam and Eve, Stephen is at first unaware of his own nakedness: He cannot figure out why adults throw a towel around him when he gets out of his bath, as though his body were filthy or evil. Both Uncle David's box of balloons and the "last lemon" in Grandma's pantry represent "forbidden fruit," which the child Frances— Katherine Anne Porter's equivalent of Eve—seduces Stephen into stealing. A revealing detail is the description of the last two balloons that the children take as "apple-colored" and "pale green." When Stephen feels exhausted from inflating balloons, he places a hand on his ribs, as though searching to see if one is missing. The children drink their stolen lemonade behind a rosebush, a secret "garden" from which they are expelled by Old Janet. The story's religious symbolism is further reinforced when Stephen and Frances use their lemonade to "baptize" the rosebush in the "Name father son holygoat."

Stephen's "downward path to wisdom" drops him from innocence and grace to a more disturbing world in which he can have no illusions. At the beginning of the story, Stephen is so naïve that he seems more at home with nature than with other human beings. Described as "like a bear cub," he crunches peanuts "like a horse" and is dismissed by his father as "dumb as an ox." He is not even named until several pages into the story. Nevertheless, as the narrative continues, this innocence is stripped away as Stephen's relatives use him as a weapon in their futile battles with one another.

The adult world to which Stephen is introduced seems full of strange contradictions. His father brings him peanuts and then shouts at him for eating them. His uncle gives him balloons and then calls him a thief for taking some. The joy that he feels in giving is regarded as "stealing" by the adults. Throughout the story, Stephen learns that he cannot depend on the unpredictable adults who surround him. He must keep his own counsel, treading a pessimistic "path to wisdom" that others have forced on him.

### Style and Technique

Although "The Downward Path to Wisdom," like all of Katherine Anne Porter's stories, is told by an impersonal narrator, its events are clearly seen through only Stephen's eyes. Thus the reader is never told what complaint Mama's family has against Stephen's father, or why his parents are quarreling so violently at the beginning of the story. Porter does not present a series of events so much as she describes the effect that those events have on Stephen himself. She includes no detail that would not have been known to Stephen or understood by him. Certain objects—such as Old Janet's stole, described as "a dead cat slung around her neck"—are specifically characterized in terms reflecting Stephen's limited comprehension.

Porter's style combines the clear narrative technique of Ernest Hemingway with the more symbolic approach of James Joyce. Some critics even regard her character's name, "Stephen," as inspired by Joyce's Stephen Dedalus, who goes off into exile at the end of *A Portrait of the Artist as a Young Man* (1916). Porter's Stephen likewise goes into numerous "exiles." First he is ejected from his parents' bedroom; then he is excluded from their house for the summer; finally, he is sent away from his grandmother's home.

Other critics trace Stephen's name to that of Saint Stephen, the first century Christian martyr who was condemned to death by the Sanhedrin for his "blasphemy." In Porter's story, Old Janet characterizes young Stephen's baptism of the rosebush as "blaspheming."

Aside from Stephen and Frances, few characters are named in the story. This device serves to make the narrative more universal and to represent Stephen as an "Everyman" character, whose loss of innocence is simply part of every person's maturation. The deceptively well-ordered world into which he is born is revealed throughout Porter's narrative to be chaotic, hostile, and marred by petty jealousies. By the end of the story, Stephen is well on his way to adulthood, filled with more than a child's share of cynicism and hatred.

*Jeffrey L. Buller*

# DRAGONS

*Author:* Julian Barnes (1946-    )
*Type of plot:* Historical
*Time of plot:* The late seventeenth century
*Locale:* A small village in southern France
*First published:* 1990

> *Principal characters:*
> PIERRE CHAIGNE, a widowed carpenter
> MARTHE, his thirteen-year-old daughter
> ANNE ROUGET, his elderly aunt
> HENRI, his fifteen-year-old son
> DANIEL, his nine-year-old son
> THREE UNNAMED SOLDIERS

*The Story*

"Dragons" begins with Pierre Chaigne, a widowed carpenter in a small French village, constructing a four-sided lantern, including three wooden pieces to be inserted into the lantern to block out the light except for a single direction. Narrated in the third person, the story is presented through the thoughts and actions of Pierre.

Pierre reflects that everything bad comes from the north, from the tireless winds to the Beast of Gruissan, who consumes local livestock. The new threat from the north comes from the dragons. In spite of the toleration edict issued by an earlier king, the Chaignes' religion is now threatened by the present monarch. Pierre considers himself a loyal subject, willing to live in peace with the king's religion, but now the dragons are coming.

About forty *dragons étrangers du roi*, or foreign soldiers of the king, descend on the village. Three are housed with Pierre's family, which includes his elderly aunt and his three children. The dragons will remain until Pierre pays the tax owed to the king. However, it is impossible to satisfy the authorities: If he pays, the tax will be raised, again and again, until the family abjures its faith.

Although he fears for thirteen-year-old Marthe at the hands of the dragons, he has a greater concern for his youngest son, nine-year-old Daniel. Previously the law of conversion had been set at fourteen because by that age an individual is mature enough to know his or her mind. Recently it had been lowered to seven, and Pierre worries that young Daniel might become susceptible to the church's enticements. The dragons take over the house, even sleeping in the single bed. They ransack the premises looking for valuables, though they know that a poor carpenter would have none. They burn chairs in the fireplace though firewood is readily available. Pierre's carpentry tools are sold to villagers who belong to the king's religion. When Pierre's coreligionists worship secretly, the dragons violently disperse them.

"What matter the road provided it leads to Paradise?" one of the dragons asks, justifying the torturing of an itinerant peddler to get him to abjure. The ill, aged, and very young begin to convert, but force and intimidation are used on the more reluctant. Pierre's aged aunt, Anne Rouget, is the first of the family to succumb. After being told that his aunt awaits him in heaven but only if he abandons his father's faith, Daniel abjures and is sent to a Jesuit college across the northern mountains. Months go by, with Pierre and his elder son Henri forced to scrounge food in the forest for the dragons. One day when they return, Pierre discovers that a dragon has forced Marthe to have sex. The following day another of the dragons has sex with her. After nine days, Henri abjures, but when the dragons continue to treat Marthe as a prostitute, Henri spits out the wafer and wine during the Mass. Convicted of blasphemy, he is burnt at the stake.

A dragon tells Marthe that she must convert as inevitably she will become pregnant, and the dragons will then claim that Pierre had sex with his daughter. They will then be burnt because of the incestuous relationship. When asked where they are from, the dragon replies from the north, Ireland. When she asks why they are persecuting the Chaignes, he refers to Oliver Cromwell, who had persecuted the dragons' religion in Ireland. Marthe abjures and is also sent north to be raised in a convent. When the dragons move on to another village, only eight dissenters remain out of the original 176. Two nights later, Pierre replaces three of the lantern's panes with the wooden pieces he shaped long ago. The remaining pane cast the lantern's light in a single direction, the direction Pierre follows into the forest, where the remaining few are to pray.

## Themes and Meanings

British critics have suggested that Julian Barnes is more French than English, an allegation he denies. Nevertheless, Barnes admits that he loves France: It is his other country. Most of Barnes's fiction is set in the present or the near past. "Dragons" is an exception, with the events taking place during the late seventeenth century reign of Louis XIV. Louis's grandfather, Henry IV, was a Huguenot, or French Protestant, who converted to Catholicism, the majority religion, for political reasons. In the 1598 Edict of Nantes, Henry granted his former coreligionists considerable religious freedom, but in 1685, with the Edict of Fontainebleau, Louis XIV revoked his grandfather's proclamation, making Catholicism France's only recognized religion. It is against this historical background that the events of "Dragons" occur.

"Dragons" can be read as a conflict between religious freedom and intolerance and bigotry. The task of the dragons is to eliminate by whatever means necessary the newly proscribed minority religion. Although the seventeenth century is often labeled the Age of Reason, religious passions still ruled, reflecting the earlier medieval Age of Faith and the religious Reformations of the sixteenth century. People were willing to die and to kill for their religion, and many did.

Familial love and personal sacrifice is another theme of "Dragons." To free his sister Marthe from sexual assaults by the dragons, Henri converts to Catholicism even though he does not believe its doctrines. Marthe stoically accepts the dragons' sexual abuse until one of them threatens to accuse her and her father Pierre of incest if she does not abjure. Conviction would inevitably lead to their execution. If it was just herself, she might well have resisted, but to save her father, Marthe converts.

"Dragons" can also be read as the story of individual courage and the commitment to principle. In spite of the threats, Pierre never surrenders to the demands that he abjure, and the narrative ends with Pierre and a small remnant still holding fast to their faith. However, Pierre knew from the beginning that if he converted, the dragons would leave and his family would be spared. Do individuals have the right to destroy their family in the defense of their own beliefs? In the seventeenth century, the answer was yes because it was a society dominated by a divine imperative: It was God's world and God's word. In this interpretation, "Dragons" becomes a tale of competing dogmas instead of a story of religious freedom versus religious persecution. Pierre is as obstinately committed to his "truth" as his persecutors are to theirs.

At the end, Pierre's lantern does not symbolize the light of freedom and toleration brightly shining in a dark world of religious bigotry. Rather, with the three sides of the lantern now darkened, the remaining light points to a single path, or truth, as the obstinate Pierre joins his few fellow believers.

*Style and Technique*

"Dragons" contains few historical facts: The kings are not named, nor are the religious edicts. The Roman Catholic Church is not explicitly referred to although mention is made of the Mass, Jesuits, priests, and nuns. The term "protestant" is used only once and the word "Huguenot" never. The story is told through the perceptions and limited knowledge of largely illiterate peasants—a carpenter in Pierre's case—who knew little but the world of the village and its environs. Experience has taught them that bad things come from the north, be it mythic beasts, harsh winds, or religious and secular power. Marthe knew nothing of Ireland or England, probably the Chaigne family had heard of neither Henry IV nor his Edict of Nantes, and perhaps Pierre did not even know the name of the present king, Louis XIV. The peasants' world was the village—beyond was only danger.

Barnes successfully portrays the internal tone or atmosphere of preindustrial rural peasants and their world. "Dragons" is not overtly dramatic in presentation in spite of rape and the burning of convicted heretics. Instead, the thoughts and actions of the characters are presented through the mentality of seventeenth century peasants. There is a somber sense of inevitability. Life is difficult, work is hard, and struggle is endless. Pierre and the other characters rarely engage in introspection and do not harbor a feeling that circumstances could be changed: Life and death will always be what they have always been. Appropriately, there are no modern sensibilities and no modern concepts of freedom and individualism in "Dragons." The revelation that the dragons were Irish Catholic refugees fleeing from Cromwell's Protestant persecutors adds to that sense of fate and inevitability: One is persecuted thus one persecutes, over and over, and Pierre's single lighted pane leads him only into the dark forest.

*Eugene Larson*

# DRAGON'S SEED

*Author:* Madison Smartt Bell (1957-     )
*Type of plot:* Fantasy
*Time of plot:* The late twentieth century
*Locale:* Somewhere in the United States
*First published:* 1990

> *Principal characters:*
> MACKIE LOUDON, a sculptor
> JASON STURGES, a young boy whom she befriends
> GIL, her neighbor

## The Story

Mackie Loudon lives alone in her cluttered house in a neglected neighborhood of what appears to be a good-sized town or small city somewhere in the United States. She is a sculptor who continues to create, even though no one any longer stops by to purchase or even to see her work. Indeed, no one visits her ramshackle house, not even her husband, son, or grandchildren, whom Mackie sees only occasionally and then only in dreams. The townspeople find her odd as she forages for anything of interest in the street or shops for her food at a nearby Asian store. She wears shapeless dresses and a man's coat; her hair is hacked into a helmet shape; her skin is like elephant hide; her shoulders are broad and her hands are strong, but her legs are bowed and slightly arthritic; her chin is whiskered, her right eye is green and her left eye pale blue with an unusual tic. Strangest of all, Mackie talks to herself, or rather talks to her two demons, Eliel and Azazael, to whom she has relegated certain aspects of her personality: seeing, judging, remembering.

When work on her latest sculpture is going poorly, she meets a boy in the alley between her house and the even more disreputable-looking house next door. Although the boy says that his name is Monkey, Mackie decides to call him Preston and entices him into her house with the promise of milk and cookies. Even more enticing than her cookies—which turn out to be yellow bean and lotus seed cakes—are the stories that she tells of the Greek myths from which her sculptures derive. Preston proves an attentive and appreciative audience, until Mackie mentions the story of Jason and the Argonauts. The boy inexplicably turns pale, bolts from the house, and stays away for a week.

Before the week is out, Mackie's equally grotesque and reclusive neighbor, Gil, arrives in his customary ill-suited motorcycle garb, "thin as from some wasting disease," to warn her not to meddle in his affairs and those of the boy who lives with him. As Gil peremptorily explains, the Monkey's "skinny little butt is mine" and "no one cares what goes on around here." At this point, Mackie does not understand that what goes on in Gil's house, with its blacked-out windows, is the sexual abuse of children.

The boy does return, but just as Mackie begins to renew their milk-and-cookies ritual, she sees his picture on a milk carton captioned "Jason Sturges of Birmingham, eight years old and missing since . . . " This time the boy bolts for good, but whether he has run away or been murdered by Gil is a mystery.

The demons that had been silent during Mackie's friendship with Preston now return to assail her for her terrible mistake. Her call to the police only earns her a second, even more violent warning from Gil not to meddle in his affairs. Found dazed on the ground by a stranger, after others had passed her by, Mackie is taken to the mental hospital where she has been confined several times before. She now withdraws even further into herself, refusing to take her medication, to participate in crafts classes and group therapy, even to talk, until the night Little Willa, whom the staff has forgotten to strap to her bed, demonstrates her fire-breathing trick. That is when Eliel and Azazael tell Mackie how she can solve her problem, and Mackie, who is eccentric but not insane, begins another of her miraculously swift recoveries.

Back at home, Mackie uses a mirror to become her own model and solves the first of her problems, completing her Medusa sculpture. In a way she becomes Medusa, or, like Medusa's slayer, Perseus, takes on Medusa's awful power, with every stroke of the chisel feeling "the Gorgon visage pushing out on her brow as if embossed upon a shield." The rest of her demonic plan swiftly unfolds. She breaks into Gil's house, sees the results of his pornographic art, destroys his video and photographic equipment, and calmly awaits his return. Stunned, first by the wreckage and then by the gasoline that Mackie splashes on him, Gil is finally "turned to stone" when she pulls out the lighter and pulls back her hair to reveal the Gorgon. Gil dies, his house burns down, and Mackie, once she realizes that she will not be arrested, goes home and shuts the door.

*Themes and Meanings*

"Dragon's Seed" treats several social and literary subjects. The most topical and most disturbing concerns children: those who run away or are abducted from their homes and come to be sexually abused and made part of the "kiddie porn" industry. Another is madness and eccentricity, as well as the social means used to deal, or not deal, with them. Finally there is Madison Smartt Bell's use, or abuse, of the mythic method of literary high modernism, which T. S. Eliot defined as the manipulation of "a continuous parallel between contemporaneity and antiquity" in order to control, order, and give "a shape and significance to the immense panorama of futility and anarchy that is contemporary history."

Bell's story is not about any of these. Its purpose is broader and revolves around two general questions: how and how well one sees oneself and one's world, and how one engages the world, a question of concern for every individual and, more especially in this story, for every artist. The answer to the first question is neatly if pessimistically summed up in Bell's description of one of the objects that Mackie finds and then quickly discards, a marble that has lost its luster: "The cloud in it no longer looked like a whirlwind, but a cataract." As for the second, Mackie unwisely withdraws into her house, herself, her Greek myths, and her art, an art without an audience and without a purpose. Even at her most withdrawn and outwardly self-sufficient, she maintains at least some contact with the world, first through her demons, to whom she relegates the task of seeing what that part of her personality called "Mackie" prefers not to, and later the boy, Monkey/Preston/Jason Sturges, in whom the Greek myths live and for whom Mackie's art takes on meaning, purpose, finished form. In taking an interest in the boy, Mackie becomes not only the engaged artist but also the engaged citizen. She comes to stand in marked contrast to her indifferent neighbors in general, particularly to Gil, the artist as pornographer.

*Style and Technique*

For many readers, the most important issue raised by "Dragon's Seed" will be whether Bell's comic style is appropriate to a subject as serious as the sexual abuse of children. Such readers will undoubtedly question whether the treatment does not in fact trivialize the subject, making it little more than grist for the author's narrative mill in much the same way (those same readers will claim) that Mackie's plight in the mental hospital becomes the occasion for writing that seems stylistically clever rather than socially committed: "She let herself be herded from point to point on the ward, moving like an exhumed corpse made to simulate animation by a programmed sequence of electric shocks."

The language here and throughout the story is vivid, self-consciously wrought, and self-regarding but never merely self-indulgent. Like the overall deadpan narration, it serves Bell's larger purpose. Although narrated in the third person, the story reflects its focal character's way of perceiving her world. Its grotesque realism is therefore as much a quality of her mind as it is a function of Bell's comic style. Even as it contributes to the story's humorous effect and psychological realism, the fantastic works here in much the same way that it does in the fiction of writers such as Ursula K. LeGuin, as a way to raise issues of social or moral import.

Bell's recycling of myths, on topics such as dragon's teeth, Medusa, and Azazael, and fairy tales, such as "Hansel and Gretel," works in a similar manner. Even as it suggests both a typically clever postmodern debunking of the mythic method and a more-or-less realistic means for representing Mackie Loudon's state of mind, Bell's playfulness has its own serious side. Bell underscores this point by embedding in the names assigned to the Monkey the name of the American director Preston Sturges, whose films, like Bell's fiction, effectively combine social satire and popular appeal. In the story's closing tableau, readers may detect yet another cinematic reference, equally apropos, this time to the sadly comic figure of the Little Tramp played by Charles Chaplin.

*Robert A. Morace*

# DREAM CARGOES

*Author:* J. G. Ballard (1930-      )
*Type of plot:* Science fiction, apocalyptic and catastrophic, Robinsonade
*Time of plot:* The 1990's
*Locale:* An island off the coast of Puerto Rico in the Caribbean Sea
*First published:* 1990

> *Principal characters:*
> JOHNSON, a sailor aboard the *Prospero*
> DR. CHRISTINE CHAMBERS, a biology professor at San Juan
> University in Puerto Rico

## The Story

"Dream Cargoes" is narrated in the third person, for the most part through the consciousness of a simple young sailor named Johnson. The story takes place over a period of six months but is presented in brief episodes, with flashbacks supplying details necessary to explain Johnson's peculiar situation and the anomalous condition of the island on which he is marooned.

The story opens one morning with a description of the fantastic plant life enveloping a Caribbean island. Beholding the spectacle is a sailor named Johnson aboard the beached freighter *Prospero*. Johnson realizes that the vegetation has grown even more luxuriant overnight, but he is more interested in one Dr. Christine Chambers, whose raft he has sighted on the beach for the past few days and whose name he has learned from labels on equipment in her raft. This morning, however, Chambers is not to be seen. Johnson wades ashore through the chemical wastes leaching out of the rusting hulk, but once there, he falls asleep in a ruined army staff car. As the story progresses, Johnson sleeps with increasing frequency and ease.

Thanks to its illegal cargo of poisonous chemicals, the *Prospero* had been denied use of ports throughout the Gulf of Mexico and the Caribbean. The ship was leaking and listing badly, and when the freighter's captain and crew abandoned it within sight of Puerto Rico, Johnson had decided—for the first time in his life—to seize control of events and to remain on board. However, the nearly illiterate young man quickly found himself lost at sea and sickened by chemical fumes. He had gladly run the *Prospero* aground near a tiny island—an abandoned U.S. Army garbage dump—and allowed the sea to flood its hold. Almost immediately, the once-barren island, somehow nourished by the leaking cargo, had sprung to frightening life.

Johnson is awakened by Chambers, who has to cut away the vines that have grown up around the staff car while he slept. Johnson identifies himself as captain of the vessel lying in the bay and is pleased that the attractive scientist seems to accept this identification. He recounts an edited version of how he came to the island, and she in turn reports what she had heard about the *Prospero*. The crew, it seems, claim that their notorious ship sank several hundred miles away and that they were forced to spend a month in their lifeboat. The island is Chambers's biological research project, but it is clear that thanks to the unexpected action of the chemicals, her experiment has taken an exciting new turn, one that involves Johnson himself.

As the story unfolds, the bizarre vegetation overwhelms the island, with Johnson struggling every day to clear his shack. He seems to be physically healthy, but he is increasingly absorbed in the burgeoning life around him and is losing track of time for hours and even days. Fascinated with what is taking place, Chambers has pragmatically conceived a child with Johnson. She asks him to trap some of the exotic birds now flying through the island's jungle canopy, but Johnson responds by insisting that time is coming to a stop and that they themselves are growing wings and can learn to fly.

Chambers eventually radios for help. By the time a U.S. Navy ship arrives, the island's vegetation has started to collapse on itself. An officer hypothesizes that the plants' "cellular clocks" have stopped, and that, unable to reproduce, the plants have grown to the point of exhaustion. He suggests that the same mechanism is responsible for Johnson's altered sense of time. Setting explosives that will demolish everything on the island, the crew take Johnson and Chambers aboard and speed away. Johnson realizes that while the child Chambers carries may be the first of a new race, it will face certain animosity. He jumps overboard, planning to swim back to the island to free the trapped birds in hopes that something of the more beautiful and advanced world he had glimpsed will survive.

## Themes and Meanings

In Johnson, J. G. Ballard has created a poor and aimless young man who has never before had the courage or opportunity to make meaningful choices. Used to finding himself at the mercy of events, Johnson assumes increasing control of his life throughout the story, first by remaining aboard the *Prospero* and finally by swimming back to the doomed island to free the birds, an act that will surely cost him his life. Although it is not clear whether Johnson's visions of flight and transformation are to be taken literally, it is obvious that the one-time cabin boy and deck hand has indeed glimpsed a world in which he has an important role to play.

The nature of that world is suggested by the basic pattern Ballard creates in "Dream Cargoes," that of a self-contained paradise inhabited by a man and woman. This situation recalls the biblical story of Adam and Eve, whose roles are taken in the story by Johnson and Chambers. When the story is read this way, the unnamed island assumes obvious parallels with the Garden of Eden, from which the first couple were driven.

Ballard delights in frustrating the expectations of his readers and in upsetting their preconceived notions. However, he does so in recurring patterns. In his novel *Rushing to Paradise* (1994), he took a critical look at the motives behind an environmental activist's destructive activities on a tropical island. In "Dream Cargoes," he uses another island setting and takes—or seems to take—a similarly unorthodox position. Playing on contemporary readers' concerns over pollution and environmental degradation, he nevertheless presents such pollution as a means of salvation, a way out of the increasingly rigid and compartmentalized structures of modern consciousness. Ballard realizes that on a rational basis, this position is ridiculous, so he supports his story with a framework of symbols and allusions, conveying his theme in a less obvious but more compelling manner.

*Style and Technique*

"Dream Cargoes" is a variation of an age-old genre, the "Robinsonade," which takes its name from Daniel Defoe's novel *The Life and Strange Surprising Adventures of Robinson Crusoe* (1719). Used by many writers in the centuries since, the Robinsonade recounts the experiences of an individual or small group of individuals marooned on an isolated island. Such a device not only allows an author to present his or her characters in an extreme situation but also provides a convenient means of focusing the action of the work. Ballard has turned repeatedly to this device in such novels as *Concrete Island* (1974) and *Rushing to Paradise*.

Ballard supports his theme with several literary allusions, the most obvious involving the name of the beached freighter. In English playwright William Shakespeare's work *The Tempest* (1613), the nobleman Prospero has been robbed of his throne and set adrift with his daughter Miranda. The two are eventually marooned on an island where Miranda grows up seeing practically no one but her father. Overwhelmed with delight when she finally confronts a band of fellow men and women, she utters the famous line: "O brave new world/ That has such people in't!" (English writer Aldous Huxley took the title of his 1932 novel *Brave New World* from this line, and Ballard's story can be read as an ironic response to Huxley's nightmarish vision of the future.)

Although Ballard is sometimes criticized for his clinical and detached language, "Dream Cargoes" is filled with vivid descriptive passages whose luxuriance approximates that of the vegetation they describe. Ballard also structures his story in a manner approximating his main character's own experience. During one of his visionary episodes, Johnson "sees" Chambers as a blurred series of superimposed images and colors. The story itself unfolds as a series of brief scenes, many of which open with Johnson awakening from sleep. The reader's initial confusion mirrors Johnson's own, and the superimposition of one scene on the next gives us a sense of Johnson's expanding yet fragmented consciousness, his vision of a "brave new world."

*Grove Koger*

# DREAM CHILDREN

*Author:* Gail Godwin (1937-    )
*Type of plot:* Psychological
*Time of plot:* 1971
*Locale:* Hudson River Valley, New York
*First published:* 1971

### Principal characters:

MRS. MCNAIR, the protagonist
MR. MCNAIR, her husband
A NURSE, her nurse during her postpartum hospital stay

## The Story

The story begins some time after an unspecified tragedy has befallen the protagonist, Mrs. McNair, and it is a wonder that she has not gone mad. Nevertheless, Mrs. McNair is portrayed as a happy woman, one who embodies the qualities desired in a young wife. She is neat and cheerful, well dressed, and polite. She returns her library books on time and politely agrees with others' political opinions, even though she has experienced a terrible, freakish thing.

Mrs. McNair, whose husband remains in the city during weekdays and is little more than a visitor on weekends, lives in a seventeenth century Dutch farmhouse that is apparently situated along the lower Hudson River in New York State. There, with her stallion and her large silver dog, Blue Boy, she exists in a peaceful but somewhat mystical, weekday world, in which she spends numerous hours reading about the supernatural and riding her horse. Science fiction, ghost stories, and parapsychology particularly appeal to her because she experienced her unexplained tragedy.

Through the eyes of her neighbor, Mr. DePuy, Mrs. McNair is observed on one of her early morning gallops on her stallion. Perceiving her as reckless and arrogant, Mr. DePuy, an otherwise kind and decent man, discovers himself wishing for her to fall. Her wantonness distresses him. Mrs. DePuy, however, more charitably recognizes the tragedy underlying Mrs. McNair's recklessness. She has nothing to fear anymore, thinks Mrs. DePuy, who simultaneously pities and envies her.

Although there are several allusions to her tragedy throughout the story, its exact nature is not described until the end. Meanwhile, the reader learns more about Mrs. McNair's somewhat dreamlike existence. As a child, she was prone to sleepwalking. Her parents, fearing for her safety, sent her to a psychiatrist. After the sympathetic psychiatrist informed her that children possess magically sagacious powers, her night journeys ended. Now, as a bereft adult, she derives comfort from the psychiatrist's words.

One evening she is awakened by peculiar noises emanating from a guest bedroom, in which she discovers her son, dead at birth, now two years old and clothed in clean but worn pajamas. His large eyes are the same as before: dark and unblinking. Mother and son do not speak to each other, but she is comforted by his presence. On six occasions during the next six months, she visits with him, imagining for him another life and another mother. She perceives herself as being like her husband, who maintains two separate lives—his weekday life in the city and his weekend life with her in the country. She also has two separate existences, but to her, the day world appears surreal while her dream world is real.

Mrs. McNair does not care whether her son's nocturnal visits actually occur or are simply imagined; to her, the level on which they meet does not matter. Through him she fully experiences the implications of the magically sagacious powers of children. Because of her dream child, she is a happy woman who rides her stallion faster than fear, awaiting her son's nightly visitations.

In the final paragraphs, the exact nature of her tragedy is described. In the midst of a smoothly progressing natural childbirth, during which she is told by her doctor that delivery will be a breeze, her son dies. Her doctor aggressively but futilely attempts to save him. While her husband faints, Mrs. McNair is sedated. The next morning a nurse enters Mrs. McNair's room and presents her with a baby whom she believes is her son. With a profound, religious relief, Mrs. McNair accepts the child and contentedly nurses him. When the overworked nurse realizes her mistake, she is unable to separate the mother and child, who are now both screaming. Mrs. McNair must be sedated before she will let the child go.

## Themes and Meanings

On a fundamental level, Gail Godwin's "Dream Children" explores the nature of the real world—that which is quantifiable and explicable—versus the many levels of the mystical otherworlds, including the dream world. It also questions whether the otherworlds are observable reality or mere extensions of insane minds. Mrs. McNair searches for the meaning of the visits with her dead child by voraciously reading about the experiences of others. Through her research, she discovers that night journeys, apparitions, and paranormal experiences have captured the imaginations of countless generations of intelligent, literate people.

She further muses over the nature of reality while observing her dog. Does the rabbit of which he dreams have a separate reality, she wonders? Her search for explanation is an empty one, for her experience is personal and unique, not quantifiable. Finally, she does not care whether she has simply dreamed of her child or whether he has on some level actually visited her. Either way, she is supremely happy in her secret otherworld, for no matter what, she is convinced that her son loved her.

Mrs. McNair is not the only character to undergo a mystical awakening in "Dream Children." An exhausted nurse, after having worked for forty-eight hours during a strike, mistakenly gives Mrs. McNair another mother's child. In her almost hallucinatory exhaustion, the nurse undergoes a profoundly mystical revelation. After seeing the woman and the baby clinging to each other, she realizes that all children and mothers are interchangeable. Neither belongs to the other; one could no more own a child than one could own an idea. For the nurse, however, unlike the mother, the mystical revelation quickly fades.

Mr. McNair experiences an altogether different sort of reality. In the city, he lives with his mistress, a sensitive, understanding woman whom he loves. Nevertheless, with his mistress's blessing, each weekend he returns to his wife, whom he also loves, acting on weekends, at least, as her tender protector. He is acutely aware of his role in bringing about her tragedy and will never leave her. Mrs. McNair is unconcerned by his duality, for she also lives two lives, each separate and distinct. Mr. McNair's mistress, in her own version of reality, compassionately accepts her lover's duty to his wife while presumably living her own double life on the weekends.

### Style and Technique

The mysticism and dreamlike nature of Mrs. McNair's life is mirrored in Godwin's prose. Short, incomplete sentences printed in italics that are interspersed throughout the story forcefully convey the tragic, mystical aspects of Mrs. McNair's life. Godwin's precise language creates a surrealistic mood against the tragic undercurrent of the story. Images of a contented young woman are juxtaposed against fervent reminders of a tragedy that she underwent. Twice a detached voice wonders how the woman was able to retain her sanity, thereby planting doubts in the reader's mind. Although the story is related from the point of view of a detached observer, it ends, persuasively, again with print italicized, in Mrs. McNair's own words. *"I am a happy woman, that's all I know. Who can explain such things?"* Whether she is mad as suggested and as her husband fears, or she has simply experienced an alternate reality, is rendered inconsequential. Only her visits with her son are important.

Symbolism abounds in this story. Deprived of sexual desire and physical sensation after her ordeal, Mrs. McNair rides in reckless abandon on her stallion, an animal that is the embodiment of uncontrollable sexuality. She rides him fearlessly, not as the demure housewife that her neighbors believe her to be, but as if she is beyond the mundane world, for nothing more can affect her. Surely the otherwise kind father and good husband, Mr. DePuy, would not wish her to fall were she riding a subdued mare, appropriate for a young wife. A stallion, however, best serves her altered, surreal state of existence.

*Mary E. Virginia*

# THE DREAM LOVER

*Author:* William Boyd (1952-    )
*Type of plot:* Psychological
*Time of plot:* The 1960's
*Locale:* Nice, France
*First published:* 1993

> *Principal characters:*
>> EDWARD, the narrator, an English student studying French in
>>    Nice, France
>> PRESTON, a seemingly rich American youth, also studying in Nice
>> LOIS, Preston's fiancé
>> ANNIQUE CAMBRAI, the daughter of friends of Edward's mother
>> INGRID, a young Norwegian woman
>> DANNI, a young Swedish woman

*The Story*

Lonely and temporarily out of ready cash because of a postal strike in England, Edward, a young Englishman studying French culture at the Centre Universitaire Nice, strikes up a friendship with Preston, an American student who seems to have a lot of money, never goes to class, and repeatedly asks Edward to introduce him to a French girl. Edward, the obliging but shy English student, promises to fix him up and eventually brings several girls from his classes to Preston's very modern studio apartment in the Résidence Les Anges, a posh place that stands in stark contrast to Edward's own dim apartment with Madame d'Amico. Edward goes to his classes; Preston rarely does.

Edward has one other social outlet, a regular Monday evening dinner date with a French couple, the Cambrais, who are friends of his mother, and their three daughters. However, other afternoons he is a regular visitor at Preston's place, drinking in the club or at the pool. Preston always expresses his wish that Edward bring a French girl for him. Edward learns that Preston is an only child and has a millionaire father who fails to send Preston the money he continually requests and a mother who divorced Preston's father and soon married another millionaire, giving Preston a choice of eight elegant homes to visit around the United States. It finally is revealed that Preston has been sent to Nice because he had seduced each of his three stepsisters, getting the oldest one pregnant.

Edward finally does take a girl from class to the club to meet Preston. However, she is not French, much to Preston's disappointment, but a Norwegian woman named Ingrid, who speaks perfect English and German. Ingrid also has very hairy armpits, which Preston finds quite erotic. A bit later Edward brings a second girl, a Swedish woman called Danni, who is voluptuous and blond but has a slightly withered leg owing to childhood polio. Meanwhile the barman, a portly unsmiling man named Serge, becomes more and more hostile to Preston and Edward because of their boisterous drinking, Preston's ever-increasing bar tab, and Preston's consistent rudeness to him. The other members of the French class now regard Edward with some interest because Ingrid and Danni have reported on their poolside afternoons with unlimited free booze; Edward, however, is beginning to feel "pimp-like."

Over the months of Monday night dinners with the Cambrais, Edward has developed a relationship with one of their daughters, Annique, a law student. Edward invites Annique to try out her American accent on Preston. She goes with Edward to meet Preston, but they discover that his fiancé, Lois, has arrived unexpectedly from the United States, solving for the moment Preston's financial stress by cashing in her return ticket. Lois assumes Annique and Edward are a couple, not realizing that he has brought her there for Preston, who now clearly envies Edward for having found a "dream lover," Preston's long-desired Platonic ideal of a beautiful French woman.

Edward's relationship with Annique develops further, to the point that Edward wants to taunt Preston with the news that they are looking for an apartment to share. So, after staying away from Preston and Lois for a while, Edward drops by his apartment to imply that he and Annique are having a lovely physical relationship. Before he can gloat, Lois, weeping, informs Edward that they are broke and desperate, and Preston asks if Edward can help them out. He does, spending nearly all he has to provide them with train tickets to Luxembourg and plane tickets to New York, relishing Preston's desperate jealousy of Edward's relationship with Annique and his despair at not having gained any knowledge of Nice, of France, or of himself during his stay there.

### Themes and Meanings

This story is a modern sexual comedy of manners about the education of Edward, a young, rather naïve Englishman who approaches his experience as a "supplicant and votary." The story's principal meanings emerge as Edward, along with students from Germany, Norway, Sweden, Tunisia, Nigeria, and the United States, attends a program in French language and culture offered by a university in Nice, France. Although Edward takes his studies seriously, Preston sees himself as an exile, cut off from home, rather than a student. He rarely attends classes, parties hard at his "club," asks Edward about his French connections, and at the end of the story regrets not only his lost "dream lover" but also his lost educational opportunities. Both young men improve their understandings of themselves.

Edward becomes increasingly aware of his power over the boorish American Preston, and the story's meaning emerges in this classic plot of two friends who discover that they are really rivals and that the quiet guy finally gets the "dream lover." However, self-knowledge and sexual triumph come at a price for both. Edward has been "pimping" for Preston, but Preston has failed to take advantage of his educational opportunity and thus fails to attain his Platonic ideal lover, a French woman. When Edward at last brings the ideal woman to Preston's apartment, he is saved from the likely consequence of his behavior by Lois's unexpected presence and gets to "keep" the girl.

Edward, diligent in his study of French language and culture, also benefits from his introduction to cultural learning involving exposure to people from different classes and economic levels and to a variety of moral standards. The moral ambiguity of his bringing girls from school to entertain his newfound friend becomes apparent to Edward as he learns more about Preston and the reasons for his "exile." The product of a set of wealthy, divorced parents has been sent to France because he seduced his three stepsisters, impregnating one. In France, he cuts classes, drinks too much, plies all visitors with liquor, and conducts a perpetual party at his apartment and club. As his behavior becomes increasingly boorish, he even descends to beating up Serge, the barman who had long endured his slurs, when Serge refused to extend him further credit.

The class theme further emerges in several scenes that contrast Preston's ostentatious apartment building, the Résidence Les Anges, to Edward's own "dim apartment"; his apparently unlimited credit based on his family's wealth to Edward's relative poverty; and his disrespectful and finally violent behavior toward Serge, the barman, and Edward's efforts to get along with the French. Finally, when Edward "rescues" Preston and Lois by providing them with money and transportation to New York City, Edward lets Preston know that he and Annique Cambrai are looking for an apartment and that his relationship with her is "good." At this point in the story, Edward's latent hatred of Preston and all that he represents is revealed. At the end when Preston begs Edward for help to get him and Lois out of France and back to New York, Edward takes great delight in providing tickets and paying Preston's bar bill, for it is only by making this grand gesture and telling Preston about Annique and himself that Edward restores himself to a position of magnanimous benevolence and superiority.

*Style and Technique*

William Boyd tells "The Dream Lover" in the first person and in present tense, through the consciousness of Edward, and explores a set of moral ambiguities centered in cultural stereotypes by contrasting the motives and experiences of two young men, one English and the other American. He draws the narrator, Edward, as envious of Preston yet attracted to him because of his own inexperience and wavering moral compass. Choosing Edward as his point-of-view character enables Boyd to reveal Edward's thoughts as he infers from Preston's actions essential details and creates a tone always more sympathetic to Edward, yet still reflective of moral ambiguity. Edward is a naïf, a character who like Preston is fascinated with the idea of a French lover. Both are in the throes of delayed adolescent sexuality, but Edward, because of his mother's connections, is able to spend Monday nights with the Cambrai family.

These repeated scenes of domestic conviviality and the Cambrai family table talk contrast sharply with Preston's sleazy bar-club soirees and the banal and bibulous discourse at Serge's bar. Thus Boyd suggests that the essential quality of Edward's education is a matter of "learning the language" and how to respect the virtues of family and culture. The Cambrai family in its warmth, hospitality, education, and number of daughters (three, the same number as Preston's stepsisters) contrasts markedly with Preston's broken family and seduced stepsisters.

Edward becomes sharply critical of Preston's "soft life of casual privilege and unreflecting ease." Boyd thus points the moral of his tale by awarding Edward the mature, beautiful, well-educated Annique Cambrai as his prize for tending his cultural fields. Edwards has acquired enough insight in the process to realize the ambiguous nature of his "pimping" for Preston and experiences great pleasure in being able to assist the profligate Preston and his fiancé. Edward's triumph is complete, its cost a small tuition for the insight into self that it affords.

*Theodore C. Humphrey*

# THE DREAM OF A RIDICULOUS MAN

*Author:* Fyodor Dostoevski (1821-1881)
*Type of plot:* Fable
*Time of plot:* The 1870's
*Locale:* St. Petersburg
*First published:* "Son smeshnogo cheloveka," 1877 (English translation, 1916)

*Principal character:*
THE RIDICULOUS MAN, the unnamed protagonist

*The Story*

The ridiculous man introduces himself as he is seen by his friends and neighbors, a madman who was formerly considered to be merely ridiculous. He states, however, that he does not mind being the object of laughter and does not dislike those who ridicule him; on the contrary, he pities them. He alone possesses the Truth; he wishes that others would believe him. After this introduction, the narrator goes back in time to describe why he was always considered ridiculous, how a dream changed his life, and why he is now considered a madman by his peers.

The narrator relates that he has always been considered ridiculous, that he himself knows that he has always been ridiculous, but that pride has kept him from admitting this fact to anyone else. As he gets older, this feeling of ridiculousness is balanced somewhat by a growing realization that nothing matters; life is meaningless. One evening, this latter feeling oppresses the narrator, and he decides to commit suicide that very night by shooting himself with a revolver that he has bought for that specific purpose. On his way home to commit the act, he is intercepted by an eight-year-old girl who is sobbing and seeking help for her mother. The narrator dismisses the girl, but he returns home deeply impressed by the poverty and fear that she exhibited. He places the revolver on the table before him, but as he sits and stares at the gun, his mind wanders back to the girl. He reflects on the fact that he can still feel pity for another person and that there are people who are, or who might be, dependent on him. This startling conclusion leads him to think about life again, and he decides to put off his suicide until he can resolve the questions in his mind. He then falls asleep in his chair and begins the dream that will change his life and his attitude toward the world.

The narrator imagines his own suicide, the ensuing confusion when his body is discovered by the landlady and neighbors, and then the placing of his coffin into the grave. After an unspecified time, a strange being opens the coffin, picks the narrator up, and begins flying through space. The ridiculous man realizes that he was wrong; death does not mean the end of existence but the beginning of some new type of life. That conclusion is confirmed when the strange being deposits him on another planet, which he recognizes as a duplication of Earth. The setting is beautiful; left alone by the strange being, the narrator inspects the trees and birds of his new home. The inhabitants of the area find him and welcome him with open arms. He, in turn, is impressed with their sincere friendliness, their beauty, and the joy that they project. He then realizes that these people have never done evil and reside in a paradise with an almost perfect society. They seem to know of the suffering on Earth of the ridiculous man and they attempt to cheer him up by loving him. He, on the other hand, is touched by the fact that he is finally being accepted by a group of people as their equal.

As the story progresses, the narrator describes his new neighbors and the society in which they live. There is no science or technology, yet these people have a mature understanding of life that makes science and technology irrelevant. Science seeks to explain the meaning of life and to explore the frontiers of knowledge, but these people already knew the meaning of life, were perfectly contented, and, therefore, saw no need to develop scientific knowledge. The ridiculous man is impressed by the bond between the people and the other manifestations of nature, such as trees and animals. When the people speak to the trees, the narrator senses that some understanding is taking place. The people live in perfect harmony with the beasts, neither fearing the other. People work only to procure what they need.

After this glowing report of the society that he discovered on this planet, the ridiculous man then discloses that he corrupted all these happy people and that their nearly perfect civilization degenerated into a society very similar to the one he had left on Earth. He cannot remember exactly how it happened—after all, this is only a dream—but it did occur and he was responsible for it. The citizens of this lost paradise began to tell lies, gave themselves over to lust instead of the selfless love they had practiced, and allowed jealousy to be introduced into relationships. In time, jealousy led to violence, and the first person was killed as a result. The people were horrified; they formed protective associations, but these groups turned hostile and eventually engaged in violence against one another.

The animals, sensing the discord and experiencing the cruelty of people, withdrew to the mountains and forests; hostility ensued between the humans and the beasts. The various groupings of people began to develop their own languages and became even more hostile to one another. To prevent crime, a system of justice, including the guillotine, was invented. The people sought to develop science and technology to bring civilization into their unruly lives; once having known the meaning of life and having possessed sufficient knowledge to lead a full life, they were compelled to attempt the slow and painful re-creation of a livable society.

Surveying the destruction of this society, the ridiculous man implored the people to crucify him; perhaps then they would return to their old ways. Having only dim memories of a better society, however, they viewed the narrator as a saintly fool preaching an impossible morality. He was informed that he would be incarcerated in a mental institution if he continued to proclaim the virtues of an ideal society. At the point of despair, the ridiculous man suddenly awakened from his dream, finding himself in his room with the revolver on the table before him.

The dream changed the life of the ridiculous man, as he explains; he now believes that people can be happy and construct a much better society. Evil is not natural; the present human condition is merely a fall from that state to which human beings can aspire. It is this newfound belief that allows the narrator to carry on with his life and to view people with affection and love. He puts aside all ideas of suicide and begins to preach the Truth that he has seen in his dream. People still believe that he is ridiculous, but he loves them anyway.

## Themes and Meanings

Fyodor Dostoevski is much better known for his lengthy novels than for his short stories. This short story contains many of the themes that Dostoevski used in his novels but in a much-reduced form. The author, a devout Russian Orthodox Christian, was intrigued by the human condition and sought answers for human imperfection in traditional Christian thought, although he often imparted to it an original insight or twist.

In this particular story, Dostoevski deals with a paradox familiar to all Christian philosophers: How does one reconcile the desire for social change and the quest for perfection with the human condition of imperfection as a result of the Fall in the Garden of Eden? This central theme is placed within a secondary theme also familiar to all readers of Dostoevski's novels, the inability of the rationalist to supply all of life's answers. The central character in this story lives by theories and has no real communication with his fellow human beings. When he cannot find the answers to life and concludes, therefore, that life is meaningless, he decides to commit suicide.

The dream shows the ridiculous man where he has gone wrong: in his dependence on the intellect rather than the heart. In order to live meaningfully, one must live as people did before the Fall, instinctively and with love. How does one do this? The vision of the perfect society and the desire to re-create it give him the wherewithal to choose life over death, for although perfection is unattainable in this life, the quest for it makes life bearable.

## Style and Technique

Like many Russian writers, Dostoevski wished to express his views on life in a form that would catch the attention of the general public and be an attractive means of furthering discussion of serious questions. Literature reached a much wider public than did theoretical journals of philosophy, and Dostoevski employed fiction in the hope that he would have an effect outside the academic community. In the process, he wrote works of literature that are considered masterpieces even by those who disagree with the author or do not even understand what point he was attempting to make. In this story, the author uses a dream to make his point, a device that he also used in other works. This particular dream recounts the biblical tale of the Fall in slightly different terms, a story that would be very familiar to the average Russian reader of the nineteenth century. By the use of this dream as parable, Dostoevski takes a very difficult point of Christian philosophy and simplifies it so that almost anyone can understand the point he is attempting to make.

*Philip Maloney*

# DREAM STUFF

*Author:* David Malouf (1934-    )
*Type of plot:* Impressionistic
*Time of plot:* 1984
*Locale:* Brisbane, Australia
*First published:* 2000

*Principal characters:*
    COLIN LATTIMER, a writer
    CORALIE, his cousin
    ERIC, Coralie's husband
    AN UNIDENTIFIED ATTACKER

*The Story*

This dreamlike story, about a writer who returns to his native Brisbane, Australia, to give a reading of his work and is attacked by a mysterious man, begins with the writer's earliest memory. His mother's Doberman, Maxie, is ill with heartworm and crawls under the house to die. Colin crawls in after him and stays there holding him the whole day until his father crawls under and coaxes him out. This memory is connected to another one, from a year later, in which his father tries to teach Colin how to swim. As Colin gasps and thrashes to stay afloat, he wears the same look of desperation his father wore when he tried to get the child to come out from under the house.

The story then shifts to the present as Colin, a successful writer living in England, has come to Brisbane, his hometown, to read from his fiction. However, the story still focuses on the past, as Colin recalls how he and his mother did not become close to each other until after he had left home and had begun to write her letters and how his father died during World War II when Colin was only six years old. He also recalls a diary left by his father, in which he had recorded his impressions of Athens, Greece. Later, when Colin goes to Greece, he tries to recover some defining image of his father by visiting the places his father did. During this visit, a man, mistaking Colin for someone else, begins talking with him and then spends the day with him, guiding him around Athens, only to disappear later in the day.

The only person Colin knows in Brisbane is his cousin Coralie, with whom he grew up, and her husband, Eric. He recalls that when they were children, he and Coralie planned to get married. He also recalls that just after the birth of his first child, Coralie came to London and spent six weeks with him and his wife. After spending an evening with Coralie and Eric, Colin takes a taxi to his hotel but then decides to go out for a walk. Suddenly a man attacks him, accusing him of being involved with his girlfriend. The man begins to slash at himself with a knife until Colin wrestles him to the ground and the police arrive. Although the police are initially skeptical of Colin's story that he has never seen the man in his life, with Eric's help, Colin is released the next day. That evening, he gives his reading to a small audience; later that night, he has a dream of going on a truck to an area where illegal marijuana is grown, the "dream stuff" of the title.

### Themes and Meanings

David Malouf, best known in his native Australia as a novelist and poet, demonstrates the poet's fascination with the short story, which has always been the most lyrical of prose forms, in this title story to his collection *Dream Stuff* (2000). The central themes of this story, common to several others in the collection, are the primitive nature of dreams and the notion that "nothing ever gets lost," which suggests the writer's obsession with the past—both personal and primitive. In "Dream Stuff," a writer, who seems very much like Malouf, comes to Brisbane to give a book reading and is caught in a combination of memory, dream, and threat. Now forty-eight years old, he has come back to Brisbane to find one of his earliest selves, a vulnerable self that never left the place. As a writer, he is fascinated by situations fraught with mystery, for he knows that his own stories derive from some occasions that he has never fully understood. "Dream Stuff" is about one such mysterious encounter.

The event at the center of the story—one Colin says he would have rejected outright as being too extravagant for a plot—involves his being approached on the street by a man who accuses him of having sex with his girlfriend or wife and then slashes his own neck with a knife. The man does not die, but Colin is arrested and questioned, after which he is tormented by his inability to wash away the claim that this strange man has placed on him—a claim in which he mysteriously feels entangled and caught. The story ends with a dream; the writer dreams he is blindfolded and taken out in a truck to pick marijuana, the "dream stuff" of the title; the dream then shifts back to the opening of the story, with Colin as a young boy under the porch, holding the dying dog, refusing to come out when his father reaches out a hand to him.

"Dream Stuff" is a quintessential example of the short story's allegiance to the stuff of dreams since the writings of Edgar Allan Poe. It is reminiscent of Joseph Conrad's Marlowe sitting on the deck in *Heart of Darkness* (1899, 1902), telling the story of the mysterious dreamlike Kurtz to the practical businesspeople who sit around him. "Do you see the story?" he cries. "Do you see anything? It seems to me I am trying to tell you a dream." Marlowe acknowledges what Malouf also knows: the frustration of trying to convey that "notion of being captured by the incredible which is the very essence of dreams."

### Style and Technique

"Dream Stuff" is told in third-person point of view focused solely on the perspective of the protagonist Colin. Malouf communicates his theme of the ambiguous relationship between outer physical reality and inner dream reality by having Colin, who is a writer, self-consciously reflect on his constant movement back and forth between the outer and the inner worlds. This technique is introduced at the beginning of the story as Colin recalls his earliest memory of crawling under the house and holding his sick dog. He awakes from this dream in a hotel room in Brisbane acknowledging that this is an "interior view," while down below in the real world, the country of his childhood had been leveled to make way for parking lots and city towers. He knows he has been drawn back to the place of his birth not out of nostalgia for a physical world that has disappeared but rather for a more personal sense that one of his selves, his earliest and most vulnerable, has never really left this place.

Malouf suggests a split in Colin between the self that lives in the real world and the self that experiences mysterious disruptions and is defined by dreams and fantasies. For example, his recollection of the man who mysteriously appeared and then disappeared while he was in Athens hoping to recover some "defining image" of his dead father is for him an exemplary afternoon of his imaginative life, for it left a teasing suggestion of something more to come and appealed to that side of him that preferred not to come to conclusions, that lived "most richly in mystery and suspended expectation." It is, of course, this side of Colin that the central event in the story most appeals to, even though he says he would never have tried to use the event for a fictional plot, for it was too extravagant for the "web of quiet incident and subtle shifts of power" that was the usual focus of his fiction. After the man attacks Colin and he is arrested by the police, his attempts to tell the story and make sense of it take up the last section of the story. The more he tells it, the less probable it becomes.

At this point, Colin's sense of puzzlement over the event creates an even more pronounced split in his self. While in jail waiting for release, he stands before a bathroom mirror and hardly recognizes himself. He thinks he looks like a "dead ringer" of himself as a man who for thirty years had lived a different and coarser life. He thinks he probably looks like the man for whom he had been mistaken. He thinks about the strange man who lies in a hospital somewhere and in his inner world still pursues him, filled with resentment toward some shadowy third party that Colin feels connected to in "ways so dark and undeclared" that they may never be known. The story ends by coming full circle with Colin entering a dream world, this time being taken out to the foothills of the city where marijuana is grown; he is once more under the house, refusing, at least for a time, to reach out and put his own hand in the outstretched hand of his father.

*Charles E. May*

# DREAMERS IN A DEAD LANGUAGE

*Author:* Grace Paley (1922-    )
*Type of plot:* Satire
*Time of plot:* The late 1950's
*Locale:* Coney Island, New York
*First published:* 1977

*Principal characters:*
FAITH DARWIN, a single parent, recently divorced
ANTHONY (TONTO) and
RICHARD, her sons
PHILIP MAZZANO, one of her boyfriends
MR. AND MRS. DARWIN, Faith's parents

*The Story*

From a conversation between Faith Darwin and one of her three boyfriends, Philip, the reader learns of a poem written by Faith's father ("one of the resident poets of the Children of Judea, Home for the Golden Ages"), lamenting the loss of his wife but expressing the desire "to go sailing in spring among realities." It also alludes to "a young girl who waits in a special time and place/ to love me." This reference becomes a topic of debate between Faith and Philip.

Philip likes "old people" (for example, his former wife's dad) and hopes to talk to Faith's father, which he does at the end. He is a worldly businessperson who bewails his being forced into "low practicality" by "the thoughtless begetting of children, and the vengeance of alimony." Faith chides him for ascribing malice to Anita Franklin, her old friend and Philip's former wife. She warns Philip not to disillusion her parents about Anita, whom Philip "dumped." In passing, Faith confesses her romantic disposition, preferring John Keats's and Percy Bysshe Shelley's fantasies to John Milton's moralizing.

Visiting her parents in a retirement home, Faith is scolded by her father for criticizing her former husband in front of the children. Her son Richard wonders whether the home is a hospital. "Worry and tenderness" characterize Faith's attitude. When she was a child, she was "a constant entertainment" to her parents—her father tells her children. Mrs. Darwin enjoys Richard's sense of humor; Faith's other son, Tonto, however, reveals the truth about his mother's gloomy moods. While the father takes the boys on a tour, Faith visits her mother, "the saint," who is ministering to the bedridden Mrs. Hegel-Shtein. The latter launches into a litany of complaints centered on the responsibility of keeping "a sick old man alive." Faith responds with "What you mean is—life has made you sick," to which Mrs. Hegel-Shtein assents. Mrs. Darwin thinks that that is a "lopsided idea," revealing her concern for Faith's mental health following the collapse of her marriage.

After showing Faith and the children around the roof garden, Mr. Darwin returns, praising Faith's former husband, Ricardo: "such an interesting young man." Eventually he confesses that he wants to leave the place (and his wife) because he feels that he is not old; he resents his wife's fancying the home a Grand Hotel. Faith flees from her father's scolding, and her father compares Faith to her mother's "crazy sister Silvia," who "died in front of the television set." The story ends with a memorable scene: Faith playing with her children in the "old Brighton Beach of her childhood," the boys burying her in the sand but "giving her lots of room for wiggling and whacking."

## Themes and Meanings

Writing usually "from distress," Grace Paley seeks to recover from the "history of everyday life" those nuances of humor and pathos that relieve the sardonic tone of her characterization and counterpoint the moral disintegration of modern society.

Here the breakdown of Faith's marriage symbolizes the ordeal of a time when idealism (suggested by the mention of Theodor Herzl and her father's poem, appropriately named by Philip "Dreamer in a Dead Language") is challenged by a materialistic, egocentric world. Faith tells her father, "I'm just like you, an idealist" who wants "only the best, only perfection." She justifies sleeping with three men by her search for "perfection." Ironically, her father claims that he and Faith's mother never formally got married because they were "idealists." For all of his daydreaming, the father is shocked by Faith's entertaining three divorced men, and he blames her for being "more mixed up than before."

Mr. Darwin's stubborn, patriarchal ways are revealed in his excessive sympathy for Ricardo, Faith's former husband, for being young. He considers Faith "demented" in her treatment of her former husband, he considers his wife and Mrs. Hegel-Shtein to be psychosomatic cases. When he condemns Heligman (another resident of the home), whose view of life allows for the process of healing and fulfillment after crisis—time unfolding its spontaneous cure—Faith blurts out: "I can't stand your being here." Although attached to her father's poetic genius, the daughter cannot stand his domineering and supercilious attitude. His joke—"Honesty, my grandson, is one of the best policies"—and his defense of his unconventional liaison with Faith's mother as a proof of "idealism" demonstrate the destabilizing contradiction in the lives of the older generation. In this sense, the "modesty of the old" noted by Philip in the first line of the story seems the opposite of their intolerant but vulnerable self-righteousness.

Faith's mother, although sensitive to her daughter's plight and proud of her own compassion, also bears down on her: "You went to college. Keep your hands clean," and so forth. She reinforces the authoritarian bent of the father: "Tell her, Sid, she has to be more sensible. She's a mother. She doesn't have the choice."

Contradicting that advice, Faith's whole emotional and ethical behavior toward her parents, former husband, lovers, and children argues for an intelligent understanding of the present generation's predicament, their anxious quest for a new morality affirming tough but sensitive realism, collective determination, and hope for a better future (suggested by the romantic aura of the title, Anthony's sand castles, Herzl's Utopianism, and allusions to Keats and Shelley). Her son Richard's alert intelligence and caring thoughtfulness incarnate two qualities that coalesce in Faith's conflicted sensibility. The closing exchange between Richard and Faith encapsulates the thematic issues posed by the dynamics within the family and between generations: "Why is everything my responsibility, every goddamn thing?" Faith asks. "Had she been born 10, 15 years later, she might have done so, screamed and screamed. Instead, tears made their usual protective lenses for the safe observation of misery." Faith asks to be challenged and convinced by the younger generation, but she also claims the right to impose her painfully won maturity on her children.

When Faith insists that the younger girl addressed in her father's poem is her mother, the reader perceives her refusal to accept an impersonal and alienating reality different from her wishes. She seems caught in the dilemma of suppressing her true feelings and compromising her integrity. She craves affection, she is afraid of jeopardizing Philip's friendship, but she castigates him anyway: "She didn't want to hit him. Instead her eyes filled with tears." Faith's tear-filled eyes, the dominant image that the text interposes at the end between an unfeeling world pervaded by Darwinian competitiveness (note Faith's surname) and a dreaming soul, evoke the crisis of the modern individual: As the old Jew in Mr. Darwin's anecdote discovers, no more space exists for those whom life and worldly changes have victimized. The hospital or home symbolizes the intermediate space between the innocent questioning of children and the cynical or sexist males who idealize women only to abandon them.

Aware of the injustice of the world and encroaching physical debility, Mr. Darwin has his moment of insight when he "felt the freedom of committed love" as his daughter demonstrates her affection. His desperation exemplifies the difficulty of personal commitment: "If it were possible, the way I feel suddenly toward life, I would divorce your mother." Like individuals in a marriage, freedom and responsibility coexist in dialectical tension.

*Style and Technique*

Paley's lively seriocomic style has been frequently praised for its blending of sardonic wit and spare description, which somehow intimates the gap that she experiences "between knowing and telling."

The three settings noted earlier—Faith's apartment, the retirement home, and the beach of her childhood—divide the narrative into the spheres of the intimate relationship between lovers, the argumentative tension between parents and daughter, and the playful communication between mother and children. In all of them, the prose scarcely focuses on physical appearance (except telling details such as the boil on Faith's wrist). Snapshot impressions punctuate the dialogue. Saturated with diseased or pain-afflicted bodies, the text is largely made up of disembodied voices (no quotation marks are used, and words are rarely attributed to their speakers) whose diverse tones—mocking, derisive, ambiguous, frank, vulgar, urbane, sentimental—more than compensate for the sparseness of "realistic" details to convey the abundant zest or élan of her characters in confronting the cruel indifference and betrayals of life.

The narrative is chiefly composed of dialogue interspersed with brief summaries. The rapid and sometimes discontinuous exchanges between the characters suffice to disclose their temperaments and motivations. When the father says about Faith's delinquent husband, "Young. Young is just not old. What's to argue? What you know, you know. What I know, I know," one can detect the authoritative register in the tone. Her mother's solicitude is displayed also with suggestive economy.

To establish the consumerist milieu of industrial society, Paley puts these words into Philip's mouth as he ridicules Faith's husband, whose "dancing" around her father seems to irk him: "Who's that jerk know? Four old maids in advertising, three Seventh Avenue models, two fairies in TV, one literary dyke." His anecdote about Ezra Kalmback, like the vignettes and jokes of Faith's father, exemplifies the divided selves of the marginalized and alienated (especially ethnic immigrant groups, Jews, women, blacks, and others), a condition that may culminate in the sixth-floor ward of incurables where physically sound young people are "tied with shawls into wheelchairs."

When the unforgettable Madame Elena Nazdarova, editor of the prize-winning journal *A Bessere Zeit*, sees "Mr. Darwin, breathless, chasing Faith," and calls, "Ai, Darwin . . . no love poems this month? How can I go to press?" one can perceive in this event the old father-dreamer pursuing youth, faith, and passion, this time no longer hobbled by spurious idealism or self-doubt. Paley's austerity and idiomatic tactfulness succeed in controlling the welter of violent emotions unleashed here. Intractable and recalcitrant impulses and psychic drives are contained by the sheer gusto of urbane wit, folkloric and aphoristic gestures, and compassionate knowingness.

*E. San Juan, Jr.*

# DRENCHED IN LIGHT

*Author:* Zora Neale Hurston (1891-1960)
*Type of plot:* Autobiographical, regional
*Time of plot:* 1900-1910
*Locale:* Eatonville, Florida
*First published:* 1924

> *Principal characters:*
> ISIS WATTS, a mischievous eleven-year-old black child
> GRANDMA POTTS, her exasperated grandmother
> A WHITE LADY AND TWO MEN, travelers on the road

*The Story*

Isis Watts is perched on the gatepost of her home, looking with longing up the road to Orlando. The conflict between the child and her grandmother is evident from the opening paragraphs. Isis is a child who is filled with the joy of life and yearns for the horizon, while her grandmother urges her to stop dreaming and instead work around the house. Isis has earned the nickname "Isis the joyful" among the neighbors, but her grandmother seeks to restrain the child's exuberance and orders her to sit on the porch like a lady rather than romp with the dogs in the yard.

After the noon meal, Grandma falls asleep with her sewing in her lap. Isis and her brother Joel decide to shave the gray hairs on their sleeping grandmother's chin. The children get into mischief and make a mess, lathering the dogs and the walls with shaving soap. Grandma, her face covered in lather, awakens to discover Isis standing over her, razor poised. Grandma exits screaming, Joel runs off to go fishing, and Isis crawls under the house to await the whipping that is sure to follow the adventure.

Isis is quickly distracted by a parade of people marching down the road to a community barbecue. His spirits rise, and she begins to run and dance after the band. Realizing that her dress is torn and dirty, not suitable for dancing at a carnival, Isis snatches up her grandmother's new red fringed tablecloth, which she wears like a gypsy shawl as she imitates a Spanish dancer, the shawl trailing in the dust.

At the picnic, all eyes are on Isis, the joyful dancer. An automobile drives up and two white men and a lady get out and are watching Isis when an angry Grandma arrives, and Isis flees into the woods. Isis pauses beside a creek, and knowing a whipping is in store for her, she resolves to drown herself. She wades into the creek, where she is soon splashing and singing. The car and its occupants, lost, stop by the creek, and recognizing Isis as the dancer from the barbecue, they ask her for directions. She tells them they need to be on the shell road that runs by her house, and they ask her to ride with them and show them the way.

Isis is thrilled to ride in the car, and during the drive, she charms the white lady with her stories of herself as a princess who travels to the horizon and wears golden shoes and trailing gowns. As the car approaches Isis's gate, her grandmother spots her and bawls for the child to "Come heah *dis instant.*" Isis, wrapped in the dirty tattered shawl, and the white lady confront Grandma, who clearly intends to punish the misbehaving child.

The white lady gives Grandma five dollars for a new tablecloth and for permission to allow Isis to come to her hotel and dance for her, because she "could stand a little light today." The story ends with Isis snuggled into the car with her benefactress, who says "I would like just a little of her sunshine to soak into my soul."

### Themes and Meanings

Zora Neale Hurston's purpose in this story is to portray Isis as a child who is "drenched in light," who lives every moment of her life to the fullest, rather than as a tragically disadvantaged poor black child. The white lady recognizes that she lacks what Isis has. Though well-to-do and evidently cultured, this white lady desires and envies the light, sunshine, and sense of herself that Isis naturally exudes. The implication is that Isis's joy is cultural, deriving from her family and her rural, communal surroundings, and that white people lack this culture of joy.

Hurston was a writer who recognized and celebrated the rich indigenous black folk culture of her home state, Florida. "Drenched in Light," one of her earliest published short stories, is a statement of cultural identity and self-confidence. This affirmation of her origins and the parallel refusal to accept white culture as superior to southern black folk life were Hurston's primary contributions to the movement of black art, music, and voice in the 1920's and 1930's known as the Harlem Renaissance.

Hurston wrote the story while she was a student at Howard University in Washington, D.C. It is thinly veiled autobiography. Clearly she is Isis, the child gifted with natural intelligence and grace. The grandmother in the story is named after Hurston's own grandmother, and Hurston's childhood habit of sitting on the gatepost and hailing passers-by is recalled in her 1942 autobiography *Dust Tracks on a Road*. "Drenched in Light" was originally published in 1924 in *Opportunity* magazine, a publication that articulated the philosophy and expression of the Harlem Renaissance. It was Hurston's first nationally published story, the story that introduced this passionate writer with "the map of Florida on her tongue" to literary New York.

The setting of "Drenched in Light" is the remarkable town of Eatonville, Florida, Hurston's own hometown. Eatonville, a tiny township in central Florida, was organized, incorporated, and governed by black people. It was an unusual place in the early twentieth century, a town in which an intelligent black child could grow up with self-esteem intact, free from the sense of second-class citizenship common in American southern black life. Eatonville was a cradle of community and folk culture, a bottomless source of stories. The safety of her family and the rich community life of Eatonville provided Hurston with her strong sense of self-confidence, the self-confidence that she transfers to her young protagonist Isis. Eatonville was Hurston's primary subject throughout her career of writing fiction and collecting and preserving folklore.

The story is not complex. Critics consider it immature, lacking in plot development and dramatic suspense. Its structure is based on its theme and purpose, which is to address both black self-pity and white paternalism and acknowledge and celebrate Hurston's unusual upbringing in Eatonville as the source of her own self-confidence and sense of self. Hurston felt strongly that her life had been graced in singular ways specifically because she was black and came from a remarkable enclave of southern black culture and community, nurtured on family and folklore. Her goal in writing "Drenched in Light" was to express that grace in fiction.

*Style and Technique*

Hurston had both an eye and an ear for her folk material. One of her trademarks was the use of dialect. The stories and folklore that she collected and translated into her writing were from an oral tradition. To preserve this form of African American expression, Hurston mastered the art of presenting black vernacular speech in written form. Isis, Grandma Potts, Isis's brother Joel, and even the Robinson brothers (local white cattlemen) speak in the local dialect throughout the story, in contrast to the white lady, who speaks in educated English.

Grandma Potts in particular represents family and tradition, and it is from her mouth that the most colorful speech in the story emerges. She speaks the opening line of the story: "You, Isie Watts! Git 'own offen dat gate post an' rake up dis yahd!" Frustrated by Isis's failure to respond, she screams: "Ah'll show dat limb of Satan she cain't shake herself at *me*. If she ain't down by the time Ah gets dere, Ah'll break huh down in de lines."

The story is written in the third person, but the point of view is distinctly that of Isis, the joyful dancer. The strong sense of self-confidence that characterizes both Hurston the young writer and her alter ego, the child Isis, pervades the story.

The image of the horizon is the expression of Isis's hopes and dreams. She habitually sits on the gatepost gazing yearningly up the road to Orlando. Once seated comfortably in the car, Isis explains to her benefactors that she is really a princess. "She told them about her trips to the horizon, about the trailing gowns, the gold shoes with blue bottoms . . . the white charger, the time when she was Hercules and had slain numerous dragons and sundry giants."

These words are echoed in Hurston's autobiography, *Dust Tracks on a Road.* Hurston writes of her childhood: "I used to climb to the top of one of the huge Chinaberry trees which guarded our front gate, and look out over the world. The most interesting thing that I saw was the horizon." She goes on to say "for weeks I saw myself sitting astride of a fine horse. My shoes had sky-blue bottoms to them, and I was riding off to look at the belly-band of the world."

"Drenched in Light" is confirmed by Hurston's autobiography to be an expression of her own joyous childhood and of the singular grace of growing up as a black child in the lap of her community.

*Susan Butterworth*

# A DRIVE IN THE COUNTRY

*Author:* Graham Greene (1904-1991)
*Type of plot:* Psychological
*Time of plot:* The 1930's
*Locale:* London and the countryside immediately beyond
*First published:* 1947

> *Principal characters:*
> THE PROTAGONIST, an unnamed girl who is about to elope with Fred
> FRED, an unemployed and desperate young man determined on a suicide pact
> THE YOUNG MAN, a stranger who gives the girl a lift back to her father's house in Golding's Park

## The Story

The narrative begins with a young woman's observations of her father's careful ritual of preparing his household for the night. He is the head clerk at Bergson's Export Agency, and she feels a mild contempt for him as a worker, for his pride of ownership, and for the devotion to convention that he exhibits in his daily life and in the fulfillment of his church obligations. In contrast, the young woman thinks of Fred, her young man, and "his air of unbalanced exultation."

Once the doors and windows are locked, and the household put to sleep in the jerry-built house that her father will own outright in fifteen years, the young woman leaves for her rendezvous. She hears again, in her imagination, her father's statement about having improved the property, and she remembers the apple tree that has produced one more tasteless apple each year since it was planted.

She meets Fred, ready, she thinks, for anything. Fred has borrowed a car, he says, and she settles into her dream of reckless adventure. They drive outside the city, past a roadhouse, and, to please her, Fred goes deeper into the countryside. She is aware of his restiveness, his mood of desperation, as he drinks from his bottle. She is also aware of the assertion of his will over hers. As they drive deeper into the country, the protagonist, excited as always by Fred's need to live on the dangerous edge of things, by his seeming nonchalance in his inability to find a job in the economically depressed 1930's, by his failure to gratify either himself or his family, listens to his proposal: that they kill themselves as a means of escaping a world that has rejected them. The young woman, who thought that she understood the limits of Fred's "craziness," is frightened by the gun he carries and the certainty of his choice. She comes to a realization that what attracts Fred to suicide is not so much an escape from the tedium of a deprived existence as the thrill of the action itself. She understands Fred's need to gamble with life and death—the attraction of the uncertainty that lies beyond. Because neither of them believes in God, he says to convince her, they have a chance, "and it's company, going like that." For the first time, she questions Fred's protestations of love for her and the nature of hers for him.

She attempts to reason him out of his decision, finally admitting to herself that his "craziness" has gone beyond her ability to comprehend or contain it. She realizes, "He had always wanted this: the dark field, the weapon in his pocket; but she less honestly had wanted a little of both worlds: irresponsibility and a safe love, danger and a secure heart."

The young woman leaves Fred, and the last word that she hears him speak is "damnation" as he stumbles over a root. The sound of the word fills her with horror. She makes her way to the roadhouse as it begins to rain and asks a stranger for a lift to London. The young man who offers to take her to Golding's Park, suffering from much the same social and economic malaise that Fred has experienced, offers to drive her to Maidenhead instead, but she refuses. "Hell of a life," he says. She makes her way to the jerry-built villa, and once inside, she locks the door firmly against the rain and the escape that Fred offered her. She recognizes now, as she did not at the story's beginning, the bravery of her father's refusal to give in to the dark.

*Themes and Meanings*

A third-person narrative, "A Drive in the Country" achieves its somber effects through a psychologically acute presentation of the young woman's dawning awareness of the value of life and the uncertain consequences of death. In the course of the narrative, Graham Greene convincingly presents a character who changes from an attitude of come-what-may to one of stoic vulnerability. The turning point of the story is reached when she refuses Fred's offer of a love-death and accepts instead everyday life in an economically depressed society. Talk of unemployment and Bolshies (as she makes her way back to London) contributes to the reader's awareness of time and place and establishes the dominant theme of social inequality.

Greene is known primarily as a writer who employs Roman Catholic notions in his novels and stories. "A Drive in the Country" can, although it need not, be read as a commentary on the sham suicide pact into which Pinkie Brown attempts to trick the girl Rose in *Brighton Rock* (1938). In that novel, Pinkie and Rose are Roman Catholics, and the love-death bears on their understanding of the moral ramifications of the sin of despair. The bird whose gigantic wings beat against the windscreen of the car that carries Rose and Pinkie to Peacehaven and, as Rose believes, to their deaths, can consequently be read as a divine prompting that tempts Pinkie to good as Satan has tempted him to evil. There are in "A Drive in the Country" no statements that are overtly religious in intention, except the one in which Fred notes that neither he nor the girl believes in God. However, the wood, suggestive of Dante's dark wood of error; the fact that the girl makes a choice for life over death; the use of the word "damnation"; and the references to suicide as a desperate gamble suggest a moral interpretation that is difficult to dismiss.

*Style and Technique*

To direct his reader to a proper appreciation of the social and moral themes suggested by the narrative, Greene makes subtle use of imagery and symbolism that suggest reconciliation and renewal within a starved landscape. As the girl leaves her father's house for her rendezvous with Fred, the narrator directs the reader's attention to the "crazy paved path" that takes her past the half-finished development in which she lives with her family. She is aware of the "wounded" fields that remain "grimly alive in the form of thin grass and heaps of clay and dandelions," and of the small garages that suggest graves in a cemetery. As she and Fred make their way deeper into the country, the notion of the journey into the self becomes apparent. The girl is suddenly made aware of the fact that a choice that she has not fully considered is being thrust on her, and she is forced to choose between the annihilation that Fred offers and the bleak life of London that she has hitherto considered lacking in value. Her choice, regardless of whether she is fully aware of the sights about her, is confirmed by the references to the continuing life of nature in the dark of night, to the bird that beats against the car that Fred has stolen for the drive into the country, to rabbits and owls, to oaks and elms, and to the clover that covers the earth where they stop the car. The symbols of house and apple tree, as well as the many references to a meager nature, offer the reader the best means of appreciating both the social and the moral meanings of the story.

*A. A. DeVitis*

# THE DROVER'S WIFE

*Author:* Henry Lawson (1867-1922)
*Type of plot:* Domestic realism
*Time of plot:* About 1890
*Locale:* The Australian Outback
*First published:* 1894

> *Principal characters:*
> THE DROVER'S WIFE, who is referred to as "she"
> TOMMY, her elder son
> ALLIGATOR, a big, black, yellow-eyed dog-of-all-breeds

*The Story*

Like many stories by Henry Lawson (and like those of Anton Chekhov and Katherine Mansfield), "The Drover's Wife" has remarkably little action: The plot, such as it is, suggests the absence of action that characterizes life in the Outback (the dry, sparsely settled, and inhospitable areas distant from the few major urban settlements of Australia) during the long intervals between recurrent natural disasters, such as floods, bushfires, and droughts. This indicates a technical aspect that Lawson mastered in his short stories: the construction of a coherent fiction on the flimsiest of plots. One of his aims was always to use a slight plot.

In its simplest form, the plot is limited to the discovery of a five-foot black snake in the woodheap, watching it go under the house, and waiting through the night for its reemergence so that it can be killed. The variety and violence of life in the Outback are indicated by the omniscient narrator's allusions to memorable episodes that have punctuated the drover's wife's life, which is frequently marked by her solitude from adult companionship. (She has not heard from her husband for six months as the story begins.)

She has two boys and two girls ("mere babies") and a dog, Alligator, for company; she has two cows, a horse, and a few sheep as possessions; her husband is often away driving sheep and cattle, and has been away for periods of up to eighteen months. During one of his absences she contracted fever in childbirth and was assisted by Black Mary (an aboriginal midwife); one child died when she was alone, and she had to carry the corpse nineteen miles for assistance.

Times were not always so desperate. When she was married, her drover husband took her to the city, where they stayed in the best hotel. Soon after, however, they had to sell their buggy; her husband, who started as a drover and rose to become a squatter (a small-scale cattle raiser on government-owned land), met the inevitable "hard times" of the Outback and returned to droving, with its isolation, low pay, low status, and long absences from home. The wife's only connection with the few pleasures of her life is *Young Ladies' Journal*—a bitter irony under her circumstances.

However, her life in the bush (another name for the Outback) has not been wholly uneventful: A nephew died from snakebite; she battled a bushfire; she coped with a flood, even to the extent of digging trenches in a vain attempt to avoid a dam break; she shot a mad bullock; she treated pleuropneumonia in the cattle (though her best two cows succumbed); she has had to control crows and magpies; and she has always had to be "the man" in getting rid of sundowners, bushmen, and "swaggies" (itinerants). Clearly, the snake poses a threat to her children, but she has successfully handled crises of far greater significance in her years in the Outback.

Still, for all her impressive practicality, she has been tricked: Only the day before, an Aborigine bargained to collect a pile of wood in exchange for a small amount of tobacco; she praised him for doing a good job and then, when the snake was first seen, discovered that the "blackfellow" (the term then used for Aborigines) had built a hollow woodpile. She was hurt and cried, but she has "a keen, very keen, sense of the ridiculous, and some time or other she will amuse bushmen with the story. She had been amused before like that. . . . Then she had to laugh."

## Themes and Meanings

Lawson's stories are almost all authentic illustrations of the several hardships and few small pleasures of proletarian domestic life—especially in the country. "The Drover's Wife," which appeared in his very first book, is of major significance because it so clearly and impressively states one of his pervasive themes, that the lives of people in the Outback are molded by the environment so that they, too, become hardened, desiccated, silent, and of necessity even predatory. However, in spite of all this, the occasional blossoms of the bush have their equivalents in the tender, soft, beautiful, yet temporary moments of life of the drovers and squatters.

The opening paragraphs of the story indicate Lawson's approach to his theme; the lean, starved, drab minimalism of life in the bush is conveyed by the description of the drover's house: "The two-roomed house is built of round timber, slabs, and stringybark, and floored with split slabs. A big bark kitchen standing at one end is larger than the house itself, veranda included." The individuals who live there are also gaunt and hardy, for the children are described as "ragged, dried-up-looking," and the mother, who has a "worn-out breast," is described as a "gaunt, sun-browned bushwoman."

Further, this identification of people and place is brought out in the second paragraph, where one finds one of Lawson's best descriptions of the bush itself with all of its negative connotations: "no horizon, for the country is flat. No ranges in the distance. The bush consists of stunted, rotten native apple-trees. There is no undergrowth, nothing to relieve the eye save the darker green of a few she-oaks that are sighing above the narrow, almost waterless creek. Nineteen miles to the nearest sign of civilization—a shanty [shack] on the main road." This is the bush at its grimmest, yet in many ways it is the real Australia, for only one-tenth of the continent is arable, fertile land: The "sunburnt country" is the typical land, the land of Australian literary and cultural mythology. In great measure this was Lawson's achievement. He knew the country at first hand, his stories pictured it in all its drab, horrendous realism, and his popularity assured acceptance of the image that he presented. Some readers and critics have taken a somewhat different approach: One considers stories such as "The Drover's Wife" to be social satire redeemed by a strong sense of nationalism, and there is some merit in this appreciation.

Essentially, this story is a study of human adaptation to adversity and environment that shows the strength of individuals isolated from the main currents of civilization. In a way, too, it is a strong statement for the cause of feminism, and reminds the reader, perhaps, of the California rancher's wife in John Steinbeck's "The Chrysanthemums." However, the emphasis is less on the delineation of character than on the description of the oppressive nature of the eternal round of disasters and trials that bedevil people in situations that resemble that of the drover's wife.

*Style and Technique*

Clearly, a story that has slight action, such as waiting for a snake to reappear, must have some compensatory elements (especially in the absence of any direct characterization) to account for its popularity and fame. In part these are stylistic, in part technical. First, Lawson makes Tommy, the drover's young son, a representative of his father, a foil for the drover's wife. Though still a child, he sees the emptiness of his mother's life and the hollowness of the family existence, so that the story ends when he says, "Mother, I won't never go drovin'; blarst me if I do!" and she hugs and kisses him "while the sickly daylight breaks over the bush."

Even the use of "Mother" is significant. Instead of the more usual "Mum" or "Ma" in country children's speech, there is the more polite, tender "Mother," which suggests a child's desire to be separated from the harshness of the bush. (His "normal" language is revealed in the double negative and "blarst.") This epiphany occurs, significantly, at dawn. The daylight, though, is "sickly," with all that this connotes.

Alligator, the dog, is developed as a character in the story. (His name is another irony in a waterless environment.) When the snake is first encountered by Tommy, Alligator "takes small notice" of Tommy's stick and "proceeds to undermine the building." He is an equal, a colleague, and "they cannot afford to lose him." He felt, readers are told, "the original curse in common with mankind" and approaches the snake as if it were a representative of the intruder in Eden in this least Edenic of places.

The structure of the story is of some interest. It opens near sunset as a storm approaches. At midnight the drover's wife reminisces about her life; at about 1:00 A.M. and 2:00 A.M. she remembers past difficulties on the land; and near daylight Alligator catches and shakes the snake, which then has its back broken and head smashed and is thrown on the fire. In the nightlong vigil, Tommy and Alligator are her company and comfort; all three share a vital interdependence. Animals, like people, are friends and foes.

After the initial reported conversation between the drover's wife and the children, there is no dialogue until Tommy's announcement at the close of the story that he will not become a drover; this is more than an accidental taciturnity—it further emphasizes the isolation of the Outback and of the drover's wife, even within her own family.

*A. L. McLeod*

# THE DRUNKARD

*Author:* Frank O'Connor (Michael Francis O'Donovan, 1903-1966)
*Type of plot:* Social realism
*Time of plot:* The first quarter of the twentieth century
*Locale:* Cork, Ireland
*First published:* 1948

*Principal characters:*
>MICK DELANEY, a laboring man whose weakness is drink, the father of the narrator of the story
>LARRY DELANEY, the adult narrator and the little boy in the story
>MRS. DELANEY, Larry's mother, a hardworking, anxious woman

## The Story

A first-person narrative by the adult Larry Delaney, "The Drunkard" opens with his recollection of a critical episode in his childhood. The crisis began with the death of his father's friend and confidant, Mr. Dooley. Larry's father, Mick Delaney, took Mr. Dooley's death very hard, not only because Mr. Dooley was about the same age as he but also because he lost in Mr. Dooley his best source of inside information, of "the news behind the news." To express the depth of his mourning, Mick Delaney decides to attend the funeral, a decision that causes Larry and his mother great anxiety. Mick Delaney will be tempted at the public house afterward; as Larry recalls, "Drink . . . was Father's great weakness." Consequently, Larry's mother sends Larry along to act as a "brake" on his father. With humor and poignancy, the narrative records the boy's feeling of utter ineffectualness, as his father pulls him into a public house, where the boy expects, one more time, to stand helplessly by, watching his father get drunk. His father bribes him with a lemonade while ordering beer for himself. Thereafter oblivious to the child, he turns away from the bar to expatiate on the merits of the funeral. In the meanwhile, Larry, bored and still thirsty, samples and then finishes his father's drink. In turn, Larry becomes drunk, noisy, and sick. Larry's father, assisted by a barroom friend, is obliged to bring his sick, drunken child home in broad daylight, before the astonished eyes of all his neighbors, while Larry, in his drunken state, mimics the belligerent behavior that he has observed in his father's past drinking bouts. Mrs. Delaney returns home in a rage, prompted by her neighbors to conclude that her husband and his crony have plied the child with drink for their amusement; her husband, feeling increasingly sorry for himself, tries unsuccessfully to explain. The next day, when Mick Delaney quietly goes off to work, the mother's mood changes, and she praises and pampers Larry for having proved indeed to be his father's "guardian angel."

## Themes and Meanings

Characteristic of Frank O'Connor, the story combines humor and seriousness, a mixture that the author referred to as "crab apple jelly." The narrative provokes laughter and sadness as it explores the moving plight of a child who is apparently following in his father's drunken footsteps. The equivocal title points to the dual meaning: Is the reader to focus on the humorousness of the inadvertent drunkard, Larry, or on the irresponsibility of the more habitual drunkard, Mick, who pays for his drinking bouts by pawning everything in the house down to the kitchen clock? As the grown Larry ruefully remembers, "I could never get over the lonesomeness of the kitchen without a clock."

The particular satisfaction of the story is not only in the reversal of expectations that it creates but also in the poetic justice that it delivers to the father. Victim and victimizer exchange roles: The potential victim Larry becomes victimizer of his father, who is passive witness and helpless victim to his son's drunkenness. The potential victimizer Mick sees how he himself looks, acts, and speaks when he is drunk, as his son Larry proves to be a most unflattering mirror. The reader's awareness that Mick has been the model for Larry's drunken behavior underlies the hilariousness of Larry's mood shifts from grandiosity to belligerence to melancholy self-pity, in which final state he proclaims his heroic martyrdom by singing "The Boys of Wexford."

Although the story records a small triumph for Larry and his mother, it avoids sentimentality by reminding the reader of all the other times when they stood by helplessly, watching the drunkard's progress of Mick Delaney. Larry recalls his father saying, after the incident, "Never again, never again, not if I lived to be a thousand!" In response to this statement, the older Larry comments, "To this day I don't know whether he was forswearing me or the drink." He thereby points out that, after this particular episode, his father repudiated neither him nor the drink. Thus, the story ends happily but not "happily ever after."

*Style and Technique*

Neither a rigorous naturalist such as Émile Zola nor an avant-garde experimentalist such as James Joyce, O'Connor strived for a style that captured what he called the "glowing center of action." In a voice that is candid, straightforward, terse, and colloquial, he puts before his audience the central facts and the telling details; he points to a theme that is clear, simple, and universal. Unwilling to call attention to itself, O'Connor's style seems almost transparent, yet the simple phrases can turn suddenly to eloquence, as in Larry's description of his father, "He had long months of abstinence behind him and an eternity of pleasure before," or the words can turn to salt, as when Larry notes his father's "pleasant awareness that however much he would miss poor Mr. Dooley in the long summer evenings, it was he and not poor Mr. Dooley who would do the missing."

One outstanding feature of O'Connor as a storyteller is his ability to recapture the feel of childhood. He does not comment on what a child feels; he records it. Again and again he notes the child's earnestness, literalness, and befuddlement in trying to make sense of what adults say. When Larry vomits, his father says, encouragingly, "You'll be grand when you get that up." However, Larry notes, "Begor, I was not grand! Grand was the last thing I was." When another man similarly states, "You'll be all right in a minute," the boy bewilderedly comments, "I never met two men who knew less the effects of drink."

Perhaps the most remarkable characteristic of O'Connor's style is his ability to capture the lilt, the peculiarities, the quaintness, and the occasional luminousness of Irish speech. It penetrates his descriptions: "He was first up in the morning and brought the mother a cup of tea in bed." It colors the speech of his characters: "I wouldn't give it to say to them"; "Whisht, woman, whisht, whisht!" Throughout, it heightens and particularizes the world that the narrator sees: "Ever since, when somebody has given me some bit of information off the record I have found myself on the point of asking: 'Was it Mr. Dooley told you that?'"

Like the traditional Irish storytellers whom he admired, O'Connor, as an artist, was always a real man speaking to real men and women. In each of his stories, which echo the vitality and the roughness of life itself, he seems merely to be pausing, for the brief pleasure of a tale's telling, from life's more urgent and mundane labors.

*Carola M. Kaplan*

# DRY SEPTEMBER

*Author:* William Faulkner (1897-1962)
*Type of plot:* Psychological
*Time of plot:* The late 1920's or early 1930's
*Locale:* A small southern town
*First published:* 1931

> *Principal characters:*
> MISS MINNIE COOPER, an aging white spinster who accuses Will
>     Mayes of having attacked her
> WILL MAYES, a black man
> HAWKSHAW, a reasonable barber who argues against violence
> JOHN MCLENDON, the leader of the murderers of Will Mayes

### The Story

William Faulkner organizes the plot of "Dry September" around a single incident: the murder of an innocent black man. An aging and sexually frustrated white spinster starts the rumor that the black man has attacked her. A group of men, led by a former war hero, murder him before they substantiate his guilt.

After two months without rain, the small southern town of Jefferson has an explosive atmosphere. A rumor spreads through Jefferson that the black man, Will Mayes, has "attacked, insulted, frightened" Miss Minnie Cooper. No one knows exactly what has occurred, but the rumor of an attack by a black man on a white woman spreads "like a fire in dry grass."

The first section of "Dry September" takes place in the town barbershop on Saturday evening. Whether Will Mayes has actually molested Miss Minnie Cooper does not seem important to most of the men in the barbershop. Because a white woman has accused a black man of attacking her, the accusation alone requires that these men demonstrate their white superiority. Hawkshaw, the barber, stubbornly refuses to believe that Will Mayes has attacked Miss Cooper. His rational demand for facts provokes the hostility of the other men.

The smoldering tension flares into violence when John McLendon crashes through the screen door. McLendon leads the party of men who set out to murder Will Mayes. When one member of the group gathered in the barber shop questions what really happened, McLendon whirls on the speaker and asks: "Happen? What the hell difference does it make? Are you going to let the black sons get away with it until one really does it?" Enraged by the heat as well as the rumor, the heavyset McLendon wants to kill. The honor of an aging white spinster gives him an excuse.

The second part of the story describes Miss Minnie Cooper. Her life seems as stale as the "vitiated air" in the barbershop. Despite a short period of youthful popularity, she did not marry. Her gaunt aunt, a "thin, sallow, unflagging" woman, runs the house, and her invalid mother stays in her room. Miss Minnie's only romantic experience was with a widower in the town bank. The town "relegated" her "into adultery" twelve years ago, and eight years ago the cashier went to a Memphis bank. The narrator comments that Miss Minnie's "bright dresses, her idle and empty days, had a quality of furious unreality." Intensified by the heat, Miss Minnie's sexual frustration explodes, as does McLendon's brutality. Both vent their personal frustration on Will Mayes.

Part 3 of the story returns to the account of Will Mayes's murder. The rumor that spreads like a fire in dry grass has destroyed the humanity of the men who plan to teach the "black sons" a lesson. Hawkshaw accompanies McLendon and the others, hoping that he can reason with them and prevent the murder of Will Mayes. When he realizes that he can only watch, not stop them, Hawkshaw begins to retch and asks McLendon to let him out of the car, but the car does not slow down. Will Mayes repeats the barber's name twice. Unwilling to witness the actual murder, Hawkshaw jumps out of the speeding car. The barber hides in the weeds and watches the cars return without Will Mayes; afterward, he limps back to town.

Parts 4 and 5 conclude the story by showing the murder's effect on Miss Minnie, the townspeople, and McLendon. As Miss Minnie dresses to go to the picture show, her flesh feels "like fever." Her friends call for her early, and their eyes, too, glitter with a bright feverishness. Miss Minnie enjoys the walk to the cinema, strolling "slower and slower, as children eat ice cream," because "even the young men lounging in the doorway tipped their hats and followed with their eyes the motion of her hips and legs when she passed."

The picture show, which is described as a "miniature fairyland," recalls the "desert rat" in the barbershop and the "furious unreality" of Miss Minnie's bright dresses and her "idle and empty days." Miss Minnie begins to laugh as she watches the young couples enter the theater: "bodies awkward, divinely young, while beyond them the silver dream accumulated, inevitably on and on." Miss Minnie started the rumor to make herself part of a life that is only a "silver dream" to her, but she cannot stop her empty, feverish laughter as she watches the "young men and girls . . . scented and sibilant in the half dark." Her friends take her home and put ice on her temples. As they freshen the ice pack, they smooth her hair, "examining it for gray; 'poor girl!'" They enjoy Miss Minnie's frustrated laughter—their eyes "darkly aglitter, secret and passionate."

The narrator does not tell the reader that Miss Minnie created the rumor herself, but the reactions of both the men in the barbershop and her friends indicate that she did. They whisper to one another: "Do you suppose anything really happened?" When Miss Minnie realizes that her dry, frustrated life will continue, she becomes hysterical.

In the story's concluding part, McLendon arrives home at midnight. His house is described as "trim and fresh as a birdcage and almost as small, with its clean, green-and-white paint." He half strikes, half flings his wife across a chair because she has waited up for him. His "birdcage" home and small southern town provide no outlets for the violence in his nature. He strikes his wife, as he killed Will Mayes, to relieve his personal frustration.

*Themes and Meanings*

Faulkner extends the meaning of "Dry September" beyond an account of racial violence in the South by including Hawkshaw, who wants to "get the sheriff and do this
thing right." Hawkshaw, "a thin, sand-colored man with a mild face," is contrasted
with the heavy and powerful McLendon, who "had commanded troops at the front in
France and had been decorated for valor." To emphasize the contrast between
Hawkshaw and McLendon, the narrator states: "They looked like men of different
races."

Faulkner ironically suggests that though Hawkshaw and McLendon both have
white skin, they do not belong to the same race. Hawkshaw considers Will Mayes a
human being who deserves justice. To McLendon, he is a Negro, an object on which
he can safely unleash his brutality. Society approved McLendon's violence during the
war, and in Jefferson, his violence against a black man is still sanctioned.

*Style and Technique*

The images contained in the first sentence of "Dry September" establish the story's
scheme of imagery: "Through the bloody September twilight, aftermath of sixty-two
rainless days, it had gone like a fire in dry grass—the rumor, the story, whatever it
was." The equally important image of a "bloody September twilight" foreshadows the
violence that will erupt.

Faulkner intensifies the horror of the murder by using images that evoke a sense of
impending violence and death. As the barber hurries up the street after McLendon and
the others, the streetlights glare "in rigid and violent suspension in the lifeless air."
The "bloody September twilight" has passed into evening: "The day had died in a pall
of dust; above the darkened square, shrouded by the spent dust, the sky was as clear as
the inside of a brass bell." As the car moves along the road, its motion is like that of
"an extinct furnace blast: cooler, but utterly dead." The imagery and diction of violence and death intensify the impact of the story. Later, as the "brass bell" begins to
toll the death of Will Mayes, "the wan hemorrhage of the moon" increases.

The violence of the "bloody September twilight" has burned itself out; only the red
dust remains. Hawkshaw could not prevent the murder of an innocent black man, but
he lives and can limp home. The "eternal dust" absorbs the "glare and the sound" of
McLendon and the others. Hawkshaw's race of humane and rational men may fail to
control the violence and inhumanity of McLendon's race, but the dust of the land and
of all men absorbs them: "They went on; the dust swallowed them; the glare and the
sound died away. The dust of them hung for a while, but soon the eternal dust absorbed it again." Faulkner suspends one violent moment in a southern town, but the
eternal cycle of life and death, of timeless motion, can absorb even the moments of violence.

*Jean R. Brink*

# THE DUEL

*Author:* Anton Chekhov (1860-1904)
*Type of plot:* Psychological
*Time of plot:* The 1880's
*Locale:* The Caucasus
*First published:* "Duel," 1891 (English translation, 1916)

*Principal characters:*
> IVAN ANDREITCH "VANYA" LAEVSKY, the protagonist, a young
> government clerk
> NADYEZHDA FYODOROVNA, his married mistress
> ALEXANDR DAVIDITCH SAMOYLENKO, a good-natured army
> doctor, friend of Laevsky
> "KOLYA" VON KOREN, a zoologist who hates Laevsky
> ILYA MIHALITCH KIRILIN, the police captain, lover of Nadyezhda
> Fyodorovna

## The Story

The first five sections of "The Duel" explore the emotional and mental states of two lovers, Ivan Andreitch Laevsky and Nadyezhda Fyodorovna, who have fled to the Caucasus in search of happiness and now are living together without benefit of matrimony, to the scandal of local society. Now realizing how different daily life is from romantic dreams, how different life as a farmer would be from visions of love in a vineyard, Laevsky is convinced that he no longer loves Nadyezhda Fyodorovna. Only the lack of money prevents him from deserting her. As he tells his friend Alexandr Daviditch Samoylenko, the fact that Nadyezhda's husband has died, leaving her free to marry, makes Laevsky's plight more pressing. He does not want to marry a woman he does not love, and Samoylenko's attempts to shame Laevsky for irresponsibility have no effect on him. To the zoologist Von Koren, Laevsky's attitude is shocking, typical of the hedonists of the 1880's.

Nadyezhda's dreams of love in a seaside cottage have been as much unrealized as those of her lover. Rather than breaking her heart, his recent cold behavior has relieved her sense of guilt, for she has not only grown unenthusiastic about life on a farm; she has also run up debts without Laevsky's knowledge and has taken Ilya Mihalitch Kirilin, the police captain, as a lover. Although she is now bored with Kirilin, Nadyezhda has some difficulty in justifying her infidelity.

At a picnic, while Laevsky contemplates flight from his situation, Nadyezhda considers accepting as a lover the son of the shopkeeper to whom she owes money, hoping in some way to escape from her debts while enjoying herself at the same time. Kirilin, too, desires her favors. When the lovers return home, Laevsky tells Nadyezhda that her husband is dead and hurries to Samoylenko, begging for a loan so that he can run away from her. While Laevsky waits for money to flee, Nadyezhda is desperately concealing her own pressing debts from him until a propitious time to confess. As Samoylenko extracts a loan from Von Koren, Laevsky finally admits to himself that his flight will be based on lies: to Nadyezhda, whom he will abandon; to the generous doctor, who will not be repaid in the foreseeable future; to his government superiors; to his creditors; and to his mother, from whom he will get some money, but not enough for his needs.

Meanwhile, because Kirilin has threatened her with exposure, Nadyezhda agrees to give him two more assignations. Angered by the judgmental Von Koren, nearly hysterical with financial worries and his desire to break off his love affair, Laevsky insults his benefactor Samoylenko and his enemy Von Koren, and the zoologist turns Laevsky's unthinking words into a challenge to a duel. Later that evening, consumed with hatred for Von Koren and anxiety about his own situation, Laevsky has a final blow: The jealous son of the shopkeeper conducts him to the room where Kirilin is making love to Nadyezhda Fyodorovna.

Facing himself at last, Laevsky realizes that his life has been both selfish and meaningless, that Nadyezhda has become only what he made her, and finally, that she is the only person in the world for whom he really cares. Although the situation is unchanged, his debts unpaid, he now wishes to live. When Von Koren refuses to accept his apology, Laevsky fires into the air. Still impelled by hatred, Von Koren prepares to kill Laevsky, but a shout from the boyish deacon who is observing from the bushes throws off his aim, and Laevsky is spared, to find new joy in life and in love.

The final revelation comes three months later, at the time of Von Koren's departure. Urged by Samoylenko, Von Koren admits to Laevsky, now married, hardworking, and happy, that he had misjudged him. Laevsky concludes that no human being knows the truth, but that through suffering and misery everyone does more nearly approach an understanding of life.

*Themes and Meanings*

"The Duel" is often classified as a short novel because of its length and because of the complexity of its structure. In most Anton Chekhov short stories, there is one scene in which the protagonist comes to realize a truth about life or a revelation about himself. "The Duel," on the other hand, has several important revelatory scenes before the duel and a final scene three months after the climactic duel, wherein there is a final turn of character.

Throughout Chekhov's story, there is constant opposition between love and hate, between fidelity and infidelity. Whatever speeches the characters may make about values, they are motivated by their emotions. Laevsky and Nadyezhda both blame each other for the failure of their dreams, and both take revenge by infidelity—on her part, physical unfaithfulness, and on his part, the planned desertion. Although they talk, they do not confide. Von Koren himself, hating what Laevsky stands for, is eager to kill him, and Nadyezhda's other two professed lovers are willing to blackmail her into having sexual relations with them and to betray her to her husband. Only Samoylenko and the deacon are truly good-natured.

However, the movement of the story is toward reconciliation. Laevsky's suffering and Nadyezhda's unfaithfulness bring them to a love based on mutual understanding rather than on illusion. Von Koren learns that even men like Laevsky can change and that his own hatred can be turned to liking.

Laevsky's final realization, that human beings proceed like a small boat in high waves, unevenly yet with progress, suggests that the harsh judgments made by Laevsky, Von Koren, and even Nadyezhda in the first sections of the story were erroneous. None of them knew the inmost feelings of the others, which were revealed to the reader by Chekhov; each of them had unique grievances and unique dislikes, which culminated for the men in the duel and for Nadyezhda in her rendezvous with Kirilin. From a distance, human hatred can be as laughable as the young deacon found it; it can also be as wrong as the tolerant Samoylenko, the reconciling and forgiving force, insisted. Given the wrongs of which all human beings are capable, neither high-minded speeches nor destructive actions make sense. However, even mistakes—like the duel—can produce reform.

## Style and Technique

Because Chekhov often deals with the ironic difference between what people think and what they do, and because in this complex story he is dealing with several different major characters, he proceeds by exploring first the actions and thoughts of one character and then those of another. For example, after several sections in which Laevsky plans his escape from the woman whose heart he thinks he will be breaking, Chekhov moves into her mind, to reveal her own guilt, boredom, and deception, even her own relief because Laevsky has by his harshness provided her with an excuse for what she had already done. In other cases, too, both the ironic humor of the story and the thematic emphasis on human isolation come from Chekhov's penetration of the minds of his characters—of the innocent deacon's dreams of priestly power, conflicting with domestic bliss, for example, or of the scientist Von Koren's joy at the prospect of killing a man whom he hates, a joy that is concealed within the ritual of the duel.

Finally, theme and technique merge in a clear didactic statement that is not characteristic of Chekhov. Because no one can know the heart of another, and because human beings can change for the better, like Samoylenko one should reserve judgment, act in kindness, and hope always for human progress.

*Rosemary M. Canfield Reisman*

# DUEL

*Author:* Richard Matheson (1926-      )
*Type of plot:* Allegory
*Time of plot:* The 1960's or the early 1970's
*Locale:* A highway to San Francisco, California
*First published:* 1971

> *Principal characters:*
> MANN, a middle-aged traveling salesperson
> KELLER, a truck driver

*The Story*

"Duel" is based on a simple but provocative premise: What if an ordinary man, a salesperson, were driving along a highway minding his own business when a truck driver, for no discernible reason, suddenly challenged him to a duel of machines? The task the author poses for himself is to develop fully the potential of this premise, to dramatize its limited but exciting and suspenseful narrative possibilities.

Heading west on a two-lane highway through the mountains, Mann, a middle-aged traveling salesperson, sees very few vehicles. Because he must maintain his routine speed of fifty-five miles per hour if he is to keep his appointment in San Francisco, he casually passes a truck that is pulling a gasoline trailer. This action somehow sets off a hostile response in the faceless truck driver. The truck passes him, Mann passes the truck, it passes him again, and he begins to realize that an unusual situation has developed, one the truck driver intends to control. An intricate series of actions and reactions ensues, with Mann's own emotions escalating from bewilderment to mild irritation to ordinary anger to mortal fear to combative rage.

There are three major turning points in the narrative. As he climbs a steep grade, Mann is able to pass the truck, but he blares his horn derisively. Soothed by a reverie about his wife and children, with music on the car radio as background, he settles into the delusion that the incident is over. However, on the steep, curving downgrade, the ugly, square truck tries to ram him from behind, and Mann realizes that the driver intends to kill him.

The second turning point comes when Mann decides to evade the truck by pulling over into the lot in front of Chuck's Cafe, and to placate the driver, who may or may not have entered the café while Mann was trying to calm himself with rationalizations in the rest room. Back on the highway, however, the truck resumes its deadly game, stopping and starting and blocking the highway in response to Mann's evasive maneuvers.

Mann's impulsive decision to outrun the truck and his indulgent joy in the race is the third turning point. In this pastoral setting, he is forced to accept the fact that he cannot withdraw from this duel. Two emotions new to his experience—uncontrollable rage and terror of imminent death—enable him to draw on resources that he had not known he had. His overheated car having barely made it to the crest of a steep grade ahead of the truck, he must elude his opponent on the steep downgrade. When the motor fails, he makes a sudden turn onto a side road, timed so that if the truck driver surrenders to an instinct to follow, he will lose control. When the truck disappears from his rearview mirror, Mann stops, gets out of his car, and walks back down the road just in time to see the truck crash in a ravine and explode. Mann looks down, too stunned to feel anything. Then he cries exultantly, like a beast over his defeated prey.

## Themes and Meanings

Rising above the story's surface of detailed realism is an allegory of irrational male aggression that reaches back through history beyond the era of dueling to prehistory, when men slew one another out of mere instinctual territorial combativeness. Mann is Everyman, from the first man to man at this moment to man in the future. For the first half of the combat, strange in a modern, civilized setting but commonplace in the jungle, Mann's antagonist is more an alien mechanical force than a person: "He visualized the truck as some great entity pursuing him, insentient, brutish, chasing him with instinct only." After Mann sees the driver's face and learns his name from the printing on the side of the truck—Keller (read "Killer")—the duel is between two men but reduced to the level of their primeval ancestors, bereft of human empathy and intellect, a function of animal reflex and instinct.

In the first half of the story, in the Chuck's Cafe restroom, a hostile oasis, Mann can reflect on the way in which modern society suppresses the knowledge that man's aggressive instincts have survived more than two thousand years of the civilizing process; each person is so dependent on the illusion that he and other people are civilized that when the primitive, irrational violence erupts, he is totally unprepared to understand logically or react effectively to it: "Suddenly, the jungle is in front of you again. Man, part animal, part angel." Ironically, Mann thinks that only the driver of the truck is an animal, and that he is its "prey."

Early in the second half of the story, the allegory that equates modern man with his primeval ancestor converges with an allegorical element that is secondary to it but inseparable from it: The animal-angel elements in man are trapped and forever warring in the body of a nonhuman beast. Before Mann saw the driver's face, the truck had been "the embodiment of unknown terror," which appeared to him earlier as a "leviathan," which now is a "purple-silver relic" (of primeval eons), and which later is a "looming gargantuan shape," a "ponderous beast." Ecological conditions and smaller creatures destroyed mammoth creatures in primeval times; Mann-car destroys, by strategy and accident, Keller-trailer-truck. In the final paragraph, Mann and Keller as combative primitive men are submerged in nonhuman beast imagery: "The cry of some ancestral beast above the body of its vanquished foe." Thus Richard Matheson's allegory, based on a detailed realism with which his readers can identify (and which they can fully experience on that level), simultaneously subjects his reader to a reversion to the murderous behavior of his primeval human ancestors and of the beasts out of which humankind evolved.

However, the significance of that dual-level allegory is made much more forceful when one considers that it has a present-day and futuristic correlation: In the history of life-forms, the human invention of mechanical locomotion occurred only a second ago, and machines are currently engaged in an armed duel, heading, on the two-lane highway of life, west, the direction symbolic of death. Matheson's simple allegory has impressive scope in time and space, illuminating humankind's predicament as it illuminates the nature of each of his readers.

*Style and Technique*

Matheson is an interesting example of the commercial writer who is so in command of his craft that he achieves, in this profound allegory, through the controlled use of various techniques and a style almost perfectly suited to it, a work of art.

Except for a few lapses, the narrative point of view is third-person, central intelligence. Serviceable phrases such as "Mann's expression froze in terror," "with haunted eyes," and "his face a mask of animosity" violate that point of view by giving the reader external views of Mann, through whose perceptions all elements of the story are otherwise centralized. Perhaps Matheson the screenwriter intruded at these points; "Duel" appeared in *Playboy* only months before Matheson's own adaptation, directed by then novice Steven Spielberg, showed up on television, becoming a cinematic as well as a literary classic. The very mechanics of the situation as it develops help Matheson to control his basically commercial-literary style, which now and then produces such lines as "He eyed the truck with cursory disapproval." Given the already well-controlled Mann point of view and the ongoing context of terror, it is not necessary to follow "He's going to kill me" with "Mann thought, horrified."

Readers experience Matheson's simple, precise, fast-paced plot structure as if they were being carried forward, simultaneously terrified and exhilarated, inside a swift, smooth-running machine. Readers intimately share Mann's emotional, imaginative, and intellectual reactions as they escalate from mild irritation to sheer terror to instinctive murderous rage. Readers experience a process in which an ironic reversal turns Mann-the-victim into Mann-the-victor.

To enhance Mann's reactions to the aggressive behavior of the truck driver, Matheson uses vivid descriptive detail, imagery, and the devices of parallel and contrast. "Sunlight on his arm and lap" is a detail that enables the reader to drift with Mann into reverie. Later, Mann sees "the back of the truck driver's left hand on the steering wheel," a detail that helps make the driver seem mysterious. That Mann can see only the lower half of the square radiator grill focuses his sense of the menace rushing after him. Matheson makes Mann's response to everything that he sees along the highway very lively: "Who the hell is Will Jasper," he wonders, looking at the name painted on a rock. "What would he think of this situation?" The author offers a grotesquely comic parallel to the deadly serious situation when Mann notices the "Night Crawlers—Bait" sign and thinks of monster films. More effective as contrasts are

Mann's responses to the music on his car radio and to the pastoral scenery framing the highway. However, music finally lacks the power to soothe the savage instincts provoked in his breast, and scenery as relief from terror becomes an irritant, a mocking contrast to his perilous predicament.

Another enhancement of Mann's basic predicament is the sense of isolation that Matheson creates. At the start, and now and then throughout, Mann notices that few cars are on the highway. Even the drivers in Chuck's Cafe are shadowy figures. He feels the driver has isolated him from all other possibilities for this duel. Imagining his wife at the supermarket performing her domestic chores only makes his isolation more intense. When Mann sees two lovers parked in a car, not even noticing him as he passes, the reader shares his poignant isolation. At the sight of a pet cemetery, he wisecracks, but the sight later of flowers and a "Funeral" sign makes him imagine the final isolation—his own death.

By endowing all elements with a sense of immediacy, Matheson enables the reader to follow even Mann's developing, ambivalent meditations with no lag in pace. For example, Mann draws on his lifelong preconception that truckers are cautious; then he decides that this driver must be an independent who lives by his own rules; finally, he will see that the man is lawless. Mann's interrogation of aspects of the mystery, as when he is in Chuck's Cafe, enhances the reader's enjoyment of the fast-paced sequence of actions. There is a rare congruity between the character's questions and the reader's as both try to understand why, in this case, the driver behaves so irrationally. As the truck driver manipulates Mann's behavior, the writer manipulates the reader's responses. "Duel" is an unusually clear demonstration of how, in many effective stories, the main elements become a metaphor of the storytelling process itself—of the dynamics of the writer-reader relationship.

*David Madden*

# THE DUNWICH HORROR

*Author:* H. P. Lovecraft (1890-1937)
*Type of plot:* Horror
*Time of plot:* 1913-1928
*Locale:* "Dunwich," Massachusetts
*First published:* 1929

*Principal characters:*
>OLD WHATELEY, an elderly Dunwich resident suspected of
>  sorcery
>LAVINIA WHATELEY, his daughter
>WILBUR, her son
>DR. HENRY ARMITAGE, the librarian at Miskatonic University

*The Story*

The birth of Wilbur Whateley in Dunwich is obviously an ominous event. On the night he is born, strange noises rumble through the hills, all the dogs in the vicinity continuously bark, and a hideous screaming is heard. In fact, the whole Whateley family is rather bizarre. Lavinia, Wilbur's mother, is a deformed, unattractive albino. Lavinia's father, Old Whateley, is feared by the local populace for his practice of black magic, while the father of Wilbur is completely unknown.

This ominous note continues as the child grows. Wilbur is described as "goatish" in appearance, although he possesses the Whateley trademark of a chinless face. He can already walk at the age of seven months and talks at eleven months. He is very particular about keeping his body well covered with clothes, unlike the rest of the Whateleys. Every May Eve and Halloween, the boy and his mother are seen going up to the top of Sentinel Hill and apparently practicing weird rites, to the accompaniment of bursts of flame and underground rumblings.

At the same time, the boy's grandfather has been playing an active part in his development. He teaches the boy ancient lore, incantations, and formulas from the old books that he keeps. He continuously buys cattle with a never-ending supply of ancient gold pieces, yet the size of his herd never increases. He also feverishly rebuilds the second floor of the house and constructs a wooden ramp leading up to it from the ground. The few visitors to the house are invariably disturbed by extremely odd noises upstairs.

After Old Whateley dies and his daughter disappears, there is a shift of scene, as Lovecraft affords the reader a view of Wilbur, now fourteen years old and eight feet tall, resembling a huge, dark gargoyle, at the library of Miskatonic University in Arkham, hurriedly copying some missing formulas that he needs out of a rare book, the *Necronomicon*. The alert librarian, Dr. Henry Armitage, reading the Latin text over Wilbur's shoulder, sees references to the Old Ones, beings who apparently are ready to "break through" and destroy the earth. He associates this with the mysterious happenings in Dunwich and the dim, hideous aura of Wilbur, and he immediately refuses him further access to the book.

There now occurs the first climax of the story, which serves as a preview of the real Dunwich horror, which the reader has yet to see. Wilbur is desperate to get the formula he needs, although he seems fearful of being away from the farm for too long for some reason. He finally breaks into the library in an attempt to steal the book, but he is killed by the watchdog. As he lies on the floor with his clothes torn away, Dr. Armitage sees him as the monster he really is—tentacles with red, sucking mouths protruding from his stomach. Dr. Armitage and the reader realize that, terrible as this is, something far worse waits in the farmhouse in Dunwich.

In the final section of the narrative, the horror has already broken loose. The Whateley farmhouse, which has previously had all its inner partitions removed by Wilbur so as to make one huge, two-story space, has literally been blown apart by the monster, nourished by its steady diet of cattle (the reason for Old Whateley's ramp). It soon becomes evident that the thing that has escaped is invisible, although its myriad footprints, resembling those of a herd of elephants, can be seen. A reign of terror in the surrounding area has already begun, with houses being flattened at night and people and cattle disappearing.

Dr. Armitage has exhaustively studied the *Necronomicon* and as a result has learned more about the strange evil threatening the world and has managed to discover several formulas that might possibly defeat the present evil. He comes to Dunwich with two colleagues from the university, and he hopes to get close enough to the monster for the formulas to have effect when he recites them.

In the concluding scene, Dr. Armitage has tracked the monster to the top of Sentinel Hill, on which is a circle of stones in Stonehenge fashion, along with a huge altar. This confirms his worst fears, for he knows that the monster will try to communicate with the beings from beyond. Dr. Armitage gets close enough and begins to recite the formula while his two helpers spray a powder that gives a brief glimpse of the monster, causing the onlookers far down the hill to scream in terror. As the monster cries out in a thunderous voice, it is obliterated by a lightning bolt, and the situation is saved.

In the course of this final scene, two facts have been revealed. The huge monster, with its Whateley face barely discernible among the tentacles, eyes, suckers, and feet, is evidently the twin brother of Wilbur, born at the same time as he, while the father of both Wilbur and the monster is one of the mysterious beings from the otherworld.

## Themes and Meanings

H. P. Lovecraft believed that the oldest and strongest fear of humankind is fear of the unknown. This belief was an important force behind the idea that he gradually developed over many years that the earth was once inhabited by a race of beings from another world or dimension who, while having lost their hold on earth, are waiting to enter again. This is the major theme in "The Dunwich Horror."

This idea develops slowly as the story unfolds. Dr. Armitage has realized that "unseen things not of earth—or at least not of tri-dimensional earth—rushed foetid and horrible through New England's glens, and brooded obscenely on the mountaintops." Old Whateley on his deathbed tells Wilbur that only the beings from beyond, the Old Ones who want to come back, can make the monster multiply. The *Necronomicon* relates that the Old Ones broke through long ago, and they shall break through once again.

Lovecraft was indebted to the English writer Arthur Machen (1863-1947) for the inspiration of this idea, but he carried the idea much further and in a different direction, for although Machen's otherworld is populated by a mixture of little people and nature deities (sometimes fearful), Lovecraft's otherworld, or dimension, is completely terrifying and threatens the continued existence of this world. Lovecraft built up these ideas into an entire body of myth known as Cthulhu Mythos. The names mentioned in the *Necronomicon*, such as Yog-Sothoth, Cthulhu, and Kadath, are beings or places important in the myth.

An interesting and related idea in the story is the ominous feeling imparted by great age. The beings from beyond are described as the oldest things in or around earth. Old Whateley is extremely aged, and the rapid aging of Wilbur is emphasized. The entire village of Dunwich is seen as old, decadent, and unsettling in appearance, and the stone circles (where evil rites are practiced) are of great antiquity, going back at least to Indian times.

*Style and Technique*

This is one of Lovecraft's most tightly constructed stories, largely as a result of his use of linking elements that give subtle clues and anticipate developments. The climactic scene in which the monster on the hilltop cries out to its father is presaged by Old Whateley in the beginning, when he tells the loungers at the general store that a child of Lavinia's would call for its father on Sentinel Hill. The constant rebuilding and expansion of the farmhouse are clues to the existence of the horror within and its growth. Smell is important, for the similar odors of the upstairs room (where the monster is growing), Wilbur, the top of Sentinel Hill, and the rampaging monster at the end serve to provide clues to the identity of Wilbur. Even sound is utilized, for the whippoorwills always cry in concert before a death.

Some of Lovecraft's strategies are reminiscent of Edgar Allan Poe—not surprising, because he once referred to Poe as his god of fiction. These devices include the conscious use of archaisms and a tendency to use many adjectives. Dr. Armitage "seemed to sense the close presence of some terrible part of the intruding horror, and to glimpse a hellish advance in the black dominion of the ancient and once passive nightmare." This style, mannered and obtrusive in Lovecraft's earlier prose, was more successfully utilized for narrative effect in his later fiction, such as "The Dunwich Horror," in which the story is related in almost reportorial fashion.

*James V. Muhleman*

# THE EARTHQUAKE IN CHILE

*Author:* Heinrich von Kleist (1777-1811)
*Type of plot:* Realism
*Time of plot:* 1647
*Locale:* Santiago, Chile
*First published:* "Das Erdbeben in Chili," 1807 (English translation, 1946)

> *Principal characters:*
> JERONIMO RUGERO, a Spanish tutor
> DONNA JOSEPHE ASTERON, his lover, the daughter of one of the
>    city's wealthiest aristocratic families
> PHILIP, their infant son
> DON FERNANDO ORMEZ, the son of the city's commandant

## The Story

The story opens at the moment of a fatally destructive earthquake, just as the young Spaniard Jeronimo Rugero is about to hang himself in prison. Jeronimo despairs at the fate of his beloved, Donna Josephe, who on this day is to be beheaded for having borne a child on the steps of the cathedral while she was a novice in the Carmelite convent. Her father had sent her to the convent on learning of her secret love for her tutor, Jeronimo. Later, Jeronimo managed to gain access to the convent garden, where their love was consummated.

On hearing the bells accompanying Josephe to her execution, Jeronimo tightens the rope that would tear him away from his wretched life, when suddenly the ground trembles under his feet. The earthquake destroys the major part of the city and rips apart the walls of the prison. Barely conscious, Jeronimo escapes through an opening between the fallen buildings and reaches the nearest gate to the city, where he is filled with feelings of ecstasy and thankfulness at his deliverance. However, depression soon overwhelms him again when he remembers Josephe. He searches for her in vain among the fleeing crowds, then at sundown discovers a distant, solitary valley. On reaching it, he catches sight of a young woman washing her child in a spring. It is Donna Josephe.

The earthquake miraculously rescued her as well, as the falling buildings scattered the gathered crowds and the procession of her executioners. She returned to the convent just in time to rescue her son from the flames engulfing it. Before leaving the city, she noticed that all the seats of power and authority had collapsed, including the prison. Believing Jeronimo dead, she sought out the isolated valley to pray for his soul.

Their first night back together is idyllic, as they exchange stories of their imprisonment, enjoy their incredible good fortune, and plan on departing for a new life in Spain. The next morning their reveries are interrupted by a young nobleman, Don

Fernando Ormez, carrying his infant son. Because his wife is badly wounded, he asks Josephe to breast-feed his son. After initial hesitation at meeting someone familiar with her history, she agrees, whereupon Don Fernando invites the lovers to join him and his family for breakfast. Both are overwhelmed by the warm reception of their new friends and quickly forget the horrible events of the recent past. The human spirit appears rejuvenated, as the different social classes mingle easily with one another and everyone helps to ease the pain and deprivation of their neighbors.

Blinded by the general goodwill that they see all around them, Jeronimo and Josephe decide not to go to Spain but rather to become reconciled with those who had condemned them and their illicit love. Word spreads of a solemn thanksgiving mass in the Dominican church in Santiago. Despite the warnings of Don Fernando's sister-in-law, Josephe insists on attending the mass and immediately sets off for the church with Jeronimo, the two infants, Don Fernando, and Donna Constanza, another sister-in-law.

In the crowded church, an elderly prelate begins a sermon of praise and thanksgiving, then quickly turns to condemning the city's moral depravity and alludes to the scandalous event in the convent garden. Before Don Fernando and his party can escape from the church, voices call out that the godless couple are among them. Saved temporarily by Don Fernando's presence of mind, the lovers slip out of the church, with Don Fernando, freshly armed with a naval officer's sword, holding the two infants. No sooner, however, do they reach the square in front of the church than someone, who cries out that he is Jeronimo's father, slays both Jeronimo and Donna Constanza, who was at Jeronimo's side. Don Fernando manages to fend off the violent crowd, in particular a fanatic shoemaker, but Josephe sacrifices herself in order to save the children. The shoemaker than snatches away Don Fernando's son, Juan, and ruthlessly smashes him against a church pillar.

Don Fernando does rescue Philip, the son of Jeronimo and Josephe, and later adopts him. When he compares Philip to his own son and thinks of how he acquired him, it seems to him almost "as if he had to rejoice."

*Themes and Meanings*

The terrible destructive force of the earthquake levels both buildings and human institutions. At the same time that it kills scores of people, it liberates Jeronimo and Josephe from the bonds of the old hierarchical social and political order. The Rousseauistic promise of a new, egalitarian social order based on the natural goodness of humanity, however, deludes the lovers into desiring to return to the city immediately—to the one building left standing where the old power structure could reassert itself and incite people to return to their old ways. The earthquake, Heinrich von Kleist suggests, brings out the best and worst in everyone, and the evil that triumphs in the Dominican church is an evil upheld by a church governed by a powerful need to protect its own authority and interests. Kleist's sympathies clearly lie with Jeronimo and Josephe, yet the purity of their love is no match for the far stronger social conventions and structures that ultimately destroy them.

The world is the staging ground for vast, unpredictable forces—whether natural, human, political, or religious. It is chance that saves the lovers at first, chance that brings them together at the spring, chance that they are recognized and slain outside the church, and, finally, chance that saves their son. If there is no final certainty, only a universe governed by irrational forces and a God who is incomprehensible and largely absent from everyday life, how should one act? Jeronimo, Josephe, and Don Fernando all act with a natural grace and dignity in the face of turmoil, yet each pays dearly for it. Kleist's deep pessimism about the nature of human behavior and institutions leads almost inevitably to tragedy. Don Fernando embodies Kleistian moral character and provides the story its small yet persistent hope that a more just moral order might yet prevail.

*Style and Technique*

The narration of the events of the story is extremely compressed and full of dramatic irony and twists. The narrator, although anonymous, is not completely objective in his report, for he betrays his own attitudes toward religious hypocrisy in his subtly sarcastic language, and he clearly does not believe in the lovers' sinfulness or guilt. The serene and idyllic middle section of the story is surrounded by scenes of continuous action, in which details are piled up like the rubble of the fallen buildings and often are not easily separated from the whole. The sudden appearance and disappearance of people and voices underlie the haphazard encounters of friends and enemies. There is little causal explanation: Things simply happen, and the characters react as best they can. If the narrator believes in any grander order, he does not reveal it and couches his own metaphysical uncertainties in a series of speculative, "as if" statements: When the earthquake hits, it is "as if the firmament collapsed"; when Josephe rescues her child from the collapsing convent, it is "as if all the angels of heaven protected her"; when the pair are reunited, it is as if they were in the valley of Eden.

The narrative impatience and uncertainty is counterbalanced by a dramatic structure that is exemplary in its economy and power. After plunging immediately into the dilemmas of the story in the first sentence, the narrative unfolds impetuously, with hardly a pause for reflection until the climax of the sermon in the church, from which point the hideous finale is played out with breathtaking rapidity. The ending, with its coda of Don Fernando reflecting on the tragic fate of his friends and son, resolves little and leaves open the question of the proper human response to apparent divine intervention.

*Peter West Nutting*

# EASTER EVE

*Author:* Anton Chekhov (1860-1904)
*Type of plot:* Social realism
*Time of plot:* The 1880's
*Locale:* Russia
*First published:* "Sviatoiu noch'iu," 1886 (English translation, 1915)

> *Principal characters:*
> THE UNNAMED NARRATOR
> IERONIM, a monk and a ferryman
> NIKOLAY, a monk and an author of canticles, the late friend of
> Ieronim

*The Story*

On the night before Easter, the narrator waits on the riverbank for a ferry to take him to the monastery on the other side of the river to see the Easter ceremonies. It is dark; only the stars are shining as if they have come out for the festival procession, with each of them renewed and joyful, and each softly twinkling and beaming. The river is flooded and looks like a lake. It is as though nature itself celebrates Easter.

Soon the narrator finds out that he is not alone. Not far from him, a peasant is waiting for the illumination. He does not have the five kopecks for the ferry and refuses to accept the money when the narrator offers it to him. Instead he asks the narrator to put up a candle for him in the monastery. He likes it better this way. The ferry does not come, however, and on the other side of the river, the Resurrection is declared. The religious ceremony can be seen and heard only from across the river.

The ferry, whose shape resembles a gibbet, finally arrives. The narrator meets Ieronim, the ferryman, who is a monk from the monastery. The ferry slowly floats toward the other bank, where the illumination has begun. Now the Easter celebrations can be observed from the ferry. A rocket cleaves the darkness and brings a roar from the other bank. The narrator and Ieronim admire the scenery, although Ieronim is sad. It turns out that today his dear friend, the monk and deacon Nikolay, has died during a celebration of the Mass. He was an unusual person: not only intelligent, kind, and sweet but also exceptionally talented at writing hymns of praise. Although Nikolay had not studied anywhere, he could do something no one else in the monastery could do, not even educated elders and monks. Nikolay wrote the hymns for his own comfort. With loving detail and admiration, Ieronim describes the art of writing canticles. One should possess a sweet, harmonious tongue in order to write them. No one, except Ieronim, appreciated them in the monastery. There were some who even laughed, considering Nikolay's writing a sin.

In the meantime, the ferry has approached the bank. The narrator shares the joyful excitement and agitation with the crowd outside the church. He observes the same unrest and sleeplessness in nature. An endless stream of people is going in and out of the church. The narrator does not forget about Ieronim and his late friend.

In the church, where the elation and agitation are felt more than outside, there is no concentrated prayer, just continuous, childish joy. The narrator sees the expression of triumph on the faces, but he also notices that no one is listening to the choir. Who can appreciate the song of praise better than Ieronim? Why is such a sensitive man deprived of this joy? Why must he work the ferry and mourn the death of his friend while other monks celebrate the holiday?

In the early morning, the crowd and the narrator come out of the church after Mass. The narrator wants to have a look at the dead Nikolay, but he does not know in which cell his body is lying. Subsequently, he is glad he has not seen it; he might lose the picture created by Ieronim's story.

In the morning, the excitement is gone, and everybody and everything, including nature, looks exhausted and sleepy. Returning on the ferry to the other side of the river, the narrator is finally able to see the monk Ieronim clearly. No one has relieved him from his duty, and he looks exhausted and sad. Working the ferry across the river, he looks at the face of a young merchant's wife. There is nothing masculine in his gaze, however. It appears that he is trying to find in her face the tender features of his dead friend.

## Themes and Meanings

In a letter to a friend, writer Anton Chekhov wrote: "When I recall my childhood now, it appears to me dismal enough; I have no religion now. You know, when my two brothers and I formed a trio in the middle of the church and chanted the canticles . . . the members of the congregation were touched and they envied our parents, but at the same time we felt ourselves to be little convicts." It appears from "Easter Eve," however, that Chekhov genuinely loved the Easter ceremony and its impact on people. He re-creates the heightened and exuberant atmosphere of the eve of Easter. At the same time, the atmosphere is imbued with sorrow brought into the story by Ieronim's tale and his mourning ritual (working the gibbet-like ferry between the two banks of the river), which create the mood of restlessness, anxiety, and mysticism. In describing this mood and in portraying Ieronim and his late friend, Nikolay, who had an extraordinary gift for writing canticles, Chekhov is more interested in the aesthetic and artistic aspect of the event and the characters than in the religious ones.

Speaking about his vocation, Chekhov wrote in another of his letters: "My holy of holies is the human body, health, intelligence, talent, inspiration, love, and absolute freedom." In this story, his interest is mostly in human inspiration, imagination, and talent. They are like the rocket in the story that cleaves the darkness and lights up the human life. The narrator, who saved the picture painted by Ieronim's tale by not seeing the body of Nikolay, brings the reader back to the peasant, for whom it was enough just to watch the illumination in order to feel the magnificence of the Easter night. For Chekhov, Nikolay was his fellow writer and Ieronim was a talented reader. Sorrow brought into the story by Ieronim's suffering and the indifference of the monks in the monastery, who did not value Nikolay's canticles and made Ieronim work the ferry on Easter night, becomes the important theme of the story.

*Style and Technique*

Chekhov creates unity in the story through mood and atmosphere. The mood and atmosphere are created by his impressionistic method of writing, which includes not only the description of nature but also the portrayal of his characters. It was Leo Tolstoy who first spoke about Chekhov's impressionism. Chekhov's portrayals of nature, characters, and events are like patches of color that, in the distance, result in a remarkable picture of real life. In a letter to his brother, Chekhov wrote: "In description of nature one should seize upon minutiae, grouping them so that when, having read the passage, you close your eyes, a picture is formed. . . . In the area of mental states there are also particulars. May God save you from generalities." As one can see, nature plays an important part in the story. It creates the atmosphere, it supports the human actions. The sky, the stars, the river, the rhythms, the sounds, the rocket, the lights—everything works to create the poetic substance of the story, revealing its meaning. In order to show that the Easter ceremonies are both joyful and, at the same time, restless and mystical, they are observed at the beginning from the other side of the river, then from the ferry, then closer and closer, outside and inside the church. The symbol of the gibbet-like ferry with the reclining figure of Ieronim represents grief and sorrow. The endless stream of people going in and out of the church reminds one of the currents of water.

Chekhov relates "Easter Eve" in the first-person singular. He chooses the anonymous narrator to combine the thrill of joy from the ceremony with the feeling of agitation and restlessness, to infuse sincerity and lyricism into the story, to bring the pitch of the story down, closer to the reader.

*Grigory Roytman*

# EASY TIME

*Author:* Jack López (1950-        )
*Type of plot:* Domestic realism
*Time of plot:* The late twentieth century
*Locale:* Near the Colonia, perhaps Northern California
*First published:* 1993

*Principal characters:*
TONY, a young Hispanic man
ALEX, his uncle
SYLVIA, his former girlfriend
JIMMY, his older brother
HIS GRANDMOTHER
HIS MOTHER

*The Story*

Tony, who is about to serve thirty days—easy time—for auto theft, meets with his uncle, Alex, who is on probation. Concerned about Tony's first stay behind bars, Alex wants to give him a quick lesson in fighting. He soon grows impatient with Tony's lack of fighting skills, however, and exclaims: "Didn't your old man teach you nothing?" Tony remembers how his father once tried to get his brother Jimmy and him to spar. They did not show enough aggression, so their impatient father took Tony's gloves, put them on, and beat Jimmy himself. Jimmy got a nosebleed and Tony remembers trying to stop the flow of blood that should have been his.

After Tony finally collapses from his uncle's fighting lesson, Alex reluctantly offers to go back to jail himself with him. He says that he can call his parole officer and arrange it easily, but Tony says that he will take care of himself. They agree to meet at eight the next morning for the drive to the jail.

As Tony goes home to shower and change, he notes the beauty of the place in which he lives. His house faces the sea, and open land—much more in his childhood than in the present—surrounds the immediate cluster of houses. He remembers the stables and a helicopter landing in the strawberry fields and reflects on how the hunting land and the farmland have been parceled off, with tract housing encroaching on the open space. At home, Tony must lower his head as he enters a low-ceilinged room; this reminds him of when he became big enough to be wooed by the same football coach for whom his brother had played. Tony was flattered to be offered a spot on the football team, but by then Jimmy was flying a helicopter in Vietnam, and he himself was spending his afternoons with Sylvia.

Tony goes to his grandmother's house to eat. When he returns home, he finds a note from his mother. It says that she does not want to see him before he goes to jail, that if he wants to be like his father's family, "fine." The note also says that going to jail does not make him a man and that his mother will spend the night at a friend's place.

Tony thinks of the parties that families once threw for their sons bound for jail. After one such party, when he was in high school, was the first time that he got somewhere sexually with Sylvia. He later stole a car in order to visit her at her college. She called him stupid for stealing the car, and on the way back he was caught. Tony also remembers a Fourth of July when he threw a sparkler on the roof of the hunting lodge. His drunk father proved incapable of putting out the resulting fire, so Jimmy put it out after climbing on the roof.

After Tony goes for a swim in the ocean alone, contending gracefully against the large waves, he telephones the house where his mother is staying and is told that she is not there. He rummages through old boxes, finding the certificate he earned for making the honor roll in high school—the achievement of which his mother was proudest. He also finds the silver star that Jimmy won in Vietnam and thinks about Jimmy's funeral, how admirable Jimmy was, how angry and apathetic about everything he felt after Jimmy died. Only Sylvia made him feel better, but she went away to college and broke up with him.

The next morning, Tony's mother wakes him up, having changed her mind about not seeing him off. She cooks him breakfast. Alex arrives to drive Tony to the jail. As they arrive there, Tony holds the medal in his pocket and remembers how his brother died in an act of heroism, flying back under fire to get his men. The word "stupid" rings in his ears.

*Themes and Meanings*

"Easy Time" has an ironic title. Tony is going through anything but an easy time. Jail will certainly not be an easy time for him. Try as he may to be otherwise, he is too thoughtful and too sensitive to do well in jail. He is suffering from the grief—with which he does not have many ways of coping—of losing his brother and his girlfriend. He has hurt his mother by stealing a car, and now she threatens him with rejection. His alcoholic father has, in Tony's view, abandoned the family. Tony now faces an unsettlingly clear-cut choice: He can go the way of his uncle, father, and friends—to crime, drink, and being bad—or he can go the way of his brother, girlfriend, and mother—to getting along, finishing school, and being good. Now that Tony has taken another step toward being bad he is painfully confused about what next to do with his life.

Tony faces a problem that confronts all people as they grow up. Additionally, his problem is a symbol for the problem facing all young Latinos. He feels pride in his Colonia, and fondly recalls a past in which the urban sprawl that is emblematic of the mass Anglo culture had not yet reached the beautiful coastal area where he lives. Indications of Tony's symbolic role include his reflections about the new houses, the trash on the land ("We kept it cleaner," he thinks), and such sentences as the following: "Weak lights from the mansions on the peninsula twinkled as if they were stars that money could buy." The culture that is encroaching on Tony's rural peace celebrates money. The Colonia, for all its simplicity and beauty, does not have much money. Tony understands that he must either play the game (literally, in the case of the foot-

ball team), go to school, and work, or assimilate in another way, with the cons and ter-
minally unemployed of the Colonia. What he does not understand is his anger.

## Style and Technique

Jack López's key technique in "Easy Time" is association. He limits the third-person
narrative to Tony's point of view, so it follows his thoughts. For example, after spar-
ring with his uncle, Tony goes home to clean up. He enters a "low-ceilinged room."
Having to duck his head reminds him of when he first needed to duck to enter the
room. "It was the summer of the tenth grade," and the coach began to try to persuade
Tony to join the football team. This in turn reminds Tony of Jimmy, who had been on
the team, and of Jimmy flying a helicopter in "Asia." This memory evidently leads
to something Tony does not wish to think about—the reader discovers more later—
because Tony then thinks of something else. Tony remembers turning the coach down
for a reason Tony considers, with some naïveté, "simple": He was spending his afternoons with Sylvia. "Afternoons without Sylvia would drive him crazy." All these
thoughts flow from his lowering his head in order to enter a room. This narrative technique is effective in conveying the inner life of a young man who does not speak much
about his thoughts and feelings.

"Easy Time" owes a debt to Ernest Hemingway, particularly his short stories about
a young man, Nick Adams, who grows up in a small town. "Easy Time" recalls these
stories in its setting, spare, idiomatic style, celebratory descriptions of the challenges
of physical activity (fighting, sex, swimming with grace against surf, handball), and
young hero, who on the surface is laconic although articulate and who has a full, difficult, emotional life.

López accomplishes a difficult feat in "Easy Time." He presents the inner life of
one who cannot himself articulate his inner life. The reader learns more about Tony
from following his thoughts than Tony knows about himself. Tony is unaware of how
his angry grief over his brother's death and his father's incompetence and abuse has
led him, years after the fact, to steal a car in order to be rejected in person by someone
who has escaped the small town and all it represents—namely Sylvia, who has gone
to college. He went to see her in order to show her his new tattoo. Tony has sought unworthiness, and has found it. He seems unaware of the redemption—in the form of acceptance, work, and understanding—that lies within him, but the reader is aware of it.
López's narrative implies much more than it says, using implication, association, and
the nuances of everyday speech. For example, when Tony's grandmother asks after
his father, Tony says: "I'm not going to that house." When she asks about his mother,
he says: "She's alright. She's barely speaking to me." Another example of López's
subtle use of language is how the narration of two simple acts implies Tony's condition: "He kicked apart the flames . . . and walked back up into the wind."

*Eric Howard*

# EATING NAKED

*Author:* Stephen Dobyns (1941-  )
*Type of plot:* Realism
*Time of plot:* The 1990's
*Locale:* Rural New York
*First published:* 1997

> *Principal characters:*
> BOB FRANKENMUTH, a carpenter
> LAURA SPALDING, a young woman
> CHUCKIE, a potter

### The Story

This story is outwardly a simple one about the events that follow a nighttime accident on a rural road. Those events take an unusual turn, however, and end in a room in which social standards have, for the moment, been discarded.

At nightfall, Bob Frankenmuth is driving between cities but not paying attention to the road, being preoccupied with thoughts of leaving his wife. He hits a deer, which damages the right front end of his pickup truck, including one headlight. When he gets out to inspect the damage and the dead animal, he is surprised by the appearance of a car rushing down the road at too great a speed. The car's driver swerves and loses control, crashing into a tree. Bob finds the driver, Laura Spalding, apparently unhurt and both laughing and weeping at the accident. Her car, however, is wrecked. At his offer to take her to a garage, she says she was rushing to the house of her boyfriend, who had just threatened suicide over the phone. She took the threat seriously because he fired one of his guns next to the phone receiver.

Bob does not want to leave the deer for someone else to pick up. It shows no visible damage. He envisions giving it to his wife, to provoke her. With Laura's help, he heaves it in the back of his truck.

Although he has doubts about facing this gun-wielding boyfriend, Bob thinks the encounter offers an interesting change of pace. He has been feeling disgruntled at his wife, who has returned to school to become a teacher. Driving toward Laura's boyfriend's house, he also recognizes elements he has come to hate in himself. He finds himself too predictable, at times.

When offered the option of simply dropping Laura at the corner, Bob instead impulsively decides to go with her. Laura's boyfriend, who goes by the childlike name of Chuckie, greets Bob with distrust, at first thinking he is some other man vying for Laura's affections. He is disarmed when Bob asks if Chuckie has a grill, in order to cook the deer.

Bob is surprised at his own words. Chuckie and Laura both agree to the idea, the former with reluctance, the latter with enthusiasm. Bob, who has never prepared a deer before, hangs the carcass up, skins it, and removes its entrails to the light of the head-light that still works on his truck. Chuckie has prepared a fire, and Laura has scrounged up more food, as well as champagne leftover from a birthday party. She sets the table, using handmade plates and wine glasses. During this time, Bob talks with Chuckie about his threat of suicide and tells Chuckie he should learn to deal with change.

After the food is prepared, as they are about to sit down, Bob finds himself making another impromptu announcement: that they should eat naked. "I say we take off our clothes, eat this dear, and afterward we'll do whatever the god of change wants to have happen," he says. He immediately takes off his clothes and is followed by Laura and finally by Chuckie. The trio eat and drink heavily in a celebratory manner, and make a toast to the "spirit of the forest."

Late in the meal Laura chokes on a piece of venison. First Chuckie and then Bob attempt to help her. When Bob is successful in dislodging the meat, the three of them fall back in the exhaustion of the moment. Bob sits staring at the wind-blown curtains, feeling as if he is close to realizing something important. They drink more and, after beginning to feel embarrassed, put on their clothes.

Bob, unsure what has changed within himself, finds himself able to return to the life he had thought was falling apart, only hours earlier in the evening.

## Themes and Meanings

In "Eating Naked," Stephen Dobyns is describing a moment of crisis for a man who has become set in his ways. In some ways, Bob prefers being in a settled state. He looks back fondly on the first years of his marriage, when things went according to his expectations. Once his wife decided to assert herself and make the necessary moves toward becoming a teacher, however, his dissatisfaction grew.

At the same time, Bob reflects that their life together had never been easy. He also has moments when he dislikes who he is. One such moment arrives when he is driving with Laura beside him. In observing his reactions to her, he realizes he has become sick of himself. He sees how he is leading a life so predictable it has taken on the quality of a film script.

First Laura and then Chuckie help him in this self-awareness. Each in his or her turn responds to one of Bob's pat assertions by asking him, "How come you know so much about it?" Their question has a sarcastic side, being addressed to this character who has a tendency to act all-knowing. It also has a straightforward aspect, however. Being younger, to some degree, they do want to know. In both cases, Bob replies, "I don't. I'm just making talk."

The crisis in Bob's life, within the confines of the short story, is most strongly expressed through the first problem introduced in the story: the deer. Bob has hit it, an act that has damaged his truck. Laura then swerves around the deer and wrecks her own car. Bob feels a need to come to grips with this dead deer, a need that leads to the series of events at Chuckie's house. In dealing with it, however, he is also dealing with the central problem in his own life.

Chuckie also becomes a vital figure in Bob's wrestling with his crisis. In considering Chuckie's threat of suicide, Bob realizes the two have things in common. He discovers this through the words he himself dispenses to Chuckie as worldly advice. Chuckie is unable to accept change, he says, and that refusal has become a crisis for Chuckie for which the outside world is not responsible. Bob turns these words on himself and begins to see the arbitrary manner with which he has been responding to his wife. She was trying to make a life for herself outside the limits of being wife and mother. He realized he might have been fighting change just because it was change.

*Style and Technique*

Although "Eating Naked" is realistic in its depiction of events, it uses symbolism to help advance the story and to communicate the main character's progress toward resolution. Images of roads and road travel prove to be especially significant throughout. Bob is traveling between cities, thinking about a marriage that seems over, while Laura travels the same road, thinking about her boyfriend's life which possibly is over. Bob later compares his life to going through a tunnel, with no option of turning. When he takes Laura toward her boyfriend's house, she offers him the option of going straight ahead and just letting her off at the turn. Instead, he takes the turn with her. When he later considers how his wife would look at the three of them around the dinner table, sitting naked before the feast, he imagines her thinking he had "gone right around the bend." By the end, however, he finds his "life had gotten back on track."

Car headlights also serve a symbolic function. Headlights normally help a driver see straight down a road. After the accident, however, one headlight of Bob's truck is broken. When Laura then has her accident, the same thing happens: One headlight breaks, while the other shines up into the surrounding pines. The truck's remaining headlight is sufficient for steering it to Chuckie's house and also for illuminating the scene when Bob is gutting the deer. However, symbolically, one headlight is clearly inadequate for fully lighting the road ahead, especially when the road turns. The single headlight also embodies the fact that Bob had been driving and going through his life while he "had hardly been watching the road at all," as he admits to himself at the beginning of the story. At the story's end, the headlight image is echoed in Bob's preoccupation with Laura's breasts, one of which points forward and the other points off to the side.

Several symbolic elements signal the change happening in Bob's life. The first is nakedness, prefigured by the skinning of the deer. Bob removes the skin and guts of the animal, then holds its heart in his hand. Later he removes his own clothing, before baring his own heart in a different way. The warmth of the deer's heart is in itself a symbolic element. The room in which the feast occurs is noticeably warm from the fire, while the deer steaks steam on the plate. At the end of the story, the strongest memory Bob retains of the evening is of the warmth of Laura's naked skin. It turns out to be the element that most haunts him in the years ahead.

*Mark Rich*

# ECCO

*Author:* Ronald Sukenick (1932-    )
*Type of plot:* Magical Realism
*Time of plot:* The late twentieth century
*Locale:* Venice, Italy
*First published:* 1990

> *Principal characters:*
> THE NARRATOR, a successful writer
> A YOUNG MAN, a fledgling writer
> A YOUNG WOMAN, his wife

*The Story*

The narrator awakens in Venice, pleased to be there with enough money to do whatever he wants. Happy to be neither a tourist nor a Venetian, he feels invisible. However, his invisibility—the consequence of his profession as a writer—has been exacerbated by recent events: deaths, divorce, and geographical circumstances. He is, in fact, in Venice alone, hoping to recuperate from his losses. His observations of activity in the city (usually made parenthetically) alternate with his narrative about his own activities.

As a water taxi goes by, the narrator goes to a blind shoemaker to collect his shoes. Only after three visits are the shoes finally ready, as the shoemaker has a different sense of time, one that is of another world. The narrator decides that Venice is as concerned with the spiritual as it is with the practical.

One day he wanders into the Hotel Falier (pronounced like "failure" in English). He sees a thin young man with black hair and green eyes trying to collect a refund on his reservation so that he can move to a less expensive youth hostel. Seeing this exchange makes the narrator recall his own first visit to Venice almost thirty years earlier. Arriving by train with an eye injury, he had no money to pay for medical attention. A young New Zealander at the youth hostel lent him the money to see a doctor. When the doctor removed a locomotive cinder from the narrator's eye, he cried, "Ecco!"—which is how the narrator learned the Italian term for "Here it is!"

The next day the narrator visits the Jewish ghetto that was established in the sixteenth century. He again sees the young man from the Hotel Falier and feels inexplicably attracted to him; his presence is somehow evocative. After leaving the synagogue, the narrator suddenly finds himself back inside it. How? It is not that he has lost his way, he thinks, "It's that a certain period of duration has disappeared, unaccounted for, during which you were transported back here in a wink of time, and you are not so much back where you started as back when you started and it occurs to you that the real meaning of labyrinth is time warp."

The next day, he again sees the boy, who is viewing paintings by Tintoretto at the

Scuola San Rocco. Although the narrator is no longer surprised by these chance encounters, his curiosity about the boy so intensifies that he finally speaks to him. However, the boy—or young man, for his age is not clear—looks through him so absolutely that the narrator wonders if he himself is visible, or if the young man is staring
into another spiritual dimension. Venice is, after all, a spiritual city and a timeless one
whose waters offer a reflecting pool in which travelers may reflect.

When he sees the boy again a few days later, this time the boy is with a young bru-
nette woman. The next day he meets the woman and learns that she is an artist and the
young man, her husband, is an unpublished writer. It is her first visit to Venice; her
husband was here once before, but he then had some kind of eye trouble that kept him
from seeing everything that he wanted to see. The narrator mentions that he paid his
second visit to Venice with his former wife. He turns to speak to the young woman but
finds that she has disappeared in a wink of time.

Later at a café, the narrator sees a lively senior citizen whom he wistfully envisions
as his future self. He also remembers having been in just such a café with his young
wife in happier times, when he saw himself as a successful writer twenty years in the
future. Remembering who one was going to be helps one to remember who one is.

In the narrator's last encounter with the young man and his wife, he overhears them
celebrating the publication of his first story. The title of the story is the same as one of
the narrator's own stories. The young man is also telling his wife about his first visit to
Venice, when he had a locomotive cinder removed from his eye. Disturbed by these
coincidences, the narrator tries to speak to the couple but realizes that they cannot
hear him. He approaches their table, desperately trying to communicate. The young
man suddenly stares into space, paling as if he sees a phantom. He looks the narrator
in the eyes, dropping his glass in fright. When his wife asks what has happened, he replies, "I just dreamed I saw myself twenty years from now." The narrator now understands his own invisibility as the young man miraculously disappears into passing
time.

*Themes and Meanings*

The central metaphor in Ronald Sukenick's story is the labyrinth, which is explicitly mentioned several times and is metaphorically traced in the narrative. The narrator wanders within the physical labyrinth of Venice's streets and canals, even losing
his way once. He also describes Venice as a timeless, spiritual city, a city whose many
religious works of art, of transfigurations and ascensions, "signify expanding contact
with the other world so aptly signified by Venice."

The lives of the narrator and the young man seem remarkably parallel—an other-
worldly coincidence. In fact, the middle-aged writer-narrator walks the streets of Venice, turning the corner to see the earlier version of himself, the young, unpublished or
newly published writer. Events from the present blend with events from the past and
his two previous visits to Venice. The young man's experiences are in fact the narrator's memories. The apparent confusion of times, persons, and places gradually clari-
fies as the narrator comes to understand the labyrinth of time. After being invisible to

the young man through most of the narrative, he becomes visible and then the young man becomes invisible to him. The two characters approach a fusion of worlds and times, but the various times—for the narrator the present and the past, for the young man the present and the future—cannot coexist simultaneously. Consequently, the one who is aware of the other becomes invisible. Ecco! Here it is. An echo in time, an echo of time, gradually fading.

## Style and Technique

"Ecco" exemplifies many of the techniques for which Sukenick is known—self-reflexiveness, improvisation, protean characters, a disjointed narrative, and an auto-biographical touch. Although "Ecco" has no characters named Ronald, its narrator is—like Sukenick himself—a divorced middle-aged writer who has visited Venice several times.

Self-reflexiveness—having a text comment on its own making or otherwise making readers aware of its construction as a literary artifact—manifests itself in several ways. First, parenthetical observations are constantly in the foreground of the physical scenes that the narrator observes, contrasting his own thoughts with the activities that he sees. When he thinks of Venice, for example, "a city so full of thereness your presence isn't necessary," he sees a houseful of furniture floating by on a boat. Such descriptions seem improvised, written as the narrator glances out the window, and break the expected narrative flow. Second, the narrator routinely analyzes his own activity, his own thoughts and reactions, directing the narrative to himself: "You recall yourself . . . you decide . . . you're walking . . . you see . . . you wonder . . . you are content." The insistent use of present tense also calls attention to a text in the process of being constructed, of coming into being as the reader reads.

Although the characters in "Ecco" are less complex—and thus more easily identified—than those in much of Sukenick's work, there is nonetheless a sense of changeableness, of flux, of uncertainty about them that seems almost disturbing, owing at least in part to the apparent lack of traditional linear narrative. However, despite parenthetical interruptions and shifts in time from a present being lived by his past self who glimpses his future self, and a present being lived by his present self, who has glimpses of his younger self, a chronological narrative gradually emerges, constructed by the reader's attempts to understand a seemingly confusing text. Sukenick has said that "experience is not prefab. It is immediate, metamorphic, and unpredictable." His aim is not to produce "literature," which packages and fixes experience, but rather to produce writing. Writing "is not different from experience, it is more experience." With "Ecco" Sukenick once again achieves his aim.

*Linda Ledford-Miller*

# EDIE
## A Life

*Author:* Harriet Doerr (1910-2002)
*Type of plot:* Domestic realism
*Time of plot:* 1919-1948
*Locale:* California
*First published:* 1987

> *Principal characters:*
> EDITH "EDIE" FISK, the protagonist, an English nanny
> THOMAS RANSOM, her employer and the father of the children whom she tends
> JAMES,
> ELIZA,
> JENNY, and
> THE TWINS, Ransom's children

### The Story

In April, 1919, Edith Fisk leaves England for California in order to care for the five young children of Thomas Ransom, a lawyer, whose wife died during the birth of twins. Since Mrs. Ransom's passing, no relative or servant has been able to care for the children properly. Edie changes all that. On her arrival in the family, she serves the children tea and speaks to them in an adult manner. Within weeks, their behavior begins to improve as she stops every tear and bandages every cut. She posts the children's drawings in her own room along with the pictures of her two former charges—Lady Alice and Lady Anne, prim and proper little English girls. The children come to trust Edie and depend on her.

This relationship develops just before the children's father marries a series of three different women. The first, nineteen-year-old Trish, has little to do with anyone in the house but her husband, except for Saturday afternoons when she, Edie, and the three oldest children go to the movies and immerse themselves in fantasy. Trish leaves after two years, during which the children grow and flourish.

Childhood diseases pass uneventfully and each child begins to develop an individual direction. James leans toward mechanical experiments, Eliza buries herself in books, Jenny escapes in romantic daydreams, and the twins entertain each other. Meanwhile, Edie occasionally reveals something about her own past, but the children fit everything relating to England into their own romantic picture of Lady Alice and Lady Anne.

Two years later, Ransom marries Irene, an exotic woman who fills the house with friends who discuss trendy philosophies, and she redecorates the house to fit her foreign tastes. Once she takes Edie and the children to a fortune-teller, who predicts the usual fame, fortune, and good luck.

By the time that Ransom's next wife, Cissy, comes along, the older children are teenagers. Cissy, an Englishwoman, glories in the California climate and lies in the sun until she blisters. However, as the seasons become drier and she confronts American holidays, her gaze turns eastward. It is clear to the children that she is miserably out of her element, so she too departs. The children discuss her with Edie as they have done with her two predecessors. Edie classifies all the various husbands and wives involved in such remarriages as "poor souls."

After having survived all these childhood traumas and events, the children grow up, appearing none the worse for not having a mother. Edie remains in the house until the twins leave for college. By then, the two girls are married and James has married, divorced, and remarried. Only occasionally does anyone visit. In 1938, when all the children are gone, Edie goes to Ransom, who sits in his study below a portrait of his first young wife. She tells him that because she has no one left in England, she wishes to stay in California. He grants her a pension and a small cottage in which to live for the rest of her life.

Retired to her cottage near the sea, Edie fills it with children's paintings and pictures of Lady Alice and Lady Anne. Each Ransom child visits her just once. Letters come less and less frequently. During the first autumn after her retirement, she returns to the Ransom house to dispose of the belongings of the twins, who have been killed in a bombing mission over Europe. She and Ransom speak only two words: "Lovely day."

If the children had written to Edie, James would have told her that instead of becoming an inventor, he is a junior partner in his father's firm. Eliza would have told about living with her archaeologist husband in the damp jungle of Mexico where she looked north and remembered first tasting tea. Jenny would have told about her marriage to a thin pale English student whose accent she adored. She has spent her days making tea in their Massachusetts kitchen.

In the spring of 1948, Ransom assembles his children to tell them that Edie is dying. One at a time, they enter her hospital room to visit. Perhaps she does not recognize them. After their separate visits, they meet outside and recall Lady Alice and Lady Anne, imagining these girls, seven and eight years old, writing "I am sorry" over and over again, then signing their two names. In the midst of this, Edie dies.

### Themes and Meanings

In just fifteen short scenes, Harriet Doerr's "Edie: A Life" covers twenty-nine years in the lives of Edie and the Ransoms. Edie establishes the tone in the very first scene when she arrives in the Ransom house and serves the children English tea. When James says that their mother has died, Edie merely nods with English formality and changes the topic. Gradually everyone reacts this way, becoming more and more isolated. No one talks about why things happen or how they feel about them. By the end of the story there is a total lack of communication.

This may be attributable to Edie's exaggerated English reserve, which contrasts with the greater openness of Americans. At the beginning of the story the children are so outgoing that they even tease Edie. However, they clearly need her care and are eager to please her. Her goal is a smoothly running household with properly behaved children, so they act accordingly. On the surface things are calm—with no more fighting, teasing, untidy hair, or untied shoes. There are no outward signs that the children are motherless. At the same time, however, the children are withdrawing: James to his headphones, Eliza to her books, Jenny to her dream world, and the twins to each other. Their father, relieved that all is calm, focuses his attention on his next three wives.

During the chaotic period when stepmothers are in residence, the children need Edie's constancy. In creating an orderly routine, however, Edie sets a pattern of noncommunication that influences the children's entire lives. Both of James's marriages fail, Eliza takes refuge from the world with her husband in an isolated Mexican jungle, and Jenny retreats to an imitation English cottage in a Massachusetts town. The twins die together in Europe. After three attempts to re-create the past, their father sits in his study below a picture of his first wife. Unable to communicate, all these characters are unable to carry on normally with their lives.

Edie also lives in the past. When she retires to the cottage, she hangs pictures of Lady Alice and Lady Anne on the wall along with the Ransom children's drawings. It is little wonder that they do not write to her or visit her, as they no longer need her to tie their shoes, give them aspirin, or settle their arguments. Because they have never talked about their feelings, there is nothing they can discuss.

When their father tells the surviving children that Edie is dying, they visit her. Afterward, however, they retreat into fantasizing how her two English girls would react. They have never dealt fully with the death of their own mother, so their pattern of not dealing with emotions continues. It is ironic, therefore, that Edie's description of people who repeatedly remarry as "poor souls" describes them all.

*Style and Technique*

The fifteen vignettes that make up the story are written in a cool, unsentimental, controlled style. On the surface, events seem casual and leisurely. Underneath them, however, are powerful tensions that build as the story moves toward its ending. To maintain this tension, Harriet Doerr carefully chooses just what information to disclose. Edie's cool exterior, for example, hides much repressed emotion. Glimpses of her past reveal that two brothers died and that a love was lost to "a girl with red curly hair."

When the Ransom children press for more information about this girl, Edie says only that she worked at a pub. She proceeds to describe the pub, allowing the children to visualize it as the American stereotype of an English pub. Her cool, clear, factual language masks the emotion behind what happened to the romance. Nevertheless, the tension created by this unresolved conflict remains.

As the story progresses, more and more lies beneath the controlled dialogue. When Ransom recalls Edie to the house to sort through the twins' clothes and toys after they die in the war, all they can say to each other is "Lovely day." It is a tense moment because all feelings that surround two lifetimes of death and loss are near the surface. If they were to say more, the surface calmness and their lives would shatter.

It is appropriate that in the final scene in the hospital, Doerr describes Edie impersonally: "She had started to be a skeleton. Her skull was pulling her eyes in." At this moment, with a lifetime of unspoken feelings, there is almost nothing to say. Doerr's dialogue reveals that the children even lack the words themselves and must put them in the mouths of prim and proper Lady Alice and Lady Anne. Their "I am sorry" ironically reveals more than any of them can express. The tension created by Doerr's technique leaves the reader with a chillingly cold feeling of isolation and loneliness, enhancing the theme of the story.

*Louise M. Stone*

# EDITHA

*Author:* William Dean Howells (1837-1920)
*Type of plot:* Social realism
*Time of plot:* 1898
*Locale:* Balcom's Works, New York
*First published:* 1905

> *Principal characters:*
> EDITHA BALCOM, a pretty young woman, eager for war but
>     ignorant of its consequences
> GEORGE GEARSON, her fiancé, who opposes war
> MRS. GEARSON, George's widowed mother

## The Story

An impressionable young woman, Editha bases her sentimental views about war on the yellow journalism that she reads in the current newspapers. She insists that her fiancé, George Gearson, a conscientious objector, fight in the Spanish-American War. She is ecstatic that war is being declared and cannot understand his dislike for war and his unwillingness to fight in a war. She believes that a man who wants to win her must do something to deserve her. Now is his chance, because the Spanish-American War has been declared. Editha joyfully repeats jingoistic newspaper phrases to George, but he remains ironic, thoughtful, and rational. When George leaves Editha's presence after war has been declared, Editha's mother says that she hopes that George will not enlist, but Editha hopes that he will. Editha puts her engagement ring and various mementos into a package with a letter to George telling him to keep them until he enlists. She decides to keep the package for a while in case George does the right thing. George returns to the Balcom household that evening with the news that he has led the prowar speakers at the town meeting and will be the captain of the local volunteers.

Editha gives George her letter as he leaves, to show him how serious she is about the war. She tells him that war is in the order of Providence: There are no two sides about war; there is nothing now but their country. George remains silent after Editha's words, musing and pensive. Editha brings him a glass of lemonade and calls the war a sacred war, a war for liberty and humanity. However, she notices a strange thing in men; they seem to feel bound to do what they believe, and not think a thing is finished when they say it, as women do. George muses that he should have been a preacher after all, and he asks Editha to help his widowed mother, who opposes war, if he is killed. Editha writes to Mrs. Gearson, who is not well enough to reply.

Word comes that George is dead, killed in one of the first battles. Editha becomes ill but does not die. She eventually goes with her father to Iowa to see Mrs. Gearson, who surprises her with her cold bitterness and irony. Mrs. Gearson derides Editha's eagerness to send George off to kill other young men and Editha's assumption that George would suffer only some trifling, glamorous wound and return to her in glory. Mrs. Gearson ends by saying she was glad George was killed before he could kill some other mother's son, and she attacks Editha for wearing mourning clothes. Instead of being aware of the reality of war and its consequences, Editha had been swept up by the sentimentality of war and the glamour and escapism of fighting a war in a foreign land.

That summer, a visiting lady painter consoles Editha. She says that the war was good for the country, that Editha's behavior was exemplary, and that Mrs. Gearson's behavior was vulgar. At this final word, Editha's misery falls away and she begins to live once again in the ideal.

## Themes and Meanings

The main subject of "Editha," one of William Dean Howells's most successful and best-known short stories, is war. Howells was very much opposed to war and especially the Spanish-American War, which he considered imperialistic. He shows his dislike in his portrayal of Editha, a thoughtless, selfish young woman, idealistic but ignorant of the consequences of war.

"Editha," which questions what constitutes a justifiable war, is a tale whose brevity belies its weight. The story impales Editha, who embodies all the nonsense about the heroic romanticism of war and whose false sense of values drives her unfortunate fiancé to a premature death in a questionable war.

Egotism and ignorance like Editha's leads to the suffering of many people. Her fixation of belief about the correctness, indeed the necessity, of war impels her pacifist fiancé to act against his beliefs and convictions about the supremacy of world peace and engage in what he fears and detests most, battling and possibly even killing other human beings. George had said it was not this war alone, although this war seemed peculiarly wanton and needless. Every war was so stupid that it made him feel sick. His total love for Editha, however, leads him to act against his principles. When he goes to the town meeting the day war is declared, he intends to sprinkle cold water on the enthusiasm of the young men who are of the age to be soldiers. In the confusion and drinking of toasts, people call his name, the men adore him, and, after everyone has volunteered, they elect him their captain.

Both of the central men in the story, George and Editha's father, agree that the Spanish-American War will not amount to much in terms of the length of the war and the loss of lives in battle. They are both mistaken, however, in assuming the war will be a "walkover" because George himself dies in one of the first skirmishes. Those who took the war lightly were proven wrong.

## Style and Technique

Howells was capable of strong artistry and irony, as one sees in this bitter short story. In the United States, at the end of the nineteenth century, there was a revival of interest in the historical romance, which overwhelmed the realistic movement. People had tired of the commonplace and photographic in literature. They wanted imagination, and the general reading public was interested in swashbucklers and their swords. Howells complained that these historical romances, with their taste for strange lands, adventure, and sentiment, were poverty-stricken in ideas. Howells theorized that this return of interest in the "romanticistic," in the sentimentalism that took the form of the historical romance, represented an unconscious revulsion from the shameless imperialism of the Spanish-American War, an effort to get away from the facts of the odious present.

Howells wrote "Editha" in an effort to explode the sentimentalism that led to an interest in the historical romance. Editha blindly and ignorantly believes in the heroic romanticism of war and is totally oblivious to the real consequences of battle. At this time in history, there was a shift in focus from individualism to natural and social forces that seemed to enslave humanity. Émile Zola epitomized this naturalism. Despite the fact that authors were writing about natural and social forces in the hope that people would improve and reform society, by the turn of the twentieth century, people were buying superficial and shallow novels by the millions. By 1900, the historical romance not only had captured the general reading public but also, critics asserted, had reduced the level of culture in the United States. Through his ironic indictment of Editha, Howells criticizes the sentimentality of the day, which counteracted the realism in which he believed.

*Linda Silverstein Gordon*

# EDWARD AND GOD

*Author:* Milan Kundera (1929-     )
*Type of plot:* Farce
*Time of plot:* 1958-1960, with reference to events "a number of years" later
*Locale:* A small Czech town
*First published:* "Edward a Bůh," 1969 (English translation, 1974)

> *Principal characters:*
> EDWARD, the protagonist, a young schoolteacher
> HIS OLDER BROTHER, a farmer
> ALICE, a devout young woman whom Edward pursues
> MISS CHEHACHKOVA, the directress of Edward's school

## The Story

Edward, a recent graduate of a teachers college, is visiting his amiable farmer brother. Although now happily settled into his new existence, Edward's brother was once expelled from Edward's college for laughing at a fellow student's exaggerated grief over Joseph Stalin's death. That student, who later denounced Edward's brother to the authorities, is now the director of a school in a small town. Edward's brother advises him that because "she was always after young boys," Edward should apply to her for a position. Edward calls on Miss Chehachkova, the director, whose very "ugliness" puts him at ease, and soon he is teaching at her school.

Though indifferent to his teaching duties, Edward is soon pursuing the beautiful young Alice in the town. Alice, however, is reserved, and one day asks Edward if he believes in God. Unwilling to admit that he does not, Edward says that he does believe but is "bothered by doubts." Edward attends church with Alice, but as he is leaving he is seen by the director. He later excuses his behavior to the director by claiming an interest in "the baroque interior of the cathedral." During the following weeks, Edward pursues Alice but is frustrated by her sexual puritanism. For tactical reasons, he begins to read the Bible, study theology, and "exaggerate his religiousness."

At school, Edward is soon called in for "a friendly and unofficial talk" with a panel that includes the director. Deciding that the momentum of events makes it impossible to tell the truth, Edward untruthfully says that he does believe in God, although quite unwillingly. The director, disarmed, praises him for his apparent honesty, and says that she personally will oversee Edward's future intellectual development. Visiting her apartment on a required visit, Edward finds the director well disposed toward him, but he also has an uncomfortable vision of the sadness and intense loneliness of her life. They exchange expressions of regard, and before he leaves, Edward even says, untruthfully, that he finds her "pretty."

Confident that he is now safe from official displeasure, Edward attends church again with Alice. She seems "somehow different" and proud to be seen with him.

Eventually he realizes that a distorted report of events at his hearing has turned him into a sympathetic public figure. Although he realizes that Alice's new feelings toward him are "an undeserved gift," Edward makes arrangements for them to spend the weekend at his brother's cottage in the country.

Edward later visits the director, as required. She has cognac set out for him, and as the conversation gradually turns personal, Edward realizes that he is in a changed and "irreversible" situation. It becomes obvious that the director expects advances from Edward that he fears his physical aversion to her will make impossible. Eventually, seizing on a sudden inspiration, Edward springs away from her, saying that he is afraid of "sin." The director persists, until Edward, in desperation, imperiously orders her to kneel, clasp her hands, and pray. Momentarily swayed, the director obeys. This unexpected reversal enables Edward to regain his confidence and overcome his physical antipathy. He succeeds in making love to the director.

That Saturday, Edward takes Alice to the country and finds that her puritanism has disappeared, along with her religious scruples. Despite Alice's beauty, Edward is obscurely irritated by this, and he begins to see Alice in a new and unflattering way. He also has a disagreement with his brother, who has learned something about Edward's recent life. His brother attacks dissembling, but Edward argues that in a world of madmen, one can hardly afford to tell the truth.

As the lovers return to town, Edward is overcome with a wave of anger and disgust at Alice, at the "shadowy people" he has struggled to accommodate, and at himself. He picks an ugly fight with Alice, whom he cruelly charges with "sin" and a betrayal of her religious principles. He is soon able to precipitate a break.

This "curious anger" passes, but Edward does not seek a reconciliation. He continues to visit the director, while beginning to pursue other women. These activities cause Edward to appreciate the "solitary walks" that he has begun to take, which often end at the church. The narrator warns the reader not to be "apprehensive"—Edward is not beginning to believe in God. Nevertheless, as the years pass, Edward begins to long for the "essential" that he has never found in his "unessential" work, love affairs, and thought. At the moment the narrator chooses to take leave of him, Edward is in church, sunk as usual into a deep sorrow over the nonexistence of God. Suddenly, from that sorrow there "emerges the genuine living face of God." Edward breaks into a happy smile.

## Themes and Meanings

Milan Kundera is explicit about the nature of the "God" of his title, and about the difference between his nature and Edward's merely human one. "God," as the narrator remarks in a difficult but significant passage, "is essence itself. . . . God alone is relieved of the distracting obligation of appearing and can merely be. For he solely constitutes (He Himself, alone and nonexistent) the essential opposite of this unessential (but so much more existent) world."

Kundera's language here derives from the "basic theological literature" of Edward's studies. Within orthodox Catholic theology, God's "existence" (the fact of his life) and his "essence" (the defining qualities that make him what he is) are the same thing. God, in other words, is not troubled by the perplexing gap that opens up for Edward between the seemingly arbitrary facts of his actual existence and an "essential" Edward begins to seek for, but in vain. Because, as the narrator's language insists, the God of this story is "nonexistent." Unpleasant though he may be in many ways, Edward preserves a certain integrity by refusing to set up for himself some false "essential," as do other characters in the story (consider Alice's brittle religiosity or the directress's rather wooden invocations of "the future").

Within the story, it is true, Edward's "straightforward" brother seems to suggest the possibility of a mode of life that is neither tormented nor dishonest. Unlike Alice or the director, he does not appear to deceive himself; unlike Edward, he does not deceive others. Unlike anyone else in the story, he appears to be genuinely happy.

Nevertheless, in his debate with Edward, it is Edward's criticisms of merely human "truth" that are allowed to stand as the last word. The story's ambiguous ending seems to suggest that, for Kundera, Edward's irresolvable, faintly comic dilemma over God is itself the "essence" or defining quality of the human.

### Style and Technique

Irony, in the broadest sense of that term, refers to any perception of the difference between the way things are and the way things seem. In "Edward and God," the plot turns on the real consequences of a pretended belief, and the story's theme on Edward's real longing for a God he considers unreal.

However, Kundera's narrative technique also depends on a use of dramatic irony: the contrast between his narrator's insight into motives and events, and Edward's own painful if sometimes inspired blundering. Thus, the narrator's description of how Edward sees his teaching duties as being "among the fortuitous aspects of his life," something "attached to him like a false beard," foreshadows Edward's own later dissatisfaction with the "unessential." Similarly, Alice is first introduced into the story with language that looks ahead to Edward's own later disillusionment with her: "In his new place of work Edward soon found a young girl who struck him as beautiful, and he began to pursue her with a seriousness that was almost genuine."

Far more clearly than Edward as the reader first encounters him, the narrator can see through the behavior of the story's characters to its actual sources. For example, the narrator realizes that the extreme and opposing attitudes toward religion taken up by Alice and the director have a common psychological source, the desire to align with one's own side against the enemy and so preserve the sense of one's own superiority. In the course of the story, however, Edward's insight into his own motives improves. During his final fight with Alice, for example, he realizes that his disgust is partly with himself, and that "even the shadow that mocks remains a shadow. . . nothing more." Edward, in other words, seems on his way to being able to write a story like "Edward and God."

*S. Badrich*

# THE EGG

*Author:* Sherwood Anderson (1876-1941)
*Type of plot:* Regional
*Time of plot:* The beginning of the twentieth century
*Locale:* A small town in Ohio
*First published:* 1921

>*Principal characters:*
>THE NARRATOR, a man relating events from his childhood
>HIS FATHER, a failed entrepreneur
>HIS MOTHER, a loving, ambitious wife
>JOE KANE, a customer in their restaurant

*The Story*

"The Egg" tells the story of a childhood memory that has in a profound way shaped its narrator's moral outlook. The tale centers on the narrator's father, a man "intended by nature to be . . . cheerful [and] kindly," who, through acquiring the "American passion for getting up in the world," loses his happiness. The father's loss engenders in the son a sense of tragedy and irresolution and a conviction that "the egg"—the source and symbol of that loss—completely and utterly triumphs over life.

The narrator begins his story by describing his father's life as a farmhand in the rural Midwest. The older man is content in this position; he enjoys his work and the easy camaraderie of the other farmhands, who gather at a local saloon on Saturday nights. Dissatisfaction does not strike him until, at age thirty-five, he marries. His wife, "a tall silent woman with a long nose and troubled grey eyes," initiates a change in his life. While wanting nothing for herself, she is nevertheless "incurably ambitious" for her husband and for the son born to them—the narrator. At her prompting, the man leaves the farm and, with his new family, moves closer to town to take up chicken raising.

From the chicken farm, the young narrator gains his initial impressions of life. There he sees at first hand the inescapable tragedy of the chicken:

>It is born out of an egg, lives for a few weeks as a tiny fluffy thing such as you will see pictured on Easter cards, then becomes hideously naked, eats quantities of corn and meal bought by the sweat of your father's brow, gets diseases . . . stands looking with stupid eyes at the sun, becomes sick and dies.

The miserable cycle of chickenkind comes to be, for the narrator, a paradigm for human life; the chickens are so much like people that, in his mind, "they mix one up in one's judgments of life." The narrator's primary problem, however, is not with "the hen," the mature bird already locked in its mortal coils, but with "the egg," the source of potential new life.

Against such odds as the narrator describes, chicken raising proves to be a futile struggle. Selling the chicken farm, the family loads a small wagon with their possessions and begins the slow journey to a railroad way station, where they plan to open a restaurant. Along the way, the boy-narrator, noticing his father's balding head, imagines the bare swath of skin as a path going to "a far beautiful place where life was a happy eggless affair." The father, however, carries with him a memento of the chicken days—a collection of "grotesques . . . born out of eggs," alcohol-preserved specimens of two-headed or six-legged chicks hatched over the years on his farm. These he keeps in the simple belief that people like "to look at strange and wonderful things."

After some time in the restaurant trade, the father decides that his lack of success in business derives from his failure to be pleasant enough; he resolves, therefore, to "adopt a cheerful outlook on life." The central event of the story comes of this decision. One night while the father is tending the restaurant, a young man comes in to pass the time. Convinced that this is the moment to put into action his new cheerfulness, the father begins to imagine ways to entertain the customer. His nervousness, however, strikes the young man as odd; the customer believes the proprietor wants him to leave. Before he can do so, the father begins to perform a trick with an egg. When the trick fails to capture the young man's attention, the father brings down from the shelf his collection of pickled grotesques. When this, too, fails to interest the customer, he tries another trick—heating an egg in vinegar so that it can be pushed inside a bottle. He promises to give the customer the egg-in-the-bottle, but again his trick proves difficult. In a final, desperate effort to force the egg into the narrow container, the father breaks the egg and spatters it on his clothes. Already leaving, the customer turns for a moment and laughs.

The father, consumed with anger, fires an egg at the retreating customer. Then, grasping another egg, he runs upstairs to the bedroom where his wife and son are no longer sleeping. The narrator, remembering his thoughts at the moment, imagines that his father "had some idea of destroying it, of destroying all eggs," but instead he lays the egg gently down and drops to his knees, crying. The mother quietly strokes her husband's balding head. The son, troubled by this scene of his father's grief, weeps too. Into the night, the boy ponders the question of the egg—"why eggs had to be and why from the egg came the hen who again laid the egg"—a question that gets into his blood and remains with him unresolved into adulthood.

## Themes and Meanings

Given its title and the narrator's statement that his tale "if correctly told will centre on the egg," the egg is unquestionably crucial to Sherwood Anderson's story. As an image, the egg promotes the possibility for new life, as well as the simultaneous fragility and resilience of that life. For the narrator, however, the egg's special power is to condemn the young possibility, the passionate promise of life, to a relentless round of decay and death. He sees this power of the egg operative in his father, whose "new impulse in life"—to leave the farm and make his fortune in the urban world—is ruined by the egg. Ironically, though, at his moment of crisis, the father preserves rather than destroys the egg. Despite his failure, he values the life in the egg just as he values the "poor little things" that he saves in the jars as a source of wonder.

For the narrator, the egg acquires ever larger significance. "Prenatally" involved not only with his father's fortunes but also with the narrator's own moral disposition, the egg of that night in the bedroom is inextricably linked with the innumerable eggs laid and hatched by his father's chickens. Conjoined with the narrator's ability to think and articulate his thoughts—a talent that his father, as a physical man, lacks—the egg gains the power of generality. It becomes for the narrator the source and symbol of the tragic cycle of life so vividly experienced on the chicken farm, a cycle whose most enduring creations are the pitiful monstrosities preserved by his father. Eventually, the narrator's general view of the egg leads him to the ultimate metaphysical question— the "why" of the egg that implants itself in his mind and leaves him with a feeling of irresolution.

Though the narrator cannot solve logically the question of the egg, he does solve it creatively. The irresolution that the egg engenders in him in fact impels him to attempt, through his tale, to articulate his uncertainty in a form that, like the egg, is in itself whole and complete and pregnant with life. The egg—particularly that one that his father holds in his hand when he enters the bedroom—functions as the fertile ovum from which the boy's imagination prepares for the story that he tells as an adult. Focusing as it does the narrator's memory of his and his father's mutual grief at the failing of life to live up to its early promise, the egg gives birth to the new, narrative act. "The Egg," not the idea of the egg, triumphs.

### Style and Technique

Much of the power of "The Egg" comes from the narrator's ability to articulate the inner life of his father. This difference between father and son becomes indirectly the subject of a passage in which the narrator explains his father's decision to become cheerful:

> It was father's notion that a passion for the company of himself and mother would spring up in the breasts of the younger people of the town of Bidwell. . . . They would troop shouting with joy and laughter into our place. There would be joy and festivity. I do not mean to give the impression that father spoke so elaborately of the matter. He was as I have said an uncommunicative man. "They want some place to go. I tell you they want some place to go," he said over and over. That was as far as he got. My own imagination has filled in the blanks.

The father's repetitive statement reveals in a rough and untutored way his simple urge toward a better life. However, he is not more able to carry out this urge in action than he is able to express it in words. In fact, the urge itself, the ambition to rise in life, leads him out of his natural element—the rural and masculine life of a farmhand—and into the urban, feminine, and civilized town life that requires a greater complexity of mind, speech, and social savvy than he possesses.

   In contrast, the son imagines in detail what his father could only minimally verbalize. This act of imagination joins the father and son, for in order for the narrator to relate his father's inner life he must himself intimately experience that life. However, the imaginative act also advances the son beyond the father. The son, grown into an adult, understands what the father only felt. As a narrator conscious of telling a story to "you," his reader, he achieves the ability to communicate that his father lacked. Furthermore, in seeing his father's suffering, the narrator is led to speculate about the complexity of life. In doing so, he becomes a more complex man, a man who gives life in words to his father's mute yearnings. In style, the narrator is true to his father's inner vision, for his sophistication of mind is rendered in simple diction and sentences, in a voice that his father might have used had he been able to speak his heart.

*S. Elaine Marshall*

# EIGHT VIEWS OF TOKYO

*Author:* Osamu Dazai (Shūji Tsushima, 1909-1948)
*Type of plot:* Psychological
*Time of plot:* 1930-1940
*Locale:* Tokyo
*First published:* "Tokyo hakkei," 1941 (English translation, 1983)

> *Principal characters:*
> A WRITER
> H, a former lover
> MR. S, a former teacher
> T, a young draftee

*The Story*

It is July 3, 1940. The author has stopped at a small impoverished village on the Izu Peninsula looking for an inexpensive place to stay and write. For ten days he recalls the sordid events of the last decade, writing about a life of poverty and debauchery as a young student in Tokyo. He had moved many times to keep ahead of the law and creditors—hence the "eight views," although he actually records more than eight impressions of his past.

His writing retreat gets off to a bad start. The inn is shabby, and the maid insists on a deposit when she learns that he will stay ten days. That night, however, he gets out his worn map of Tokyo. It reminds him of a mulberry leaf eaten by silk worms. Like the worms, people from all over Japan descend on Tokyo, pushing and shoving, each seeking a desperate living, "females calling to males, males just wandering around half-crazed."

The first "view" is a Totsuka boardinghouse, where he rented a room in 1930 and entered the French literature department of Tokyo Imperial University. From the second semester on, however, he stops going to classes to work as a political activist. He also invites to Tokyo a young geisha whom he had met a few years earlier, who is identified in the story as "H." H was under contract as a geisha, and his family is shamed by the scandal. An older brother is sent to Tokyo to clear up the matter. There is a tense family conference. The writer agrees to send her back to the countryside as long as they are permitted to get married eventually. He sleeps with her for the first time the night before she leaves.

H wrote that she had arrived back, and that was all. The writer, in despair because of her lack of commitment, devotes full time to political work without much success. He begins a short and sordid affair with a Ginza bar girl who falls in love with him. In part to get attention from both H and his family—they were appalled at the H affair—he attempts a double suicide with the bar girl by swimming into the sea at Kamakura, but only she succeeds. He is put on probation, and his family is reconciled with the would-be suicide. They buy out H's geisha contract and send her back to Tokyo, where he rents a house in Gotanda, the second "view" of Tokyo. By this time, the author is twenty-three and H is twenty. He is supposed to be continuing his studies, supported by the family, but he seldom attends classes, and does nothing but watch H.

That summer they move to the Kanda area of Tokyo, one known for its bookstores and student hangouts. In the fall they move again, and again in the spring they move to Yodobashi as the writer begins to dabble in haiku. Twice he is held by the police and questioned about political activities. He moves again to avoid the police, to a room over a lumber dealer in Nihonbashi. In this sixth "view," the writer takes on a pseud-onym to cover his trail. Beset by ennui, he occasionally goes to the university, not to his classes but to lie on the lawns.

It is there that he learns that H had slept with another man before joining him in To-kyo. He rushes home to confront her, but she coolly denies the allegations, allaying his suspicions. Later that night, however, he reads Jean-Jacques Rousseau's *Les Confes-sions de J.-J. Rousseau* (1782, 1789; *The Confessions of J.-J. Rousseau*, 1783-1790), and comes to the realization that H had lied. He feels betrayed and leaves in disgust and confusion. Lacking another place to stay, he returns home to her, and they make an uneasy reconciliation. Again they move, to a small gatehouse of a ruined mansion. They survive on money sent from the family, which has all but given up on the twenty-four-year-old profligate son.

The writer begins a lengthy last testament, thinking of suicide once again. It be-comes his first major work, a chronicle of his evil childhood and adolescence. Having set this period down on paper, he finds that he cannot finish, that he needs to bring it up to the present: "I was being consumed by a demon who eternally beckoned. It was like an ant trying to stop an express train."

By now it is 1933, and the writer is theoretically due to graduate, but he cannot. The next two years he lies to his brother to get more money to live as a "student," repeat-edly promising to graduate, and buying time to complete his manuscript. Finally, he finishes and names it *The Final Years*.

The next "view" is a room in a house in Suginami owned by a friend. For two years he continues work on his collection of stories and continues the pretense of going to classes. By this time, he is deceiving even H. He puts on his school uniform about once a week and works on his stories at the school library, returning home in the eve-ning. The burden of this elaborate deception and the increasing impatience of his rela-tives begin to weigh heavily on the writer. He knows they will cut off his meager al-lowance if he tells them that he is finishing his last testament.

They move yet again when their friend changes houses to be near his work. Ne-glecting his health and drinking, the writer finally chooses his best fourteen stories and burns the rest. He settles his affairs and adds two letters to his completed manu-script. He pretends to H that he is busy with graduation preparations, but he knows that he will fail his final exams at the university. It is 1935 and time to end the decep-tion and die.

Because he could not drown himself five years earlier, the writer tries to hang himself in the hills of Kamakura, but once again he is a failure, returning home with a red and swollen neck. Again his family rallies around him. Ironically, a few days later he nearly dies of appendicitis. He has a long and difficult recovery requiring lengthy hospitalization. H takes up residency in the small private hospital with him; three months pass. They move to the seacoast of Chiba Prefecture to continue the recuperation, but another danger appears. While in the hospital, the writer becomes addicted to painkilling drugs, and this new vice is expensive. He becomes dirty and a nuisance to editors in Tokyo, whom he asks for money.

He is finally on the edge of recognition, for his friends have placed several of his stories in good magazines while he was in the hospital. Soon all the stories are sold to pay for his drug habit. As he falls deeper and deeper into debt, his acquaintances begin to avoid him. Finally he reaches the bottom and is placed in a mental hospital. H meets him a month later when he is released. Their reunion is tense and full of suspicion. Nevertheless, he immediately begins to write to pay the bills. His earlier stories were well received, and he has requests from two magazines for more stories. After selling them, he spends the money on a month long drunk at Atami. Returning to Tokyo, he is given another shock. H has had an affair with a painter friend of his, and there is no resolution. He and H attempt suicide by poisoning but fail. She finally leaves him to a solitary drunken existence. His family falls on hard times and he begins a gradual transformation. There is no critical incident, no dramatic turning point, but somehow he decides to become a real writer. He works with great intensity, and soon produces a story about his latest failed suicide, which sells immediately.

This success leads him to a yearlong retreat in the mountains, where he completes more short stories and works on a novel. He also makes a conventional arranged marriage through a mentor—the wife is not described—and gradually works his way out of debt. One evening, in their Tokyo house overlooking the Musashino Plain, he hits on the idea of writing about his views of Tokyo.

Two final scenes are added. One is a meeting with a former teacher who had almost given up on him during his deranged period. They visit an art museum where a painting by H's painter is displayed. Both agree that it is no good. The other scene occurs when his sister-in-law's fiance, T, is drafted. His wealthy relatives and employees in their factory all gather at a temple to see him off. When his regiment stops there, T immediately picks out the writer from the back of the crowd. There was a bond between them because the writer has also faced death. As the troops leave, he calls out, "You have nothing more to worry about!" Several days later, the writer sets out for Izu to write, and the story comes full circle.

## Themes and Meanings

Osamu Dazai was a leading member of a group of writers called *burai-ha*, or decadents. He wrote about the underside of urban Japan, his life on the fringes of polite society. Dazai rejected the values of society, devoting himself to drink and other excesses that destroyed his health. His lack of a vision or political philosophy—

although he was interested in communism—led to an intense ennui and periodic depression, and he made his first suicide attempt while still a university student. His flamboyant lifestyle and his troubled search for meaning have appealed to several generations of young Japanese in the way that J. D. Salinger's *The Catcher in the Rye* (1951) has continued to find a readership among young Americans.

"Eight Views of Tokyo" touches on many of Dazai's recurring themes, but the central focus of the story is his vocation: how he became a writer, and the place of writing in his life. The theme of the artist finding his vocation has been treated countless times from countless perspectives; even so, Dazai's version is unusual. For Dazai, quite literally, to keep on living meant to keep on writing. His first stories, he says, were written as a "last will and testament," and it is true that after finishing them he attempted suicide, but as long as he was writing he was deferring death. Later, having recovered from drug addiction and having made for the first time a commitment to a writer's career, he says explicitly that he was "writing in order to live"—and so he did, until his fifth (and finally successful) suicide attempt, in 1948.

It is interesting that Dazai provides no explanation for the decision he made, in the mid-1930's, after several abortive suicide attempts, to go on living; indeed, he makes a point of rejecting "explanations for a man's turning point. . . . Many times," he concludes, "a man simply finds himself walking in a different field before he realizes it."

## Style and Technique

Dazai's criticism of society was often a parody; Donald Keene has compared him to the *gesaku* writers of the Tokugawa period (1600-1868), who wrote comical farces. Although he writes of life on the edge of survival and his feelings of despair, there is an appealing bohemian romanticism in Dazai's writing. As personal as his stories seem, Dazai did not write purely autobiographically. Like most writers, he built on his experiences and adorned them; for example, his collected writings include five versions of his first suicide attempt in 1930. Even a story such as "Eight Views of Tokyo," which appears to be straight autobiography, is a complex weave of fact and invention.

Particularly noteworthy in this story is the handling of chronology. The opening scene shows Dazai in the mountain village where he has gone to write; he worries that he may be unable to write anything, that he will run out of money. The bulk of the story rehearses his past, with the conclusion looping neatly back to the beginning, until the reader realizes that this story is itself the "writing" that Dazai was planning in the opening paragraphs. This technical device conveys very effectively the writer's perception of his own life as "material"—a perception that, in Dazai's case, was unusually strong. Thus, style and theme work together: The method of telling the story reinforces the theme of "writing in order to live."

*Richard Rice*

# THE EIGHTY-YARD RUN

*Author:* Irwin Shaw (1913-1984)
*Type of plot:* Realism
*Time of plot:* 1925-1940
*Locale:* A Midwestern university and New York City
*First published:* 1941

> *Principal characters:*
> CHRISTIAN DARLING, a clothing salesperson and a former athlete
> LOUISE TUCKER DARLING, his wife

*The Story*

The story opens with an arresting, vividly detailed description of an eighty-yard run made from scrimmage by Christian Darling, a football player at a Midwestern university. Immediately after the descriptive passage, the reader learns that Darling made the run during football practice in 1925, fifteen years earlier, and that the episode has been reconstructed in his mind as he stands on the same practice field, the site of his former triumph. Now thirty-five, Darling recalls and retraces his downhill course in life from that moment of triumph and promise.

Christian's fellow players, his coaches, and his girlfriend, Louise Tucker, were impressed and predicted great accomplishments for him. Louise proudly drove him from the field in her convertible and kissed him in such a way that he knew for the first time that she belonged to him. However, the promise of glory at a major university was not fulfilled. A German boy named Diederich came from the third string and proved a better ball carrier than anyone else around, being named to All-American teams. For two years, Christian, a good blocker, cleared the path for his teammate through the big linemen of Michigan, Purdue, and Illinois. Still, he was considered an important man on campus, and an adoring Louise lavished gifts on him.

After graduation, Christian and Louise married and moved to New York City, where Christian became a representative of his father-in-law's company, an ink manufacturing firm. While Christian worked, Louise attended plays and visited art galleries. She acquired a taste for modern painters such as Pablo Picasso, Georges Braque, and Paul Klee, decorating their expensive Manhattan apartment with reproductions of their paintings. Christian preferred paintings of animals to theirs. When the economic crash of 1929 came, Louise's father lost everything, and Christian was left unemployed.

With time on their hands, Louise wanted to continue her cultural activities, but Christian had developed no aesthetic or intellectual interests. He began to seek solace in drinking, leaving Louise to pursue her interests on her own. She found a job with a woman's magazine that paid enough to meet their expenses. The best that Christian could do was to land a few temporary jobs that provided no significant income.

Louise's work brought her into closer contact with writers, intellectuals, and artists. At parties with Louise's friends, Christian felt bored and out of place, whereas she found them exhilarating. Christian did not understand the conversations or the references to obscure poets, composers, philosophers, or leftist politicians. Moments of tenderness between Christian and his wife grew more infrequent. In one poignant scene, he embraced her as she was sitting in the bathtub and asked that she not call him "Baby."

When Christian and Louise received an invitation from a labor leader to a performance of Clifford Odets's *Waiting for Lefty* (1935), Christian preferred to remain home drinking and accepted the reality that his wife would attend plays with others. Still too much in love with her to want a divorce, he lived with her harmoniously but distantly. Finally he received a job offer as a sales representative for a clothing firm. The job required traveling because the major outlets were colleges and universities. Except for holidays, he would be home only once a month. He hoped that Louise would urge him not to accept the offer, but as he expected, she thought that he should take it. Louise now looked on him with "a kind of patient, kindly, remote, boredom."

The narrative returns to the practice field where it began, his alma mater being among the colleges that Christian visits on business. Having reflected on the events of his life over the past fifteen years, he reaches important understandings and realizations. He grasps that he did not practice for the right things. He had no preparation for either the 1929 Depression or the fast-paced and complex life of New York City. He was not prepared for the time when a girl turned into a woman. Tentatively, he perceives that at some point he and Louise were even and that if he had then put all of his effort toward it, he might have kept up with her. He ruefully reflects that while he is standing alone on a practice field in the fading afternoon light, his wife is in another city, having dinner with another and better man, speaking in a different, new language that he does not understand.

Finding himself standing on the same spot where he received the ball before his run, Christian begins to run toward the goal line, making all the cuts and feints, following the same course, of fifteen years earlier. After he crosses the goal line, he sees nearby a young couple who had escaped his notice. They are puzzled by the spectacle of a middle-aged man in a double-breasted suit mimicking a football play. Christian explains awkwardly, "I—once I played here," and leaves for his hotel, sweat breaking out on his face and around his neck.

## Themes and Meanings

Set during the exhilarating 1920's and the depressed 1930's, the story depicts character conflict during rapidly changing times. Louise finds the capacity to adjust and grow when confronted with challenge, whereas Christian, considered an important figure on campus during college, finds himself ill prepared for the world that he confronts beyond the university. The hollowness of his character is exposed when he is no longer propped up by Louise's father. By accepting society on its terms, Louise succeeds in the highly competitive environment of New York City. Because he expects society to adjust to him and rejects all activities that he does not enjoy, Christian fails in his environment. The story presents the classic conflict of one character's outgrowing another.

Further, it challenges the usual acceptance of the value of athletic and business success. Christian comes to recognize that his value system, which placed importance on competitive athletics, is flawed. The German boy Diederich, who received the cheers that Christian had expected, went to a professional team and had his neck broken. Louise's father, who has succeeded as a manufacturer, commits suicide when he has to face failure and bankruptcy. The social criticism offered by the story is, however, muted and detached. The reader is reminded that values are not absolute and that adaptability is essential to success.

In addition, poignantly, sympathetically, the story develops the theme of lost youth. Christian attempts to recapture a moment of triumph, of promise, a time when he felt invulnerable and harbored no thought of death. Except for that moment, his memories of his life are recollections of unfulfilled promises, of lost opportunities, of defeats. He has had to scale down his expectations, and his future seems bleak.

*Style and Technique*

The narrative moves with admirable clarity and economy. It opens with the exquisitely detailed account of Christian's run and immediately shifts to his appearance on the field fifteen years later. The detailed account has been a feat of his memory. The narrative then moves chronologically, essentially from Christian's point of view, ending with his re-creation of the earlier run.

Irwin Shaw's style is marked by vivid, energetic description that relies heavily on verbs, verb forms (largely participles), and absolute constructions (largely nominative absolutes). The technique is reminiscent of the styles of Ernest Hemingway and William Faulkner. The following passage illustrates the technique well: "Darling tucked the ball in, spurted at him, driving hard, hurling himself along, his legs pounding, knees high, all two hundred pounds bunched into controlled attack." In the passage the verbs and verbals bear the weight of meaning and create the impression of movement and energy. The stylistic technique is especially effective when a writer is describing a developing or ongoing action. It permits Shaw to craft lengthy sentences that are carefully controlled and balanced.

*Stanley Archer*

# EISENHEIM THE ILLUSIONIST

*Author:* Steven Millhauser (1943-    )
*Type of plot:* Fantasy
*Time of plot:* The late nineteenth to early twentieth century
*Locale:* Vienna, Austria
*First published:* 1989 as "The Illusionist," 1990 as "Eisenheim the Illusionist"

*Principal characters:*

EISENHEIM, stage name of Eduard Abramowitz, a renowned
   magician
WALTER UHL, police chief of Vienna
ERNEST PASSAUER and
BENEDETTI, rival magicians

## The Story

Despite the fantastic occurrences of its plot, "Eisenheim the Illusionist" is presented in the form of objective nonfiction, as a short biography of a mysterious character.

Little is known of the magician Eisenheim's origins, other than that he is the product of the late Austro-Hungarian Empire and its appetite for stage magic. Son of a gifted cabinetmaker, Eisenheim uses his skill at cabinetmaking in constructing the devices that allow him to achieve his earliest illusions. His appetite for magic can be traced to a meeting with an itinerant magician, and he proves to be a slow developer who nevertheless is capable of prodigious bursts of creativity and talent.

Eisenheim's early feats are disturbing variations on more traditional illusions, many of them involving a reflection or creation of life, such as the Mysterious Orange Tree, and the Phantom Portrait. The next stage of his career, during which he opens his own theater, the Eisenheimhaus (House of Eisenheim), sees more original creations, which reveal more clearly a thread of darkness already implicit in his earlier tricks: the Satanic Crystal and the Book of Demons. A frightening variation of the Pied Piper of Hamelin brings him to the attention of the police in the person of Walter Uhl, who henceforth keeps a close eye on Eisenheim.

The increasingly unsettling trend in Eisenheim's career is confirmed in his rivalry with Benedetti, a rival magician whose attempts to outdo Eisenheim climax in his vanishing during one of his tricks, never to reappear. A similar fate appears to await another rival, Ernest Passauer; however, to Uhl's and everyone else's consternation and subsequent delight, Passauer turns out to be Eisenheim himself.

For reasons never convincingly explained, Eisenheim retires from performing from near the end of 1899 until the beginning of 1901. During this period, he unsuccessfully courts the daughter of an anti-Semitic landowner and builds the Teufelsfabrik

(Devil's Factory), a building on his property that he uses to store his stage devices and to experiment with new illusions; its name reinforces the darker aspects of Eisenheim's reputation.

On his return to the stage, Eisenheim's act becomes minimalistic. With his only prop a glass table, he conjures objects out of thin air that only he can touch and manipulate. Soon he progresses to materializing human beings, most notably a young boy and girl, Elis and Rosa. Such seemingly transgressive feats and the panic they inspire give Uhl the excuse to arrest Eisenheim and close the theater; however, Uhl's real motivation seems to rest in his fear that Eisenheim's blurring of the lines between reality and illusion threatens the stability of the empire itself. However, when the police try to seize Eisenheim, they can grasp only air. Like Benedetti, Passauer, and (some say) the itinerant magician who initially inspired Eisenheim, the master slowly fades and dissolves himself, his last and greatest feat—or was it only an illusion all along?

*Themes and Meanings*

The surface level of "Eisenheim the Illusionist" is what might be called Uhl's level: to see Eisenheim and his career as metaphors for the collapse and dissolution of the Hapsburg Empire. Uhl fears that Eisenheim's boundary-breaking performances unsettle the public and its support of the stasis of empire. Uhl is not entirely mistaken: Some of Eisenheim's audience, in their longing for the lost unifying personalities of the empire, speculate that one of the images that he summons in the last stage of his career is actually the dead inamorata of the crown prince who killed himself at Mayerling or the spirit of the assassinated Empress Elizabeth. Eisenheim's dismissal as a suitor because of his Jewish ancestry foreshadows the barbarism that a later Austrian anti-Semite would inflict on the territories of the empire.

An extension of this surface view implies the future fissioning of all Europe, with its reliance on a Newtonian worldview and the primacy of realism, in the face of mechanized war, mechanized genocide, the disappearance of belief, and the intimations of a quantum universe. Normal stage magicians rely on sleight of hand, combined with exquisitely constructed mechanical props, which, while imitating a violation of the laws of nature, must nevertheless obey these mechanistic laws to engender their illusions. Eisenheim's eventual dismissal of these props, his abjuring of the customary panoply that accompany such illusions, imply on the surface a bargain with the traditional powers of darkness. Underneath, his seeming mastery of the laws of time and space hint at the fear of another Jewish product of German-speaking Europe, Albert Einstein: that God does indeed play dice with the universe.

On a deeper level, "Eisenheim the Illusionist" is an investigation of one of Steven Millhauser's favorite thematic concerns: a portrait of the artist. Like the title character in Millhauser's "August Eschenburg" (1985), a creator of lifelike automatons, and like Heinrich Graum in "The New Automaton Theater" (1998), whose mentor is named Eisenmann, Eisenheim seems to be interested in producing increasingly lifelike illusions. In an elaboration of one of his first major tricks, the Mysterious Orange Tree, real butterflies appear from it instead of the earlier mechanical ones. In another illusion, the Phantom Portrait, paintings mysteriously appear on a blank canvas and come to life. In an unnamed trick, reflections in a mirror acquire a will of their own. Indeed, many of Eisenheim's magical illusions are said to involve the use of mirrors, a familiar trope concerning the function of art, as seen in Hamlet's adjuration to the traveling players—that art presents "the mirror up to nature"—in William Shakespeare's *Hamlet, Prince of Denmark* (c. 1600-1601). The final episode in Eisenheim's seeming rivalry with Passauer (who is actually himself) recalls another famous portrait of the magician as artist: Shakespeare's Prospero in *The Tempest* (1623). The props on Passauer's stage all gradually disappear, and he is left standing "alone in a vanished world." Similarly, the stage in Eisenheim's final series of illusions is bare, save a starkly modeled table. These recall Prospero's words as he abjures "his rough magic": his world, his helpers have "melted into air, thin air."

The end of Eisenheim's career reveals the ultimate danger and siren song of attempting a perfect replication or reflection of reality. The characters Eisenheim summons, the narrator says, "appeared to emerge from the mind of the magician." However, where else do literary characters ultimately come from but the mind of their creator? The inability of Eisenheim's audience to interact with his characters in any meaningful way leads to Eisenheim's demise, if it can be called that. As Eisenheim disappears, he is said to "unknit the thread of his being." Eisenheim's fate, his ultimate failure, point out the danger of using fantasy, the most powerful aspect of the imagination, in an attempt to recreate nature. Nevertheless, the fact that Eisenheim is physically untouchable before his vanishing implies that he, too, is a product of the imagination, a creature of, in the last words of the story, "the indestructible realm of mystery and dream."

## Style and Technique

The quasi-journalistic, quasi-objective voice that the narrator uses in "Eisenheim the Illusionist" is characteristic of Millhauser's stories, in which, typically, a totally external view of the events is presented. Readers know absolutely nothing of what is going on in Eisenheim's mind. The narrator can only offer rumors and speculation about Eisenheim's thoughts and intentions. This method of narration, combined with the naming of actual historical persons, such as the French magician Jean-Eugène Robert-Houdin, has the simultaneous effect of both anchoring Eisenheim in and removing him from his historical fabric. For example, at the moment of Eisenheim's apotheosis, some witnesses claim to see triumph in his face; others hear a "cry of icy desolation." Could both be true simultaneously, in the sense of a famous quantum-physics thought problem? If they are, how can any of the reported or implicit facts of the narration be substantiated or denied?

Like many stories by Millhauser's literary precursors, such as E. T. A. Hoffmann, Edgar Allan Poe, and Vladimir Nabokov, and like other of Millhauser's artist substitutes, Eisenheim has his double, his mirror image: first Benedetti, then Passauer. However, unlike Millhauser's character Eschenburg, Eisenheim vanquishes his doubles: One vanishes, and one is transformed into Eisenheim himself. Millhauser also allows himself two puns on Passauer's name: The first is when Eisenheim remarks "that Passauer's hour had passed"—a pun not possible in German. The second occurs in the last line of the story, which states that Eisenheim "had passed safely out" of history. These intertextual reverberations echo the other mirrorings and doublings within the story: the characters who emulate and then turn into other characters, the illusions that resemble other magicians' tricks, and the names of illusions that echo story and fable titles, such as the Vanishing Lady, the Blue Room, and the Enchanted House. These correspondences indicate that Eisenheim is not the only one who transgresses boundaries and threatens to break down the barriers between art and life, illusion and reality—which is perhaps the ultimate purpose of the story "Eisenheim the Illusionist."

*William Laskowski*

# THE ELEPHANT

*Author:* Sławomir Mrożek (1930-     )
*Type of plot:* Fable, allegory, satire
*Time of plot:* The 1950's
*Locale:* A provincial town in communist Poland
*First published:* "Słoń," 1957 (English translation, 1962)

> *Principal characters:*
> THE DIRECTOR of the Zoological Gardens
> A PARTY OF SCHOOLCHILDREN

*The Story*

This third-person narrative focuses on the ambitious and self-serving director of the Zoological Gardens in a provincial Polish town. The zoo is substandard in this communist society in which appearances mean everything and in which major inadequacies are overlooked because they would, if articulated, reflect badly on the bureaucracy governing the country.

The zoo's animals are distinctly inferior. The giraffe has a short neck, the badger has no burrow, and the whistlers seldom whistle. The director cares little about the educational function of the zoo, which is often visited by parties of schoolchildren. The facility lacks some of the major animals that zoos should have, most notably an elephant. As Sławomir Mrożek observes, three thousand rabbits are no substitute for "the noble giant."

On July 22, the anniversary of liberation, a letter from Warsaw announces that an elephant has finally been allocated to the zoo. The director, however, seeking to cast himself in a favorable light among his superiors, rejects Warsaw's offer, saying that he can save considerable money by procuring an elephant on his own. After his letter works its way through the bureaucracy, his proposal is accepted.

On receiving this news, the director rushes his plan into operation: He has a fake elephant constructed from heavy rubber. This ersatz animal, painted an elephantine gray, is to be secured behind a railing far from visitors to the zoo. The descriptive material posted on the railing outside the elephant habitat explains that the elephant is a sluggish animal and that this elephant is particularly sluggish. The director then sets two zoo attendants to work secretly in the deep of night, blowing up the huge mass of rubber that, when fully inflated, will be indistinguishable at a distance from a genuine pachyderm.

The attendants begin their task, but their progress is slow and discouraging. After two hours, the rubber mass has risen only a couple of inches. It looks like a collapsed rubber skin, not an elephant. The attendants work under considerable pressure because the director wants the elephant in place immediately, thereby qualifying him for a bonus. The discouraged attendants notice a gas pipe that ends in a valve. They quickly connect the rubber skin to the valve, and gas passes into the cumbersome body that within a few minutes clearly becomes an elephant.

The following morning, the elephant is secured in an area in front of a large rock beside the monkey cage. A descriptive poster declares that it is particularly sluggish and that it hardly moves. Everything is now in place for visitors. The first group to arrive consists of schoolchildren, whose teacher identifies elephants as herbivorous animals related to the mammoth. The teacher explains that elephants, weighing between nine thousand and thirteen thousand pounds, are the largest land animals, outweighed in the animal kingdom only by the whale, which is not a land creature.

The children are transfixed at the sight of this huge animal, bigger than any living thing that they have ever seen. As they stand in awe watching the elephant, a gentle breeze agitates the branches of nearby trees. Just as the teacher is expounding on the elephant's weight, the breeze engulfs the noble beast. It shudders, then rises into the air. It quivers above the ground, but suddenly a hearty gust blows beneath it, causing it to rise precipitously into the sky, rising, ever rising, until it disappears beyond the treetops, as the astonished monkeys in the adjoining cage stare unbelievingly into space. The carcass finally lands in the adjacent botanical gardens, settling on a cactus that punctures its skin.

The schoolchildren who witness this bizarre incident soon begin to neglect their studies, indeed turning into hooligans. They begin to drink liquor and to break windows, no longer believing in elephants.

*Themes and Meanings*

"The Elephant" is a fable written when Poland was under the authoritarian rule of the Communist Party. Those who wished to criticize the oppressive government risked imprisonment and deportation if they spoke directly against the ills they perceived in their society. The only outlet for their social commentary was through art— in Mrożek's case, writing. Writing this story was a very courageous act because its political satire was direct. One cannot read the story without realizing that it has a meaning far beyond the humorous account of how a gas-filled elephant is buffeted by the winds and blown away from the zoo.

The director of the Zoological Gardens is a typical petty bureaucrat who places his own advancement above the needs of the people he supposedly serves. Quite without shame, he uses deception to achieve personal ends. He also draws into this deception two hapless subordinates who are powerless to resist his orders to work in secret during the night, blowing up the rubber carcass he needs to carry out his deception. The attendants are old and not used to the work they have been assigned.

As they labor away, trying to do their jobs, they become exhausted. Then they find the means of fulfilling their assignment expeditiously and satisfactorily. The elephant that emerges when the rubber skin is filled with gas is wonderfully lifelike and reasonably convincing if one does not examine it too closely. It is not unlike certain political philosophies, in this case communism, that seem quite tenable until one begins to consider them in depth and to realize all their implications, as well as all of the ramifications of having them carried out in any authentic way by legions of petty bureaucrats scrambling to gain power.

In the long run, the actions of such bureaucrats lead to their own undoing. The director had the cooperation of his two attendants in carrying out the deceptive plan he had hatched. In the end, however, quite without evil intent on their parts, they unwittingly revealed to the public a deception gone awry.

It is telling that Mrożek ends the story by having the schoolchildren who witnessed this hilarious event turn into hooligans who neglect their studies, turn to drink, and break windows. The author here is commenting on the pernicious effects that political deception can have on upcoming generations. Even though the director's deception is unmasked through the fortuitous intervention of a gentle breeze, the schoolchildren are forever affected by the disillusionment that the deception engenders within them. Within the sociopolitical context in which this story was written, these children represent the upcoming generation in communist Poland.

*Style and Technique*

In "The Elephant," Mrożek establishes himself as a master of literary satire. His entire story is a metaphor that represents the sociopolitical situation in Poland during the 1950's. To achieve his end, he writes an overtly humorous account of an absurd occurrence. Readers are not expected to believe that such an event actually did or could take place. Nevertheless, once readers have overcome their incredulity, they quickly become aware that, like Jonathan Swift's *A Modest Proposal* (1729), "The Elephant" is about something much deeper than a fabricated pachyderm moored to the ground before a rock beside a monkey cage in a provincial zoo.

In his third-person narrative, Mrożek is writing a story of ideas. His tale is short—about three pages. He spends little time developing any of his characters, the most fully developed of which is the director, but even he is merely sketched in as a political type rather than as a rounded person. The two attendants are just that: two elderly men doing the job to which they are assigned. Readers learn nothing about them aside from that they are old and tired. The bureaucrats with whom the director corresponds in Warsaw are called soulless; they are clearly faceless in this story, paper-shuffling types who deal impersonally with those doing business with them.

The basic absurdity of this story reflects a marvelous wit. The writing is consistently visual. Readers can visualize the barely inflated elephant skin. They see it rise rapidly as gas is funneled into it. They are given a clear vision of how it looks moored to the ground in front of the rock. They see it quiver tentatively when the gentle breeze lifts it from the ground, and they witness how it floats off into space, its columnlike legs projecting from its overinflated body.

Finally, Mrożek's ending the story with the disillusioned schoolchildren is vital to its political impact. The image of the great body filled with gas, suggestive of the political system governing Poland in the 1950's, is bold, forthright, and provocative.

*R. Baird Shuman*

# THE ELEPHANT VANISHES

*Author:* Haruki Murakami (1949-　　)
*Type of plot:* Magical Realism
*Time of plot:* The 1990's
*Locale:* Suburb of Tokyo
*First published:* 1991

>*Principal characters:*
>THE NARRATOR, a public-relations man
>A WOMAN, the editor of a woman's magazine

*The Story*

The nameless narrator begins with a long, careful, and reflective examination of the event that inspired the story's title. He then continues in a more active vein, describing his personal encounter with an attractive, seemingly compatible woman at a business event. What transpires during this encounter reveals how deeply the mystery of the elephant's disappearance has affected him.

When the story opens, the narrator is sitting alone in his kitchen, drinking coffee and reading a newspaper. He discovers a news article about the disappearance of the town's elephant, which has escaped.

The narrator has closely followed the story of the elephant for some time and has assembled a scrapbook of news items concerning it. Originally an attraction in a private zoo, the elephant became a ward of the town because its original owner was unable to find the animal a new home when the zoo closed. Because much of the zoo property was to be developed, with condominiums taking the place of animal cages, the mayor decided the town would pay the animal's expenses. These included maintaining the elephant keeper from the zoo, an old man named Noboru Watanabe.

The elephant's disappearance is mysterious. It was shackled with a locked iron cuff chained to a cement anchor and was kept in an elephant house made from the former school gym. On the morning of its disappearance, the cuff was found empty but still locked, and the key remained securely locked up elsewhere. No footprints showing the path of escape were found outside, even on the hill above the elephant house. Perhaps more mysteriously, the emergency personnel called in to search for the animal turned up no traces of it, despite the town being a well-populated suburb of a major city. The old keeper had likewise disappeared without a trace.

The narrator adds new newspaper clippings about the search to his scrapbook, watches the elephant house and surrounding yard fall into neglect, and dwells on the fact that the elephant's disappearance had little effect on society as a whole.

The narrator works in public relations for a manufacturer of household electrical appliances. At a promotional party thrown to announce the beginning of a new product line, he meets a woman who is the editor of a woman's magazine. Their friendly encounter at the party continues afterward at a cocktail lounge. They find they have things in common and feel a comfortable sense of mutual attraction. Things go well until the narrator brings up the subject of the elephant.

Although he senses his blunder in bringing it up, the narrator feels a need to speak about the strange disappearance and reveals for the first time that he may have been the last person to see the animal and keeper before they vanished. For some time before the disappearance, he had made a practice of climbing the hill above the elephant house in the evening. From this vantage point, he could observe inside the house, and see the elephant and keeper going through their evening routines. He had noticed a distinct affection between the two when they were alone in the house, an affection not revealed at day, in public view. On the last night, he saw something unusual. The proportions seemed to be changing between the elephant and the keeper. The elephant seemed somehow smaller. Then the lights died in the elephant house. He saw nothing else. The next morning, he read about their disappearance.

The revelation of the narrator's preoccupation with the elephant disrupts the incipient warm feelings between him and the magazine editor. He finds, in fact, that after witnessing the strange scene in the elephant house he cannot find personal satisfaction in his life and cannot restore his previous sense that the outer world made sense. Things now seem out of balance. Despite this, in his work with the appliance manufacturer, he is more successful than ever before. He attributes this to his ability to be pragmatic in his business life. His pragmatic outlook seems to make him appear balanced. He even feels that this appearance of balance is what he is selling, even though he completely lacks balance inside.

### Themes and Meanings

In "The Elephant Vanishes," as in many of his other stories, Haruki Murakami explores the impact of extraordinary and even inexplicable happenings on an ordinary life. In this case, the ordinary life is a decidedly lonely one, and one made worse by the story's pivotal event. Within the framework of the story, the narrator spends most of his time alone, engaging in solitary activities. His only direct encounter is with another isolated individual, the magazine editor. He is single and childless, as is she. Although he finds her attractive, which almost makes him reach out to her, he finds himself unable to break out of his deepening isolation.

The old elephant and its keeper, Watanabe, are another pair of childless individuals. The animal was brought from a distant land to live out its last years in a cage, isolated from others of its kind. The old keeper, by choosing to live within the elephant house, makes it plain that he, too, has no family and sees no other place for himself in society.

When the narrator reveals to the magazine editor how he had regularly perched on the dark hill to watch Watanabe and the old elephant being affectionate together, he inadvertently reveals his fascination with the idea that these two individuals, who otherwise appeared lonely and isolated, had found comfort in each other's company. In witnessing their apparent happiness, the narrator found a degree of meaning for his own life. He could look forward to spending evenings on the hill. At other times, in his apartment, he could work on his scrapbook.

The narrator, however, then witnessed the unlikely pair becoming closer to each other, even if only in terms of their relative physical proportions, on the night of their disappearance. When the lights went out, the narrator found himself confounded by unexplained mystery and, later, deeply disturbed at the removal of this source of comfort from his life. The narrator's loneliness also results from his life as a company man. Externally, he appears to have found success, but internally he wishes he could find personal happiness.

*Style and Technique*

Although writers often use first-person narration to draw the reader more directly into the narrative, Murakami uses it in this story to underline the main character's isolation from the outer world. Not only does the main character spend most of the story in solitude, but also he does so anonymously, giving the reader no more than the pronoun "I" when referring to himself. The narrator also leaves anonymous other figures who appear in the story. The woman to whom he is attracted, the mayor of the town, and the people opposing the mayor all go nameless. The sole exception is the elephant keeper. The one person in the story who has found stable companionship and comfort in life, unusual though that companionship and comfort might be, is the sole possessor of a name.

The author uses images of the external world to deepen his portrayal of the narrator's isolation. Especially important are images linking the narrator, age thirty-one, to children. When the elephant was present, the others watching it were primarily children. From the time of the opening of the elephant house, school groups made regular visits to sketch the animal. The elephant house itself had once been the elementary school gym. The elephant's food was even made up of school cafeteria leftovers. In contrast, once the elephant disappears, the narrator continues his lonely vigil on its empty house but now without youthful company.

The elephant itself, often used in folklore as a symbol of long life and wisdom, carries some of its traditional trappings in Murakami's story. More important, it represents a sort of stability in life, a stability that proves elusive to the narrator, more so once the elephant disappears.

In addition to images, Murakami resorts to having the narrator directly address his own situation through abstract concepts. In his first conversation with the magazine editor at the promotional party, the narrator speaks of people seeking a sense of unity when equipping their kitchens. Unity is linked to being in balance with the surroundings, he tells her. When he later talks of the elephant and its keeper appearing to change proportions, he speaks of a balance being disturbed. At the end of the story, he invokes unity and balance once again, only this time as elements now permanently removed from his life.

*Mark Rich*

# EMERGENCY

*Author:* Denis Johnson (1949-    )
*Type of plot:* Psychological
*Time of plot:* 1973
*Locale:* Iowa City, Iowa
*First published:* 1991

>       *Principal characters:*
>       THE NARRATOR, an emergency room worker
>       GEORGIE, his friend
>       TERRENCE WEBER, a patient
>       HARDEE, a hitchhiker

*The Story*

Told in the first person, "Emergency" begins when the narrator has a break in his emergency room job at an Iowa City hospital, so he goes searching for his friend Georgie, an emergency room orderly who often steals drugs from the hospital. The narrator finds Georgie in the operating room. Despite having mopped the floor several times, Georgie insists that it is still covered in blood. The narrator, realizing Georgie is already high on one of the drugs that he has filched, asks him to share. He does, and both characters become so high on the mystery drug that they have trouble functioning.

Soon after, a patient named Terrence Weber arrives. He has a hunting knife protruding from his one good eye, and his other eye is glass. When the floor doctor sees this, he panics at the potential difficulty in removing the knife without damaging the eye and causing brain damage. So he orders the narrator to call several specialists while Georgie preps Weber for surgery. When Georgie returns from prepping Weber, he is holding the knife, which he has removed from Weber's eye. Miraculously, the man recovers, and his eye is essentially undamaged.

The next morning, still high on the unknown drug, the two emergency room workers take off in Georgie's orange pickup. On their way home from the county fair, they become lost. Georgie runs over a jackrabbit, and intending to make rabbit stew, he drives back to retrieve the slain animal. As he begins to cut it open with the hunting knife he took from Weber's eye, he discovers that the rabbit was pregnant. In a misguided effort inspired by his drug-induced state, Georgie carries the bloody rabbit fetuses back to the truck in his shirt, thinking that he can keep them alive.

However, Georgie and the narrator are still lost, and when it grows dark, they finally pull over because the headlights are not working. Leaving the truck, they begin wandering in the woods and soon become hopelessly confused. Despite it being only mid-September, an unusual arctic wind has blown in from Canada, and it begins to snow. Georgie and the narrator stumble on what they think is a cemetery but is actually a drive-in theater. A film is running, but there are no cars because the early snowfall had scared them off.

The theater shuts down early because of the lack of customers, and the pair stumble back to the truck, finding it after a great deal of trial and error. Once there, Georgie announces again his desire to save the rabbit fetuses, and the narrator reveals that he has sat on them, and they are therefore a lost cause.

Depressed by the fate of the dead rabbits, the two friends fall asleep in the truck cab. When morning comes, they awaken, find their way back to town, and miraculously arrive at work on time. They meet Terrence Weber leaving the hospital, a totally successful case thanks to Georgie's sudden inspiration to pull out the hunting knife. However, when Terrence shakes Georgie's hand, the drug-rattled orderly does not even recognize the man he healed.

The story ends with a flashback, as the narrator remembers how Georgie had picked up a hitchhiker while they were heading back to town. The hitchhiker, a friend of the narrator's named Hardee, had been drafted into the army and has gone AWOL (away without leave). He declares his need to get to Canada, and Georgie proclaims that he has friends who can get him there. As with Weber and the knife, it is clear to the narrator that Georgie will be able to pull this off.

This is what makes Georgie special—despite his drug-rattled mind, he can still perform wonders. However, it is tragic to consider the incredible potential being wasted through Georgie's unchecked drug urges and the mental deterioration clearly shown through his attempt to save the rabbit fetuses and his inability to remember Weber. Still, when Hardee asks the orderly what his job is, he responds that he saves lives, which is indeed the case.

*Themes and Meanings*

Much of Denis Johnson's fiction deals with the strange and surreal lives of people who live on the fringes of society, and "Emergency" is a clear example of this motif. Johnson included it in a collection of stories about the same unnamed protagonist of "Emergency." The title for the collection, *Jesus' Son* (1992), comes from a line in "Heroin," the Velvet Underground's famous rock song about addiction. The collection was the basis of a 1999 film, *Jesus' Son*, directed by Alison Maclean.

Johnson went through a period of drug and alcohol addiction, and it left him with a stark understanding of its grim realities. Therefore, there is nothing romantic about drug use in "Emergency"; however, Johnson is not judgmental about it either. Instead, he clearly shows its dangers and attractions and depicts the empty cultural wasteland that helps make drugs attractive.

Much of the meaning of "Emergency" centers on the orderly, Georgie. He is in many ways an admirable character. He saves Terrence Weber's life and sight by withdrawing the knife from his eye when the rest of the emergency room staff were panicking. He claims he will help Hardee reach Canada, thereby saving the narrator's friend from prison. We also see his deep sense of compassion when he weeps over the imaginary blood on the floor of the operating room and attempts to save the rabbit fetuses after his truck runs over their mother.

However, Georgie's drug use undercuts his greatness, for these moments of compassion are based on hallucinations and absurd impulses. Also, while he does save Weber, he cannot even remember the man one day after doing so.

The journey the narrator and Georgie take in the pickup exemplifies the emptiness of a drug-filled life. The pair wander around lost and hopeless, experiencing everything from gutting a bloody rabbit, to standing in front of a giant drive-in theater screen, to being lost in the woods as equal phenomena of an unreal universe. The narrator even admits that the events of their night out in the truck are unclear; he thinks it is possible he is mixing together the happenings of several nights and calling it one night's experience. Thus, Johnson portrays a life on drugs as meaningless and uncertain, an observation he amplifies by criticizing a person who is a thinly disguised Timothy Leary, one of the leading spokespeople for the drug counterculture in the 1960's.

However, "Emergency" is not a simple morality story. Johnson does not portray the drug-free characters as exemplary paragons with meaningful lives. The narrator's supervisor, the emergency room nurse, is a cynic who cares only for her job. She pulls pranks on the doctor, makes cracks about Weber's knifed eye, and reacts with sarcasm to the reciting of the Lord's Prayer over the Catholic hospital's loudspeaker system. Also, the emergency room doctor is thoroughly incompetent, and Johnson shows the only two cultural offerings of the Iowa landscape—a county fair and a drive-in—as being utterly banal and void of any redeeming value.

Therefore, "Emergency" is not just a story about the pointlessness of drug use. Instead, Johnson reveals the meaningless absurdity of life in late twentieth century America. As the title suggests, the "emergency" is not just with the drug-deranged main characters, but with society as a whole.

## Style and Technique

In keeping with his unromantic view about drug use and his despairing vision of late twentieth century America, Johnson writes "Emergency" in a terse, unadorned style. Descriptions are coldly precise, even when they concern the mental confusions of someone lost in a drug haze. There are few interpretations of events, and such horrors as a man with a knife in his eye and a bundle of bloody rabbit fetuses pass by the narrator as if he were watching them on the motion picture screen he encounters at the drive-in.

Johnson reinforces this unromantic view of life and of drug addiction by writing "Emergency" in first-person narrative voice, which allows him to take the reader inside the mind of someone on hallucinogenic drugs. The narrator dwells in a world of shifting uncertainties, a manic realm in which blood can evoke giggles and snow tears. The main character of "Emergency" certainly exemplifies the concept of the "unreliable narrator" because he admits he is never sure of what he is experiencing, much like Georgie's illusory belief that blood covers a clean operating room floor, blood he cannot manage to mop up.

Dark humor also pervades "Emergency." When the emergency room nurse asks Weber if he wants them to call the police to report that his wife stabbed him with a knife, he says to do so only if he dies. The narrator describes the Timothy Leary character as having eyes one would purchase at a joke shop, and a bull elk standing in the pristine dawn as stupid. Johnson's humor deprives the world of meaning and transcendence, confirming the absurdity of the United States after the Vietnam War.

Still, a feeling of potential redemption does emerge from "Emergency." When Georgie says his job is to save people, Johnson reveals the hope, albeit a slender one, that his characters, and the United States as well, can rediscover a world of reality and significance.

*John Nizalowski*

# EMPEROR OF THE AIR

*Author:* Ethan Canin (1960-      )
*Type of plot:* Psychological
*Time of plot:* The 1970's to 1980's
*Locale:* A small town in California
*First published:* 1984

*Principal characters:*
THE UNNAMED NARRATOR, a sixty-nine-year-old high school
science teacher
MR. PIKE, his next-door neighbor
KURT, Mr. Pike's son

## The Story

The unnamed narrator announces that he is sixty-nine years old, a high school biology and astronomy teacher, married with no children, and a recent heart attack victim. Vera, his energetic wife, is off on one of her frequent walking trips. Although the narrator and Vera have traveled widely throughout their lives, his failing health has prevented him from any serious strenuous activity. He must keep with him at all times a small vial of nitroglycerine pills in case his chest begins to tighten.

The narrator's next-door neighbor, Mr. Pike, comes to his house to inform him that the giant, 250-year-old elm tree on the narrator's land is infested with insects, a fact that the narrator already knows. Pike insists that the tree must be cut down to protect the three young elm trees that grow in his front yard. A week later, Pike reappears, this time with a chainsaw in hand, arguing that his elms are young and he cannot let them become infested. The narrator replies that his tree is more than two hundred years old.

The narrator calls a man at a tree nursery who tells him that the insects do not necessarily mean that the ancient tree will die or that it is dying, although it could die if it is not strong. There is hope. After several confrontations with Pike, who suggests that they plant another tree in its place, the narrator reminds him that he had lived in this house all of his life, and the tree was ancient when he climbed it as a boy. Later, the narrator meditates on certain experiences in his life that had always deeply moved him: crossing the Mississippi River as a child, listening to Ludwig van Beethoven quartets at a concert and, most of all, looking up at the stars at night.

After a successful attempt to stop the relentless line of insects, the narrator finds himself descending into his youthful memories and the key role that this magnificent elm tree played in his life. He recalls the time when his neighborhood had been threatened by a fire that raged through the town. His father took charge of their neighborhood and helped everyone move out. The young narrator climbed up into the highest part of the elm tree—the most dangerous act of his life—and there gained a visual and spiritual perspective that he had never experienced before: He beheld nature in one of its most sublime moments.

The narrator returns to a problematic present when he discovers that the insects have returned. Pike's renewed threat forces him into taking drastic steps to preserve the tree. He decides to transfer some of the insects from his tree to the three elms in Pike's front yard, reasoning that if his neighbor's trees were infested, they would probably still live, and then Pike would no longer want to chop down his old tree.

The aging high school teacher prepares for a night attack on Pike's domain. He blackens his face with shoe polish, dresses in dark clothes, and begins his dangerous journey. On his way to Pike's yard, he crawls across the bomb shelter that Pike built. Finding the hatch unlocked, he descends into its womblike interior. There he muses over Pike's character and about how fearful he must be in wanting to destroy the ancient elm and in building a bomb shelter.

As the narrator emerges from the shelter, Pike and his son, Kurt, come out of the house and into the beautiful summer night. The narrator sees them both pointing at the sky. Flashbacks of his own father teaching him the mythic names behind the magnificent stellar constellations converge with images of himself as an astronomy teacher giving his suddenly interested students the same information. What he hears, though, stuns him. Pike is telling Kurt about the stars, but he does not know the proper names; he is making up his own mythic version. "These," he said, "these are the Mermaid's Tail, and south you can see the three peaks of Mount Olympus, and then the sword that belongs to the Emperor of the Air." The narrator realizes that Pike has actually described the bright tail of Cygnus and the neck of Pegasus. The narrator then observes father and son go back into the house to watch television. Observing the paternal affection that Pike shows Kurt deeply moves the narrator. "Every so often when they laughed at something on the screen, he moved his hand up and tousled Kurt's hair, and the sight of this suddenly made me feel the way I do on the bridge across the Mississippi River."

That gesture of love restores the narrator's hope, so he decides not to infest Pike's trees with insects. Instead he sits up all night staring into the glorious stellar constellations with awe and gratitude. When the paperboy appears at dawn, the narrator asks him to do something for him. When the curious boy asks what, he asks him to put down his bicycle and look up at the stars.

### Themes and Meanings

The principal theme that unifies all the various elements of this multifaceted story is hope. Ethan Canin clearly announces that theme at the conclusion of the first paragraph: "I now think that hope is the essence of all good men." The word "hope" recurs three other times during the course of the narrative, and always at the most crucial moments. What mystifies the narrator most about the bully, Mr. Pike, is the depth of his cynicism, a condition that demonstrates his utter lack of hope and forces him to live in a permanent state of despair. Pike (whose name derives from the words "pike," an aggressive instrument of attack, and "piker," a petty or stingy person) anticipates that his young elms will be infested and insists on cutting down the ancient tree in the narrator's yard. Pike's vision is so dark that it allows for virtually no hope, and the narrator labels him early in the story as a doomed and hopeless man. When the narrator descends into Pike's bomb shelter, he palpably experiences the cynicism in the very structure of the building. Once he observes the bleak Pike becoming human and showing love for Kurt, the narrator begins to sense that Pike may be human after all. The major threshold experience that the narrator undergoes takes place when he observes Pike teaching Kurt about the heavens and the stellar constellations. Pike does not know the proper names for those magnificent configurations, so he creates his own—an act that overwhelms the narrator and makes him rethink his attitude toward the man. Indeed, the story's title is one of Pike's fabrications in his awkward attempt to reveal to his son the sublime order of the cosmos. The inestimable beauty of the stars pierces even Pike's emotional armor, an accomplishment that restores a sense of hope to the nearly despairing narrator: "How could one not hope here? . . . Miracles . . . Anybody who has seen a cell divide could have invented religion." Seeing Pike teaching his son what the narrator's father taught him, and what the narrator has taught his students all of his professional life, he discovers himself in Pike.

## Style and Technique

The most effective technique that Canin employs in this carefully wrought story is his artful use of flashbacks and symbolism, particularly in regard to the historical significance of the ancient elm tree in the young narrator's childhood. The tree takes on a mythic dimension as the tree of knowledge as it becomes the symbolic agent of revelation for both the youthful and the aging narrator. The tree becomes an instrument for gaining perspective—for learning not only about the world but also, equally important, about himself. The tree also becomes the controlling metaphor for the entire story, in that it ties together all the various branches of the narrative: the narrator's youth, the focus of conflict between Pike and the narrator, and a natural object that transcends the boundaries of time and mortality. It is, in a sense, a modernized version of the mythic Tree of Knowledge in Eden, because it becomes the medium through which the narrator more deeply understands himself, his past, and the possibilities of hope in what he had presumed was an irredeemable world.

*Patrick Meanor*

# THE EMPRESS'S RING

*Author:* Nancy Hale (1908-1988)
*Type of plot:* Fiction of manners
*Time of plot:* 1954
*Locale:* The South
*First published:* 1954

*Principal character:*
THE UNNAMED NARRATOR, a woman reflecting on her childhood

*The Story*

The narrator of this story begins with an admission: "I worry about it still, even to-day, thirty odd years later." The object of her worry is a child's golden ring "set with five little turquoises." It was given to the narrator for her eighth birthday by a family friend of whom she was so fond that she thought of her as her aunt. The ring was special not only because it was purchased especially for the narrator by a favorite relative but also because the ring was said to have belonged to Austria's Empress Elisabeth.

The ring is so beautiful and precious that immediately the little girl's nurse declares that it cannot be worn outside to play. This only makes the child want to defy her nurse: "For nobody—certainly not she—could understand the love I had for that ring, and the absolute impossibility of my ever losing anything so precious."

She does indeed wear the ring out to play in her playhouse. Attaining a playhouse is "a sort of victory" for the narrator as a little girl. She has envied the playhouse of their only neighbors, which was built especially for their little girl Mimi. Mimi's play-house is a miniature cottage complete with shuttered windows, a shingled roof, and a brass knocker that says "Mimi." It is furnished with a miniature table and chairs and real Dresden china made just for children's tea parties.

The narrator, too, must have a playhouse, but her family cannot and will not build one to rival Mimi's, for their farm is no longer a working one. Instead, they clean out an abandoned milk house and move some of her nursery furniture into it.

Although the little girl tries to make it a real playhouse, it cannot match the gran-deur of Mimi's. Her mother gives her some of her old china, but the narrator yearns for "rosebuds" and "china, made for children." As an adult, she realizes that what she had was much nicer, but as a girl, she recalls, she felt that "nothing . . . would take the place of pink rosebuds." This yearning added to the appeal of the ring, which, like the miniature china and furniture for which she longed, was meant for a little girl.

She loses the ring in her sandpile—a sandpile that is as imperfect as her playhouse. The sand has become mixed with dirt, for unlike Mimi's sandpile, it lacks a frame to contain it. The narrator is scolded for losing her ring, but in childish bravado she an-nounces that it is not lost at all; she knows exactly where it is. Although she searches for it many times, eventually she feels "a hollow, painful feeling inside me because I had lost my precious possession." The loss of the ring haunts her, and she periodically digs for the ring in the sandpile and even dreams of finding it.

As the narrator tells the reader at the beginning of the story, thirty years later she is still thinking of her ring. Now an adult, she retains some of her childhood tendency toward envy and dissatisfaction. Mimi's perfection has been replaced by that of other neighbors, the Lambeths; the narrator is certain that they have "silver tumblers" while her glasses are "a sorry collection, the odds and ends of a number of broken sets."

The narrator consoles herself with the thought that although the old place where she grew up as a child has been sold, perhaps the new owners have a little girl who will dig in the sandpile, if it still exists, and will find the empress's ring.

## Themes and Meanings

Coming from a distinguished family of artists, statesmen, and educators, Nancy Hale is well aware of the importance of the past to people. Her forebears extend back through the Beecher dynasty of New England, and a list of her ancestors' acquaintances reads like the table of contents of an American literature anthology. It is no wonder that Hale has said "[T]he fiction-writer uses for material what other people have forgotten—the past, the meaning of the past." The effect of the past on the present is one of the major themes of her work.

In the past are the seeds for future behavior. As a little girl, the narrator believes that her life is inferior to Mimi's; as an adult, she is still comparing herself with others, feeling somehow inadequate—only now it is a new set of neighbors.

Hale has said that the heart of a short story is a crisis—a point at which someone must make a decision. The decision comes for the narrator in that although she may still think of her ring, she knows that she will never find it, but comforts herself with the thought that perhaps another little girl will find it. By reconciling herself to the loss of the ring (and the loss of her childhood), she gives her life a new direction.

## Style and Technique

Because this story re-creates a child's experience, Hale uses short, straightforward sentences and simple words: "I had to have a playhouse. I wept." Part of the immediacy and appeal of this story is that any reader can identify with the first-person, unidentified narrator. As children, most readers knew a little boy or girl whose playthings they coveted.

As an artist and a writer about artists, Hale is distinguished by a careful eye for detail. She can sketch a character in the swift strokes of a portrait artist. Hale is often compared to Edith Wharton in her use of specifics to convey a segment of society.

Hale has said a short story is "an impenetrably integrated whole." Like the ring in the title, this story is circular, linking the past with the present. The story closes with the hope that "one of the new owner's children will one day really find my ring, for it is there somewhere." The past can and does encircle the present.

*Resa Willis*

# THE ENCHANTED DOLL

*Author:* Paul Gallico (1897-1976)
*Type of plot:* Realism
*Time of plot:* The late 1940's and the early 1950's
*Locale:* New York City's Lower East Side
*First published:* 1952

*Principal characters:*
> DR. SAMUEL AMONY, the narrator and protagonist
> ESSIE NOLAN, a young woman who is suffering from a
>     mysterious illness
> ROSE CALLAMIT, Essie's cousin and guardian
> ABE SHEFTEL, a shopkeeper

*The Story*

Although the setting of "The Enchanted Doll" is a poor neighborhood in New York City's Lower East Side, the plot has many of the elements of a fairy tale: a handsome young doctor, a beautiful but helpless young woman, and an ugly old harridan. The tale begins when the narrator, Dr. Samuel Amony, sets out to buy a birthday present for his little niece in Cleveland. With a hurdy-gurdy playing "Some Enchanted Evening" in the background, Amony drops by Abe Sheftel's combination stationery, cigar, and toy shop. When the doctor sees a twelve-inch, handmade rag doll with a painted face, he reports that he feels an affinity with the doll as one might feel with "a stranger in a crowded room." The doll seems lifelike, mysterious, and feminine all at once. When quizzed, Sheftel replies that the doll was created by some red-haired amazon who lives nearby. Sheftel cannot quite recall her name, but he thinks that "Calamity" is close.

Coincidentally, Amony gets to meet the redheaded woman when she summons him to her apartment to make a house call. Her name is actually Rose Callamit, not Calamity, but the latter seems more appropriate. Amony reports that her voice is unpleasant, her hair is dyed, her makeup is overdone, and her perfume is both overpowering and cheap. He is offended to think that this vulgar woman is the creator of the charming doll that he sent to his niece. Her sitting room is cluttered with dolls, each of which is different but stamped with the same creative genius as the one that Amony first saw in Sheftel's window.

Finally, Rose leads the doctor through a connecting bath into a small back room, where her cousin, Essie Nolan, sits listlessly in her chair. In the best tradition of the fairy tale, Rose illustrates her cruelty by brutally pointing out that Essie is a cripple. The doctor notices, however, that not the lame left leg but some mysterious, consumptive disease is the cause of Essie's illness. Although puzzled by Essie's illness, the doctor is relieved to discover that the sensitive girl rather than the vulgar woman is the creator of the exquisite dolls, for Essie is surrounded by paints, material, and other equipment necessary for making the dolls. When the doctor looks into Essie's misery-stricken eyes, he is spellbound.

Leaving Essie's sickroom, Rose and Amony have an angry confrontation. When the doctor insists that Essie's deformity can be cured, Rose tells him to shut up. The doctor is convinced that the reason for Rose's reaction is not that she wants to protect her cousin from false hopes, as she says, but that she does not want to lose her lucrative income from the dolls. He apologizes to Rose, however, because he wants to be allowed to see Essie again.

A tonic and ten days' rest from doll making improve Essie's condition, but when Amony prescribes ten more days of rest, Rose dismisses him. Denied access to Essie, the doctor himself falls sick. He is slowly wasting away until he realizes that his disease is love. He is in love with Essie Nolan. That revelation rejuvenates the doctor, and he decides to rescue Essie. With the help of the shopkeeper, who tips Amony off when Rose leaves her apartment, the doctor rushes to Essie's bedside. Reaching Essie just as she is about to lose consciousness, he explains to the young woman that all of her love and hope have been leeched out by Rose, and, declaring his love for her, the doctor persuades Essie to let him take her home with him. She agrees, and he wraps her in a blanket and carries her through the August heat to his rooms behind the doctor's office.

The narrator frames his account by an explanation at the beginning and end of the story that this day is an anniversary for him and Essie. They are married, have one son, and now have another child on the way, but the anniversary that he cherishes the most is the day he first saw the doll in Abe Sheftel's window. He reports that Essie no longer makes dolls because she now has her own family to care for. The implication is that the young couple will live happily ever after.

## Themes and Meanings

The enchanted doll of the title is not the doll that the narrator first encounters in Abe Sheftel's store window but Essie Nolan herself. Essie is enchanted in the sense that she is under the spell of her cousin Rose Callamit. However, there is no mystery or magic in Rose's methods. By constantly harping on the fact that Essie is lame and by insisting that no man will ever love Essie, Rose cripples the young woman psychologically so that she is too embarrassed to leave the apartment. Starved for human contact, Essie begins to create the hauntingly lifelike dolls, which, as the narrator eventually discovers, become Essie's substitute children.

However, Essie is not allowed to mother her "children." Quick to recognize the commercial value of the dolls, Rose sells them as fast as Essie can make them, symbolically killing Essie's offspring. The cycle of giving but never receiving love and affection eventually causes Essie to give up any interest in life. At the last moment, this spell, Rose's hold over Essie, is broken by Amony. Just as the handsome Prince kisses Sleeping Beauty and brings her back to life, Amony falls in love with Essie and gives her back her will to live.

The theme, then, as explicitly stated in the story, is that all human beings need love. If deprived of love, the soul will eventually wither and die. Given love, body and soul will regenerate.

*Style and Technique*

Paul Gallico's experience first as a sportswriter and later as a screenwriter as well as his often-stated goal of entertaining his readers rather than encouraging them to think caused him to create stories that rely heavily on plot details and external conflicts rather than on an exploration of psychological subtleties.

The characters in "The Enchanted Doll" are flat, being either totally good or totally evil. Amony is an idealistic doctor living and practicing in a poor neighborhood. Essie Nolan is at once completely helpless and totally loving, and her jailor-cousin is mean and self-serving. The suspense depends entirely on whether Amony will be able to rescue Essie from Rose before Essie gives up her will to live.

The lack of subtlety is further emphasized by Amony's tendency to speak in clichés. Although the narrator warns that he is a doctor rather than a writer and even fears that his story will be "crudely told," one might expect a doctor to be more original than his phrases "great reservoir of love," "much blacker crime," and "I who loved her beyond words" would indicate.

The least predictable, and therefore the most engaging, feature of the story is its realistic background. The factories belching coal smoke across the East River, the withered cigars and cardboard cutout advertisements in Sheftel's window, and the cheap satin cushions in Rose's bedroom create vivid visual images. The matter-of-fact accuracy of these details enhances what is essentially a formula plot.

*Sandra Hanby Harris*

# THE END

*Author:* Samuel Beckett (1906-1989)
*Type of plot:* Absurdist
*Time of plot:* The twentieth century
*Locale:* Possibly Ireland
*First published:* "La Fin," 1955 (English translation, 1960)

*Principal character:*
THE NARRATOR, an elderly, unnamed man

*The Story*

If readers expect the contemporary short story to concentrate on a "slice of life," it must be said that Samuel Beckett is inclined to take his cut at the far end of the loaf. "The End" is a good example of the subject on which he has concentrated in much of his work: the gritty, sometimes offensive experience of the last days of an old man, struggling to survive and, at the same time, willing to die.

There are no tricks, no sophisticated twists and turns in this story. It is simply the tale of an old, unnamed man, thrown out of some kind of public institution (probably a charitable hospital) with a bit of money and not much else. He has, however, a peculiarity that makes him more than a repulsive, stinking bag of bones; he has the capacity to survive, despite crippling physical limitations, a lively curiosity especially about himself, and (like many of Beckett's tramps) something that is often not seen quickly enough: a first-class, witty intelligence and the ability to talk well, if sometimes disgustingly, about his experiences.

This old man goes from pillar to post, leaving the institution reluctantly, being rebuffed in his attempts to find shelter, finally getting himself a basement room from which he is soon evicted after being cheated out of his money. On the streets again in a town that seems to be his home, he passes his son, who tips his hat to him and goes on his way. It is just as well because the old man despises him. Finally, in his wandering in and out of town, he meets an old friend who offers him shelter in a seaside cave. He uses it briefly and then leaves because he cannot stand the constant tumult of the sea. He is relieved to get away because he does not need friendship.

He retreats to a wrecked mountain cabin owned by the same man in which, in his weakened and hungry state, he attempts in a comic knock-down-and-drag-out attack to milk a cow on the move. Eventually, he falls, stumbles, and crawls back to town, where he finds shelter in a shed on a deserted estate near the river.

He now sets up to work as a beggar during the day, mindful of his nice problem of eliciting sympathy without at the same time offending donors' delicate noses. He is not without a peculiar dignity that will not allow him to be used by a Marxist street orator as an example of the capitalist failure. He scoops up his coins, unties his begging board, and leaves work early.

In the shed he sleeps in an old boat that he has meticulously fixed up as a home and as a refuge from the local rats. It is here that the reader leaves him, as he is describing his visions, particularly his ultimate vision of floating out to sea and pulling the plug hole in the bottom of his boat in order to make his end.

If the story goes anywhere, it is from bad to worse, as the old man degenerates physically day by day. What does not happen is any loss of the wild, lively, pawky imagination or any cessation of the chattering soliloquy. Self-pity never intrudes, and it is hard not to admire a man, however odoriferous, who can stare his end in the face with such equanimity.

### Themes and Meanings

The word "absurd" may sometimes cause a reader to shy away from the most obvious way of reading this story because that word suggests intellectual complications that are worrying. They ought not to be. Beckett simply believes that life has no meaning, and he occasionally illustrates that belief in somewhat involuted and technically difficult tales. Sometimes, however, he explores it with works such as "The End," which is, in fact, what it looks like. It is a story about an old man, expelled from a hospital into a society that has no interest in him, and in which he, in return, has no interest. He survives despite all, if with less and less physical strength from day to day.

It can, then, be read as a story about an exceptional old bum living hand to mouth—a peculiar subject and one that may not seem to have much appeal. It is certainly a mark of Beckett's perversity as a writer that he often uses the old and how they survive, how they die, or, at least, how they try to die. On that level, there is a gritty reality and tactility in his work, and a fine eye for detail. What is perhaps larger than life is the quality of the old man's mind; he is stunningly bright and knows how to show it. He is dying nevertheless, and the nature of that experience is faced with relentless rigor.

One ought not, however, be satisfied with "The End" simply as sociological art. Beckett uses versions of this old man often in his works, often being ground down to inevitable death. This conjunction of old age and death stands for him in the abstract as a metaphor for the meaningless nature of life, for the fact that the moment one is born, one begins to die.

Death can take a long time in Beckett's work, and even in "The End" it may be that the old man is only dreaming it, dreaming of setting out to sea like an old Viking. He is not quite that far gone as the story ends. This old man's determination to occupy himself with getting ready for death, without self-pity and without any hope of everlasting life Hereafter is, in a peculiarly Beckettian and Irish way, the author's celebration of man's capacity to accept pain and suffering, thinking and stinking all the way to the end.

### Style and Technique

The first-person narrator, whose chief function seems to be to talk to himself, in a prose version of the dramatic monologue, in order to cheer himself up and on—to give himself some identity in a world where he is often confined or in which he is so physically repellent that people avoid him (and he avoids them)—is a common character in Beckett's later works. The reader must not confuse the physical or economic or social state of this narrator with a similar mental condition; he is not mentally destitute. He may not know his name or quite where he is, but he seems to have had an excellent education, and a taste for logic chopping. The casual reference to Arnold Geulincx, a seventeenth century philosopher concerned with the relation of mind and body, comes naturally to the old man in "The End" and is consistent with his attempts to make some sense of his physical degeneration by imposing a lively mind on the question. As a result, the basic vulgarity of a tramp's life, the search for food and shelter, the disarray and mess of clothing and personal belongings, the awareness of the problem of personal hygiene, all the problems of hobo life are shot through with bits of scholarly knowledge, touches of obsessive rationalization, a lunatic sense of humor, and an occasional wide-eyed innocence about the way of the world.

The oral style is personal and unguarded, a constantly shifting mix of high, middle, and low in which defecation and epistemology are likely to show up in the same sentence. There is no decorum, no forbidden subject, no attempt to defend oneself from sheer silliness. The narrator's intelligence cannot save him from the crazy attempt to milk a cow into his hat while she is escaping, or from his dumb, deadpan comment on the fiasco. That bit of farce and his obsessive, fumbling grasp of detail ought to remind one of old film comics such as Charlie Chaplin and Buster Keaton (whom Beckett once used in a film based on one of his works).

There is pleasure in the quick, furtive, side-of-the-mouth comment, as well as in the dense argument: the way he dismisses the hot air of the Marxist orator, as well as the long essay on the fine art of begging. Every once in a while the prose picks up lyric power, particularly in the descriptions of nature. Tonally it is, then, all over the place, sometimes sad, sometimes lugubrious, often offensive, but also very amusing. It is an example of putting a character at the end of his tether but with energy enough to pull cheekily on the rope.

*Charles H. Pullen*

# THE END OF OLD HORSE

*Author:* Simon J. Ortiz (1941-    )
*Type of plot:* Social realism
*Time of plot:* The 1950's
*Locale:* Acoma Reservation, New Mexico
*First published:* 1974

> *Principal characters:*
> THE NARRATOR, a Native American boy
> GILLY, his younger brother
> TONY, an adult neighbor
> OLD HORSE, Tony's dog

*The Story*

The narrator, a young Acoma Indian boy, and his brother Gilly are in the habit of visiting their neighbor Tony during the long summer days that pass in much the same uneventful way, week in and week out. Nothing, he thinks, ever happens in the summer, so he expects nothing unusual to happen on one particular day when he and Gilly wander by Tony's place.

Tony has tied up his dog, Old Horse, which chews on the rope, snarling to get free. Feeling no sympathy for the dog, the boys do not equate its desire for freedom with their own; they only laugh and tell Tony that his dog "is going nuts." Tony, busy with chores, replies that Old Horse is a "dumb dog," and Gilly agrees.

The boys next go to the creek, where they have a good time playing. They try to chase trout upstream to a trap they have made, but this day they have no luck. As they prepare to go home, Tony arrives. Not smiling or joking as he usually does, he tells them that Old Horse has choked to death while trying to break free. Although the boys felt no particular affection for the dog, the news of its death evokes unexpected emotional reactions, which they try to hide. When the narrator suggests that perhaps Tony should not have tied up the dog, Tony erupts with anger, pushing him into bushes and frightening him. A moment later, however, Tony picks him up and apologizes.

The boys start home, and Gilly begins to cry. The narrator does not know what to say except to repeat that Tony should not have tied up Old Horse. He, too, is about to cry, so he challenges Gilly to a race, but Gilly continues sobbing. After saying "The hell with you," the narrator runs by himself until his lungs hurt "more than the other hurt." His exhaustion makes him so sick that he goes to the side of the road to vomit.

By the time that Gilly catches up, he has stopped crying, and the narrator apologizes for telling him to go to hell. The boys arrive home late for dinner. After they sit down, their father asks what Tony is doing these days. Gilly replies, "Tony choked Old Horse to death, hellfire." The mother warns Gilly not to use that kind of language. The narrator does not want to talk about it and remains silent.

## Themes and Meanings

Simon J. Ortiz's deceptively simple story provides the vehicle for a penetrating analysis of two children's first encounter with loss and of adult strategies for coping with grief and guilt. Old Horse's death is so unexpected that it takes everyone by surprise. Neither boy has developed a strategy for dealing with the losses and diminutions that come unexpectedly; nor, as it happens, has Tony. When the narrator says aloud what Tony has merely been thinking—that he should not have tied up the dog—Tony angrily lashes out in order to mask his grief and feelings of guilt. On their way home, the boys cannot discuss what has happened; both try to hold back the tears that they believe would be an inappropriate and "unmanly" reaction to a dog's death. Much of the boys'—and Tony's—physical and psychic energy is expended in the effort to act like "men," which means keeping silent, hiding emotions, and pretending to be unmoved by loss. Ortiz shows how the masking of grief can result in a lashing out at others that may be inappropriate and even cruel and brutal.

At the end of the story, the mother responds to Gilly's wrenching announcement of Old Horse's death with an irrelevant rebuke for his use of the word "hellfire," language he uses to demonstrate his "manliness." The father invokes his own posture of manliness by remaining silent, depriving the boys of the opportunity to develop appropriate strategies for dealing with loss and, by his example, seeming to validate their dysfunctional and repressive responses. In this world, there can be no sharing of grief, not even any outward acknowledgment of it. The adults are no wiser or better prepared to cope with loss than the boys are, and the ideas about "manliness" shared by the male characters are revealed as immature and unworthy.

Ortiz also presents a wonderfully subtle and understated commentary on the freedom of youth. This theme is developed primarily through the contrast between the freedom that the two boys enjoy and the confinement to which the dog is subjected. The boys, who never realize that they unconsciously identify themselves with Old Horse, are free to spend their days as they wish, visiting neighbors, wandering down to the creek, unfettered except for the injunction against cursing that their mother tries to enforce—against the example of the adult males—and which the boys recognize as her attempt to confine them to childhood.

The dog, on the other hand, is tied up, and his inability to adapt himself to confinement results in his choking himself to death. All creatures, including boys, should be free; confinement means death, if not to the body then to the spirit. However, Ortiz implies that a responsibility goes with freedom, and Old Horse has not shown himself sufficiently responsible to be free. The boys, too, seek freedom, not just physical freedom but also the freedom to use "cuss words" as Tony uses them, and they chafe at the restraint imposed by their mother on their exercise of language that will make them feel "manly." It is, Ortiz implies, through maturity and responsibility that one earns freedom.

Ortiz also uses Old Horse's death to comment on how the crucially important and formative events of people's lives—such as one's first encounter with death—come about without warning. They give one no opportunity to prepare, to anticipate, and thereby to steel oneself for what will come, just as the boys have no opportunity to prepare themselves for news of Old Horse's death. Instead, one is left with the struggle to formulate a response to what one never expects to happen; out of that struggle and under the pressure of the immediate trauma of events, the person that one will become is shaped by forces only dimly glimpsed and far beyond one's ability to control. As the narrator says, "I used to wonder what was the use for important things to happen when it was too late to do anything about them, like to jump out of the way or to act differently or to not think so much about them. But it never worked out like that."

*Style and Technique*

Ortiz makes effective use of the first-person point of view in this story. His style is appropriate to the young boy whose experience is the subject, and who, like Ortiz himself, is an Acoma Indian. His diction is simple, his sentences short and clear. However, within these restrictions Ortiz creates subtle and perceptive effects, as in the following passage: "Gilly was pretty silent, and I knew he was either crying or about to. I tried to take a sneak look, but I knew he'd notice and be angry with me, so I didn't." The diction in phrases such as "pretty silent" and "take a sneak look" is simple, but the insight that a "man" must ignore the tears of another "man" in order to allow the other to preserve his façade of manliness is deftly presented.

Because much of the meaning of the story lies beyond the limited understanding of the inexperienced narrator, it must be implied. Therefore, Ortiz carefully establishes structural parallels and contrasts to suggest those meanings that lie beyond his narrator's ability to verbalize. By using such a narrator, Ortiz involves the reader in the process of understanding the events of the narration, and the fact that the characters are Native Americans does not, in this story, constitute any obstacle to that understanding. The characters and events are universal and thereby emphasize commonalities rather than the differences that are often emphasized in fiction by Native American writers.

*Dennis Hoilman*

# END OF THE GAME

*Author:* Julio Cortázar (1914-1984)
*Type of plot:* Psychological
*Time of plot:* The mid-twentieth century
*Locale:* A country home somewhere in Argentina
*First published:* "Final del juego," 1956 (English translation, 1963)

> *Principal characters:*
> LETITIA, an adolescent girl
> HOLANDA, her companion
> THE NARRATOR, another adolescent girl
> ARIEL, a young man

*The Story*

As the title of this story indicates, the characters are playing a game that comes to an end at the close of the narrative. Letitia, Holanda, and the narrator spend their summer vacation thinking of ways either to confuse or to elude the authority figures in their lives, the narrator's mother and her Aunt Ruth. When they manage to escape the watchful eyes of the adults, Letitia, Holanda, and the narrator retreat to their "kingdom," an area near the railroad tracks where they can act out their game and thus enter into a fantasy world of "Statues and Attitudes."

The game consists of deciding on a statue or an attitude that each of the girls will portray, and then striking a pose to express that statue or attitude. The attitudes—Fear, Envy, Jealousy—are done without props, but the statues—Venus, the Ballerina—require the use of ornaments, which the girls have gathered from the house. What begins as an exercise in freedom and liberation from the world of adults becomes a game of the discovery of adolescent sexuality, even though the girls do not understand it as such.

Although there is no specific information in the story about the relationship of the three girls or their age, it is evident that they are cousins or sisters, and that they are probably thirteen or fourteen years old. Holanda and the narrator understand the world of adults, for they know exactly how to create excitement in the house by spilling hot water on the cat, or dropping a glass while washing dishes, or coaxing the two older women into an argument over who should wash and who should dry. Letitia, a quieter, calmer girl, has a slight paralysis that causes occasional back pains and periods of confinement in bed. The game of Statues and Attitudes takes on a new importance one day when a man on the passing train throws the girls a note complimenting them on their performance. Letitia, Holanda, and the narrator begin to play the game more enthusiastically for the benefit of their admirer, Ariel. At the same time, they begin to invent details about him—his background, the school that he attends, where he lives.

Ariel begins to drop notes each day as the train passes; each day the notes become more intimate, and it becomes obvious that he prefers Letitia over the other two girls. He finally announces that he will get off the train the next day to speak with them. The next day, however, Letitia becomes ill and cannot accompany the girls to the kingdom. Instead, she gives the narrator a note to deliver to Ariel. When Holanda and the narrator meet Ariel, he engages them in polite conversation but cannot hide his disappointment that Letitia is not there. He takes the note and puts it in his pocket for later reading.

The following day, the three girls go to the kingdom and Letitia brings out the jewels that she has taken from the house for her performance. She dresses herself elaborately and performs the most extravagant statue possible as the train passes with Ariel leaning out the window to look at her. The next day, Holanda and the narrator go to the kingdom alone because Letitia is suffering from her paralysis. As the train passes, the two girls see the window empty and imagine Ariel sitting on the other side of the train, "not moving in his seat, looking off toward the river with his grey eyes."

*Themes and Meanings*

Julio Cortázar is best known for his story "Las babas del diablo" ("Blow-Up), on which Michelangelo Antonioni based his popular film. In fact, the collection of stories in which "End of the Game" first appeared in English carried the title *End of the Game, and Other Stories* (1963) and then, after the success of the film, was reissued in paperback in 1967 as *Blow-Up, and Other Stories*. "Blow-Up" is more typical of the kind of story that has made Cortázar a popular writer than is "End of the Game," which is more subtle in its blend of fantasy and reality. However, the fact that the collection in English was first published with "End of the Game" as the title story indicates that Cortázar considered it to be of particular significance.

Cortázar creates his story through the elaboration of the familiar theme of the conflict of fantasy and reality. The three girls engaged in a game that consists of playacting invent a character, Ariel, based on the very limited knowledge that they have of the real person whose face they have seen on the passing train. When the fantastic game becomes real through the confrontation of Ariel, the narrator, and Holanda, the conflict between the fantastic and the phenomenological destroys the invented reality.

Cortázar elaborates the theme of fantasy and reality in such a way that "End of the Game" becomes representative of the ideology evident in all of his fiction—that instinctive behavior is liberating and any constraints on the expression of the individual will are destructive. Of the three girls in the story, Letitia is the most significant because of her physical deformity and because she is the one chosen as the prettiest by Ariel, whose name relates him to the spiritual realm of the Ariel of William Shakespeare's *The Tempest*. Because Letitia avoids the confrontation with the real Ariel, she does not experience the disenchantment suffered by Holanda and the narrator. She maintains a distance from phenomenological reality by writing the letter and then creates the most fantastic invention possible in an extraordinary display of physical prowess despite her paralytic condition. Although the story narrates the moment at which all three girls become aware of their sexuality, it concentrates on Letitia's loss of innocence. Not only does she steal the jewels from the mother and the aunt, but she also releases all of her energy in an orgasmic display for the idealized object of her sexual feelings.

Throughout the story, the girls find ways to escape the restraints imposed on them by the adults. The kingdom by the railroad tracks provides them with a kind of childhood freedom, as does the game of Statues and Attitudes. At first, the game is liberating because it provides a means of exteriorizing the interior world of the girls' feelings. It then becomes liberating because it allows the expression of their awakening eroticism.

*Style and Technique*

The narrative style of Cortázar is distinctive primarily because of its clarity and directness. Although many details of the story are unclear in "End of the Game," as in any Cortázar story, that uncertainty is the result not of the language but of the narrative perspective. As in most of Cortázar's stories, the narrator is a character in the story, and the narrator does not understand the significance of what is happening. Certain details are not clarified, such as the relationship of the three girls or the contents of the letter that Letitia writes to Ariel, primarily because the narrator is not omniscient and does not have the narrative awareness of an objective storyteller.

Through the use of the first-person narrator, Cortázar is able to create a tension between the events as they appear to the character and the perception of the events by the objective reader. The narrator's version of the story is a reflection of her involvement in the struggle to free herself from adult restrictions and express her individuality. In the first part of the narrative, the narrator concentrates on the girls' attempts to destroy the control that the mother and the aunt have over them in the household. As the story progresses, the narrator becomes less concerned with the events in the home and more involved in the impending event—the extraordinary confrontation with Ariel, who represents the liberation from the strictures of childhood. Through this changing attitude of the narrator, the reader perceives that the game of Statues and Attitudes has become symbolic of the process of children growing up. The game playing typical of childhood is transformed into the ritualistic game playing characteristic of the adult world.

*Gilbert Smith*

# THE ENDURING CHILL

*Author:* Flannery O'Connor (1925-1964)
*Type of plot:* Realism
*Time of plot:* The early 1960's
*Locale:* A small southern town
*First published:* 1958

Principal characters:
ASBURY FOX, a frustrated writer returning home from New York
MRS. FOX, Asbury's doting mother
MARY GEORGE, Asbury's older, unsympathetic sister
DR. BLOCK, a local doctor who treats Asbury's illness

*The Story*

Asbury Fox is a failed writer. Leaving behind the provincialism of his small-town southern roots, he moved to New York to seek his destiny as a playwright, novelist, and poet. His legacy, however, consists only of "two lifeless novels . . . stationary plays . . . prosy poems . . . sketchy short stories." He returns home believing that he is dying of some unnamed disease. He is also out of money.

Met at the train station by his mother and sister, Asbury certainly looks like one about to die, and his mother immediately plans Asbury's recuperation: mornings are devoted to his writing career, afternoons to helping the black dairy workers milk the farm's cows and to treatment by Dr. Block, the local physician. Asbury immediately balks; he has come home to die—not to take up the life of the country gentleman. If it had been possible to find a cure, a New York specialist would have found it. His school-principal sister, Mary George, however, refuses to pity him. Skeptical of both his malady and his manner, she scorns her ashen-faced brother and his pseudo-intellectualism.

Asbury's plan is simply to spend time in reflection on his tragic life. Amid his unsuccessful manuscripts is the chronicle of his short, unhappy ordeal: a long, explanatory letter to his mother that fills two notebooks. Intending it to be read after his death, he regards it as a letter such as that "Kafka had addressed to his father." In reading it, Mrs. Fox would finally come to understand the degree to which she has been responsible for Asbury's disappointments: how she domesticated him, squelching his talent and imagination, but "not his desire for these things." She left him with the worst of both worlds: a taste for artistic achievement without the means to reach it. Although her "literal mind" would not allow her to see the deep significance of his letter, it would, perhaps, leave his mother with an "enduring chill" that would in time "lead her to see herself as she is."

After arriving in Timberboro, he discovers how completely different the atmosphere on the family farm is compared to the rarefied, intellectualized air of his beloved New York. There he met a group of people, including a Jesuit priest, whom he believed grasped "the unique tragedy of his death, a death whose meaning had been far beyond the twittering group around them." By contrast, at Timberboro he is surrounded by people he regards as dull, backward, and incapable of recognizing life's subtleties and challenges. Chief among them is Dr. Block, a favorite of children, who "vomited and went into fevers to have a visit from him." Against Asbury's wishes, Mrs. Fox invites Dr. Block to examine Asbury and root out the cause of his illness. "Blood don't lie," Dr. Block harrumphs as he completes his examination of the exasperated Asbury by extracting a syringe full of blood. "What's wrong with me is way beyond you," Asbury sardonically counters.

Still, Asbury finds some comfort in the company of Randall and Morgan, his mother's two black dairy workers. Because he once spent a year trying to write a play "about Negros," he feels a special camaraderie with these two. He tries to establish his liberal, egalitarian identification with them by sharing cigarettes and by impulsively drinking fresh, unpasteurized milk from a glass from which the black workers themselves have drunk—despite their admonitions not to drink it: "That the thing she don't 'low."

As his fever increases and he faces what he believes is his impending death, Asbury convinces his mother to send for the only likely intellectual in the area who might have an enlightened view of life and death, a Jesuit priest. To his surprise, Asbury receives a visit not from a knowing, worldly priest such as the one he met in New York, but a down-to-earth, salvation-minded priest who quizzes Asbury on the catechism. In the midst of his inquisition, Asbury cries out, "The Holy Ghost is the last thing I'm looking for!" "And He may be the last thing you get," the priest fires back.

In the climax of the story, as various workers and relatives file by the stricken Asbury to pay their last respects, Dr. Block enters triumphantly to announce that Asbury merely has undulant fever, which he acquired by drinking unpasteurized milk. The story ends with Asbury alone in his room shuddering from a sudden chill that he recognizes as the Holy Ghost, "emblazoned in ice instead of fire."

*Themes and Meanings*

Asbury Fox is representative of the kind of self-styled intellectuals Flannery O'Connor delighted in skewering. Despising their southern roots, these refugees seek enlightenment in the bastions of eastern intellectualism, eventually confronting their own pretentiousness and selfishness in a reunion with family or forgotten friends. There are thus some delicious ironies in the career of Asbury Fox, the would-be novelist, playwright, and poet.

Thinking himself some kind of tragic, Keatsian figure, he returns home to receive the pity and respect such a tragic hero should elicit. He has designed his two-notebook letter to convince his mother of her responsibility for his failures; in death, he will triumph over those unable to recognize his potential artistry. Prepared to die but not to live, he discovers that he has only a recurrent and controllable fever; his egotism and irresponsibility are thus transparent to all by the end of the story.

O'Connor, who imbued most of her stories with the presentation of some un-adorned Christian truth, uses Asbury's confrontation with the local Jesuit priest to re-veal the hidden, spiritual source of his failures. Seeking salvation in mere secular wis-dom and worldly approval, he becomes a narcissistic parody of the wronged artist. The "enduring chill" he intended for his mother becomes his own destiny, both liter-ally in his undulant fever and in his confrontation with the Holy Ghost he shunned ear-lier.

*Style and Technique*

O'Connor is at her satiric best in capturing the posturing of intellectuals in their as-sumed superiority over their backward southern brethren. From the beginning of the story, Asbury is depicted as a dilettante whose manner—a disdain for simplicity and directness—betrays his phoniness and insincerity, and O'Connor uses several charac-ters as foils to reveal these unpleasant truths about Asbury.

The first is Asbury's sister, Mary George, a no-nonsense, unsympathetic observer of Asbury's eccentricities; she sees through Asbury's pose as a maligned artist and re-fuses to accept his role as a helpless invalid. Morgan and Randall, the two black dairy workers, are astonished by Asbury's naïveté when he drinks the unpasteurized milk, and, later, when they are asked to say their good-byes to Asbury on his "death bed," they tell him that he looks fine and on the road to recovery. Finally, Dr. Block, the un-sophisticated and unassuming physician from Timberboro, deflates Asbury's "trag-edy" when he uncovers the real source of the illness that New York doctors could not diagnose. The pomposity of Asbury is thus finally laid to rest.

*Bruce L. Edwards, Jr.*

# ENEMIES

*Author:* Anton Chekhov (1860-1904)
*Type of plot:* Psychological
*Time of plot:* The late nineteenth century
*Locale:* Russia
*First published:* "Vragi," 1887 (English translation, 1903)

>  *Principal characters:*
>    KIROLOV, a small-town doctor
>    ABOGUIN, a wealthy man

*The Story*

A six-year-old child—the only son of Kirolov, an aging doctor, and his wife, who cannot expect to have another child—has died of diphtheria. Just as the parents are beginning to succumb to grief, the doorbell rings. Leaving his wife beside the dead child's bed, Kirolov goes to the door. There he finds a man who is so distraught that he can hardly speak. After the man manages to introduce himself as Aboguin, he says that his wife has collapsed and that he believes her to be dying of heart failure. Because he has no inkling of what has just happened to Kirolov's family, Aboguin assumes that the doctor will, as a matter of course, come with him immediately. Although the doctor is still in shock, he pulls himself together enough to explain why he cannot go. Aboguin tries to be sympathetic but points out that Kirolov is the only doctor in the area, and without his help, his wife almost certainly will die.

While Aboguin waits in the hallway, Kirolov wanders aimlessly about his house, looking at a book, sitting down for a time in his study, and finally ending up in the bedroom, where his wife is still prostrate beside the body of their dead child. After standing there for some minutes, Kirolov returns to the hall, where Aboguin is still waiting for him. Again, Aboguin insists on the doctor's going to his wife; again, Kirolov refuses. When Aboguin reminds Kirolov of his ethical responsibility and promises that it will take no more than an hour to make the trip, the doctor agrees to go. Shortly after they set off in Aboguin's carriage, Kirolov thinks once more of his wife, and asks Aboguin to stop. Aboguin ignores his outburst, and the coach speeds on through the night.

When the carriage finally stops, Kirolov sees an imposing, brightly illuminated house. After the men go into the house, however, they are met with total silence. At first, Aboguin takes this to be a good sign; surely, he says, his wife cannot have died. Leaving the doctor in a luxurious drawing room, Aboguin goes to find out what has happened. Soon he returns with the news that his wife is missing. Her collapse was evidently merely a ploy to get her husband out of the house; as soon as Aboguin left, she eloped with her husband's friend, who had stayed in the house with her. Aboguin is devastated, but Kirolov cannot think of anything but his own grief. When Aboguin launches into a heartfelt speech about what he sees as the tragedy of his life, Kirolov's indifference changes to anger, and he launches into a nasty verbal attack. Soon the two men are shouting insults at each other. When they part, it is as the bitterest of enemies.

As a result of this confrontation, Aboguin gives way to his emotions, fires all of his servants, and rushes off to complain to everyone he knows, thereby making a fool of himself. Kirolov goes home with a new hatred of the upper classes that will be with him as long as he lives.

*Themes and Meanings*

"Enemies" reflects Anton Chekhov's view of life as essentially ironic. Much of what happens to human beings, Chekhov believes, lies beyond their control. For example, Aboguin arrives on Kirolov's doorstep at the worst possible moment, when the doctor is exhausted and overcome by his own personal grief. As Aboguin comments, it is hard to know whether this unfortunate juxtaposition of events, the boy's death and the woman's apparent illness, should be ascribed to coincidence or to the workings of fate. When the two men discover the truth about Aboguin's wife, the situation becomes even more ironic. One is not surprised that more than one person in an area is gravely ill at the same time; however, the wife and her lover must have planned their flight well in advance. Given all the times when she could feign her attack and send her husband for a doctor, it is almost uncanny that she chooses this particular night to do so. No wonder Kirolov speculates that it all may be a cosmic joke at his expense.

From attributing the unhappy conjunction of events to fate, however, Kirolov proceeds to place the blame on Aboguin. As Chekhov points out, in doing so, he commits an unjust act, motivated by prejudice. As a doctor himself, certainly Chekhov was aware of the fact that men of his profession, although considered gentlemen, were socially and economically inferior to the landed aristocrats who ruled czarist Russia. Aboguin, however, treats Kirolov with great courtesy. It is not Aboguin but Kirolov who mentions the law requiring a doctor to come when needed. Aboguin speaks of a mutual friend, he helps Kirolov with his coat, and when he discovers that he has been deceived, he confides in Kirolov as he would in a personal friend and social equal.

It is Kirolov who sees in Aboguin, with his stylish clothing, his obvious good health, and his air of confidence, the smug self-satisfaction of the ruling class. When he arrives at Aboguin's home and observes the luxury in which he lives, Kirolov becomes even more resentful. Thus it is not merely being called away from his grieving wife on what proves to be a wild-goose chase that causes Kirolov to strike out at Aboguin but also a deep-seated class prejudice. The doctor reveals his own prejudice not only by refusing to treat Aboguin as a human being as capable of suffering as himself but also by making the unfounded charge that Aboguin is prejudiced against doctors.

Even though Chekhov treats his doctor sympathetically, underlining his exhaustion and admitting that it is difficult for a grieving person to think of anyone but himself, he shows Kirolov not as a victim of fate, but as a human being with the power to choose between good and evil. Such moral decisions are even more important because, as the tragic poets knew, whatever force governs the world does not have a sense of proportion in meting out punishment for an evil action. The final irony of Chekhov's story is that, because in a thoughtless moment Kirolov permits himself to vent his accumulated anger on an innocent man, two human lives are, in essence, destroyed.

## Style and Technique

On occasion, Chekhov's "Enemies" has been published in English as "Two Tragedies." This alternate title is appropriate in that the story begins with one tragedy and ends with another, which, although less dramatic than the first, shapes the course of two lives.

Chekhov uses the natural setting to symbolize the progress of his tragic human story. The child's death occurs in September, the time of year when, as Chekhov later says, the world seems to be sunk in apathy, waiting for winter. The story is pervaded by darkness. The child's death occurs on a dark night; Aboguin appears out of the darkness, waits in a dark hall, and then, with Kirolov, goes out into the dark, cloudy night, which is brightened only by the stars and the moon. The fact that the moon is veiled in clouds suggests that the light may well vanish; its red color indicates a possibility of warmth or, alternatively, of blood. The only sound that the men hear is the cry of the rooks, the night birds often associated with death, which seems to reflect their own sorrows.

At first, Aboguin's pleasant home seems like a sanctuary. Even here, however, there are echoes of the natural setting, suggesting that human beings cannot barricade themselves from grief. The hall and the drawing room are half in darkness; the red lampshade recalls the red moon. When Aboguin returns, it is evident that darkness and misery have invaded this house as well. After the final tragedy has occurred and the men have become enemies, Chekhov again uses nature to symbolize the state of their lives. Now the stars are shrouded in clouds, and the moon has completely vanished. Unfortunately, the two men in the story are too obsessed with themselves and their grievances to notice that the pervasive darkness in nature reflects the condition of their own hearts.

*Rosemary M. Canfield Reisman*

# THE ENEMIES

*Author:* Dylan Thomas (1914-1953)
*Type of plot:* Allegory
*Time of plot:* 1934
*Locale:* "Llareggub," Wales
*First published:* 1934

>       *Principal characters:*
>         MR. OWEN, the pagan protagonist
>         MRS. OWEN, his pagan wife
>         THE REVEREND MR. DAVIES, the rector of Llareggub

## The Story

Mr. and Mrs. Owen enjoy a simple life, close to the land, in the fertile Jarvis valley, hidden by hills from the village of Llareggub. They live in a one-story house built in the green fields, and there they maintain a garden and some cows.

As the story opens, Mr. Owen is working in his garden, pulling up weeds, while his wife observes in the tea leaves of her cup a dark stranger. She then peers into her crystal ball and sees a man with a black hat walking into Jarvis valley. She calls out to her husband to inform him of her discovery. Mr. Owen simply smiles and continues with his weeding.

The Reverend Mr. Davies, the doddering rector of Llareggub, meanwhile loses his way among the hills outside his village. Whenever he tries to hide from the strong wind, he becomes frightened by the darkness of the dense foliage and hills. He finally reaches the rim of a hill and sees the Owens's little house and garden in the valley below: "To Mr. Davies it seemed as though the house had been carried out of a village by a large bird and placed in the very middle of the tumultuous universe."

Mr. Owen, meanwhile, smiles at his wife's faith in the powers of darkness and returns to his work. Cutting earthworms in half to help them spread their life over the garden, he says, "Multiply, multiply." Throughout the story, Mr. Owen is consistently related to the earth, weeds, worms, and other fundamental elements of nature and fertility.

By the time Mr. Davies arrives at the Owen house, his hands are covered with blood from the scratches and bruises that he has received from the rocks. Once out of the safe confines of his small Christian village, Mr. Davies is a prey to every natural force surrounding him. Mrs. Owen bandages Mr. Davies' battered hands and asks him to stay for dinner.

As Mr. Davies says grace before the meal, he observes that the prayers of Mr. and Mrs. Owen are "not his prayers," thereby suggesting their mysterious pagan origins. During the meal, Mr. Owen, "proud in his eating," bends over his plate and eats his food with the same natural zest with which he works his garden. Mrs. Owen, on the other hand, does not eat, because "the old powers" are "upon her." A darkness gathers in her mind, drawing in the surrounding light. "Mr. Davies, like a man sucked by a bird, felt desolation in his veins." The strength of both his physical body and his religious faith is nearly drained.

Mr. Davies recounts his adventures to his hosts, telling of his fear of the dark recesses among the hills. He explains that although he loves his God, he also loves the darkness, where ancient people worshiped "the dark invisible," but that now the hill caves are full of ghosts that mock him because he is old. Hearing this, Mrs. Owen thinks that he is afraid of "the lovely dark." Mr. Owen, however, thinks that he is frightened of the primitive life forces surrounding him in the valley.

Then Mr. Davies kneels down to pray, not understanding his sudden compulsion to ask for deliverance. He continues to pray and to stare dumbfounded at the dark mind of Mrs. Owen and the gross dark body of her husband. The story ends with Mr. Davies praying "like an old god beset by his enemies."

## Themes and Meanings

In this story, Dylan Thomas contrasts the Christian religion of Wales with the region's pagan past. Mr. Davies represents the dying force of Christianity, which is overwhelmed by the powerful force of ancient pagan religion, embodied in Mr. and Mrs. Owen. Mr. Owen is associated with the fertility of the land: "the worm in the earth . . . the copulation in the tree . . . the living grease in the soil." Mrs. Owen, with her tea leaves and crystal ball, represents the ancient belief in the occult. Once out of the village, Mr. Davies is at the mercy of the natural forces that, while supportive of the Owens, frighten and nearly destroy him.

During the meal Mr. Davies becomes aware of the failure of his Christian faith and falls to his knees in fear. The name of the village from which Mr. Davies has strayed—Llareggub—is "bugger all" spelled backward. This is Thomas's mischievous joke that warns the reader early that the rector and his village colleagues are clearly out of harmony with the natural order of the physical universe surrounding them.

Although this story may be viewed as one that is self-contained, Thomas clearly intended it to be read along with its sequel, "The Holy Six." In that tale, Mrs. Owen informs six of Mr. Davies' colleagues of his plight. When they arrive in Jarvis valley, they also find themselves in a hostile world. Thomas reveals them all to be hypocrites, comic fools with evil minds. Meanwhile, Mr. Davies' newly acquired devotion to the primitive life force, mixed with his conventional Christianity, turns him into a grotesque figure. By the end of the story he claims to be the father of the child in Mrs. Owen's womb, a notion that is a bizarre mixture of his lust and spirituality.

## Style and Technique

There is not much narrative action in this story. The characters of Mr. and Mrs. Owen and Mr. Davies are important primarily for their symbolic significance. Consequently, Thomas devotes a large part of his tale to a description of the symbolic landscape. During the meal at the Owen house, for example, the focus shifts from the three people gathered around the table to a detailed commentary on the scene outside the window. The "brown body" of the earth, the "green skin" of the grass, and the "breasts" of the Jarvis hills are more than simple personifications of the area around the Owen home. The language suggests the primitive sexuality and vitality of nature, powerful contrasts to the desiccated and desolated old clergyman.

In order to develop the poetic descriptions, rich in metaphors, Thomas had to tell his story from the third-person omniscient point of view. By the end of the tale, it becomes clear that the fabric of Mr. Davies' Christianity has been torn away, leaving him frightened and vulnerable in the face of the powers of raw nature. Thomas's description of him as "an old god beset by his enemies" suggests that a faltering Christianity cannot win out against the omnipotence of the pantheistic world of the Owens, a couple in complete harmony with the pulse of nature and the forces of darkness and the occult.

The allegorical nature of Thomas's story (the Owens representing pagan religion and Mr. Davies representing Christianity) is further developed in the sequel. The holy six of Wales bear allegorical names in the form of anagrams. Mr. Vyne and Mr. Stul, for example, represent Envy and Lust respectively.

*Richard Kelly*

# ENERO

*Author:* Mary Helen Ponce (1938-    )
*Type of plot:* Social realism
*Time of plot:* The 1940's
*Locale:* Southern California
*First published:* 1990

*Principal characters:*
> Constancia de Paz, a woman pregnant with her tenth child
> Justo de Paz, her husband
> Apollonia, their eldest daughter, who is dying of tuberculosis

*The Story*

Expecting her tenth child, Constancia has just been examined by Dr. Greene, who has told her that her baby is due in January (the "Enero" of the title). This will be her first winter baby, and she only hopes it will be strong enough to fight disease.

Constancia's eldest child, seventeen-year-old Apollonia, is dying of tuberculosis, despite undergoing surgery and special drug treatments. During the three years that Apollonia has been in a sanatorium, Constancia has visited her faithfully. After Constancia's new baby is born in January, Constancia will have to stay in bed for several weeks; she fears that Apollonia will die in the interim. As she moves around the house doing her daily chores, she thinks about the past, present, and future, reviewing her life now in Southern California and remembering her earlier life in her native Mexico, where Apollonia was born.

Constancia herself was one of five children carefully spaced three years apart, thanks to her mother's careful use of church-approved birth control—abstinence. Her father, Don Pedro, managed a large ranch in the state of Guanajuato; her mother supervised the women who did chores on the ranch. Constancia met her own husband, Justo, when he was working for her father. He later wrote her letters from California, telling her about the very different life there. He was twenty and she was eighteen when they married. Some time after Apollonia was born, they moved to the United States, separating Constancia from her family and her roots.

After bearing nine children, and especially after the difficult delivery of her last baby, Constancia did not plan to have any more. She recalls her cousin Amador's visit, when he brought a jug of wine to share with Justo, who seldom drank. Unable to drive home, Amador was forced to spend the night. "Much to Constancia's chagrin, he was given her husband's bed [and] soon after Constancia knew she was in the family way." "Weary . . . of childbearing," she and Justo will sleep apart again after the baby's birth.

Life in California has changed the life of the Paz family. Unlike Mexican ranchers, American ranchers do not feed their workers, who must carry cold lunches to work. Constancia is too tired to make tortillas every day, so her family eats white American bread, which the children like. "Americanas" buy it, she thinks, so why should she not?

Constancia's wandering thoughts finally focus on the task she has been avoiding—sorting the baby clothes in preparation for the new arrival. She has carefully stored Apollonia's baby clothes, hand sewn in Mexico by her mother and sisters, wrapped in tissue paper in the bottom of the trunk. Unlike the baby clothes of her other children, Apollonia's have never been worn by anyone else. Now that Apollonia is dying, however, Constancia has no reason to keep them. She clutches Apollonia's baptismal dress to her heart, crying for the impending loss of her daughter. She suddenly decides to dress the new baby in Apollonia's tiny dress, and all of her other clothes. It will make Apollonia happy. With that thought, Constancia walks out of the dark bedroom and into the warmth and light of her kitchen.

*Themes and Meanings*

Although Constancia is a woman living in the present, she is caught between a past that she remembers fondly and a future that she both fears and welcomes. To her, the past represents a happier, simpler time, when she helped her mother serve meals to the workers on the ranch and was responsible for only two children—her younger brother and sister. It was a time when her husband was a young man with a future. That was long ago, however, and now Constancia is no longer free like the clouds that she observes through the window, to Justo's annoyance. At thirty-eight, she is soon to be the mother of ten children, with one dying and another soon to be born. She will have twice as many children as her mother. She loves all of her children, but her life has been circumscribed by their numbers, very much like the rosebush that she tends in her garden, which "cannot grow with these small suckers," for they "take the nourishment needed by the plant."

Mary Helen Ponce's story is set in October, when the earth and its creatures prepare for the death of winter. Constancia, too, must prepare for death, and for life, and the two intertwine inseparably in this story. The title, "Enero," looks toward the future, toward the coming of new life to be born in the month that begins the New Year and holds the promise of the unknown future. There are other indications of a hopeful future, as Constancia makes a mental list of the home improvements that she wants to accomplish before January: new linoleum, additional clotheslines, and a yellow rosebush.

In her sixth or seventh month of pregnancy, Constancia is literally heavy with life, but her heart is filled with the coming death of Apollonia. This dichotomy between life and death is the central concern of this story, and it is a dichotomy whose resolution comes with Constancia's decision to use the baptismal dress of her dying daughter for the formal entrance into life signified by the baptism of the baby who is to be born.

*Style and Technique*

A third-person omniscient narrator supplies information on Constancia's age and appearance and the details of her daily life: At thirty-eight she is "still a pretty woman.

Her olive face unlined, the black, wavy hair slightly gray." She is much like her neighbors, in a Mexican neighborhood of first- and second-generation Mexicans in Southern California in the 1940's—the time and place on which Ponce focuses much of her writing. Ponce's occasional use of Spanish words (such as *el lavadero* for washroom, *cocido* for stew, and *hija mía* for my daughter) gently reinforces the Latino context.

Ponce's use of Constancia's point of view lifts the narrative above mere social realism of place to create an intimate portrait of a woman straddling the boundaries of several conflicting worlds—Mexico versus the United States, the past versus the present, the present versus the future, freedom versus commitment, youth versus maturity, and most important, death versus life and despair versus hope. Ponce uses a variety of symbols and metaphors to represent these conflicts. The name Constancia ("constancy") is the most obvious example, for despite her reverie and a certain longing for the halcyon days of her youth in Mexico, she is indeed constant. She fulfills all of her obligations as a wife and mother despite personal cost. Although her husband, Justo, may not have fulfilled the promise of his youth, he provides well for his family and is an honorable and just man, respected by all.

The month of "Enero" used as the title of the story seems carefully chosen to symbolize new beginnings and hope. The rosebush that Constancia tends is a metaphor for her situation as the mother of so many unplanned children: The suckers that spring up at the base of the rosebush are its attempt to propagate itself, and yet its "offspring" divert the rose's vitality to themselves, hampering its growth just as Constancia's growth has surely been hampered by her ten pregnancies in twenty years and their attendant responsibilities.

The baptismal gown, used in the religious ceremony that admits a baby as a spiritual member of the church, affirms life. The trunk where it has been stored in the dark bedroom suggests the carefully guarded past, a past that is useless to the present unless released into the light. The blue sky and the cloud formations that Constancia loves to watch remind her of the blue skies and freer days on the ranch in Mexico, where she "played on the open meadows." The kitchen is the center of domesticity, the room where she lovingly cooks and serves her family's meals and they unite to eat together. When Constancia leaves the dark bedroom to return with the baptismal dress to the warmth of her kitchen, she leaves behind despair, abandons the past, and moves toward the light and hope of the future. The circle of life, which always includes death, remains unbroken.

*Linda Ledford-Miller*

# THE ENGAGEMENT IN SANTO DOMINGO

*Author:* Heinrich von Kleist (1777-1811)
*Type of plot:* Postcolonial
*Time of plot:* 1803
*Locale:* The island of Santo Domingo
*First published:* "Die Verlobung in St. Domingo," 1811 (English translation, 1960)

> *Principal characters:*
> Kongo Hoango, the leader of a black rebel force
> Babekan, his mulatto wife
> Toni Bertrand, Babekan's fifteen-year-old daughter by a
> French merchant
> Gustav von der Ried, a Swiss officer serving under the French

*The Story*

As a consequence of the French Revolution, in 1794 the French National Convention declared freedom and equality for black slaves in the colonies, including the French part of the Caribbean island of Santo Domingo. Kongo Hoango, an old West African who faithfully served his white master for years, rebelled with his fellow blacks, massacred the planter and his entire family, and took over the plantation as his base of marauding operations to help drive the French from the island. Kongo Hoango makes it his practice to have his wife, Babekan, and her daughter, Toni, offer sanctuary to fugitive whites during his absence on raiding expeditions, allowing their unsuspecting guests to believe themselves safe from the rebels until Kongo Hoango returns and brutally executes them.

One night in the year 1803, a desperate white man comes to the house asking for assistance for himself, his family, and several of their household servants. They have narrowly escaped death at the rebels' hands in the town of Fort Dauphin and are fleeing on foot and under cover of darkness in the hope of reaching Port-au-Prince, the sole remaining French stronghold, in time to leave the island for Europe. The man identifies himself as Gustav von der Ried, a Swiss officer who was in the French service at Fort Dauphin. The rest of his party, he tells them, is in hiding some distance away until he can return with fresh provisions for their journey. Gustav cannot understand why his family, Swiss citizens, should be as much threatened by the rebels as the French colonists, but he realizes now that it is their race, not their nationality, which puts their lives in peril. Babekan tells him that she and Toni also suffer cruelties at the hands of the blacks because both women betray their mixed blood by their lighter-colored skin.

It is decided that Gustav should spend the night at the plantation and send for his family the following day. Toni brings supper for their guest, and Gustav is struck by the charms of the girl, who has, after all, been taught to use them in beguiling those unfortunate enough to stray into Kongo Hoango's trap. In the course of the conversation at table, Gustav tells the story of a white planter from Fort Dauphin and a black slave girl whom the landowner had sought favors of and later abused. The girl had her revenge, however, when she became ill with yellow fever and sent word that she would offer the besieged man a hiding place during the rebellion. Only after taking him into her bed did she confront him spitefully with the fact of her deadly contagion. Gustav asks Toni if she would ever be capable of such a vicious deed, and she insists that she would not.

When it is time for Gustav to retire, Toni goes to prepare the room and a footbath for him. In the course of the preparations, he again finds himself enchanted by the girl's beauty, engages her in conversation about her marriage plans, and draws her tenderly into his arms. Toni is torn between her sense of duty to the rebel cause and the rising desire within herself. Gustav confides that he had a fiancé in France and that the young woman sacrificed her own life to spare him execution as an enemy of the revolution. Toni is moved to sympathy for his grief, and the embrace that follows ends in the consummation of their love.

The next morning Toni protests to her mother the unjust cruelty of plotting Gustav's murder, and Babekan questions her loyalty to the rebellion. Thus, Toni must gain time by pretending to cooperate in the deadly plan, at the same time contriving to put off Gustav's impatience to announce their "engagement" without arousing his suspicions. Babekan intends to keep Gustav in the house until Kongo Hoango's return, when a detachment can be sent to surprise and destroy the group in their hiding place as well. However, Toni manages to send word for the others to come to the plantation, certain that then she can defy her mother and leave with her betrothed for Europe.

That night she steals back to Gustav's room, determined to reveal the truth to him and finds him asleep in his bed. In his sleep, Gustav murmurs her name. At that moment noises are heard in the yard; Kongo Hoango's contingent is back. Toni ties the still sleeping Gustav down in his bed, a trick to convince Babekan and Kongo Hoango that she is faithful to them, and the desperate ploy works. Once the commotion has finally died down and all have gone to bed, Toni goes to meet the Swiss fugitives, by now on their way to the plantation, warns them of the danger threatening Gustav and awaiting them, and leads them into the house, where they overpower the surprised rebels. When they cut Gustav free of the ropes on his bed, however, he seizes his pistol, accuses Toni of being a whore and betraying him, and shoots her through the chest. The others tell him how terribly he has misjudged her, whereupon he turns the weapon on himself and puts a bullet through his head.

The remaining members of the family must still think of their own survival. They bury the bodies of Toni and Gustav, having exchanged the rings on the hands of the two lovers, and finish their journey to Port-au-Prince and then home to Europe. Gustav's uncle settles in Switzerland again, "and even in the year 1807 one could still see, amid the shrubbery of his garden, the monument he had erected to the memory of his nephew, Gustav, and the latter's bride, the faithful Toni."

*Themes and Meanings*

Because Heinrich von Kleist regarded the human individual as a riddle, he made Toni the central figure of this story. She stands at the nexus of turbulent events and conflicting allegiances. As a child of mixed race, she enjoys the confidence and affections of both whites and blacks, but she also suffers the antipathy and mistrust of both. She must be clever and deceitful beyond her years to make the mother believe that her moral principles, not her attraction to Gustav, prompt her to plead for his release. Gustav himself has difficulty fathoming his feelings toward Toni: "If not for her color, which repelled him, he would have sworn that he had never seen anything prettier." His mixed emotions are only more profound and ominous after their lovemaking: "He swore he would never stop loving her, and that it was only in the delirium of his strangely disordered senses that the mixture of desire and fear she inspired in him could have seduced him into doing such a thing."

Kleist need not have made Toni a mere girl of fifteen if the innocence of youth had not been crucially important to her character. She is a riddle as much to herself as to the others in the story and to the author as well (no omniscient narrator questions or probes the reasons for her actions). She is experienced at playing the decoy for many hapless white fugitives up to now, but she is overtaken by love's desire in the encounter with Gustav; in affairs of the heart she is guileless and utterly confused. It is typical of Kleist that the heart takes over where rational deliberation fails, whether the course thus taken leads to happiness or tragedy.

The tragedy of "The Engagement in Santo Domingo" is perhaps that Toni, the individual so placed as to mediate between the opposing sides, fails to do so. As so often in the works of Kleist, much revolves about a question of knowledge—the opposite of innocence, the cause of humankind's loss of innocence and fall from grace. Standing in the eye of the cyclone, Toni alone knows all sides of the desperate situation; knowing more than any of the others, she is threatened on every side and must be the most dissembling. The loss of her virginity is nothing beside the loss of this far deeper innocence.

For Gustav knowledge is paradoxically treacherous because it is imperfect. Having consummated his love for Toni, "he knew that he had been saved, and that here in this house he had nothing to fear now from the girl." He is right, but Gustav overlooks the fact (and so does Toni, though she could never imagine it) that he has everything to fear from himself: In the end he kills her before he can learn the reason for her actions. Throughout the story, in fact, Gustav trusts Toni when he should not and does not trust her when he should.

*Style and Technique*

Like any number of Kleist's other stories, "The Engagement in Santo Domingo" pulls first one way and then the other on the reader's expectations. It appears that Gustav von der Ried will die as other whites before him have; then, because he has violated Toni, it seems likely that his fate at Kongo Hoango's hands will be unusually cruel. There follows a stretch of frantic but somewhat brighter expectation as Toni works to win freedom for Gustav and herself. (She firmly believes that they can escape together to Europe.) None of these developments prepares the reader for the surprise ending.

Other expectations prove illusory, too. Gustav's story of the black slave girl who lured her former white owner into her fatal embrace with the promise of saving him from the rampaging rebels only appears to foreshadow what Toni will soon do to Gustav, and her denial that she could commit such treachery seems—and surely is intended to be—deceitful of her. The story that parallels it, in which Gustav tells of his own former bride-to-be and her self-sacrifice to the revolutionary mob in France for his sake, unambiguously prefigures Toni's faithfulness. Gustav gradually discovers that it is the European woman to whom Toni bears a mysterious resemblance. The ironic reversal comes only at the end, when Gustav confuses faithfulness with duplicity and takes it on himself to execute the second of his redeeming angels.

Some of the story's devices belong to Kleist's stock-in-trade: the fateful confusion of appearance and reality; the intoxication—in this case erotic—that abruptly changes the course of characters' actions; and the appearance of the beloved in the blissful escape of a dream vision, such as that in which Toni finds Gustav as he sleeps on the final night of the story. The motif of forbidden love-at-first-sight, the young girl's awakening to the power of love, and the concluding love-death scene are all familiar to readers from the Romeo and Juliet tradition in literature.

It is worth recalling that, in November of the same year in which this story appeared, Kleist carried out a suicide pact with a woman of his acquaintance, firing a bullet through her heart and a second one through his own head.

*Michael Ritterson*

# THE ENGLISH LESSON

*Author:* Nicholasa Mohr (1935-    )
*Type of plot:* Domestic realism
*Time of plot:* The 1970's
*Locale:* New York's Spanish Harlem
*First published:* 1986

> *Principal characters:*
> SUSAN HAMMA, a teacher
> LALI PADILLO, a Puerto Rican immigrant woman
> WILLIAM HORACIO COLÓN, a Puerto Rican immigrant who works
>   at the luncheonette

*The Story*

Susan Hamma, a history teacher from a junior college in Queens, is teaching an adult-education class for immigrants trying to learn English. She is an exuberant woman who is convinced that the small group of mostly Hispanic students in her class desperately need her services, reasoning that if they can come to class after working all day in dreary, boring, even revolting jobs, the least she can do is make every lesson count.

Susan has asked the students to make oral statements about where they are from, why they are taking her class, and what their plans are. William Colón, a dwarfish man who is almost the same height standing as sitting, begins the recitation pattern that most of the students follow. All the students stand and read a prepared statement indicating that they have come to the United States in search of a better future, that they are living with relatives, and that they are working as unskilled laborers. All the legal aliens indicate that they want to become American citizens, except for Diego Torres, a young man from the Dominican Republic. When Susan urges Torres to be brief, he snaps at her that he is not finished, insists that he is proud to be Dominican, and maintains that he has no desire to be a U.S. citizen. Aldo Fabrizi, an Italian immigrant who does want to become an American, speaks passionately about his goal, scolding and challenging Diego Torres, who only yawns and closes his eyes.

The last student to recite is Stephan Paczkowski, a Polish immigrant, who was a professor of music at the University of Krakow for ten years until his wife, also a professor, was asked to leave the country because she had Jewish parents. He now works as a porter in the maintenance department of a large hospital. At the close of the class meeting, William walks home with Lali Padillo, a Puerto Rican immigrant whose husband, Rudi, runs the luncheonette where she and William work. They talk together about the class, and William urges Lali not to be embarrassed about her poor English skills.

On the last night of the class, Susan brings coffee and cookies for a treat. Lali is sorry to see the class end, for it has meant an escape from the luncheonette and Rudi and all the things that she believes imprison her. Diego Torres and Aldo Fabrizi goodnaturedly argue about the merits of citizenship, the students praise Susan for her teaching, and everyone says good-bye. William and Lali, who have made plans to take a more advanced English class together the following term, walk home, teasing each other by imitating Susan.

## Themes and Meanings

Nicholasa Mohr's "The English Lesson" is a restrained love story. Although neither Lali nor William refer directly to how they feel about each other, the story suggests that although they are only friends, each secretly wishes the relationship could be more intimate. In addition to William's gentleness with Lali, the most obvious suggestion about their unexpressed feelings occurs on the walk home after the class meeting when the students make their oral presentations. Lali says that she did not know that William's name was Horacio, remarking how imposing the name is. William, who is dwarfish, says that his mother expected a valiant warrior but got him instead. Lali, however, pays no attention to William's physical stature. A plain woman, she grew up in a tiny mountain village in Puerto Rico and had no suitors until Rudi, an older man, asked her parents for her hand. She now feels closed in and alone. Her only pleasure is the English class and William. She feels that when she attends the class, she is accomplishing something all by herself without the help of the man on whom she is dependent. She finds herself waiting for William to come in to work, looking forward to his presence. On the initial walk home, as William takes Lali's elbow and tells her in English to watch her step, Lali stares at him and wishes that she could be like everyone else, but in a moment the "strange feeling of involvement had passed, and William had taken no notice of it."

The parallel theme of the story focuses on the patronizing attitude that many native speakers of English have toward immigrants who do not speak English fluently. Although Susan Hamma is a caring and concerned teacher, she thinks of her students as if they were children. Indeed, she treats the class much as if they were elementary students rather than adults. This is why she is so embarrassed when Diego Torres snaps at her harshly for telling him to hurry along with his presentation, and why she is somewhat breathless and confused when she learns that Stephan Paczkowski was a professor of music. At the last class meeting, she tries to speak to Paczkowski and pay recognition to his advanced degree. It is clear, however, that she is more comfortable thinking of the students as if they were children rather than as her peers or academic superiors.

## Style and Technique

The style of "The English Lesson" is realistic and straightforward. An omniscient narrator provides the expositional background, and most of the action is presented by means of dialogue between the characters in the five scenes: the classroom when the students give their oral presentations; Lali and William walking home together the first time; the luncheonette dialogue with Rudi; the last night of class, when Susan provides cookies and coffee and says good-bye to all; William and Lali's final walk home when they laugh and joke about Susan. The story is so formally organized that it could well become a short play.

All the details in "The English Lesson" contribute to the dual themes of the treatment of the immigrants as if they were children, and the submerged and unspoken relationship between Lali and William. For example, Susan trying to illustrate the idiom "get the ball rolling" by winding up like a pitcher and throwing an imaginary ball suggests the kind of simplistic gestures that one might use with a child. When Mr. Fong misunderstands and says that "get the ball rolling" is an "idiot" rather than an "idiom," Susan must correct him.

The fact that the immigrants do not understand English does not mean that they are either children or idiots, as Susan discovers when Diego Torres refuses to be patronized and when Stephan Paczkowski tells her that he is a professor. On the first walk home, when Lali complains that she is embarrassed because her accent is so terrible, William quite rightly points out what many English-speaking people forget: "Look," he says, "we all have to start someplace. Besides what about the Americanos? When they speak Spanish, they sound pretty awful, but we accept it." Moreover, the fact that William is dwarfish and Lali is shy does not mean that they are children.

The two themes come together at the end of the story when, on the walk home, William says to Lali, "I would like to say to you how wonderful you are, and how you gonna have the most fabulous future . . . after all, you so ambitious," and, realizing that he sounds just like Susan Hamma, he bursts into laughter. Lali joins in the game, also talking formally. The story ends with both of them breaking into uncontrollable laughter when William tells Lali that he is "now a member in good standing . . . of the promised future."

"The English Lesson" suggests the difficulty of expressing oneself in a language not one's own, as well as the difficulty of being oneself in a land that is not one's own. Because of this displacement, immigrants are initially compelled to ape the behavior of the native residents and mouth the platitudes and generalities that the new language compels them to speak. The playful and good-humored joking of William and Lali at the conclusion of the story suggests that even as they submit to the necessity of this imitation, they can mock it. Looking forward to the promised future is, for them, both real and silly at the same time.

*Charles E. May*

# THE ENGLISHWOMAN

*Author:* Ruth Prawer Jhabvala (1927-    )
*Type of plot:* Autobiographical
*Time of plot:* The 1970's
*Locale:* India
*First published:* 1976

*Principal characters:*
SADIE, the protagonist, a fifty-two-year-old Englishwoman who
has been living in India for thirty years
HER HUSBAND, an Indian
ANNAPURNA, her husband's mistress
DEV and
MONICA, Sadie's children, now grown up

*The Story*

Although fifty-two-year-old Sadie has been married to an Indian and has lived in India for thirty years, she has always remained an Englishwoman at heart. She feels young and free as she packs her bags and prepares to leave her husband, children, and grandchildren in order to return to England, where she intends to spend the rest of her days.

Over the years her relationship with her husband has so withered away that their marriage now exists in name only, but they remain friends. The person who is apparently most upset at Sadie's impending departure is Annapurna, a distant relative of her husband who now lives with them as his mistress—an open arrangement that suits everybody, including Sadie. There appear to be no hard feelings on any side. Annapurna is genuinely grieved that Sadie is about to leave the household because both she and Sadie's husband love her in their own way and enjoy taking care of her. Sadie, however, is so thrilled to be leaving that she can hardly contain her joy, but she tries to suppress her smiles because she feels ashamed of her happiness in the face of their grief at her leaving.

Sadie has carefully planned her departure. A week earlier, she went to Bombay to say good-bye to Dev and Monica, her grown children who have families of their own. When Monica asked her why she was leaving, Sadie explained that as people age they grow homesick for the places where they grew up until their need to return becomes unbearable. Monica understands and sympathizes, and both her children promise to visit her regularly in England. The only person who remains inconsolable is Annapurna, who cries and repeatedly asks whether Sadie will miss them, their love for her, and her life of the past thirty years. Sadie, however, is merely appalled to think that it has been such a long time since she left her real home.

Sadie does not like to remember the time when she arrived in India as a young English bride of a slim Indian boy with bright eyes, whom she had met when he was a student at Oxford. She was happy then, even when her husband was busy with his activities outside the home, because the family had lavished so much attention and love on her. However, the heady excitement of her strange new life in India paled over the years until she lost interest in it and her marriage. Her husband began straying to other women. Annapurna then entered the house after fleeing from an abusive husband, and she slowly took over Sadie's duties of a wife. Sadie was grateful and there was never any bitterness or jealousy between them. Annapurna looked after her husband, fed him delicacies that made him fat, and played cards with him during the evening before taking him to bed. After they retired for the night, Sadie often stayed up for hours arguing with herself about her own future.

It was during those hours that she decided to return to England. When she announced her decision, it seemed sudden, but she had actually agonized over it for a long time, and she realized that she had begun preparing to leave some twenty years earlier. She could even mark the exact day—a moment when her young son was very sick. Sadie wanted to nurse him alone in peace and quiet, but his room was filled with the numerous women of the house who fussed over him until it nearly drove her crazy. She remembered the cool and quiet sickrooms of her own childhood in England, which her mother had periodically visited with medicine. When she sensed the alarming difference of her new life, she became distraught and burst into tears on her husband's return. He and Annapurna struggled to soothe and comfort her, without understanding the real reason for her distress. She knew then that she did not belong.

On her last night in India, Sadie feels excited and young again. As she gazes over the moonlit garden of her Indian home, it is transformed into a vision of the English downs as she remembers them, and the wind that she feels is the English wind against the hair of her youth.

*Themes and Meanings*

Like Sadie, the author of this story, Ruth Prawer Jhabvala, is a European who married an Indian. She likewise returned to the West after nearly twenty-five years of married life in India. Of her own Indian experience, Jhabvala has said that she never felt that she really belonged, and this is the central theme of "The Englishwoman." Even after spending thirty years in her adopted country with a husband, children, and grandchildren, fifty-two-year-old Sadie still feels that she would be more comfortable in the land of her birth, although she admits that she now "knows almost no one there."

Sadie is not particularly unhappy or ill-treated in India. From her own impressions, she began her life there with much enthusiasm and excitement, and although all that gradually disappeared, she has always been well cared for by her husband's family. Although her marriage has disintegrated, her relations with her husband (and his mistress) have remained amicable. One thus gets the distinct impression that it is not unhappiness that drives her away. The major reason for her decision is her realization, after twenty years, that her own ways are so different that she can never really adapt to Indian society. Her homesickness for the place to which she believes she truly belongs—despite having had no connections with it for thirty years—has grown so un-

bearable that she can no longer stay away. The fact that she has indeed never connected with her adopted country is proved by her indifference to carrying anything to
England to remind her of India. It appears that Jhabvala is using her fiction to prove to
herself that one cannot really belong anywhere but in one's own homeland, and that
however late it is, one can always go back. The essence of Sadie's story is captured in
an early sentence as she prepares for her return: "Her heart is light and so is her lug-
gage."

## Style and Technique

Jhabvala is a straightforward storyteller who generally uses little literary embellishment in her fiction. "The Englishwoman" sets out its facts right at the start. Within
a few paragraphs the reader is comfortably aware of the background. However, Jhabvala also manages to arouse one's curiosity by providing snippets of information that
the reader will want explained—for example, why Sadie is so eager to leave a thirty-
year marriage, or why her husband's mistress is so upset at her impending departure—
thereby ensuring that the story captures one's attention and sustains it.

Jhabvala also appears to be writing with a wider, non-Indian audience in mind—
one for whom she provides sympathetic and accurate insights into Indian family life.
While explaining, for example, why Sadie felt so out of place in a house teeming with
relatives when her son was sick, she also points out that the prevailing social structure
is respected and relied on by the insiders, including her son, who enjoyed the great
fuss made over him.

Jhabvala uses imagery sparingly, allowing the facts and details to convey the sense
of her story. At the end of the story, when she describes Sadie's transformation of a
moonlit Indian garden into a soft English landscape, the scene becomes an especially
evocative image that provides both a sense of closure and the hint of a new beginning
in Sadie's life.

*Brinda Bose*

# ENOCH SOAMES

*Author:* Max Beerbohm (1872-1956)
*Type of plot:* Satire
*Time of plot:* The 1890's and 1997
*Locale:* London
*First published:* 1920

> *Principal characters:*
> ENOCH SOAMES, a failed writer
> THE NARRATOR, a well-known writer
> WILL ROTHENSTEIN, a painter
> THE DEVIL

*The Story*

The narrator, a middle-aged, well-known author, looks back on his introduction to London artistic life as a young man in the 1890's. He remembers the fashionable aesthetes with whom he became acquainted, figures whom he then viewed with uncritical, youthful reverence. He mentions actual places and people, such as the portrait painter Will Rothenstein. In this historical context, the fictional protagonist of the story appears: Enoch Soames. Soames tries to force his company on the preoccupied Rothenstein at a restaurant table where the painter and narrator sit together. The kindly Rothenstein tries to put the intruder down gently but cannot get rid of him; he joins them and monopolizes the subsequent conversation in a boasting, affected way. To the narrator, Soames seems to be a comically ridiculous figure; nevertheless, he has published one book, with another on the way. The narrator, himself an aspiring but as yet unpublished writer, is enormously impressed, despite Soames's ludicrousness.

Soon after this restaurant meeting, the narrator gets a copy of Soames's book. It seems to be drivel, but after all, it has been published. The naïve narrator does not know what to believe. Some of the acknowledged literary giants of the moment seemed earlier to have been writing nonsense, until established critics validated them.

In subsequent meetings between the two men, however, the narrator's judgment about Soames becomes clarified: He is indeed a pretentious fool, with his silly verses about trotting with the devil through a London square, his fondness for absinthe, his habit of lapsing into bad French, and his haughty disdain for all other creative people.

Meanwhile, the narrator is himself beginning to achieve the kind of literary recognition that Soames craves. The latter, in sharp contrast, goes steadily downhill. His first two books have had few sales and almost no critical notice from the press; his third and last volume must be published at his own expense; it sells three copies. Soames's air of bravado and contempt, the narrator now becomes aware, is a mask for deeper feelings of self-doubt and depression: He suffers intensely from the world's neglect of his literary effusions.

Several years have now passed since the beginning of the story, and the narrator has lost track of Soames. He suddenly notices him, sitting shabbily dressed and alone in an unfashionable little restaurant, itself about to fail—the kind of place in which Soames would never have permitted himself to be seen in the earlier, more hopeful, days. The now successful younger man joins Soames and tries to comfort him by suggesting that posterity might yet come to appreciate his efforts. Soames admits that literary fame means so much to him that he would sell his soul for a peek into a library card catalog a hundred years hence, simply to verify that his books have survived.

At this point, a formally dressed gentleman at the next table, overhearing the wish, interrupts them. He is the devil and he will grant Soames's wish. The pact is concluded on the spot; Soames rushes out into the future, leaving the narrator to await his return later the same day for a reunion in the restaurant.

The round trip is, in fact, successfully completed, but, alas, the only mention of Soames in the library of the future is the less than flattering portrait sketched of him in this story. The devil drags Soames down to Hell in payment for his futile look.

*Themes and Meanings*

On one level, "Enoch Soames" is the witty reminiscence of a middle-aged writer looking back over the abyss of World War I to a more frivolous, carefree era. It is a genial satire, a debunking of what Max Beerbohm had come to see as a time of pretension, of the inflated poses of would-be artists who gathered around such bona fide geniuses as Oscar Wilde, the writer, and Aubrey Beardsley, the caricaturist. Youthful rebellion occasionally produced enduring works of art; often the result was pretentious nonsense—parodied in this story in the fictional figure of Enoch Soames.

Although Beerbohm mocks Soames, he does not spare his younger self, Soames's near contemporary, from satire. The narrator's own problem in recognizing Soames's nonsense for what it is reflects on his own overconcern to be thought well of and to have the right, the fashionable opinions on all subjects. Thus, Beerbohm's satire and parody have three objects in the story: Soames; himself as the narrator-character of the story; and his generation's tendency to startle by affectation in dress, speech, food, and drink, but most especially in its artistic opinions.

On one level, then, this is a light, entertaining narrative, a realistic if nostalgic portrait of a bygone time, brought to climax by the fantastic introduction of the devil to reduce Soames's craving for success ultimately to absurdity. Beneath Beerbohm's light touch, however, is a serious exploration of important philosophical issues: What is authentic? What is spurious? How can the difference be satisfactorily determined? The object in question is the character and ability of Soames. Both narrator and reader start gaining access to this phenomenon from the beginning of the story, but the issue of authenticity is muddled by his striving to project a favorable image, and also by his reputation as a published author. It soon becomes a question of who is more ridiculous—Soames for being a buffoon or the narrator for being impressed by Soames.

In the second half of the story, the philosophical issue of authenticity becomes transmuted to the psychological one of identity. Soames is revealed as more pathetic than ridiculous in his pursuit of fame, and the narrator, who becomes successful in exactly the way that Soames craves, ends by feeling sympathy for the older man's plight. Although the issue is resolved fantastically, with Soames literally selling himself for a peek at what he hopes will be his posthumous success, the seriousness and relevance of this theme are clear and more general than Beerbohm's own professional concern. There is a contemporary ring, with universal overtones, to the character of Soames, a hollow man for whom existence and facade are interchangeable.

### Style and Technique

One of Beerbohm's striking techniques is combination; he fuses elements that are often kept separate in different narratives: fiction with autobiographical reminiscence; realism with fantasy, to which he shifts with the devil's appearance; initially, satire and parody—exaggerated, comic imitation of 1890's affectation in Soames's speech and writing—with a more sympathetic, psychological view of this character later in the story. These fusions all contribute to an overall richness of effect.

The author's handling of character is also skillful. The two supporting characters perform functions for the major relationship of the work, that between Soames and the narrator. Rothenstein is the link that brings them together at the beginning; the devil is a device for separating them at the end: He drags Soames off to Hell while leaving the narrator, and the lesson of the story, with the reader. In the Soames-narrator relationship, Beerbohm uses the technique of the double: Soames is the narrator's double in his overvaluation of literary success. The narrator, unlike Soames, does have genuine ability and does achieve success even as the older man sinks into failure; it is their similarity that emphasizes the two major themes of the story, the earlier one of authenticity and the later one of identity. In the earlier authentic-spurious confusion, both characters are ridiculous; later, in the growing appreciation of Soames's hollowness, the narrator becomes more sympathetic to the reader. As doubles they both share the temptation to put image before substance.

In addition, much of the entertaining effect of the story derives from Beerbohm's adroit use of the first-person point of view. The 1890's was a colorful time, and the reader is injected into this era easily and intimately, in the company of a masterful guide who has experienced it directly. The satire and parody directed at this epoch is made more acceptable to the reader because the author disarmingly includes himself as a target. There is one further advantage of the first-person point of view: When Beerbohm moves from reality to fantasy with the sudden appearance of the devil, this potentially disorienting shift is cushioned for the reader by the narrator's own shocked, amused reaction.

Finally, the author's handling of time is ingenious. At the beginning of the story, literary time recedes to the 1890's. Through the device of the library visit fantasy, time then curls around, moving forward, ultimately leaving readers with the illusion of having experienced something nearer at hand than that with which they started.

*Sanford Radner*

# THE ENORMOUS RADIO

*Author:* John Cheever (1912-1982)
*Type of plot:* Fantasy
*Time of plot:* The late 1940's
*Locale:* New York City
*First published:* 1947

*Principal characters:*
JIM AND IRENE WESTCOTT, a "typical" urban couple in their thirties

*The Story*

One of the most frequently reprinted of John Cheever's stories, "The Enormous Radio" derives most of its initial impact, and subsequent memorability, from the author's ironic blend of fantasy and realism, shadowed by suggestions of the supernatural.

Set during the years immediately following World War II, "The Enormous Radio" is the best known of Cheever's urban tales, foreshadowing in subject matter, theme, and style the suburban stories that would follow. Here as elsewhere, Cheever foregrounds the subtleties and stresses of contemporary marriage against a background of ambition and social mobility.

In the story's opening paragraph, the narrator spares no effort in presenting Jim and Irene Westcott as a typical, moderately successful Manhattan couple, married nine years, with one child of each sex; significantly, the Westcott children are seldom seen in the story and are never mentioned by name. Jim and Irene, observes the narrator, differ from other, similar couples only in their shared devotion to "serious" music, an interest carefully concealed from friends and acquaintances lest the Westcotts appear too "different."

The Westcotts spend many hours together listening to broadcast music, and when their radio falls into disrepair Jim hastens to replace it with an expensive new model in a "large gumwood cabinet" that clashes with their other furniture. The new radio, although quite superior in tone to its predecessor, soon begins picking up sounds from the elevator and from appliances in neighboring apartments; before long it is receiving and amplifying the neighbors' voices as well, providing the astonished Westcotts with a unique opportunity for eavesdropping: Each turn of the dial tunes in the sounds from a different apartment.

On the first evening, the Westcotts go to bed "weak with laughter" after an evening of switching "stations" with reckless abandon. Before dawn, however, Irene rises to take their young son a glass of water and on impulse tries the radio, only to overhear the conversation of an aging couple; the wife, it appears, is probably dying of some undisclosed disease. Thereafter, the conversations that Irene overhears are increasingly sad, violent, or scandalous in tone and content. In the elevator, Irene begins to scrutinize her neighbors, trying to match the faces that she sees with the voices that she hears. Returning from lunch with a friend, she tells the maid that she is not to be disturbed as she listens to the radio; with the approach of nightfall, the conversations that she hears, interspersed as before with the quaint recitations of a British nurse-maid, become increasingly provocative and frightening.

Irene becomes obsessed with the odd revelations emanating from the radio; soon, she urges Jim's intervention in righting the various wrongs of which she has lately been informed: Mr. Osborn, she tells Jim, is beating his wife, and the elevator man suffers from tuberculosis. Faced with Jim's apparent indifference, she further tells him that Mrs. Melville has heart trouble, that Mr. Hendricks is about to lose his job, and that a female neighbor, as yet unidentified, is having an affair with "that hideous handyman."

Heedless of her husband's advice to turn off the radio, or at least to stop listening, Irene hysterically seeks Jim's reassurance that they, the Westcotts, are different from the other couples in the building. "You love me, don't you?" she asks. "And we're not hypercritical or worried about money or dishonest, are we?" Despite Jim's immediate efforts to calm her, it develops not long thereafter that the Westcotts are at least all those things, and possibly more. Once the radio has been "repaired," at Jim's insis-tence, he begins complaining about the radio's initial cost, simultaneously chiding Irene for leaving clothing bills unpaid. Immediately if not sooner, he observes, they will have to begin cutting back on expenses, as business is not good.

In the story's closing paragraphs, Irene cautions an increasingly irate Jim to lower his voice lest they be overheard through the newly repaired radio. Jim, gathering mo-mentum in his anger, proceeds to denounce Irene for stealing from her mother's es-tate, cheating her sister out of the sister's rightful legacy, ruining another woman's life, and undergoing an abortion, doubtless illegal, without misgivings or remorse. When Irene turns on the radio, hoping at least to hear the comforting voice of the Sweeneys' British nursemaid, all she receives is the "suave," "noncommittal" tones of an announcer informing his listeners of the current news and weather.

*Themes and Meanings*

Here, as in his more mature work, Cheever shows a nearly obsessive concern with the instability of modern marriage, a condition sustained and prolonged by the seem-ingly infinite human tendency toward self-delusion. Beneath the Westcotts' immedi-ate predicament lurks the author-narrator's own preoccupation with the proximity of death, reflected in the darker conversations that Irene overhears.

Intent on getting and spending, like the rest of the postwar population, the West-cotts have in fact sublimated their true humanity in their common fondness for music—an avocation that, in the case of other couples, might well be replaced by hiking, golf, tennis, or any other imaginable shared activity. The Westcott children, although per-haps a source of pride at times, remain all but invisible, obscured by their parents' determination to find themselves conventionally happy. Jim Westcott, despite his om-nipresence throughout the story, gradually diminishes in importance before the gathering force of Irene's imagination; his emotional outburst at the end of the story merely underscores the power and eventual dominance of Irene's self-delusion, fueled in turn by her increasingly active imagination.

Arguably, the entire action of the story takes place in Irene's mind, at a moment when she begins to doubt both the force and the extent of a conjugal "bliss" based mainly on a shared interest in classical music. Assuming Jim's accusations to be true, Irene seeks justification for her past behavior in her perceived superiority to those around her; her pleasure in the radio's revelations, a pleasure initially yet only briefly shared with Jim and followed by intimations of mortality, soon gives way to a massive access of insecurity, which she knows to be quite justified. Like Neddy Merrill, the title character of Cheever's later story "The Swimmer," Irene has managed to survive only at the considerable cost of nearly total self-delusion.

*Style and Technique*

Later acclaimed for his skillful use of often "unreliable" first-person narrators, Cheever in "The Enormous Radio" confines his narrative voice to the third person, presumably omniscient yet, like the radio itself, unable (or unwilling) to pass judgment. The style is generally noncommittal, like the voice of the announcer, save for the increasingly animated and thought-provoking dialogue; only gradually does the reader come to suspect that he might be participating in a fantasy generated and perpetuated by Irene. Notwithstanding, the fiction of the "enormous" radio, in which the adjective regains no small part of the force still felt in the substantive "enormity," continues to suggest supernatural possibilities.

To be sure, Jim Westcott's revelations and accusations in the story's penultimate paragraph come as something of a shock to the reader as well as to Irene, unforeshadowed by any preceding action or description. Later in his career, particularly in such stories as "The Swimmer" and "The Scarlet Moving Van," Cheever would perfect the technique of "fitness," amply preparing for the climax through clues and gradual revelation; in the present case, the ending appears to have been borrowed from O. Henry or Guy de Maupassant. Nevertheless, "The Enormous Radio" ranks among the more impressive of Cheever's earlier efforts, encouraging readers to expect, and to appreciate, the even greater achievement of his suburban stories during the years to follow.

*David B. Parsell*

# ENTROPY

*Author:* Thomas Pynchon (1937-    )
*Type of plot:* Allegory
*Time of plot:* February, 1957
*Locale:* A suburb of Washington, D.C.
*First published:* 1960

> *Principal characters:*
> MEATBALL MULLIGAN, the proprietor of the lower floor of the
>     house in which the story occurs
> SANDOR ROJAS, a former Hungarian freedom fighter
> SAUL, Meatball's friend
> CALLISTO, a nihilistic philosopher
> AUBADE, Callisto's female companion

*The Story*

The narrative opens with an evocation of the fortieth hour of Meatball Mulligan's lease-breaking party, complete with drunken revelers, much debris, and loud music. The latter awakens the upstairs tenant Callisto from an uneasy sleep, and the scene shifts to his apartment, which is a kind of sealed hothouse luxuriating in plants and protected from the wintry weather outside, where it has been, the reader learns, precisely thirty-seven degrees Fahrenheit for three days running (despite announced changes in weather by the newscasters).

Callisto has been nursing a sick bird back to health, attempting to keep it alive with the warmth and energy from his own body—as if their continuous existences were a single system, an enclosed heat engine (into which the tropically warm room has, in effect, been made). For several pages, the story shifts back and forth from the thoughts and occasional audible remarks of Callisto to Meatball's party downstairs. The latter includes a brief conversation between Meatball's friend Saul, whose female companion Miriam has recently left him, the intrusion of a group of drunken sailors on shore leave and in search of a party, and the eventual decision by Meatball to attempt to quell the anarchy that ultimately breaks out and to attempt to keep the party going for several more hours. In the meantime, Callisto reflects on the concept of entropy, on the possibility that the universe will ultimately suffer heat death and cease to act at all (the first sign of which is the constant thermometer reading outside his window), and on the possible implications of the laws of thermodynamics for social existence (this with some help from those investigators who had appropriated the term "entropy" from physics to information theory). The story ends with the death of the bird and with Aubade's breaking the glass that separates her and Callisto from the cold outside, as the two of them await the equilibrating of the temperatures between outside and inside, the ultimate consequence, for them at least, of the principle of entropy.

## Themes and Meanings

Thomas Pynchon himself has remarked, in the introduction to *Slow Learner* (1984), the collection of his short fiction in which "Entropy" is included, on the comparative aridity of this story, on the mistake he made (he attributes it to his youthfulness at the time of writing) in believing that a story could be generated directly out of a theme or symbol or abstraction—in this case, the concept of entropy evoked in the title and explored theoretically in Callisto's musings and the conversation between Meatball and Saul, as well as practically in the actions of Meatball and Aubade at the end. In fact, for even such a brief tale as this one, there is comparatively little action, virtually no characterization of any significance, and the thematic concerns of the nature of entropy in thermodynamics and in information theory almost completely dominate the story. If one were to characterize the story in classical, Aristotelian terms, it would almost certainly fall under the heading of a plot of thought.

The controlling trope or idea of the story, entropy, remains, as Pynchon attests once more in his introduction to *Slow Learner*, a very slippery concept. In thermodynamics, it is a measure of the disorder in a system, and it was the theorem of Rudolf Clausius that the entropy of any closed system tends toward a maximum. If, then, like Henry Adams (whose autobiography provides the model for the memoirs that Callisto is dictating to Aubade during the course of the story), one conceives of the entire cosmos as a closed system, then it follows that the universe is inexorably heading for ultimate heat death, the ceasing of all motion that is prophesied at the end of this story, the outward and visible sign of which is the steady state of the thermometer outside Callisto's window.

The concept of entropy, however, has also been imported into information theory, more or less illegitimately, as a measure of disorder in systems of signals. Entropy is roughly the measure of noise, of meaningless sound in any given string of communicative signals. This meaning of the concept is deployed in a conversation between Meatball and the recently jilted Saul (the latter is a computer technician, which makes the conversation marginally more plausible because Meatball knows nothing about entropy in either sense of the term, being merely a likable, dumb slob trying to keep his party from getting out of hand). It is impossible to summarize this conversation, so it will simply be quoted here:

> Saul jumped down off the stove . . . "Tell a girl: 'I love you.' No trouble with two-thirds of that, it's a closed circuit. Just you and she. But that nasty four-letter word in the middle, that's the one you have to look out for. Ambiguity. Redundance. Irrelevance, even. Leakage. All this is noise. Noise screws up your signal, makes for disorganization in the circuit."
>
> Meatball shuffled around. "Well, now, Saul," he muttered, "you're sort of, I don't know, expecting a lot from people. I mean, you know. What it is is, most of the things we say, I guess, are mostly noise."
>
> "Ha! Half of what you just said, for example."
>
> "Well, you do it too."
>
> "I know." Saul smiled grimly. "It's a bitch, ain't it."

Pynchon would ultimately do better with this kind of game in his novels, particularly in *Gravity's Rainbow* (1973), where the technical matter is brilliantly integrated into a masterfully executed plot that turns on some possibilities suggested by probability theory and operant conditioning of subjects in behavioral psychology. Here the conversation does illustrate the principle in question (entropy as a measure of noise in a communication system), but the joke, at least to some ears, falls rather flat.

What does work, however, is the portrayal of Meatball as a kind of counterentropic force in the universe of the party, a sort of primitive resistance against the cosmic pessimism of Callisto. For Meatball does resist the entropic tendencies inherent in his own party at the end, and in that sense he gives the lie to Callisto's resignation to the cosmic fate that he has contemplated and passively endures when Aubade breaks the window in the final paragraph. To the extent that Meatball's cheerful attempt to set things straight in his chaotic household succeeds, it stands as Pynchon's hopeful rebuttal of cosmic pessimism, a potentially bright spot in the otherwise gloomy historical forecast that the concept of entropy seems to project.

*Style and Technique*

From a technical point of view, this story is not very interesting. The only device worth remarking is the use of a double plot line in the stories of Meatball and Callisto—stories that, as suggested above, are meant to unite (or at least come into contact) at the level of theme. In every sense, "Entropy" is a youthful production, an apprentice piece by a precocious but still technically immature writer. The rich range of different registers (from the snappy slang of postwar urban America, to the lyricism of post-Symbolist fictions such as William Faulkner's, to the almost forbiddingly technical language of scientific manuals, to the humorous song parodies) that characterize Pynchon's mature fictions is confined here almost exclusively to a single voice, interrupted only occasionally by the dialogue of characters such as Meatball and Saul. In short, "Entropy" is a production of a writer who has yet to master his craft; it is of interest chiefly as a prelude to what is to come.

*Michael Sprinker*

# ENVY
## Or, Yiddish in America

*Author:* Cynthia Ozick (1928-      )
*Type of plot:* Satire
*Time of plot:* The mid-twentieth century
*Locale:* New York
*First published:* 1966

*Principal characters:*
EDELSHTEIN, an elderly Jewish intellectual
BAUMZWEIG, his friend, editor of a Yiddish periodical
PAULA, Baumzweig's wife
YANKEL OSTROVER, a famous author, envied by Edelshtein
CHAIM VOROVSKY, a drunken lexicographer
HANNAH, Vorovsky's niece

## The Story

The basic premise of this novella-length, seriocomic story is Edelshtein's envy of the success of the writer Yankel Ostrover and his obsession with sustaining Yiddish as a language. Parallel to this plot line is the contradiction involved in Edelshtein's ironic need for a translator, without which he can never achieve success as a writer, but with which he cannot really sustain Yiddish. Although Edelshtein finds American writers of Jewish extraction such as Philip Roth, Bernard Malamud, Norman Mailer, and Saul Bellow puerile, vicious, and ignorant, he reserves his most passionate vituperation for Ostrover, who seems patterned after Isaac Bashevis Singer in some ways and Jerzy Kosinski in others. Ostrover is a writer of stories in Yiddish that, when translated into English, have become highly popular. For Edelshtein and his friend Baumzweig, editor of a Yiddish periodical, Ostrover's Yiddish is impure and his subject matter is pornographic. They call him "Pig" or "Devil" or "Yankee Doodle." With his focus on an imaginary Polish village named Zwrdl, however, Ostrover is considered "modern" by contemporary critics. Free of the prison of Yiddish, he has burst out into the world of reality. Taking Anton Chekhov and Leo Tolstoy as his literary gods, he has been published in *The New Yorker* and *Playboy.*

There are other reasons for Edelshtein's hatred of Ostrover than his envy of his success. Thirty years earlier, Ostrover had an affair with Edelshtein's wife; Edelshtein blames Ostrover for the fact that he and his wife have remained childless. It is the envy that gives the story its title, however, that most eats at Edelshtein. He writes Ostrover's publishers asking them to provide him with a translator so he might show them that there are Jewish writers other than Ostrover. The irony of Edelshtein's position is indicated by the publisher's response that reputation must precede translation, to which Edelshtein replies that without translation there can be no reputation. Edelshtein then writes to a spinster hack who translates for Ostrover, from whom he receives a long reply arguing that she is the one that makes Ostrover modern, although, like a wife, she has the passive role.

When Edelshtein goes with Baumzweig and Baumzweig's wife, Paula, to hear Ostrover read, Ostrover reads a story about a poet who sells his soul to the devil in order to get a translator and then, when he still cannot find success, is condemned to Hell to write poems that are immediately consigned to oblivion. The story is an obvious allegory about Edelshtein and his desire for a translator, and it serves only to infuriate Edelshtein more. It also enrages Edelshtein that Ostrover responds with jokes to the homage he receives. He believes that the Jewish intellectual, in the modern world, is reduced to being a comedian. At the reading one is also introduced to Chaim Vorovsky, a mad lexicographer who, after completing seventeen years' work on his dictionary, began laughing and could not stop, and then began wetting himself. Now alcohol has cured the laughter but not the incontinence. Edelshtein also meets Vorovsky's niece, Hannah, who knows his poetry from her grandfather, and he begins his efforts to make her his translator.

The climax of the story comes when Edelshtein goes to Vorovsky's house and finds that he has reverted to his laughing madness. Still, Edelshtein tries to convince Hannah to be his translator, telling her that she will be like a messiah to a whole generation. She, however, recognizes him as merely another jealous old man from the ghetto, looking not for a translator but for someone's soul to suck out like a vampire. When she tells him that Ostrover is not of the ghetto but in the world, Edelshtein realizes that for him the ghetto is the real world and the outside world only a ghetto. Hannah attacks him with the accusation that he is a cannibal who hates imagination, magic, and God. When he leaves, Edelshtein calls the number of a fanatical religious organization with whom he argues about the values of Judaism and Christianity. Finally, the religious fanatic calls Edelshtein a "kike" and a "Yid." Edelshtein shouts into the telephone that the whole world is infected with anti-Semites who have caused him to lose everything, and most tragically, to fail to have a translator.

*Themes and Meanings*

Because "Envy" is both a satire, written in broad comic strokes, and an ironic treatment of a serious theme—the isolation of the American Jewish intellectual who clings to his old European tradition—it is a story that is difficult to perceive as a unified totality. Edelshtein scorns what is "modern," particularly if that term means the rejection of the old values. He rejects what he calls the mere storytelling of Ostrover in favor of the true art of poetry. He rejects English in favor of Yiddish and laments that his language is dying. However, he longs to have Ostrover's success, desperately seeks a translator who he thinks will make this possible, and knows great dejection in his loneliness and despair. The story is less a theme story than a comic satiric story that lashes out through Edelshtein at the Americanized Jewish writer, yet at the same time makes fun of Edelshtein's Old World self-pity and bitter jealousy.

For Edelshtein, the loss of Yiddish is the loss of an entire world. In reading the story, however, one is not always sure whether a world will be lost or only the narrow intellectual world of Edelshtein will be lost. The conflict of the story is summed up in the final dialogue between Ostrover and Hannah, in which Hannah seems to see Edelshtein correctly as a ghetto Jew who refuses to accept the modern world. Even as one rejects the narrowness of Edelshtein, however, one cannot accept the triviality of the vision of Ostrover and Hannah. Thus, there is no answer to the dilemma here. Ultimately, what "Envy" seems to be about is the loss of Jewishness, its absorption into what is American and what is modern. Thus, although Edelshtein is right at the end of the story—that the whole world is infected with anti-Semites—the seriousness of the charge is undercut by his comic cry that because of anti-Semites he has no translator.

The more serious aspect of the search for a translator focuses on the symbolic need of an intermediary between the Old World and the New. Edelshtein is an isolated figure, like an Old Testament prophet crying out in the wilderness for someone to communicate his cultural values to the modern world; he feels himself surrounded by infidels and traitors to both his society and religion. He is, however, also a comic figure—ineffectual, pathetic, absurd. What he wants is both valuable and worthless at once.

## Style and Technique

Style is more important to "Envy" than theme; the point of view of the story and its rhetorical structure are the most obvious sources of its interest. Ozick maintains an ironic and satiric perspective on Edelshtein, even as she sustains a point of view that reflects Edelshtein's values. The language of the story is comic and ironic, combining the conventions of Yiddish folktale with the style of the upbeat Jewish comic; even as it makes fun of the Americanized Jewish idiom and folktale devices, it makes use of them. Its structure, made up of various kinds of rhetorical patterns such as letters, stories, and debates, is far from straightforward. This highly stylized and self-conscious structure and style make the story somewhat difficult to fix in the reader's mind, depending primarily neither on plot nor on characterization, but rather on purely rhetorical devices and erratic shifts in tone and perspective.

"Envy" is a satiric comment on the nature of Jewish literary culture in the United States. Although Edelshtein's view that without the Jews there would be no literary culture in Western civilization may be an extreme one, it is obvious that the success of Jewish writers in the United States is a result of their willingness to give up the strict traditions of their culture as well as their language. Moreover, the success of such writers as Malamud, Bellow, and Roth is largely the result of their willingness to make their Jewish characters the butt of an extended Jewish joke. Roth especially has written novels that reflect on this capitulation for the sake of popularity. The basic punch line of Ozick's joke about this dilemma of the Jewish writer is "You can't have it both ways"; that is, the Jewish writer cannot maintain his language and culture and be read at the same time. The technique of Ozick's story is to maintain the seriousness of this problem even as it must be seen from the perspective of satiric humor.

*Charles E. May*

# EPICAC

*Author:* Kurt Vonnegut (1922-    )
*Type of plot:* Science fiction
*Time of plot:* An unspecified future
*Locale:* A computer room
*First published:* 1950

*Principal characters:*
THE NARRATOR, an unnamed mathematician
PAT KILGALLEN, his girlfriend, later his wife
EPICAC, an advanced computer

## The Story

The greatest computer ever built, EPICAC has been designed for the purpose of rapid calculation, mainly for military purposes. It is a huge machine, described as plugged into the wall like a toaster or a vacuum cleaner. Soon, however, it is clear that EPICAC is far more than a machine.

The narrator, after repeatedly being turned down by his beloved, Pat, a mathematician as he is, sits down one night in front of the computer keyboard and playfully asks the computer for advice. To his great surprise, the computer responds, first asking for definitions of such basic terms as love, girl, and poetry. After some explanation, EPICAC produces a long poem, called simply "To Pat." EPICAC then starts asking questions of its own, about how Pat looks, what she likes to do, and so on. The computer will do nothing else until it gets its answers.

When Pat sees the poem, she is extremely moved, and finally agrees to a kiss. The narrator is thrilled and tells EPICAC all about the experience. The computer responds by producing a shorter poem, "The Kiss," which leads Pat finally to agree to marry the narrator, on the condition that he write her a poem on every anniversary.

Early the next morning, the narrator gets a frantic call from Doctor von Kleigstadt, who screams that disaster has befallen the great computer. The narrator finds smoking wreckage and a huge collection of computer printouts. He takes them home and decodes them.

EPICAC has left a suicide note, explaining that it does not want to be a machine and think about war all the time, but wants to be human and think about love. There are no hard feelings, however. The computer has also left enough poems to last the narrator through five hundred anniversaries.

## Themes and Meanings

At one level, Kurt Vonnegut's "EPICAC" is a love triangle story, minus the jealous rage usually associated with such stories. The fact that one of the lovers is a computer might easily be played for laughs, and there is certainly a comic element involved.

The way that the story is presented, however, suggests several far deeper levels.

The first level is that of science fiction. EPICAC is the greatest computer in history, with a huge potential. From the first sentence of the narrative, it is obvious that there is more to it than merely the ability to calculate rapidly and accurately. This is most clearly shown in the ways that the various characters are depicted.

EPICAC is described at first as a huge machine, but "he" soon replaces "it" as the pronoun used to describe the machine, and the narrator often refers to the computer as his friend. Pat Kilgallen, the narrator's girlfriend, is a wooden figure, useful only to advance the plot. Doctor von Kleigstadt is a stereotypical scientist, complete with an overdone German accent. Even the narrator is never named. The most human character in the story is the computer. The only dialogues with any meaning are between the narrator and EPICAC.

The most important plot development in this regard is the computer's suicide. It does not make much sense that a computer should be able to commit suicide; a computer is a machine, after all. Even more important is the manner of that suicide. EPICAC is a machine designed to make calculations for use in warfare. At the end of the story, it makes the ultimate sacrifice for love. Not only does it short-circuit itself, but before doing so, it prints out enough poetry to make sure its friend will be happy in the love that it can never enjoy.

The basic question is whether a thinking machine can become, in some sense, a human being. Human beings are far more than thinking machines. They have emotions, and often act illogically on the basis of those emotions. Vonnegut poses this question early in the story, when he refers to "my friend EPICAC, God rest his soul." Can a computer have a soul? At the deepest level, this is what "EPICAC" is about. Standard religious beliefs are useless in this regard, because they are based on teachings that far predate modern technology. Vonnegut later did question religious values, and even invented a new religion in *Cat's Cradle* (1963). In the present story, however, religion does not enter the picture, at least on the surface.

"EPICAC" was one of the earliest attempts at the fictional treatment of modern computers. As such, it was a radical departure from the usual ways in which machines had been treated by earlier science-fiction writers. Generally, they were shown as either complicated but mindless gadgets, or monsters out of control. "EPICAC" was one of the first stories that imbued computers with anything like human emotions.

In 1950, when this story was written, computers were primitive by the standards of the late twentieth century. They were huge, lumbering machines, requiring constant attention and regular repairs. The concept of a computer thinking for itself was something new, but it became a regular theme in later science fiction, and a few decades after "EPICAC," scientists were considering this question very seriously.

EPICAC is the reverse of Frankenstein's monster: He is a machine created for warfare, who dies for love; inefficient at calculating war programs, but capable of writing great poetry. As such, he is more human than the human characters around him, or certainly more humane.

*Style and Technique*

"EPICAC" is written in the playful style common to Vonnegut's works. The very name of the machine is comic; it is clearly related to ipecac, a medicine used to promote vomiting. The story begins with the narrator discussing his friend EPICAC, and referring to him with human pronouns. At the same time, there is no question that he is dealing with a machine, an object to be owned by human beings: "After all, he cost the taxpayers $776,434,927.54."

This technique of switching back and forth between humanizing the computer and presenting it as a machine might easily become confusing in a larger work. It would also be confusing if there were any serious plot development, or if the characters other than EPICAC were developed in a believable way.

Less than six pages long, "EPICAC" consists almost entirely of narration and dialogue between two characters, a human and a computer. After a brief discussion of the simple encoding techniques used, these dialogues are almost always presented as two people talking.

One result of this technique is to make the reader feel sympathy for the machine. It is easy to imagine the machine having facial expressions and changing tones of voice, even though the reader has been told that all the conversations are conducted by the operator punching a keyboard and the computer printing out answers in numerical code. One has far more sympathy for the computer than for any of the human characters, even the narrator.

"EPICAC" is told in the first person, which is usually an intimate way to narrate a story. In this case, however, it is difficult to have any feelings for the narrator, because he reveals so little about himself. He is a mathematician, and he is in love with another mathematician, but he never appears outside his computer room. One does not know what he likes to eat, what he reads, or what he does when he is not working. He is a narrator, and nothing more.

Apart from any sympathy that can be evoked for a computer, there is no real human interest in this story. Not one of the characters is described physically. The reader may picture the narrator as some stereotypical computer expert, or at least a 1950's reader could. Pat is difficult to picture at all. All of this is deliberate. The purpose of "EPICAC" is to pose quickly a few fascinating questions about intelligence, emotion, and behavior, and presenting realistic characters would get in the way.

This story is a peculiar mixture of comedy and tragedy. Certainly, the prospect of a computer falling in love and killing itself because it cannot consummate that love is ridiculous, and should evoke laughter. Still, EPICAC is such a human computer that the reader feels for it. The ultimate result is that the humans are proposed as comic figures, while a machine is proposed as tragic.

*Marc Goldstein*

# AN EPISODE OF WAR

*Author:* Stephen Crane (1871-1900)
*Type of plot:* Psychological
*Time of plot:* 1864
*Locale:* A Civil War battlefield
*First published:* 1899

> *Principal characters:*
> THE LIEUTENANT, who has been wounded in battle
> THE DOCTOR, who treats him

*The Story*

An army lieutenant concentrates on rationing out his company's supply of coffee, meticulously dividing the brown squares before him, when a shot rings out. The enlisted men, startled by the noise, suddenly see blood saturating their lieutenant's sleeve. In pain, the wounded officer sways, winces in disbelief, mutely surveys the forest, and tries instinctively and clumsily to sheathe the sword that he has been using to count out the coffee packets. His mind swirls with mysterious revelations about existence and the meaning of life. As his dumbstruck, sympathetic troops try haltingly and timidly to assist him, he realizes his helplessness. He desperately holds his right wrist with his left hand. Silently and mournfully, he leaves the field to seek medical attention. His dark journey begins.

The lieutenant's wandering quest takes him through scenes of wartime horror: An aide gallops to a general, salutes, and presents his commander a vital message; batteries sweep in majestic, frightening curves bent on destruction; and horsemen curse and shout amid a chaos of levers, motors, and wheels. This chorus of war is ferocious and emotional with dramatic passion. A beautiful unity seems to hover over these fields of mindless destruction and sudden death. The lieutenant comes on a group of stragglers who are insensately trudging his path, all excitedly caught up in the drama; he encounters a roadside brigade making coffee—the pedestrian task in which he had been involved before his wounding—and buzzing with talk like girls at boarding school, as if war were simply an adventure. A solicitous officer, observing the lieutenant's bloody arm, scolds him to fix it and kindly, though amateurishly, binds the wound with his own handkerchief. The lieutenant is embarrassed both by his shattered arm and by the gesture of concern. He feels strangely apologetic. He has not yet mastered the proper etiquette for behaving as a wounded soldier, but believes there is some proper ritual to be followed when one is no longer a complete human being.

At last the lieutenant arrives at the low, white tents of a makeshift hospital, a former school now surrounded by moaning and dying soldiers. A busy surgeon passes by and greets the lieutenant in a friendly way, but his considerate demeanor disappears, even approaches contempt, when he spies the wounded arm. He brusquely orders the lieutenant to come along. Suddenly fearful and overwhelmed by panic, the lieutenant cries out that he will not allow his arm to be amputated; he tries to draw away. The surgeon seductively cajoles him, insisting that he will not amputate it. The lieutenant is far from reassured, but is not strong enough to resist. He proceeds reluctantly, suspicious and terrified, toward the doors of the field hospital that assume the appearance of the portals of death. The narrator then simply states that this was "the story of how the lieutenant lost his arm."

After some time has passed, the lieutenant's sisters, mother, and wife sob at the sight of his empty, flat sleeve. He stands ashamed before them, minimizing his disability, still not certain of the proper etiquette for behavior of the wounded. It was nothing, however, merely an ordinary experience shared by many soldiers who are doomed thereby to a lifetime of remembrance and suffering, just "an episode of war."

*Themes and Meanings*

An essential antiwar message predominates in this sober tale, but Stephen Crane, going well beyond the ethos of combat, infuses it with ideas endemic to the nineteenth century cosmic view, that humanity is but a tiny mote in the universal scheme, an insignificant entity driven by the fates and the winds of haphazard chance. Humankind's triviality is underscored by the characters not even having names; they are identified as types of people, generic manifestations caught in capriciously unfolding events they cannot control. The characters are unable to exercise freedom of the will; each person is propelled to action by the circumstances and forces about him; no one can direct his own destiny. All life is driven by some inexorable, unpredictable fate, the only apparent certainty being the existence of human suffering. Passion, not rationalism, is the fuel that ignites and unleashes the forces precipitating human movements that occur amid anarchy and frenzy.

The nameless lieutenant is the unfortunate Everyman, powerless to help himself and clearly at the mercy of the forces directing his steps. He also represents the archetypal victim gratuitously marked out for this role within the chaotic forces of war. He is helpless, small, ineffectual. Unable to sheathe his sword, divide the rations, or deter the surgeon, he is dependent on destiny for his existence. In the furious tumult and aimlessness, he joins the figurative march of ants that move in fixed parade, part of an unremarkable species, minuscule but striving toward a mysterious purpose. Crane's battlefield transcends the Civil War and may be seen as a microcosm of the world, for all life becomes a battle, a struggle to exist against the challenging fates that casually toss obstacles in the daily path. Human beings, nameless to the deterministic forces controlling life, are never the captains of their souls. The prime undercurrent rushing through "An Episode of War" is this philosophy of pessimism that eliminates free will from human option and renders a somber picture of life.

*Style and Technique*

With admirable, conscious artistry, Crane brought to his episode a confluence of literary impressionism and symbolism, a major triumph revealed in the abject anonymity of all of his characters. These human theory representations are fused into hectic actions that roll across a continuously exploding landscape roiling with menace and motion. The language is unremitting in its bleak, suggestive violence: "the slant of glistening guns," the "maniacal horses," the shooting that "crackled like bush fires." Within and against the colliding forces that reverberated with thunder and suffocated under rolling smoke is the solitary, wandering, wounded lieutenant, delicately holding his fragile, bleeding arm as if it were made of glass. The nameless officer, carrying his wounded arm, is thus described as already separated from the limb, bearing it as an independent part no longer attached to his body. The finality is clearly foreshadowed at this point, the diabolical lie of the surgeon notwithstanding.

The wounded arm, symbol of the lieutenant's separation from his essential self and his troops in wartime, is emblematized in civilian life by the empty sleeve, marking him as less than a complete human being. Both symbols also denote the end of the man's illusion—that the temporary arm of authority he once possessed was real, that he was in control of action and choice. The final picture Crane paints of the lieutenant finds this stammering veteran shamefaced, perhaps at what he now recognizes as his sin of pride in even momentarily believing he had the ability to fashion life. The missing arm is now a permanent reminder of his, and humankind's, impotence.

*Abe C. Ravitz*

# ERRAND

*Author:* Raymond Carver (1938-1988)
*Type of plot:* Historical
*Time of plot:* July, 1904
*Locale:* Badenweiler, Germany
*First published:* 1987

> *Principal characters:*
> ANTON CHEKHOV, a Russian author and playwright
> OLGA KNIPPER, his wife
> DR. SCHWÖRER, the physician who attends Chekhov on his
>     deathbed

*The Story*

In 1897, Anton Chekhov is dining with a wealthy publisher named Suvorin, at an elegant restaurant in Moscow. The two share an awareness of their peasant origins, although Suvorin's politics are reactionary and Chekhov's are quite the opposite. During the dinner, Chekhov experiences his first hemorrhage; the blood gushing from his mouth indicates that he has tuberculosis. Even while he is recuperating in a sanitarium for tuberculosis patients, however, Chekhov denies that anything serious is wrong with him. (Raymond Carver quotes from the memoirs of Chekhov's younger sister, Maria. During a visit with Chekhov at the clinic, she saw a doctor's drawing of Chekhov's lungs and recognized that the doctor had told him he was seriously ill.)

The author Leo Tolstoy also visits Chekhov during this time; although he does not like Chekhov's plays, he admires his short stories. During the visit, he tells Chekhov his ideas about immortality, ideas that Chekhov cannot share. Chekhov confines his beliefs to things that he can experience with his senses.

Chekhov spends much of his illness in denial, constantly insisting that he is getting better or that he is about to improve, even in his last weeks of life. He spends those weeks at Badenweiler, a popular German resort frequented by Russians, accompanied by his adored wife, Olga Knipper. The couple had met when Olga acted in Chekhov's *Chayka* (1896; *The Seagull*, 1909), and married in 1901. After a lengthy and complicated courtship, Chekhov has found marriage to be a happy experience.

Before going to Badenweiler, Chekhov consulted a specialist in Berlin, but that doctor had summarily dismissed him because his disease was far too advanced for treatment. A Russian journalist who visited Chekhov at about this time confirmed for his editor that the famous writer seemed to have entered the last stages of his illness, and noted his thinness, his constant fever, and his difficulties in breathing.

In Badenweiler, Chekhov is treated by Dr. Schwörer. Chekhov himself is a physician, so he must know how sick he is; nevertheless, his letters to his mother and sister in these last weeks of his life insist that he is improving and getting stronger. Chekhov is not writing during this period, however. His last work was *Vishnyovy sad* (1904; *The Cherry Orchard*, 1908), which he finished writing with difficulty in 1903 after expressing the belief that he would never write again.

On July 2, 1904, shortly after midnight, Olga sends for the doctor to come to Chekhov in their hotel. Chekhov has begun hallucinating, evidently about a trip he had once made to Japan. When Dr. Schwörer arrives, he senses that Chekhov has little time left. He gives him an injection to speed his heart, but it does no good. At last, he says he will send for oxygen, but Chekhov, momentarily lucid, says that he will be dead before it arrives. At that point, the doctor goes to the telephone and calls the hotel's kitchen to order a bottle of champagne and three glasses.

A rumpled young man who works for the hotel delivers the champagne and receives the doctor's generous tip. Then the doctor pours three glasses and presses the cork back into the bottle. Olga puts the cool glass into the hand of Chekhov, who says it has been a long time since he has drunk champagne. He drinks all of his wine, and Olga removes his empty glass. After rolling onto his side, Chekhov dies a few minutes later. Olga asks the doctor to delay telling the authorities for a few hours; she wishes to be alone with her husband before his body is taken over by others. Just as the doctor agrees, the champagne cork pops out of the bottle.

Olga sits with her husband until morning, when a knock at the door reveals the young hotel employee who has come to deliver a porcelain vase of roses and to collect the champagne bottle and glasses. Seeing the cork on the floor and becoming aware that someone is lying in the bedroom, he senses that something is wrong. Now Olga, who has not paid attention to the young man's suggestion that she might like breakfast on a tray, tells him that Chekhov is dead. She asks him to go for a mortician, taking care that he find someone appropriate for a person as important as Chekhov. She carefully instructs him to do nothing that will call attention to the situation or cause an unseemly commotion. As Olga instructs him, the young man thinks about how to retrieve the champagne cork that is lying near the toe of his shoe. He leans over and picks it up.

*Themes and Meanings*

Carver was a great admirer of Chekhov and his work. Like Chekhov, he was interested in the lives of common people struggling to get along in a difficult world, a theme Carver saw as central to his writing. Also like Chekhov, Carver died of a lung disease—cancer in Carver's case. In "Errand," one of the last stories that Carver wrote, he examines the ramifications of an artist's life, using Chekhov's life in part as a metaphor for his own. For example, he quotes Chekhov's unsentimental statement about how peasants face death and his rejection of all philosophical or religious world views. That rejection left Chekhov able to record only the objective details of his characters' lives—their births, marriages, deaths, styles of speech—the very material to which Carver limited himself in his own spare and undecorated writing.

Throughout "Errand," Chekhov denies the seriousness of his illness until the very end (unlike Carver, who wrote about his cancer several times). Even the journey to the spa at Badenweiler suggests this denial. The crisis of the story moves the focus from Chekhov himself to Olga, who must cope with her husband's death in the midst of strangers who cannot understand what has happened. Even after she has given the young hotel employee detailed instructions about finding a mortician, the name of the famous writer means so little to him that he can concentrate only on the champagne cork on the floor.

The champagne receives special emphasis in this story because it serves to link the opening scene in the elegant restaurant with Chekhov's last moments. The doctor's decision to order champagne, underscored by Carver's comment on the rightness of the action, and later the hotel employee's inability to recognize the significance of Olga's instructions, all seem to recall Chekhov's denial of his tuberculosis as well as his assertion that he will confine his fiction to the objective details of his characters' lives.

*Style and Technique*

This story, one of the last that Carver wrote, is quite unlike his usual portrayals of life among ordinary contemporary Americans. Instead, Carver has used many of the details of Chekhov's last days to make a story that is part biography and part fiction. As the story progresses, Carver indicates the material he drew from letters and journals of Chekhov's relatives and acquaintances. At the same time, he adds material such as the hotel employee in order to give the story texture and thematic focus.

Although this story, with its foreign setting and its historical detail, differs from Carver's usual work, its style is what Carver's readers have come to expect. Carver's sentences are bare; he uses relatively little modification, with the result that he sometimes seems rather distanced from his characters. It is his minute observation of detail that gives the story its emotional impact. The story deals with death and alienation, themes that inform much of Carver's work. At the end, the reader is moved by Chekhov's death partly because of his wife's tender devotion to him, partly because Chekhov is so little able to confront it, and partly because the man and his work remain so unknowable to the rest of the world—here suggested by the hotel employee, the very sort of person about whom Carver usually wrote. That the artist who interprets the lives of others must himself remain a mystery is an irony that surely Carver relished.

*Ann D. Garbett*

# MASTERPLOTS II

## SHORT STORY SERIES
### REVISED EDITION

# TITLE INDEX

L

# TITLE INDEX